D1274477

ABORTION: Choice & Conflict

ABORTION: Choice & Conflict

An Editorials On File Book

Editor: Oliver Trager

Facts On File
New York

ABORTION: Choice & Conflict

Published by Facts On File, Inc.
© Copyright 1993 by Facts On File, Inc.

Library of Congress Cataloging-in-Publication Data

Abortion: choice and conflict / edited by Oliver Trager.
    p.   cm. — (An Editorials on file book)
  Includes bibliographical references and index.

  ISBN 0-8160-2872-9
  1. Abortion—North America.   I. Trager, Oliver.   II. Series
HQ767.5.N7A26 1992
363.4'6—dc20   92-32300

Printed in the United States of America

9 8 7 6 6 5 4 3 2 1

This book is printed on acid-free paper

Contents

Selected Bibliography

Garfield, Jay L., Hennessey, Patricia (eds.), *Abortion: Moral and Legal Perspectives*, The University of Massachusetts Press, 1984.

Harrison, Beverly Wildung, *Our Right to Choose: Toward A New Ethnic of Abortion*, Beacon Press, 1983.

Petchesky, Rosalind Pollack, *Abortion And Women's Choice: The State, Sexuality, and Reproductive Freedom*, Northeastern University Press, 1984.

ABORTION: Choice & Conflict

Preface

Judges, legislators, doctors, philosophers, feminists and theologians, among others, have pondered the meaning and consequences of abortion. They have examined its bearing upon the individual and upon a democratic society; its medical risks; and its political impact. Their extensive deliberations, augmented by scholarly insight and constitutional expertise, have failed to resolve the many issues of the abortion conflict. If anything, protracted discussions on abortion have only broadened the scope of debate and further complicated the conflicts of interest involved.

The U.S. Supreme Court's 1992 ruling in the Pennsylvania abortion case has perpetuated the controversy ignited nearly two decades ago by *Roe v. Wade*, the 1973 decision establishing an inherent right to abortion for women under constitutional protections of the right of privacy. The fundamental issues raised by abortion continue to tear at the fabric of U.S. politics, law, medicine, religion and education. In recent years, the conflict between freedom-of-choice advocates and right-to-life supporters has grown more heated and more complex.

As the abortion debate intensifies, *Abortion: Choice and Conflict* explores the issues that surround this divisive topic and the questions it provokes: How have Supreme Court decisions of recent years eroded *Roe v. Wade*? What are the controversies surrounding the Bush administration's ban on abortion counseling in federally funded clinics? How has abortion been used as a political campaign issue? Do the methods of right-to-life groups such as Operation Rescue infringe on other constitutional rights? What legislative initiatives have been undertaken on the state and local level, and what are their implications? Are parental notification rules desirable, and how do they affect our youth? Should abortion be explained in the schools as a part of a sex education curriculum? What role does religion play in the nation's perception of abortion? What are the social ramifications of new birth technologies, and should the U.S. government permit medical research using fetal tissue obtained through abortion?

In *Abortion: Choice and Conflict* the nation's leading newspaper editorial writers and cartoonists examine the variety of searing issues stemming from the fundamental conflict over abortion.

November 1992   Oliver Trager

1

Part I: Abortion & the Courts

The legal status of abortion in the U.S. became a heightened national issue with two 1973 Supreme Court rulings that severely limited states' rights to control the procedure. The Court's decisions in the cases of *Roe v. Wade* and *Doe v. Bolton* found that a woman's right to limit childbearing was constitutionally guaranteed. The majority decision, based on the inidividual's constitutional right to privacy, stated that the government cannot interfere with the doctor-patient decision on abortion during the first three months of pregnancy.

The 7-2 ruling, in *Roe v. Wade*, divided the nine-month term of a normal pregnancy into three trimesters, narrowing the choices of the pregnant woman as she moves nearer to full term. The majority opinion, authored by Justice Harry Blackmun, found that "a woman's decision whether or not to terminate her pregnancy" was guaranteed, during the first trimester, by the right of privacy granted by the Fourteenth Amendment. During the final trimester, however, when the fetus "presumably has the capability of meaningful life outside the mother's womb," Blackmun wrote, the state may protect its legitimate interests in "protecting potential life" by banning abortions "except when it is necessary to preserve the life or health of the mother." In between, during the second trimester, the state could intervene to protect the health of the woman, regulating the procedure through licensing and other measures, but the woman's right to choose remained. This highly controversial ruling overturned restrictive abortion statutes in 44 states. In more than half of those states, abortion had been a crime.

The vast majority of the abortions now performed in the U.S. take place before the 13th week of pregnancy, or during the first trimester. But recent developments in neonatal care have moved the time when a fetus can be expected to survive outside the womb, known as viability, earlier into the second trimester than ever before. Critics of the *Roe v. Wade* ruling have argued that these developments have placed the reasoning behind the 1973 decision, which is largely dependent upon then-current medical technology, on shaky ground.

As the elder Supreme Court justices retired in the late 1980s and early 1990s and were replaced by justices appointed by the Reagan and Bush administrations, the high court approved some state limits on abortion, but has adhered, at least in part, to the fundamental view that women have a constitutional right to obtain abortions. Most notable among these rulings are the 1989 *Webster*, 1991 *Rust* and 1992 *Pennsylvania* decisions upholding state restrictions on abortion counseling and availability.

In *Webster v. Reproductive Health Services*, a bitterly argued 5-4 decision, the Supreme Court upheld a restrictive Missouri abortion law and, according to pro-abortion advocates, set the stage for the dismantling of *Roe v. Wade*. Though the decision stopped short of overturning *Roe v. Wade*, the ruling was seen as a victory for anti-abortion forces. The Missouri law upheld by the court prohibited public employees from performing abortions unless the mother's life was in danger, barred use of public buildings for performing abortions unless the mother's life was in danger, and required doctors who were about to perform abortions after 20 weeks to conduct tests to determine whether the fetus could live outside the womb.

Chief Justice William H. Rehnquist wrote in his majority opinion that, "the key elements of the *Roe* framework – trimesters and viability – are not found in the text of the Constitution, or in any place else one would expect to find a constitutional principle."

Justice John Paul Stevens, in his dissenting opinion, said the court could have declared the preamble to Missouri's abortion law unconstitutional because it declared that human life began at conception. Stevens said this reflected a religious view and violated the First Amendment's prohibition against establishment of religion.

The Supreme Court's 1991 ruling in the case *Rust v. Sullivan* upheld, 5-4, federal regulations that barred federally funded family planning clinics from providing information about abortion. The regulations, issued in 1988 by the Department of Health and Human Services, concerned clinics funded and regulated under Title X of the Public Health Service Act of 1970. The law prohibited funding of programs "where abortion is a method of family planning." Before the 1988 regulations were issued, the law had been interpreted as applying only to abortions, not to abortion counseling.

The *Rust* ruling affected up to 4,500 federally funded clinics across the country, which served between four million and five million women each year. The clinics would be required to direct all pregnant women to prenatal-care facilities. If a woman asked about terminating a pregnancy, the regulations instructed the clinic to tell her, "The project does not consider abortion an appropriate method of family planning." The decision allowed clinics to advise a woman of the abortion option if continuing the pregnancy posed a threat to her life. The 1988 regulations had prohibited abortion counseling in such cases.

In one of the the three dissenting opinions, Justice Harry A. Blackmun said the regulations were an "intrusive, ideologically based regulation of speech."

In another 5-4 decision, the Supreme Court's 1992 ruling in *Planned Parenthood of Southeastern Pennsylvania v. Casey* upheld most of the stern provisions of a Pennsylvania law that imposed limits on a woman's ability to obtain an abortion. But the majority also reaffirmed that a woman's basic right to choose an abortion was "a rule of law and a component of liberty we cannot renounce."

The decision effectively gave states broad powers to restrict abortions. But by explicitly reaffirming a woman's right to terminate her pregnancy, the ruling also surprised observers who had believed that conservative justices on the court would more thoroughly weaken – if not overturn – *Roe v. Wade*.

Leaders and spokespersons for both sides in the national debate over abortion expressed their dissatisfaction with the ruling. Opponents of abortion complained that the High Court's ruling did not offer sufficient protection to the unborn. Wanda Franz, president of the National Right to Life Committee, called the ruling "a loss for unborn children and a victory for pro-abortion forces." Randall Terry, the leader of the anti-abortion group Operation Rescue, complained that "three Reagan-Bush appointees stabbed the pro-life movement in the back" by upholding *Roe v. Wade*.

Leading abortion-rights advocates charged that the restrictions upheld by the court would create severe obstacles for poor women and teenagers who sought abortions, and would enable and encourage states to restrict abortion rights still further. Their sentiments were perhaps best expressed by Patricia Ireland, president of the National Organization for Women, who said: "*Roe* is dead."

Racketeering Judgment Upheld in Case Against Demonstrators

A federal appeals court in Philadelphia, Pa. March 2, 1989 upheld a judgment against a group of anti-abortion demonstrators under the federal Racketeer Influenced and Corrupt Organizations Act (RICO).

The protesters had been found liable under RICO in 1987 for destroying property and harassing patients and staff during a series of protests at the Northwest Women's Center in Philadelphia. They had been ordered to pay $43,000 in damages, plus $65,000 in legal costs.

The three-member appeals panel ruled that the racketeering judgment had been appropriate because the protesters had gone beyond merely expressing their opinion and had engaged in criminal conduct during the protests.

Civil liberties groups said the decision was the first at the appeals court level that expanded the use of RICO to cover acts of civil disobedience.

The RICO statute said that individuals or groups could be held liable for damages if they had engaged in "a pattern of racketeering activity" that involved at least two serious crimes or threats of serious crimes.

The law had come under increasing fire from some lawyers, businesses and other organizations who said that prosecutors were using RICO too broadly, in cases that had nothing to do with organized crime.

Abortion-rights groups praised the appeals court decision. "It's time that [anti-abortion activists] are held accountable for their violent acts and their efforts to interfere with women's rights to health care," said a spokeswoman for the National Rights Action League. "This decision is a big victory."

Abortion foes blasted the RICO verdict, however. "It takes away the right to assembly, the right to free speech and the right to redress a grievance," said Joseph Scheidler, director of the Pro-Life Action League. "I think the Supreme Court will overturn it. The racketeering law, RICO, is being overused these days."

ST. LOUIS POST-DISPATCH

St. Louis, Missouri, March 6, 1989

The Racketeer Influenced and Corrupt Organizations Act of 1970, better known as RICO, was written specifically to thwart organized crime. But a federal appeals court in Philadelphia, in a clear abuse of the law's purpose, has just upheld its use against anti-abortion advocates in that city. Since not only the appeals court, but the federal courts in general and the Supreme Court in particular have been strangely reluctant to limit RICO's scope, Congress must step in and do the job.

Several leaders of Philadelphia's anti-abortion movement were convicted of engaging in an organized attempt to put an abortion clinic out of business by harassing the staff, terrorizing patients and destroying property. That the defendants committed these acts and that such acts exceed the constitutionally protected right to free speech isn't in doubt. But while adequate statutes exist under which such behavior may be punished, RICO isn't one of them.

Unfortunately, the law is vague. In seeking to arm prosecutors with special powers to fight organized crime, the law defines a pattern of racketeering as only two or more acts — and they can be virtually any kind of

crime — occurring in a 10-year period.

Once defendants are indicted, their assets may be seized before trial to prevent their disappearance, and a conviction isn't required to subject defendants to civil suits in which plaintiffs can seek triple damages. These extraordinary tools are appropriate to attack what society commonly understands as "racketeering" — most notably, criminal control of legitimate business. But they have no place outside that sphere.

When the courts are reminded of this distinction, which is clearly evident in the legislative history of the statute, they have responded that since the law's language contains no explicit restrictions, they can apply none.

Such an uncharacteristically strict reading of the law now permits anti-abortion protesters to be branded as racketeers, as well as many white-collar criminals whose offenses, serious though they are, should not be lumped into the overall category of organized crime.

The issue is now up to Congress. It should strictly define racketereering to restrain prosecutors from using the law in ways for which it was never intended.

Richmond Times-Dispatch
Richmond, Virginia, March 20, 1989

Is it legitimate to use the Federal Racketeering Influenced and Corrupt Organizations Act not just against organized crime, as originally intended, but against protest groups practicing civil disobedience? Yes, recently concluded the 3rd U.S. Circuit Court of Appeals in Philadelphia — at least in the case of the anti-abortion protesters who have been demonstrating at abortion clinics around the country.

Curiously, the American Civil Liberties Union, which had been fretting about RICO's becoming a threat to First Amendment rights, took a pass on this one. An ACLU spokesman said that, well, maybe such lawsuits would be OK in some cases — that is to say, when the targets are people who oppose abortion on demand.

Another great defender of freedom, the National Organization for Women, has been busy filing racketeering suits of its own against anti-abortion groups. Wonder how loudly NOW would yell if it were hit with a RICO suit for engaging in its own advocacy activities?

When anti-abortion protesters seek to block entrances to public facilities or even physically to prevent individuals from entering clinics, they break any number of common laws and they should be subject to prosecution. However, a protester who pushes or yells at someone does not, ipso facto, become an extortionist or a racketeer. A charge of simple assault should cover such a situation.

In the recently decided case of *Fort Wayne Books vs. Indiana*, a divided U.S. Supreme Court found that RICO sanctions could be imposed against those who engage in a pattern of distributing obscenity through "adult bookstores." However, the majority declined to permit use of a key RICO feature — pretrial seizure of materials for later forfeiture. RICO, said Justice White, "may not be used against materials presumptively protected by the First Amendment."

It could well be that if the Supreme Court accepts the anti-abortion RICO case for a review (and pro-life groups have promised to pursue an appeal), it will decide that free-speech rights similarly must be safeguarded. But don't expect the ACLU or NOW to applaud First Amendment rights for protesters they detest.

THE BLADE
Toledo, Ohio, October 1, 1991

THE anti-abortion zealots may think they have created a masterstroke by opening so-called copycat abortion clinics where no abortions — but plenty of anti-abortion advice and propaganda — are dispensed. But what they've managed to do is make an already difficult decision for women that much harder.

These clinics have been opening all over the nation in recent weeks; one estimate by pro-choice forces is that there are 2,000 of them. The scenario is to place ads into the Yellow Pages, suggesting that such clinics offer abortions when in reality they do not.

Young women are given anti-abortion "advice," including graphic pictures of destroyed fetuses. The point is to dissuade women from visiting legitimate abortion clinics and win more converts to their cause.

For the moment this process appears to be legal, and it will undoubtedly divert more than a few women from going ahead with an abortion. But judging from the manner in which some of the people who oppose abortion have comported themselves, it may well do more harm than good.

Scare tactics used against a woman who is facing an abortion will inflict additional emotional distress. Women deserve to have the right to make a decision about abortion in something other than the kind of charged and coercive atmosphere that exists in some of these "clinics."

Women can make up their own minds on this issue. But they should not be victimized by such underhanded tactics. Deciding to have an abortion is an excruciatingly difficult time for a women — and that decision is made all the more traumatic if they are ensnared in a phony clinic.

THE SPOKESMAN-REVIEW
Spokane, Washington, March 4, 1989

The timing of Friday's anti-abortion protest in Spokane appears to have been coincidental. It came just a day after a federal court in Philadelphia issued a ruling which, on its surface, likens such protests to organized crime.

Regardless of one's view on abortion, or on the customarily overbearing tactics employed by anti-abortion protesters, the U.S. Appeals Court's ruling Thursday requires an elastic imagination.

The federal Racketeer Influenced Corrupt Organizations (RICO) Act was passed in 1970 because Congress and President Nixon wanted a tool for dealing with gangsters who hid behind seemingly legitimate business fronts to engage in gambling, drug-running, prostitution and other lucrative criminal enterprises.

It is most improbable that members of the House and Senate ever would have approved such legislation had they thought it would be directed against confederations based on social protest.

Indeed, experience shows that anti-abortion demonstrations can be ugly affairs. People going innocently about their business may be subjected to vulgar and unsettling taunts. Children, nervous enough about a visit to the doctor, suffer heightened anxieties in the face of chants about babies being murdered.

Accordingly, the courts intervened, not to silence the protesters but to place appropriate limits on where they could air their views without infringing on others' rights. Friday's demonstrations resulted in several arrests, based in part on violation of earlier court orders. The disturbance didn't last long and the perpetrators will be held accountable.

The Spokane experience shows that the normal channels can work.

In Philadelphia, the circumstances of the case were not dramatically different. There were no bombs, no weapons, no serious injuries. True, while the Spokane incident resulted in no physical confrontations between protesters and employees or patrons of the building, the series of demonstrations at a Philadelphia clinic did involve some pushing, shoving and tugging. But none of that prompted police, who were on hand, to charge anyone with assault.

Nevertheless, in taking legal action in 1985, the clinic invoked RICO, arguing the activity constituted a conspiracy to destroy its business and property. A federal trial court in 1986 dismissed the charges, saying the demonstrators had caused unpleasantness but no irreparable harm.

Unfortunately, the appellate ruling which overturned that decision Thursday has elevated the kind of spontaneous unruliness that can break out during an emotional protest demonstration to the level of thumb-breaking goons dispatched by underground crime lords to terrorize anyone bold enough to stand in their way.

Attempting to harm the Philadelphia clinic's business? That's probably a given, just as civil-rights boycott leaders in the 1960s were trying to harm the business at segregated lunch counters in the South. They weren't racketeers either.

Already there is strong sentiment in Congress to refine the RICO Act because of the belief it is being abused in civil cases filed against legitimate businesses by competitors intent on harassing them. The Philadelphia ruling, should it hold up in the face of an expected appeal, should give impetus to that congressional movement.

DESERET NEWS
Salt Lake City, Utah, March 5, 1992

Anti-abortion protesters who break the law in picketing, harassing and otherwise intimidating women clients or those who work in abortion clinics should be prosecuted under laws relevant to such acts.

But they should not be prosecuted under such stringent measures as the federal Racketeer Influenced and Corrupt Organizations Act, known as the RICO Act.

A three-judge panel of the 3rd U.S. Court of Appeals in Philadelphia ruled this week that 27 protesters violated the federal measure in their attempts to shut down a Philadelphia abortion clinic.

While the strong-willed protesters, bent on closing down such facilities, may have been guilty of collusion, assault, disturbing the peace and a variety of other statues, it is unlikely they were guilty of laws aimed at curbing organized crime.

The case, being followed closely by both sides of the abortion dispute, marked the first time use of RICO by the pro-choice movement against anti-abortion activists. It isn't likely to be the last.

The RICO Act has most often been used against organized crime figures. An attorney for the abortion center said the act was applicable because protesters used extortion, in the form of threats and force, to deny the center its right to operate and to deny women their right to use the center.

Appeals court judges said center videotapes shows demonstrators pushed, shoved and tugged on patients as they tried to approach the center. The tapes apparently showed that the protesters knocked over and crossed police barricades and blocked the movement of cars.

None of this activity is justified and should be dealt with under the law, but charging the activists with racketeering is a total misapplication of the meaning of the word.

An official of the Pro-Life Coalition of Southeast Pennsylvania says that pushing, for example, doesn't constitute racketeering or extortion. That ought to be obvious.

What do disruptive acts at abortion clinics have to do with organized crime, even if the acts were plotted in advance? Until that can be explained, the use of the RICO law in this instance makes no sense.

American Bar Association Backs Abortion Right for the First Time

The American Bar Association voted for the first time February 13, 1990, to support a constitutional right to abortion.

The measure was adopted by the ABA's house of delegates, 238–106, at the association's midwinter meeting in Los Angeles following a heated debate.

The resolution declared that the ABA "opposes legislation or other governmental action that interferes with the confidential relationship between a pregnant woman and her physician or with the decision to terminate the pregnancy at any time before the fetus is capable of independent life."

The policy decision meant that the ABA would be able to file friend-of-the-court briefs in abortion cases in front of the Supreme Court or any other court indicating that it supported legalized abortion.

However, the ABA's president-elect, John Curtin, who opposed abortion, said he would refused to sign his name to any ABA briefs supporting abortion during his one-year term of office, which was scheduled to begin in August.

The ABA, reversing a position it had adopted in February, voted August 8 to abandon its support of abortion rights. Instead, the ABA declared itself neutral on the issue of abortion.

The Washington Post
Times Herald
Washington, D.C., August 9, 1990

THE AMERICAN Bar Association, the national organization of lawyers which has 365,000 members, routinely takes positions on any number of issues before the courts and Congress. Its views are sought or proffered on matters as diverse as the merits of changes in the antitrust laws and the government's role in combating discrimination against homosexuals. These, like most public issues, are legal as well as policy matters, and the professional opinion of this body of lawyers, whether in briefs or testimony, is usually welcome.

Yet the ABA has a problem in this role as commentator on policy questions in that it is also called upon from time to time to play a conflicting, more detached role which it also cherishes. That is, of course, that it is asked to evaluate candidates for federal judgeships, including for the appellate and Supreme courts. The problem that arises is a simple one of potential conflict of interest that any lawyer might counsel a client to avoid: What happens when a candidate for an important judgeship, whatever his other qualifications, has taken a policy position with which the ABA vigorously disagrees? How, in these moments of extreme controversy, does it assure all sides—and itself—that its view of the candidate is independent of its view of the policy question, that it is not affecting a purely professional pose when advancing what is essentially a political agenda?

The organization has had to confront its dilemma and much more this week; it met in Chicago to debate, among other things, the question of whether to take a position on abortion. This is a legal matter but plainly also a political, personal and moral one. In February, the policy-making board of the association voted to endorse the position that a woman's right to abortion was guaranteed by the Constitution. This provoked a strong reaction within the membership. More than 1,400 lawyers, including some officers, resigned; the elected leadership of the ABA voted 21 to 9 to stay neutral on the question; and earlier this week those attending the convention also voted 885 to 837 for neutrality.

But the debate is of particular interest because of the ABA's quasi-official role in the judicial confirmation process. Abortion was a major issue in the debate on Judge Robert Bork's qualifications for the Supreme Court two years ago and could become the same in the case of Judge David Souter. If the ABA has strong views on abortion, might these influence it in taking a position on Judge Souter, or could it be objective? How would we know? No nominee for the Supreme Court is likely to be confirmed without the ABA's endorsement, so much is at stake.

We think the professional association should evaluate only a candidate's scholarship, legal experience and integrity, not his political philosophy and certainly not his views on a matter of great controversy that is continually before the court. The ABA as a private association is free to take whatever stand it chooses on public matters. But yesterday it backed off its stand on abortion. Though the members who voted doubtless had many motives, we think the organization was wise to do so. The ABA needs to understand that its special role in the judicial confirmation process will be challenged if it is thought to be governed even in part by policy positions on such questions as abortion. The organization has to choose whether it wants to be above the fray or part of it.

The Register-Guard
Eugene, Oregon, August 21, 1990

The American Bar Association, which regularly offers opinions on constitutional issues, has chosen a position of neutrality on one of the most prominent issues of the day: abortion.

In February, by a 2-1 margin, the ABA's policy-making House of Delegates adopted a resolution opposing any government interference "with the confidential relationship between a pregnant woman and her physician." The resolution basically endorsed the Supreme Court's 1973 Roe vs. Wade decision. This month, by a razor-thin vote of 200-188, the delegates rescinded that resolution.

What happened between February and August? Political pressure happened. Financial pressure as well.

After the February action, anti-abortion groups launched a $50,000 lobbying campaign on ABA members. And U.S. Attorney General Dick Thornburgh, reflecting the Bush administration's anti-abortion position, weighed in by saying that the ABA's pro-choice stance compromised its impartiality in evaluating nominees to federal judgeships.

The heat also was turned up by the resignation of 1,500 of the ABA's 360,000 members in protest against the group's pro-choice stand. The resignations reportedly cost the ABA $300,00 in annual dues, and many more were threatened.

The bar association's retreat to neutrality on the volatile issue of abortion is disappointing. But proponents of neutrality argued that the issue is simply too "personal" and "divisive" for the organization to deal with.

Said The Baltimore Evening Sun: "The Bar Association's retrenchment deflates its august, professional image and clearly exposes it as just another trade organization whose main concern is not principles but protecting the position and economic interests of its members."

That may be too harsh. But if the organization intends to pronounce judgment on all constitutional questions except those that are personal and divisive, its opinions will not be widely sought or respected.

Richmond Times-Dispatch
Richmond, Virginia, August 11, 1990

The American legal profession has long since become an irritant to the rest of society, with lawyers having somehow found a way to make large numbers of people despise and distrust them as a class. Much of this is attributable to the lawyer's common penchant for extraordinary and calculated self-interest, an unfortunate aspect famous well beyond America and in fact highlighted by history's most prominent commentators, including Shakespeare and Jesus Christ.

The situation is so bad that we would feel great sympathy for lawyers, if not for the fact that they may well have it all coming. Lawyers control the court system and it is a frightening mess. The criminal courts are a slow, inefficient tragicomedy, where outlaws enjoy the benefits of slap-dash plea bargaining, unbridled defense attorneys and routine suppression of valid evidence. The civil courts are full of overdrawn, redistributionist lawsuits, fanciful causes of action with demands for damages so huge that new product development is driven down to a crawl and the cost of medical care driven up to the stars. Meanwhile the legislative branch continues to mismanage national affairs, nourish the omnipotent welfare state and spend the greatest nation on Earth into a humiliating, emasculating debt. And who dominates the Congress? Lawyers.

The common man has good reasons for his deepening contempt for the legal profession, and the profession therefore has much to do to redeem itself with the public. And so what do you suppose commanded the full attention of the 365,000-member American Bar Association at its Chicago convention this week? Why, abortion, of course.

In February the ABA House of Delegates, a representative policy-making body in that organization, voted to lend ABA endorsement to abortion as a fundamental right guaranteed by the Constitution. There was little significance to this action, except to members of the ABA who

had not realized they were paying dues to support abortion rights. Some 1,500 ABA members resigned in protest, costing the organization about $300,000 in fees and leading to a reconsideration of the policy at this week's meeting.

The policy has been abandoned and the ABA restored to a position of neutrality on abortion, but not by much. The vote was 885-837 for a neutrality resolution in the Assembly, which consists of any member who pays to register for the meeting and casts a vote. In the House of Delegates it was 200-188 against the pro-abortion position the same body had adopted by a 2-1 margin in February. The losers, emboldened by the closeness of the votes, have vowed to fight on, despite warnings from some officers that continuing internal bickering about abortion will harm the ABA's reputation and call into further question the organization's practice of passing judgment on the qualifications of judicial nominees.

Truth be told, the ABA has for some time been a liberal-left outfit, and so it comes as no surprise that abortion rights would find a prominent place on its agenda. It is absurd, though, for any of its members to insist on a formal endorsement in favor of abortion, no less so than if a national association of plumbers or accountants were similarly prevailed upon to enter a profound moral debate. The big difference, of course, is that there are a lot of woman lawyers now; in many law schools at least half the enrollment is female and many of these have grown up to see abortion as the legal issue most vital to their professional lives. "I'm practically the only one of my friends who hasn't had an abortion," said Sandra J. P. Dennis at the convention. "We're talking about lots of women in this room …." And so while the feminist element among lawyers may be relatively new, certainly it has caught on fast, picking up in no time at all that capacity for extraordinary self-interest that has so long distinguished the profession.

ST. LOUIS POST-DISPATCH
St. Louis, Missouri, August 11, 1990

The American Bar Association has now voted that the abortion issue is so divisive that neutrality is the better part of valor. In a dramatic turnabout, it is rescinding its February resolution that supported the constitutionality of abortion.

It is not neutrality per se that caused the controversy. If the ABA typically refrained from taking positions on social issues, the decision wouldn't merit any attention. Or, if the ABA were just taking up the abortion issue, the temptation to avoid dissension by adopting neutrality could be understood.

But the ABA adopted a resolution supporting abortion rights in February; now, following complaints from many of its members and a large number of resignations, the association has retreated from that position. The reversal is what is at issue, but neutrality looks more like a rejection of abortion rights than a decision not to take sides.

Conservative supporters of neutrality raised the red herring of credibility. They, as well as Attorney General Dick Thornburgh, suggested that the ABA's

endorsement of legal abortion rendered it incapable of impartial assessments of judicial candidates.

The ABA has, in the past, taken stands on controversial legal issues — civil rights legislation and gun control, for example. Those stances don't seem to have impaired its capacity to make professional evaluations. Why should abortion be any different?

Beyond that, though, it is intellectually erroneous to assume that people or organizations with opinions cannot make fair judgments. Nothing in the abortion-rights resolution suggested that abortion be made into a litmus test; and no evidence indicates that judicial candidates disagreeing with other ABA positions were summarily rejected.

The ABA's retraction stands in stark contrast to the American Medical Association's announcement in June that it supports the testing of RU-486, the abortion pill, in the United States. It's too bad that the nation's most prestigious group of lawyers didn't stand up for social justice the same way the AMA stood up for medical advances.

The Register
Santa Ana, California, January 28, 1990

The other day the trustees of the Los Angeles County Bar Association approved a measure affirming the *Roe v. Wade* ruling that legalized abortion, implicitly condemning any attempts to tinker with that ruling. The vote was overwhelming, but not without controversy. Several bar members protested that the resolution was ramrodded through — that the entire organization, not just the trustees, should have been allowed a say on the measure.

Whatever the merits of that complaint, the action is interesting because it calls attention to a question now before the US Supreme Court: Should the State Bar of California force lawyers to fund blatantly political lobbying campaigns?

Granted, no lawyers are required to pay dues to the LA County Bar Association, so the abortion vote didn't represent compulsory use of attorneys' money to support a cause some of them might disagree with. But don't be surprised if the same resolution, backed by some of the activists who sponsored it in Los Angeles, isn't soon put to the State Bar for its consideration.

If it passes, it would hardly be the first example of political meddling by the State Bar. The organization has lobbied the Legislature on issues ranging from criminal penalties to comparable worth to environmental policies. It filed "friend of the court" briefs attacking prison conditions in California and challenging the Victims' Bill of Rights initiative. It went to bat for former Chief Justice Rose Bird before her unsuccessful retention election.

None of these activities might rate censure if it weren't for one fact: Under California law, all attorneys have to belong and pay yearly dues to the State Bar if they want to practice in California, the rationale being that the Bar sets standards for the practice of law.

Some observers argue that compulsory membership is itself unjust. Many libertarians go further and assail the legal profession's monopoly over legal services. But even if you think a professional class of lawyers, with mandatory membership in a professional organization, is a good thing, has the Bar discharged its duties responsibly?

The state Constitution says the organization's purpose is to "further the administration of justice." That shouldn't be a license to butt into political issues on which the membership has widely differing views.

A group of attorneys has brought a court challenge to the use of their dues to grind ideological axes. The state Supreme Court largely rebuffed their argument that they should get back their money when the Bar stoops to politicking. But the fat lady hasn't warbled yet: the US Supreme Court has taken the case on appeal. If justice prevails, the Bar will be ordered to either stop the political shenanigans or stop seizing mandatory dues.

Rule Limiting Abortion Counseling Challenged

The Reagan administration March 3, 1988 suspended its effort to prevent federally funded family planning clinics from engaging in abortion-related activities. Rules barring such activities were to have gone into effect that day.

The administration acted hours after a federal judge in Boston issued a nationwide injunction permanently prohibiting enforcement of the new policy.

U.S. District Judge Walter Jay Skinner acted in a lawsuit in which the plaintiffs were the Commonwealth of Massachusetts and two national groups, the National Family Planning and Reproductive Health Association, which represented most family planning clinics in the U.S., and the American Public Health Association, which represented some 50,000 public health professionals.

In issuing his injunction, Judge Skinner said it applied to all members of the plaintiff groups nationwide. The proposed rules, Skinner said, would "as a whole violate both congressional intent and rights protected by the Constitution."

Preliminary injunctions barring enforcement of the anti-abortion policy had been issued in February by federal judges in Denver and New York City. But the Denver ruling applied only to clinics affiliated with the Planned Parenthood Federation of America, and the New York decision applied only to New York State.

A Department of Health and Human Services spokesman March 3 said that regional HHS offices had been notified to take no action to implement the new policy until the permanent injunction issued in Boston by Judge Skinner had been studied.

The Miami Herald
Miami, Florida, October 12, 1988

PREDICTABLY and rightly a Federal court has barred the state from enforcing its obnoxious new "snitch law." The law bars women under the age of 18 from obtaining an abortion without the consent of a parent or judge.

After listening to arguments that the law unconstitutionally restricts the rights of women, U.S. District Judge John H. Moore II held that the law falls "woefully short of Constitutional requirements." He issued an injunction to prevent enforcement until the Florida Supreme Court implements rules to expedite abortion petitions and protect the women's confidentiality.

That the Florida Court must establish such rules indicates the influx of cases expected — by some estimates one-third of 9,100 teen-agers who annually seek abortions. It also reflects the legal complexity of mixing religious views with the civil laws that guard women's rights.

Florida's law passed amid an emotional frenzy and election-year threats. No candidate wants to be picketed by zealous anti-abortionists. Moreover, its advocates argue, if minors must have parental permission to have their tonsils removed, why not for an abortion?

Why, indeed? Never mind that the minor became pregnant without the family's permission and would bear sole legal responsibility for the child she doesn't want. Never mind, either, that the question presumes a loving family ready to rally around a daughter in trouble.

But what happens to the daughter who is the victim of incest? The girl with no father? Whose mother is a drug addict or alcoholic? Who faces a beating when posing a problem? Who's been locked out of the house? Who quit school to marry an abusive man? Young women who find their way to abortion clinics — alone — are women already bearing hellish burdens.

As a state, Florida has never fully faced its obligation to protect and nurture young people. It has one of the nation's highest school-dropout rates and one of its lowest levels of health and social services. When it comes to sex and young women, however, the Legislature finds it easy to muster moral outrage and add to a punishing burden.

Once again a Federal court has proved itself women's last, best refuge. Legislators who resent what they call "interference" from the judiciary should look to their own irresponsibility.

THE PLAIN DEALER
Cleveland, Ohio, August 22, 1988

Earlier this month a federal appeals court in Cincinnati struck down Ohio's law requiring doctors performing abortions on teen-age patients to first inform the parents of those patients. The U.S. Court of Appeals (6th Circuit) correctly read the law for what it is—an attempt to limit abortions, not a means to improve communications between parent and child. Because the right of a woman to an abortion is protected by the Constitution, broad limitations such as Ohio's law—passed in 1985 but unenforced because of the legal challenge—cannot be acceptable.

Unfortunately, another federal appeals court, the same week as the Cincinnati court, acted otherwise. In St. Paul, the U.S. Court of Appeals (8th Circuit) upheld a Minnesota law similar to the Ohio law that was struck down. That means sooner or later the issue will get a hearing before the Supreme Court, which with new Justice Anthony M. Kennedy is expected to be more cordial to reconsidering some aspects of the 1973 Roe vs. Wade ruling that legalized abortion.

Does that mean the court will uphold parental notification laws? Not necessarily. There's ample evidence backing the argument that such laws are not necessary and that they victimize the very teen-agers they are supposed to help. A lower court in Minnesota, in earlier voiding that state's law, found that: "Parental notification of a pending abortion can only add to the magnitude of the problem of family violence, which in turn intensifies the distress and anxieties of the abortion decision confronting the pregnant minor."

In the vast majority of families, parents have been able to nurture good relationships with their offspring; notification laws simply aren't needed in such cases. And in families where mutual trust has not been established? Chances are the children of abusive or alcholic parents, victims already, will be further hurt, as the Minnesota judge indicated, if they are required to confess to having become pregnant.

The appeals court in St. Paul nonetheless overruled the judge's ruling, even though it recognized "considerable questions about the practical wisdom of this statute." Obviously the court, loaded by President Reagan with anti-abortion judges, was looking for a way to put in place the administration's anti-abortion views.

Ironically, parental notification laws are promulgated by legislators who in most other areas resent the government's intrusion into personal affairs. The lawmakers claim the best intentions, saying they only want to ensure that parents know when their children are about to undergo a medical operation. Yet there's no Ohio law that requires physicians to notify parents before performing other medical procedures on children. Why the need for a law regarding abortion?

The answer is that many lawmakers still are unwilling to accept the Supreme Court's 1973 abortion ruling. They're grasping at whatever way they can to limit the reach of that decision. Their mischief not only wastes legislative time, but also plays a cruel trick on young women already traumatized by unwanted pregnancy and insensitive parents.

▣ The Cincinnati Post
Cincinnati, Ohio, October 18, 1988

The federal courts can't seem to agree on whether minors seeking abortions may be required by law to notify their parents. Conflicting rulings from around the country show how divided society is.

A three-judge panel in the 6th U.S. Circuit Court of Appeals here last Friday affirmed a lower court ruling, which held unconstitutional Ohio's law requiring the person performing an abortion on anyone under 18 to inform a parent. Just four days earlier, a federal appeals court in a 7-3 decision upheld a similar law in Minnesota.

Court battles over parental notification laws have produced a patchwork of rulings across the nation, demonstrating how difficult it is for courts to settle fundamental social issues.

Between 26 and 30 states have passed parental notice laws. One third of these laws have been declared unconstitutional, but another third have been challenged and upheld. The rest are in some stage of litigation.

It seems obvious the U.S. Supreme Court will have to decide whether states may act to prevent children from having abortions without telling their parents. The justices split 4-4 on an Illinois notification statute last December, while the ninth seat on the court was vacant. Justice Anthony M. Kennedy had not yet been appointed, and at this stage no one is sure how Kennedy would vote.

Whatever the courts rule, most parents feel they should be involved with their minor children in a decision as serious as having an abortion. Schools, of course, will not even send a child to a doctor for a cut on a finger without authorization from parents.

Pro-choice proponents argue that informing unsympathetic parents can create even more problems for the pregnant teen-ager. That is why many notification laws provide for exemptions; Ohio's statute allows a juvenile court to waive notification.

But as Judge John Gibson of the 8th U.S. Circuit Court wrote in the majority opinion in the Minnesota case: "Although some parents may be abusive, or at best unhelpful to their minor child faced with the decision of whether to have an abortion, that is hardly a reason to discard the pages of experience teaching that parents generally do act in their child's best interests." Those pages of experience should be reflected in our laws.

The Miami Herald
Miami, Florida, May 16, 1988

ABORTION opponents cannot muster the votes simply to ban abortion; the issue is too complex. But that does not stop opponents from harassing women who seek, or might seek, abortions.

In the latest political skirmish, Florida's abortion opponents are picking on girls under 18, estranged from their families. To get an abortion, these women — say 25 Florida Senate members — must have "permission" from a parent, guardian, or judge.

How smug of them, in a state that can't find foster homes for abused children, that tells welfare mothers with three children to live on $324 a month, and that proposes "to squeeze the fat out" of the welfare budget by cutting food allowances for pregnant women.

Political debates over these "snitch bills" portray the women involved as daughters of loving and understanding families. What a terrible thing it is to bar a concerned parent from a decision such as abortion, cry proponents. In fact, daughters of *concerned* families do turn first to them, and their families give them understanding and support.

But what happens to the daughter

AN ANTI-ABORTION RUSE

who is the victim of incest? The girl who has no father? Whose mother is a drug addict or alcoholic? Who is raising herself — and perhaps a sibling? Who faces a beating when she presents a problem? Who's been locked out of the house? Who's selling drugs or working as a prostitute? Who quit school to marry an abusive man?

"Dysfunctional" is a sterile word to describe such families and the hellish burdens that they place on young women who find their way — alone — to abortion clinics. Florida lawmakers have no legal or moral right to add to those young women's burden.

The issue before the Senate was the re-enactment of expiring regulations intended to assure that abortion clinics are medically safe. Sen. Marlene Woodson of Bradenton attached her snitch amendment, declaring it "not anti-abortion"; other backers made it clear that halting abortion is exactly their intent.

The Florida Senate played along with the ruse. The House should not.

Minneapolis Star and Tribune
Minneapolis, Minnesota, August 11, 1988

Minnesota's abortion-notification law is meant to coax teen-agers to sit down for a family chat before having an abortion. But as a three-judge panel of the Eighth U.S. Circuit Court of Appeals noted last year, forcing pregnant minors to confide in their parents has spawned more family strife than unity. Now the full appellate court has disregarded that insight, unwisely voting 7-3 to reverse the panel and uphold the law.

In the best of worlds, every pregnant teen-ager would consult both her parents before seeking an abortion. Most teen-agers do. Minnesota's 1981 notification law is aimed at the unfortunate few who feel they cannot discuss such delicate matters at home: It instructs doctors to alert both parents 48 hours before a minor's abortion; a teen-ager can skirt the rule only by convincing a judge that she's mature enough to act on her own.

In the eyes of the appellate-court majority, the notification law simply recognizes parents' "significant interest" in a child's well-being. But that finding overlooks the hardship a forced family chat can inflict. For teens from troubled homes, it can incite parental hostility or even violence. For the four in 10 Minnesota children who live with just one biological parent, it sometimes entails tracking down an estranged or unsympathetic parent. For teens who hope to avoid all such anguish, it prescribes an intimidating court process.

Yet the initial trial before Judge Donald Alsop in 1986 made clear that the court process works like a rubber stamp: From 1981 to 1986, Minnesota judges granted all but 15 of the 3,573 petitions for abortions without parental notification. Because it fails to distinguish mature adolescents from those who need parental guidance, Alsop concluded, the law serves mainly to aggravate family discord and to hinder teen-agers from exercising their prerogative to choose abortion.

In overturning Alsop and its own three-judge panel, the court has revived a law that fails to fulfill its proclaimed goal and obstructs a constitutional right. The U.S. Supreme Court likely will be asked to review the ruling next term. But Minnesota lawmakers can make the matter moot by at last facing a fact: that legislating a parent-child chat neither strengthens families nor helps troubled teens. The notification law should be repealed.

ST. LOUIS POST-DISPATCH
St. Louis, Missouri, August 11, 1988

The 8th U.S. Circuit Court of Appeals has upheld a Minnesota law requiring women under the age of 18 who seek abortions to notify both parents or to get special approval from a state judge. In doing so, it has further eroded women's tenuous hold on reproductive rights.

Twenty-five states, including Missouri, require minors to notify or obtain consent from one parent or to get judicial approval before an abortion is performed. Minnesota's law, however, requires notification of both parents, even in cases of divorce, separation or desertion. Only 48 hours after the woman can prove that this has been attempted can she seek judicial review. A similar Ohio law has just been struck down by the 6th U.S. Circuit Court of Appeals, setting the stage for Supreme Court review.

The Supreme Court has upheld laws requiring parents be notified when minor daughters seek abortions so long as prompt, confidential access to court review is available if consent is withheld.

But Minnesota's law goes further. In the best of circumstances, young women who become pregnant unintentionally are under terrible stress; the Minnesota notification law places those who come from broken homes under even greater stress.

Rather than bringing families closer, it could induce young women to cross state lines, to lie about their age or, if they decide to bear the child, to risk sealing off opportunities to complete their education and become productive citizens.

Those who would withhold reproductive freedom from women have gained an edge in the Reagan years; six of the seven judges in this case were appointed by President Reagan. But when the fruits of their labor are weighed against the despair it visits on pregnant, disadvantaged minors, their victory seems bitter indeed.

Post-Tribune
Gary, Indiana, August 14, 1988

A recent spate of court decisions — one in a federal appeals court that upheld a Minnesota law requiring parents of pregnant teen-agers to be notified of pending abortions — has focused renewed attention on a woman's right to an abortion.

In addition to the Minnesota ruling, recent father's rights cases have been orchestrated throughout the country by anti-abortion groups seeking ways to increase the emotional din that surrounds abortion. In Indiana on three occasions, fathers attempted to go to court to bar the mothers from having abortions. Fortunately, the courts have consistently ruled for the woman.

The Minnesota federal court decision upheld a state law that is similar to Indiana's. Both laws attempt to undercut court rulings that give the right to decide to the mother of the child, regardless of age.

In Indiana only one parent has to be notified; in Minnesota, both need to be. Both laws allow the courts to waive the notification requirement under extenuating circumstances. On the surface, notification laws seem reasonable, as long as there is a legal out for unusual cases. Whether they work is another question.

Reputable local family planning counselors, who have tried it, have found that it doesn't work well. It takes too long and is often too traumatic an experience for the teen-ager. Rather than go to court they tend to refer those girls to states without such a law.

Ideally any person having a sexual relationship and not wanting to become pregnant would use a contraceptive. But this country has failed miserably in developing safe contraceptives and in effectively promoting their use. Many of those who disapprove of abortion also disapprove of the distribution of birth control devices, particularly to teen-agers.

The country also has failed to educate society about the normality of human sexuality and to develop healthy attitudes about sex.

If that were accomplished, it would drastically cut not only abortion rates, but also reduce divorce, murder, suicide and mental illness.

Women suffer the brunt of this failure.

The bottom line is that the decision to have an abortion must be made by the woman who is pregnant. No one can make the decision for her. No one should have the power to force her to have the baby or to abort it.

DAILY NEWS
New York City, New York, August 15, 1988

ONE OF THE WORST DREAMS of the pro-choice movement has come true. The U.S. Eighth Circuit Court of Appeals, voting 7 to 3, upheld the constitutionality of a Minnesota law that requires women under the age of 18 to notify their parents before getting an abortion.

What makes this case so important is that the next stop, if the plaintiffs appeal, is the U.S. Supreme Court, which split 4 to 4 last year in a similar case.

Since that case was heard, Anthony Kennedy has joined the court. He has yet to vote in an abortion-related case. Nobody knows what he thinks. But it's no secret that four of his brethren want to take a fresh look at the question of the legality of abortion.

The greatest fear of the pro-choicers is that the Supreme Court might reconsider Roe v. Wade, the 1973 case that struck down anti-abortion laws throughout the country. Their fear is reasonable.

Opinion is passionately divided—and will remain so—on whether abortion ought to be legal. But there is a growing feeling among legal scholars, both liberal and conservative, that Roe v. Wade, considered solely as an exercise in constitutional law, doesn't add up.

Justice Harry Blackmun's decision stated flatly that fetuses do not become "viable" until the third trimester of pregnancy—a view that has become hopelessly outdated since 1973 by advances in neonatal care.

For this and other reasons, many legal scholars now feel that Roe v. Wade ought to be reconsidered. One of those scholars was Robert Bork. His position on Roe was one of the reasons why the Senate voted down his Supreme Court nomination. The fact that Anthony Kennedy has expressed no views on Roe is one of the reasons why his nomination got through.

Four other justices—Rehnquist, Scalia, White and O'Connor—have voted in various cases to carve away at or abandon altogether judicial protection of the right to have an abortion. For the last few years, those cases have been coming out 5-4 in favor of abortion rights. With the retirement of Lewis Powell from the court, the balance shifted.

THE AMERICAN CIVIL LIBERTIES UNION took the State of Minnesota to court over its parental notification law and lost on appeal. If the Supreme Court upholds the Minnesota law, it will create the most significant legal precedent for restricting abortion rights since Roe.

That's why the ACLU may not appeal the circuit court decision. Says ACLU lawyer Rachael Pine: "On the one hand, we have a very powerful case here. On the other hand, we're a little worried about the current Supreme Court."

But if the ACLU decides not to appeal, it will be doing a disservice to everyone who is concerned about the question of legalized abortion—pro-choice or pro-life.

Roe v. Wade and the subsequent decisions that flowed from it polarized the American people. The controversy continues to rage. That's why it's essential that the U.S. Supreme Court be given an opportunity to review the Minnesota law. If it isn't this case, it'll be another one. There's no reason to delay on a question of such vital importance.

Richmond Times-Dispatch
Richmond, Virginia, August 11, 1988

Half the states have laws requiring that minors notify or secure consent from at least one parent before having an abortion. Virginia doesn't. In several recent General Assembly sessions, the Senate has been the final resting place for House-passed notification or consent bills. Opponents have bought the argument of the American Civil Liberties Union and other "abortion-rights" groups that such legislation would be "unconstitutional."

Actually, the federal judiciary's opinion as to the constitutionality of laws giving parents at least limited rights in their underage, unmarried daughter's decision about having an abortion is a big question mark. Last December, a 4-to-4 Supreme Court deadlock had the effect of upholding an appellate court decision invalidating portions of an Illinois notification law. A tie sets no precedent, however; and the legal pendulum shifted back in the other direction Monday when the 8th Circuit Court of Appeals in St. Paul upheld, by a 7-to-3 margin, a similar Minnesota statute.

What this apparently means, then, is that the newest Supreme Court justice, Anthony M. Kennedy, in effect could decide the constitutionality of parental notice laws should the high court be as it is currently constituted when the next case, whether from Minnesota or some other jurisdiction, reaches it on appeal. As for Virginia, advocates of parental rights should be encouraged in the interim to try yet again when the General Assembly convenes in January.

Ultimately, however, the American electorate may settle the issue Nov. 8, for the next president may have an opportunity to nominate at least one or two new justices before the Supreme Court next reviews this issue. President Reagan's appointment of relatively conservative jurists has played a crucial role in advancing parental rights this far. Six of the seven jurists voting to uphold the Minnesota statute were Reagan appointees. Vice President George Bush can be expected to continue the conservative trend on the federal bench. Massachusetts Gov. Michael Dukakis, an ACLU member and abortion-rights advocate, cannot.

The Atlanta Journal
THE ATLANTA CONSTITUTION
Atlanta, Georgia, June 6, 1988

Happily, Georgia is finding it no simple matter to limit or curtail abortions. For the second year in a row, it faces a legal challenge that could keep a possibly unconstitutional "parental notification" law from taking effect indefinitely.

However, this is only a temporary setback in the state's attempt to impose unnecessary delays of up to three weeks on teens seeking abortions.

The legislators, the lawyers and the women involved deserve something more conclusive from the U.S. District Court this time: an outright condemnation of the ongoing effort to discourage abortions.

It has been more than a year since a federal judge declared a 1987 law, which would have required a parent or other adult to accompany the girl to an abortion facility, unconstitutional. But his ruling left so many issues unresolved it is still under appeal, contributing to confusion about the validity of the 1988 law.

In its zeal to pass an anti-abortion measure in 1988, the Legislature once again failed to take critical questions about waiting periods, confidentiality and judicial bypass procedures (found unconstitutional elsewhere) into account.

The new law, scheduled to go into effect July 1, dropped the "adult attendant" provision but would impose 24-hour waiting periods on all girls under 18 and force those lacking parental permission into a cumbersome Juvenile Court procedure that could take up to three weeks — long enough to throw them into the next trimester and turn a safe, legal procedure into a risky one. In 1983, a federal appeals court in Illinois declared even a 24-hour waiting period to be an impermissible infringement on the right to abortion established in 1973 by the Supreme Court. Planned Parenthood had no choice but to file a second suit.

It is not enough to delay the imposition of one law after another that flies in the face of the Supreme Court. The questions raised by the lawsuits have got to be answered once and for all.

The Kansas City Times
Kansas City, Missouri, August 10, 1988

The makeup of the U.S. Supreme Court, particularly since the addition of Justice Anthony M. Kennedy in February, has been cause for concern among Americans who believe in abortion rights.

The latest evidence is a federal appeals court's decision which upheld a restrictive law regarding the ability of minors to get abortions. The court said the Minnesota law is constitutional in its requirements that teenagers under 18 years old must obtain consent from both parents for an abortion or get special judicial approval.

The Supreme Court has upheld other parental notification laws in the past, including Missouri's, while requiring that there must be an alternative procedure available, such as a judge's consent. This is the first case where the challenge has been to a law already in effect.

State laws can throw up unnecessary restrictions to the right to obtain an abortion, and parental consent laws are the perfect opportunity for that to happen. That is why it is imperative that the Supreme Court not uphold laws with undue restrictions to the constitutional rights outlined in the court's historic Roe vs. Wade decision.

The current make-up of the court presents a dilemma in this case and others. If the American Civil Liberties Union appeals the lower court ruling, it runs the risk of receiving an adverse ruling which would further erode abortion rights for minors. Justice Kennedy never has ruled on an abortion case, but his conservative views lend credence to the theory that he might provide the vote which would put the court on the road to overturning Roe vs. Wade. The court also could use this appeal as an occasion to look at other aspects of Roe vs. Wade.

This dilemma would not have occurred, of course, had President Reagan not put on the court justices who are inclined to limit abortion rights. The fears of many that this president's legacy will be the outlawing of abortion may be closer to fulfillment than ever before.

Newsday
New York City, New York, August 10, 1988

A federal appeals court has upheld a Minnesota law that puts onerous restrictions on the rights of girls under 18 to have abortions. It will also have the unfortunate effect of making the procedure riskier by delaying it.

Girls wishing to terminate their pregnancies in Minnesota won't just have to tell one but *both* of their parents even if they haven't had any contact with them in years. You can imagine the conversation:

"Hi, Dad, this is Sue... Yes, I know you haven't seen me since I was a baby, but I'm pretty grown up now... In fact, I'm calling to tell you I'm pregnant and about to have an abortion... Well, nice chatting with you, too."

If a girl can't track down an absent parent, she has to get special approval from a court. Then she must wait at least 48 hours before actually having the operation. By the time all these requirements are met, it may be too late to perform a simple first-trimester procedure.

The 7-3 ruling by the full Eighth Circuit Court of Appeals reversed an earlier one by a three-member panel and a district court order barring the state from enforcing the law. Six of the seven judges in the majority were appointed by President Ronald Reagan, evidence of the strong conservative imprint he is leaving on all levels of the federal bench.

The American Civil Liberties Union, which brought the suit, is debating whether to appeal to the Supreme Court, which split 4-4 on a similar case. The views of the newest justice, Anthony Kennedy, are unknown.

It seems to us that the case should be appealed despite the risk that this misguided ruling might be upheld. About half the states have already enacted laws requiring parental notification in some form. And the ruling is binding on those of the seven midwestern states in the circuit that require parental notification or might do so in the future.

Because the Minnesota requirements are so extreme and the health and emotional effects on young girls potentially so severe, the Supreme Court may have real difficulties sanctioning them. So the Minnesota law might provide as good a test case as any.

Supreme Court Hears Missouri Abortion Case

The Supreme Court April 26, 1989 heard oral arguments in the case of a Missouri law restricting abortion.

The Bush administration had joined with Missouri officials in urging the court to use the case as an opportunity to overturn the 1973 *Roe v. Wade* decision that recognized a woman's legal right to an abortion.

During the hour-long arguments, Missouri Attorney General William L. Webster tried to persuade the justices that much of the state law was not unconstitutional and that a controversial provision declaring that life began at conception was "an abstract, philosophical statement" that did not need to be overturned because it "doesn't affect anyone."

Former U.S. Solicitor General Charles Fried also argued on behalf of the Missouri law. He insisted that the court could overturn *Roe v. Wade* without engineering other constitutional protections of privacy. "We are not asking the court to unravel the fabric of unenumerated and privacy rights which this court has woven in [previous] cases," Fried said. "Rather, we are asking the court to pull this one thread."

Attorney Frank Susman, arguing on behalf of abortion rights, took issue with Fried's metaphor. "It has always been my personal experience that when I pull a thread, my sleeve falls off," he declared.

He noted that the Missouri law made some forms of birth control illegal, because the intrauterine device acted to prevent implantation of a fertilized egg in a woman's uterus.

Susman argued that abortion was a moral decision that should be made by a woman in consultation with her doctor.

The Missouri case had drawn intense public scrutiny and had attracted a record 78 friend-of-the-court briefs, submitted by organizations on both sides of the issue, as well as doctors, scientists, public officials and historians.

The Chattanooga Times
Chattanooga, Tennessee, May 4, 1989

It will be at least a month, probably longer, before the Supreme Court renders a decision in the case of Webster vs. Reproductive Health Services after hearing arguments last week. The case is important, both for those who oppose abortion and those who favor the right of choice, because it is widely viewed as the vehicle by which the court could overturn, or at least severely restrict Roe vs. Wade, the landmark 1973 decision that set out a woman's constitutional right to obtain an abortion, except under limited circumstances.

However, a reading of the arguments presented to the justices and their questions in response suggests that it is not a foregone conclusion that the court will overturn Roe. The justices seemed more concerned about the constitutional issues at stake than ideological ones. More to the point, one key factor in this issue is privacy, and even the more conservative justices evinced no desire to restrict it drastically.

The dilemma was framed clearly in an exchange in which it became clear that the opponents of Roe wanted it both ways: a restriction of the right to privacy in deciding whether to have an abortion, but no restriction on the same right in other personal decisions.

Both lawyers arguing for the Missouri law, for example, agreed that the state should not prohibit couples from obtaining contraceptives for the simple reason that the decision whether or not to have a child is a private one that should be made only by the man and woman. Yet although that right is guaranteed by a 1960s Supreme Court decision, justices reasonably asked, if the right to privacy were removed in abortion decisions, could not a similar right to privacy be ultimately disallowed for other issues equally as personal?

Former Solicitor General Charles Fried tried to minimize the threat to privacy should the court effectively overturn Roe. The government, he said, was "not asking the court to unravel the fabric of unenumerated and privacy rights"; rather, it was "asking the court to pull this one thread."

But as Justices Sandra Day O'Connor and Anthony Kennedy made clear in their questioning, curtailing the right to privacy in one area raises the possibility that the government could some day curtail another type of privacy. Justice O'Connor wondered, for example, whether the government could some day order women to have abortions if the country faced a disastrous overpopulation problem. While improbable, it is the flip side of an argument that says the government has the right to tell women what they may not do in this area.

There is no denying that Americans are profoundly ambivalent over the issue of abortion, as a recent *New York Times*-CBS News poll showed. One reason for that seems to us a reflection of the terms of the arguments frequently invoked. Abortion opponents often describe as "pro-abortion" those who favor allowing the woman to decide whether or not to undergo the procedure. In fact, many who favor the right of choice also oppose abortion on moral and health-related grounds. Pro-choice advocates are not entirely blameless for the confusion surrounding the issue. Many have made the issue a definition of feminism, thus offending those who take a more moderate position.

It's always foolish to predict how the court will rule on any issue, much less one as controversial as Webster. One thing that's clear, however, is that a citizen's right to privacy emerged as the key issue during the arguments, and is thus likely to be the point on which the court's decision turns.

The Honolulu Advertiser
Honolulu, Hawaii, May 1, 1989

Oral arguments on abortion before the Supreme Court have come and gone. A ruling is expected in late June or July.

Predictions are risky, but there are three possibilities:

The court could reaffirm Roe vs. Wade, leaving abortion decisions largely up to individual women, at least through the first two-thirds of pregnancy. It could narrow the scope of that ruling by upholding parts of a contested Missouri law before it, giving the states more power to restrict abortion. Or, it could throw Roe vs. Wade out entirely, leaving the legality of abortion up to each state.

Hearing the justices' questions last Wednesday, some court watchers believe at least the three newest Reagan-appointed justices are ready for a broad review of abortion rights.

Other observers doubt the closely divided court will overturn Roe vs. Wade, but will whittle away at it slowly for now.

While millions of women would be affected by more restrictions on abortion after nearly a generation of the right to choose, the greatest impact would certainly be on poor women, unmarried women (many of them teenagers) and minority women — and, of course, on the millions of children these women would bring into the world.

Some believe technological advances in saving premature infants have set Roe vs. Wade "on a collision course with itself," in the words of Justice Sandra Day O'Connor. But over 99 percent of abortions are still performed before the 20th week of pregnancy.

According to a court brief from 167 scientists (including a dozen Nobel laureates), "The earliest point of (fetal) viability has remained virtually unchanged at approximately 24 weeks of gestation since 1973, and there is no reason to believe that a change is either imminent or inevitable."

Also unchanged are the many deeply personal reasons women find themselves forced to seek abortions. Nor will those disappear, no matter what the court decides.

DAYTON DAILY NEWS
Dayton, Ohio, May 21, 1989

The abortion issue is particularly distressing and intractable. Abortion's widespread use — for reasons other than to terminate a pregnancy for extraordinary reasons such as rape or incest — is too often a symptom of moral and sexual carelessness. That is not true in the case, say, of an older woman who gets pregnant when her contraceptive fails, but it is often the case among the sexually promiscuous.

Abortion is a drastic procedure that, if regarded too casually, diminishes sensitivity to life. The pro-life people are right about that.

The abortion dilemma is complicated by the fact that the emerging life is within the body of the mother. Government control over a woman's body has to be limited. The pro-choice people are right about that.

The official middle ground has to be on the side of the right of a mother to choose what to do with her body in the earliest stages of pregnancy.

Society should also use non-coercive means to prevent the unwanted pregnancies that give rise to abortion.

The basic case against legalized abortion holds that the fetus is a human life and that, therefore, abortion is murder. Acceptance of this notion is largely a matter of instinct and of the teachings of some religions. There appears to be no way to reconcile different views on what degree of humanity an embryo or fetus represents, at least not if the issue is giving it citizenship rights that would prevail against the rights of the mother.

That being the case, the proper role for the government in a philosophically and religiously diverse society that claims to be devoted to individual rights and limited government — especially in private matters — is to stay out of abortion decisions involving the earliest stages of pregnancy.

The best in American tradition calls for:

(1) Allowing the people who are against abortion to practice their values, and allowing others to practice theirs;

(2) Denying public funding for abortions, out of concern for the people who are aggrieved by the thought of their tax money going for that purpose. There are other ways to fund abortion, anyway.

(3) Slanting public efforts to help people find alternatives to abortion. That includes offering teen-agers the guidance, example, education and value-guided channels for growth that might do more to encourage abstinence and responsibility than does preaching. It includes encouraging the sexually active to use birth control. It includes the promotion of adoption, especially of children that families are reluctant to take.

A woman should have control of her own body, but the widespread use of abortion is a serious matter and an appropriate social concern. Abortion is not an acceptable primary form of birth control.

Even some pro-choice advocates find problems with Roe vs. Wade, the U.S. Supreme Court decision that is now the law of the land on abortion.

Fundamentally the decision was correct: Abortion should be legal, because it is a private matter, and the Constitution implicitly recognizes the right to privacy. The rights to free press, religion, and expression make no sense if there isn't also a right to privacy. It's a more basic right.

What's wrong with Roe vs. Wade is primarily that it reads much like legislation. It says that in the first third (or trimester) of pregnancy, a state may not refuse a woman the right to an abortion, but that the state has more rights in the second trimester and still more in the third.

This scheme was based on some technical information about when a fetus becomes "viable" outside the womb. But viability is a dubious standard. Suppose someday science figures out how to sustain and bring to term an embryo outside the womb? Would the woman be forced to carry it to term?

Despite its flaws, however, Roe should not be overturned. Inconsistency on the court is a fairly serious matter. It tends to undermine the legitimacy of court decisions. Moreover, for the court to undo or loosen up on Roe now would cause turmoil across the country. Any court should be given pause by that prospect. Periodic judicial reshaping of the country's practices is difficult to square with the concept of judicial restraint, a concept espoused by some of the anti-abortion members of the court.

Whatever happens to Roe now, instability seems to be in the cards for the American abortion situation, because of the possibility of technological change. Already a pill exists to terminate pregnancy in its earliest stages. It's difficult to imagine that pill remaining inaccessible to American women indefinitely.

For the courts to foster a redefinition of the abortion situation even as another re-definition — fostered by technology — looms would be dubious.

If the court completely or partially undoes Roe now, the battle would go back to the 50 states. Some states would go one way, some another. People who want abortions would go where they have to, so long as they could find the money and opportunity to travel. In the end, the total number of abortions might not be reduced significantly. All that's certain is that there will be much political fighting.

Roe, whatever its flaws, at least has the merit of being a national standard.

AKRON BEACON JOURNAL
Akron, Ohio, April 30, 1989

IT IS NOT likely that many minds were changed on the abortion issue last week, either by the boisterous demonstrators on both sides of the issue outside the U.S. Supreme Court building in Washington, or by the orderly deliberations inside court chambers. But public opinion wasn't the issue. The issue is whether the court, which was moved to the right by Ronald Reagan's appointments, is ready to overturn or dilute the landmark 1973 Roe vs. Wade ruling.

The vehicle is a Missouri law, already struck down by lower courts but appealed to the high court by the state and the Bush administration. That 1986 law says that life begins at conception, and it bans public health professionals, including doctors, from performing or suggesting abortions.

The case involves several crucial issues. One is state control. Roe vs. Wade legalized abortion and, in effect, removed regulation from the states. If overturned, abortions still would occur, legally or illegally. The controversy simply would go from the national level to the states. Some states would outlaw or restrict abortion; others would not. In such cases, the denial of choice would most affect poor women.

A second issue is the constitutional right to privacy, a basis of Roe vs. Wade. Court questioning Wednesday focused on whether limiting abortions would undercut the whole question of privacy. Even Justice Antonin Scalia, who has criticized Roe vs. Wade, had to admit pro-choice attorney Frank Susman had a "very good point" in saying the Missouri law's contention that life begins at conception also jeopardizes modern methods of birth control. There is a real fear that the decision in this case also could affect the right to privacy in other aspects of American life.

This leads into the crux of the whole abortion controversy: When does human life begin? And if religious, legal and medical experts can't agree on an answer, should the government inject itself into this highly personal decision? Roe vs. Wade says no, and we agree.

No one can say how the Supreme Court will rule, probably this summer, on the Missouri case. Yet no matter what the decision — to preserve Roe vs. Wade, to limit its influence, or to overturn it entirely — the argument won't go away.

St. Louis Review

St. Louis, Missouri, April 28, 1989

In its current session, the U.S. Supreme Court will have the opportunity to review the fundamental principles behind its 1973 ruling in Roe vs. Wade that legalized abortion in the United States. The occasion for the review was given by pro-abortionists who challenged the constitutionality of a 1986 Missouri law which stipulated that the life of each human being begins at conception and laid a foundation for the protection of certain of the rights of the unborn. The Missouri law also denied the use of public funds to perform abortions.

In a series this week, the St. Louis

Post-Dispatch has provided more dispassionate information about the background to the 1973 decision than we have seen in the media over the past 16 years.

It is just this kind of information that the public at large across the country has needed to provide a basis for a meaningful discussion of the issues at stake in this national crisis. As with other decisions of the Supreme Court, the public has been deprived, by and large, of an in-depth discussion of the real issues involved, in this case not the right of the mother to decide but rather the right of the unborn fetus to

live.

Thorough reporting of the Roe vs. Wade decision reveals the serious legal misgivings of its author and the highly questionable legal foundation on which it stands.

The pro-life movement was completely accurate from the beginning in emphasizing the need for education of the public if the decision was ever to be successfully challenged. Whatever the outcome of the Missouri case now before the court, it has been a major milestone in persuading the court and the country to re-examine the entire abortion issue.

Newsday

New York City, New York, April 30, 1989

If the Supreme Court reverses Roe vs. Wade, abortion will still be legal in New York State — at least for a while. But how long it stays that way will depend on the action and activism of the pro- and the anti- forces.

So if the high court decides in the Missouri case it heard this week to send abortion back to the states, New York's pro-choice advocates had better dust off their bumper stickers and crank up their fax machines. This will be a fight to the finish. If abortion is to be kept safe and legal here, pro-choice forces must win.

The United States will probably become a crazy quilt of conflicting abortion laws if the 1973 Roe decision is reversed. A handful of states have already enacted "trigger" laws

that will automatically forbid abortions if Roe is scrapped. At the other extreme, New York is among about 20 states with liberal "abortion on demand" laws that will continue to operate. As it was before Roe, New York will probably become a magnet to women needing abortions who hail from more restrictive states. (Between them, New York and California already account for about one-third of the abortions performed nationwide.)

Since New York already has its own permissive abortion law, why worry? Because the anti-abortion forces have proved themselves, in the 16 years of Roe, to be zealous, untiring and well-organized. They have a majority in the State Senate. And any relaxation of Roe

by the Supreme Court will fire their determination to drive abortions back underground.

After Wednesday's oral arguments, which dwelled upon legalisms rather than sweeping change, experts are predicting that the Supreme Court may chip away at — rather than reverse — the Roe decision when it rules near the end of June. Even if that happens, states will become battlefields, as legislatures move to embrace the court's new constrictions.

As long as Roe was the law of the land, people who support the right to safe and legal abortions could afford to be complacent. Now that it may be revised, perhaps even reversed, New York's pro-choice forces have no choice but to prepare for battle.

The San Diego
Union-Tribune.
San Diego, California, May 7, 1989

More than 15 years after the Supreme Court legalized abortion as a woman's constitutional right of privacy, Americans are still ensnared in an emotion-rending national debate: Is the human fetus a life which deserves protection by the state, or should the interests of the unborn be subordinated to the free choice of the mother?

Roe v. Wade, the 1973 decision that continues to send seismic shocks through American life, cleaved a wide swath through longstanding legal, societal, and moral standards. The court's current review, in *Webster v. Reproductive Health Services*, attests to the unresolved dimensions of abortion a decade and a half after it became commonplace in every state.

Basically, the *Roe* ruling forbids states to prohibit abortions during the first 24 weeks of pregnancy. The justices allowed legislatures to restrict abortions during the last 12 weeks, on the premise that, at this advanced stage, the fetus is "potential life" which the states have a legitimate right to safeguard.

The seeming arbitrariness of this distinction, the fine line on different sides of which abortion becomes either a constitutional right or a crime, presents a moral dilemma that is impossible to untangle in the minds of most Americans. Scientists, theologians, philosophers, and lawyers have all failed, certainly, to agree on when human life begins.

At the same time, though, millions who believe abortion is morally wrong also oppose a flat ban. Opinion surveys demonstrate that, for a majority of Americans, the circumstances prompting an abortion are crucial determinants in whether it should be permissible. This ambivalence illustrates the lack of national consensus amid the fervent, polarizing battle between pro-life and pro-choice forces in the streets, courtrooms, and legislative corridors.

The latest polling data, compiled by The New York Times/CBS News, show that solid majorities of Americans back legalized abortion in cases where the mother's health is threatened (87 percent) or where the baby is expected to suffer serious birth defects (69 percent).

But support declines drastically when abortion becomes a backstop for unintended pregnancies. Only 26 percent of Americans approve of abortion in cases where the child would interfere with the woman's career or education — the classic choice so ardently defended by women's-rights groups. Even many doctors object to abortions simply because the baby is not of the preferred sex.

In spite of these lingering reservations, it is indisputable that abortion has become embedded in American society. Some 1.6 million abortions are performed each year; thus, 30 percent of all pregnancies in this country are voluntarily terminated. This places the United States near the top of industrialized nations in the percentage of aborted pregnancies. In Canada, the figure is 14 percent. In the Soviet Union, where contraceptive technology is often ineffective and not widely available, the rate soars to 68 percent of pregnancies.

The Supreme Court, having usurped with *Roe v. Wade* the legislatures' historical responsibility to sort out complicated social, legal, and moral problems, now must grapple with the abortion issue on constitutional grounds again. Does the 14th Amendment right of privacy bar legislators from declaring, as in the case of the Missouri law in question, that life begins at conception?

Regardless of what the justices rule, legalized abortion will not be swept away overnight, if ever. Even if the court overturns the 1973 decision, the roiling national debate would merely shift back to the legislatures, where it should always have been. Then lawmakers would be required to search for a Solomonic solution that balances the rights of women against the rights of the unborn. Under any circumstances, the agonizing impasse engendered by *Roe v. Wade* will endure for years, possibly decades, to come.

THE SPOKESMAN-REVIEW
Spokane, Washington, April 23, 1989

In the 16 years since the landmark U.S. Supreme Court decision legalizing abortion — a decision the court will be reconsidering this week — everything has changed, and yet, nothing has changed.

Long before 1973, there were abortions in America. If a woman had the money, getting an abortion meant a trip to another country where the procedure was legal; if she didn't, it meant cash first and no questions asked of a nameless abortionist in a boarded-up building. The Roe vs. Wade decision changed that, allowing women who opt for abortion the use of clean, sanitary hospitals and their attendant medical care.

The historic, controversial 7-2 court ruling, which was based on the 14th Amendment right to life and liberty, sought a balance between a woman's right of choice and the state's duty to protect human life. It left the decision about an abortion up to a woman and her doctor during the first three months of pregnancy; it allowed the state to apply medical regulations between the third and seventh months and to forbid the procedure after the 26th or 27th week of pregnancy unless an abortion was essential to save the mother's life or health.

The justices buttressed their decision with experts' knowledge of "the point of viability" — 24 to 28 weeks — when an infant could exist independently outside its mother's body. Later advances in medical technology have resulted in a higher percentage of babies being saved who are born more than eight weeks prematurely. But a brief filed by 167 scientists and doctors, including 11 Nobel Prize winners, says medical science continues to be unable to save younger preemies.

In fact, most of the 1.6 million abortions performed in the United States each year are done well before the date of viability — 90 percent during the first trimester and less than 1 percent after 21 weeks.

Just as medical technology has changed since 1973, so has the makeup of the Supreme Court. The nine sitting justices apparently fall into two equal opposing camps, with one swing vote, Justice Sandra Day O'Connor.

This polarization reflects the continuing and perhaps increased polarization of the American public on the abortion issue. Both sides have taken a more visible stance in lobbying and staging protest marches and also have bombarded the court with letters as the time has neared for arguments to be heard Wednesday in a case involving Missouri abortion law.

Whether the court ultimately upholds, overturns or modifies Roe vs. Wade will be a moot point in a few states such as Washington, whose law legalizing abortion predates that court decision. Back in 1970, Washington voters gave strong approval to Referendum 20, allowing abortion during the first 16 weeks of pregnancy in a hospital or clinic when performed by a licensed doctor. However, women in the many states without such laws will contend with an inequity if Roe vs. Wade is overturned. Those who can afford it would have to travel to states where abortion is legal; others, once again, would resort to illegal abortionists with the attendant risks of infection, sterilization or death.

No matter what the court decides, individuals' minds probably will not change appreciably on this divisive issue. The most productive course would be to refocus the debate, asking the question: What are stalwarts on both sides doing to lessen the likelihood that a woman will choose abortion? Reproductive freedom must be linked with reproductive responsibility, but, ironically, some of the same forces who rail bitterly against abortion are just as adamantly opposed to sex education in the schools.

And if abortion is no longer legal in most states, who will care for all the unwanted children? Raising that question doesn't justify abortion in the name of expediency, but failure to consider it is unrealistic and irresponsible. Reducing the demand for abortion means finding ways to help women cope with the choice to keep a child or to offer it for adoption.

Everyone can — and must — deplore abortion. Many of those strongly supportive of a woman's right to make that choice feel personally uncomfortable with abortion itself. Still, it is an intensely private decision that a woman must wrestle with and make her own peace with, as 1.6 million women in this country do each year.

Rather than accuse and harass, we ought to be asking ourselves what we are doing to reduce the necessity to make that choice.

Supreme Court Upholds Missouri Abortion Restrictions

The Supreme Court, in a bitterly divided 5–4 decision, July 3, 1989 upheld a restrictive Missouri abortion law and set the stage for the dismantling of *Roe v. Wade*, the 1973 decision recognizing a constitutional right to abortion.

The current ruling, *Webster v. Reproductive Health Services*, stopped short of overturning *Roe v. Wade*. Chief Justice William H. Rehnquist said in the majority opinion that the case presented "no occasion to revisit the holding in *Roe*," but, he said, "to the extent indicated in our opinion, we would modify and narrow *Roe* and succeeding cases."

The court, acting on its final day of the current term, accepted three new abortion cases for its next term in the fall. One of them, *Turnock v. Ragsdale*, concerned strict standards for facilities and equipment available at outpatient abortion clinics. Two others, *Ohio v. Akron Center for Reproductive Health* and *Hodgson v. Minnesota*, involved state laws requiring parental notification prior to abortions for minors.

Justice Harry A. Blackmun, the author of *Roe v. Wade*, warned in a dissent in the *Webster* case that "I fear for the future...The signs are evident and very ominous, and a chill blows."

The latest decision was seen as a critical victory for anti-abortion forces. While restricted in application to Missouri, movement was immediately made for matching the court-approved restrictions in other states.

The Missouri law upheld by the court prohibited public employees from performing abortions unless the mother's life was in danger, barred use of public buildings for performing abortions and required doctors, before performing abortions after 20 weeks, to perform tests to determine whether the fetus could live outside the womb.

Rehnquist said that "the rigid trimester analysis" employed in *Roe v. Wade* made "constitutional law in this area a virtual Procrustean bed."

The 1973 ruling held that no restrictions on abortions could be imposed by the state in the first three months of pregnancy, but that regulations in the interests of the mother's health could be set at the start of the third trimester, when the fetus was deemed to have attained viability.

Rehnquist said "the key elements of the *Roe* framework – trimesters and viability – are not found in the text of the Constitution, or in any place else one would expect to find a constitutional principle."

Blackmun, in a sorrowful reading of his dissent, acknowledged that "the plurality repudiates every principle for which *Roe* stands."

"Thus," he said, "'not with a bang, but a whimper', the plurality discards a landmark case of the last generation and casts into darkness the hopes and visions of every woman in this country who had come to believe that the Constitution guaranteed her the right to exercise some control over her unique ability to bear children."

Stevens, in his separate dissent, said the court could have declared the preamble to Missouri's law unconstitutional because it declared that human life began at conception. Stevens said this reflected a religious view and violated the First Amendment's prohibition against establishment of religion.

Leaders of anti-abortion groups hailed the court's ruling as a victory. "This is what we were hoping for," John Wilke, president of the National Right to Life Commission, said July 3. He called the ruling "the first step to eliminating *Roe v. Wade*."

Randall Terry, head of Operation Rescue, an anti-abortion group, predicted an "avalanche of new legislation" by states on the issue.

Abortion rights advocates were dismayed. "There is no longer a majority on the court to support *Roe*," said Janet Benshoof, director of the American Civil Liberties Union's reproductive freedom project. "Now it's just a battle over details."

Judith Lichtman, director of the Women's Legal Defense Fund, viewed *Roe v. Wade* as "well on the way to unraveling."

Molly Yard, president of the National Organization for Women, called the decision "a total disaster." Essentially, she said, "They have begun to dismantle *Roe v. Wade*."

Minneapolis Star and Tribune
Minneapolis, Minnesota, July 12, 1989

Though still digesting the words of last week's Supreme Court ruling on Missouri's abortion statute, some Minnesota legislators are already hungry to duplicate the law. But if lawmakers truly want to serve the citizenry, they will curb their appetites. Once hearings are held and facts become clear, tightening the state's abortion regulations is likely to look less delicious.

Even longtime abortion foe Gov. Rudy Perpich is wisely wary of a change. Speaking to reporters last week, he expressed reservations about mimicking the part of Missouri's law that bars state-funded facilities from offering abortion services. "I have some real concerns that we don't end up being a two-class society," said Perpich, "like you have in South America."

That prospect does not seem to vex state Rep. Steve Wenzel, DFL-Little Falls. Anxious to translate the court's ruling into law, Wenzel is developing legislation to ban abortions at all "public or taxpayer-supported hospitals." He also wants to forbid public employees from recommending abortion as a solution to unwanted pregnancy — a policy the high court did not specifically approve. Though the import of these changes depends on just which facilities and employees the Legislature considers "public," the outlook for indigent women is grim. Minnesota already bars use of Medicaid funds for abortions; prohibiting even the mention of abortion in the public-health agencies they frequent could deter poor women from securing the services they need.

That, of course, is Wenzel's objective: to hinder as many women as possible from opting for abortion. In that quest, his proposal to require doctors to perform viability tests on any fetus more than 20 weeks old is bound to be helpful. Experts note that fetuses born before 23 weeks have virtually no chance of survival; the odds increase to one in 10 at 24 weeks. Doctors can readily determine a fetus's age by measuring its size, but tests of lung maturity — the marker of viability — are generally useless until after 28 weeks. Wenzel's plan thus would raise abortion costs by requiring pointless tests on fetuses certain to be nonviable.

Just because the Supreme Court has served up permission for new abortion restraints is no reason for Minnesota to gulp them down. As long as abortion is a constitutional right, it should remain available to women of all incomes. Blocking its exercise with discriminatory and irrational rules would serve no admirable end.

The Houston Post

Houston, Texas, July 12, 1989

THE SUPREME COURT of the United States on Monday traded one battle for 50, in effect telling the states they are free to impose restrictions on abortion that have been banned since the court's landmark 1973 *Roe vs. Wade* decision.

The ruling — another of the close votes that are becoming the hallmark of this court under Chief Justice William Rehnquist — turns on fine points of the law cited in the Missouri case that the court had before it. That is another commonality of rulings issuing from this court. It seems unwilling to grasp large issues — even to the point of simply overturning its 1973 ruling, which some of the more conservative justices plainly would prefer to do.

That is the court's privilege — and indeed, several of the justices must be torn between their disdain for *Roe* and their dislike of judicial activism. But whatever the case, they certainly have given state-level officials and hopefuls interesting times, not to say outright turmoil. For it is likely that no state's politics will be untouched by abortion politics in the next election cycle.

In fact, here in Texas there exists the outside chance that the matter could be brought up in the current special session of the Legislature.

The Austin rumor mill says it won't happen, but technically nothing stands in the way of it. If not, look for it to be *the* issue of the 1990 governor's and lieutenant governor's races, to say nothing of a host of others farther down the ballot.

For now — except perhaps in Missouri — nothing is changed about the legality of abortion in America. But the tug-of-war in the nation's statehouses between the pro-life and pro-choice forces will be frenetic in the coming months and years. And, back in Washington, look for more sharp adjustments to *Roe* this fall, when the Supreme Court takes up related cases from Ohio, Illinois and Minnesota. One likely outcome is to dismantle the rigid trimester-criteria method of gauging abortion rights, an artifact of the 1973 case.

It is important that people understand that the court has not outlawed abortion. What it did, by and large, was say that the states don't have to be partners to it. Also, importantly, it allowed Missouri to require that doctors test the fetus to determine if it could survive outside the womb. That makes sense.

In Monday's ruling, neither side won big or lost big. But that may change as the fall cases come up.

The Honolulu Advertiser

Honolulu, Hawaii, July 4, 1989

The Great Abortion Rights Battle of the 1990s has now been joined, and no one can clearly predict how it will be resolved.

Given the U.S. Supreme Court's more conservative makeup, yesterday's ruling was as predictable as it was disappointing to those of us who believe it is a woman's right to terminate her pregnancy.

True, this case on a Missouri law leaves intact the high court's landmark 1973 Roe vs. Wade ruling which nationally leaves such decisions up to women. But this was also a change in direction by the court, approving restrictions in Missouri and virtually inviting other states to clamp down as well.

The Supreme Court will hear three more abortion law cases next year. And, while the Missouri ruling did not go to the heart of Roe vs. Wade, it seems only a matter of time before another case does.

Meanwhile, since the 1973 decision clearly no longer has majority support of the Supreme Court, the abortion-rights battle effectively goes to the state legislatures. There it will be fought with strong legal, medical and moral arguments on all sides.

Abortion has been legal in Hawaii since 1970. Polls indicate it still has strong support as a necessary alternative. But that does not mean Hawaii will be immune from our version of the emotional national debate to come.

In fact, some feel such debate on one of the ultimate human rights issues will be healthy for the nation, although its potential to bitterly divide people and detract from other public questions is obvious.

A story in Sunday's paper told how the late Governor Jack Burns, a devout Roman Catholic who abhorred abortion, let the 1970 bill become law because of changing community standards and his feeling our laws should be silent on the subject.

Now, almost two decades later, we still feel Burns was right — and courageous. But there won't be silence on this subject and the debate will be a test of our present community standards.

LAS VEGAS SUN

Las Vegas, Nevada, July 5, 1989

The long-awaited decision of the U.S. Supreme Court on abortion came Monday — fortunately, two days after the Nevada Legislature closed the doors on its longest session in history.

What fortuitous timing! Can you imagine what would have happened had the decision come down while the Legislature was still in session?

Now we can be sure that abortion and its regulation will be a ready-made campaign platform for the 1990 elections and one of the main issues of the 1991 Legislature.

We certainly don't advocate calling a special session to consider the subject. For one thing, the present bunch of lawmakers has shown what damage they can do in the nearly half-year they were in Carson City, but more importantly such action would be premature.

Along with its decision giving states more leeway to regulate abortions, the court also announced it will consider three more abortion cases during its next term, so the matter has not yet been put to rest. Those cases should be decided in plenty of time for Nevada's next legislative session.

It appears that the pro-life activists have gained ground with the high court's split decision in the Missouri case, *Webster vs. Reproductive Health Services.* The pro-choicers lost a battle, but so far not the war. *Roe vs. Wade* was battered considerably, but it was not overturned.

The battleground now moves to the states, for the most part, although there will also probably be congressional activity, and of course arguments on the new abortion cases the Supreme Court has agreed to hear.

There are some who believe the latest ruling by the Supreme Court is another step backward, as they do other recent decisions such as those affecting the flag and civil rights.

And there are those who foresee the abortion

ruling as marshaling the pro-choice advocates, whose voices sometimes have been drowned out by more vocal pro-life groups.

The National Abortion Rights Action League has compiled a list of how the states view the abortion issue. It says the legislatures of 24 states favor making abortion illegal, were it not for the still-standing *Roe vs. Wade.* In only nine states and the District of Columbia do the legislative bodies favor keeping abortion legal.

Twenty-three governors favor making abortion illegal; 16 governors and the mayor of the District of Columbia favor keeping abortion legal; and 11 governors have unknown or unclear positions on abortion rights.

And 35 states have laws restricting the access of minors to abortion, including Nevada, but our law requiring parental notification or district court consent was ruled unconstitutional by a federal judge. It is on appeal before the 9th U.S. Circuit Court of Appeals in San Francisco.

Issues that were decided in the *Webster* case should not impact the state of Nevada, but the question elsewhere of public funding for abortions, or to help educate about having an abortion, will lead to many intense and emotional debates.

Bitter battles over abortion can be expected in every state capital, new legislation will undoubtedly emerge from many legislative halls, and lawsuits can be expected to work their way through the courts.

There is no clear course ahead, and the path is certain to be difficult. But when the smoke has cleared, when the analysts have analyzed the *Webster* decision to death, when tempers have cooled and rationality prevails, maybe then Nevadans will be prepared to legislate the abortion issue according to the will of the majority of its people.

The Oregonian

Portland, Oregon, July 4, 1989

The U.S. Supreme Court's anxiously awaited abortion decision Monday was neither a bang nor a whimper. This was an evolutionary, not a revolutionary, ruling.

Indeed, what may be most surprising is how little this court, increasingly described as conservative, departed from the 1973 court, usually called liberal, in the benchmark Roe vs. Wade decision.

In his opinion for the 1973 Roe vs. Wade majority, Justice Harry A. Blackmun said: "We need not resolve the difficult question of when life begins. When those trained in the respective disciplines of medicine, philosophy and theology are unable to arrive at any consensus, the judiciary, at this point in the development of man's knowledge, is not in a position to speculate as to the answers." However, considerable speculation was evident in the court's delineation of periods of pregnancy.

The high court Monday did not bind the nation to a decision of when life begins. And it did not profoundly alter the earlier court's balance of the mother's right of privacy in abortion decisions during the first trimester and the state's increasing right to regulate that decision in later trimesters as the fetus approaches independent viability.

What the court did do in the case at hand was to tell the medical community to use available technology to search harder into the question of the viability of the fetus from the 20th week. This could advance, by about six weeks, the time when under Roe vs. Wade the states were given authority to take steps to protect fetal life as opposed to regulating abortions only to protect the woman's health.

This is not an about-face. It is a recognition of advances in medical technology and what information is needed so that the state can make informed decisions regarding its regulatory authority.

However, this decision will not be neutral in its effects, for it will be played out in the sovereign decisions of the 50 states on how to implement it. Not all states, like Oregon, fund voluntary abortions for the poor under Medicaid. So, in states that do not do so, the cost of additional testing requirements inevitably will narrow the scope of choice of poor women.

On this issue, The Oregonian continues to believe that the state should provide its full medical support to pregnant women on welfare who decide to have their children, to raise themselves or to offer for adoption. To those who decide to terminate the pregnancy, the state should provide the same medical options available to those who can pay for their treatment themselves.

Richmond Times-Dispatch

Richmond, Virginia, July 5, 1989

Legal scholars will comb for nuances and hints of future direction the five separate opinions — totaling 78 pages — in the landmark abortion decision the U.S. Supreme Court finally released on Independence Day Eve. But this much seemed certain Monday on the basis of first news accounts of Webster vs. Reproductive Health Services:

● While not (yet) reversing the 1973 Roe vs. Wade decision that made access to abortion a woman's constitutionally protected privacy right, the high court majority has returned to states greatly increased power to regulate and restrict abortion. States which choose to follow Missouri's lead now may assert an interest in protecting unborn life.

● State legislatures now become the battlegrounds for determining abortion policy. We'll have more lawmaker-made law, less judge-made law in this area.

● Virginia will be a hotbed of abortion debate, at least initially. That is because Virginia is one of only two states electing a governor this year. In addition, Virginia has had some of the most liberal abortion laws in the nation, a situation that now seems less tenable than ever.

● Justice Anthony M. Kennedy, a Reagan nominee, provided the crucial fifth vote for a series of 5-4 votes modifying Roe. Thus, the pro-abortion liberals who thwarted Judge Robert Bork's nomination with a smear campaign of horrendous proportions were thwarted in one of their chief objectives.

We find these developments, on the whole and in a word, salutary. Roe created a constitutional right where none existed before. It was a bad decision. Further, its practical effect has been to trigger a holocaust of the unborn, as abortion became, in effect, a routine method of birth control rather than a procedure used only in extreme circumstances, such as when the mother's life was imperiled. Webster gives Americans, through their elected representatives, a chance to protect life and to encourage adoption instead of abortion.

Justice Antonin Scalia penned a stinging rebuke of his colleagues for not just going ahead and rescinding Roe. With at least three abortion cases on the high court's docket next year, he may yet get his wish. But Justice Sandra Day O'Connor had a point when she noted that there was no urgent reason to re-examine Roe, practically speaking, because "the court today has accepted the state's [Missouri's] every interpretation of its abortion statute and has upheld, under our existing precedents, every provision of that statute which is properly before us." Thus, Roe was put to rout.

As Virginia lawmakers consider what to do, they ought, at a bare minimum, resolve to enact a measure requiring parental consent before a minor may obtain an abortion. Such legislation has passed the House by wide margins in recent years, only to be bottled up in the Senate. But other, more basic provisions of Missouri law, now given judicial clearance, will deserve a close look. These include: (1) a required gestational age, weight and lung-maturity test when a physician believes that a fetus may have achieved "viability," the ability to live outside the mother's womb; (2) a prohibition on use of public funds or public employees to counsel a woman to choose an abortion; (3) a ban on use of public employees or facilities in performing or assisting abortions.

The Webster decision will force the candidates for 43 contested House of Delegates seats and the two candidates for governor, Republican Marshall Coleman and Democrat L. Douglas Wilder, to define their positions on abortion with greater precision, a process that began only hours after the Supreme Court handed down its ruling. That's good. That's democracy. If the past is any guide, most voters will not make a decision on the basis of a single issue. But abortion is one concern, among others such as drugs, family life education, state mandates, taxes, transportation and state spending, that will be a hot topic of debate this fall.

The Boston Globe

Boston, Massachusetts, July 5, 1989

The Supreme Court decision upholding the legality of restrictions on abortion will lead to widely varying laws on abortion, state by state. Women seeking abortions may find their options depend on where they live or how much travel they can afford.

Massachusetts – despite a 1986 referendum in which voters supported using public funds for abortions sought by poor women and rejected banning abortions in all but extreme circumstances – is vulnerable to abortion restrictions. In recent years, abortion legislation has been determined by a one-vote margin in the state Senate.

Justice Blackmun, in his dissent, said the decision invites every state to enact more restrictive regulations until abortion rights are undone. He said, "For today, at least, the law of abortion stands undisturbed.... But the signs are evident and very ominous, and a chill wind blows."

Massachusetts women have a slight edge on which to pin their hopes for retaining access to abortion: the stronger protection afforded abortion by the state constitution. The legality of public funding for abortion was upheld by the state Supreme Judicial Court in the 1979 Moe v. Hanley case, based on the state constitution's due-process clause.

That ruling is expected to protect public hospitals in Massachusetts from the US Supreme Court decision, which allows states, based on funding restrictions, to make it illegal for public hospitals or their employees to perform abortions.

One ominous segment of the decision is its affirmation of states' rights to protect "potential" human life throughout pregnancy, rather than only from the point of viability. Although not precisely saying that life begins at conception, the decision allows jurisdiction from that point on, and raises the specter of laws against forms of contraception.

Three more abortion cases will be reviewed by the Supreme Court this fall; these cases are part of the "mansion" of abortion rights that Justice Scalia says "must be disassembled doorjamb by doorjamb." The Legislature must preserve women's right to abortion choices from such assault in this commonwealth.

"COULD I GET A SECOND OPINION?"

The Sun Reporter

San Francisco, California, July 5, 1989

The United States Supreme Court's decision Monday to limit abortions does not make them illegal, but does give more power to the states to regulate them.

In their 5-4 decision, the high court touched off political and social turmoil throughout the nation, and pro-abortionists and anti-abortionists are gearing up for an all-out political campaign in various state legislatures.

The court made it easier for states to restrict abortions, but rejected the Bush administration's plea to take the drastic step of overturning the 1973 *Roe v. Wade* decision, which legalized abortions in the U.S.

In their controversial ruling, the court restored key provisions of the restrictive Missouri law that the lower court invalidated for unduly interfering with women's constitutional right to abortion.

The provisions:

● Ban the use of public hospitals and other tax-supported facilities for abortions not necessary to save a woman's life.

● Prohibit any public employee, doctor, nurse or health care professional from performing or assisting in an abortion.

● Forbid using taxpayer money for "encouraging or counseling" women to have abortions.

● Require doctors to determine through medical tests, including tests of the lungs, whether a fetus — thought to be 20 weeks old — is capable of surviving outside the womb.

The decision effectively makes abortions more expensive, and virtually bars them for low-income women, minorities and the poor in Missouri.

The only woman on the court, Justice Sandra Day O'Connor, was the swing vote on the issue. She said that it wasn't necessary for the court to accept the state's invitation to re-examine *Roe v. Wade*, but rather "the court accepted the states every interpretation of its abortion statute and has upheld, under our existing precedents, every provision of that statute which is properly before us."

While the high court did not vote to make abortions illegal, their decision to limit abortions is a great threat to women's rights, and can open doors to state legislators to restrict a woman's right to choose.

California, for two decades, has ruled abortions legal, and the law provides for the poor and people on welfare have abortions paid for through state funds. However, with the high court's ruling, California will see a new struggle escalating over the issue.

All people of good will must not abandon in this struggle, to preserve the right to choose.

Portland Press Herald

Portland, Maine, July 29, 1989

The political battle to retain abortion rights now moves to the state legislative level following the Supreme Court's recent ruling. As it does so, pro-abortionists would do well not to emulate the polarizing tactics of anti-abortion activists.

The signs of a burgeoning militancy among women's groups angered by the court's weakening of abortion rights are unsettling. One group calls for threatening state legislators with political retribution — "Take our rights, lose your jobs" — if they vote to ban abortions.

But that's a self-defeating approach. For one thing it seeks to persuade lawmakers to make a decision for exactly the wrong reasons.

Furthermore, it is a strategy which virtually invites failure. The likelihood that such groups can muster the political clout to drive anti-abortion legislators out of office is extremely slim. In the game of intimidation politics, fear without follow-through counts for nothing.

A far better approach is being urged by some abortion rights leaders who recognize that confrontation will not work. Instead, they advocate building public support by reaching out to the millions of Americans who may feel uneasy about abortion but who feel even more uneasy about the government deciding who shall have one.

Education and persuasion is a lot harder than sloganeering, to be sure, but it is also a lot more effective and durable.

TULSA WORLD

Tulsa, Oklahoma, July 9, 1989

GOV. Henry Bellmon gave legislators some good advice this week. He urged them to wait awhile before tying up the House and Senate in a protracted abortion fuss in light of the latest U.S. Supreme Court decision on that subject.

There isn't much hope the advice will be heard. Never mind that the new ruling is not the court's final word on the subject. Never mind that it doesn't seem to be in great conflict with existing Oklahoma law.

Some legislators have strong religious feelings on the subject. They see a moral imperative to give the state maximum authority to regulate pregnancy. The court's latest ruling — upholding the state's power to ban abortions by public employees or in public facilities — is all the incentive they need.

Some others, who have no strong personal convictions, see a chance to make hay with a zealous minority of citizens whose votes hinge on this one issue. Still others are simply political cowards, ready to do whatever is required to keep a noisy pressure group off their backs.

Polls invariably show a majority of citizens tolerate abortion under at least some circumstances. But in politics, numbers are offset by zeal. The anti-abortionists have shown that they will give not only their votes but their time and money as well to politicians who support their religious views.

The political equation may be changing.

Many citizens who disagree with the absolutist views of the "pro-life" crowd simply haven't paid much attention. Certainly, they have not seen abortion as the single issue upon which all political decisions must be made.

The court's latest decision — with its implied threat to a woman's right to make her own decisions about pregnancy — has undoubtedly raised concerns among many people not previously heard in the abortion debate. They are not fanatics, but believe in the right to privacy in matters of sex and reproduction. They don't want Big Brother in their bedrooms or meddling in their relationship with their doctors. Aroused, they could be a real political force.

Call it wishful thinking, but lawmakers hoping to turn an easy political profit on a new round of demagoguery on abortion may be in for a surprise.

St. Louis Review

St. Louis, Missouri, July 14, 1989

Men and women of good will everywhere have hailed last week's Supreme Court ruling on Webster vs. Reproductive Health Services as a major victory for the pro-life effort. Even those who espouse a pro-choice position readily concede that the decision is a serious blow to what has been for 16 years a right to abortion on demand.

At first glance the court's decision may appear to have done little. Essentially the justices upheld Missouri's current legislation on abortion in our state. Specifically, the Supreme Court ruled that Missouri is within the law in prohibiting the use of public employees and facilities to perform abortions that are not considered necessary to save the life of the mother. While this falls far short of overturning the Roe vs. Wade ruling that legalized abortion, it allows the states to greatly restrict the number of abortions.

Perhaps the most significant thing that has emerged from the deliberations of the court is clear evidence of a change in thinking, a change represented by the newest additions to the court. The majority of the justices had the opportunity to act on their anti-abortion beliefs — and they did so. They have signalled the states that they may proceed in pro-life legislation. Gov. John Ashcroft has already called for a task force to make recommendations as to what initiatives Missouri might take toward greater restrictions on abortion. Other states will be doing the same in the months ahead.

Although it has no immediate legal impact on the abortion problem, it is noteworthy that the justices allowed the preamble to the Missouri law to stand. That is the declaration that "life begins at conception." It is an important philosophical principle that currently allows Missouri to protect the unborn with all the rights due a citizen of the state — except protection from abortion. As long as Roe vs. Wade stands, no state may absolutely prohibit abortion. But, because Missouri legislation is pro-life, the door is now open to greater educational efforts on the part of the state.

The Supreme Court has invited more cases to test Roe vs. Wade. The Missouri case was not sufficient to allow the court to reverse the 1973 legalization of abortion. It is the hope of all concerned with the life of the unborn that many more states will begin to restrict abortions, and eventually the Supreme Court will be able to restore the right to life to all human beings.

Newsday

New York City, New York, July 8, 1989

If the Supreme Court's decision upholding Missouri's restrictions on abortion signals an all-out attack on a woman's right to have an abortion, at least Gov. Mario Cuomo has his priorities straight.

The state will not go down the same slippery slope that the court has, Cuomo said this week, promising that he would reject any legislation that limited abortion the way the Missouri statute did. "Nothing in [the decision on the Missouri law] changes my opinion about the right to abortion or the right of poor people to receive funding," he said.

Thus, despite the court's clear invitation to abortion opponents to continue this divisive battle at the state level, the anti-abortion movement is going to have to overcome a gubernatorial veto to impose new restrictions in New York, at least in the immediate future.

This is Cuomo at his best. Under enormous political pressure, he has refused to cave in to the proponents of the death penalty. Now he has pledged himself to stand by the liberal abortion law enacted by the Legislature in 1970 and signed by Nelson Rockefeller. That law was passed only after years of emotional struggle and what many considered the most wrenching debate of their political careers. The Supreme Court has made a terrible mistake by forcing all this to the fore again.

Cuomo, a former law professor, emphasized that the poor must not be singled out because of the Missouri decision. He said New York has a "higher standard" than the Supreme Court's: a due-process clause in the state's constitution that requires "you must treat poor people fairly, and that means you must give Medicaid funding for abortion."

If we have any concern, it's with the governor's failure squarely to confront the issue of what he'd do if legislation requiring parental consent for abortions for minors came across his desk. That would be as intrusive a move on a young woman's ability to control her destiny as any part of the Missouri statute.

The Union Leader

Manchester, New Hampshire, July 8, 1989

The Supreme Court justices may have given the unborn a faint ray of hope in their recent decision, but little more. Whether due to cowardice, or otherwise, they still refuse to face the basic issue, to answer the unanswered question. They ducked and ran over admitting the scientific reality that life begins at conception, for that would necessitate recognizing that abortion is murder, pure and simple.

LAS VEGAS REVIEW-JOURNAL

Las Vegas, Nevada, July 5, 1989

Lawmakers in many states — Nevada being no exception — are pondering what course of action to take, if any, in light of the U.S. Supreme Court's ruling upholding a Missouri law restricting abortions.

The strident voices on both sides of the issue are sure to turn the matter into a divisive political struggle. We would counsel patience.

While there are bound to be calls from the anti-abortion forces for a special session in which Nevada lawmakers could match the restrictions now legally imposed in Missouri, this would be premature.

Between now and the next regular session in 1991 — assuming there is not a special session — there is time to engage in review and to listen to the people of Nevada and to whatever additional word is to come down from the Supreme Court.

The high court has not yet written the final, definitive chapter in this issue. It plans to hear abortion cases from Minnesota, Illinois and Ohio when it meets again in October. One involves a law requiring a minor seeking an abortion to have permission of her parents or a judge. Nevada already has a similar law on its books, but it is not being enforced while the courts mull over its constitutionality.

Monday's court ruling basically did two things: It allows states to bar the use of public money, employees and facilities in performing abortions or counseling about abortions when the life of the woman is not in jeopardy. It also allows states to require testing after the 20th week of pregnancy for whether a fetus can survive outside the womb.

The decision also let stand a declaration in Missouri law that "the life of each human being begins at conception," but only because it carried no enforceable restrictions against abortion and thus was meaningless in a practical sense.

The ruling does not allow states to ban abortion, though the author of the 16-year-old Roe vs. Wade ruling that made abortion legal fears the camel's nose is under the judicial tent.

Justice Harry Blackmun's Roe vs. Wade ruling said abortions in the first trimester of pregnancy are up to the woman and her doctor, but permitted states to regulate second- and third-trimester abortions. The 1973 ruling said the state has no right to interfere with a woman's decision to obtain an abortion so long as the fetus cannot survive outside the womb.

With abortion now likely to be the most hotly debated issue in the next session of the Nevada Legislature, there could be a trend in the 1990 state elections for one-issue candidates to step forward from both sides of the debate. We hope that the voters will choose candidates with a broader agenda and not let this single, though very important, issue be the sole determining factor in selecting legislators.

Those who seek office with only one burning issue in mind seldom can do justice to the more mundane matters involved in keeping a state running.

Both the rhetoric and the action already are heating up. In Nevada, we hope this heat also provides light by which the Legislature can act in 1991.

The Supreme Court members, within the security of their marble halls, safe in the power of their office, have placed themselves so far above humanity that they can no longer hear the voices.

Can these black-robed figures hear even one small voice that says:

"**I was supposed to be born to feel the sun, warm upon my face, and breathe the air of an early summer morning, to explore the world around me and to love and be loved. I was to be a citizen of a great land, a nation based on a Constitution which promises me an unalienable right to life, as well as liberty and the opportunity to pursue happiness.**

"**However, through no fault of my own, I was considered an inconvenience, an embarrassment. I was supposed to have a mother to love me, but now she is demanding control over her body, while she failed to have that control when I was conceived.**

"**I was supposed to be your future, to preserve and protect this land after you are gone, to work and to create and to care for my fellow man. I am here, though you cannot or will not hear me.**

"**I am here for the moment only, because you will shape the laws so that I might be destroyed.**"

No matter how the Supreme Court justices might try to hide behind their black robes, sooner or later they will have to listen. The simple, basic question must be faced and the Supreme Court has failed to fulfill its duty to define the Constitution by refusing to answer it.

The question remains: "Is this unborn baby alive from the moment it was conceived?" If so, the destruction of that life must be murder.

The Seattle Times

Seattle, Washington, July 10, 1989

POLITICIZATION of abortion is inevitable in light of the recent U.S. Supreme Court decision. But how and in what arenas that debate should occur is crucial both for good government and for enlightened responses to the emotion-laden debate.

The last thing the debate needs is for either pro-choice or anti-abortion activists to turn abortion into a test in all political races.

The recent request from several King County Democratic leaders and pro-choice advocates, that the King County Labor Council endorse only pro-choice candidates for office, is simply wrongheaded.

■ First, a single-issue litmus test is a shortsighted way of choosing elected officials — particularly since experience shows that a litmus test invites crass demagoguery on both sides.

■ Second, not all public offices involve abortion. Candidates for school boards, the Port Commission, and the county assessor's office, for example, need not declare their stands on abortion.

■ Third, there is no fear that the abortion issue will be swept under the rug in races where it does count. Candidates for the Legislature and Congress, who may shape new abortion policy, should be prepared to face thorough grilling on the topic.

Pro-choice forces and liberals have, in the past, rightly denounced fundamentalist right-to-lifers for pushing a narrow orthodoxy. The Supreme Court's abortion decision is an ominous sign for the future of privacy and women's rights. Distressing as that may be, it is still no reason to take the low road.

AKRON
BEACON JOURNAL
Akron, Ohio, July 4, 1989

THE U.S. Supreme Court did the states no favor in a ruling Monday that chips away at a woman's right to an abortion. Abortion rights is perhaps the most divisive and emotional ongoing issue in American life. The states will now have to deal more with that contention, and a crazy-quilt pattern of abortion laws is likely to be the result.

The court did not scrap its 1973 ruling in *Roe vs. Wade*, which holds that a woman has a constitutional right to an abortion, based on the right of privacy. Those opposed to abortion hoped to overturn that ruling, but didn't really expect it — this time. But the court opened the door for more direct challenges to *Roe vs. Wade* as more prohibitive state laws are passed and brought before the court on appeal.

Monday's decision, mostly in 5-4 votes, restored provisions of a Missouri law that had been rejected by lower courts. Basically, those provisions deny the use of tax money for abortions, including bans on the use of public hospitals or other facilities, public employees and public funds to counsel women on abortions.

Lower courts, citing *Roe vs. Wade*, held that these provisions interferred with a woman's constitutional right to an abortion. The practical effect will be that poor women, who need help most, won't get it.

The high court also allowed the Missouri law to declare that life begins at conception. It's hard to predict whether that will change the legalities of the issue, but it probably won't affect public opinion. A recent poll for the Beacon Journal by the University of Akron found that 56 percent of Ohioans believe that life begins at conception; but a majority of those voicing an opinion still believe abortion should remain legal.

Abortion does remain legal, even after Monday's decision. The reasoned *Roe vs. Wade* says that during the first three months of a pregnancy, the decision on an abortion must be left to the woman and her doctor; states may regulate in the second trimester only to protect the woman's health; in the third trimester, the state can protect fetal health.

Where the Missouri ruling confuses the issue is in the second trimester, and in Missouri's ban of public money in cases not necessary to save life. Many state legislatures will now plunge into that confusion. The result, given the current "Reagan court," is likely to be bad news for this most basic of women's rights.

Now, wrote dissenting Justice Harry A. Blackmun, author of *Roe vs. Wade*, "the women of this nation retain the liberty to control their destinies. But the signs are evident and ominous, and a chill wind blows."

THE ARIZONA REPUBLIC
Phoenix, Arizona, July 4, 1989

THE U.S. Supreme Court stopped short of repealing *Roe* vs. *Wade*, the 1973 decision legalizing abortion, but not by much. Constitutionally speaking, *Roe* is now without props.

Like many Americans, the court clearly is troubled by the widespread use of abortion as a means of birth control. Since *Roe*, abortions have reached 1.5 million a year, or 4,000 a day — a shocking figure by any standard. To be sure, most Americans support abortion in cases of rape and incest, where the life of the mother is at risk, or in instances of severe fetal deformity. But they also oppose the abortion-on-demand that the *Roe* decision legitimized, and they do not suppose that 4,000 abortions a day are therapeutic.

While yesterday's 5-4 ruling left the *Roe* decision standing, it also left it teetering. The court, it seems obvious, cut savagely at the reasoning of *Roe*, even as it recoiled — in the interest of narrowing the decision to the case at hand — from delivering the coup de grace. The Missouri law before the court prohibits abortion after the 20th week of pregnancy — the point of presumptive fetal viability — and bars the use of state funds, facilities and employees for abortions or abortion counseling.

In upholding the Missouri statute, the majority held that the state had a compelling and constitutionally sanctioned interest in protecting potential human life. Then, in a direct repudiation of *Roe*, the court went further. The Missouri law, it ruled, "is a reflection of the fact that *Roe*'s rigid trimester analysis has proved to be unsound in principle and unworkable in practice."

The *Roe* decision, wrote Chief Justice William Rehnquist for the majority, "is hardly consistent with the notion of a Constitution like ours that is cast in general terms and usually speaks in general principles." The decision's "trimester" and "viability" criteria, he said, "are not found in the Constitution's text and, since the bounds of the inquiry are essentially indeterminable, the result has been a web of legal rules that have become increasingly intricate, resembling a code of regulations rather than a body of constitutional doctrine."

The majority, moreover, could find no reason why the state's compelling interest in protecting human life should not extend throughout pregnancy, rather than commencing with viability. "The *Roe* trimester framework should be abandoned," Mr. Rehnquist declared.

In a strong dissent, Justice Harry Blackmun seemed to fault the majority for not reversing *Roe*, as he thinks is their intent and as Justice Antonin Scalia would have done. But since Justice Sandra O'Connor balked at basing so sweeping a decision on a Missouri law of limited scope, *Roe* survived — for now.

But the court did invite further challenges and has agreed to hear three more abortion cases in the fall, when it is almost certain to chip away further at the *Roe* decision. Indeed, by recognizing the state's power to regulate abortions, it already has greatly attenuated the constitutional right to abortion that *Roe* established.

The Kansas City Times
Kansas City, Missouri, July 5, 1989

What the Supreme Court has said, in effect, is that the legal right to an abortion holds, but that the states can enact laws to make it more difficult to secure that right. Given the composition of the court, the complicated fragmentation of Roe vs. Wade was aptly described by Justice Harry Blackmun:

"For today, at least, the law of abortion stands undisturbed. For today, the women of this nation will retain the liberty to control their destinies. But the signs are evident and very ominous, and a chill wind blows."

The court emphasized that states can restrict the use of public money and personnel in facilities that perform abortions. The immediate practical effect would be to strictly limit the availabilty of abortions to the poor.

The logic of politics suggests that the state legislatures will be the arena of fiercest contesting in the immediate future. For anti-abortionists the matter has been the only issue. The pro-choice majority may be so amorphous as to preclude such steady attention.

Many anti-abortionists are moved by religious conviction. Many who would be pro-choice if polled in the matter become involved only from the experience of need. Yet unless legislatures are to inundate states with restrictive laws, pro-choice forces will have to turn to single-issue politics and show much more interest in state and local elections. Abortion already is the litmus test for those who would outlaw the procedure. Whether it can become that for the other side is problematical.

The court has stepped into the past. It seems determined to parallel the post-Civil War crazy-quilt of states' rights laws that depressed minorities for so many decades with poll taxes, literacy tests and other subterfuges that kept people from voting despite constitutional guarantees of citizenship. Conceivably, the court could let the right to abortion stand but allow the states to so clutter the health professions and institutions with regulations and exceptions that the right becomes hollow.

The sad fact remains that this devastatingly divisive issue would hardly exist if contraception education and materials were universally available. If anti-abortion forces would devote half their energy to that cause, the incidence of what they insist are "baby murders" would drop dramatically. They will not do that, for many oppose contraception. Unfortunately, the organizations and institutions that distribute knowledge and materials for birth control are the very ones that could be most crippled by the action this week.

So the issue remains and the raging goes on. It will spread through government and the body politic like a fever. It is difficult not to wonder whether it will obsess society to the extent that very little else will matter in choosing those who conduct public policy.

"...and this is my Lamaze coach..."

MARGULIES
©1989 HOUSTON POST

DAILY NEWS

New York City, New York, July 5, 1989

THEY WERE ONCE known as the "Nine Old Men." No longer. Not since they became eight men and a woman. And, besides, to call them old might be considered a violation of their sacred preserve, the Constitution, which frowns upon age discrimination.

So they are accepted, hailed if you will, as the Supreme Court, the highest of the highest, who, hopefully, are smart enough and brave enough to preserve the freedom that makes this country different.

Monday, the day before our ultimate celebration of freedom, the court rendered its decision on abortion, an issue that could appropriately and cynically be called a child of freedom.

The decision preserved the 1973 landmark Roe vs. Wade ruling, barely, but delivered a flat-out invitation to the states to make abortion difficult and, for the poor or uninformed, possibly impossible.

Unsurprisingly, the decision was hardly unanimous. Chief Justice Rehnquist held that abortion was not a fundamental constitutional right. Justice Blackmun, dissenting, held that the constitutional right remains but that "a chill wind blows." No way to argue with Blackmun on that point. Legislators, here and elsewhere, are already climbing over each other on the way to the anti-abortion barricades.

You will read and hear about the details of the ruling upholding the Missouri law — public employes can't perform abortions except to save a mother's life; a fetus must be tested for viability after 20 weeks of pregnancy; no public buildings or public funds can be used for abortions, but doctors' offices and clinics may be used. But the quintessential questions remain.

Forget our sainted legislators, what possible right does a court of law have to tell a woman what or what not to do with her body?

Conversely, should a healthy fetus — a potential supreme court justice — be destroyed, assuming it poses no danger to the mother?

Hundreds of thousands have marched and fought — literally and otherwise — in response to this issue of issues. Some of the most brilliant and imbecilic arguments have been made on both sides of the debate.

At bottom, however, stripped of rhetoric and judges and legislation, abortion is a profoundly personal matter *and* a major social concern. If it weren't such a bedeviling mixture, the Rehnquists and the Blackmuns and those who went before them would have resolved the issue long, long ago.

At this stage it is hard to see how the July 3 Supreme Court decision contributes much beyond paving the way for legislative mischief across the land.

The Seattle Times

Seattle, Washington, July 4, 1989

IN YESTERDAY'S abortion decision, the conservative controlled U.S. Supreme Court once again displayed a chilling philosophy. As shown in its recent capital-punishment rulings, the Rehnquist bench is in full retreat from the court's traditional role as protector of individual rights against the will of the majority. Or — in the case of the anti-abortion movement — a politically powerful minority.

One effect of yesterday's ruling in the watershed case, Webster v. Reproductive Health Services, will be to allow state legislatures to enlarge their role in regulating abortions and, therefore, in limiting access to them.

Five of nine justices upheld the constitutionality of a Missouri law which:

■ Bars abortions in public hospitals (even if the procedure is paid for by the patient.)

■ Prohibits public employees from counseling women on abortions.

■ Requires doctors to perform tests to determine the viability of fetuses in women more than 20 weeks pregnant. (A law drafted by local anti-abortion groups with no intent other than to discourage abortions.)

The ruling in this case does not eradicate the fundamental right to have an abortion. But an abstract right means next to nothing if states are now free to throw up obstacles to make obtaining abortions difficult for poor women and rural women, whose medical-care choices always are limited.

For the Missouri women who will be denied the option of abortion, the court's cold analysis of the state law's fine points will be irrelevant.

The court's states-rights ruling shifts the abortion battle to the heated arenas of legislatures. A barrage of proposals for similar anti-abortion statutes no doubt will surface in every state capital, including Olympia. Lawmakers of every stripe will now face the abortion litmus test from both anti-abortion and pro-choice camps.

Justice Harry Blackmun, who wrote the Roe v. Wade decision in 1973, wrote yesterday's impassioned dissent. He rightly criticized the majority's silence on their decision's far-reaching impacts as "profoundly disruptive of this court as an institution."

Indeed, the court's majority ruling decision will be profoundly disruptive of American lives and politics. The question now is what state legislators will be hearing from the majority of Americans, who continue to support a woman's fundamental right to make her own decision about an abortion.

ST. LOUIS POST-DISPATCH

St. Louis, Missouri, July 4, 1989

The Supreme Court has said that in upholding Missouri restrictions on abortion, it has not reversed *Roe vs. Wade*, the 1973 decision affirming a woman's right to obtain an abortion. That right survives, but by only the thinnest of threads.

For even as the justices in the majority were paying lip service to that right Monday, they were inviting states to undermine it by making it more difficult, costly, cumbersome and dangerous for women to end unwanted pregnancies. Most significant, they have served notice that they would welcome a case that, unlike the Missouri statutes, directly challenged *Roe*.

The provisions of Missouri law at issue in *Webster vs. Reproductive Health Services* were overshadowed by the court's lack of a strong commitment to the underlying principles of *Roe vs. Wade*. The ban on state participation in nontherapeutic abortions, the Legislature's "finding" that life begins at conception, the requirement that doctors determine fetal viability before performing abortions after the 19th week of pregnancy — all were deemed constitutional and in keeping with court precedent by the majority of justices. As Justice Harry Blackmun noted in his dissenting opinion, the court did not make "a single, even an incremental, change in the law of abortion."

That fact should not obscure what it has done, however. In one of the most blatant examples of judicial activism in recent memory, the majority stated it would, should the proper case arise, "modify and narrow *Roe* and succeeding cases," and acknowledged that "our holding today will allow some governmental regulation of abortion that would have been prohibited under the language" of previous rulings.

In a chilling indication of the court's frame of mind, the plurality opinion written by Chief Justice William Rehnquist questioned "why the state's interest in protecting potential human life should come into existence only at the point of viability" — suggesting the court might approve restrictions on abortion from the moment of conception.

In effect, the court for the moment has upheld *Roe vs. Wade* not because of any love for that case or because the majority of justices believes deeply that the Constitution implicitly grants women the right to have an abortion, but because the Missouri case wasn't a good enough vehicle to challenge it. The decision is disingenuous, coy and, as Justice Blackmun points out, "foments disregard for the law and for our standing decisions."

He added: "The plurality opinion is filled with winks and nods, with knowing glances to those who would do away with *Roe* explicitly, but turns a stone face to anyone in search of what the plurality conceives as the scope of a woman's right . . . to terminate a pregnancy free of the coercive and brooding influence of the State."

Abortion opponents will cheer the court's decision. Those who cherish the constitutional right to privacy and its corollary, the right to reproductive freedom, must redouble efforts to guard them. It will be an uphill battle, but, as the celebrations of this Independence Day should remind us, the job of protecting freedoms has never been easy.

DAYTON DAILY NEWS

Dayton, Ohio, July 9, 1989

The abortion question is gradually being returned to the states, and this is seen as a conservative, anti-abortion triumph of historic proportions.

In 1972, George McGovern ran for president as a left-of-liberal. His position on abortion: leave it up to the states.

That, in fact, was the most common position of liberal politicians. At the time, states were generally moving in the direction of legalizing abortion, and some conservatives were appalled and were calling for national legislation to ban abortion or for a constitutional amendment to do so.

Just noted for the record.

The San Diego Union

San Diego, California, July 4, 1989

In what is described as the decision of the decade, the U.S. Supreme Court did not decapitate its precedent in *Roe vs. Wade* that effectively legalized abortion in the United States 16 years ago. Instead, the eagerly watched ruling handed down yesterday in the case known as *Webster vs. Reproductive Health Services*, upheld significant portions of a Missouri law regulating abortion, without explicitly overturning the 1973 ruling. This, it appears, is the first of numerous cuts that will likely bleed *Roe vs. Wade* to death.

In the closely divided 5-4 decision, the constructionist, conservative views of Chief Justice William Rehnquist and Justices Anthony Kennedy, Byron White, Sandra Day O'Connor, and Antonin Scalia prevailed. What they did was to change the site of the raging abortion battle from the courts to the state legislatures. They acknowledged, in effect, that the Warren Court in *Roe vs. Wade* had created law instead of interpreting it.

Specifically, the Roe decision prohibited states from regulating abortions during the first three months, or trimester, of pregnancy. States were granted the right to interfere with abortions in the second trimester only to protect the mother's health. And states were allowed to protect the fetus only in the final three months of pregnancy.

Writing for the majority, Chief Justice Rehnquist went to the heart of the Roe rationale by denouncing its rigid framework as being " . . . hardly consistent with the notion of a constitution cast in general terms, as ours is . . . The key elements of the Roe framework — trimesters and viability — are not found in the text of the Constitution or in any place else one would expect to find a constitutional principle . . . "

And Chief Justice Rehnquist boldly tackled Roe's perplexing question of fetus viability — when does the fetus become a human being with human rights? Like the ancient argument about the number of angels on a pinhead, the viability mystery has frustrated definition by scientists and theologians.

Without bogging down in such an impossible technicality, the Chief Justice cut the knot with this compelling statement: "We do not see why the state's interest in protecting the potential human life should come into existence only at the point of viability, and that there should therefore be a rigid line allowing state regulation after viability but prohibiting it before viability." Such logical reasoning would make a lot of sense to a lot of Americans.

What this most significant decision portends is best suggested by the highly articulate reaction of the case's involved principals. Speaking for the dissenters, Justice Harry Blackmun, who wrote the 7-2 Roe majority opinion, acknowledged " . . . the women of this nation . . . retain the liberty to control their destinies. But the signs are evident and very ominous, and a chill wind blows."

And Molly Yard, head of the National Organization or Women, opined: "It's a black day for women's right to control their lives. It opens up the door for every state legislature to greatly restrict women's right to choose, and I personally think it's war against women."

On the other side, Randall Terry, head of the anti-abortion Operational Rescue, praised the decision and said "the court is sending very clear signals to the states to pass legislation to protect children. The writing is on the wall. Roe is going to go down — there's no question about it."

Suggesting that very scenario, the court announced its acceptance of three new abortion cases from Illinois, Minnesota, and Ohio, each apparently offering abortion aspects not covered in the Missouri case.

Understandingly, the agonizing divisiveness of the abortion issue has torn at Justice O'Connor, the first woman ever to serve on the high court. Although she concurred with the majority judgment, she declined to join in the portion of the chief justice's decision dealing with the Roe trimester scheme. Consequently, that portion of the ruling became a plurality consisting of just four members. Such decisions are not as weighty as a majority opinion, but are law nonetheless.

Yesterday's ruling will have no immediate effect in California, where women's abortion rights are already fixed in law. But the momentum generated by *Webster vs. Reproductive Health Service* to restrict abortion on demand is certain to rage here as an inflammatory issue in forthcoming politics as it will in all the other states across the country. In a more perfect world, the pro-life and pro-choice antagonists would confront each other in this new arena with restraint and decency, confident in the logical force of their causes. The reality is that the unrequited controversy that Roe loosed in the country is not likely to be resolved without a great deal of pain and anguish.

The Evening Gazette
Worcester, Massachusetts, July 5, 1989

ANTI-ABORTION leaders, as well as pro-choice supporters, should be disturbed and offended by the violent turn anti-abortion protests have taken.

Last April, an anti-abortion group called Operation Rescue held a peaceful protest near Planned Parenthood's Boulder clinic. Some protesters were arrested for minor infractions, but there were few overt hostilities. Even pro-choice supporters respected Operation Rescue's right to gather and make its views known.

But what happened Saturday in Denver bore little resemblance to the April gathering. About 300 Operation Rescue demonstrators converged on Planned Parenthood's Vine Street clinic. They grabbed, mauled, shoved and bit clinic workers and the women who were trying to enter the facility. They charged police lines and disobeyed police orders. Police had to use a modicum of force to quell a violent situation. About 60 protesters were arrested.

Despite lame threats to sue the police for supposed "brutality," it appears that Operation Rescue participants owe the police and the public an apology. The group repeatedly has promised that its actions would be nonviolent. That promise was blatantly broken.

Saturday's events may stiffen the resolve of pro-choice supporters. Abortion clinics and pro-choice groups will come to expect increasingly physical attacks by anti-abortion forces, and will take appropriate measures. But the violence also may undermine the public sympathy Operation Rescue attempted to garner.

Had police not been on the scene, Saturday's fracas easily could have resulted in death or injury to clinic workers or patients. For example, suppose a protester tripped or shoved a woman on her way to the clinic. She could have fallen, struck her head on the pavement and died. Or, if she had been pregnant, she might have had a miscarriage.

Anti-abortion advocates steadfastly claim they want to prevent violence to the unborn. They cannot maintain that moral position while committing violence against human beings outside the womb.

THE DENVER POST
Denver, Colorado, July 11, 1989

Women's rights advocates can take some solace in the fact that the U.S. Supreme Court has declined to overturn or even reconsider the court's landmark, 16-year-old decision in Roe vs. Wade, which affirmed that choosing to abort a pregnancy is a woman's right.

Make no mistake about the unspoken impact of Monday's ruling on Missouri's abortion law. It opens the way for what will doubtlessly be an extended battle over abortion rights on both the state and federal levels.

Overall, the effect of Monday's decision was to allow Missouri to restrict the use of public money, medical personnel or facilities in performing abortion procedures. Specifically permitted are: Bans on use of tax money for "encouraging or counseling" women to have abortions not necessary to save their lives; bans on any public employee from performing or assisting an abortion not necessary to save a woman's life; and bans on use of any public hospital or other taxpayer-supported facility for performing abortions not necessary to save life.

Missouri law bans all abortions of viable fetuses, and the court upheld the Missouri requirement that doctors determine viability by testing lung capacity and conducting other tests, when possible, of fetuses at least 20 weeks old.

Although the central principles of Roe vs. Wade stand, the majority opinion was criticized bitterly in a dissent by Justice Blackmun: "For today, at least, the law of abortion stands undisturbed. For today, the women of this nation will retain the liberty to control their destinies. But the signs are evident and very ominous, and a chill wind blows."

That assessment is almost certainly correct. Although the court failed to return the abortion issue to local lawmakers, it opened the way for Missouri-style restrictions at the state level nationwide. Anti-abortion activists are already gearing up for a long campaign. Expected to be among the first states targeted are Pennsylvania, Wisconsin, Minnesota and Ohio. In addition to the public-funding issues covered in Monday's decision, anti-abortion groups say they will attempt to introduce parental consent and notification laws and measures to give fathers more say in abortion decisions.

The eventual outcome of the national debate over abortion is not only important to women of reproductive age, but to all Americans. At the center of the controversy is the right of individuals to privacy and freedom from undue interference from government.

The right of individuals to make their own life choices has long been the bedrock of American democracy, and that right stands for now. We can only hope that the court will continue to affirm it as the abortion debate moves into its next phase.

The Chattanooga Times
Chattanooga, Tennessee, July 5, 1989

In its long-awaited abortion decision on Monday, the Supreme Court stopped short of overturning Roe vs. Wade, the landmark 1973 ruling that established a woman's right to that procedure. The ruling was a splintered one that included several opinions, yet public anticipation was so high that both sides in the controversy read more into the decision than it actually contained.

States may now have more authority to restrict elective abortions — those not considered medically necessary to save the woman's life — and that is likely to ensure controversy in state capitals. There is no guarantee, however, of a drastic reduction in the number of abortions performed each year. Neither is there any doubt that Monday's ruling is merely a prelude to more controversy over this issue. The court has already agreed to hear three more abortion cases in its fall term, and undoubtedly additional challenges will arise when state legislatures attempt to conform with the court's ruling on Monday.

Under that ruling, states are free to bar the use of tax funds to encourage or counsel women to have' abortions not necessary to save their lives; forbid public employees from performing or assisting in such abortions; and prohibit the use of tax-supported facilities for performing abortions. The ruling is not insignificant, even though in several states public facilities have already stopped performing abortions.

The key ruling in the Missouri case requires doctors to determine, when possible, whether a fetus at least 20 weeks old can survive outside the womb, by conducting certain tests. That ruling implicitly recognizes advances in the field of obstetrics and pediatric medicine that have saved the lives of prematurely born babies. But pushing the viability standard back to 20 weeks is an arbitrary act that cannot be applied across the board, for the simple reason that each fetus is different. Moreover, it is this ruling that made clear the court's unwillingness to void the three-trimester standard it established in Roe vs. Wade.

That standard said that in the first trimester, the decision to have an abortion is one to be made strictly by the woman in consultation with her doctor. As the fetus develops, however, the court allowed the state to assume a greater role in the second and third trimester because with each passing week, the fetus' likelihood of viability increases. However, since 90 percent of abortions are performed in the first trimester, well before the 20th week, the viability ruling does not ensure a dramatic reduction in the number of abortions.

Even so, the court has dramatically strengthened those who oppose abortion and made the task facing pro-choice advocates much more difficult. With the battle shifting to state legislatures, pro-choice forces may have an advantage in public opinion.

Polls have consistently shown that a majority of Americans believe that abortion should be legal under all or certain circumstances. But that support is slippery; other polls have reported substantial uneasiness with the moral implications of abortion, and for good reason: Stripped of rhetoric about rights, abortion involves the taking of a human life. The impact of this 16-year-old issue on American society flows directly from the debate over competing rights: those of the woman vs. those of the developing child.

Despite its limited scope, the court with its ruling Monday clearly strengthened the position of those opposed to abortion. At the same time, it sounded the opening salvo of a battle now shifting to the states. Legislators now find themselves on the front line in the campaign to decide whether the court's latest ruling can be translated into state laws. The process will be politically charged and therefore messy. The legislators' ability to chart an independent course will be severely tested.

Supreme Court Upholds Ban on Abortion Counseling

The Supreme Court, in a 5–4 ruling, May 23, 1991 upheld federal regulations that barred federally funded family planning clinics from providing any information about abortion. The case was *Rust v. Sullivan*.

The regulations, issued in 1988 by the Department of Health and Human Services, concerned clinics funded and regulated under Title X of the Public Health Service Act of 1970. The law prohibited funding of programs "where abortion is a method of family planning." Before the 1988 regulations were issued, the law had been interpreted as applying only to abortions themselves, not to abortion counseling.

The Supreme Court decision would affect up to 4,500 federally funded clinics across the country, which served between four million and five million women each year. The clinics would be required to direct all pregnant women to prenatal-care facilities. If a woman asked about terminating a pregnancy, the regulations instructed the clinic to tell her, "The project does not consider abortion an appropriate method of family planning."

The Supreme Court's decision would allow clinics to advise a woman of the abortion option if continuing the pregnancy posed a threat to her life. The 1988 regulations had prohibited abortion counseling in such cases.

The U.S. 2nd Circuit Court of Appeals in New York had upheld the regulations in 1989. Both the 1st Circuit Court of Appeals in Boston and the 10th Circuit Court of Appeals in Denver had found the regulations to be unconstitutional. The Bush administration had supported the rules.

The regulations, which had been delayed during three years of court challenges, went into effect immediately following the Supreme Court's decision.

In the case before the court, the American Civil Liberties Union had represented Planned Parenthood of New York, one of its medical officers, Irving Rust, and the state and city of New York against Louis Sullivan, secretary of health and human services. The American Civil Liberties Union argued that the regulations violated a woman's right to an abortion and the free-speech rights of women and health-care providers.

Chief Justice William H. Rehnquist, writing for the majority, rejected every argument raised against the regulations. He wrote, "The government has no constitutional duty to subsidize an activity merely because the activity is constitutionally protected and may validly choose to fund childbirth over abortion." Justices Byron R. White, Anthony M. Kennedy and Antonin Scalia joined the opinion. Justice David H. Souter, the court's newest member, also joined the majority in the case. It was the first time Souter had indicated his opinion on an abortion-related issue.

In one of the three dissenting opinions, Justice Harry A. Blackmun said the regulations were an "intrusive, ideologically based regulation of speech." Blackmun had written the majority opinion in the Supreme Court's 1973 landmark *Roe v. Wade* decision upholding a woman's right to an abortion.

The Supreme Court's decision May 23 drew strong reactions from both abortion-rights supporters and anti-abortion groups.

Planned Parenthood Director Faye Wattleton, whose clinics received $37 million of the $150 million annual Title X appropriation, May 23 said her group would not withhold information on abortion only from its clients. Under the regulations, clinics were permitted to provide information on abortion if they set up their own, privately funded programs in buildings separate from those receiving federal funds.

THE DENVER POST

Denver, Colorado, May 26, 1991

THE U.S. Supreme Court has sanctioned a policy crafted by anti-abortion forces in the Reagan and Bush administrations, designed to keep as many American women as possible ignorant of their rights.

The court, in one of its patented 5-4 rulings, claims that Congress authorized the Department of Health and Human Services to draft rulings that forbid even mention of the word "abortion" in publicly subsidized family planning clinics. If a woman asks about abortion, she must be told only that "abortion is not an appropriate method of family planning" — even when the doctor believes an abortion may be her best recourse.

The ruling is a travesty, a mandate for doctors to lie to their patients to promote the political agenda of militant anti-abortionists. It's true that Congress has denied funding for poor women's abortions. But Congress surely did not intend to go so far as to order doctors to deceive their patients.

Three things can be said about the new decision.

✔ It is wrong as a matter of law and disastrous as social policy.

✔ It is the first sign of the abortion attitudes of the court's newest member, Justice David Souter, who provided the decisive vote for this mandate to lie. You blew it, Justice Souter.

✔ Congress should draft a clear law ordering the Department of Health and Human Services to stop lying to patients and give them honest and unbiased medical advice, even when the questions concern abortion.

It is unfortunate that the court has given so much force to a bureaucratic interpretation of a law. But now that it has, there is nothing to do but for Congress to make its intent clear, effectively making the court ruling void.

Political pandering should never be allowed to go so far as ordering a doctor to lie to a trusting patient.

The Boston Globe
Boston, Massachusetts, May 24, 1991

In a devastating defeat for five million impoverished American women who depend on federally funded family planning clinics, the Supreme Court says they cannot so much as be informed that abortion is an option to pregnancy. Not even if they ask about it; not even if ill health warrants it.

The decision came on a sharply divided 5-4 vote in which the newest court member, Justice David Souter, an appointee of President Bush, sided with the conservative majority. Bad enough in itself on family planning constraints, the lineup of votes bodes ill for cases directly concerned with the protection of choice on abortion.

The vote upholds what is known as the gag rule, a Department of Health and Human Services regulation issued in 1988, which for the first time prohibited abortion counseling in tax-supported clinics. Before that, although no abortions could be performed at such clinics, abortion could be discussed. About $200 million in federal funds partially support 4,000 clinics across the country.

Clearly, the court has handed responsibility for reversing the rule to the Congress. A bill filed by Sen. John Chaffee of Rhode Island would restore the guidelines that encouraged family planning clinics that receive Title X money to provide pregnant women upon their request information on all legal medical options, including abortion.

"It is wrong for federally sponsored programs to censor vital information about a legal healthcare option, simply because some people disagree [with it]," says Chaffee, who pledged to push for enactment of his bill, which previously won Senate support, contending that Congress will not stand by while its intent is ignored.

Souter's vote was key. And it was singularly disappointing because last October he had voiced concern that denying doctors freedom to mention abortion impeded their responsibility to patients. During public argument on the case, Souter said to Solicitor General Kenneth Starr, the Bush administration's top courtroom lawyer: "You are telling us the physician cannot perform his usual professional responsibility. You are telling us [the government] in effect may preclude professional speech."

Yet, yesterday's majority opinion by Chief Justice William Rehnquist held that the government, in choosing how to spend taxpayer money on family planning, may legally ban mention of abortion. "Here, the government is not denying a benefit to anyone but is instead simply insisting that public funds be spent for the purposes for which they were authorized," Rehnquist stated. Souter, evidently, agrees with that point.

Though the restrictions on domestic family planning programs were issued in 1988 at the behest of the Reagan administration, they were spawned at the 1985 UN International Conference on World Population in Mexico. President Reagan's special ambassador to the conference, former US Sen. James L. Buckley, startled the meeting by announcing that the US would not fund family planning services overseas if abortion was mentioned in any way. That ban remains in effect.

Just as Reagan courted campaign support from anti-abortion factions, so does Bush. Both have tried to outlaw abortion, with Bush making only weak concessions to rape or life-threatening conditions as a justification.

Thus, the portent of yesterday's decision reaches far beyond the family planning issue. And it comes in the aftermath of decisions in which the Supreme Court has chipped away at the historic 1973 ruling that legalized abortion.

Those decisions returned to states the right to ban the use of public money for abortions and upheld laws requiring teen-age girls to obtain permission of a parent before undergoing abortion. Other cases narrowing options on abortion are to be heard later this year.

Among the more dangerous precedents set by yesterday's decision is its tacit permission to treat poor women differently in a medical situation – to limit their access to medical advice concerning legal procedures. Congress must act swiftly and surely to ensure that poor women, dependent upon tax-supported medical services, have full information upon which to make reproductive decisions.

The New York Times
New York City, New York, May 24, 1991

The Supreme Court has now ruled that the Government has the power to pressure clinics to hide information or even mislead poor pregnant women about their right to choose whether or not to bear a child. That's bad enough as a moral and constitutional matter, but the Court did more. It held that Congress has actually authorized the Department of Health and Human Services to promote this coercive, unprofessional assault on a woman's rights.

By a 5-to-4 vote the Court upheld regulations of the Reagan and Bush Administrations claiming to implement Congress's program subsidizing family planning clinics. Those rules forbid even the mention of abortion in such clinics. If a woman directly asks whether abortion is an option for her unintended pregnancy, she must be told that "the project does not consider abortion an appropriate method of family planning," even if the doctors in fact believe it is an option.

Surely Congress had no intention, when it passed the 1970 Family Planning Act or any time since, of forcing doctors and clinics to give such skewed advice. Even when it denied funding for poor women's abortions, Congress never contemplated gagging doctors from giving full, honest answers to trusting women.

Justice David Souter, the newest member on the Court and yesterday's swing vote, had it right during oral arguments last fall when he asked whether the H.H.S. regulations didn't interfere with a doctor's professional advice. Yet he joined Chief Justice William Rehnquist's opinion that denied any such interference. Their captious reasoning: Since the patient has no reason to rely on the clinic for *complete* medical advice, she will not be misled. Nor is the doctor forced to say anything he does not believe because he is only stating clinic policy.

Is the Court countenancing a two-tier system of health care, one for the rich, who use private doctors, and one for the poor, who rely on the clinics?

The Chief Justice argues defensively, cynically and contrary to experience, that poor women are no worse off under the H.H.S. rules than if Congress had never supported any clinics at all. Tell that to the patient who sees the clinic as her only source of information or help.

Congress now must respond with legislation so clear that the Supreme Court will honor its intention to provide honest information with family planning services for the poor. A simple bill negating the H.H.S. rules is the right place to start.

THE LINCOLN STAR
Lincoln, Nebraska, May 27, 1991

The U.S. Supreme Court's decision on federally funded family planning clinics is a dangerous erosion of free speech.

Last week, the court ruled that clinics which receive federal funds cannot discuss the option of abortion with pregnant women nor tell them where they can get an abortion.

The court said that the ban, contained in regulations issued during the Reagan administration, does not violate free speech rights or women's right to end their pregnancies.

But Justice Harry A. Blackmun, one of four dissenters, accurately described the serious free speech problems.

Until this decision, the high court has never said that government can supress speech about a certain viewpoint as a condition for accepting public money, he said.

"In its haste to further restrict the right of every woman to control her reproductive freedom and bodily integrity, the majority disregards established principles of law and contorts this court's decided case to arrive at this preordained result."

Obviously the decision will put an additional roadblock between women who want an abortion and a safe abortion.

Family planning clinics are often one of the few places in communities where women know they can get information about where to get safe, legal abortions and now to make those arrangements.

But the most serious problem with the Supreme Court ruling is not the practical results. It is the potential the decision creates for using federal funds to curb free speech.

If government can link federal funds to a ban on discussions about abortion, what other speech can be banned and for which federal dollars?

Will there be language bans tied to other federal funds?

For universities which depend on an assortment of federal dollars

For physicians who earn any money through federal programs — Medicare and Medicaid.

For students who receive Pell Grants for college education.

For farmers who earn a living with the help of federal dollars.

And what other legal but morally controversial issues or behavior will be put on the banned speech list.

Having an abortion is not illegal, at least not yet. The federal government should not get in the business of censoring discussion, and in particular discussion of perfectly legal activities.

And the Supreme Court should be protecting free speech not allowing slices of censorship.

The TENNESSEAN
Nashville, Tennessee, May 26, 1991

WITH one decision this week, the Supreme Court assaulted free speech, intruded on patient-physician relationships, and limited the ability of poor women to receive a legal abortion.

Justice David Souter joined the slim majority in the 5-4 ruling that federally funded family planning clinics can be restricted from mentioning abortion or referring a person who asks about abortion to a clinic that performs them. If a woman asks a clinic staffer directly about abortion, the staff members can only say that the clinic "does not consider abortion an appropriate method of family planning."

The decision should trouble all Americans, regardless of where they stand on the abortion issue, because it unnecessarily intrudes on the relationship between patient and physician.

The ruling is the first indication that Souter may be less independent than he seemed. It was Souter who raised the issue of professional speech when the case was argued last year. In a question to Solictor General Kenneth Starr, Souter said, "You are telling us the physician cannot perform his usual professional responsibility. You are telling us government may, in effect, preclude professional speech."

Yet Souter joined in the opinion, written by Chief Justice William Rehnquist, that would restrict speech in family planning clinics.

Justice Harry Blackmun, in writing the four-member dissent, noted it was a chilling first for the court. "Until today, the court never has upheld viewpoint-based suppression of speech simply because that suppression was a condition upon the the acceptance of public funds."

Abortion is legal in this country. And, it is an accepted practice — indeed, a sworn medical obligation — for doctors to give patients all the medical options that are available to them. A woman who went to a private doctor could get those options. A woman who relied on a family planning clinic, funded in part with federal funds, wouldn't get that information.

For some clinics, the ruling will mean disruption and the additional cost of separating family planning services from abortion services.

But the ruling's full force comes down hardest on poor women. Poor women can't pay for private doctors. They have to go to family planning clinics. And now, their poverty will be made that much more vicious because the clinic doctors won't even be able to give them a hint of where to go to get a legal abortion.

Some members of Congress now promise swift congressional action to overturn the federal regulation. Americans should hope Congress has the stamina to stand up for free speech and professional responsibility under the heat of a debate that is certain to center solely on abortion.

But regardless of what Congress may do, Americans should be frightened by a Supreme Court that is willing to censor physicians and deny women medical information. ∎

The ARIZONA REPUBLIC
Phoenix, Arizona, May 29, 1991

AMID all the fury over last week's U.S. Supreme Court decision upholding anti-abortion regulations governing the use of federal funds in family-planning clinics, it is important to keep in mind what the 5-4 ruling was *not* about: *Rust* vs. *Sullivan* was not about the First Amendment, free speech, women's "rights" or any other issue ginned up by the abortion industry.

This issue is about money, plain and simple. At stake is $150 million in federal family-planning funds. The biggest single recipient of these funds — about $37 million annually — is Planned Parenthood.

Nothing in the court's ruling prevents Planned Parenthood or any other organization from doing what it is presently doing with regard to offering women abortion counseling at family-planning clinics. The decision means only that family-planning centers must give up some federal funding if they wish to continue offering counseling and referrals for abortion.

The 1970 Public Health Service Act, passed three years before *Roe* vs. *Wade* legalized abortion on demand, states that the federal government regards abortion as an unacceptable method of family planning. In 1988 the Reagan administration promulgated guidelines for the use of Title X funds, thereby provoking a lawsuit.

As Chief Justice Rehnquist notes in his majority opinion, "Here the Government was not denying a benefit to anyone, but instead was simply insisting that public funds be spent for the purpose for which they were authorized . . . ." As Mr. Rehnquist points out, nothing in the regulation forces Title X recipients to give up abortion-related speech; it merely requires that the grantee keep such speech separate and distinct from Title X activities.

This is not a case of the government suppressing speech, but of a prohibition on an organization receiving public funds while engaging in activities outside of their intended scope. Justice Rehnquist drew a parallel to the National Endowment for Democracy, saying that the First Amendment does not require the endowment to subsidize the promotion of communism or fascism.

Abortion advocates have dredged up all manner of fanciful arguments against the court's decision in *Rust*. Some have suggested that countless women, being denied access to abortion information, will die due to complications in pregnancy. This is unadulterated nonsense. As the court notes, the regulations provide an exception for abortion counseling in a medical emergency when the life of the mother is in imminent peril.

Others argue that the decision denies women complete information about their 'family-planning' choices. In this scenario women will be turned away in droves from family-planning clinics, condemned to carry unwanted fetuses to term because they were never told of the abortion option.

Few will take this argument seriously. Can there be a person in America who is as yet unaware that abortion is legal, nay, common. Of the 1.5 million abortions done every year in the U.S., approximately half are performed on women who already have had one or more abortion. Surely these women are not unmindful of their options.

Moreover, it is precisely the use of abortion as a means of post-conception birth control that the guidelines stand against. To cite Mr. Rehnquist once again, "The Title X program is designed not for prenatal care, but to encourage family planning." Title X recipients now have to decide: are they interested in sound family planning, or are they in the abortion business?

Los Angeles Times
Los Angeles, California, May 24, 1991

Read between the lines of the U.S. Supreme Court's decision Thursday banning mere whisper of the word *abortion* at federally funded family planning clinics. Knowledge is dangerous, says the high court. Do the justices fear that some poor, pregnant woman who learns about abortion might choose to have one? No matter that all women still have a constitutional right to abortion. The court says it's against "public interest" for a poor woman to even be told about abortion if she's at a federally funded clinic.

Chief Justice William H. Rehnquist, writing for the slim 5-4 majority, upheld regulations issued in 1988 forbidding discussion of abortion in clinics funded through the federal government. The family planning program funds about 4,000 clinics serving more than 4 million low-income women each year. The clinics have always been banned from using federal money to perform abortions. But until 1988, clinic staffs could tell women about all options, including abortion, and make referrals. In 1988 the Reagan Administration clamped a lid on all such information. Court challenges kept the the ban from being enforced virtually everywhere. Not any more.

Now, when a woman specifically asks about abortion, the clinic can only say it does not consider abortion an appropriate method of family planning. And the clinics will only refer patients to physicians who do not perform abortions. Rehnquist said this is not "a case of the Government 'suppressing speech' but of a prohibition on a project grantee . . . from engaging in activities outside of its scope."

More troubling is Rehnquist's facile argument: "The doctor-patient relationship established by the [federal] program . . . does not justify an expectation on the part of the patient of comprehensive medical advice." Is the court condoning a dual standard: full medical information for those who can pay but only court-approved medical information for those who can't?

This cruel ruling is part of a slow erosion of the federal right to a legal abortion. The court is signaling that while it has not yet been willing to reverse the Roe vs. Wade ruling that made abortion legal, it is more than willing to whittle away at it.

The News and Observer
Raleigh, North Carolina, May 26, 1991

The U.S. Supreme Court has gone somewhere it doesn't belong — into the doctor's office, where it has disrupted a historic, sacred and confidential relationship by limiting doctors in what they may tell their patients.

Allowed to stand without congressional intervention, this court ruling could be dangerous. In saying that federally funded family-planning clinics may be prohibited from giving any information about abortion, as the court did Thursday, some doctors in those clinics will be stopped from giving what they believe to be the best medical advice.

What if, for example, a pregnant woman goes to a family-planning clinic and an examining physician determines that without an abortion, her health may be in jeopardy? According to the Supreme Court, if he or she discusses with that woman the possibility of abortion, the clinic can lose its federal funds. That is an intolerable restriction on a doctor's freedom to act in the patient's best interest.

Anti-abortion forces, who have made family-planning clinics a prime target, don't like to acknowledge that abortion sometimes is a sound medical choice. But it should be acknowledged by the Supreme Court, a body that is supposed to stand for the Constitution — in this case, freedom of speech — and for good sense in ruling on the letter and spirit of the law. This time, the majority in a 5-4 decision failed miserably on both counts.

The practical effect of the ruling is that affluent women will continue to get abortions on demand from their doctors. But some women, predominantly poor, will not take advantage of their right to abortion simply because they were never advised that it was a prudent option. And in some cases, sad to say, women may be placed at undeserved and unnecessary risk.

Now there is but one alternative, and that is for Congress to do its duty as the balancing branch of government. It must enact laws protecting all women, rich and poor, and ensuring that doctors, not judges, make vital decisions about women's health.

The Phoenix Gazette
Phoenix, Arizona, May 24, 1991

The abortion issue continues to divide the nation and the nation's highest court. By a 5-4 vote, the Supreme Court ruled that federally funded family planning clinics may not discuss abortion with pregnant women or tell them where to get one.

Under 1988 regulations, clinic staff are not permitted to engage in abortion counseling or refer patients to abortion clinics.

In the court's view, the regulations do not violate free-speech rights or women's right to end their pregnancies.

Federally funded family planning clinics always have been banned from using federal money to perform abortions, but until 1988 clinic staffs were permitted to tell women about the abortion option and make referrals.

Writing for the court, Chief Justice William H. Rehnquist said, "In these circumstances, the general rule that the government may choose not to subsidize speech applies with full force." The decision does not alter the 1973 *Roe v. Wade* ruling that legalized abortion.

Rehnquist was joined by justices Byron White, Anthony Kennedy, Antonin Scalia and David Souter. Sandra Day O'Connor, Thurgood Marshall, Harry Blackmun and John Paul Stevens dissented.

The Gazette is not comfortable with regulatory intrusion into the relationship between health care providers and patients. It certainly is within Congress' power to determine which medical procedures will be funded with federal money; it doesn't necessarily follow that Congress should determine legislatively what medical advice doctors should give patients.

However, the decision is consistent with the legislative intent of Title X of the Public Health Service Act, which is to provide pre-pregnancy family planning services. The legislative intent was a clear product of abortion politics rather than any medical problem.

The ruling also follows on a series of decisions in which the court held that government has no obligation to assure citizens' access to the means for enforcing constitutional rights, even when those rights have been foreclosed because of expense.

The best that can be said of the decision is that it is an uneasy compromise between a woman's right to obtain abortion counseling and care and abortion opponents' desire not to be required to have their taxes promote a service they find repugnant.

The Washington Post
Washington, D.C., May 24, 1991

IT IS NOW clear that there is no longer a majority on the Supreme Court dedicated to protecting abortion rights against the onslaughts of hostile legislators and retrogressive regulation-writers. Only a few years ago, the court spelled out its conviction that government actions designed to inhibit the exercise of the right—by requiring, for example, waiting periods and lectures on the perils of abortion—were unacceptable. There has been a gradual retreat in recent years, but yesterday the extent of the drift from that strong stand was apparent when the court approved federal regulations that bar doctors and health workers even from mentioning abortions in government-funded family planning clinics. Justice David Souter, whose first vote on the issue was eagerly awaited, cast the deciding vote.

At issue were regulations promulgated in 1988 that changed a practice at the 4,000 family planning clinics funded, in part, under Title X of the Public Health Services Act. One section of that law provides that "[n]one of the funds appropriated under this subchapter shall be used in programs where abortion is a method of family planning." So from its inception the program never funded abortions. But staff routinely *discussed* abortion as an option and referred women to providers when appropriate. The Reagan administration regulations banned this counseling and referral and, where Title X recipients used their own money to provide abortion services, required that these services be separated both physically and financially from the family planning operations. The regulations have not been enforced during the time they have been challenged in court, but now they will go into effect.

The four dissenters on the court, Justices Marshall, Stevens, Blackmun and O'Connor, write that the regulations go far beyond the plain meaning of the statute. One dissenting appeals court judge styled them "arbitrary and capricious," which they certainly are. They are also an unconstitutional restriction on free speech and on a woman's ability to exercise her right to abortion. But the persuasive arguments of dissenters are now history, and the task ahead is to plan an alternative challenge.

President Bush, who did not propose the regulations, could, of course, tell Secretary of Health and Human Services Louis Sullivan to revoke them. But he won't, and so the task falls to Congress. The votes are there. Last year, the Senate voted 62 to 36 to overturn the regulations, and House leaders believe that body could do the same. But veto-proof majorities are probably needed, and that measure of support will be much more difficult to organize. Yesterday's decision, allowing the government to prohibit recipients of federal funds from even mentioning the option of abortion to poor women seeking advice, should cause a backlash sufficient to mobilize Congress.

The Oregonian

Portland, Oregon, May 25, 1991

When a pregnant woman visits a health clinic, she should be able to get information that accurately describes all the medically safe and legal options open to her — including abortion.

But because of Thursday's U.S. Supreme Court ruling, that is now too much for her to expect when the clinic receives federal funds.

The court allowed unfair restrictions on a low-income woman's access to medical advice when it upheld Reagan and Bush administration efforts to bar federally funded clinics from providing abortion information and referrals.

Planned Parenthood, whose clinics nationwide receive $37 million in federal funds, says it will continue to provide information on abortion even if that means losing the federal support. That is a commendable decision; complete medical advice should be the basis of any health clinic's operation.

The court's ruling applies to 4,500 clinics that serve nearly 4 million women each year. In Oregon, more than 70 health clinics are affected. None of those clinics performs abortions, but they have been providing information about abortion, adoption and keeping the child as options to pregnant women.

Under the now court-approved regulations, abortion will not be mentioned as an option if a clinic continues to receive federal funds. If a woman asks about abortion, she will be told that "the program does not consider abortion an appropriate method of family planning."

The regulations were issued by then-President Reagan's Department of Health and Human Services in 1988 and were immediately challenged on the grounds they exceeded Congress' intent and violated the free-speech rights of clinic doctors and workers and a woman's right to an abortion.

It's troubling that a court majority didn't see the free-speech implication: How can a doctor or other health worker be denied the right to tell a patient anything professional judgment says is appropriate?

Since the Supreme Court failed to prevent this misguided federal intrusion, Congress needs to step in. Legislation to undo this rule should be passed immediately, even though the outlook for overriding a presidential veto is uncertain.

In the meantime, Planned Parenthood's decision to forgo federal funds in order to continue to provide women with complete information should be applauded.

Richmond Times-Dispatch

Richmond, Virginia, May 26, 1991

The U.S. Supreme Court's 5-4 decision upholding a Reagan-era regulatory ruling that federally funded family planning clinics may not dispense information about or promote abortion has rekindled the nation's passionate debate over abortion rights. Further, it has sparked fear or hope, depending on one's perspective, that new Justice David Souter's siding with the majority presages the overturning of the 1973 *Roe vs. Wade* decision that made abortion a constitutionally protected right.

In reality, however, Thursday's decision in *Rust vs. Sullivan* turned on separation-of-powers and governmental administration issues. Obviously the abortion culture, so extensively represented in the news media, is sorely displeased, and anti-abortion activists are emboldened. But this ruling does not reach or even hint at any determination whether *Roe* was a bad precedent. The heart of the issue is the ability of the executive branch, through its regulatory agencies, to control the scope of governmental programs so long as the clear intent of Congress is not flouted.

The program in question is Title X of the Public Health Service Act of 1970, which provides for subsidies and regulation of family planning clinics. The law contains a prohibition on federal appropriations being used "in programs where abortion is a method of family planning ..." For the first 17 years, federal regulators interpreted that language as a ban only on actual abortions, not on advice or information about abortion. However, the Reagan administration, in its final year, issued more stringent regulations holding that to use federal support to counsel a woman to have an abortion is to impermissibly exalt abortion as a family-planning method.

The most basic question for the high court was whether the Reagan regulators had abused their discretion by violating congressional will. Writing for the majority, Chief Justice William H. Rehnquist said the congressional record was "ambiguous and unenlightening" and noted that "we customarily defer to the expertise of the agency" in such instances. And he found unpersuasive plaintiffs' contentions that their constitutional rights of free speech somehow had been violated by the government's choosing to support childbirth over abortion. That is the kind of "value judgment" properly authorized program administrators may make, the chief justice said.

In sum, this is not a matter of government's discriminating on the basis of viewpoint; rather, government "has merely chosen to fund one activity to the exclusion of the other. ... " Because Washington supports a National Endowment for Democracy does not mean, the chief justice noted wryly, that it is constitutionally required to underwrite the views of those who think communism or fascism ought to be promoted around the world. Pro-abortion activists are free, on their own time and own dime, to advocate their cause.

The majority's support for the right of the executive to "define the limits" of grant programs, as opposed to letting them become open-ended grab bags for special interests, is a highly welcome exercise in judicial restraint, one that we hope will be applied more widely than just in the abortion context. As for those clinicians who equate planning a family with destroying a budding member of that family, they have a right to lobby Congress for change or to continue their advocacy without the support of taxpayer dollars, as some are threatening to do.

The Record

Hackensack, New Jersey, May 26, 1991

The U.S. Supreme Court's reasoning in its latest decision on abortion is pretty hard to figure out. Even though abortion is perfectly legal, the court's majority ruled, federally funded health clinics may not give women any counseling about abortion. In fact, the court said, the clinic must tell women that it does not consider abortion an appropriate method of family planning and therefore does not counsel or recommend abortion.

Isn't there an inconsistency here? Since abortion is legal, isn't it only logical to conclude that federally financed clinics have an obligation to at least explain to pregnant women that abortion is a lawful option?

The court, with its 5-4 decision, raised another inconsistency. In effect, it said that women who can afford to go to private clinics not covered by the high court's ruling are entitled to abortion counseling, but poorer women who use the federally funded clinics are not. Ironically, it is poor women, who don't get much information from newspapers and magazines, who probably know the least about abortion to begin with. Especially poor teenagers. Is this ruling fair for them?

Finally, the court's ruling means that doctors and other trained advisers at the federally funded clinics will be barred from providing information on abortion, even if they consider it an advisable option for the patient. During arguments on the case, Justice David Souter suggested to a lawyer that this would mean physicians could not perform their usual professional responsibilities. "You are telling us [the government] in effect may preclude professional speech," Mr. Souter added. Ironically, Mr. Souter went on to vote with the majority in upholding the restriction.

Consider this, however: Would the federal government even consider forbidding doctors to offer treatment or advice on a legal option for any other condition? Would the government proscribe a legal treatment for, say, glaucoma or cancer? Obviously not.

•

Now that the court has ruled, there's only one thing to do. Congress should pass legislation restoring to federally financed clinics their right to offer abortion counseling. If President Bush were to veto such legislation — as he has indicated he would — the question should be debated in the 1992 presidential campaign.

On an issue as important and sensitive as this, there can be only one final arbiter: we, the people.

The Hartford Courant
Hartford, Connecticut, May 24, 1991

About 4,000 family planning clinics, serving more than 4 million low-income women each year, receive funds from the federal government under a 1970 law commonly called Title X.

These clinics, which have never used government money to pay for abortions, were ordered by the Reagan administration in 1988 to purge even the word abortion from their vocabularies. No facility using federal funds may tell women about abortion as an option, or make referrals, the administration's zealots decreed.

On Thursday, a sharply divided U.S. Supreme Court affirmed the government's right to prohibit all talk of abortion between pregnant women and physicians and other professionals at family planning clinics.

Justice David H. Souter, the court's newest member, voted with the 5-4 majority, even though he had pointed out when the case was argued in October that the restrictions interfered with a doctor's "professional speech."

Writing for the court, Chief Justice William H. Rehnquist tried to make fine distinctions: By prohibiting any talk of abortion, government "is not denying a benefit to anyone, but is instead simply insisting that public funds be spent for the purpose for which they were authorized."

In other words, a woman may go to private clinics and received the most comprehensive advice possible — if she can afford it. But if she's poor and her only option is a federally aided family planning facility, then she's entitled to limited information about family planning; clinicians must pretend that abortion does not exist, that it is not legal.

The clinicians may talk extensively with their clients, of course, about prenatal care and various social services for women who choose to have babies.

So family planning clinics now have a choice: They may pull out of Title X or succumb to federal dictates about what to tell their clients.

It's a cruel choice.

Title X has been the mainstay of the nation's effort to promote the use of contraceptives and hence to eliminate the need for abortion. Clients also receive a variety of health-screening services at the clinics. More than 1 million additional unintended pregnancies would occur each year without the government-supported family planning programs, according to the experts. In Connecticut, about 48,000 women may be affected by the court's decision.

Patients must not be denied relevant medical information about pregnancy or anything else. Government must not interfere with a woman's right to choose a legal abortion and with medicine's obligation to discuss options on request or make referrals.

When Congress approved Title X, it did not intend for regulators to write these absolutist anti-abortion rules. Congress now has the obligation to leave no doubt about its intention by enacting legislation to reverse the court's decision.

If Mr. Bush vetoes the legislation, the issue will be taken to voters next year. Most Americans would support the proposition that a pregnant women should be informed by her doctor of all the legal options available.

Arkansas Gazette
Little Rock, Arkansas, May 25, 1991

As feared and expected, the Supreme Court has further undermined a woman's right to an abortion. In a 5-4 decision Thursday, the court majority attacked the most vulnerable prey — the poor.

The court upheld federal regulations that bar government-subsidized family planning clinics from discussing abortion with pregnant women or telling them where abortions are performed. Some 4,000 of these clinics serve millions of low-income women, but they will not serve them nearly as well under the court's decision.

The decision conforms with the policies of the Reagan and Bush administrations to weaken abortion rights and family planning programs. It is significant that Justice Sandra Day O'Connor, the only woman on the court, joined the Court's three most liberal members in dissenting. O'Connor is normally found in the conservative bloc, but she knows the injustice of the court's decision and the administration's policies.

Justice Harry A. Blackmun, author of the 1973 Roe vs. Wade decision that legalized abortion, said in a dissenting opinion Thursday that the Court now was taking away a poor woman's right to abortion.

"This [decision] is a course nearly as noxious as overruling Wade directly, for if a right is found to be unenforceable, even against flagrant attempts by government to circumvent it, then it ceases to be a right at all," Blackmun wrote.

Federally subsidized family planning clinics are prohibited by law from performing abortions or paying for them, but until 1988, the clinics were allowed to discuss abortion with clients and to make abortion referrals. That year, the Reagan administration issued regulations forbidding even this assistance. The regulations say that if a woman asks about abortion, she is to be told that the clinic staff "does not consider abortion an appropriate method of family planning." The regulations are not only anti-women, they're anti-free speech. Since the court majority is anti-individual rights generally, this presented no problem. It probably firmed up the consensus.

Court challenges have kept the regulations from being enforced in most parts of the country. The Supreme Court decision unleashes the enforcers.

The right-wing ideologues infesting the court press on, toward a reversal of Roe vs. Wade. The Rehnquist Court could make history by denying a personal freedom that a previous court had recognized. What sad and divisive history it will be, what oppression of women.

DESERET NEWS
Salt Lake City, Utah, May 27, 1991

Though opponents of abortion won an important round in this continuing battle Thursday, both sides of the dispute are attributing too much significance to it.

That's because the new ruling from the U.S. Supreme Court will only make it harder for some women to get information about abortion but not impossible.

In a 5-4 ruling that reflects the extent to which the nation as well as the court is divided over this highly emotional issue, the justices upheld the federal government's controversial regulations barring federally funded clinics from giving patients abortion advice. The regulations were written in 1988 but were not enforced until the courts could finish ruling on them.

The decision against using taxpayer funds to pay for abortion advice is simply a logical extension of the longstanding rule against using taxpayer funds to perform abortions themselves.

Even so, the fight on this score is still a long way from over. The battle now shifts to Congress, which is being asked to overturn Thursday's Supreme Court ruling.

As the nation's lawmakers consider such legislation, they would do well to remember that the new ruling is no aberration but simply puts the Supreme Court in line with previous rulings from federal district court in New York, where this week's case originated, and the Second Circuit Court of Appeals.

Keep a few other points firmly in mind, too.

First, though federal funds may not be used to provide information about abortion, including the names and addresses of clinics, the location of such services is still readily available to anyone who knows how to use a telephone and a phone directory.

Second, if the new ruling results in fewer abortions, so much the better. The appalling fact is that more abortions are performed in this country than any other surgical procedure except tonsillectomies. This situation strongly suggests that abortions are often being used not out of necessity but as a convenience.

Third, though poor women are the ones affected most by the new ruling, the Supreme Court is not necessarily saddling them with unwanted children. Abortion never was the only option in family planning. Far more couples are looking for children to adopt than there are children available.

Meanwhile, abortion itself is still as legal as ever — and as controversial. That means Americans had better brace themselves for more fights over just about every aspect of this issue for many years to come.

The Washington Times
Washington, D.C., May 28, 1991

Last week the House of Representatives and the Supreme Court took opposite points of view on two separate but similar abortion-related issues. The House passed an amendment to the fiscal 1992 defense bill that will allow military medical facilities overseas to effectively ignore the Hyde Amendment, which bans federal subsidies for abortion except in cases where the life of the mother is in danger. The Supreme Court ruled that federally funded "family planning clinics" must adhere to federal regulations that prohibit them from promoting abortion or referring clients to abortion providers.

Congressional supporters of the amendment to allow the Pentagon to provide abortions overseas argue that female officers and military dependents deployed in remote areas of the world, where medical practices are not up to American standards, could endanger their lives seeking abortions in local clinics. The amendment, they point out, only allows women seeking abortions to "prepay" for such services and then have them performed by a military doctor in a military facility. They would like to ignore the implicit subsidy here and disparage the idea that there will be any damaging moral or cultural impact from using military personnel, equipment and property, which exist specifically to preserve the lives of American soldiers, to instead terminate the lives of unborn children.

In the Supreme Court's case of Rust vs. Sullivan, the regulations for federally funded family planning clinics were opposed by Planned Parenthood (chief recipient of federal family-planning subsidies), the American Civil Liberties Union and the National Abortion Rights Action League. These groups argue that the regulations not only violated the First Amendment rights of clinic employees and clients, but also violated what they believe is the Fifth Amendment right of all Americans to procure abortions. A 5-4 majority properly rejected that tortured interpretation.

The congressmen arguing for military abortions have a better case. After all, they have been elected to legislate. In Congress, the question of federal subsidies for abortion can and should be debated as a matter of national policy. But the weakness in the case made by the supporters of military abortions is that they simply don't want to grapple with the question of subsidies directly. That is why they chose a hard case: We are beckoned to conjure up in our mind's eye female soldiers seeking the services of shady Third World doctors.

But Pentagon spokeswoman Susan Hansen says that during a period in the 1980s when "prepaid" abortions were allowed as a matter of internal Pentagon policy (in 1988 the Pentagon changed its policy to comply with the Hyde Amendment) there were only 12 to 15 such abortions per year. The Pentagon, moreover, does not know how many of them were performed in Europe, where the vast majority of female soldiers posted overseas are stationed. Germany, Italy and Great Britain may or may not hold to medical standards that match D.C. General's, but neither do their standards replicate those currently in existing in Bangladesh.

Rep. Henry Hyde argues that the amendment will create an abortion "entitlement" for military personnel. Once the wall that prevents the military from performing abortions is breeched, the litigational tide will come rolling in, and it will be adjudged discriminatory to allow a pregnant Pfc to abort her child at a military facility in Athens, Greece, but not Athens, Ga. Mr. Hyde also objects to the idea of "making abortionists out of military doctors."

This gets right to the point. Abortion, even if it is performed in outer space by an alien doctor, is a moral evil. That abortion is allowed at all is regrettable. But even though it is, taxpayers should no more have to pay for anybody to have one, be counseled about one or be referred to one than they should have to pay for congressmen and government officials to use government airplanes for personal trips at public expense.

The Courier-Journal
Louisville, Kentucky, May 24, 1991

TELLING doctors and counselors in federally funded family planning clinics not to brief pregnant women on certain legal options may not be unconstitutional, but it's unsound policy. And dangerous. Following yesterday's ruling by the U. S. Supreme Court, however, only Congress can undo damage done by the Reagan administration.

At issue is language adopted in 1970 that prohibits federal funds from being used "in programs where abortion is a method of family planning." For years, federal regulators said those words had no bearing on the right of medical professionals to present information about abortion. Indeed, they expressly required clinics to provide information about abortions.

But that changed when President Reagan needed to buttress his standing with right-wing supporters. To appease them he drafted a regulation prohibiting clinics receiving federal money from "assisting" a woman in obtaining an abortion. Workers couldn't mention the word "abortion" or even refer patients to clinics listed in the Yellow Pages, regulators said.

Until yesterday's ruling, those regulations were not enforced in many of the 4,000 clinics that receive federal aid. But now they can be — giving constitutional authority to rules that are a disturbing intrusion by government into the physician-patient relationship. By keeping women in the dark about some options, they interfere with their right to make informed decisions. The intrusion stems from political — not health — considerations. Furthermore, they're arbitrary, since women who don't use federally-funded clinics aren't affected by them.

The Court's ruling could have a detrimental bearing on future decisions about federal funding in the arts, education and libraries. If, for example, regulators decided that libraries receiving federal money shouldn't have information about abortion, would the Court go along with that, too?

Those affected are women without health insurance. They rely upon non-profit clinics for family-planning services, which perform services of incalculable value to the poor and help this country contain health costs. Making it more difficult for the clinics to fully serve them is unsound policy.

This week Congress reversed a Department of Defense directive forbidding military health clinics overseas from performing abortions. Now, it must undo another bad regulation.

DESERET NEWS
Salt Lake City, Utah, May 24, 1991

Though opponents of abortion won an important round in this continuing battle Thursday, both sides of the dispute are attributing too much significance to it.

That's because the new ruling from the U.S. Supreme Court will only make it harder for some women to get information about abortion but not impossible.

In a 5-4 ruling that reflects the extent to which the nation as well as the court is divided over this highly emotional issue, the justices upheld the federal government's controversial regulations barring federally funded clinics from giving patients abortion advice. The regulations were written in 1988 but were not enforced until the courts could finish ruling on them.

The decision against using taxpayer funds to pay for abortion advice is simply a logical extension of the long-standing rule against using taxpayer funds to perform abortions themselves.

Even so, the fight on this score is still a long way from over. The battle now shifts to Congress, which is being asked to overturn Thursday's Supreme Court ruling.

As the nation's lawmakers consider such legislation, they would do well to remember that the new ruling is no aberration but simply puts the Supreme Court in line with previous rulings from federal district court in New York, where this week's case originated, and the Second Circuit Court of Appeals.

Keep a few other points firmly in mind, too.

First, though federal funds may not be used to provide information about abortion, including the names and addresses of clinics, the location of such services is still readily available to anyone who knows how to use a telephone and a phone directory.

Second, if the new ruling results in fewer abortions, so much the better. The appalling fact is that more abortions are performed in this country than any other surgical procedure except tonsillectomies. This situation strongly suggests that abortions are often being used not out of necessity but as a convenience.

Third, though poor women are the ones affected most by the new ruling, the Supreme Court is not necessarily saddling them with unwanted children. Abortion never was the only option in family planning. Far more couples are looking for children to adopt than there are children available.

Meanwhile, abortion itself is still as legal as ever — and as controversial. That means Americans had better brace themselves for more fights over just about every aspect of this issue for many years to come.

Detroit Free Press

Detroit, Michigan, May 27, 1991

The principle underlying the decisions of Planned Parenthood and others no longer to accept federal family-planning funds in light of last week's U.S. Supreme Court ruling is an important one. Women seeking help must be able to so do with confidence that respect for them as individuals, and professionalism, not politics, are guiding those to whom they've turned.

In vowing to sidestep the court's 5-4 ruling that the government can prevent them from telling poor pregnant women of their full range of medical options, the clinics are acting responsibly. So, too, are members of Congress who quickly responded by saying they would seek to reverse the impact of the court's ruling.

The Supreme Court, for its part, acted with recklessness by choosing to ignore questions of free speech, medical ethics and the right of a woman to decide without government interference whether or not to bear a child. Despite what Chief Justice William Rehnquist acknowledged was the ambiguity of Congress' intent, the court upheld regulations of the Reagan and Bush administrations that prohibit even the mention of abortion in clinics receiving funds under the 1970 Family Planning Act. Instead, the chief justice said the court should defer to the expertise of the Secretary of Health and Human Services, who can — he wrote — "without violating the Constitu-

tion, selectively fund a program to encourage certain activities (he) believes to be in the public interest . . ."

Far more persuasive, we think, is Justice Harry Blackmun's dissent, which was joined, in part, by the sole woman on the court, Sandra Day O'Connor, as well as by Justices Thurgood Marshall and John Paul Stevens. In it, Justice Blackmun ominously warned that the majority opinion for the first time in the court's history upheld "viewpoint-based suppression of speech simply because that suppression was a conditional upon acceptance of public funds."

Equally troubling is the court's naive assertion that the regulations have no impact on "a doctor's ability to provide, and a woman's right to receive, information concerning abortion and abortion-related services."

What, in effect, the court has done is perpetuate and extend a dual system of health care. Women of means can — and should — expect private physicians to discuss fully their options. Information, though, would be withheld from women who go to publicly subsidized clinics.

No government should tolerate, much less *require*, that sort of conduct by healthcare professionals. And surely that was never Congress' intent.

Members of that body must move quickly to undo the damage done by the court.

The Seattle Times

Seattle, Washington, May 26, 1991

IF YOU'RE one of 4 million poor women seeking help at a family planning clinic, the Supreme Court has ruled that you don't have the right to complete medical advice.

The court upheld a federal regulation that forbids doctors in 4,500 government-subsidized family planning clinics from mentioning abortion even when they are asked.

The 1988 regulation, issued by the Department of Health and Human Services under Title X of the Public Health Services Act, was devised by the Reagan administration to restrict free speech and abortion rights.

Title X, which has funded family planning services since 1970, expressly provides that "none of the funds appropriated under this subchapter shall be used in programs where abortion is a method of family planning."

Accordingly, no Title X money has ever paid for abortions. The new regulation goes a lot further. It requires doctors to refer all pregnant patients to prenatal care whether or not the doctor believes that is the right course, and prohibits doctors from giving information on abortion to those seeking help.

When asked about abortion, doctors are permitted only to answer that "the project does not consider abortion an appropriate method of family planning."

This is a crude gag order. Chief Justice William Rehnquist's garbled majority opinion cynically argues that the regulation does not "significantly impinge on the doctor-patient relationship" because patients should not expect "comprehensive medical advice," anyway.

Since the five-member majority — including Justice David Souter, who cast the deciding vote — is willing to let the government erode a woman's right to choose by denying her basic medical facts, it's time Congress stepped in.

Last year the Senate voted, 62 to 36, to strike the regulation. The bill should be reintroduced now that appeals to the courts have ended. Very likely, such a measure will have to be vetoproof, making passage tougher. Even so, what lawmaker in good conscience could oppose dispensing accurate, neutral medical information?

THE SPOKESMAN-REVIEW
Spokane, Washington, May 24, 1991

If you want to talk about abortion, go somewhere else. That, in essence, is what family planning clinics that receive federal funds must begin telling their clients in light of the sharply divided U.S. Supreme Court's 5-4 ruling on abortion counseling Thursday.

We're not talking here about demanding that no federal dollars be used to pay for abortions; that's already on the books. We're talking about the court's affirmation of a Reagan-era regulation that denies young or poor women access to legally available information.

The court said federally subsidized clinics cannot advise women about the option of abortion or make a referral. It puts such clinics — of which there are about 4,000 serving more than 4 million low-income women each year — in the foolish position of saying to women inquiring about abortion: "That's for me to know and you to find out."

What the court really said Thursday is that, in this country, women still — for the moment, at least — have the legal right to an abortion. But women are going to get no help through any federal resources figuring out how, when, where and even *if* it is the best option for them.

These clinics' patients will be denied information about the procedure, feelings during and after, risks and long-term effects. The right to choose is hollow without information on which to base a choice.

Requiring these clinics to deprive women without private resources of an opportunity to explore all the legally available family planning options sets them up to act irresponsibly. The clinics must give women full and complete information, about everything from prenatal care to adoption to pregnancy termination.

What is most clear is that the season of worry for women — and for men concerned about protecting women's rights — has begun in earnest. The fate of Roe vs. Wade, which since 1973 has given American women the right to choose abortion, is scary in the hands of this court. At a time when the women's movement has appeared to be dormant, largely because of the many strides that have been made, comes a sharp reminder of how quickly the cornerstones of that progress can be chipped away.

The Bronx, New York, clinic that challenged the federal ban on abortion counseling and lost vows to get by without the federal money — more than a quarter of its annual budget — rather than sell women short. That clinic, and others like it, say they will continue to inform women of their choices — all of them — in the event of unwanted pregnancy.

But, ultimately, less money to operate with means less service. That, in turn, can mean more unwanted pregnancies and ultimately more abortions — something no one wants.

The Honolulu Advertiser
Honolulu, Hawaii, May 24, 1991

The Supreme Court ruling forbidding abortion counseling in family planning clinics that receive federal funds denies help to those who need it most.

These are poor women who are among the least likely to use other birth control, who due to poor health and nutrition find themselves and their offspring at greatest risk, and who are least able to care for an unwanted child.

Clinics always have been banned from using federal money to perform abortions. But it's hard to imagine any other health situation in which a legal alternative may not even be mentioned, much less advocated, because some people object to the procedure.

About 4,000 clinics, including five in Hawaii, are affected. What do they do now?

They can obey the rules, at great disservice to clients. They can refuse federal funds. They can set up physically and financially separate facilities for abortion counseling. They can hope Congress overrides the regulations.

But will enough legislators be willing to buck the noisy anti-abortion minority? Most Americans favor leaving to women the decision on abortion (though many are dismayed at the large number performed versus other less drastic birth control). But anti-abortionists tend to be one-issue voters.

The bigger test may be ahead. The court's 5-4 ruling — relying on the newest justice, David Souter — suggests the time is nearer when the Roe vs. Wade abortion-rights ruling may be overturned. That will throw the issue back to individual state legislatures.

Minneapolis Star and Tribune
Minneapolis, Minnesota, May 30, 1991

The U.S. Supreme Court's abortion decision last week will undercut the ability of many women to make informed, coercion-free decisions about whether to continue their pregnancies. That's the central damage, but the court also inflicted severe collateral distress. In its zeal to get at the abortion issue, the five-man majority stepped all over the professional responsibilities of doctors and treated the Constitution with appalling flippancy.

In its decision, the court upheld Reagan administration regulations, issued in 1988, that prohibit staff members of federally funded family-planning clinics from discussing abortion with patients, most of them low-income women without resources to seek advice elsewhere. If a woman asks about abortion, the regulations stipulate, staff members must respond that the clinic "does not consider abortion an appropriate method of family planning" — whether or not that actually is true. In effect, the regulations require clinic staff members to deceive patients and withhold information from them — serious violations of medical ethics.

When it authorized federal funds for family-planning clinics in 1970, Congress stipulated that none of the money "shall be used in programs where abortion is a method of family planning." Although that language is legally ambiguous, a common-sense reading suggests that Congress intended to prohibit federal funding for programs involving abortions, not discussion of the procedure. For 18 years that common-sense view prevailed in the implementing regulations. Then the Reagan administration rewrote them.

To uphold those new regulations, the court majority had to find that they did not violate free-speech rights guaranteed by the First Amendment or abortion-related privacy rights guaranteed by the Fifth. With alarming casualness, it found that neither set of rights was violated. That's what upset Justice Sandra Day O'Connor. When a statute contains ambiguous language and the court is called to decide between two plausible interpretations, the court by long tradition has chosen the interpretation that avoids raising serious constitutional questions, O'Connor pointed out. If the court had followed that tradition, it would have disallowed the Reagan family-planning regulations and avoided Chief Justice William Rehnquist's shallow dip into important issues of personal rights.

Rehnquist's majority decision has the priggish tone of a parent who, confronted with an injured child, focuses on cause rather than on comfort. Many of the points he makes appear technically correct but ignore the real world that patients of family-planning clinics inhabit. Congress should quickly enact legislation that would explicitly allow the clinics to continue answering women's questions about abortion and referring them elsewhere if they choose to pursue that option.

TULSA WORLD

Tulsa, Oklahoma, May 29, 1991

A PEEK at how the newest Supreme Court justice, David Souter, would vote on abortion-related issues came last week. He cast the tie-breaking vote to uphold the government policy that bans abortion counseling and referrals at federally subsidized family planning clinics.

Anti-abortion forces cheered and pro-choice supporters began to worry out loud about the ultimate question: Will he vote to rescind Roe vs. Wade, which gave women the legal right to an abortion?

It's probably all a little premature. The closeness of the Supreme Court view parallels the divided opinions of Americans on this sensitive issue. But the unmistakable trend on the high court in recent decisions has been to restrict access to abortion.

This decision prohibits doctors from mentioning abortion, even if there is a clear medical reason for it. If during an examination a physician discovered a life-threatening pregnancy, he could not even refer the woman to another facility.

That type of muzzling is an outrage. The government is saying to the poor: Don't expect complete, candid and unbiased advice from our facilities.

The ruling places further difficulty on professional clinics, such as Planned Parenthood, which must continue to forfeit federal funds.

The last chapter has not been written but the abortion battle is entering another stage as the conservative court becomes more activist.

LAS VEGAS REVIEW-JOURNAL

Las Vegas, Nevada, May 26, 1991

Thursday's U.S. Supreme Court ruling — hailed by right-to-lifers and denounced by pro-choicers — was, interestingly, not fundamentally about abortion. Rather it was about whether the federal government has an obligation to finance clinics that advertise abortion as a "family planning" option.

In a 5-4 ruling, the justices said, essentially, that while women may indeed have a constitutional right to secure abortions, it is not the government's duty to make it easier to get one. The government can deny taxpayer money to clinics that counsel abortion, the high court said.

Abortion rights activists flailed away at the decision as an infringement on the free-speech rights of doctors and clinic workers. But it represented nothing of the kind.

We see a clear parallel here to the recent controversies involving federal financing of art works through the National Endowment for the Arts. Let it be known that artists in this country have a perfect, iron-clad right to paint or write or film anything they want: They *do not* have a consequent right to receive taxpayer money while doing so, despite protestations to the contrary from the arts community. If Andres Serrano wants to stick a plastic crucifix in a vat of urine and call it art, fine. That does not mean the government has to pay for it.

The notion that Thursday's ruling deprives doctors and "family planning" clinics of their First Amendment right to push the abortion option is erroneous. It doesn't. The doctors and clinicians are free to advocate anything they want: But they do not have a parallel right to receive federal money while doing so.

Along with many other pro-abortion organizations in the country, Planned Parenthood of Southern Nevada plans to relinquish the federal tax-funded portion of its budget rather than quit supplying abortion advice. That is its choice.

In the majority opinion, Chief Justice William Rehnquist wrote: "When the government appropriates public funds to establish a program it is entitled to define the limits of that program. In so doing, the government has not discriminated on the basis of viewpoint; it has merely chosen to fund one activity to the exclusion of the other."

He is exactly right. In cruder terms: Those who would feed at the federal trough must eat what's on the menu.

The Star-Ledger

Newark, New Jersey, May 28, 1991

Family planning clinics were conceived with the purpose of counseling expectant mothers on matters of health and the size of their families. That advice might well include the possibility of abortion, especially in a deprived social environment where the termination of a pregnancy could be a matter of crucial importance for a poor woman who could ill afford to have an infant.

But that useful maternal counseling, unfortunately, no longer will be available to millions of poor pregnant women if the planning clinics they attend receive federal subsidies. That vital aspect of family planning will be barred under a backtracking decision by a deeply divided U.S. Supreme Court.

In a 5-4 vote, the court held that a 1988 ban contained in regulations issued by the Reagan administration does not violate free speech rights or a woman's right to end her pregnancy. Primarily, the harshest impact would be on women with low incomes who are dependent on 4,000 family planning clinics that receive federal grants.

For pro-choice advocates, the court ruling is a critical setback, not only immediately but also in unsettling long-term implications of further inroads on a woman's right to terminate pregnancies. Particularly unsettling for the future was the crucial tie-breaking vote cast by the newest court member, Justice David Souter. He could be a decisive force in abortion challenges before the high court that are certain to be accelerated by the latest ruling.

The court decision was sharply assailed by Justice Harry Blackmun, who drafted the landmark 1973 Roe vs. Wade decision legalizing abortion. While the court's latest ruling does not affect the Roe decision, Justice Blackmun was concerned over the adverse social effect it would have in depriving low-income women of their abortion right.

"While technically leaving intact the fundamental right protected by Roe vs. Wade," Justice Blackmun said, the court had, for all practical purposes, made that right worthless. "This is a course nearly as noxious as overruling Roe directly, for if a right is found to be unforceable, even against flagrant attempts by government to circumvent it, then it ceases to be a right at all."

Besides the unsettling constitutional breaching of a woman's free speech right and right to abortion, the ruling has the socially regressive effect of setting up a two-tier system of reproductive health care—one class of women able to afford a private physician who can advise them on choices, the other, a deprived class of women who no longer will have access to federally funded clinics for this essential counseling.

This is, indeed, a poor choice in basic social terms.

Abortion Case Accepted on Eve of *Roe v. Wade* Anniversary

The Supreme Court January 21, 1992 agreed to a limited review of the constitutionality of a Pennsylvania law that restricted a woman's access to abortion. In October 1991, the U.S. 3rd Circuit Court of Appeals in Philadelphia had upheld all but one of the law's key provisions. The case was *Planned Parenthood of Southeastern Pennsylvania v. Casey.*

The timing of the Pennsylvania case, with a decision expected by July, began to force abortion to the forefront as an issue in the 1992 U.S. presidential campaign. In the current case, the Supreme Court would decide the scope of restrictions that could be placed on the constitutional right to abortion. The high court had first recognized the right in its 1973 *Roe v. Wade* decision.

The Pennsylvania law in question was passed in 1989, after the Supreme Court's *Webster v. Reproductive Health Services* decision had allowed states greater authority to restrict access to abortion. The Pennsylvania law was one of the strictest in the country.

In accepting the case, the Supreme Court limited the scope of its consideration to the legality of several of the restrictive provisions of the Pennsylvania law, including a provision that required a married woman seeking an abortion to notify her husband before the procedure, in most cases. The appeals court had declared that provision unconstitutional.

The other key provisions under review required doctors to give women seeking abortions state-prepared information about the alternatives to abortion, the risks of both abortion and pregnancy, and access to materials about the fetus and state agencies offering abortion alternatives. The law required a 24-hour waiting period between receiving information and obtaining an abortion. The law also required women under 18 to receive parental or court consent.

The high court, in its order accepting the case, also said it would consider the law's definition of medical emergency, under which the restrictions on receiving an abortion could be waived. In addition, the court said it would review the reporting requirements that the law imposed on abortion providers.

Anti-abortion demonstrators January 22 held their annual March for Life in Washington, D.C., to mark the 19th anniversary of the Supreme Court's landmark 1973 *Roe v. Wade* decision legalizing abortion. As in past years, President George Bush addressed the marchers via telephone from the White House as they assembled on the Capitol Mall.

The March came one day after the Supreme Court had agreed to review the restrictive Pennsylvania abortion. It had been widely anticipated that the court might use the case as a vehicle for reconsidering *Roe v. Wade.*

In his address, Bush told the anti-abortion groups to continue to seek alternatives to abortion. He said, "The most compelling legacy of this nation is [Thomas] Jefferson's concept that all are created equal – he doesn't say 'born,' he says 'created.' From the moment the miracle of life occurs, human beings must cherish that, must hold it in awe, must preserve, protect and defend it."

A small but vocal group of abortion-rights advocates joined the rally and exchanged angry remarks with the anti-abortion marchers. Police estimated that some 70,000 people, on both sides of the abortion debate, attended the rally.

Several hours before the March for Life, dozens of anti-abortion activists from the national anti-abortion group Operation Rescue had attempted to block access to two Washington-area abortion clinics. More than 100 were arrested. The clinics remained open. Protesters had staged similar blockades at other area clinics Jan. 21. The blockades were similar to ones Operation Rescue had staged in Wichita, Kan. in July and August 1991.

The Philadelphia Inquirer
**Philadelphia, Pennsylvania,
January 23, 1992**

Theoretically at least, the Supreme Court has just made it possible that the presidential election could be decided by its ruling — expected by mid-summer — on Pennsylvania's restrictive abortion law.

We had hoped, instead, to hear if anyone out there had a clue about how to strengthen the economy over the long haul, to improve education, to realistically rein in health costs and make medical care available to all.

So far, the candidates *are* dutifully addressing the Big Issues. But we suspect the very nature of the campaign will be transformed if the high court goes beyond what it said Tuesday it would do — narrowly rule on the notice and consent provisions of the Pennsylvania law.

We suspect that, if it goes to the heart of the matter, if it indeed answers the question that abortion rights activists want clearly and definitively answered, then abortion will move front and center in the election — and, possibly, swing it one way or the other.

On the one hand, as editorialists are wont to say, that would have a clarifying quality. Instead of weaseling and chipping and fulminating and twitching, the court would have declared itself on *Roe v. Wade,* the 19-year-old decision that a since-departed majority once ruled a fundamental right.

If it voided it (as it apparently is poised to do at some point), the battle would be joined: The Bush administration would have to defend its record of court appointees; the President would be held accountable for his pep talks to anti-abortion activists such as those who gathered yesterday on Washington's Mall; the silent majority that tells pollsters it supports abortion rights would be mobilized to vote its preference — presumably one of the Democrats who have cast their lot solidly on that side of the issue.

On the other hand, it would be a pity if an election that was shaping up as a full-fledged discussion about where this nation is headed were to be suddenly overshadowed — hijacked, almost — by a grudge match on abortion.

If that occurs, to be sure, it will not be the fault of abortion-rights advocates in Pennsylvania who challenged the burdensome and punitive provisions of the state's unnecessary law.

It will be the fault of the statute's architects, of a court that was chosen — in part — with this end in mind, and of two Republican presidents who have kept the fuse burning.

The Courier-Journal
Louisville, Kentucky, January 23, 1992

NOBODY who has followed the legal and political history of the battle over abortion rights should have been surprised Tuesday when the U. S. Supreme Court announced that it would decide the constitutionality of a highly restrictive Pennsylvania law.

And nobody deserves more credit for the likely outcome — which probably will erode much further the right of a woman to make a choice about abortion in the early months of pregnancy — than President Bush. Since he joined Ronald Reagan's ticket in 1980, Mr. Bush has been one of the most vocal foes of abortion rights. In the last dozen years, federal courts — stocked with Reagan-Bush appointees — have whittled away at the basic premise of the 1973 *Roe v. Wade* decision, which said states could not interfere with the right of a woman to an abortion during the early months of pregnancy. With the recent changes in the high court's composition, the opportunity to topple *Roe* is real.

Yet surveys show that abortion rights are important to voters, especially younger suburbanites who helped fashion GOP victories in the last three presidential elections. An NBC-*Wall Street Journal* poll has found that voters are twice as likely to oppose an anti-abortion candidate than to oppose someone favoring abortion rights. In Kentucky's last major election, Gov. Brereton Jones, the pro-choice Democrat, won by a landslide against Larry Hopkins, who tried to sell voters on an anti-abortion platform.

By agreeing to review the Pennsylvania law, which requires a waiting period and spousal notification before an abortion can be performed, the high court has essentially guaranteed that abortion will be on the front pages this summer — at convention time. And the Republicans are likely to split over the abortion plank of their platform.

Still, Mr. Bush — whose position on abortion flip-flopped when he abandoned moderate Republicanism for the Reaganite wing in 1980 — deserves this dilemma. He has opportunistically exploited this issue for a long time, and it will be just indeed if it ultimately punishes him.

The tragedy, though, is that the real victims will be those persons for whom *Roe* has meant a legal, safe alternative. Mr. Bush knows, as do those who back him on this issue, that abortions won't end if *Roe* is repealed. They'll just move back to the shadows, available at a price that many can't afford in circumstances that may bring disease or death.

Pro-life indeed.

ILLUSTRATION BY ELEANOR MILL

The State
Columbia, South Carolina, January 29, 1992

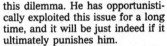

PRESIDENT BUSH, reeling from a huge drop in popularity, surely was unhappy to learn that the Supreme Court he has packed with conservatives will rule in July on the legality of a Pennsylvania law restricting access to abortions. The timing ensures that abortion rights will become a hot issue in the 1992 Presidential campaign.

The Pennsylvania law seeks to limit abortions with a number of regulations, including a mandatory 24-hour waiting period, parental or judicial consent for minors and the notification of husbands by women intending to have an abortion.

It appears unlikely the high court will overturn its 1973 ruling in *Roe vs. Wade*. Instead, the court is likely to chip away at *Roe* by allowing states to erect more obstacles to an abortion. It will decide whether the 3rd Circuit Court of Appeals was correct in upholding most provisions of the Pennsylvania law. The appellate court said state abortion regulations are constitutional unless they impose an "undue burden" on a woman's rights.

Activists on both sides are mobilizing. Democratic Presidential candidates favor choice, while Mr. Bush opposes it and wants *Roe* overturned. Choice advocates believe that, if the economy is still in the doldrums by election time, the President's anti-abortion stand could become a second campaign negative. Abortion opponents say their rank-and-file will support Mr. Bush, regardless of his positions on other issues.

Congress may also force the President's hand. The American Civil Liberties Union and Planned Parenthood are pushing a bill, the Freedom of Choice Act, which would protect women's abortion rights. If this passes, it could add to Mr. Bush's woes.

Mr. Bush's approval rating is at an all-time low of 40 percent. A veto of the pro-choice bill could erode it even further.

The Phoenix Gazette
Phoenix, Arizona, January 26, 1992

YOU can hear staple guns fixing placards to wooden handles. You hear the ripple of cardboard as it is fashioned into signs. You hear the barking calls of protesters. You hear the testing of core dogma. You hear the sounds of political vacillation, of demagoguery and, yes, courage. You hear . . . abortion.

Vast armies of conflicting beliefs and passions are mobilizing once again for conflict, provoked last week by the Supreme Court's decision to review a 1989 Pennsylvania law requiring doctors to tell their pregnant patients about development of the fetus and inform them of the alternatives to abortion, including adoption.

In addition, the law includes a 24-hour waiting period for abortions, parental consent for minors and pre-abortion notification of the husband — all restrictions that are contrary to the court's landmark 1973 *Roe v. Wade* decision.

Roe v. Wade fittingly gave to women the constitutional right to have stewardship over their own bodies, leaving to women and their doctors decisions about abortions. But more recent court decisions have begun to unravel the rights to which women are entitled, and the court's intention to rule in the Pennsylvania case indicates the unraveling is likely to continue.

Will that stop abortions? Of course not.

It will simply make outlaws of the women who have them or the physicians who seek to serve their patients with courageous dissent from governmental edict. Tucked away in the Arizona criminal code, for example, are laws that say the physician or person who performs an abortion in Arizona faces two to five years in prison, and the woman who obtains the abortion can receive one to five years in prison.

If women are forced to opt for coat hangers or back-alley butcher shops, maternal and infant death rates will overwhelm the national conscience. You will hear yet again staple guns fixing placards to wooden handles and the ripple of cardboard to be fashioned into signs. The signs will say, in searing outrage of understanding, "See what the anti-abortionists have done."

Rockford Register Star
Rockford, Illinois, January 24, 1992

The only great mystery surrounding the U.S. Supreme Court's impending review of a Pennsylvania law restricting access to abortion is whether the court will use this case as a vehicle for overturning the *Roe vs. Wade* decision of 19 years ago. Otherwise, there is little doubt that a majority of the justices will uphold the Pennsylvania statute, at least for the most part.

The law at issue requires a 24-hour waiting period, parental consent for minors and notification of husbands by women who are planning to have abortions. While most Americans might find some or all of these restrictions acceptable, polls also show that most do not want to see *Roe* overturned, which would leave the basic legality of abortion up to the individual states.

This general pro-choice attitude among the public makes the high court's impending ruling in the Pennsylvania case potentially problematic for President Bush. Since becoming Ronald Reagan's vice president 11 years ago, Bush has paid at least lip-service to the anti-abortion cause. But many people in Bush's re-election campaign are less than eager to see abortion rights diminished by the Bush-Reagan court in the middle of a presidential election year. Even if the court doesn't completely negate abortion rights, the president's opponents on this issue will try to make political hay of anything less than a ringing affirmation of *Roe*.

If the *Roe* ruling is overturned, it will be the first time in American history that the high court has negated a previously established constitutional right. It will also be a tragic mistake which will only invite politicians to stick their noses where they don't belong — that is, into the reproductive affairs of women. The ensuing backlash from such a ruling could well doom Bush's re-election prospects as well as those of numerous other anti-abortion candidates.

Thus, it just might be that Bush is secretly hoping the court doesn't go whole-hog in heeding the rhetoric he's been peddling ever since he switched from a pro-choice position for reasons of political convenience. It is doubtful that he wants to be a martyr for this cause.

The Honolulu Advertiser
Honolulu, Hawaii, January 24, 1992

It is no surprise that a national survey recently found Hawaii among the states most likely to protect a woman's right to an abortion if the U.S. Supreme Court overturns or further limits Roe vs. Wade.

Sooner or later it will likely be up to individual states to extend or withhold that right, which has been protected for almost 20 years by the landmark Supreme Court decision. The addition of Justice Clarence Thomas gives court conservatives a 6-3 majority on most issues, probably including abortion.

Bainum

The high court's decision to review Pennsylvania's restrictive abortion law this year could make it far easier for states to limit abortions, if not to outlaw them altogether.

The National Abortion Rights Action League weighed several factors — including legislative history and political leaders' views — in deciding which states are most likely to protect abortion rights.

Hawaii was the first state to completely legalize abortion. A bill introduced in this year's Legislature by Waikiki Rep. Duke Bainum, a physician, would strengthen Hawaii women's right of choice.

Overturning Roe vs. Wade will make the country a crazy quilt where what is legal and safe in one state is illegal and dangerous in the next. That will be especially hard on the poor and young.

Efforts will probably continue even in Hawaii to have government dictate to women what may or may not happen within their own bodies, and it will take continued vigilance to protect rights women here now take for granted.

The Virginian-Pilot
Norfolk, Virginia, January 24, 1992

The U.S. Supreme Court's announcement that it will review the constitutionality of Pennsylvania's law raising obstacles to abortion came on the eve of the 19th anniversary of *Roe vs. Wade*, the Jan. 22, 1973, decision legalizing abortion nationwide.

No one can forecast how much of the Pennsylvania law the Supreme Court will uphold. That law mandates parental consent for teen abortions, a spousal-notification requirement, extensive record-keeping, counseling and a 24-hour waiting period designed to discourage abortion. A federal appeals court has ruled all but the notice-to-spouse provision constitutional.

But the court has scheduled arguments for and against the law in April. The betting is that it will uphold most, if not all, of the law's provisions and release its decision in June or July, shortly before the 1992 presidential campaign gets into full swing.

That will create difficulties for many Republicans. Another court ruling sanctioning state barriers to women's access to abortion will stimulate pro-choice forces to work to defeat the likely Republican ticket of President Bush and Vice President Dan Quayle, both of whom favor repeal of *Roe vs. Wade*.

Many women who otherwise are expected to vote Republican next November may switch to the Democratic ticket if the Pennsylvania case goes against the pro-choice side. Many women did exactly that in the 1989 Virginia and New Jersey gubernatorial races, tipping those elections to the pro-choice Democratic candidates. Their protest votes were spurred by the court's 5-4 decision in *Webster vs. Repro-*

ductive Services, which approved Missouri legislation restricting access to abortions by, among other things, forbidding them in public hospitals.

Four justices — Chief Justice William H. Rehnquist and Justices Anthony M. Kennedy, Antonin Scalia and Byron R. White — who found the Missouri restrictions constitutional, signaled their readiness to overturn *Roe vs. Wade*. Justice Sandra Day O'Connor, the swing vote on the court, did not, asking only if provision of the Missouri law placed an "undue burden" on the abortion access that *Roe* established as a fundamental constitutional right. Of the four justices who found the Missouri statute unconstitutional, two — Thurgood Marshall and William J. Brennan Jr. — have retired. They were succeeded by Justices David H. Souter and Clarence Thomas, both of whom are suspected of hostility to *Roe*.

The court has indicated that it will not use the Pennsylvania law to repeal *Roe*, but placement of the case on the court's docket is enough to add heat to the political scene. All the contenders for the Democratic presidential nomination are pro-choice. That frees pro-choice advocates to concentrate their fire on the anti-choice Republicans. If the recession still lingers in November and the Democrats have fielded a credible candidate, the Republicans will be on the defensive. Energized pro-choice sentiment could, as it did in Virginia and New Jersey, tip the balance against the GOP.

Whatever happens, this is sure: Repeal of *Roe* wouldn't end the fight over abortion; it would intensify and broaden it — indefinitely.

Portland Press Herald
Portland, Maine, January 19, 1992

Next Saturday women from throughout Maine will travel to Augusta to form a living circle around the State House. They will be there for themselves and for their daughters. Their mission: to demonstrate they intend to retain the freedom to choose safe, legal abortions spelled out 18 years ago by the U.S. Supreme Court in Roe vs. Wade.

We support both their right and their determination to keep it.

In the days ahead, a very different Supreme Court will take up challenges to Roe vs. Wade. It is to those judges, as well as state lawmakers, that this week's affirmation from women is directed.

Like most far-reaching social decisions, Roe vs. Wade did more than move abortion out of a dingy and dangerous netherworld into hospitals and medical clinics. Over 18 years of controversy, it has also taught supporters that rights, once won, must be vigorously defended to be kept.

Reproductive rights are neither a distant nor an insignificant issue in Maine. Between 4,000 and 5,000 women in this state, for their own private and personal reasons, choose abortion yearly. They are among the more than 1.5 million women who do so in this country. The numbers neither rise nor fall dramatically. And that shouldn't surprise us. Choosing abortion is a serious decision that women approach in a serious manner.

Their right to do so deserves the full protection of state law and the U.S. Constitution.

Not just for 18 years, but forever.

Pittsburgh Post-Gazette
Pittsburgh, Pennsylvania, January 22, 1992

Last fall, when opponents of Pennsylvania's latest Abortion Control Act asked the U.S. Supreme Court to give the law expedited constitutional review, the request almost took the form of a dare.

In announcing the appeal of a lower-court decision upholding several sections of the act, an attorney for the American Civil Liberties Union called upon the Supreme Court "to determine whether Roe vs. Wade remains the law of the land." If the court's answer were no, the ruling would come down in time to influence this year's presidential election — presumably in a pro-choice direction.

•

Yesterday, on the eve of the 19th anniversary of the Roe vs. Wade decision, the court agreed to hear arguments on the Pennsylvania law. But in defining the questions in the case for attorneys, the court did not say that it would re-examine Roe vs. Wade; rather, it indicated that it would confine its inquiry to the constitutionality of the provisions of the Pennsylvania law.

That seemingly narrow focus confounds the immediate political strategy of pro-choice groups. But it raises hopes that even this conservative Supreme Court is unwilling to return to the days when abortion could be banned and punished as a crime.

In upholding Pennsylvania's law, the 3rd U.S. Circuit Court of Appeals did not profess to overturn Roe vs. Wade, which discovered a right to choose abortion in the privacy protections of the Constitution. The appeals court did, however, find in a series of post-Roe Supreme Court decisions a legal standard that allowed states to impose restrictions on abortion so long as they did not pose an "undue burden" on the abortion right and were rationally related to a legitimate state interest. (The "undue burden" terminology comes from Justice Sandra Day O'Connor, who is regarded by some legal observers as disinclined to overturn Roe vs. Wade.)

The specific controls upheld by the appeals court were a requirement that a woman give "informed consent" before receiving an abortion; that she wait 24 hours before an abortion could be performed; and that minors contemplating an abortion receive parental consent — although a judge could waive that requirement. The appeals court struck down another section of the law requiring pregnant women to notify their husbands of a planned abortion.

Unlike the appeals court, we believe that the 24-hour waiting period does pose an "undue burden" on the right of abortion, particularly for women in rural areas who must travel a long distance to obtain an abortion. But, like the other provisions of the Pennsylvania law upheld by the appeals court, that section falls far short of prohibiting abortion. A Supreme Court decision upholding the Pennsylvania law would not be a repudiation of Roe vs. Wade.

We understand why some pro-choice groups would have preferred to have the Supreme Court, for good or ill, decide whether Roe vs. Wade is still the law of the land. For one thing, such a reckoning may be inevitable because of recently enacted laws from Guam and Louisiana that, unlike Pennsylvania's statute, are impossible to reconcile with the Roe decision. Better, one might argue, to have Roe vs. Wade repudiated openly so as to embolden supporters of efforts to enshrine the abortion right in state and federal legislation.

But it is far from certain that the Supreme Court is bent on repealing Roe vs. Wade. It is possible that the Supreme Court will go no further than did the 3rd Circuit in upholding Pennsylvania's law. (It is also possible that in doing so the Supreme Court might define "undue burden" so loosely that all manner of truly onerous restrictions on abortion would pass muster. That would be alarming.)

•

The Post-Gazette long has supported the basic holding of Roe vs. Wade — that abortion should be legal in the first six months of pregnancy. But we have expressed concern about the number of late abortions (which would be more stringently policed under the Pennsylvania law) and we have recognized that the issue of parental consent for minors' abortions involve more than one interest.

For that reason, we are glad that in agreeing to review Pennsylvania's law the Supreme Court has not assumed that Roe must go if the law is upheld.

The Boston Globe
Boston, Massachusetts, January 22, 1992

The Supreme Court seemed highly political yesterday, rather than judicially free of politics as it is meant to be, in choosing to limit its review of abortion – during this presidential election year – to state laws imposing restrictions on abortion. The decision leaves untouched the central federal question of whether abortion should remain legal.

For now, the court will rule only on appeals from drastic new Pennsylvania restrictions on abortion. Coming on the eve of the anniversary of the 1973 Roe v. Wade ruling guaranteeing constitutional protection to a woman's right to abortion, the court's agreement on a limited review fuels the already white-hot flames of controversy about abortion.

Activists on both sides of the abortion question had counted on a decision on the broader issue of the validity of Roe v. Wade. The decision would have come down, under the court's regular schedule, by mid-July – the height of the political season for nominating presidential candidates.

The political importance of the abortion dispute is undeniable. President Bush has called for an overturn of Roe v. Wade, and the Republican Party platform opposes choice on abortion. The Democratic candidates and party platform support the right to choice and the legality of abortion. Nor would anyone deny the conservative makeup of the current Supreme Court.

Four members – Chief Justice William Rehnquist and Justices Antonin Scalia, Byron White and Anthony Kennedy – are on record as opposing the 1973 ruling. Justice Sandra Day O'Connor, the only woman on the court, has voiced reservations about it. And though the views of the newest members – Clarence Thomas and David Souther – are not known, they are political conservatives.

What the court did is postpone action until after the November election on the fundamental issue of a woman's right to choose abortion. However, that delay could boomerang politically.

The Pennsylvania law markedly restricts the process for seeking an abortion. Teen-age girls would have to obtain parental consent or court approval. A 24-hour waiting period is also mandated. The most intrusive requirement is that a wife must obtain the consent of her husband.

Faye Wattleton, president of the Planned Parenthood Federation of America, assailed the legal basis of that law yesterday. She called it "an undue burden" for a teen-ager to have to face an abusive parent or for a poor woman traveling a long distance to an abortion center to have to come back a day later. For women to again be made subject to the will of their husbands, Wattleton said, reduces them to the status of chattel.

In the long run, it may not serve the political interests of the administration to have these restrictions in the news at convention time. Nor can it help President Bush to have the basic question of abortion rights held hostage for another year by a Supreme Court dominated by his appointees.

The Washington Post

Washington, D.C., January 22, 1992

THE SUPREME Court will hand down a major decision on abortion rights before the end of its term in July, and supporters of *Roe v. Wade* are already organizing to respond to what they fear is coming. Yesterday, on the eve of the 19th anniversary of the landmark ruling, the court announced that it would hear arguments this spring in a case from Pennsylvania. No matter what the court decides, the fate of *Roe* will be a major issue in the coming presidential election. Litigants on both sides sought accelerated consideration of this case for that reason.

In the Pennsylvania case at issue, the U.S. Court of Appeals for the 3rd Circuit abandoned the reasoning in *Roe*—that abortion is a fundamental right so firmly grounded in the Constitution that it can only be regulated by the state for a compelling reason—and adopted a new test allowing regulation that does not put "an undue burden" on the exercise of the right. The court went on to sustain those parts of the statute that require parental consent, extensive record-keeping, pre-abortion information sessions and waiting periods. A spousal notice requirement, however, was found to be unconstitutional. In announcing Tuesday that it will hear this case, the court said it would limit its ruling to the Pennsylvania law and not directly consider overturning *Roe*. But as abortion rights advocates point out, affirming this decision will require a finding that the right is no longer fundamental and will open the door to extensive new state regulation.

A political campaign on this issue is about to begin. Kate Michelman, executive director of the National Abortion Rights Action League, has already announced that her aim is to secure the election of a president committed to abortion rights—all announced Democratic candidates take this position—or at least to elect a veto-proof Congress. Abortion opponents, of course, will want to retain an administration that appoints people sympathetic to their cause to the Supreme Court and vetoes any attempts to make abortions more accessible here and abroad.

But as the campaign begins, it is important to understand exactly what is at stake: Even in what we regard as the worst case—that is, even if *Roe* is overturned—there will not necessarily be a nationwide return to back-alley abortions or a wholesale criminalization of the procedure. Abortions will not automatically become illegal. In the absence of *Roe* safeguards, each state will be free to regulate abortion in its own way. A few will enact repressive laws, as Utah, Guam and Louisiana, whose statutes are now being challenged in court, have done. A great many others will continue to protect abortion rights fully, and some will impose restrictions like parental notification that burden but don't eliminate the right. We hope that none of this becomes necessary and that the court continues to uphold what we consider to be this fundamental right. But all is not over if the court does not, for the political struggle will be carried to every state legislature, and abortion rights forces will concede nothing.

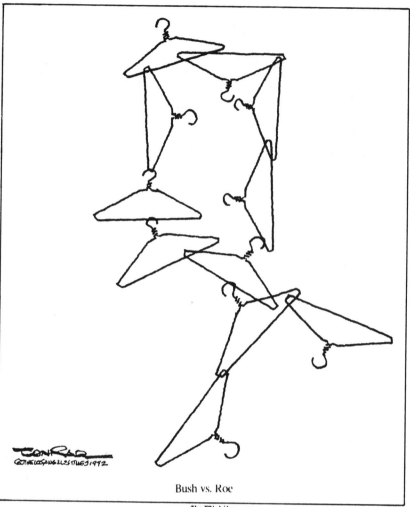

Bush vs. Roe

The Wichita Eagle-Beacon

Wichita, Kansas, January 28, 1992

It's bound to strike some Kansans as strange that a group of pro-choice Democratic and Republican House members is proposing restrictions on abortion — requiring teens younger than 16 to seek counseling before obtaining abortions, for instance, and banning abortions after the fetus is viable. It's usually pro-life members who propose abortion restrictions.

Unusual though their proposal may be, the pro-choice group is practicing good politics — and proposing good public policy. The U.S. Supreme Court last week made clear that it intends to take another run at Roe vs. Wade, the 1973 decision that barred states from denying women the right to an abortion.

The justices said they don't intend to use a Pennsylvania abortion law now under review to overturn Roe vs. Wade outright. But they left the door open to further abortion-rights restrictions that could have the same effect.

Like other states, then, Kansas has to get ready for the post-Roe era. It makes sense for the Legislature to decide now what the post-Roe environment will be, rather than wait to see what the Supreme Court does.

Accordingly, the pro-choice representatives, led by Rep. Kathleen Sebelius, D-Topeka, are proposing a state abortion policy in keeping with a majority of Kansans' sentiments on this difficult subject. In polls, Kansans have repeatedly said they don't think it's the government's place to exert control over a woman's body.

But Kansans also think that some women too easily choose the abortion alternative, and that late-term abortions are wrong. The teen counseling requirement and the ban on abortions after viability — except in cases of fetal abnormality or threats to the health of the mother — would address those concerns.

The representatives also would bar cities and counties from passing abortion restrictions — they may use their home-rule powers to do so now — and stiffen the penalties for blocking access to medical facilities. Those restrictions are certain to be well received in Wichita.

Not surprisingly, the pro-life lobbying groups have declared war on the bill. Many Kansans had hoped that the 1992 session of the Legislature would be free of major battles over abortion so members could concentrate on cleaning up the school finance and property tax messes. But the Supreme Court's decision to review the Pennsylvania abortion law has added urgency to the need for a sensible post-Roe state abortion policy. If there must be a 1992 abortion fight, so be it.

The pro-choice representatives were right to bring the matter up now. The Legislature should pass their bill.

MILWAUKEE SENTINEL

Milwaukee, Wisconsin, January 27, 1992

The U.S. Supreme Court's decision to review a controversial Pennsylvania abortion law threatens to shift the focus of the 1992 presidential campaigns from the issue of the economy.

The court has indicated that it will review provisions in the Pennsylvania law requiring a 24-hour waiting period for abortions and mandating that women tell their husbands if they plan to have such an operation.

Also under review could be provisions mandating that doctors keep detailed records on abortions and that they provide counseling on alternatives to women who seek abortions.

Those considerations all open the door for provocative debate. But the failure of the court to make clear whether it will actually consider overturning Roe vs. Wade, the 1973 decision that legalized abortion, also could leave an opening for arguments on that most controversial matter on the campaign trail.

Should the justices undo Roe vs. Wade or shouldn't they?

President Bush already has validated the Republican Party's strong anti-abortion position in a telephone speech to thousands of anti-abortion advocates. About the same time, Sen. Don Nickles (R-Okla.), a staunch opponent of legalized abortion, was named head of the committee that will draft the GOP platform.

Democratic candidates probably will try to make hay out of the focus the abortion issue will get while the court ponders its decision.

In any case, what voters should keep in mind is that the decision is not in the hands of the candidates or the president, all of whom should be tested instead on what they are going to do about the sluggish economy, the deteriorating state of public education and the plight of the homeless and hungry.

The high court's decision, it should be noted, probably won't come down until July, when all the primaries are over and the nominating conventions are about to begin. There will be plenty of time for discussion on abortion then.

The News Journal

Wilmington, Delaware, January 23, 1992

The issue of abortion splits our nation. It is a base line issue with roots in ethical and religious convictions and beliefs. Our position is that women should have the right to chose abortion.

The U.S. Supreme Court in recent years has nipped at the edges of its landmark 1972 ruling, Roe v. Wade, which gave abortion constitutional protection. Now the court has agreed to rule on the constitutionality of a new Pennsylvania law that places a number of restrictions on abortion.

It is significant that the court will rule on the law this year, an election year.

The courts should interpret, not make, law. Abortion is an issue demanding legislative action. The men and women in Congress or in state legislatures should decide whether abortion is legal and they, not the courts, should establish whatever conditions should be imposed.

Abortion draws on emotions as well as intellects and for that reason many who sit in legislative bodies are terrified of it. They have been willing to dodge the issue, relying on court rulings to do their work for them.

If, as is expected, the conservative majority on the Supreme Court upholds the Pennsylvania law, there will be a firestorm of legislative proposals in Washington and in state capitals.

A major debate on abortion in an election year is perfect justice. No one will — or should — be able to hide. Legislators will be forced to take a position. And, in short order, they will have to face the voters with their on-the-record position.

We believe women should have a right to chose abortion with as few restrictions as possible. But there is no national consensus, nor is there consensus in Delaware. Let the debate proceed.

St. Louis Review

St. Louis, Missouri, January 24, 1992

The U.S. Supreme Court has agreed to review a Pennsylvania law restricting abortion. The court limited its review to specific restrictions of the Pennsylvania law. Among other conditions this law requires parental consent for minors to have abortions. It requires notification of husbands and mandates that women be informed about fetal development and alternatives to abortion. It further stipulates a 24-hour wait before a woman can receive an abortion. Observers on both sides of the abortion debate feel it is unlikely that the court will use this opportunity to overturn its Roe vs. Wade decision of 1973.

This announcement came as pro-life proponents from around the country rallied to protest the Roe vs. Wade decision in their annual March for Life in Washington. As might be expected, politics figured large in the strategies of both pro-abortion and pro-life groups. Pro-abortion strategists had been urging this Supreme Court review, hoping that a decision reversing Roe vs. Wade would shock many undecided voters into voting for pro-abortion candidates in November. Pro-life forces see in the Pennsylvania law a good model for abortion-restrictive laws in others states.

Although the number of medical facilities providing abortions has dropped slightly from 2,680 in 1985 to 2,585 in 1988, the number of women obtaining abortions continues constant at 1.6 million each year. Since 1973 this amounts to some 26 million lives lost. Such numbers indicate the sizable numbers of American women who have been directly involved in obtaining abortions. Members of their families and friends, aware of these actions, have been indirectly involved. A lot of emotional upset has thus occurred in many people's lives. But beyond this upset we must remember that abortion is a matter of suffering and death for the fetus. A botched abortion means a live fetus.

There are indications that this message of destruction of the life in the womb is becoming better known. When even Phil Donahue presents a panel of women whose children were born disfigured as the result of botched abortions you know that the public is getting the message. Pregnant women need support and encouragement. Women for whom pregnancy is a problem should be aware of the many options open to them to preserve and nourish the life in their wombs. Now is the time to protect and promote life.

THE DAILY OKLAHOMAN
Oklahoma City, Oklahoma, January 26, 1992

OPINION polls must be used carefully to reach conclusions about public policy. A headline in *The Oklahoman* last Sunday proclaimed "Public Support for Abortion Remains Strong," after a Gallup poll found only 30 percent support for overruling Roe vs. Wade.

Those surveyed were told the controversial 1973 Supreme Court decision "ruled that states cannot place restrictions on a woman's right to an abortion during the first three months of pregnancy." That is wrong. Roe vs. Wade overturned laws in all 50 states and the District of Columbia, including relatively "liberal" provisions in several states.

Gallup finds different results when questions are worded differently. An April 1990 survey found 53 percent who thought abortion should be "legal only under certain circumstances." This "middle majority" has ranged between 52 percent and 58 percent since 1975.

Gallup last year found that 69.9 percent of respondents thought there were existing restrictions on abortion that actually are not in place because of Roe. Only 17.6 percent knew that the effect of Roe was to legalize abortion throughout all nine months of pregnancy.

Gallup has also found 86.1 percent support for laws which would require women to get information about fetal development and abortion alternatives before procuring abortions. Nearly 70 percent supported requiring parental consent for abortions performed on minors, and 69.2 percent opposed abortion as a means of birth control. A full 54.8 percent would back a requirement that a baby's biological father must consent before abortions.

Most Americans oppose most abortions. When Roe vs. Wade is overturned, new restrictions on access to abortion will be enacted. That will be no surprise, given the results of an October 1989 Wirthlin Group poll which found 69 percent popular support for the proposition that "the lives of unborn babies should be protected."

THE PLAIN DEALER
Cleveland, Ohio, January 23, 1992

Every woman has a "fundamental right" under the Constitution to choose to give birth or to seek an abortion, thanks to a landmark of liberty: the Supreme Court's 1973 ruling in the case of Roe vs. Wade. But that right is in jeopardy because of the Supreme Court's recent shifts of position, giving the government more and more power to dictate this most delicate of personal decisions.

The law of the land, unsettled by the Rehnquist Court's hostility to civil liberties, must be clarified. After all the debating is over, the issue must be calmed with the only reasonable solution: an enduring federal law, securing a nationwide abortion-rights standard that protects each individual's freedom of choice.

The Supreme Court this week, on the eve of the Roe decision's 19th anniversary, agreed to review a new Pennsylvania law that undermines Roe by imposing severe anti-abortion restrictions. The justices probably will deliver their decision in July — just in time to roil the presidential campaign. Although the court might not rule directly on Roe (if it prefers merely to continue restricting abortion rights rather than discard them completely), its decision will surely invite an election-year furor.

Ideally, such an issue of conscience should not be decided amid the turmoil of a political campaign. But it's long past time for the Rehnquist majority to clarify its position: Either Roe remains the law, or it does not. Painful as the issue may be, the nation needs to confront this debate. The court's willingness to review the Pennsylvania case is thus welcome, even if the majority's evident hostility to abortion rights is deplorable.

The justices this week said they will focus on the technicalities of the Pennsylvania statute. But even if the Supreme Court does not use this case to discard Roe completely, a majority seems ready to restrict Roe further. Even the author of the 1973 ruling, Justice Harry A. Blackmun, admits that "the votes are there" for an eventual, complete reversal of Roe.

The Pennsylvania controversy shows how the court has drifted away from America's pro-choice mainstream. In 1986, a 5-4 majority struck down a similar Pennsylvania law. But since then, three liberal justices have retired and three conservative justices have been appointed. The court now has two pro-choice votes; five justices seek to restrict Roe still further; the two most recent appointees have so far expressed no public view.

There's no use trying to pretend that the Supreme Court is somehow "above politics." All nine justices were appointed by a president and confirmed by the Senate. Presidents shape the court, so the opinions of presidential candidates on the abortion issue are fair game for election-year debate. Since opinion polls find a solid majority of the public is pro-choice, abortion-rights advocates probably stand to benefit from this controversy during the 1992 campaign.

No wonder the Republican Party is worried. There is a clear distinction between the parties' platforms on this issue, and the split may work to the disadvantage of the GOP. The Republican doctrine takes the absolutist anti-choice stance, calling for a constitutional amendment to outlaw abortion. The Democratic platform takes the pro-choice position. Every Republican candidate now in the race supports the anti-choice stance; every Democrat, the pro-choice position.

Abortion is a sad reality that cannot be wished away. Even abortion opponents who are sincere in their beliefs must realize that severe restrictions will only victimize many women by driving them to illegal, back-alley abortion mills. One way or another, abortions will occur. The only real decision is whether to keep them legal and medically supervised, or to revert to the pre-Roe era when, in most states, they were illegal and unsafe.

America must reaffirm the right to choose. If the Supreme Court will not uphold such a compassionate standard, there is only one other body that can do so: Congress. In case the court reverses Roe, some lawmakers have already prepared a Freedom of Choice Act that would codify the Roe standard. It will not be easy or painless to settle this issue. But lawmakers must not allow this most intimate of decisions to be dictated by a Big Brother government.

THE KANSAS CITY STAR
Kansas City, Missouri, January 27, 1992

The U.S. Supreme Court says it will hear arguments this term on the Pennsylvania law which restricts abortion rights. If the Pennsylvania statute is not the Supreme Court's vehicle for overturning all abortion rights under Roe vs. Wade, then it undoubtedly will be another of the various state laws headed to the Supreme Court. That is the prevailing wisdom on both sides of the abortion question.

What is uncertain is whether the court will overturn Roe vs. Wade before this year's presidential and congressional elections. It would be better for abortion rights supporters if it did. That way, the campaigns this fall to turn out anti-abortion lawmakers will attract greater support from Americans who perhaps finally will have awakened to what they have lost.

The states will be an important battleground in the campaigns. With no constitutional protections guaranteed on the national level, the attention will be on state legislators and governors to provide the rights through state laws and state courts.

The battle will be just as tough as it has been on the national level. Missouri is an example. The General Assembly has sent law after law to the nation's highest court, which has willingly — through Reagan and Bush appointees — whittled away at the rights. A recent report by the National Abortion Rights Action League put Missouri third in the nation as most likely to ban or strictly limit abortions following any Supreme Court ruling allowing that. Kansas was farther down the list.

How political the Supreme Court has become on this issue perhaps will be revealed in the timing of its decision to overturn Roe vs. Wade. Americans deserve to know what the rules are going to be.

DAILY🖼NEWS
New York City, New York, January 22, 1992

Nineteen years ago today, the Supreme Court recognized a federal right to abortion. Yesterday, the court jumped back into the fray by agreeing to review a Pennsylvania law that has become a flashpoint for the fury on both sides of this debate.

Under the legislation, women under 18 must get parental consent for an abortion. And all women must wait at least 24 hours between requesting and obtaining an abortion. Another provision under review, struck down by the lower court, would require spousal notification prior to an abortion.

By ruling narrowly on the statute — as the court has decided to do — the justices will avoid redeciding Roe vs. Wade in the midst of a presidential campaign, thereby sparing President Bush political fallout from the decision. Such fence-sitting, however, will leave millions of women in doubt about their right to terminate an unwelcome pregnancy.

Though no serious person can believe the option is one to be exercised lightly, the Daily News believes it is a right women should have. If the Supreme Court disagrees, it has a duty to make its direction clear — rather than continuing to gnaw away at the edges of a right that most Americans take for granted.

The News and Observer
Raleigh, North Carolina, January 23, 1992

Not much oil will pour on troubled waters from the U.S. Supreme Court's decision to review Pennsylvania's abortion restrictions this year. But as the Roe vs. Wade decision's 19th anniversary passes, the court's move is welcome even so.

It's welcome because the deeply disturbing abortion issue isn't going to go away until America works through it to some resolution. The Pennsylvania case could lob the issue straight into the presidential campaign spotlight. But another ruling will at least move this national marathon of moral, social and political agony another notch toward closure.

Pennsylvania's abortion law requires a 24-hour waiting period, notice from doctors about alternatives, parental consent or a court order for minors, and notification of the husband before a wife can have an abortion.

Clarence Thomas and David Souter now sit where Thurgood Marshall and William Brennan sat in 1989, when a 5-4 vote upheld Missouri's abortion restrictions. That makes it likely that today's court will uphold most of Pennsylvania's controls. It could even approve the husband-notice requirement, on grounds of a husband's interest in the fate of a fetus that was presumably jointly conceived.

Further, the court could decide this case without specifically overturning Roe vs. Wade, which rooted the right to access to abortion in the Constitution. Some pro-choice people feel that upholding Pennsylvania's law would amount to an overturning. They say that if the court finds, using Justice Sandra Day O'Connor's test, that Pennsylvania has not put an "undue burden" on access to abortion, then justices aren't very likely to find "undue burden" in any other restrictions states could dream up.

They have a point in warning that court approval of Pennsylvania's law thus could open the way for states each to stitch their own patch in a crazy quilt of abortion restrictions. That is not to be wished.

But there's still a fundamental difference between restricting the right to abortion and revoking that right. In a recent article carried in this newspaper, commentator Roger Rosenblatt wrote that three-fourths of Americans seem to agree on two things: Abortion should be available, and they personally wouldn't want to have one. That shows, he said, that a "permit but discourage" policy on abortion could find wide acceptance among both pro-choice and anti-abortion advocates.

That kind of policy may be the way out of the impasse that has wracked and divided this nation for far too long. But it is unlikely to arise from state-by-state abortion regulation. Such a policy needs to be nationwide, because if some American women have to bear unplanned, unwanted children while others do not, and the only difference is the state they live in, they will find such a situation morally and politically intolerable. And they will be right.

Since all that is predictable right now, it ought to be possible to find a way to avert it. The Supreme Court, as it ponders Pennsylvania's law, should try to find that way.

THE BLADE
Toledo, Ohio, January 24, 1992

INDIVIDUALS who support the right of abortion fear that a U.S. Supreme Court decision overturning Roe v. Wade would create a crazy-quilt pattern of state-by-state rules. Indeed, it might well resemble the kind of wildly uneven pattern that exists in Ohio when it comes to applying the parental-notification law.

For the last 15 months unwed and underage abortion patients have been required to notify a parent before an abortion would be allowed. But as Blade staff writer Nara Schoenberg reported last Sunday, judges have wide latitude in allowing exemptions to the law. In fact, they have such freedom that there is no consistency whatsoever in Ohio as to who must notify parents.

A teenage girl who wanted to win an exemption from the reporting law would best travel to Franklin (Columbus) or Montgomery (Dayton) counties, where more than 90 per cent of requests are allowed.

In Hamilton (Cincinnati) county, however, the letter of the law prevails; 100 per cent of requests for exemptions are rejected. (Lucas County Juvenile County judges refuse to disclose how many requests were approved, in an effort to protect the confidentiality of requests.)

Given the glaring and inherent dangers in any parental-notification law, there needs to be protection for pregnant teenagers who might face the excessive wrath of their parents, for example.

And the law does allow a vaguely worded exemption for girls "sufficiently mature and well informed" to make the decision themselves about an abortion. Clearly, however, personal judicial attitudes may determine how tightly or loosely the law's exemption applies. As a result of such flexibility, no sense of equal, uniform justice exists in this state — nor can there be, given the need for and the nature of exemptions.

No easy way exists to make judges in one country think like the judges in another county, obviously. And parental notification serves no useful societal purpose. Youngsters who don't fear their parents will admit pregnancies, but those who do will try anything to avoid notifying their parents.

For that reason — and given the fact that each county now seems to have its own interpretation of what notification means — it would be far more consistent and less burdensome to the courts to do away with the law in its entirety.

Wider State Abortion Limits Upheld; *Roe v. Wade* Weakened

The Supreme Court, in a 5–4 ruling, June 29, 1992 upheld most of the provisions of a Pennsylvania law that imposed strict limits on a woman's ability to obtain an abortion. But the majority also reaffirmed that a woman's basic right to choose an abortion was "a rule of law and a component of liberty we cannot renounce." The case was *Planned Parenthood of Southeastern Pennsylvania v. Casey.*

The decision effectively gave states broad powers to restrict abortions. But by explicitly reaffirming a woman's right to terminate her pregnancy, the ruling also surprised observers who had believed that conservative justices on the court would more thoroughly weaken—if not overturn—*Roe v. Wade,* the landmark 1973 decision upholding a woman's right to an abortion.

The broad terms in which the high court redefined the right to abortion appeared likely to prompt further litigation on abortion-rights issues. The ruling was also viewed by many observers as being certain to help keep abortion issues in the national political spotlight during the run-up to presidential and congressional elections in November.

The court's decision upheld most of the key provisions of the Pennsylvania Abortion Control Act of 1989, one of the strictest anti-abortion laws in the country. The provisions backed by the court had been upheld by the U.S. 3rd Circuit Court of Appeals in 1991.

The high court let stand an "informed consent" clause requiring doctors and clinics to present women seeking abortions with state-prepared information on abortion and fetal development. A mandatory 24-hour waiting period between the presentation and the abortion procedure was also upheld by the court, as was a requirement that women under 18 obtain the consent of one parent or a judge before undergoing the operation.

The court ruled that none of the provisions it upheld constituted a substantial obstacle to a woman's ability to obtain an abortion. Its decision overturned previous Supreme Court rulings that had struck down informed-consent laws and mandatory waiting periods on the basis of principles upheld in *Roe v. Wade.*

The court struck down a provision of the Pennsylvania law that required women to notify their husbands of their intent to obtain an abortion. The majority opinion stated that the provision would endanger women who suffered from physical or psychological abuse at the hands of their spouses. The court also added, "A state may not give to a man the kind of dominion over his wife that parents exercise over their children."

Justices Sandra Day O'Connor, Anthony M. Kennedy and David Souter collaborated to write a joint opinion for the majority in which they unexpectedly expressed strong support for the constitutional protection of a woman's right to have an abortion.

In an often impassioned 60-page opinion, the three justices said that they had overcome strong ethical misgivings in favor of constitutional principle in arriving at their decision. "Some of us as individuals find abortion offensive to our most basic principles of morality," they wrote, "but that cannot control our decision. Our obligation is to define the liberty of all, not to mandate our own moral code."

The justices repeatedly reaffirmed that the "central holding" of *Roe v. Wade*—that a woman had a fundamental right to terminate her pregnancy—had acquired "precedential force" within constitutional jurisprudence as a protection of a personal liberty.

Leaders and spokespersons for both sides in the national debate over abortion expressed their dissatisfaction with the ruling June 29. Hundreds of pro- and anti-abortion leaders were gathered on the steps of the Supreme Court building in Washington, D.C. as the ruling was announced.

Gary, Indiana, June 30, 1992

Anyone surprised by the Supreme Court's decision upholding many of the restrictions on abortion in Pennsylvania must have spent the past 12 months watching videotapes of the Clarence Thomas confirmation hearings. (You remember, the ones in which Thomas stated

> **Our opinion**
>
> **In the wake of the Pennsylvania abortion case, Congress must pass a law legalizing abortion.**

he'd never, *ever* discussed Roe vs. Wade, the Supreme Court ruling that legalized abortions.)

We're certain they were not watching the nation's highest court swing perceptibly and dangerously to the right in its position on civil liberties in recent years.

The only remarkable thing about the court's abortion rights ruling is that it pleased no one but infuriated everyone: To the dismay of the pro-choice movement, the conservative court affirmed states' rights to impose severe restrictions on women seeking abortions. But that didn't satisfy rabid members of the pro-life movement who want to see Roe wiped from the books.

The court's refusal to do just that was due more to a "respect for precedent" than a respect for women's right to privacy. The 5-4 vote restricting abortions but retaining Roe was not the frontal assault on this most cherished of liberal tenets the pro-life movement wanted. It does, though, nibble away at the underpinnings of Roe and weakens it for the next assault.

Ironically, pro-choice advocates may have been better served by a head-on attack on Roe. That would enable Congress to do something it should have done 10 years ago: reaffirm the principles of women's right to privacy and make legal, safe abortion the law of the land.

Pro-choice advocates — and we — fear the Pennsylvania ruling will encourage a domino-effect in which other states will attempt to "out-restrict" Pennsylvania. We urge Indiana legislators to forego that temptation: Indiana's abortion regulations are plenty strict already and have not — as Justice Anthony Kennedy said in refusing to overturn Roe — proved unworkable.

Among other things, the Pennsylvania law requires women seeking abortions to hear an "anti-abortion speech" and wait at least 24 hours before having an abortion. The Supreme Court, to its credit, struck down a portion of the law that would have required married women to get their husbands' permission before obtaining an abortion.

Displeased as we are at the court's restrictive leanings, we wish they'd rule forcefully on one side or the other and stop coyly playing with Roe the way a cat does with a defenseless mouse.

Then, we hope, Congress will do the right thing.

The Seattle Times

Seattle, Washington, June 30, 1992

THE Supreme Court's decision on the Pennsylvania abortion law is not the victory for reproductive rights that some conservatives believe. Although the Roe vs. Wade ruling that legalized abortion is not overturned, the court has made a woman's privacy rights subject to government intrusion.

The majority opinion, co-written by Justices Sandra Day O'Connor, Anthony Kennedy, and David Souter, states the court's intent to affirm the "essence" of the Roe decision. Its approach, however, departs substantially from the core principle articulated in Roe.

Either abortion is a fundamental privacy right or it is not. The O'Connor-Kennedy-Souter troika tries to split the difference, suggesting a little intrusion is acceptable. The question left unanswered is what is a little and what is too much.

The result is a compromise that erodes abortion rights, and kicks the controversy back into the political arena.

The opinion explicitly rejects Roe's trimester analysis. Under Roe, government could not restrict abortions during the first trimester of pregnancy, but could impose some restrictions in the second trimester and even severe limitations in the third trimester to protect fetal life.

The court now jettisons that approach for a weaker "undue burden" standard. Under the new standard, any state regulation that does not impose an "absolute obstacle or severe limitation on the abortion decision" would be constitutional if it is rationally related to a legitimate state purpose. The decision invites state legislatures to tinker with abortion rights from the moment of conception.

The court upholds Pennsylvania provisions that require doctors to give women detailed descriptions of fetal development by 2-week intervals and to provide lists of agencies offering "alternatives to abortion"; a 24-hour waiting period after receipt of the fetal-development information; requiring doctors to turn over to the government records on each abortion performed, and parental consent or a judge's consent for teenagers under 18 seeking abortions.

Only the husband-notification requirement was struck down as unreasonable and unconstitutional.

Forcing doctors to confront women with abortion alternatives and imposing a waiting period assumes women are incapable of making an intensely personal decision without government oversight.

Asking teenagers to obtain parental consent or a judge's consent is neither realistic nor helpful to families. Youths who have supportive families will seek parental advice without the heavy hand of the law; those who will not or cannot (for example, victims of incest) should not be coerced to do so.

Indeed, the consent provision gives parents the right to force a minor to carry a pregnancy to term against that minor's will. The judge's-consent alternative is no solution at all. Judicial intrusion will not heal a broken family, yet sets up a hurdle few teenagers can overcome.

The O'Connor-Kennedy-Souter approach is rife with problems, but it's still more protective of privacy than the approach adopted by conservative Justices William Rehnquist, Antonin Scalia, Byron White, and Clarence Thomas. All four voted to abandon Roe, allowing states to outlaw abortion altogether.

That possibility is still very much alive. In a moving opinion, Justice Harry Blackmun, author of the Roe decision, argued to uphold Roe in its entirety. In criticizing Rehnquist and Scalia's dissents, Blackmun writes: "In the chief justice's world, a woman considering whether to terminate a pregnancy is entitled to no more protection than adulterers, murderers and so-called 'sexual deviates' . . .

"In one sense, the court's approach is worlds apart from that of the chief justice and Justice Scalia. And yet, in another sense, the distance between the two approaches is short — the distance is but a single vote.

"I am 83 years old. I cannot remain on this court forever, and when I do step down, the confirmation process for my successor may well focus on the issue before us today."

Blackmun's fear may yet play out. As the nation convulses over abortion rights, the high court slouches toward a temporary resolution.

The Sun

Vancouver, British Columbia, July 2, 1992

FINANCIALLY INDEPENDENT women over the age of 18 still have the right to choose abortion in the United States, but that is hardly reason to celebrate the tenuous survival of the precedent-setting decision that guarantees that choice.

Roe v. Wade is perhaps the most famous case in American jurisprudence. It gave rise to the U.S. Supreme Court decision in 1973 that a woman — every woman — has constitutional dominion over her own body and hence the right, early in her pregnancy, to choose whether she will carry a fetus to term.

But there is a catch. The last two U.S. presidents, Ronald Reagan and George Bush, care more for their own version of morality than for the law of the land. They have worked relentlessly to pack the court with justices who will overturn Roe v. Wade.

Many people thought they had succeeded: Justice Sandra Day O'Conner's previous opinions were sufficiently critical of the landmark abortion rights decision that she was expected to tip the balance on this occasion. In siding with the defenders of Roe v. Wade Justice O'Conner has protected both the rights of women and the reputation of the court. But she may also have given President Bush enough wriggling room to avoid the issue in the coming election. If so, Roe v. Wade has merely won a reprieve.

Even aside from the bleak future, abortion rights were also compromised in this ruling when the majority upheld a state's rights to set out certain conditions — potentially onerous and expensive conditions — before the right to abortion is granted.

All this proves that the political attack on abortion rights is working. Americans should remember that at the polls in November.

THE EMPORIA GAZETTE

Emporia, Kansas, July 2, 1992

THE Supreme Court's ruling in the Pennsylvania abortion case makes us aware of how difficult it is to take a middle position on anything. The pressures to declare oneself either left or right, black or white, up or down are tremendous.

Often it is necessary to choose a side, but absolutes do not apply to some issues, and abortion is one of these.

While we have consistently supported a woman's right to choose what to do with her own body — which includes the right to have an abortion — we also know that there are many times in life when all of us make hasty decisions that we later regret.

Kansas law, which is compatible with the Supreme Court decision, now calls for an eight-hour waiting period and limits late-term abortions. For a minor who seeks an abortion, it also requires parental notification or a waiver from a judge. These requirements make good sense and help to put a check on impulsive action.

What is important about the Supreme Court's decision is that it acknowledges the merits of both sides of this issue and forces pro-life and pro-choice advocates to stop fighting each other and come up with some new solutions. Activists from both sides would be wise to take this opportunity to look at the real issues that lie behind the need for abortion, and spend their energies on preventive education and support for women and children — steps that would lessen the need for abortions.

A law needs to be enacted which protects a woman's right of choice, but which also includes some reasonable limitations.

This week's moderate decision will provide a chance for people to cool down and work together for a law that will settle the issue once and for all. — BWW

THE DAILY OKLAHOMAN

Oklahoma City, Oklahoma, July 5, 1992

SOME initial coverage of the U.S. Supreme Court's abortion decision (issued Monday) — and virtually all of the commentary from liberal "spin doctors" — was off the mark.

The court upheld restrictions on abortion access which are supported by about 70 percent of the American people. However, it left intact the core of Roe vs. Wade (a good nominee for the title of "most nonconstitutional precedent of this century.")

Much of the analysis, including items in The Washington Post, contended that now the court said that any regulations must not pose an "undue burden" (whatever that means) on abortion access. This analysis is wrong.

Only three justices (Sandra Day O'Connor, David Souter and Anthony Kennedy) joined that part of the decision which discussed "undue burden." Two justices (Harry Blackmun and John Paul Stevens) rejected any new regulations of abortion (and explicitly did not concur with that part of O'Connor's opinion dealing with "undue burden"). Four other justices (Antonin Scalia, Clarence Thomas, William Rehnquist and Byron White) made it clear they felt additional abortion controls can withstand court scrutiny.

In sum, the nine members of the court are in at least three different places. The abortion debate is not over. The court's interpretation of the so-called "fundamental" right to abortion — which is only 19 years old — remains a moving target.

THE 🌅 SUN

Baltimore, Maryland, July 1, 1992

Democrats may not be able to make the abortion issue the silver bullet that kills President Bush in the 1992 election. They had hoped the Supreme Court would confirm their worst fears and Mr. Bush's professed wishes by overturning Roe vs. Wade, thereby affronting the clear national majority, especially among women, that insists on abortion rights. Instead, one of Mr. Bush's own appointees, Justice David Souter, provided the key vote by which the right to choose was upheld, though subject to tighter state restrictions.

In political terms this muddles the issue, just as Republican strategists had wished. The Souter vote cancels the dissent of Mr. Bush's other appointee, Justice Clarence Thomas. Instead of thumping for the outright overturn of Roe, Mr. Bush now can counter Democratic passage of a Freedom of Choice Act not only with a veto but with the court's powerfully expressed compromise. GOP handlers have long considered abortion a loser for their candidate, a judgment shared by Democrat Bill Clinton and independent Ross Perot, who may split the pro-choice vote in November.

In the aftermath of the court's 5-4 decision, zealots on both sides of the abortion issue were quick to react with predictable exaggeration.

Movement conservatives, who don't like Mr. Bush anyway, assailed the "wimp bloc" on the court for betraying their cause. Their targets were Justices Sandra Day O'Connor and Anthony M. Kennedy, both Reagan appointees, plus Justice Souter. These three have combined to keep the court on a moderate path in recent decisions.

Liberals, in looking for a worse-case scenario with which to clobber the president, claimed that Roe vs. Wade really was dead and the court's seeming compromise merely a smoke screen and a facade. In this opinion, they had an unlikely ally in Chief Justice William H. Rehnquist, leader of the four dissenters (including JFK appointee Byron R. White) who wanted to overturn the 1973 decision.

It is fair to say that the court, once again, sought to reflect a national consensus — in this case the view that abortion rights should be preserved but under reasonable limitations as determined in individual states. It is also fair to say that Justice Souter (and Justice White) have shown once again that the future voting patterns of a justice cannot always be accurately anticipated, even by the president who does the appointing.

Governor Clinton, seeking abortion rights votes, said he would appointed only right-to-choose justices if he is elected. But Presidents Eisenhower, Kennedy, Nixon, Reagan and Bush could tell him, with vivid examples, that the presidential reach ends at the Supreme Court's door.

We find this healthy for our political as well as our judicial system. Abortion should be a key issue in this campaign, but it should not be the only issue. The court has ruled in a way that will allow American voters to judge the presidential candidates through many prisms.

The Chattanooga Times

Chattanooga, Tennessee, July 1, 1992

Anti-abortion forces who thought they were within striking distance of a Supreme Court reversal of Roe vs. Wade found out differently on Monday. But while this Supreme Court apparently will not overturn that landmark decision, the future of abortion rights in this country clearly hinges on the next presidential appointment to the high court.

Four members of the court have now explicitly called for a reversal of Roe, and Justice Harry Blackmun, in his own words, "cannot remain on this court forever." Justice Blackmun, who is 83, was the author of Roe vs. Wade. His successor may well determine whether it remains the law of the land. For the time being it does, though in diluted form.

In Monday's 5-4 decision, the court affirmed a woman's right to terminate her pregnancy until the time the fetus can live outside the womb. Still, it held that states can go to considerable lengths to dissuade women from exercising that right. Thus it approved restrictions on abortion previously held to be unconstitutional.

No longer must a state show a "compelling interest" to justify restrictions on abortion. It must only prove its restrictions do not place an "undue burden" on a woman's right to abortion by putting a "substantial obstacle" in her way. If they only make the process more time-consuming and expensive, the court ruled, that's permissible.

The effect of the court ruling will be felt disproportionately by poor women, who more likely will lack the means to jump hurdles state legislators put up for them. And while Monday's decision dashes the hopes of states seeking almost total bans on abortion, it invites anti-abortion forces to dream up — and legislatures to enact — new ways of making the procedure more difficult to obtain.

The tone of the majority opinion reflects ambivalence in the three writers, Justices Sandra Day O'Connor, David Souter and Anthony Kennedy. They explicitly state that their judgment in this case was not guided by their personal moral views. What was critical to the decision was the principle of adhering to precedent.

Reviewing the history of Roe, the majority found that the constitutional basis for the decision remained firm. It is established on long-acknowledged constitutional guarantees of personal liberty, autonomy, privacy and bodily intergrity.

Given those facts, the opinion said, overturning Roe now would portray the court as a creature of politics and ideology rather than principle and the rule of law. It would say to the country that even such a significant constitutional ruling can be changed merely by changing personnel on the court. Sending such a message, the majority concluded, would undermine the legitimacy of the court in the public mind.

Interestingly, the three justices who made up the core of that majority were appointed by presidents who sent the country exactly that message. Justices O'Connor and Kennedy were appointed by President Reagan, Justice Souter by President Bush. Both campaigned for the presidency on a platform calling for selection of judges with an eye to securing a reversal of Roe.

Likewise, Democratic presidential candidate Bill Clinton said Monday, "The constitutional right to choose is hanging by a thread . . . only the next election can preserve it." The political reality is that presidents appoint judges who generally share their constitutional philosophy.

That reality, and the warning from Justice Blackmun that he will not always be there to defend Roe, will keep abortion rights very much alive as an issue in the presidential race this fall.

SYRACUSE
HERALD-JOURNAL
Syracuse, New York, June 30, 1992

Neither side of the abortion controversy scored a complete victory in Monday's Supreme Court decisions. But abortion opponents clearly came out ahead. A woman's right to choose was further restricted, continuing a trend that began with the court's tilt to the right under Ronald Reagan. And while Roe vs. Wade itself was affirmed, the margin was only a single vote.

Ruling on the constitutionality of a Pennsylvania law, the court Monday refused to grant states the power to outlaw abortion altogether. But the justices did allow most of the Pennsylvania restrictions to stand, in effect authorizing the states to make it more difficult for women to get abortions.

The court said Pennsylvania is within constitutional limits when it requires that all women seeking abortions be counseled about alternatives and that the abortion not take place until 24 hours after such counseling. It also upheld a provision of the law that requires doctors to keep detailed records on every abortion, subject to public disclosure. It let stand a requirement that unmarried minors have the permission of at least one parent or a judge before having an abortion.

Interestingly, it was a Bush appointee who provided the swing vote for preserving Roe, the 1973 decision that legalized abortion throughout the United States. In an opinion accompanying his first vote on abortion, Justice David Souter wrote with Justices Sandra Day O'Connor and Anthony Kennedy:

"It is settled now, as it was when the court heard arguments in Roe vs. Wade, that the Constitution places limits on a state's right to interfere with a person's most basic decisions about family and parenthood. . . .

"Men and women of good conscience can disagree, and we suppose some always shall disagree, about the profound moral and spiritual implications of terminating a pregnancy, even in its earliest stage. Some of us as individuals find abortion offensive to our most basic principles of morality, but that cannot control our decision. Our obligation is to define the liberty of all, not to mandate our own moral code. . . ."

That part of the decision angered abortion opponents, but on the whole it was a good day for them. They are closer to what appears to be their goal: A return to a two-tiered system of abortion availability, based on socioeconomic status.

Women with money have always been able to procure safe abortions — either by paying a premium price to a doctor willing to take a risk, or by traveling to where abortion is legal. That was America's dirty little secret before abortion became legal. Roe merely opened the opportunity to women of modest means.

Contrary to popular notion, the Supreme Court cannot outlaw abortion. Only state legislatures can do that, should Roe be overturned. Many forget that abortion was legal in New York years before the Roe ruling. It will continue to be legal here — and in many other states — even if Roe is overturned.

Abortion opponents know this. They also know that if Roe were overturned and every single state subsequently outlawed abortion, women of means would go to countries where abortion is legal. The rest would subject themselves to the clumsy ministrations of amateur abortionists, or use a coathanger on themselves, or throw themselves down a flight of stairs.

That's the kind of chaos and human misery we invite when we try to "mandate our own moral code."

The Washington Post
Washington, D.C., July 2, 1992

IF THE Supreme Court had overturned Roe v. Wade on Monday, the political pressure on Congress to pass the Freedom of Choice Act would have been irresistible. If states had been freed to criminalize abortion or dramatically restrict its availability, it would have been clear, at least to federal legislators favoring abortion rights, that they had to step in and prevent such a catastrophe by statute. In fact, the ruling was not the dire edict that some had feared. The decision reaffirmed a woman's constitutional right to abortion before fetal viability. But it also authorized additional state regulation of that right. This may take some steam out of the movement to enact federal legislation, but it does not make the matter moot.

The Freedom of Choice Act would preserve abortion rights on a national basis by prohibiting, with a few exceptions, states from adopting regulations that infringe on the right. At the moment, the bill being considered in the House would allow state parental notice laws and would protect medical personnel who oppose abortion on grounds of conscience. The Senate bill has the same provisions and would also allow states to exclude abortion coverage from Medicaid programs. Other exceptions will be debated when the bills get to the floor in each house.

The bills' sponsors have both preemptive and political goals. They rightly want to preclude the possibility that the states, using the new "undue burden" test announced by the court on Monday, will chip away at abortion rights and cumulatively undermine them. They also want to make a record that will be available to the voters by Election Day, so that every member of Congress asking for reelection will be on record as favoring or opposing this limitation on state action. Voters are entitled to this knowledge and also to know whether the president will keep his promise to veto the bill.

So there is bound to be a lot of politicking concerning this legislation, as there is in fact whenever the subject comes up. We hope it will not obscure the importance of a measure that deserves the soberest and most thoughtful consideration. The court did not create an emergency by its recent ruling. But it did not settle the abortion question once and for all, either. National standards on abortion that set a cap on allowable restrictions are desirable. They would obviate the need for a state-by-state, case-by-case court hassle testing every regulation and ordinance that abortion opponents can devise. They would mercifully take the abortion issue out of the process of confirming Supreme Court nominees. Legislation with these ends is a very good idea.

Detroit Free Press
Detroit, Michigan, June 30, 1992

The U.S. Supreme Court remains unwilling — at least for now — explicitly to overturn the Roe vs. Wade decision that has wisely defined abortion rights for the past two decades. Yet the high court's ruling Monday in a Pennsylvania abortion case affirms its support for the inexorable erosion of the basic freedoms protected by that opinion.

Before the government assault on abortion rights — and attendant guarantees of privacy, choice and equity — gets much worse, Congress should promptly adopt the proposed Freedom of Choice Act, which would codify in federal law many of Roe's fundamental safeguards. And if, as seems certain, President George Bush were to veto such legislation, he should be made accountable to voters in November.

The Supreme Court declared constitutional most of the key restrictions, except in medical emergencies, of a Pennsylvania abortion law: a 24-hour wait for abortions, mandatory "informed consent" counseling (usually a government-scripted anti-abortion spiel), parental or judicial consent for minors' abortions, and detailed reports by doctors to government about the abortions they perform. Justices struck down a provision requiring most married women who sought abortions to tell their husbands.

The court fell one vote short of mustering the majority needed to scrap Roe vs. Wade entirely and effectively outlaw elective abortion nationwide. But that ostensible respect for precedent offers little long-term comfort to abortion rights advocates, since previous high courts had held that state-imposed waiting periods and informed-consent laws were invalid.

And the court majority largely replaced the durable trimester scheme of Roe vs. Wade — which permitted greater government limits on abortion in later stages of pregnancy — with a weak, vague "undue burden" test. As anti-abortion Chief Justice William Rehnquist observed, the majority opinion "retains the outer shell of Roe vs. Wade but beats a wholesale retreat from the substance of that case."

Neither President Bush nor the Supreme Court will protect abortion rights. In Michigan, Gov. John Engler and majorities of the Legislature and state Supreme Court have supported harsh restrictions on the availability of abortion as a matter of reproductive choice. Congress appears the best — and perhaps the last — hope for salvaging what remains of Roe vs. Wade.

Protecting American women's right to safe and legal abortion — preventing illegitimate governmental intrusion into their private decisions — is and ought to be a fundamental issue of this year's political campaigns, as much as timid candidates might wish to evade it.

Roe vs. Wade, we are convinced, remains good law that should continue to guide the nation. Politicians who would affirm it — and those who oppose it — should be clearly on record by November.

Minneapolis Star and Tribune
Minneapolis, Minnesota, June 30, 1992

By one vote, the U.S. Supreme Court Monday upheld its 1973 ruling that ending a pregnancy through abortion is a private matter between a woman and her doctor. Such decisions, the court said in 1973 and affirmed Monday, are governed by a constitutional right to privacy. But even as it affirmed that right, the court weakened it by upholding intrusive restrictions on abortion. Monday's decision puts women in the untenable spot of having a "right" that government can seek to keep them from exercising.

It could have been worse. Four justices — Rehnquist, White, Scalia and Thomas — would have overturned the 1973 decision, Roe vs. Wade, entirely. Courage and wisdom are evident in the judgment of three justices — O'Connor, Kennedy and Souter — who joined with Blackmun and Stevens to uphold the central tenets of Roe. "The reservations any of us may have . . . are outweighed by the explication of individual liberty," the three said. "The woman's right to terminate her pregnancy before viability is the most central principle of Roe vs. Wade. It is a rule of law and a component of liberty we cannot renounce," they wrote. That's precisely the point. For liberty to have meaning, it must apply to behavior that many find objectionable.

But Souter, O'Connor and Kennedy failed to heed those warnings in upholding restrictions on abortion imposed by Pennsylvania. The state may regulate abortion, they said, so long as the regulations don't create an "absolute obstacle or severe limitation." Thus, they approved of Pennsylvania's requirements that women seeking an abortion be told about fetal development and alternatives to abortion; that women wait 24 hours after receiving that information before undergoing an abortion; and that women younger than 18 get the consent of one parent or permission of a judge.

Deciding to abort a pregnancy involves a woman in a tangle of issues. In good circumstances, you'd hope that sensitive doctors would provide unbiased information on fetal development and the options open — including abortion. You'd hope a woman would consider all the information before making her decision. You'd hope that young women would seek help and counsel of compassionate parents.

But those ideas should not be state requirements imposed on the patronizing presumption that women aren't capable of knowing their own minds and seeking help to make such momentous decisions. In the genteel atmosphere of its chambers, the court has decided that a constitutional right to privacy can coexist with such requirements. In the real world it can't. Pennsylvania's restrictions were designed and will be used to coerce women out of abortion. Think of the irony: Doctors now can be required to discuss alternatives to abortion, but if they practice in clinics that receive federal funding, they are prohibited from mentioning the abortion option itself. For many women, the right to privacy that the court affirmed Monday will be a hollow promise.

The Augusta Chronicle
Augusta, Georgia, June 30, 1992

The 1973 *Roe vs. Wade* Supreme Court decision overturning state anti-abortion laws set off a bitter debate between advocates of "women's right to choose" and the "rights of the unborn." It has dominated this super-sensitive issue for 19 years.

Yet largely overlooked in the heated rhetoric was that *Roe* also trampled on states' rights.

If abortion had been left to the discretion of the states, it likely would never have become the seething national issue that it is today. Indeed, the Reagan and Bush administrations had the Justice Department intervene in cases pending before the High Court to urge that issue be returned to the states — even though both were also urging the outright overturning of *Roe*.

In this context, the Supreme Court yesterday gave states sweeping new power to regulate abortions by upholding most provisions of a Pennsylvania law making abortions not so quickly obtainable.

But, by a 5-4 vote, the Court said states may not outlaw all abortions. "Though abortion is conduct, it does not follow that the state is entitled to proscribe it in all instances," Justice Sandra Day O'Connor said in the court's main opinion.

O'Connor and Justices Anthony Kennedy and David Souter also adopted a significant new test for judging abortion regulation — the "undue burden test."

Under it, an abortion regulation that imposes an "absolute obstacle or severe limitation on the abortion decision" would be subjected to the highest judicial scrutiny. If the regulation is judged not to be an undue burden, then it is constitutional if rationally related to a legitimate state purpose — usually an easy test for states to meet.

Pennsylvania's governor calls the decision "a victory for the unborn child" yet the National Right to Life Committee's lawyer laments that the Court "has given us very little hope that anything can be done about abortion on demand."

From the "pro-choice" camp comes the question as to whether *Roe* is now so weakened that it really doesn't establish a constitutional right. The answer will no doubt come after the Court decides two other pending abortion cases.

The Oregonian
Portland, Oregon, July 4, 1992

Pennsylvania's 1989 law permitting public disclosure of quarterly reports from abortion providers isn't as broad as some news reports have suggested.

For example, it clearly forbids disclosing the names of women seeking abortions. But that doesn't make it much less awful.

The law's public-disclosure requirement was among provisions the U.S. Supreme Court upheld Monday. It will limit access to abortions in two ways:

● By discouraging doctors from doing abortions, knowing that their names and addresses will be available for public inspection.

● By providing a handy hit list for radical groups that fight abortion by intimidation, harassment, occasional firebombings and other violence.

Under the law, all clinics and doctors who do abortions must file quarterly forms listing their names, addresses and numbers of abortions performed, broken down by trimester of pregnancy, says Linda Wharton of the Women's Law Project in Philadelphia. And reports from abortion providers who receive funding from the state for any reason, including Medicaid payments, are open for public inspection.

Exactly the same information — although in far more detail — is compiled in confidential records on every legal Pennsylvania abortion. If the state really thirsts for public-health knowledge, which the General Assembly said is its objective, the non-disclosable records have it.

Wharton, who was co-counsel for clinics and doctors who appealed the law to the Supreme Court, is concerned that disclosure of the quarterly reports will open more doctors to anti-abortion harassment.

"The clinics are listed in the phone book," she says, "but they wouldn't necessarily know about individual physicians performing abortions."

Now they will. Sad to say, the court has all but invited other states to be just as cynically creative in hampering women's reproductive choices.

THE CHRISTIAN SCIENCE MONITOR
Boston, Massachusetts, July 1, 1992

THE Supreme Court of the United States has narrowly refused to overturn its 1973 Roe v. Wade decision that established a right to abortion for all American women. But by upholding most provisions of a Pennsylvania law restricting access to abortion, the court greatly broadened the regulatory options open to state lawmakers.

The return to a patchwork of abortion law, with the procedure restricted in some states and readily available in others, is at hand. In light of the Pennsylvania ruling, however, it's clear that only the appointment of yet another strong conservative to the Supreme Court would bring a final reversal of Roe v. Wade.

The court's slim majority, led by Justice Sandra Day O'Connor, put forward a new standard for abortion cases: whether a statute puts an "undue burden" on a woman's rights. Justice David Souter pointedly told the crowded courtroom that a reversal of Roe would threaten the court's legitimacy. Justice Anthony Kennedy emphasized the private, intimate nature of decisions regarding the formation of families.

These views herald the formation of a plurality of moderately conservative and liberal justices who want to preserve women's access to abortion, as required by Roe. But what the court saw as a reasonable burden on women – such as required discussion of the alternatives to abortion and a 24-hour waiting period – may present significant hurdles to women who want the right to make up their own minds without state interference.

A particularly intrusive requirement for women in shaky marriages – mandatory notification of husbands – was struck down by the court as too burdensome.

Concerns about privacy, equal access for women of all means, and the care of unwanted children argue for retaining unfettered freedom of choice, at least in the early stages of pregnancy.

The issue now shifts to the political realm, with abortion-rights forces in Congress poised to push for passage of a bill to solidify Roe into national law. Their efforts face an inevitable presidential veto – which is just what some in Congress are counting on to damage George Bush with pro-choice voters.

But politics – whether of the presidential or state-house variety – won't resolve the abortion issue. This issue is fundamentally addressed through moral education, character building, and spiritual development, which lead individuals toward responsible decisions in their personal lives. The 1.5 million abortions performed in the US yearly underscore the need to strengthen such processes and the institutions that nurture them.

The Virginian-Pilot
Norfolk, Virginia, July 2, 1992

Political scientists may note that the U.S. Supreme Court's decision Monday on abortion came three years almost to the day after it made its first ruling limiting women's abortion rights. That was the Webster decision, July 3, 1989, and the political fallout from it was quick and decisive.

The response from pro-choice groups to Webster, which permitted states to impose restrictions on women seeking abortions, boosted the candidacies of Democrats who were running in the only major 1989 races: the gubernatorial campaigns in New Jersey and Virginia. One major reason Democrat Douglas Wilder beat Republican Marshall Coleman in Virginia was the negative reaction in Republican-leaning cities (such as Virginia Beach) to Mr. Coleman's hardline anti-abortion stance.

For 16 years prior to the Webster decision, since the court declared in Roe vs. Wade that abortion is a fundamental right, anti-abortionists had been more active politically than pro-choice advocates. The reason was simple: The law of the land (the Roe decision in 1973) was pro-choice, so there was little apparent need to get exercised about the issue.

That changed with Webster. And today the question is whether this week's decision, which approved further limiting access to abortions but did not overturn Roe, will have a similar effect.

President Bush's political strategists sighed with relief when the court decided not to overrule Roe. On the record, Mr. Bush says that Roe is bad law; off the record, his strategists believe and hope that this week's ruling is not a severe-enough blow to abortion rights — as overturning Roe would have been — to drive more pro-choice voters away from the president.

Maybe. But if pro-choice voters look at one aspect of the decision — the court upheld Roe by just one vote, 5-4 — they will be out on the hustings, working as hard as possible to elect someone in November, Bill Clinton or Ross Perot, who won't place another anti-abortion justice on the Supreme Court.

The words spoken Monday by Justice Harry Blackmun, who wrote the Roe decision and remains its most ardent defender, are ominous:

"I am 83 years old. I cannot remain on this court forever, and when I do step down, the confirmation process for my successor well may focus on the issue before us today."

Presidential elections turn on a handful of litmus-test issues: crime, foreign policy, race, taxes. Given the 5-4 split on the court now, abortion must be added to the list. He'll never admit it, but Mr. Bush has been damaged by the court's ruling.

THE ARIZONA REPUBLIC
Phoenix, Arizona, July 2, 1992

WHILE most defenders of abortion rights were celebrating Monday's Supreme Court declaration that "the essential holding of Roe v. Wade should be retained and once again reaffirmed," Planned Parenthood was thrashing about in a frenzy.

"Don't be fooled," cried the New York chapter in a full-page ad in yesterday's New York Times. "Roe v. Wade is dead." Elsewhere in the paper, the Planned Parenthood Federation of America warned that the court's decision "threatens to put every woman right back where she was nineteen years ago — before Roe v. Wade ended back-alley horrors." It warned that, "unless you act right away, women all across the country will be forced to deal with a chaotic patchwork of frightening, unfair state restrictions on abortion." Monday's ruling, it said, means that "countless women may again be compelled to risk death."

Well now. Before joining Planned Parenthood's crusade to have Congress adopt the so-called Freedom of Choice Act — an effort to outlaw parental consent, pre-abortion counseling and other protections — it might be wise to consider just what Monday's ruling did allow by way of "frightening, unfair state restrictions."

The practical effects of the ruling are easily summarized. In addition to affirming Roe v. Wade, the court upheld Pennsylvania's requirements (1) that women seeking abortions be told about fetal development and abortion alternatives, (2) that they wait 24 hours thereafter before deciding on abortion, (3) that doctors keep detailed records, subject to disclosure, on all abortions performed and (4) that unmarried females under 18, if not self-supporting, obtain the consent of a parent or a judge before having abortions.

What is Planned Parenthood trying to say? That women should not be told about alternatives to abortion? That walk-in abortions need to be encouraged? That doctors should not keep records? That minor children should be making these life-and-death decisions on their own?

Pennsylvania has enacted reasonable safeguards to ensure that abortions are not entered into hastily or ill-advisedly. Unlike Planned Parenthood's efforts to misrepresent the effect of Monday's decision and touch off a congressional stampede, such safeguards are neither frightening nor unfair, and Congress should keep hands off.

DAYTON DAILY NEWS

Dayton, Ohio, June 30, 1992

States may not ban abortion.

That's the heart of the U.S. Supreme Court decision Monday on a Pennsylvania law that restricts abortions.

A strong court majority said Pennsylvania's law — which is similar to Ohio's approach to regulating abortion — is constitutional. But more significant, a bare majority of five said abortion can't be outlawed totally.

Three members of the court — Justices Anthony Kennedy, Sandra Day O'Connor and David Souter — joined with the two justices who opposed the Pennsylvania rules to say that abortion can't be banned outright.

That left four justices — including President Bush's most recent appointee, Clarence Thomas — saying Roe v. Wade should be overturned, that states have no obligation to allow abortions. Justice Thomas, during his confirmation hearings, said he had no opinion about a woman's right to an abortion. He does now, and his opinion surprised no one.

Most court watchers assumed that Justice O'Connor would not vote to overturn Roe. Justice Kennedy and particularly Justice Souter were the unknowns. With this vote, they've shown they're not ideologues. They're honest conservatives who believe in adhering to precedent unless there's a good reason for abandoning it.

For most women, the right to abortion isn't in jeopardy until the next justice retires.

The Pennsylvania law imposes a waiting period, requires doctors to tell women about fetal development and mandates that minors inform their parents about an impending abortion or get a judge to relieve them of that requirement. (Women cannot, however, be made to inform their husbands about their intent to have an abortion, which was another provision in the Pennsylvania law.)

The O'Connor faction didn't endorse any and all regulation. It said rules that are simply roadblocks to an abortion are unconstitutional. That view is a logical extension of Roe, which said government can restrict abortion at certain stages of pregnancy.

While the American public supports a woman's right to choose, abortion remains controversial. That's because while most Americans want to leave the decision up to women, they can imagine many circumstances under which they believe women *shouldn't* opt for the procedure. This is not a contradiction; it's a way of reconciling individual liberty with respect for potential human life.

A majority of the Supreme Court is in sync with past court decisions and the views of most Americans.

The Providence Journal

Providence, Rhode Island, June 30, 1992

The Supreme Court's decision on abortion is neither the "insulting, patronizing and condescending" ruling that the president of the League of Women Voters calls it, nor the "victory for the unborn child" claimed by the governor of Pennsylvania. It is, instead, the Court's tortured effort to arrive at some reasonable standard on the issue of abortion. We support a woman's right to an abortion, and regret that the Court has seen fit to rule as it has. Nevertheless, for those who support abortion rights, this decision contains as much good news as bad.

Of course, we would have preferred to see the question settled by *Roe v. Wade*, which, as Justice Souter said yesterday, "has not proven unworkable in practice." But that was destined not to happen.

For the past two years the Court has signaled unmistakably that it intended to modify *Roe* by allowing the states to impose certain limitations on the practice of abortion; in effect, to transfer some of the law governing abortion from the federal to the state level. That is what it has now done, upholding a Pennsylvania statute that requires women seeking an abortion to be informed about alternatives and to wait 24 hours after receiving such information. It also obliges doctors to keep records available for public disclosure, and requires unmarried minors to gain the consent of one parent, or a state judge, before undergoing the procedure. These are not onerous limitations, but we hope that the Court's decision will not open the door to further restrictions.

Some jurisdictions have already imposed them; indeed, Louisiana, Utah and the territory of Guam have banned abortion outright. Will other places follow suit? We doubt it. Legislative efforts to outlaw abortion have failed in places where success was expected — Florida, for example — and the fact that the justices struck down the Pennsylvania requirement that wives inform husbands suggests that this Supreme Court is by no means opposed to abortion in principle.

Nobody welcomes the idea of abortion, and everybody agrees that alternatives to unwanted pregnancies — through education, contraception, adoption, family planning — are essential. Nevertheless, most Americans favor the right to an abortion, and oppose the absolute banning of a fundamental option. For Rhode Island, the message is clear: The General Assembly must now take any steps necessary to guarantee for the citizens of this state that abortion remains safe and legal.

The Washington Times

Washington, D.C., June 30, 1992

"There is a limit to the amount of error that can plausibly be imputed to prior courts."

The Supreme Court
Pennsylvania vs. Casey

For example, as we learned from the controlling opinion filed by Justices Sandra Day O'Connor, Anthony Kennedy and David Souter yesterday, we may say that a prior Supreme Court erred in ruling that a woman has a "fundamental right" to an abortion; that it erred in relying on a formula involving "trimesters" to determine fetal viability; that it erred in holding that any regulation of abortion must be subjected to "strict scrutiny" by the courts and could be upheld only in cases of a "compelling state interest." We may, in short, say that the court erred in all the relevant particulars of Roe vs. Wade. But we may not, according to the O'Connor-Kennedy-Souter standard, say the court erred in Roe vs. Wade.

Because if we did that, we would be asking for trouble. We would be risking the very legitimacy of the judiciary as an institution. "The price may be criticism or ostracism, or it may be violence," the court warned darkly.

The court decided yesterday to uphold most of the provisions regulating abortion in Pennsylvania. A women seeking an abortion must give her "informed consent" prior to the procedure, and she has to be provided with information about her pregnancy and the alternatives to ending it at least 24 hours before she has an abortion. A minor must obtain the informed consent of one parent prior to an abortion (although a so-called judicial bypass is also provided for). These requirements are waived in case of medical emergency. The court held that a requirement that a married woman seeking an abortion must sign a paper indicating that she has notified her husband of her intention is unconstitutional, however.

The court's new standard for permissible regulation of abortion, derived from its ruling in Webster, is that state action is permissible so long as it does not impose an "undue burden" on a woman seeking an abortion prior to the viability of the fetus she carries (at which point the state may assert a stronger interest in protecting life, if it chooses). What is an undue burden? The court explains: "An undue burden exists, and therefore a provision of law is invalid, if its purpose or effect is to place a substantial obstacle in the path of a woman seeking an abortion before the fetus attains viability." In other words, an undue burden is a substantial obstacle.

In other words, the courts will decide. And so the tangled and bizarre Supreme Court jurisprudence surrounding abortion — much like its jurisprudence concerning the Establishment Clause discussed in this space Sunday — continues apace. We have neither Roe nor an overturned Roe. We have instead an implied promise from the Supreme Court that it will use all of the wisdom it possesses — in areas from law to medicine and science to sociology and labor-force economics — to guide our legislators in their task.

To guide, in this instance, means to overrule and second-guess. The people who elect legislators, and the legislators who are themselves the legitimate representatives of the people, continue to be held incompetent to decide matters of abortion regulation and restriction for themselves. They may get lucky and pass legislation the court believes does not impose an "undue burden" on women. Surely they are now invited to try. But the courts will have the final say.

The dubious inference that gives rise to this preemption of the people's will — namely that access to abortion derives from privacy rights articulated by the court in other cases — remains as unexamined and indefensible as it was when the court handed down Roe and gutted state laws on abortion in 1973. The O'Connor-Kennedy-Souter formulation about "a limit to the amount of error that can plausibly be imputed to prior courts" is revealing. It seems to envision a distinction between the actual amount of error the court has made and the amount of error it is acceptable for the court to acknowledge. What is that distinction? No doubt state attempts to enact abortion laws, now and into the future, will provide many occasions for the court's solipsistic if not Solomonic ruminations on the subject of what it really thinks.

REHNQUIST SCALIA THOMAS WHITE

THE ROE VS. WADE ABORTIONISTS

The TENNESSEAN
Nashville, Tennessee, June 27, 1992

CONGRESS fought its first fights on women's right to abortion last week, and the news was encouraging.

By a vote of 5-3 along party lines, a House subcommittee on civil and constitutional rights approved a measure to protect abortion rights. The Senate started its own measure with a proposal to write into federal law the guarantees expressed in past Supreme Court decisions. But the fight is far from over.

This year is already shaping up as perhaps the most important ever in the abortion rights struggle. Within days, the U.S. Supreme Court is expected to rule on a Pennsylvania law that severely restricts women from having an abortion. The court's decision could chip away or even end the protection affirmed in *Roe v. Wade* by the court in 1973.

But fear about the court's action already has galvanized the political campaigns this season. Pro-choice Republicans have forced a confrontation over the issue of abortion in their party platform. The division in the party which has traditionally opposed abortion in its platform surfaced publicly in hearings last month. But the rift is expected to widen even more in platform fights at the Republican National Convention in Houston this August.

President Bush, who has flipflopped on

Abortion battle only gets hotter

the issue of abortion in his career, faces Ross Perot and probable Democratic nominee Bill Clinton, both of whom stand firmly for choice.

Republican women who support choice have also started an effort to get abortion rights candidates in Congress. Democrats have been actively getting pro-choice candidates, too.

Congress has faced several tangential issues to abortion, including the so-called gag order on federal funded family planning clinics. For the most part, abortion protection, such as the removal of the gag order, has won Congress' support.

Abortion certainly isn't the only issue this political season. But the right of women to choose in their own health matters is in danger, and it should be concern of every candidate for public office this year. A House subcommittee and Senate supporters have affirmed the importance of that right. Voters will be looking for those candidates who share their concern about the future of the most personal decision a woman can make. ∎

The Star-Ledger
Newark, New Jersey, July 8, 1992

For almost two decades, ever since the landmark Roe vs. Wade decision by the U.S. Supreme Court, Congress has been sitting on the sidelines, insulated from the emotional political backlash of the abortion controversy. But the latest ruling by the high court that restricts a woman's right to terminate a pregnancy strongly suggests that the legislative branch's sideline role could be altered in a climactic, terminal stage.

As Justice Harry Blackmun, author of the Roe decision, noted in a personal opinion on the new abortion ruling, the decision is the law of the land only as long as the current court remains intact. The naming of another conservative justice could mean the demise of the historic abortion ruling.

In the past, the congressional role in the controversy was mainly associated with peripheral issues, such as federal funding for abortions. That detached legislative status no longer may be tenable under the court's new ruling that states can restrict access to abortion. This major change of the ground rules has raised concern among abortion rights advocates.

Rather than leaving the issue to fragmented uncertainty at the state level, pro-choice leaders are urging Congress to replace a diluted Roe by enacting federal legislation guaranteeing the right to abortion. The essential components of Roe would be preserved under a proposed Freedom of Choice Act; it would bar states from restricting a woman's right to have an abortion.

There may, however, be some problems on Capitol Hill. Similar legislation died in Congress last year, but supporters believe there is more backing for the bill now. The House Judiciary Committee approved a new version, and similar action is expected in the Senate.

House Speaker Thomas Foley is confident that there are enough votes in Congress to pass an abortion rights bill, but not enough to override a veto by President Bush, who opposes abortion.

For a Democrat-controlled Congress the timing for forcing the abortion issue with the Bush administration is enhanced by this year's presidential election. Congressional passage of the Freedom of Choice Act would significantly complicate the already tenuous Bush bid for re-election by putting him on the political hot seat before the November election.

Partisan politics aside, it should be apparent that the most feasible solution to the volatile abortion issue would be the enactment of a federal law. It would finally, in a long-term, stable manner, establish the right of choice as the law of the land, effectively removing it from the ideological vulnerability of the judicial branch of government.

The News Journal

Wilmington, Delaware, June 30, 1992

WHERE WE STAND

The General Assembly should keep hands off weakened Roe vs. Wade

For Delawareans, the most important part of the Supreme Court's ruling on abortion yesterday is that Roe vs. Wade was reaffirmed, albeit by a one vote margin. That means that abortions remain legal in every state in America, including those that have laws that tried to prohibit them.

Unfortunately, the ruling also means that abortions are now more restricted in Pennsylvania and that other states may try to follow its path as a rearguard attack on abortion rights. The relief we feel at the Supreme Court's refusal to overturn Roe vs. Wade is tempered by our concern over issues raised by its shifting to states the authority to restrict reproductive rights.

Roe vs. Wade, unrestricted, now rules in Delaware. That is because the state's old abortion law, which allowed abortions only in cases of rape and incest, to protect the mother's life or to prevent serious birth defects, was superceded by Roe vs. Wade in 1973.

That is exactly the way we want it to stay in Delaware. There should be no tinkering by the state legislature. If Roe vs. Wade is overturned in the future, the legislature should restore abortion rights at the state level. Until then, hands off in Dover.

The restrictions in the Pennsylvania law may seem on the surface to be reasonable, but in practice they are likely to cause difficulties for women most in need of abortion rights. While we agree in principle that most unmarried juvenile females are better off getting the consent of a parent before an abortion, we also know that in the real world getting parental consent for girls under 18 (who are not self supporting) is a trauma many will avoid. For those young women determined to terminate the pregnancy, their illegal alternatives could be life-threatening.

The "informed consent" clause and the 24-hour waiting period will undoubtedly become the window of opportunity for anti-abortion forces. There should be intense judicial scrutiny of anti-abortion activity to make sure they do not violate the "undue burden" test. The court held regulations that impose an absolute obstacle or severe limitation on the abortion decision are unlawful.

This ruling is more than a dark cloud on the horizon for reproductive rights, but it is not the thunderburst it might have been had Roe vs. Wade been overturned.

ARGUS-LEADER

Sioux Falls, South Dakota, June 30, 1992

Justices Clarence Thomas and David Souter received their first opportunity Monday to take a significant legal stand on abortion. Surprisingly, the two newest members of the U.S. Supreme Court stood apart.

Souter sided with a moderate majority in a highly noteworthy 5-4 decision, and Thomas sided with the minority that wanted to go further by overturning Roe vs. Wade.

More surprising, given the overall makeup of the high court, was that a majority of the nine justices reaffirmed that women have a fundamental right to obtain abortions.

Editorial

The court's decision, released Monday in a case called Planned Parenthood vs. Casey, bars states from outlawing abortion.

Abortion opponents on the court fell a vote short of overturning the landmark Roe decision of 1973, which legalized abortion nationwide. The Roe decision was based largely on a woman's constitutional right to privacy.

In its decision Monday, the court also upheld restrictions in a Pennsylvania law that gives states new power to make it tougher for women to end pregnancies.

Nationally, the decision did not satisfy abortion opponents or those who favor abortion rights. Although convoluted, the ruling strikes us as logical and reasonable.

We consider abortion a deeply personal issue — one that people should consider and resolve with their own conscience. We avoid commenting on the issue, except when it is thrust prominently onto the political or legal stage, as it is now.

Monday's decision is bound to prompt abortion opponents to lobby legislatures for tougher regulations. The majority decision was written by Justices Sandra Day O'Connor, Anthony Kennedy and Souter.

Those three acknowledged a woman's right to have an abortion without undue interference from government. They also acknowledged state government's right to "restrict abortions after fetal viability, if the law contains exceptions for pregnancies which endanger a woman's life or health."

The ruling was the result of a dispute over a Pennsylvania law that places a variety of restrictions on abortions, including a 24-hour waiting period. The law also requires parental consent for unmarried woman under 18 and counseling by a physician. The court struck a requirement that a husband be notified of his wife's abortion.

The Supreme Court has been nibbling away at the Roe decision for about 15 years. In 1986, it struck regulations almost identical to those imposed by Pennsylvania. In 1989, it it gave states more leeway to regulate abortions.

On Monday, the court reaffirmed a woman's right to obtain an abortion but also cleared the way for reasonable regulation. That's quite a feat, one we find hard to fault.

Newsday

New York City, New York, July 4, 1992

Forget all the problems this nation has — at least for today. Enjoy the midsummer holiday, let the fireworks explode and, while you are celebrating, also appreciate, for a change, what is right about this nation. And one shining example is the manner in which the Supreme Court made its decision this week to uphold a women's right to have an abortion.

No matter how you feel about the substance of the decision, no matter how bitter or how excruciating the debate has been, an extraordinary and unexpected majority came together out of a conviction that the center must

hold. Two hundred and five years after it was written, the Constitution of the United States continues to exert an authority more powerful than individual ideology, more lasting than even the most contentious issues. Just read the words of Justice David Souter:

"The root of American government power is revealed most clearly in the instance of the power conferred by the Constitution upon the Judiciary of the United States and specifically upon this Court. As Americans of each succeeding generation are rightly told, the Court cannot buy support for its deci-

sions by spending money and, except to a minor degree, it cannot independently coerce obedience to its decrees. The Court's power lies, rather, in its legitimacy, a product of substance and perception that shows itself in the people's acceptance of the judiciary as fit to determine what the nation's law means and to declare what it demands."

Some of the justices admittedly bypassed their own moral code to do what they believed necessary to protect the court's legitimacy and the Constitution itself. It is reason enough to celebrate the nation's birthday.

TULSA WORLD

Tulsa, Oklahoma, June 30, 1992

THE U.S. Supreme Court's muddled decision upholding Pennsylvania's anti-abortion law appears to be an effort to agree with both sides.

The decision clearly supports, in principle, a woman's right to decide on an early term abortion as defined in the 1973 Roe vs. Wade case. But a few paragraphs later, the ruling approves most of Pennsylvania's unreasonable and authoritarian statute.

Notwithstanding the doubletalk about reaffirming the right recognized in Roe, the new ruling is a major blow to individual choice and liberty. It reaffirms the right to abortion in one sentence and emasculates it in the next.

The Pennsylvania law approved in the 5-4 ruling places humiliating and degrading restrictions on a woman's right to choose. It requires, for example, a waiting period during which a woman must listen to unsolicited "counseling." A woman is held to be legally incapable of exercising a constitutional right without the "help" of government-required advice and propaganda. Women under 18 face even more restrictive official roadblocks in exercising their rights.

The court's decision drops the emotional but important issue squarely into the political arena. With Roe vs. Wade now all but neutered, people who believe in individual liberty have no appeal except the ballot box.

One battleground will be the regular elections. In Oklahoma's U.S. Senate races, the seriously contested congressional races and many of the legislative races, candidates already are making their pro- or anti-choice stands known. The same is true in the presidential contest. Arkansas Gov. Bill Clinton and Ross Perot are committed to leaving the decision on early term abortion largely to the individual citizen. President Bush — once an avowed advocate of choice — now takes the authoritarian line: Government should make the decision for all women; government knows best.

In Oklahoma, an even more important battle for individual liberty may be fought soon over a deceptive state question that would effectively outlaw nearly all abortions in Oklahoma.

State Question 642, an initiative petition measure now awaiting court certification, is being pushed by the Government-Knows-Best crowd as a "reasonable" middle-ground approach to abortion regulation. That's a lie. It is in fact an authoritarian measure that places such unreasonable restrictions on abortion that all but a few would be effectively outlawed.

The battle for individual rights in decisions affecting pregnancy has now moved from the courts to the ballot box.

San Francisco Chronicle

San Francisco, California, June 30, 1992

THE U.S. SUPREME Court continues to erode Roe vs. Wade, while narrowly upholding its legitimacy. The heartening aspect of yesterday's ruling was this: A majority — albeit slender — firmly upheld the core of that landmark decision giving women the constitutional right to choose to terminate a pregnancy. The depressing downside was that the court also approved a number of Pennsylvania's mean-spirited restrictions on that right.

A retreat from Roe, while preserving its essence

So the ruling constitutes a retreat from Roe, but far from a calamitous capitulation.

What gives encouragement to those, like ourselves, who believe this right to be a fundamental one for women, is that the court could have overturned Roe entirely, or skirted the question of its constitutionality.

Instead, an increasingly influential "moderate center," composed of Justices Sandra Day O'Connor, Anthony Kennedy and David Souter, held fast to the reasonable and humane precedent that is at the decision's heart.

Indeed, Justice Souter's words to the courtroom had ringing reverberation: "To overrule (Roe) would subvert the court's legitimacy beyond any reasonable question. If the court is undermined, the country would also be so ... Roe has not proved unworkable in practice."

The court, in short, listens and is sensitive to words and sounds well outside those contained in legal briefs. It is aware of the deep, emotional division in this country over choice. Souter's statement has power and reach.

AS FOR APPROVING the Pennsylvania law's restrictions — the mandatory instruction, the waiting period, the consent required from unmarried women under age 18 — these decisions dilute Roe's strength and will fall most heavily on those with least defense: the poor, the untutored, the harassed.

Such action will also serve as invitation for further state encroachment on this most personal of decisions — one that should be unfettered and made solely by the woman involved with, if needed, the assistance of unrestricted medical advice.

In California, further encroachment seems unlikely at this moment. But the fact of the slender court majority and its shifting emphasis makes passage of a federal Freedom of Choice Act all the more important. The darkness may be hovering, as Justice Harry Blackmun noted, but Roe's essential flame burns on.

Richmond Times-Dispatch

Richmond, Virginia, June 30, 1992

The secret is out. The reaction to yesterday's Supreme Court decision regarding Pennsylvania's abortion regulations affirms that the issue is not "choice." It is *abortion* — abortion simple and abortion pure.

The so-called pro-choice side argues that Pennsylvania denies women freedom of choice. Does it? Consider what the state's principal regulations authorize:

— A 24-hour waiting period between the time a woman seeks an abortion and the time she receives one;

— Parental consent (with a judicial bypass) and spousal notification (the court upheld the former, but threw out the latter);

— Requiring clinics to inform potential clients about alternatives to abortion, the facts of fetal development, and the risks the operation itself poses to the health of the mother.

Regarding adults, the approved stipulations do not diminish choice. After waiting 24 hours, a woman can choose to have an abortion. After learning about adoption programs or that abortion is not a fix-it-up on a par with piercing ears or lancing boils, she can choose to have an abortion. The choice is hers.

But — and here's the rub — while the Pennsylvania regulations would not persuade women who do not want abortions to have them, in some instances they might encourage women leaning toward abortions to change their minds.

If a woman went to a clinic in a panic, a 24-hour rest might calm her down. In a less-befuddled state of mind, she might choose not to have an abortion. After learning about adoption programs or certain health risks, she might choose to carry her pregnancy to term. The choice would be hers.

Poll after poll suggests the citizenry opposes abortion on demand. The public declines to endorse abortion without strings. Although a constitutional amendment to prohibit all but medically necessary abortions seems unlikely to pass, regulations treating abortion like other medical procedures enjoy substantial popular support. If parental consent (or a court order) is required for a minor to have a bone set or a tooth pulled, then it ought to be required for a minor to have an abortion. If the Pennsylvania law applied to, say, breast implants, then feminists would hail it as a victory for women's rights, an affirmation of "informed consent."

Yesterday the court did not overturn *Roe v. Wade*. "Choice" still exists. While not denying abortion as an option, the Pennsylvania regulations might modestly reduce abortion's frequency. The regulations are sound, and so is the Supreme Court's decision upholding them.

Part II: Politics & Abortion

Since the 1973 Supreme Court *Roe v. Wade* ruling, abortion has emerged as a key issue in American politics and legislation. Opponents of abortion have succeeded in implementing measures – at the local, state and federal levels – that restrict or regulate the availability of the abortion procedure. The curbs are designed to circumvent the High Court's decision, and some have faced court challenges.

One of the first and most significant legislative moves in this direction was the Hyde Amendment, passed by Congress in 1977. The Hyde Amendment banned Medicaid reimbursement for all abortions except those to save the mother's life – or under limited conditions to safeguard her health – and in officially reported cases of rape or incest.

In 1978, the House of Representatives approved a bill that would allow federal funding of abortions only when the mother's life was endangered by carrying the pregnancy to term. The curb was attached to the fiscal 1979 appropriations bill for the Labor and the Health, Education and Welfare departments.

In the 1980s, the Reagan administration, frustrated in its efforts to change the body of abortion law through individual court cases, and chafing under the criticism of conservative supporters, backed proposals before Congress to override *Roe v. Wade* and subsequent Supreme Court rulings on abortion through passage of a constitutional amendment.

Under Article V of the Constitution, a constitutional amendment – the only means of overturning a Supreme Court ruling – can be initiated if approved by two-thirds of both houses of Congress, and then ratified by three-quarters of the states.

The most highly publicized of these amendments, sponsored by Rep. Henry J. Hyde of Illinois and Sen. Jesse Helms of North Carolina, simply declared that life begins at conception. The fetus's life would thus be entitled to full protection under the law, and abortion at any point during pregnancy would become murder.

The stance reflected in such a measure, which pro-choice advocates say ignores any claim by the pregnant woman to rights of her own, is one that has set the tone of the abortion debate in the national political sphere. Politicians who have attempted to separate their personal beliefs about abortion from their political stance on the issue – including 1984 Democratic vice presidential candidate Geraldine Ferraro – have found it difficult to combat the black-and-white representation of this complicated issue put forth both by fervent anti-abortionists, including prominent members of the Roman Catholic Church, and the extreme fringe of the feminist movement

While abortion foes have failed to push a constitutional amendment to ban abortions through Congress, they have been successful in getting Congress to prohibit federal financing of nearly all abortions. Abortion opponents have also succeeded in implementing measures on the state and local levels to deny use of public funds for abortion.

As a result of the 1989 Supreme Court *Webster v. Reproductive Health Services* decision upholding the right of the states to restrict abortion, several key measures on this issue were presented both in Congress and in individual state legislatures.

In 1989 the House of Representatives narrowly approve a measure to restore Medicaid funds to pay for abortions in cases of rape or incest. The vote reversed eight years of House policy that had barred any use of Medicaid funds for abortions except in cases where the mother's life was endangered.

The vote was regarded by activists on both sides of the abortion question as evidence of a shifting political attitude toward abortion rights in the wake of the Supreme Court's *Webster* decision.

President George Bush, as promised, vetoed the bill. "I have informed Congress on numerous occasions that I would veto legislation if it permitted the use of appropriated funds to pay for abortions other than those in which the mother would be endangered if the fetus was carried to term," Bush said in a veto message.

In 1990 the Idaho senate voted to approve legislation that would ban most abortions in the state. The legislation, which was the most restrictive of any state in the U.S., had been designed as a vehicle to give the U.S. Supreme Court an opportunity to reconsider and possibly overturn *Roe v. Wade*.

The legislation was described as a ban on abortion as a means of birth control. Specifically, it prohibited all abortions except in cases of rape reported to the police within seven days, incest involving a woman under age 18, "profound" fetal deformity or threat to a woman's physical health. The bill had been crafted by members of the National Right to Life Committee, in the wake of the Supreme Court's *Webster* ruling.

Supporters of the legislation said it had been specifically designed to overcome the objections of Supreme Court Justice Sandra Day O'Connor, who had previously voted to uphold abortion restrictions, but whose opinions had stopped short of a declaration in favor of overturning *Roe*. Abortion opponents believed that one of her chief objections to other abortion restrictions had been that those bills had included criminal penalties for women who obtained abortions. Therefore, the Idaho bill had been crafted in such a way as to avoid holding women criminally responsible for having an abortion.

Instead, the bill penalized doctors, making them liable for a fine of up to $10,000, and allowing individuals involved in a particular abortion case – including fathers of fetuses or parents of minor children who had an abortion – to file civil lawsuits against a doctor who performed the procedure.

Abortion has played an increasingly major role in U.S. presidential politics. As the Republican Party alligned itself with the religious right, the Democrats became more responsive to the concerns of pro-choice advocates.

At their July 1992 National Convention in New York City, the Democrats adopted a platform one of the key points of which was, "Support for the right to abortion through Supreme Court decisions and law."

In addition, the platform promised "an effective system of child-support enforcement," and "family and medical leave and affordable childcare." The platform also promised to "Expand child health and nutrition programs."

On the other hand, the Republican Party's platform, issued during their August 1992 National Convention in Houston, Texas, specifically stated: "We believe the unborn child has a fundamental individual right to life that cannot be infringed. We therefore reaffirm our support for a human life amendment to the Constitution...We reaffirm our support for appointment of judges who respect traditional family values and the sanctity of innocent human life..."

States Enact Varying Abortion Restrictions

As the Supreme Court continued to redefine its 1973 abortion decision *Roe v. Wade*, individual states began enacting regulations of their own. The following developments occurred in the late 1980s and early 1990s:

■ The Florida state legislature, meeting in a special session October 10-11, 1989, voted down a series of measures proposed by Gov. Bob Martinez (R) that would have restricted access to abortion. Martinez had vowed to toughen the state's abortion laws after the Supreme Court upheld a strict Missouri abortion statute in July.

The proposals included restrictions that would have barred state employees and facilities from performing abortions, established a seven-day waiting period for women seeking an abortion, required fetal viability testing beyond the 20th week of pregnancy and mandated special licensing of abortion clinics. To the anger of anti-abortion activists, all of the proposals were rejected in committee before they were able to reach the floor of the legislature for a full debate.

Previously, the Florida Supreme Court October 5, 1989 struck down a law that required pregnant teenagers to obtain the permission of a parent or judge before having an abortion.

■ The Pennsylvania House voted overwhelmingly October 24, 1989 to approve a series of restrictions on abortion. The restrictions, if adopted by the state Senate and signed by Gov. Robert P. Casey (D), would make Pennsylvania's abortion laws among the strictest in the nation.

Pennsylvania Nov. 18, 1989 became the first state in the U.S. to enact anti-abortion legislation in the wake of the Supreme Court decision in July that gave states the right to restrict abortion.

The law banned most abortion at public hospitals, prohibited almost all abortions after 24 weeks of gestation, and required prior notification of the spouse, counseling on alternatives and a 24-hour waiting period before the procedure was carried out. The law included penalties of up to seven years in prison and a $15,000 fine for doctors who violated its provisions.

A federal appeals court panel in Philadelphia October 21, 1991 upheld most of Pennsylvania's 1989 abortion law, clearing the way for a Supreme Court challenge.

■ Illinois state officials and abortion rights advocates reached agreement Nov. 22, 1989 on an abortion lawsuit that was due to be argued before the U.S. Supreme Court on December 5.

The case, *Turnock v. Ragsdale*, had been initiated by an Illinois abortion clinic operator, Dr. Richard Ragsdale. The doctor had objected to the state's abortion regulations, which required abortion clinics to meet strict standards, similar to those for hospital operating rooms. In 1985, Ragsdale had won a court decision declaring the regulations unconstitutional.

The settlement was reached after lengthy negotiations between Illinois Attorney General Neil F. Hartigan and abortion rights advocates, chiefly the American Civil Liberties Union. The compromise regulations set up a new class of clinic – the "surgi-center" – that would be permitted to perform abortions up to the 18th week of pregnancy. After the 18th week, abortions would have to be performed in hospital-like clinics.

■ Maryland Gov. William D. Schaefer (D) February 18, 1991 signed into law a bill that was regarded by both opponents as one of the most liberal abortion laws in the U.S. The measure was designed to protect a woman's ability to obtain a legal abortion, even if the U.S. Supreme Court were to overturn its 1973 *Roe v. Wade* decision, which had recognized a legal right to abortion.

■ A panel of the Michigan Court of Appeals February 20, 1991 struck down a statewide ban on Medicaid-funded abortions for poor women.

The panel ruled, 2–1, that the ban violated clauses in the state's constitution that essentially provided a legal right to abortion by guaranteeing a right to privacy and to equal protection. The ban "has created a direct barrier to the woman's exercise of her right to an abortion," the court wrote.

THE TAMPA TRIBUNE
Tampa, Florida, July 28, 1989

Gov. Bob Martinez is taking a lot of heat from people who won't accept the suggestion of compromise on the abortion issue. His most vocal opponents reject any legislation that would limit the operation to victims of rape or incest, or to women for whom carrying a fetus to term would entail serious physical or emotional risks.

But the governor's position is squarely in the mainstream of public opinion. There is great yearning for a compromise on a subject that has long seemed beyond compromise. The extremists make everybody else uneasy. On the one hand are the pro-lifers who deem all abortions immoral and perhaps acts of murder. On the other are the pro-choicers who believe that every mother-to-be is entitled to end her pregnancy for any reason, no matter how selfish or trivial.

All Americans don't endorse the same religious values or ethical precepts. Or, for that matter, share the same intuition about the nature and value of human life. So when a profoundly important moral question becomes a political issue, with high-octane passions shaking the very air, moderate people look to reduce the noise level and find a compromise that will appeal to the great American middle.

Absolutists will remain outraged but, so long as they continue their agitation in a lawful manner, they can be safely suffered in our polyglot democracy.

The stance of Governor Martinez will make him enemies on both sides. But, politically speaking, we are not sure there is a wiser or more conscientious course.

The state dropped efforts to require counseling on alternatives to abortion and mandatory reporting of abortion and patient information to state authorities.

■ A Maryland legislative compromise adopted March 22, 1990 in an effort to end an eight-day filibuster in the state Senate failed the next day as a committee from the state House of Delegates rejected the plan.

The compromise had called for the legislature to pass two bills on abortion – one permitting the procedure and the other restricting it – and to let the state's voters decide which bill to keep. The compromise had been designed to end a Senate filibuster that had been launched on March 14 by anti-abortion legislators in an attempt to block consideration of a liberalized abortion law.

■ New Hampshire Gov. Judd Gregg (R) April 10, 1990 vetoed a bill that would have liberalized the state's abortion laws. Gregg argued that the government had an obligation to protect life, which he believed began at conception. "I obviously will not support legislation which represents a dramatic expansion of the availability of abortion as a means of terminating life in New Hampshire," he said.

The bill would have allowed all abortions until the point of fetal viability (the point at which the fetus could survive outside the uterus), and would have permitted abortions after that point in cases where the woman's life or health was jeopardized or where the fetus had a life-threatening abnormality.

■ Connecticut Gov. William A. O'Neil (D) April 30, 1990 signed legislation intended to ensure a woman's right to abortion even if the U.S. Supreme Court were to strike down the 1973 *Roe v. Wade* decision that had legalized abortion nationally.

The measure had passed the State House on April 17 by a vote of 151–12 and the Senate by a vote of 32–3. According to legal experts, it made Connecticut the first state in the U.S. to make abortion a legal right under state law rather than merely outlining the conditions under which it was permitted. In addition to guaranteeing a right to abortion, the measure also struck from the books a series of anti-abortion laws, some dating back to the 19th century, that had been declared unconstitutional in the 1970s but had never been taken off the statute books.

In a compromise designed to reduce opposition to the bill, the legislation outlawed abortion beyond the point of fetal viability "except when necessary to protect the life or health of the pregnant woman." It also called for counseling on alternatives to abortion to be given to all women under age 16 who sought abortions. A parental notification requirement had been rejected by both the House and Senate, however.

■ The Mississippi state legislature March 28, 1991 voted to override a veto by Gov. Ray Mabus (D) of a bill requiring a woman to receive information from her doctor about the medical risks of alternatives to abortion, and to wait 24 hours after receiving the information before undergoing the procedure.

■ The Utah state legislature April 19 voted to clarify an abortion law enacted January 25, 1991 that had barred abortion except in cases of rape, incest, "grave danger" to the mother's health or "grave defects" in the fetus.

■ Nebraska Gov. Ben Nelson (D) May 29, 1991 signed into law a bill requiring that at least one parent be notified in cases where a girl under age 18 was seeking an abortion. The measure had been passed by the state Legislature May 28, by a vote of 33 to 12.

The Miami Herald

Miami, Florida, July 10, 1989

FLORIDA needs a special legislative session to consider whether the state should react to the U.S. Supreme Court's decision in the *Webster* abortion case. Gov. Bob Martinez makes good sense in suggesting a special session and in voicing caution about just what it should do.

Florida already has a quite-restrictive abortion law. Few late-pregnancy abortions occur in Florida, which is as it should be. The state Medicaid program for the poor paid for only one abortion in the past year, in a life-threatening situation.

The top priority, then, is caution. The Legislature's inexperience with the actual responsibility for abortion policy is near total. Only three of the 40 senators and seven of the 120 House members were elected before the Supreme Court took that responsibility for itself with the 1973 *Roe v. Wade* decision. The governor and most legislators thus have never borne the weight of their votes and their campaign posturing.

They have discussed abortion in the abstract, separated from the reality of state funding for infants born with AIDS, or a cocaine addiction, or fetal-alcohol syndrome, or the many expensive disabilities of babies born to adolescent mothers. Until now, politicians have discussed abortion as though it

SPECIAL SESSION WARRANTED

were unrelated to the availability of contraception, to the enforcement of laws against sex with minors, or to the financial responsibility of unwed fathers. They have not faced the prospect of imprisoning reputable doctors in their districts.

That free ride is ending. The Court now has returned to the states the authority to make a few decisions, mostly affecting the ability of poor women to end unwanted pregnancies before the fifth month. Next year, if the Court continues its *Webster* swing, that authority might broaden.

All these issues must be considered now. A special session thus is a welcome opportunity for lawmakers to hear from the medical profession, from religious counselors, from social-service providers, from educators, and from state-budget experts.

However, neither the governor nor the legislators should deceive themselves that one session will resolve the matter. It will not. Rather, this will be only the first stage of a continuing debate on what the Florida Constitution calls every resident's "right to be let alone and free from governmental intrusion into his private life."

The Union Leader

Manchester, New Hampshire, April 12, 1989

If the fetus were simply, as some choose to see it, "tissue" having no right to life, no one would take serious issue with state Representative Scott Green, chief sponsor of abortion decriminalization legislation (HB 377), who on Monday told the state Senate Judiciary Committeee that *"the state has absolutely no right to dictate when a woman may or may not have an abortion."*

But if the fetus is human, and — biologically — human life is a continuum from the moment of conception until death at advanced age, unless interrupted — then the state has as much right to prevent destruction of human life in the mother's womb (such destruction is now running nationally at the rate of 1,500,000 lives a year!) as it does to prevent the unwarranted taking of human life generally. Basically, that is why, for the first 184 years of the nation's history, prior to the advent of the Warren Court, abortion was a crime in America.

The clear intent of Green's bill is to try to "jump the gun" on whatever the U.S. Supreme Court might rule in the *Webster v. Reproductive Services* case now before it. In anticipation that the high tribunal may reverse or sharply modify its controversial ruling in *Roe v. Wade,* perhaps throwing the issue back to the states, Green's bill declares "open season" on fetuses. It would promote unrestricted abortions anywhere, anytime and for any reason.

Rather than being simply a "housekeeping" measure, as some describe it, HB 377 goes beyond the Supreme Court's ruling in Roe v. Wade and declares unrestricted warfare on defenseless human life.

To vote for this bill is — in the words of Bishop Odore Gendron's reasoned statement on the issue — *"to state that abortion-on-demand for any person, for any reason, at any point in the 9 months of pregnancy is the public policy of preference of the State of New Hampshire."*

The state Senate had the good sense to pass legislation (SB 136) requiring parental consent before an abortion could be performed on a minor, only to see the House kill it and a similar measure (HB 510). Similarly, the Senate stood symbolically with traditional New Hampshire values by rejecting House-passed adultery decriminalization legislation.

It remains now to be seen whether the upper chamber will say no to the proposed "Greening" of New Hampshire, no to the proposition that, assuming a reversal or modification of Roe v. Wade, the state should nevertheless acquire a national reputation as an abortion mecca.

Manchester, New Hampshire, July 10, 1989

Pro-abortionists who vow to make Judd Gregg a "one-term governor" and who view U.S. Rep. Bob Smith as another inviting target for their enmity are either wishful thinkers or are badly miscalculating the majority view of New Hampshire people.

The fact that New Hampshire's legislators have voted pro-abortion on a number of issues does not at all mean that the voters who elected them to office are themselves pro-abortion or are about to remove from office either Gregg or Smith.

The confusion, if it is in fact honest confusion and not deliberate deceit on the pro-abortionists' part, comes from two sources.

First, votes for the state General Court, in particular the 400-member House, are often cast on the basis of knowing the candidate and his or her position on local issues. Because of the 1973 U.S. Supreme Court decision, abortion hasn't been much of a local issue. All that may change in the wake of last week's high court decision on the matter.

The higher the office, the more likely such broader issues are to be taken into account by the voters. For instance, a state senator's position on abortion means more to the voters. Liberal Democrat Wayne King may well find that out next year, when former senator and staunch abortion foe Mark Hounsell bids to regain that North County Senate seat.

This holds true for issues other than abortion. On broad-based taxes, for instance, a state senate or gubernatorial candidate must much more carefully weigh his or her own election chances based on that issue than a member of the House need do.

At the gubernatorial and congressional level, such major issues come into even clearer focus. Gov. Gregg and abortion opponents can take heart in knowing that the very strong anti-abortion stands of Bob Smith and Gordon Humphrey, to name two, have not hurt them at the New Hampshire polls.

The second source for possible confusion of the popular view of abortion comes from pro-abortionists constantly citing national polls which, they claim, put a clear majority of Americans on their side. However, what such polls really show is that the majority does not favor abortion on demand, especially when they are asked if that should include use of abortion as just another form of birth control.

Pro-abortionists are right about one thing. This battle is far from over.

San Francisco Chronicle

San Francisco, California, February 7, 1989

IN A NATION where 30 percent of pregnancies that don't end in miscarriages terminate in abortion, the United States Supreme Court's review of the practice will surely have an enormous impact on the lives of millions of Americans.

If the court returns control of abortions to the states, the California Legislature will be under extreme pressure. It is awesome to contemplate what would happen if the Legislature yielded to demands that it outlaw or impose unworkable restrictions on abortions, which now number about 300,000 a year in the state.

Many legislators expect, in fact, to face the possibility that they may have to reverse their politically comfortable position of pretending that they oppose funds for any Medi-Cal abortions They have done so with the secure knowledge that the courts will order the payments anyhow — and that, as a result, neither side in the abortion dispute will be angry with them.

The Supreme Court may change all that. The Legislature will then have the choice of having the state pay for more than 75,000 abortions a year for women on Medi-Cal or denying them the same rights as other women by forcing their pregnancies to go to term.

BY ITS NATURE, the argument over abortions is divisive, as Chronicle writers have documented in a series of reports.

At one extreme there are "pro-life" advocates who contend that the 22 million abortions in the United States since 1973, when the Supreme Court issued its Roe vs. Wade ruling, were actually 22 million murders.

Then there are those, and we agree with them, who say the court's 7-to-2 ruling legalizing abortions in the first three months of pregnancy means that such a decision is the business of nobody except the woman involved and her doctor.

Most people appear to regard abortion as a choice that may be unfortunate but is better than an undesirable birth.

A constructive approach, it seems to us, is to reduce the number of abortions by heading off undesired pregnancies in the first place. Far greater stress should be placed on birth control while retaining abortion as an alternative.

IT IS UNREALISTIC that many who oppose abortions are adamant in their opposition to contraception and even to sex education.

THE RICHMOND NEWS LEADER

Richmond, Virginia, July 21, 1989

American politics occupies the middle ground. Americans are not an ideological lot, and they cast their ballots generally for candidates professing "moderation." During a given political season, most issues before the electorate lend themselves to non-traumatic compromise. Abortion is the exception.

On abortion there is no middle, no half-way, no in-between. Although both sides — pro and anti — may make temporary tactical concessions, their ultimate goals remain unaltered. If one believes abortion reflects a woman's right to control her body, then any restrictions on abortion restrict that right. If one believes that abortion is

murder, then any exemptions to an anti-abortion statute encourage the taking of innocent life. Not since slavery has American politics seen an issue as resistant to compromise as abortion.

The Supreme Court's recent ruling returned abortion to the states, where candidates must grapple with political and moral issues they would prefer to ignore. State legislators and candidates will feel the heat.

The anti-abortion side faces the tougher political test. Although the populace remains uncomfortable with abortion and does not want to encourage it, the populace also seems unlikely to support an outright ban. Restrictions, yes. Prohibition, no. A parental-consent law would gather broad support — Doug Wilder's hasty backing-and-filling on parental consent suggests he understands that his former views are non-winners. But the best the anti-abortion side can hope for probably is a law proscribing abortion except in the cases of rape, incest, and threat to the mother's life — with the last exemption broadly defined to allow the middle classes continued access to abortion as a birth-control convenience.

There will be name-calling aplenty in the months and years to come. The extremists at Planned Parenthood already have geared up a p.r. campaign in support of abortion on demand; the anti-abortion side will continue to demonstrate in front of abortion clinics and will continue to lobby candidates. For better or worse, abortion will remain legal, with certain restrictions attached. Another thing is certain: The abortion debate will make life much more difficult for politicians of every stripe.

The Houston Post

Houston, Texas, July 8, 1989

ABORTION, OR ANY LAW regarding it, is too important a topic to be tossed into the hurly-burly of this special legislative session. Fortunately, it appears Gov. Bill Clements has seen at least part of the wisdom of this: He says he won't add it to the current session, or tack another one on right behind it for that purpose.

But a bigger question is, should it be the focus of a special session at all? The Post thinks not — and especially not soon.

The most important reason is that the U.S. Supreme Court has agreed to hear three more states' abortion cases in its term that begins in October and runs into next summer. Why put Texas legislators to the trouble of enacting laws that could quickly be dashed by a new ruling handed down from Washington? It's better to hear the high court's decisions first.

Second, our lawmakers have been in Austin (with a break between sessions) since January. Not only are they likely worn down, every day spent away from their home districts removes them further from the thoughts and attitudes of their constituents. The lawmakers need plenty of time to absorb and digest the feelings of the folks back home on a matter of this magnitude — enough time, we feel, that

the autumn is too soon for such a session.

Well, then, what about next year? That's bad, too. Because while the legislators need to know the home folks' feelings, ultimately they must use their own hearts and minds to arrive at a well-considered decision. By spring, primaries will be in the offing, followed by November's general election. The high feelings on both sides that attach to the topic of abortion are bound to make for demagoguery, grandstanding and arm-twisting. This decision deserves to be made on the highest plane of principle and conscience, and it needs to be made in a calm atmosphere. Certainly it shouldn't be dealt with while passions on both sides are as inflamed as they are now.

Texas will deal with this topic, as will most of the other 49 states. But let's leave it until next regular session. It's not as far away as you might think, and the lawmakers will have as much of the 140-day term as they feel they need to hold hearings, propose bills and amendments, and reason with one another.

Hasty votes usually make bad law. The Post calls on the governor to let this issue follow its natural path to 1991. That's the best way for Texas to get the kind of thoughtful legislation such a serious matter deserves.

The Washington Post

Washington, D.C., July 19, 1989

VIRGINIA and New Jersey are the two states with gubernatorial elections in this off political year. They provide the two most visible early tests of the Supreme Court's decision strengthening the right of states to restrict abortion. The Virginia candidates, Republican Marshall Coleman and Democrat Douglas Wilder, are already hotly debating the issue. But so far that debate has occurred in a rather narrow band.

Current law in Virginia is to place few restrictions on abortion but to make little public money available for it. Spending is restricted to Medicaid recipients who seek abortions as the result of rape, incest, gross fetal abnormalities or conditions that threaten the life of the mother. Some 33,000 abortions were performed in the state in 1987, but in the 12 months ending last March, only 53 were performed with state funds, at a cost of less than $20,000.

Several polls have shown that this hands-off mix of few limitations but little support is about what most voters in Virginia prefer—and it is where the candidates are tending as well. Mr. Wilder is not proposing to increase state funding (as we think should be done, to give rich and poor equal access to abortion); on the contrary, he would add the requirement that minors have parental consent for abortions, a requirement defeated in the General Assembly in the past.

Mr. Coleman, for his part, has abandoned the hard-line anti-abortion position he staunchly maintained throughout the GOP primary in favor of something closer to middle ground. His shift came as Mr. Wilder asked how he could "justify saying to a woman who has been a victim of rape or incest that she cannot have an abortion." That is more a debating point than a major policy issue, but when the former state attorney general tried to duck the question, the lieutenant governor posed it a second time. Mr. Coleman then said he would not propose such legislation as governor. Later in the debate he said, "I do, however, propose to support parental consent and other measures to restrict abortion on demand because I think, while those restrictions are less than ideal, that they are a giant step in the right direction."

Well, not that giant. Incumbent attorney general Mary Sue Terry, who is running for reelection, observes that the recent Supreme Court ruling "has no immediate impact on any existing Virginia law. Nor does it require the General Assembly to amend or reexamine any existing statute." She's right. So far, for all the sharp rhetoric on the issue and some genuine differences of instinct and degree, neither candidate seems prepared to take the state far from where it already stands.

THE DAILY OKLAHOMAN
Oklahoma City, Oklahoma, November 8, 1991

YOU couldn't ask for a clearer illustration of divisions over abortion than the results on an initiative in the state of Washington.

Initiative 120 was designed to put into state law the permissive abortion structure of Roe vs. Wade (the controversial 1973 U.S. Supreme Court decision). In a liberal state, it was expected to win easily.

Instead, it seems to have lost narrowly. With election day votes counted, the measure had only 49.8 percent support. However, 100,000 absentee ballots are not yet tabulated. A recount will be required if the margin stays within .5 percent. Regardless, the closeness of the vote shocked supporters of abortion on demand (in the only state to pass a Roe-like pro-abortion referendum before 1973) and illustrated that Americans remain ambivalent on this issue.

The results do not mean states — if Roe vs. Wade is overturned — will merely revert to provisions strongly restrictive of abortion, the kinds of laws that existed before 1973.

The results are another hint, however, that when and if Roe is reversed, states are likely to move toward regulations affording at least some heightened protections for unborn children — laws curbing at least somewhat the untrammeled access to abortion which has prevailed for nearly 19 years.

The Seattle Times
Seattle, Washington, October 27, 1991

A YES vote on Initiative 120 will preserve the right to choose abortion that exists today, plain and simple.

The initiative will put abortion rights, as developed in the 1973 Supreme Court case of Roe v. Wade, into state law. If passed, Washington women will retain the fundamental right to choose even if the conservative Supreme Court overturns the Roe decision. The need for certainty makes passage of the initiative important.

■ The initiative will not cost the state any additional money.

■ It allows only physicians to perform abortions.

■ It allows abortions only up to the point of fetal viability, unless a woman's life or health is endangered.

■ It maintains the constitutional status quo that has been the law in this country for 18 years.

The political shift on the Supreme Court is rapidly eroding abortion rights. Already the court has allowed a Missouri law banning abortions in public hospitals to stand. And it has upheld the Reagan administration's gag rule prohibiting doctors at federally supported family planning clinics from mentioning abortion.

Meanwhile, some states have enacted strict regulations that impose substantial obstacles to prevent women from choosing abortions. Louisiana, Utah and Guam have outlawed abortion. As these cases move through the courts, the signs are clear that Roe will be further weakened, if not destroyed altogether.

Washington voters need not wait for the Supreme Court to speak. Passing Initiative 120 will ensure that abortion rights in this state will remain intact.

The Oregonian
Portland, Oregon, October 30, 1991

Should a woman be allowed to have an abortion?

That is the question Initiative 120 puts before Washington voters on Nov. 5, although the anti-120 campaign dwells on everything but that essential issue.

The answer to that agonizing question ought to be yes.

The decision whether to have an abortion is one each woman should make for herself, with advice and guidance from her doctor and family, clergy and friends. The state should not decide.

Initiative 120 would write into state law that each woman has a fundamental right to choose or refuse an abortion, and establish that decision as a private one.

Passage of the initiative would, in fact, change nothing about the way abortion is handled in Washington now. However, the initiative provides a state standard to take effect if the U.S. Supreme Court decides that the right to an abortion is not constitutionally guaranteed and overturns the 1973 Roe vs. Wade decision.

Washington voters first approved abortion in 1970. That 1970 law is outdated. It limits abortions to the first four months of pregnancy, requires a husband's consent for a wife and a parent's consent for an underage daughter, imposes a 90-day residency requirement and requires that abortions be performed only in hospitals.

Although 90 percent of abortions in Washington are performed in the first three months, abortions now can lawfully be performed during the first six months. The U.S. Supreme Court has struck down residency requirements and spousal consent. Washington's Supreme Court has ruled that parental-consent provisions violate the state constitution. Common medical standards no longer require abortions to be performed in hospitals.

Given the uncertainty about abortion on the national level, it makes sense for Washington voters to clarify state law to acknowledge those new realities and their wishes.

In addition to guaranteeing a woman's right to decide, the initiative establishes that the state cannot attempt to influence a woman's choice through its funding policies. It declares that if the state provides maternity-care benefits, then it also must provide abortion services. That also is in keeping with the principle that the state should be neutral in reproductive decisions.

Regrettably, the campaign against Initiative 120 has avoided discussing important issues such as state neutrality. Instead, it has relied on gross distortions of the initiative's effect.

One common television advertisement, for example, says that state taxpayers would have to spend an additional $60 million on abortions and pay for abortions for rich women. Those claims are untrue.

Additional arguments that the initiative would allow non-physicians to perform abortions, limit a woman's ability to sue a physician for a botched abortion, lead to an increase in the number of late-term abortions or require high schools to provide abortions are equally spurious.

Thoughtful people disagree about abortion, but attempts to circumvent the debate in this way are cynically manipulative. They reduce the credibility of these abortion opponents, whose opinions we respect but whose tactics we abhor.

As voters go to the polls Tuesday, they should cast their votes on the fundamental question of who should make the abortion decision.

The Oregonian believes that decision belongs to each woman and her conscience. Vote yes on 120.

Portland, Oregon, November 22, 1991

Much will be made of the razor-thin margin by which Washington's abortion initiative passed. Absentee ballots counted this week gave the measure a 4,314-vote edge out of 1.5 million cast. An automatic recount is unlikely to change the outcome.

That narrow victory for abortion-rights forces in a state with a liberal reputation must trouble those who support a woman's right to choose. But Initiative 120 reached well beyond the simple question of choice. It also established the principle of state neutrality.

The initiative prevents the state from using its funding decisions to coerce pregnant women: If the state pays for prenatal care, then it also must pay for abortion.

That important principle — that the government should not intrude on a woman's private reproductive decision — has been eroded on the federal level.

A split U.S. Supreme Court decided last May that the government could restrict doctors and others working in federally funded family-planning clinics from discussing abortion as an option available to pregnant patients. President Bush is determined to enforce that rule. The House failed this week to get the two-thirds majority needed to stop him.

The federal government also won't pay for poor women's abortions, although it will pay for other medical care. Oregon voters sensibly turned down a similar attempt to cut off abortion funding as a way to steer low-income women toward childbirth.

Washington voters also likely were affected by a disgraceful anti-120 campaign that grossly distorted the effect of the initiative. When voters are unsure, they tend to vote no.

Those issues aside, Washington's decision makes it clear once again how divided the public is on abortion. It is a reminder that this is a matter that should remain an individual decision of conscience.

The Times-Picayune
New Orleans, Louisiana, July 22, 1991

The decisions of two national medical groups to cancel their conventions in New Orleans because of Louisiana's tough new anti-abortion law indicate that they rushed to judgment before carefully weighing all factors in the controversial issue.

It is unfair for business and professional groups to penalize the people of the city and the state, many of whom were opposed to the bill passed by the Legislature and supportive of Gov. Roemer's action in vetoing it. In Louisiana, as elsewhere, abortion is a deeply divisive issue, with citizens acting in good faith on both sides.

Local tourism officials are understandably concerned that the actions of the American College of Obstetricians and Gynecologists and the American Psychological Association could result in the loss of other medical meetings, the backbone of the city's convention business.

The College of Obstetricians, which held its national convention in New Orleans in May, was expected to return in May 1996, 2001, 2006 and 2011. Each meeting was expected to attract about 10,000 physicians, spouses, exhibitors, staff and other visitors, spokeswoman Kate Ruddon said in Washington.

Edward J. McNeill, executive vice president of the Greater New Orleans Tourist & Convention Commission, said loss of the four meetings will cost the New Orleans area $31 million. The figures are based on studies showing that the average convention visitor spends about $864.

The meeting of the American Psychological Association, which had been scheduled for August 1997, was expected to attract 12,000 visitors for an economic impact of $10.4 million.

Since the Legislature voted June 18 to override Gov. Roemer's veto of the anti-abortion bill, Mr. McNeill said, the Tourist Commission "has been inundated with phone calls and letters from business and professional organizations on this issue. Not one call or letter has been in support of the legislative action."

Jimmie Fore, president of the New Orleans Convention Center, said local officials will ask groups to postpone changing their plans until the Louisiana abortion law is tested in the courts. The law is scheduled to go into effect in September, but its constitutionality has been challenged, and the case may wind up in the U.S. Supreme Court.

On a brighter note, tourism officials were heartened by the recent decision of the National Education Association not to cancel its 1994 convention in New Orleans.

Despite the 2.1 million-member teachers union's pro-choice position, the 8,100 delegates to its annual meeting in Miami Beach voted against reconsidering New Orleans as the site. Some expressed doubt about the wisdom of using convention boycotts to protest social causes.

We join with New Orleans' tourism officials in urging groups who have scheduled conventions to honor their commitments. The city's appeal to convention-goers should be considered on its own merits and not predicated on what happens in the state Legislature.

Convention planners should keep in mind the reason they decided to go to New Orleans in the first place. It's pro-tourism.

The Boston Globe
Boston, Massachusetts, September 24, 1991

Gov. Weld deserves credit for his forceful action in protecting the right of all women to choose abortion. His legislative package liberalizing the state's abortion laws could not have come at a better time.

A provision that would lower the age of parental consent for an abortion from 18 to 16, though controversial, makes sense. The age of consent for engaging in sexual intercourse is 16. Teen-age girls do not need their parents' permission if they choose to carry a pregnancy to term. Why, then, are they considered incapable of making a decision not to become parents?

Weld's package also would require girls under 16 to get permission from one parent rather than two. This provision, already the norm in 34 states, protects young women who come from single-parent families or households in which one parent might be abusive.

A provision to prohibit groups and individuals from blocking the doors of abortion clinics is also sound. The decision to terminate an unwanted pregnancy is difficult enough for most women. They should not have to suffer assaults from disapproving strangers. The provision, along with one to do away with Pro-Life Month, sends a message that, unlike his predecessor, Weld will not tip-toe around anti-abortion politics.

Those who are troubled by Weld's general lack of compassion for the poor can be heartened by his insistence that all women have access to safe abortions. He hopes to remove legal restrictions to Medicaid-funded abortions and to permit public employees' health-insurance benefits to cover abortion costs.

While the nation is focused on his party's realignment of the Supreme Court, Weld seeks to ensure that Massachusetts' laws restricting abortion, dormant since Roe v. Wade, will again become constitutional.

"The hard reality is that if Roe is overturned, we suddenly revert to a situation where abortion is statutorily illegal in Massachusetts under almost any circumstance," Weld said at a State House rally a few months ago. "That is, to say the least, a chilling prospect."

Weld's actions are more consistent with conservative ideology than the policies of his counterpart in the White House. President Bush professes his interest in limiting government intrusion in daily life while continuing to meddle with women's private lives.

The Honolulu Advertiser
Honolulu, Hawaii, November 6, 1991

No matter how the 9th U.S. Circuit Court of Appeals rules after the arguments heard here Monday, Guam's extremely restrictive anti-abortion law seems headed for the U.S. Supreme Court.

Laws similar to Guam's in Pennsylvania and Louisiana are also on a fast track to the court. Others are in earlier stages of constitutional challenge in Utah and North Dakota.

One of these pending cases could be the lever to reverse the 1973 Roe vs. Wade ruling. That landmark decision said the constitutional right to privacy with few exceptions allows women to choose an abortion in a pregnancy's first six months.

With the addition of Justice Clarence Thomas, conservatives now have a clear 6-3 majority to strike down the protection for the right to abortion or to further whittle it away.

So Americans must face the likelihood that sooner, not later, what has been a right for almost 20 years will once again have no federal protection. It will then be up to individual states to decide their abortion laws. That will be unfortunate, for many reasons:

■ It will make every state legislature a battlefield in which there seems to be little middle ground.

■ Some states, probably including Hawaii, will be known as "abortion states."

■ Young and poor women, those least equipped to raise children, who cannot travel to where abortion is legal, will have to choose between unwanted children and unsafe, illegal operations.

Like many others, we worry about excessive abortions used for birth control when contraceptive methods are available. But we continue to believe that in Hawaii and the nation, abortion ought to be a private decision. The choice should belong to the woman — not the government or any group that will not bear the consequences of carrying her pregnancy to term.

The Washington Post

Washington, D.C., October 25, 1991

IN RESPONSE to a Supreme Court ruling two years ago that made it easier for states to regulate abortion, more than 500 bills have been introduced in legislatures around the country attempting, in one way or another, to restrict the right. In Guam, Utah and Louisiana, laws have been enacted that prohibit, with a few narrow exceptions, virtually all abortions. These statutes have been challenged in court and probably cannot be sustained unless the Supreme Court flatly overrules *Roe v. Wade*. Laws that restrict but do not prohibit abortions are also being challenged, and this week an appellate court ruled on the one passed in Pennsylvania. Major parts of the statute were upheld, with the court using a new standard for assessing state abortion laws. If this decision, which will probably be the first on abortion to be reviewed by the newly constituted Supreme Court, is upheld, the consequences will not be as grave as they would be if the Utah law, for example, were approved. Nevertheless, such a ruling could have a severe impact on the rights of women to choose this procedure.

The U.S. Court of Appeals for the Third Circuit abandoned the reasoning in *Roe*—that abortion is a fundamental right that cannot be abridged by a state except for a compelling reason. The judges found that the 1973 ruling has been eroded by a series of subsequent decisions and that the only standard that now commands a majority on the high court is one formulated by Justice Sandra O'Connor—that state regulation will be permitted so long as it does not place "an undue burden" that is an "absolute obstacle" or a "severe limitation" on the exercise of the right. Thus, Pennsylvania can require minors to obtain parental consent so long as there is an alternative available in the form of judicial consent. It may also require a 24-hour waiting period and a statement by a doctor to each patient outlining the facts about abortion and the alternatives available. It may not, however, require a woman to inform her husband about a proposed abortion, for that would constitute an undue burden.

Abortions remain available under these circumstances, but such limitations will surely prompt abortion opponents to press for more, for legislation of the kind enacted—and struck down—in the immediate aftermath of *Roe*. These include rules that cumulatively could make the process so expensive—elaborate laws on clinic staff credentials, facilities or insurance, for example—or so difficult—requiring repeated visits to clinics or long waiting periods—that the right to abortions would, in practice, be impaired.

The best way to prepare for this possibility is for citizens groups to press for legislation at the state level, as has already been done successfully in Maryland and Virginia, to preserve the rights guaranteed by *Roe*. The courts are no longer the preferred forum for abortion rights groups, but if opinion polls are correct, those advocates are sure to find a more receptive audience with the voters.

The Salt Lake Tribune

Salt Lake City, Utah, October 20, 1991

Utah should not turn to lawyers from national pro-life groups to represent the state, at no cost to taxpayers, in the defense of its abortion law.

If lawyers from organizations such as National Right to Life or Americans United for Life wish to provide free advice and assistance to the state's legal team, that's fine. The lawyers for these national organizations specialize in abortion law, and their help and research could be very valuable.

But the state must have its own lawyers, independent of these national groups, to serve as lead counsel. Otherwise, Utah runs the risk of losing control of its case.

It is well known that pro-life groups have criticized the Utah law for not protecting fetal rights forcefully enough. This basic philosophical disagreement with the Utah law means that lawyers from pro-life groups could face a conflict between defending the statute and advancing their organizations' national political agendas.

If the state were to be represented solely by these lawyers, and if the state were not paying them, Utah would have limited leverage over how the defense of its law would be argued in court. The attorneys would control their client. That's simply too high a price to pay for free legal advocacy.

The question that remains, then, is whether the state's lead counsel should come from the attorney general's office or from a private law firm. Here politics intrude again.

The official reason for hiring private counsel has been that the attorney general's office is too overburdened with other work and lacks specialized expertise in abortion law. But the Republican governor and Legislature also are concerned that the Democratic attorney general and his chief deputies are pro-choice and would not have their hearts in an aggressive defense of the abortion law.

That perception of Attorney General Paul Van Dam, whether true or not, cuts two ways, however. Mr. Van Dam, or lawyers he appointed from his office, could make an all-out commitment to defense of the Utah law, and if they did not win the case, or even if they lost on some important points while winning others, the attorney general's political opponents could argue that the reason was lack of ideological resolve. Since the attorney general of Utah is elected, the partisan implications are obvious.

To some degree, then, it serves the political interests of both Mr. Van Dam and the Republicans to hire outside counsel. The trouble is that both now are taking taxpayer heat for the $170,000 in legal bills rung up by the state's first private counsel, the law firm of Jones Waldo Holbrook & McDonough, which the state let go after conflict of interest questions arose.

The legal bills should be no surprise to anyone, however. Long before the Legislature passed the abortion law early this year there were warnings that a lawsuit could cost the state $1 million if it went all the way to the U.S. Supreme Court. The Legislature could have avoided this expense, to say nothing of the community divisiveness the new abortion law has caused, if it had decided simply to stay out of the abortion quagmire until other cases from other states settled the legal issues.

Gov. Norm Bangerter and the Legislature chose to do otherwise, and now it is at best disingenuous for them to run from the completely predictable legal bills.

Detroit Free Press

Detroit, Michigan, October 26, 1991

A U.S. Appeals Court ruling this week was a victory for abortion opponents who are attempting in state legislatures to regulate away abortion rights.

The Pennsylvania statute involved in this case nibbles away at rights affirmed by the landmark 1973 Roe vs. Wade decision. It is a regressive, intolerable law that deserved to have been struck down in its entirety.

Instead, the Appeals Court ruling overturned a district court ruling that two provisions of the Pennsylvania law impose an undue burden on women seeking abortions. Those provisions require that a woman wait 24 hours after abortion counseling before the procedure is performed, and that a woman under the age of 18 have either parental or court consent.

To their credit, though, two of the three members of the court panel upheld the lower court's finding that one particularly absurd requirement is unconstitutional: that a woman notify her husband before having an abortion.

The appellate panel's ruling provides the likely vehicle for a Supreme Court showdown on abortion rights. The planned appeal by the Pennsylvania attorney general would give the current court a chance to reject Roe vs. Wade's most basic premises: that abortion is a fundamental right and that a woman and her doctor — not the government — are the appropriate partners in the decision-making process.

Amid all the emotion surrounding the issue of abortion, those remain principles worth protecting — not because anyone likes abortion, but because a return to the era of deadly back-alley abortions is unthinkable.

The reassertion, which the Pennsylvania law represents, of government interest in one of the most private of decisions should not be tolerated.

The Augusta Chronicle
Augusta, Georgia, November 11, 1991

Aside from the state of the economy, another big debate going into the 1992 presidential election year involves where the U.S. Supreme Court stands in regard to its 1973 *Roe vs. Wade* ruling that declared abortion a constitutionally-protected right.

The American Civil Liberties Union and the Planned Parenthood Federation of America are asking the High Court if it still stands behind that ruling. They urge the Court to consider the Pennsylvania's anti-abortion law this term, instead of next.

They want a ruling before Election Day, 1992, because they believe if *Roe* goes down it will galvanize opposition to the Bush-Quayle re-election campaign.

Yet that may be wishful thinking.

As last Tuesday's Washington state referendum underscored, the issue may be a political wash. The measure, calling for keeping *Roe* even if the Court sends it back to the states, split 50-50 with the "nays" edging it out.

Moreover, other issues will be on voters' minds, especially if the economy is still in the doldrums. And few people share the intensity that the handful of true-believers on both sides of the abortion issue bring to their cause. The Court could also surprise and again uphold the 1973 ruling.

Despite the mischievous political reasons for the request, the High Court ought to grant it. Abortion rights advocates aren't the only people who want to know where the Court now stands. Everyone does.

The Salt Lake Tribune
Salt Lake City, Utah, November 13, 1991

If the legal profession is wondering why the public perception of lawyers is so unflattering, it need look no further than Utah's abortion case.

Consider the lawyers' fees. The private law firm the state first hired to represent it, Jones Waldo Holbrook & McDonough, charged the state $225 an hour and $150 an hour for its two lead attorneys. Jones Waldo now is off the case after being accused by the other side of having a conflict of interest. Nevertheless, in the five months it represented the state, the firm ran up a bill of $200,000, less $20,000 to bring the state's new counselors, Wood & Wood, up to speed.

As if the public weren't already scandalized by these costs, the other side of the dispute, the American Civil Liberties Union, has stepped up to make matters worse. Its lead counsel is charging $375 an hour. The ACLU's bill for work on the motion to disqualify Jones Waldo as the state's counsel amounts to $26,703. Jones Waldo has offered to pay $7,500 of that, and the ACLU says it might go after Utah taxpayers for the rest.

According to Jones Waldo, the ACLU's bill includes $357.74 for one day's worth of meals in Salt Lake City for two attorneys. Jones Waldo also isn't happy with the fact that the ACLU billing includes 31.5 hours of work done after the court hearing on the motion was over. And the state's former counsel also says the ACLU lawyers billed for time spent talking to news reporters.

Before the abortion law passed, the ACLU argued that legal challenges would cost state taxpayers a fortune, and it seems intent on fulfilling its own prophecy.

Critics of the American legal system point out that a common strategy is for each side to harass the other, bleeding the opponent monetarily during pretrial motions and discovery. Given the history of the Utah abortion case so far, with its hefty legal bills and arguments over class action certification, pseudonyms of plaintiffs and conflicts of interest, that criticism appears plausible. The case is not scheduled to go to trial until early next year.

The Utah taxpayer must realize that, yes, this is an important and complex case. It's bound to be expensive. Expert medical testimony and other evidence must be prepared in advance by both sides so that a mother's health may be weighed in the judicial balance against the same interest of the fetus. A doctor's liability and professional judgment also are important issues. Preparing the evidence is costly and time-consuming, but a court should have a full record before ruling on such delicate and far-reaching questions.

Taxpayers realize, too, that lawyers are professionals. They work hard, and they got where they are by working hard in school. Many deserve to be well paid. Some bear heavy responsibilities. Consider what's hanging in the balance in this case.

It's also unfair to tar all lawyers with the same brush. Utah lawyers donate thousands of hours of free legal work every year to indigent clients and worthwhile causes. In fact, lawyers are donating their services to represent plaintiffs in the abortion case. What's more, the state bar has established and sponsored programs at its Law and Justice Center to substitute negotiation and counseling for bitter and costly court battles.

Even taking all that into account, however, the high fees and adversarial gamesmanship of Utah's abortion case are hard for the average person to swallow. They undoubtedly are contributing to public cynicism about lawyers and the justice system.

St. Petersburg Times
St. Petersburg, Florida, October 26, 1991

Pennsylvania's Abortion Control Act of 1989 is a classic piece of paternalistic legislation. From top to bottom, the Pennsylvania law is based on the unwritten assumption that women are incapable of making basic decisions about their own bodies. They must instead defer to their legislators, their doctors or their husbands, predominantly male authority figures who know what is best for them.

The Pennsylvania statute was one of the first laws passed in response to the 1989 Supreme Court ruling that gave the states new latitude in restricting abortion. It required women seeking an abortion to undergo pre-abortion counseling (which amounts to *anti*-abortion counseling). It required them to wait an additional 24 hours after counseling before an abortion could be performed. It required adult women to notify their husbands, and required teen-age girls to receive their parents' consent, before having an abortion.

Even today's reactionary courts would strike down such condescending legislation in virtually any other context. Just imagine how the courts would respond to a state law requiring black Americans to receive permission from a white patron before scheduling surgery or conducting other personal business.

Yet a three-judge panel of the U.S. Court of Appeals for the Third Circuit has upheld the constitutionality of two of the most restrictive elements of the Pennsylvania law. Only the provision requiring women to notify their husbands before having an abortion was deemed unconstitutional, and one of the three judges was prepared to accept even that most demeaning of restrictions.

The appeals court's ruling amounts to the most direct challenge yet to the Supreme Court's 1973 *Roe vs. Wade* decision, which established a woman's constitutional right to an abortion. Louisiana, Utah and Guam have since passed abortion laws that are even more restrictive than Pennsylvania's, and they, too, are moving through the appeals process. The newly formulated Supreme Court soon will have its choice of vehicles for overturning *Roe*.

Whatever their differences, those restrictive state abortion laws all have one thing in common: Like decades of segregationist legislation that was based on the assumption that black Americans had no right to equal treatment under the law, they presume that women are second-class citizens whose rights are subordinate to those of the men with whom they live and work. If appeals courts, including the Supreme Court, are going to accept that assumption, women have the electoral strength to prevail upon state legislatures to protect the rights that the judicial system has begun to jeopardize.

The Clarion-Ledger

Jackson, Mississippi, January 23, 1990

Activists on both sides of the abortion issue have sought to make it a major debate before state legislatures since the U.S. Supreme Court unwisely upheld a Missouri statute restricting abortions.

Most legislatures haven't fallen into that trap. Mississippi shouldn't either.

Despite the demonstrations at the Capitol — and the disturbing disruptions of a radical group of anti-abortion activists at local clinics — Mississippi lawmakers should not attempt to negotiate the legal and ethical mine fields. Such efforts would only waste lawmakers' time with the only result being an intrusion on individual freedoms.

The best approach on the abortion issue this session is to leave it alone. It should remain an ethical and moral debate for individuals, not lawmakers.

ST. LOUIS POST-DISPATCH

St. Louis, Missouri, January 23, 1990

Gov. John Ashcroft has finally revealed his proposal for abortion legislation. The plan itself, which can be summarized by a phrase familiar to many shoppers, "one to a customer," is downright goofy. Yet in coming up with this proposal, the governor has perhaps inadvertently revealed something more fundamental about the current politics of abortion in Missouri: Attempts to ban abortion outright are unacceptable to voters.

How would a ban on second abortions be enforced? The governor's office makes it clear that no new enforcement mechanisms would be introduced. Clinics would apparently bear the responsibility for ensuring that patients were not "repeat offenders;" the clinics would be required to check their files. Of course, many women could slip through the cracks: women with new surnames or who had previous abortions in other states or at other clinics. Unless the state is willing to use totalitarian tactics, like Romania's former pregnancy police, enforcement could be haphazard.

Implicit in the governor's ban is a troubling message about women and morality. Second abortions, in this worldview, are the result of irresponsibility. That couldn't be further from the truth. Second abortions are, for example, more likely to be performed because of contraceptive failure than are first abortions. Equally important, though, a ban on second abortions, except to preserve the mother's health, violates the heart of *Roe vs. Wade*, which expressly forbids government interference in the first trimester of pregnancy.

The governor's proposal also includes that new canard so favored by those in the anti-abortion movement: a ban on all abortions for race and sex selection. Never mind that this provision is completely irrelevant and that virtually no abortions are performed for these reasons. This stipulation is there for only two reasons: to perpetuate the falsehood that women who have abortions do so for trivial reasons and to cloak the anti-abortion movement in the mantle of civil and equal rights.

The gaps in this proposal, particularly on enforcement, give rise to questions about such a law's real intent. Is it only meant as a novel challenge to *Roe vs. Wade*? Or does it reflect opportunism as the Republican Party tries to scramble out of its anti-abortion corner? Since the Supreme Court ruled in *Webster vs. Reproductive Health Services*, abortion has become an albatross around the GOP's neck; abortion rights is a winning issue, one that gives Democrats an edge. In this context, Gov. Ashcroft's proposal strikes an expedient note: Women have the right to choose but only once.

St. Louis Review

St. Louis, Missouri, January 19, 1990

Last summer the U.S. Supreme Court began the long trek up the hill to reverse the 1973 Roe vs. Wade decision that legalized abortion. It was fitting that a Missouri case was the occasion of this decision since the citizens of Missouri have been among the strongest advocates of the right to life.

Since that decision we have been subjected to a barrage of publicity aimed at convincing voters that their rights are under attack by a few fanatics bent on invading their bedroom and violating their right to privacy. Among the many publicity attacks to which we have been subjected are those proclaiming that all our legislators, both on the state level and nationally, are shaking in their boots when confronted by recharged pro-abortion forces.

That is one of the reasons that it is a refreshing change to read of a dedicated group of Missouri legislators, both Republican and Democrat, who are willing to stand up and be counted for life. They are seeking to push back the oppression of the pro-choice forces and they are introducing a series of bills that seek to limit abortions in various ways.

Statistics show that nearly 90 percent of women choose to end the life of their unborn baby other than for reasons of rape, incest or the life or health of the mother. A measure being put forth by State Rep. Ted House of St. Charles would address this problem. The measure would place no criminal penalties on women but would place penalties on anyone performing abortions for "reasons of convenience." Other bills being introduced are aimed at assisting pregnant women solve financial or personal problems that might lead them to seek an abortion. The bills aim for better prenatal care, employment services, housing, child care and promotion of adoption services. In this way this new legislation is not solely restrictive but also encourages women facing this situation.

No one likes to be reminded that abortion snuffs out the lives of unborn human beings. We do not relish the accusation that we are among the very few of God's creatures who have actually turned against our own young. Yet when we encourage people to make up their own minds about abortion we are agreeing to this course of action if it "seems all right." What seems all right for the mother in these cases destroys the life of the child who has no one to defend its rights.

There are many worthwhile ideas and opportunities for life in this new legislation. We urge you to keep yourself well-informed on their progress through the legislature. We are broadening horizons for life.

ARGUS-LEADER

Sioux Falls, South Dakota, September 14, 1990

Minnesota's primary produced some interesting results Tuesday.

The Independent-Republican and Democrat Farmer-Labor gubernatorial results provided satisfaction for the pro-life side of the abortion issue.

The victory by IR candidate Jon Grunseth over the better-known Arne Carlson provided some embarrassment for pollsters.

Paul Wellstone's victory in the DFL U.S. Senate primary over Agriculture Commissioner Jim Nichols provided some evidence that energetic, imaginative campaigns can overcome name-recognition disadvantage.

Editorial

So what does this all mean for the general election?

Minnesota has become a focal point for the abortion issue. In the DFL primary, Gov. Rudy Perpich stood firmly in the pro-life corner, while challenger Mike Hatch was pro-choice.

Grunseth, the underdog going into Tuesday's race, also stood in the pro-life corner, while Carlson made his pro-choice position clear.

Pollsters tripped over themselves to defend their numbers in the IR governor's race. But former Vice President Walter Mondale called it a black day for pollsters. The strategists who compile the numbers simply point out that the margins were good on the day they were taken, pointing to get-out-the-vote efforts as the reason for the turnaround between Grunseth and Carlson.

As is often the case with primaries, low voter turnouts may obscure the results, and the cause groups promise that they will speak in November.

On the abortion issue, there will be no November for the pro-choice faction since it lost both races.

The Grunseth victory had to be pleasing to Perpich. A Perpich-Carlson race offered a choice to voters on social issues. Grunseth, however, has painted himself into an ultra-conservative corner that may be tough to work out of.

Perpich's style has been characterized as off-the-wall during his nine years in the governor's mansion. His opponents call him Governor Goofy. But he prides himself on getting things done. He has brought Soviet President Mikhail Gorbachev to Minnesota. He has put Minnesota on speaking terms with high-tech business and industry.

He has made Minnesota an unlikely haven for sports events, getting both the Super Bowl and the NCAA Final Four competition in the Twin Cities.

Perpich's opponents find him tough to pin blame on. With a mistake here, and two successes there, he usually keeps one step ahead of the attacks.

Carlson would have been an even bet to beat Perpich, but Grunseth's philosophy is too narrow to be competitive. Republicans made the same mistake four years ago when they nominated Cal Ludeman. So for all practical purposes, Minnesotans re-elected Perpich Tuesday.

Sen. Rudy Boschwitz won a so-what landslide over a little-known opponent, readying him for battle with Wellstone, a Carleton College professor.

There is no poll in the world that will show Wellstone any closer than 30 points behind Boschwitz. There is little doubt that the margin will change much between now and November. But what DFLers did do Tuesday is nominate a candidate who has no fear of talking out loud about his opponent.

The oftentimes humorous Wellstone attacks can be cutting and revealing. Come Nov. 6, because of Wellstone's style, voters may know more about Boschwitz than they care to know. It won't cost Boschwitz the election, but it will raise the questions.

In the end, Minnesotans will keep their Rudys.

The Salt Lake Tribune

Salt Lake City, Utah, November 30, 1990

Right-to-life groups are massing for another battle in the Utah Legislature to severely restrict abortion. They would subject the state to a bitter political and legal war doomed to pointless stalemate or a high-stakes gamble.

Other states, notably Pennsylvania, and Guam already have enacted laws strictly limiting abortion. These statutes have been challenged in court, and the cases are working their way through the federal appeals system toward the U.S. Supreme Court. The cases will give the High Court opportunities to review the status of abortion law soon enough.

In the meantime, Utah should stay out of the fight. A legal crusade to the Supreme Court could cost $1 million, and would duplicate efforts that already are further along in the appeals process.

Utah would be better off to save itself the expense and political blood-letting. Let others pay the costs of rewriting the nation's abortion laws. This state's limited funds would be better spent educating its people, helping the poor and handicapped or strengthening the economy. The resources even could be spent on comprehensive, realistic sex education in Utah schools that would help to reduce the demand for abortions and combat the AIDS epidemic.

The most recent Supreme Court rulings on abortion, which dealt with parental notification and use of state funds, did not provide the impetus to change Utah law because the restrictions the court authorized already were in effect in this state.

No state funds go toward elective abortions in Utah, all of which are performed in private clinics and financed by private funds.

Utah already has an informed consent law and a statute that requires notification of parents when an abortion is to be performed for a minor child.

The changes the anti-abortion forces wish to enact are designed to be a head-on challenge to the holding in *Roe v. Wade*, the 1973 decision that allows women to choose to have abortions, particularly during the first three months of pregnancy.

The Legislature's Abortion Task Force has approved draft legislation that would allow abortions only to save the mother's life, or in cases of rape (if the crime were reported within five days), or incest, or if the child would be born with physical disabilities so profound that it would not survive birth.

The American Civil Liberties Union already has promised to challenge any such law in court, and so long as *Roe v. Wade* defines the Supreme Court's position on abortion, the Utah statute certainly would be found unconstitutional by a lower court. At that point, Utah either would have to drop the issue, in which case the whole exercise would have been pointless, or pursue a lengthy and expensive appeal in the hope of overturning *Roe*.

In one of their decisions last year, four Supreme Court justices virtually invited a challenge to *Roe*, but the prospect of successfully overturning that decision remains a gamble. Justice David Souter's views are unknown, and Justice Sandra Day O'Connor is seen as a swing vote.

This risky proposition is one that Utah needn't undertake, since cases already are moving through the legal system are closer to accomplishing the same ends.

The Duluth News-Tribune

Duluth, Minnesota, January 25, 1990

What may turn out to be one of the most potent political projects in Minnesota history has issued preliminary results. Unfortunately, those results are distorted.

The project is a survey of Minnesota residents being made by pro-choice groups. Final results of that poll will not be released until late spring, but a Duluth abortion rights leader characterized preliminary results this week. Mary Ellen Owens said the poll shows 65 percent of the city's registered voters favor a woman's right to terminate a pregnancy without government interference.

But no professional pollster would use the words used in this poll. The words seek to lead those who respond toward taking a pro-choice position. That's fine for the group's efforts to identify voters likely to support pro-choice candidates in the fall elections. But it's a bogus poll.

The basic poll question is: "Do you agree or disagree with the following statement: The decision to terminate a pregnancy is a private matter between a woman, her family and doctor, and not a decision to be made by government and politicians."

Other than the loaded word "politicians," it's a fairly straightforward question about abortion views — though it lacks the neutral wording of a good poll question.

Depending on their answer to the first question, respondents are asked one of two others. In these the loaded words or approaches get worse.

Those who say yes to it are asked: "In light of current government threats to safe, legal abortion, will this issue influence your opinion of politicians in the future?"

Those who say no to the first question are asked: "Are you opposed to abortion in cases of rape, incest, serious fetal deformity or to save the life of a woman?" Few abortion foes would have a woman die to save the life of her fetus. But do poll takers consider those who answer no to the last question pro-choice?

It's tough enough to find any agreement on abortion let alone resolve the dispute. Our comments today do not represent a conclusion that the pro-life cause has the angels on its side. We simply want the basic public debate on the issue to use facts when possible, not biased polls.

House Medicaid Bill Passed, Vetoed

The U.S. House of Representatives October 11, 1989 narrowly voted to restore Medicaid funds to pay for abortions in cases of rape or incest. The vote reversed eight years of House policy that had barred any use of Medicaid funds for abortions except in cases where the mother's life was endangered.

The vote came on an amendment to a $156.7 billion appropriations bill for the departments of Labor, Education and Health and Human Services and related agencies.

Every year since 1981, the House had attached the so-called Hyde amendment to the Labor, Education and HHS bill. The measure, sponsored by Rep. Henry J. Hyde (R, Ill.), had prohibited the use of federal funds for abortions. In recent years, the Senate had sought unsuccessfully to loosen the restriction in cases of rape or incest.

When the appropriations bill came up for consideration in August, the House once again approved the abortion ban, and the Senate backed a less restrictive measure, sending the bill to a conference committee.

On October 11, however, Rep. Barbara Boxer (D, Calif.) introduced a motion that the House "recede from its disagreement with the Senate." The motion passed by a vote of 216 to 206. It was then affirmed by a 212 to 207 vote on a motion to concur with the Senate in approving the use of Medicaid funds to pay for abortions in cases of rape or incest.

The votes were regarded by activists on both sides of the abortion question as evidence of a shifting political attitude toward abortion rights in the wake of the Supreme Court's July decision in *Webster v. Reproductive Health Services* upholding the right of states to restrict abortion.

President George Bush had previously pledged to veto any bill that eased restrictions on federal funding of abortions, and abortion opponents said October 11 that they planned to hold him to that promise.

The Florida state legislature, meeting in a special session October 10-11, voted down a series of measures proposed by Gov. Bob Martinez (R) that would have restricted access to abortion. Martinez had vowed to toughen the state's abortion laws after the Supreme Court upheld a strict Missouri abortion statute in July.

President Bush October 21, as promised, vetoed a spending bill that included a provision that would have allowed the use of Medicaid funds to pay for abortions for poor women who were the victims of rape or incest. The veto was upheld by a vote in the House October 25.

"I have informed Congress on numerous occasions that I would veto legislation if it permitted the use of appropriated funds to pay for abortions other than those in which the mother would be endangered if the fetus was carried to term," Bush said in a veto message released by the White House.

"This year, regrettably, the Congress has expanded the circumstances in which federally appropriated funds could be used to pay for abortions," Bush said.

The veto was sustained in the House October 25. Although the vote was 231 to 191 in favor of overturning the veto and approving the spending bill, it fell 51 votes short of the two-thirds majority that would have been needed to override the president's veto.

The vote followed a heated and largely partisan debate in which Democrats blasted the veto and Republicans lauded Bush's action.

LEXINGTON HERALD-LEADER
Lexington, Kentucky, October 13, 1989

Who would have thought it?

When the Supreme Court began to backtrack on its abortion decisions only a couple of months ago, the common wisdom was that state and federal lawmakers would stampede to limit abortion. But events on Wednesday suggest that view was more common than wise.

First, Florida lawmakers adjourned the special legislative session that Gov. Bob Martinez called specifically to limit abortion. The lawmakers met, rejected the governor's proposals and went home, leaving abortion rights intact in that conservative state.

Later on Wednesday, the U.S. House of Representatives reversed a stand taken only months ago. They loosened restrictions on publicly financed abortions for poor women.

The same forces seem to have been at work in both instances. For years, the noisy anti-abortion forces have dominated the debate on this issue. But while they have been yelling, a generation of American citizens — both men and women — have grown up believing that the Supreme Court meant what it said in its *Roe vs. Wade* decision: that the decision to have an abortion early in pregnancy is no one's business except the woman involved and her physician.

With that right threatened by the court's apparent retreat from the Roe decision, these citizens — many of whom have been silent until now — are making themselves heard. And politicians, no fools at reading public opinion, are listening.

Obviously, there will be many more fights in legislatures about abortion. Florida Right to Life leaders have already promised to turn the state's next legislative elections into referendums on abortion.

But so far, the evidence indicates that most Americans aren't interested in this single-issue, litmus test approach to politics. "A right once granted is hard to take away," a Florida lawmaker said after his legislature adjourned on Wednesday. That idea, so ingrained in the history of this country, is exactly why the common wisdom seems to have been so wrong in this case.

THE SACRAMENTO BEE
Sacramento, California, October 14, 1989

For years the Florida Legislature was among the most actively anti-abortion in the nation. But that was when it seemed politically risk-free to be so. As long as the U.S. Supreme Court was protecting the right to an abortion, Florida's legislators could safely vote to satisfy local anti-abortion activists without fear of accomplishing anything that would rouse the state's majority of pro-choice voters.

But when the U.S. Supreme Court last July began to dismantle that federal protection — as a first step, permitting the states to impose serious restrictions on the availability of abortions — the political calculus was altered. And the Florida Legislature has just demonstrated by how much. Called into special session by Gov. Bob Martinez, the Legislature took less than two days to kill eight different proposals for new restrictions, then adjourned.

Observers on all sides are calling this a turning point in the American abortion wars, but it would be a mistake to think that peace is just around the corner. If the Supreme Court's decision has stripped away the mantle of obfuscation in which the politicians used to be able to wrap themselves, it has also laid bare the underlying division. In every legislature of the country this battle will now be fought without cover; and regardless of the outcome, it will then be refought in many, maybe most, of the legislative district elections that follow. Florida's anti-abortion governor may have miscalculated in thinking he'd score political points by calling a special abortion session of his Legislature, but he most certainly was not mistaken when he announced afterward that this issue is not soon going to go away.

Poll after poll has shown that the majority of Americans think it should be up to a woman herself, and not her legislators, to decide whether to have an abortion. It should be no surprise that politicians have read those polls. The danger of the kind of single-interest politicking that the anti-abortion movement has perfected was never that it would overwhelm the majority in a head-on vote. The real concern is that it could keep the political process tied in knots when everyone else would rather move on to other subjects. That danger was not quelled; rather it was underscored by the Florida session and the political aftermath that all involved are already predicting. Quite aside from eroding the principle of privacy, which the U.S. Supreme Court should have sought to preserve, the justices have done the country no favor in throwing this football back onto the field.

The Honolulu Advertiser
Honolulu, Hawaii, October 12, 1989

The special session of the Florida Legislature is not taking the steps urged by anti-abortion forces. That's welcome news.

But the events in Tallahassee, with political debate and maneuvering inside the capitol while massive pro-choice and anti-abortion rallies go on outside, are the first act in a drama that may be replayed in many state capitols, perhaps even in Hawaii.

Last July, the U.S. Supreme Court opened the door to greater state regulation of abortion. That led Florida Governor Bob Martinez to call the nation's first special session aimed at restricting it.

The legislature refused to go along. And, in any case, last week the Florida Supreme Court unanimously ruled that the right to an abortion was fundamental under that state's constitution's right to privacy.

Unfortunately, the abortion question may not be so clear-cut in other states. But in general, polls show that perhaps three-quarters of the American people feel women have a right to choose an abortion in early pregnancy with little interference from the state, though many are uncomfortable with how often and why that right is sometimes exercised.

A minority, one-quarter to one-third of the people, believe there should be no abortion, or only in extremely limited cases.

A tiny minority hold this view so blindly they are willing to break into abortion clinics, destroy property and — worst of all — harass, intimidate and even harm clinic employees and women seeking abortions.

This self-righteous effort to impose religious and social beliefs on others may not fit most people's definition of "racketeering" — as the U.S. Supreme Court now says it does under the law — but it is certainly terribly wrong.

The good news from Florida, however, for those organizing to protect the right of women to control their bodies, is that no matter what the Supreme Court eventually rules on Roe vs. Wade, it will be harder to turn back the clock than many believed or feared.

And scientific advances, in the form of the French "abortion pill," may well make the political debate moot before long.

THE PLAIN DEALER
Cleveland, Ohio, October 15, 1989

The politics of the abortion issue have changed dramatically since the Supreme Court's July decision to limit the reach of its landmark Roe vs. Wade abortion-rights decision. Although the abortion-rights debate must now go through legislative rather than judicial channels, pro-choice advocates have ample reason to be reassured. There is a groundswell of support for many of the pro-choice positions: There should be equal access for poor women to abortion facilities, and victims of incest and rape should not also be victimized by the state.

That the pro-choice movement is getting stronger was reflected in Florida last week, when a special session of the state legislature — convened solely to weigh stronger anti-abortion laws — collapsed. It is also evident in this year's two gubernatorial elections, in New Jersey and Virginia, where polls show that the abortion issue is helping pro-choice candidates and hurting anti-choice absolutists.

Pro-choice politics got another boost in Congress when the House of Representatives voted to end a double standard that punishes recipients of Medicaid, the federal health-care program for the poor. Since 1981, the House had supported the so-called Hyde amendment, offered by Illinois Republican Henry J. Hyde, that refuses Medicaid payments for abortions except in a case when the mother's life is endangered; even in cases of rape or incest, the law now denies any public funds for abortion. In 1988, the House voted 216-166 for the extremist Hyde amendment.

But in a pro-choice triumph, the House reversed its position: It voted 216-206 to allow Medicaid payments for abortions in cases of rape and incest, as well as danger to the life of the mother. Although this would not end all Medicaid abortion restrictions, it does signal a new measure of compassion in the House. The Senate, less eager to impose Draconian abortion limits in recent years, already had approved that more flexible standard.

The House vote also signals a keen political realism: Members of Congress know that voters are newly aware of every shade of meaning in candidates' positions on abortion rights.

☐

Sadly, Cleveland voters find that one of their representatives, Mary Rose Oakar, voted again last week to impose the hard-hearted Hyde amendment. Whatever her personal misgivings about abortion, Oakar's position remains of concern: As long as abortion is legal, women of all income groups should have the same right of access. It is particularly appalling to deny abortion to low-income women victimized by rape or incest.

Oakar's wrong-headed vote on the Hyde amendment was mitigated somewhat by her open-mindedness on another abortion-related issue: She sensibly voted, as she did in August, not to block the District of Columbia from spending its own money (not federal money) for welfare recipients' abortions. Her willingness to reconsider her past position on District abortion funding shows some welcome reflection on the issue. Nonetheless, Oakar's vote for the Hyde amendment is disappointing to Cleveland voters who had hoped she might take a more compassionate position.

The Star-Ledger

Newark, New Jersey, October 13, 1989

Two highly significant developments in the emotion-charged abortion debate emerged this week from legislative venues in Washington and Florida that could be indicative of a changing political climate on this polarizing social issue.

In the nation's capital, the House voted to restore provisions of federally subsidized abortions that would allow payment to poor women to abort pregnancies resulting from rape or incest. In Florida, the state legislature rejected 10 anti-abortion measures, including five proposed by Gov. Bob Martinez, a staunch pro-life proponent.

These legislative actions loom as key factors in the volatile abortion issue that was sharply intensified this summer by a Supreme Court decision which upheld Missouri's restrictions on abortion. The ruling had the far-reaching effect of shifting any future legislative changes on abortion regulations to state capitals.

At the time it was handed down, the Supreme Court ruling was widely perceived as a major impetus for the pro-life movement, an opening wedge to wage a more effective counterattack at the state level, where political pressures were expected to heavily favor anti-abortion forces.

But the one-sided legislative setback in Florida appears to strongly suggest that pro-choice advocates have a powerful political constituency. The legislative rejection of new restrictions that the Supreme Court ruling now permits was clearly reflective of sentiments expressed in public polls.

In Florida, a poll showed 62 percent of state residents were in favor of leaving the law unchanged. This finding no doubt was a decisive factor for the legislative reasoning that Floridians can exercise their state sovereignty rights on this social issue regardless of what the Supreme Court may decide about the legality of abortion laws.

In a broader national perspective, the Florida legislative consensus on abortion could be a precursor of similar developments in other states when this issue, as widely anticipated, is joined in legislative forums.

It is, of course, unfortunate that an emotional, highly personal issue such as abortion has become embroiled in a political conflict. Nevertheless, there are factors that could serve a useful purpose, a means of clearly delineating public thinking on the right of women to make a private choice about a pregnancy.

It is reassuring that the pro-choice movement has shown it can more than hold its own against a powerful right-to-life advocacy. And it is heartening to note, too, that a sizable majority of Americans understandably disapprove any government infringement of a woman's right of free choice.

TULSA WORLD

Tulsa, Oklahoma, October 12, 1989

IT'S enough to make every legislator cringe, no matter what his or her feelings on abortion. The Florida Legislature convened in special session Tuesday, charged by the governor to consider a raft of abortion questions.

Republican Gov. Bob Martinez called the session and put a number of morally and politically difficult measures before a Democratic legislature.

Although few expect any constructive legislation — in fact, lawmakers talked of adjourning immediately — Florida and the rest of the nation will be treated to the full panoply of emotion-laded abortion arguments.

Given the recent signals of the U.S. Supreme Court, the Florida exercise is likely to be repeated in every state.

Oklahoma legislators will almost certainly face the same ordeal when they convene in regular session in February.

If the U.S. Supreme Court should ultimately knock down the controversial Roe vs. Wade case which made abortions legal under many conditions, the country could see a great variety of abortion laws as each state defines its own position on abortion.

The sad part of the coming exercise is that it is abundantly clear that abortion is an issue that is almost impossible to resolve by legislation. By its very nature, it is a conscience question that will be resolved in different ways by different citizens.

The freedom to exercise that conscience, of course, is what the debate should be about. If it were, then the law of the land would be to allow individual discretion on this most sensitive question of all those involving privacy and reproduction rights.

Sadly, that does not seem to be in the cards. Florida's anguish is a prelude of what is to come for every legislature — and every citizen — in the land.

DESERET NEWS

Salt Lake City, Utah, October 8, 1989

The Florida Supreme Court has overturned a law in that state requiring parental consent for minors to have abortions. The court's verdict appears to fly in the face of legal responsibilities that parents normally have for their children.

In this instance, a case involving a 15-year-old girl, the seven state justices ruled a state constitution privacy provision approved by voters in 1980 clearly encompasses a woman's right to abortion prior to the point where the fetus becomes viable.

Four justices went a step further, concluding that minors also enjoy a privacy right to abortion under the constitutional provision.

Pro-abortion groups and the American Civil Liberties Union are hailing the decision as a turning point in the abortion issue, one that will challenge recent U.S. Supreme Court rulings giving states more say in setting abortion standards.

The ruling defies logical application when considered in context with other legal responsibilities parents must assume for their children, responsibilities routinely enforced by judicial fiat.

For example, parents are required to provide safe and habitable residence for their children. They are required to provide food and clothing and to create an environment where the children are free from abuse, both verbal and physical. And if they don't? The state, through judicial action, takes custody.

Consider also that many states are adopting laws that make parents responsible for the actions of minor children. Utah is a prime example.

State law here makes parents financially responsible for remedying acts of vandalism by minor children. The law does not consider whether parents are making every effort possible to prevent such behavior. The law implies categorically that since they are YOUR children, YOU are totally responsible.

And in medical matters, doctors and hospitals will do little more than apply a bandage without a signed parental consent form.

Even children with serious injuries are given minimal treatment in hospital and clinical emergency rooms while clerks scurry around getting the proper forms signed by the appropriate parent or guardian. Unless its a life-or-death situation, it's a case of no signed consent form, no treatment.

With all these medical and legal obligations on parents, how can the courts turn around and say doctors can perform an abortion on a minor child and the parents do not even have to be notified?

Courts routinely affirm laws restricting the right to drive a car based on age and that require parental consent before minors can drop out of school or get married. Why? Because 15-year-olds are not deemed sufficiently wise or mature to make these decisions on their own.

Why then, do courts believe these same children are suddenly capable of making the life-or-death decisions that go with abortion — without the need for parental involvement?

Philadelphia Inquirer / TONY AUTH

The Courier-Journal
Louisville, Kentucky, October 13, 1989

EVENTS over the last several weeks suggest that a profound shift is occurring in the battle over abortion rights — one that ultimately may resolve the issue more decisively than the Supreme Court ever could.

In America, it turns out, a right once granted is difficult to rescind.

Neither side in the abortion debate can count yet on the vicissitudes of public opinion and politics to uphold its views. But that is the startling news of October 1989: Those who once believed that anti-abortion zealots held all the political aces have been proved wrong.

Twice since the conservative-dominated Supreme Court signaled in the *Webster* case that it would no longer resolve the issue on constitutional grounds, the U. S. House of Representatives has voted — albeit by slim margins — to relax restrictions on the use of tax money for abortions for the poor.

This week, the Florida legislature dealt Republican Gov. Bob Martinez a stunning blow by rejecting his package of eight bills designed to impose stringent restrictions on access to abortion.

Almost simultaneously, the Florida Supreme Court ruled that a provision in the state Constitution protecting the right to privacy precludes laws that interfere with a woman's right to choose abortion.

Across the nation, the impact of the *Webster* ruling appears to be re-fashioning the political landscape. Candidates in Virginia and other states have begun to see a "pro-choice" position as the politically savvy stance.

The explanation lies not only in the startling shift in public opinion — the awakening of huge numbers of pro-choice voters previously complacent on the issue. It lies also in a re-framing of the issue.

Many voters and, thus, many politicians believe staunchly in the right to privacy, the right of individuals to choose their own destiny, the need to limit government interference in personal decisions and the need to insure equity between rich and poor in the exercise of those rights.

Except for the last, those are classically conservative principles — testimony to the ironies that run deep in the debate over abortion.

Unfortunately, in the Kentucky delegation only Rep. Carroll Hubbard has grasped that fact. Mr. Hubbard, who has always been astute in gauging voters' attitudes, reversed his earlier stand and voted to remove federal restrictions on the use of local tax funds in the District of Columbia and to allow Medicaid to provide abortions for poor victims of rape and incest.

His colleagues should take heed. So should President Bush. The days when a strong anti-abortion stand was the politically safest course are over. A once silent pro-choice majority is making itself heard.

MILWAUKEE SENTINEL
Milwaukee, Wisconsin, October 13, 1989

House action permitting Medicaid funding of abortions of pregnancies resulting from rape or incest would remove from federal law two of the most repugnant conditions under which money for such operations is denied.

To require that women deliver children conceived under such circumstances is uncivilized and inhumane, given the psychological torment involved in either case and the potential for serious genetic problems where incest is involved.

It also must be remembered that this proscription involves poor people who would be condemned to accept a fate that can easily be avoided by the well-off, regardless of what the law says.

The measure has been perceived by some as a shift in attitude on the volatile issue in Congress that is related to more effective lobbying by advocates of legalized abortion.

That may be too quick a call. The 216-206 vote was hardly a landslide. And many anti-abortionists go along with these exceptions.

One who doesn't is President Bush, who has vowed to veto any bill expanding abortion rights. The law now permits use of federal money for abortions only when the life of the mother is in danger.

The president, understandably, has been wary of the might of the political right, particularly in his own party. His obvious philosophy has been to not make waves with his supporters. But Bush should at least show as much courage in this case as Congress.

Proponents of legalized abortion should be more encouraged by action in the Florida Legislature Wednesday where a raft of anti-abortion bills were defeated despite the support of Gov. Bob Martinez.

The last US Supreme Court ruling on this issue seemed to throw the ball back to the states, where it was expected lawmakers would respond just as did Bush. But, again, there can be no certainty that Florida is a test case that can forecast what will happen elsewhere in the country.

What would serve both sides best is a joint effort to promote birth control. That might stem the tide of hungry and ill-cared-for children in the nation's cities. These children are the ones who deserve the compassion and money being spent in the battle over the fate of the unwanted unborn.

AKRON
BEACON JOURNAL
Akron, Ohio, October 12, 1989

THE RENEWED efforts by some to restrict the rights of women to have abortions do not seem to be going well in Florida, a state where the anti-abortion movement has the strong support of the governor.

In fact, in the 50 states, only Florida's governor, Bob Martinez, has been so committed to restricting the legal right to an abortion that he called a special legislative session.

The special session has, as might be expected with this emotional issue, attracted the normal throngs of demonstrators on both sides. A majority of the legislature appears committed to ensuring that women, including poor women, are not denied the choice of whether to have an abortion.

That decision is an agonizing one for every woman who feels compelled to consider it. Many choose not to have abortions. Others do, and by law that is their right. It is a personal decision, and women seeking to make it deserve the chance to do so without many of the harassing tactics of some anti-abortionists.

Florida, of course, is only one state, and the Supreme Court's *Webster vs. Reproductive Services* decision gives all state legislatures the right to consider *some* restrictions on the rights of women. The Florida legislative actions indicate that states may properly be reluctant to do that, even when a governor pushes the restrictions in an unusual special session.

Much of the current debate could wind up becoming moot anyway as modern medical technology takes hold. The French development of an abortion pill, RU486, offers women pregnancy termination without any surgical procedures.

Some in the anti-abortion movement will seek to prohibit the use of the French pill in the United States. If early indications of its medical safety hold up, such efforts are likely to be as improbable as trying to prohibit the use of birth control pills, condoms or diaphragms.

The anti-abortion movement lost ground on another legal front when the U.S. Supreme Court declined to hear an appeal of a ruling that applied federal anti-racketeering laws, imposing triple civil damages, against anti-abortion demonstrators who committed multiple acts of intimidation against Philadelphia-area clinics.

The courts should support those who seek to prevent such repeated acts of harassment and intimidation. However, it is hard to believe that Congress intended that anti-racketeering laws would be applied in this case and in other civil suits not involving abortion. The Supreme Court may have accurately interpreted what Congress did, but Congress ought to re-examine the resulting scope of the Racketeer Influenced, Corrupt Organizations Act.

The Kansas City Times
Kansas City, Missouri, October 12, 1989

Two major victories in as many days should encourage abortion rights supporters to keep working. It is too early to think the job is done. The battle promises to be long and arduous, in nearly all the state legislatures as well as on the national level.

In two recent matters, it is clear that elected officials are reading the public sentiment to be against tighter restrictions on a woman's right to an abortion in light of the U.S. Supreme Court ruling which gave that option to the states.

In Florida, Gov. Bob Martinez, a Republican who has had problems misreading the voters before — he campaigned against taxes and then did a turnaround — misjudged again. He was rebuffed by the legislature in a special session he called for the purpose of putting state restrictions on abortion. The fact that this occurred in the nation's fourth-largest state, and one which has not been considered in the abortion rights column, is significant.

In Washington, an even more telling change from a national perspective is the House's decision to go along with the Senate in passing a bill to change part of the so-called Hyde amendment which restricts federal financing of abortions. The House vote was to accept language which permits federal funds for abortions for poor women who are raped or the victims of incest.

Although this hardly opens the door to large numbers of federally financed abortions, it is symbolic because the no-federal-money ban for abortions for these reasons has been in place on the Health and Human Services and Labor funding bill since 1981. President Bush has threatened a veto.

What is happening? The pro-choice side worked following the court decision last July. Public opinion polls show that the American public is ambivalent about abortion, but does not want to outlaw the procedure. The majority of public sentiment is on the choice side, but any organized lobbying group knows that legislators may be overwhelmed by a minority. That has been the case with the anti-abortion movement, which has dominated things for too long. Public sentiment hasn't been worth much until now.

Follow-through is important on the pro-choice side — support of and election of legislators who will not be afraid to vote for the rights of millions of constituents in the face of a strong-willed pressure group, and a continued presence in Congress and the legislative halls which shows that there is another, stronger side to the issue.

St. Petersburg Times
St. Petersburg, Florida, October 8, 1989

The Florida Supreme Court's decision that the state constitutional right to privacy provides solid protection to a woman's access to abortion makes this week's special legislative session even more unnecessary than it was to start with. Certainly it is encouraging to hear such staunch anti-abortion rights advocates as Florida Sen. John Grant concede as much.

Yet given the politically charged arena in which the subject of abortion is being debated, the court's decision also makes the outcome of the special session more uncertain.

It is essential that legislators who favor abortion rights not let down their guard.

Despite the succinct affirmation by the state high court that women in Florida have the right to obtain abortions with little interference from the government, there still is a danger of complacency. The court's ruling last week was enraging to many who oppose abortion, and desperation could strengthen their resolve even further. The power of a zealous minority to do serious harm when the majority is unaware or unprepared should not be underestimated.

Lawmakers in Tallahassee this week should be particularly wary of Gov. Bob Martinez's request to regulate abortion clinics. Expressing his horror over three unsafe clinics in South Florida, the governor produced lengthy proposed legislation to toughen clinic regulations.

If Martinez's concern for women's health were sincere, however, he would be wondering why it took a *Miami Herald* reporter to uncover the dangerous practices of unscrupulous abortion providers at the first clinic to be shut down. The swift closing of that clinic and two others by emergency state order is sound evidence that power to protect women from bad clinics already exists, if only the state would exercise it.

Insisting, as Martinez does, that "Florida has been handcuffed in its ability to make sure that abortions that are legal are also safe," is to disregard existing law. Only bad doctors will allow unsafe procedures, unsanitary conditions and a lack of proper equipment to exist at any clinics, and the state has full power to protect its citizens from such doctors by taking away their medical licenses. Inspections of all medical care facilities where unsafe conditions are suspected, as already allowed by Florida law, should be made a top priority.

Most Floridians welcome proper, thorough regulation of all medical facilities. Singling out abortion clinics for a crackdown when mechanisms already

> Lawmakers in Tallahassee this week should be particularly wary of Gov. Bob Martinez's request to regulate abortion clinics.

exist to ensure patients' safety, however, is a poorly disguised attempt to restrict women's ability to obtain abortions and to make political headlines. The fact that the Department of Health and Rehabilitative Services (HRS) recommended killing a proposed addition to abortion clinic regulations only last year further exposes the governor's theatrics.

It appears that abortion legislation is not likely to result from the special session. Substantive action on the state's troubled child protection system is in doubt as well, which is a blessing because the issue deserves far greater attention than this kind of publicity stunt would allow.

That the show at the Capitol this week is even occurring is an expensive embarrassment. Lawmakers should take seriously their responsibility to keep it from being any more damaging.

BUFFALO EVENING NEWS
Buffalo, New York, October 13, 1989

WHEN THE SUPREME COURT decided in the Webster case last July that states could clamp new restrictions on abortions, pro-life forces rejoiced and pro-choice supporters reacted with dismay and alarm.

The most significant reaction, however, may have crystallized among the great moderate majority of Americans.

And if recent decisions of Congress and the Florida state legislature truly reflect the view of their constituents, that majority does not want tighter restrictions on abortion and certainly does not want it banned.

What welcome news. Abortion occupies a field of public policy, as the Supreme Court wisely ruled some 16 years ago, where a woman's rights of privacy should not be unfairly circumscribed, much less nullified, by meddlesome and intrusive government.

What the House did this week, surprisingly, was repeal a prohibition against Medicaid funding for abortions for poor women who had become pregnant through incest or rape. That ban, the so-called Hyde Amendment, had been on the books since 1981. In that time, federal funds could be spent only for abortions to save the life of the mother.

The House vote was 216-206. By contrast, a year ago it voted 216-166 to keep the Hyde Amendment.

Regrettably, Reps. John LaFalce of Tonawanda and Henry Nowak of Buffalo, both Democrats, and William Paxon, R-Williamsville, all voted this time to retain the amendment. But at least Reps. Louise Slaughter, D-Fairport, and Amory Houghton, R-Corning, backed the heartening change. The exercise of such an intimate constitutional right, so personal for abused women, should not be denied merely because of unfavorable economic circumstance.

Then there was Florida — where pro-life Gov. Robert Martinez called a special session of the legislature in order to enact new restrictions on abortions.

No center of liberalism, Florida has earned a reputation for tough anti-abortion laws. Yet Martinez suffered a stunning rebuff. Not one of his eight proposals (higher special licensing standards for abortion clinics, for example, and prohibitions against state employees and centers being used to perform abortions) passed. The special session collapsed.

Returning home early, legislators spoke of a backlash from the Webster decision. "Once a right is established," said the speaker of the Florida House, "it is not easily removed."

Together, the events in Florida and Washington suggest a shift in the political climate on abortion. It may just be that the majority, alarmed by the Webster case, is making its long-held views better known. It may be that pro-choice forces have mobilized their supporters and their arguments more effectively.

Whatever the reason, this shift moves in an enlightened direction. No one should forget, however, that the House still has not done what it should for Medicaid patients — given them full equality on abortion. American women will get fair treatment only when all have access to this special medical care so essential to the exercise of their basic constitutional rights.

THE ATLANTA CONSTITUTION
Atlanta, Georgia, October 13, 1989

You don't need a weatherman to tell you the winds of abortion politics have shifted.

First the Florida Legislature turned thumbs down on a set of abortion restrictions proposed by Gov. Bob Martinez. Then the U.S. House of Representatives reversed course and voted to let the federal government pay for the abortions of poor women whose pregnancies result from incest or rape. Meanwhile, the Democratic gubernatorial candidate in Virginia, Doug Wilder, has shot ahead in the polls thanks to new television ads attacking the anti-abortion position of his Republican opponent.

The main credit for these developments goes to last summer's Webster v. Missouri decision, which convinced the majority of Americans favoring the right to abortion that they could no longer depend on the Supreme Court to guarantee it. They are speaking up, and their elected officials have hearkened.

For its part, an energized abortion-rights movement has finally hit upon a rhetorical device as effective as anything in the anti-abortion arsenal: The government shouldn't be able to force anyone (or anyone's wife, sister or teenaged daughter) to have a baby. That's powerful stuff for a citizenry that, since the birth of the republic, has harbored an abiding dislike of government interference in its affairs.

Ideally, none of this would have been necessary. By sweeping away state restrictions on abortion, Roe v. Wade ought to have placed a woman's decision to carry a pregnancy to term safely beyond the reach of politics. Instead, however, it brought into being an anti-abortion movement grounded in deeply felt religious convictions and dedicated to extending the protection of the state to fetuses.

Under the circumstances, the Supreme Court's desire to return abortion to the political arena has its virtues. For while questions of fundamental human rights are best insulated from majority rule, there are times when such rights require the sanction of a majority. The Bill of Rights, after all, was itself the product of majoritarian politics.

"A right, having been established, is not easily removed," said Florida House Speaker Tom Gustafson. It is now up to the American people to decide how much the contested right to abortion means to them.

As promising as the latest news is, many battles lie ahead, and it would be foolish to imagine that the anti-abortion forces will not win some of them. There are going to be states where women, and poor women in particular, will find it difficult, if not impossible, to procure an abortion.

But no longer will politicians be able to pander to the anti-abortionists with impunity. After opportunistically sowing in pro-life fields, the Republican party will soon begin to reap some bitter fruits.

The Register-Guard
Eugene, Oregon, October 15, 1989

This summer, the U.S. Supreme Court began chipping away at *Roe vs. Wade* — the court's landmark 1973 decision establishing a woman's unfettered right to abortion in the early stages of pregnancy — setting the stage for state-by-state warfare between the equally impassioned sides of the issue.

At the time, it was feared that anti-abortionists might prevail in many of those state battles because of the wave of conservatism that Ronald Reagan ignited around the country. Recent developments, however, indicate that defenders of a woman's right of choice have some political muscle too.

This week, the Florida Legislature ended an ill-advised special session called by Gov. Bob Martinez by rejecting 10 anti-abortion measures. Five of those measures had been introduced by the governor, a fervent anti-abortionist. A week ago, the Florida Supreme Court used the state constitution's rights of privacy provisions to strike down a statute calling for parental notification prior to a nonadult consenting to an abortion.

Also this week, the U.S. House of Representatives, in a significant policy shift, narrowly voted — 216 to 206 — to follow the Senate's lead and allow the use of federal funds to pay for abortions for poor women whose pregnancies resulted from rape or incest. Previously, the House had held to the view that no federal funds could be spent on abortions unless the mother's life was endangered.

This week's vote marked the second time since the Supreme Court's July decision weakening *Roe vs. Wade* that the House has shifted in the direction of abortion rights. Not a big shift, but a shift nonetheless. Earlier, the House lifted a prior ban on the District of Columbia spending its own money to pay for abortions for poor women.

While President Bush has hinted that he might veto the legislation relaxing the restrictions on the use of federal funds for abortions, the shifting politics of the issue might cause him to take another look. In addition, while the president's anti-abortion stance might play well among Republicans, it runs counter to public opinion. Poll after poll shows that the public at large favors a woman's right to decide such an intimate and personal matter for herself — without any governmental interference.

Roe vs. Wade guaranteed that right of individual choice. It's bad enough that the Supreme Court has begun chipping away at this guarantee. But the court has compounded its mistake by throwing this complex and extremely volatile issue into the unpredictable and untidy world of politics.

But even in that rough-and-tumble milieu, the developments this week and last provide welcome evidence that the pro-choicers can hold their own.

St. Paul Pioneer Press & Dispatch

St. Paul, Minnesota, October 15, 1989

The politics of abortion finally are growing as complicated as the issue. Judging from the mobilization and results gained by abortion-rights advocates since the galvanizing U.S. Supreme Court decision July 3 in Webster vs. Reproductive Health Services, the political momentum seems to be swinging.

Two major events in the last week are indicative of how well abortion-rights groups have been able to dominate the renewed debate. The House of Representatives, the congressional bastion of anti-abortion forces, voted to make rape and incest victims eligible for Medicaid to have paid abortions. In Florida, the first special legislative session in the nation called by an anti-abortion governor specifically to get more restrictive legislation ended in total failure for Gov. Bob Martinez.

But the man most on the spot right now is President Bush. And he knows it. On Friday the president said he continues to oppose even the slight expansion of Medicaid abortions in the House bill, but that he hopes for a compromise to "avoid a veto on my part." This might take the form of a 48-hour deadline for the victim to notify authorities. Mr. Bush has moved with the political tides before in taking a position on Medicaid abortions. He is pragmatic and correct to move again.

It is in elective politics where the trench warfare is gaining severity and impact. Abortion-rights groups seized the advantage the day Webster was announced, but the test will be in their ability to advance under fire along a front that extends to all 50 states.

In the three months since Webster gave states more latitude to restrict abortion, the line of fire has not been straight from the Supreme Court to Congress to the president.

The line extends to every precinct in America. So far, abortion-rights groups have been able to marshal the resources to fight the war this way. Witness the careful targeting of political contests and application of the abortion-rights litmus test. The tactic is paying off, for example, in the Virginia gubernatorial race, where Democrat L. Douglas Wilder, who is running an aggressive abortion-rights campaign, seems to have pulled ahead of J. Marshall Coleman, the anti-abortion Republican.

A wide array of old-fashioned lick 'em and stick 'em initiatives are raising the gamesmanship. In Minnesota, the massive voter attitude survey on abortion rights is the kind of targeted effort that pays off. Abortion opponents were unsuccessful in interjecting the issue into the special Minnesota legislative session last month. And, if Senate Majority Leader Roger Moe, an abortion-rights backer, decides to take on Gov. Rudy Perpich, an anti-abortion candidate, for the DFL nomination next year, the politics of abortion will weigh heavily. In Wisconsin, the Women's Political Caucus is conducting a drive, one of 10 nationwide, to back abortion-rights candidates for state office.

Unless medical science moots the whole dilemma, sustaining and directing efforts over the inevitable long haul will be pivotal. Careful observers from both sides know that what is occurring now is only a political mirror image of what happened after Roe vs. Wade.

San Francisco Chronicle

San Francisco, California, October 12, 1989

THE LESSON LEARNED so far in Florida is an instructive — and heartening — one. Governor Bob Martinez called a special session of the Florida Legislature in an effort to push through some bills restricting abortion. They were swiftly rejected.

There is considerable significance in such action, for Florida was looked on as an critical skirmishing ground: the locus of the first real political test since the U.S. Supreme Court opened the way for possible restriction on this medical procedure. As Kate Michelson, executive director of the National Abortion Rights League, noted: "It could have gone either way in Florida; this is not historically a strong pro-choice state."

At the time that the Supreme Court decision was handed down, there was a sense that anti-abortion proponents might overwhelm state legislatures with successful bids to curtail the procedure. But that has not been the case. The pro-choice protagonists have turned out, too, and presented both compelling argument and demonstrative evidence of strength.

THESE DEVELOPMENTS in the Southern state of Florida tell us that politicians are properly wary of intruding on this most-personal of decisions that surely must be available to all women — in the privacy of conscience and with appropriate medical consultation.

The Des Moines Register

Des Moines, Iowa, October 13, 1989

Anti-abortion politicians who for years demagogued the issue are breaking into a cold sweat and running for cover. They praised last summer's Supreme Court decision as giving them license to greatly restrict if not halt abortions. But the decision is doing something else: It is forcing those politicians to confront the issue at home. No longer can they gain points merely by attacking the Supreme Court's 1973 Roe v. Wade ruling that legalized abortion nationwide.

They now are forced to come up with legislation to back up their words, and they're finding out the public's not with them. While most Americans are uncomfortable with abortion, most also think government has no right to intrude on what should be a woman's personal decision. Pro-choice advocates, spurred on by the Supreme Court's decision to accept a Missouri law restricting abortion, have mobilized their forces. The anti-abortion movement is in retreat.

Consider what happened this week in Florida, a certifiably conservative Southern state. Gov. Bob Martinez, triumphant after last summer's court decision, proposed restrictions on abortion and called his legislature into special session. Not one of his proposals even made it to a floor vote.

Consider also what happened this week in Washington on the Hyde amendment, which permits Medicaid to pay for abortions only if a mother's life is in danger. Since 1981, when the amendment first was approved, efforts have been made to expand the exemption to allow Medicaid to pay for abortions for victims of rape and incest. Repeatedly, such efforts, though supported in the Senate, were rejected in the House. But Wednesday 26 House members, sensing the public mood, changed their votes from a year ago. The expansion was approved.

The changing momentum has been felt in Iowa, too. After the summer high-court decision some lawmakers and Gov. Terry Branstad expressed support for restrictive abortion legislation. But since then, all four caucuses in the Legislature have said they don't intend the issue to be part of their legislative agendas. Although Branstad opposes abortions, spokesman Richard Vohs says the governor doesn't want the issue to divide Iowans and interfere with other matters that need to be addressed.

The abortion issue is far from settled. Some states no doubt will seize upon the Supreme Court's decision and greatly restrict abortions, forcing their citizens to travel to less restrictive jurisdictions and creating once again an unjust system in which abortions are allowed only for the privileged. Pro-choice forces, as they exult in their recent successes, must continue to speak out for the right of a woman to choose.

Richmond Times-Dispatch

Richmond, Virginia, October 15, 1989

The Supreme Court's July 3 decision in *Webster vs. Reproductive Health Services* did not go so far as to overturn its 1973 *Roe vs. Wade* decision, which, in essence, legislated abortion to the status of constitutionally protected right. But it did begin a (possibly slow) process of restoring to the state legislatures and Congress the power to regulate when, how or if abortions may be performed.

Harvard Law Professor Laurence H. Tribe, who takes a dim view of this trend, predicted at a recent U.S. Law Week conference that the high court won't explicitly overrule *Roe*, but will instead just ignore it and allow it to be eroded,

trickle by trickle, in a "tyranny of small decisions." Tyranny is a curious word choice for a development that strengthens a principle undergirding the entire American system of government: federalism. States should be free to try differing solutions to problems as legally and morally vexing as abortion. Tyranny is a word we associate with an unelected judiciary making law instead of interpreting it.

Nevertheless, Professor Tribe may be on the mark with his observation about many more "small decisions" (which we take to mean on fine points) by the court. That trickling may continue during the court's new term with three abortion

cases on an unusually light docket of cases.

Illinois is seeking approval for a comprehensive plan of regulating abortion clinics. Among other things, it requires that all first-trimester abortions be performed in licensed clinics, which must meet certain physical standards. Cases from Ohio and Minnesota invite the court to decide if parental notification statutes must include a judicial bypass feature. In other words, should there be a way a minor could go to a judge confidentially to obtain permission to have an abortion without telling her parents?

As should be obvious after votes last week in the Florida legislature and the U.S. House of Representatives, last summer's *Webster* decision did not spell the end of all legalized abortions in the United States. Far from it. It simply began turning back this question for the American people, through their elected representatives, to decide. The first wave of alarm has redounded to the advantage of the pro-abortion side. Gov. Bob Martinez of Florida took a drubbing on all the abortion restrictions he proposed to a special legislative session he called. And the House voted 216-206 to restrict restrictions of eight years' standing and allow Medicaid funding of abortions for poor women who are victims of rape or incest.

The rape and incest circumstances, though accounting for a tiny fraction of all abortions performed, stir emotions that office-seekers can try to exploit. In the Virginia governor's race, Democrat Douglas Wilder has tried to use this issue to his advantage against Republican Marshall Coleman, even though Mr. Coleman has said that he would not support legislation to deny rape and incest victims access to abortions. The polls show that Virginians, with Americans in general, do favor allowing abortions in the so-called "hard cases" — rape, incest, fetal abnormality, health of the mother — but that a majority also oppose abortions of convenience — for birth control, gender selection, etc. So after the initial wave of politically fanned hysteria subsides, some legislatures may adopt carefully measured restrictions. In the Virginia General Assembly, however, the only anti-abortion bill that has a ghost of a chance in the foreseeable future is parental notification for a minors' abortion, and even that appears stymied in the Senate.

Of course, politicians who play with emotions that sizzle sometimes can get burned themselves. In reaction to Mr. Wilder's repeated invoking of this issue, Coleman researchers found that lawyer-legislator Wilder introduced a bill in 1972 that would have allowed defense lawyers to grill rape victims 13 years old and younger about their sex lives. Had it passed, such a measure would have been helpful to law firms, like Mr. Wilder's own, that had an extensive criminal defense practice. On three occasions, Mr. Wilder also opposed "rape shield" laws to limit accused rapists' lawyers in their examination of a victim's personal background.

Thus, it is fair to ask how much sympathy Mr. Wilder has really exhibited over the years for the victims of rape.

The Miami Herald

Miami, Florida, October 15, 1989

NOW THAT the din has receded from the special session on abortion, Florida lawmakers must look forward to next spring's regular session. Gov. Bob Martinez cannot be depended upon to lead responsibly on this issue, so the Legislature must be ready.

The anti-abortion lobbyists will be back, trying to amend restrictions onto any available bill in order to force the confrontations and polarization that they believe further their cause. Such skirmishes are a normal part of the legislative process.

The defenders of choice need only stand firm and refuse to allow the Legislature's regular work to be derailed. Anti-abortion lawmakers themselves have a key role; they must decide to take a fair shot on the issue, win or lose, and then get on with the rest of the state's business. Pro-choice legislators have done just that for years.

Further, the peripheral issues of child welfare, abortion-clinic safety, and adoption processes should be addressed. They do not belong in a debate on choice itself. They do belong on the state's broader agenda.

The issue of clinic regulation cannot be trusted to those who brand abortion patients as murderers and board-certified gynecologists as contract killers. Those who

frame the issue in those terms sacrifice any credibility on the safety issue. Rather, it is the leadership in the choice movement, and in the clinic industry, that must lead in assuring the safety of patients who may be young, frightened, or uninformed.

Adoption likewise deserves attention, though not in tandem with the right to choice. Private adoptions frequently are akin to baby-selling. Agency procedures may be lengthy, cumbersome, and highly restrictive. Efforts to place older or handicapped children often seem haphazard. Florida probably could do better.

Another neglected issue is pregnancy prevention. Youth programs can enhance the self-image of at-risk adolescents and thus delay early sexual experience. Unmarried fathers can be forced to take responsibility for their sexual adventuring. Broad dissemination of birth-control information can prevent conception among the sexually active. Anyone who sincerely wishes to curtail abortion should be eager to help prevent unwanted pregnancies.

Florida stands now as the national leader in the resurgent movement for choice and privacy. Now it should take the lead as well in meeting the associated human needs.

Miami, Florida, October 13, 1989

TALLAHASSEE held the national-news spotlight yesterday, and the Legislature did the state proud. Forced on Tuesday into a special session on abortion, members in one of the world's most open legislatures showed their mettle.

Systematically, in the normal process by which proposals pass or fail in Florida lawmaking, the Legislature batted down Gov. Bob Martinez's doctrinaire efforts to restrict the abortion rights of Florida women. It adjourned yesterday afternoon with the memorable achievement of having passed no new laws.

If the call had been broader, the session might at least have enacted tighter safety rules for licensed abortion clinics. However, anything passed under the rubric of this anti-abortion session rightly would have drawn court scrutiny as an effort to harass abortionists rather than to protect patients.

That issue can and should be treated in next spring's regular session, after state health authorities, pro-choice legislators, and responsible abortion clinics have an opportunity to review present law and practice. Likewise, a proposal to establish a state adoption center belongs in a later ex-

amination of child-welfare issues, not in an abortion session.

For now, congratulations and thanks are due Senate President Bob Crawford of Winter Haven, House Speaker Tom Gustafson of Fort Lauderdale, and their respective leadership teams. Highly emotional bills were introduced. They would have banned the use of public financing and facilities for abortion, required costly viability testing after 20 weeks of pregnancy, imposed a week-long waiting period and mandatory counseling on abortion patients, created an adoption center, and expanded regulation of abortion clinics.

The leadership resisted the temptation to adjourn without hearing the issues. Instead, it referred all 10 bills to the appropriate committees, where they died by lopsided votes in public hearings. It rightly refused to distort its own procedures by acceding to anti-abortionists' demands that every bill go to the floor for a vote in spite of the committee decisions.

No thanks to Governor Martinez, Florida now leads the national movement to bar government from intruding into individuals' personal lives. Floridians can be proud.

The Boston Globe
Boston, Massachusetts, October 18, 1989

Two decisions made by President Bush yesterday illustrate his myopic view of the nation's health concerns. He seems preoccupied with the politics of abortion, while the public anguishes over the larger issues of access to medical care and its funding – issues that apply not only to abortion but to the gamut of health problems besetting the nation.

Bush chose to satisfy antiabortion factions on two fronts. He will veto Congress's expansion of Medicaid to pay for abortions sought by poor women made pregnant through rape or incest. And he has selected a nominee who opposes abortion as his candidate for surgeon general.

Congress's concession on Medicaid abortion funding amounted to a pittance. In 1979, the last year incest and rape were included under such funding, 72 women were helped. However, the expansion was seen as a politically symbolic gain for abortion rights because it eased a provision that limited Medicaid payments for abortions to cases in which a mother's life was at stake.

Bush mulled over a vacuous compromise that would have retained payment for abortions in rape and incest pregnancies if the assaults were reported within 48 hours. His veto in behalf of one Republican faction is certain to alienate others. Sen. Robert Packwood (R-Ore.) predicts it will hurt Bush, the party and GOP candidates.

To placate women, Bush selectively sought a woman to nominate for surgeon general and has picked Dr. Antonia Novello, a specialist in childhood kidney disease. She would be not only the first woman to serve in that post, but also the first Puerto Rican – a pleasing as well as politically convenient choice since Puerto Rican-American voters traditionally oppose abortion.

Novello's choice did not turn on her impressive credentials. To be nominated for surgeon general, says Dr. Burton Lee, Bush's personal physician, candidates had to pass the president's litmus test for the job – opposing abortion. That test is a shabby yardstick for the health leadership that the job requires.

The Honolulu Advertiser
Honolulu, Hawaii, October 18, 1989

So much for George Bush's "kinder, gentler America." The president says he will veto a bill allowing Medicare to finance abortions for poor women pregnant due to rape or incest. It does not affect victims who can afford private abortions.

President Bush has been accused of excess caution, even timidity, for inaction on Panama. So now he has decided to stand tall on the bodies of women who have been horribly victimized once already.

This from a man who — at first blush, during the presidential debates — said he would have to think over what punishment would be proper for women who had abortions, should they become illegal. That was before his handlers soft-pedaled his views.

This might be called one of Bush's thousand points of *spite*. It seems to be a sop to anti-abortion forces who suffered a major setback last week when the Florida legislature rejected measures to restrict abortion.

The House of Representatives passed the Medicare measure 216 to 160, not enough to override the president's veto. Although not a major change in the House's attitude on abortion, it did reverse an eight-year stand against federal funding which is now restricted to situations that endanger a woman's life.

The president's veto is a reminder that, despite the outcome in Florida (and the unexpected House vote), the battle over abortion is far from ended. The next skirmish will be later this month in Pennsylvania, where the legislature has long been adamantly anti-abortion.

And it will likely be an issue in Bush's choice to replace C. Everett Koop as U.S. surgeon general if views on abortion are used as a "litmus test" for the acceptability of the nominee.

Koop was personally opposed to abortion, but he was a principled scientist who never allowed his office to be politically misused.

The Charlotte Observer
Charlotte, North Carolina, October 23, 1989

Refusing to be cowed by the threat of a presidential veto, Congress last week voted for a significant liberalization in restrictive rules that have virtually ended federally financed abortions for poor women. If Congress prevails — as it should — federal money could be used not only when the pregnancy endangers the life of the woman, but in cases of rape or incest.

Congress was understandably unimpressed with the president's arguments. "That such a child may have been conceived through an unconscionable act of violence makes this question difficult and indeed agonizing," Mr. Bush wrote. "It does not, however, alter the basic fact that federal funding is being sought that would compound a violent act with the taking of an unborn life."

That high moral language rings false, for two reasons. First, it came only after days of plainly political dancing in which the president sought a compromise that would not outrage his supporters in the anti-abortion movement. His advisers frankly said that his objections to the bill were practical, rather than ideological or moral.

Second, though his language would suggest otherwise, the president's position is that he does *not* oppose abortion itself in cases of rape or incest. What he opposes is the use of federal funds. So why does he say such federal funding of such abortions "would compound a violent act"?

He's got the morality backwards. What compounds the violent act is forcing the woman involved, already raped or victimized by incest, to then bear the rapist's child — that is, if she is poor. The president's utter deafness is appalling.

Government is not obliged to finance everything that is allowed, of course. The anti-abortion forces are not the only ones who deeply oppose use of their tax dollars for actions they deem immoral. Witness the persistent opposition to government expenditures for such deadly instruments as nuclear weapons and the planes and missiles that would deliver them in event of war. But taxation presumes society's right to claim funds from its citizens for uses decided by the government, and not necessarily approved by every individual paying the tax.

This case doesn't involve incidental matters. It involves women already at the bottom of the social and economic ladder who are dependent on federal assistance for basic medical care and services. At the moment they most need to have that door open, the president and his allies insist that it be closed. If the president prevails, the rapist's violent act will indeed be compounded for thousands of poor women.

THE SACRAMENTO BEE
Sacramento, California, October 24, 1989

Surely President Bush could have found a better peg on which to hang his hopes for being seen as tough and decisive — the budget, Panama, education, Eastern Europe. But no: On all those issues, Bush has ducked, feinted and wavered like a parody of himself. Instead, it's on the question of paying for the abortions of impoverished victims of rape or incest that he's decided to stand firm and say nay. What a mockery.

How Bush arrived at this peculiarly heartless position demonstrates something less than intellectual integrity. From an abortion moderate, he turned himself into a hardliner for the duration of the Reagan administration, then slipped back into a kindler and gentler mode during his 1988 election campaign, by the end of which he had pronounced himself once again opposed to outlawing abortion in cases of rape and incest. But Saturday's veto of a bill to fund abortions for indigent women so victimized effectively denies them what his "moderation" would allow the affluent. And somehow Bush expects the nation to see this position as principled.

It's not. It isn't even expedient. A majority of the public, since the Supreme Court's abortion decision last summer, has shown an unmistakable preference for leaving abortion decisions to the woman involved. Congress, in hesitant response, voted recently to allow the poor that same choice, although only in the most heartbreaking cases. Republican politicians reportedly begged the president to let this one slide, for reasons of politics if not compassion. But Bush's political vision seemed to extend no further than his rightmost flank — and even there, ironically, his efforts were mostly seen as a demonstration not of fortitude but rather of appeasement.

There have been closer calls in federal policy-making, as, for instance, when two expert panels recommended funding what looks like an extraordinarily promising line of medical research involving the transplant of fetal cells to treat Parkinson's disease. But Bush showed no appreciation of the moral complexities of that issue either: He simply banned all funding for research using fetuses. And when the call wasn't even close — when the United Nations Fund for Population Activities turned somersaults to accommodate Washington's strictures against using U.S. funds for abortions in China — there shouldn't have been any problem about restoring a paltry $15 million for that agency. But again, the president's determination to show off his single-subject intransigence led him to threaten still another veto.

The world is full of difficult moral decisions and complicated political considerations. Bush is stymied by them on any number of fronts. But not on abortion. There, he is at pains to prove that he knows his mind — and it is without nuance. Why he thinks that should enhance his public image is puzzling indeed.

THE 🌊 SUN
Baltimore, Maryland, October 26, 1989

It was to be expected that the House of Representatives would fail yesterday to override President Bush's veto of the act liberalizing federal payments for some abortions. There was a solid majority in favor of the act, but it takes a two-thirds vote to override a veto.

More disturbing was the vote the day before in Harrisburg, Pa. The state House of Representatives voted lopsidedly to restrict abortions in several ways, including ways the Supreme Court has ruled unconstitutional in other states in the past. Clearly the Pennsylvania legislators have accepted the invitation in the Supreme Court's July decision (*Webster vs. Reproductive Health Services*) to begin re-limiting abortions.

What the Supreme Court did with *Webster* was to prompt a crazy-quilt of state regulations of this most private and intimate decision. It makes no sense for a nation like ours to forbid abortions except under varying sets of circumstances in various states. Yet that is exactly what will happen.

These regulations won't necessarily reflect the will of the people, either. Consider the fact that in conservative Florida a legislative attempt to enact new post-*Webster* restrictions on abortion failed, but in moderate Pennsylvania such restrictions passed overwhelmingly. (The state Senate is expected to pass the bill next month, and the governor says he'll sign it.) Why? Because the pro-abortion rights groups were better organized in Florida and the anti-abortion rights groups were better organized in Pennsylvania.

That sort of determinative politicking may be acceptable when it comes to setting insurance rates or speed limits — but do Americans really want lobbyists, fund raisers, public relations firms and campaign advisers determining who can have an abortion and under what circumstances? We don't think so.

Even some advocates of abortion rights may not strenuously object to the specific restrictions in the Pennsylvania bill, but those restrictions grow out of a belief that the state can pass *any* regulations it wants — even proscribe abortion. The bill's supporters believe it is written in a way that the Supreme Court could use it to overturn *Roe vs. Wade*, the 1973 decision that said the constitutional right to privacy includes the right to an abortion in most circumstances. Some justices are eager to overturn *Roe*. They are being urged to by the Bush administration's solicitor general. Surely the spectacle of legislatures going off in all directions in what one Pennsylvania representative calls "the post-*Webster* world" will give the court pause. On such an important issue, a woman's rights should not depend on whether she lives in one state or the state next door or a state a thousand miles away.

THE DENVER POST
Denver, Colorado, October 26, 1989

PRESIDENT George Bush won a costly victory yesterday when the House voted 231-191 to override his veto of Medicaid funding to help victims of rape and incest get abortions. Bush "won" because the pro-choice majority was 51 votes short of the two-thirds margin necessary to overturn the veto. But his "victory" may be a very expensive one, politically.

Republican Rep. Bill Green of New York, who voted to override the veto, said bluntly "President Bush may well have stumbled on the one issue that could cost him re-election."

It may indeed. The once-quiescent pro-choice majority has been galvanized since the U.S. Supreme Court's *Webster* decision threatened abortion rights. Millions of American women decided that if the court wouldn't protect their rights, they would do it themselves. Since that decision in July, they've been putting mounting heat on Congress and state legislatures to recognize their freedom of choice.

That message wasn't lost on Colorado Democrats Pat Schroeder, Ben Nighthorse Campbell and David Skaggs, who voted to override the veto. Republicans Joel Hefley and Dan Schaefer, in contrast, voted to withhold help from victims of rape and incest.

Republican Hank Brown, who is leaving his House seat to run for the U.S. Senate, showed he really means what he says about limiting the role of government in citizens' private lives by voting to override Bush's veto.

Colorado's growing pro-choice majority won't forget this vote when Schaefer and Hefley come up for re-election in 1990. For his part, Bush must be wondering how much the Faustian bargain he cut with anti-abortion militants to win the presidential nomination will cost him in 1992.

Before becoming vice president, Bush had a pro-choice record. But he sold out those views to court anti-abortion votes in quest of his own nomination. Now he finds himself on the wrong side of a strong and growing tide of public opinion.

By abandoning principle in quest of expediency, Bush draped himself in extremist colors that are proving to be neither principled nor expedient.

HHS Funds Vetoed over Abortion 'Gag Rule'

President George Bush November 19, 1991 vetoed a $205 billion fiscal 1992 appropriations bill for the Departments of Human Services, Labor and Education. An attempt to override the veto the same day failed in the House by a vote of 276 to 156 or 12 short of what was needed.

Bush cited as his reason for vetoing the measure an amendment that would have nullified an administration rule banning doctors and other workers at federally funded clinics from giving advice to their patients on abortion. The regulation, dubbed by opponents the "gag rule," had been upheld by the Supreme Court in June 1990.

The House vote was a victory for the Bush administration and a setback for Democrats in Congress, who had launched an intense lobbying campaign in support of an override.

Democratic leaders had expressed optimism that in the vote on the appropriations bill they would be able to halt Bush's unbroken string of 23 successful vetoes. In addition to the gag-rule provision, the measure contained funding for a variety of popular programs, and gag-rule opponents had had some success in casting the issue as one of free speech rather than of abortion. Even many abortion opponents were sympathetic to the argument that the rule interfered with doctor-patient relationships.

In his veto message, Bush denied that the regulation was a "gag rule" and said doctors would still be able to inform patients fully about their condition.

The Des Moines Register
Des Moines, Iowa, November 8, 1991

Some cynical final-hour moves by President Bush may have succeeded in lowering the vote count on a congressional bill that would forestall imposition of the reckless abortion "gag rule." Although the appropriations bill, which imposes a one-year ban against using federal funds to enforce the rule, passed both houses, the House vote fell short of the two-thirds majority that would be needed to overturn an almost certain Bush veto.

Despite Bush's recent effort to put the best face on them, the regulations remain as deplorable as ever. Promulgated in 1988 and upheld by the Supreme Court last May, they effectively muzzle doctors at all federally funded family planning clinics from even discussing abortion with patients. The idea so flies in the face of the privileged doctor-patient relationship, and of the First Amendment, that even some abortion opponents in Congress have come out against the measure. So has the American Medical Association.

Bush's memo clarifying his position was distributed this week in an obvious attempt to avoid what could be an embarrassing first-time veto override. But far from reformulating the rules, the memo seems to reinterpret them in a way that is at odds with what they say.

A physician can, according to the memo, inform a pregnant woman about "her condition." If the woman has a medical problem, says the memo, she may be referred for medical care even if it results in termination of the pregnancy. And although all pregnant women seen in Title X clinics must be referred to prenatal care providers, Bush's interpretation says it is all right if those providers also perform abortions as a secondary function.

The fact is that prenatal care providers don't generally perform abortions — abortion clinics do. And under the regulations, the only time a physician can refer a woman for an abortion is in the case of an imminent medical emergency — not if a pregnancy is medically inadvisable.

The memo probably succeeded in confusing just enough representatives to keep the House vote under a two-thirds majority. The issue has been further clouded by a Bush bid to Republicans to oppose the appropriations bill for budgetary reasons.

Some gag rule opponents still are hopeful they can muster enough votes for a veto override. But if that doesn't happen, and if the stay that has prevented enforcement of this insidious measure finally is lifted, the losers will be many: freedom of choice, freedom of speech, the doctor-patient relationship, and about four million low-income women who rely on Title X clinics for unbiased medical advice.

The Providence Journal
Providence, Rhode Island, September 16, 1991

We applaud the Senate's 78-22 vote last week to revoke a ban on abortion counseling in federally financed clinics, and to end a prohibition on government payments for abortions on women who are victims of rape or incest. President Bush has promised to veto these provisions, already passed by the House. We hope he doesn't; but if he does, Congress should override him.

The counseling ban improperly extends federal controls into what should be a confidential medical advisory process, and violates principles of free speech in the process. It also unfairly penalizes poor people. As for the incest and rape provisions, they have simply gone too far in limiting the choices of poor women whose pregnancy is the result of their victimization. In short, these restrictions are cruel and unfair.

When the Supreme Court upheld the counseling ban as constitutional last May, Congress began writing legislation to rescind it. The new measure, crafted by Senator Chafee, carefully specifies that women with unwanted pregnancies who go to a federally financed clinic are to receive "non-directive" counseling on their choices in their situation. Nobody would be coerced into having an abortion, but at least women would receive balanced medical advice on this agonizing personal question. That strikes us as the just and humane approach.

But surprisingly, the senators also approved an amendment to the same bill — were they looking? — that shifts money for a $10.1 million government survey on adult sexual practices to a program that counsels woman youngsters to avoid premarital sex.

These priorities are upside down: The fact is that the problem of sexually transmitted diseases — especially AIDS — makes additional information about sexual practices more useful, indeed more necessary, than ever. And abortion foes should note that such a study might permit advances in the campaign against premarital pregnancies, and so reduce the incidence of abortion, legal and illegal, in the process.

This shift, engineered by Sen. Jesse Helms, could be seen as an admirable reminder about the dangers of promiscuous adolescent sexuality, especially in the age of AIDS. But its distance from contemporary reality is considerable. The legislation containing it now must go to a House-Senate conference committee which, we trust, will return the money to the place where it might do the most good.

Richmond Times-Dispatch
Richmond, Virginia, November 22, 1991

The House's failure to override President Bush's veto of legislation that would have allowed workers at federally funded family-planning clinics to dispense advise about abortion has set off the expected howls from the abortion industry. But the persons whose lives will be spared by Mr. Bush's veto someday might want to thank Mr. Bush.

Under Title X of the Public Health Service Act of 1970, the federal government provides grants to clinics which provide "family-planning" services to the poor. The key issue in the legislation vetoed by the president is what constitutes "family planning." The abortion industry, which like some artists claims the existence of a constitutional right to subsidies, would like that definition to include the killing of future family members.

Inasmuch as the Bush administration believes that the government has an interest in promoting childbirth over abortion, the administration does not place abortion under the heading of family planning. The administration supports regulations that restrict abortion counseling at family-planning clinics. Last May the Supreme Court agreed that the executive branch may choose to "fund one activity to the exclusion of another."

Contrary to the contentions of the abortion industry, parrotted by a supportive media, the regulations do not constitute a "gag rule." In a memo to the assistant secretary of health obtained by the Times-Dispatch, Health and Human Services Secretary Louis Sullivan outlines the president's four basic guidelines to implementation of the Title X regulations. The regulations are to permit a woman to receive "complete medical information about her condition from a physician." Furthermore, he says, "Title X projects are to provide necessary referrals to appropriate health-care facilities when medically indicated." If a pregnant woman is found "to have a medical problem, she should be referred for complete medical care, *even* if the ultimate result may be the termination of her pregnancy" (emphasis in the original).

But Dr. Sullivan draws an important distinction among health-care providers: "Referrals may be made by Title X programs to full-service health-care providers that perform abortions, but not to providers whose principal activity is providing abortion services."

This is a reasonable restriction. Because abortion clinics make their money by killing fetuses, they are much more likely than full-service health-care providers to recommend abortion. A pregnant woman referred to a full-service facility is more likely to be told all of the options available to her.

The sum of Mr. Bush's veto and Dr. Sullivan's memo is this: Federally subsidized family-planning clinics may provide information about abortion, but the counseling must be provided by a licensed doctor. According to Americans United for Life, this restriction strikes directly at the 80 percent of direct abortion referrals made by clinic workers who are not doctors. Those clinics which cannot live with such a mild restriction on the use of taxpayer funds have an option: forgo federal funding.

Abortion industry spokesmen are right about one thing: Mr. Bush's veto and Dr. Sullivan's memo probably will combine to reduce the number of fetuses killed by saline solution, dismemberment and suction, the three most popular abortion methods.

Those members of the House who voted to sustain Mr. Bush's veto cast a vote for life. Among Virginia's delegation, we are sad to say, only three, all Republicans, did so: Reps. Thomas Bliley, Herbert Bateman and Frank Wolf. Newly elected Rep. George Allen voted to override, consistent with his misguided belief, stated during the campaign, that the regulations constitute a "gag rule."

The primary federal interest in "family planning" for the poor is to encourage citizens to behave responsibly by abstaining from sexual intercourse outside of marriage and to prevent unwanted pregnancies. Once a woman has gotten pregnant, it obviously is a bit late for "family planning." The family is on its way.

The Oregonian
Portland, Oregon, November 4, 1991

Congress has a chance in the coming weeks to lift the Supreme Court-approved gag order on federally funded family-planning clinics. It should do so.

The gag order represents an unwarranted government intrusion into the doctor-patient relationship and a backdoor attempt to interfere with a woman's right to choose whether to have an abortion.

In a 5-4 decision last May, the court upheld an administrative directive first put forth by President Reagan and continued by President Bush that forbade doctors in federal clinics from mentioning abortion as one of the medical options open to pregnant women. Additionally, clinics could not make abortion referrals. The federally funded clinics do not perform abortions.

The gag rule has never been enforced because of the constitutional challenge. Fortunately, it isn't likely to be anytime soon because the Senate and House have agreed to a Health and Human Services spending bill that provides no money for enforcement of the gag order for at least a year.

But the suspension of enforcement money is only a temporary solution. The House and Senate should add language to Title X of the Family Planning Act of 1970, which comes up for reauthorization this fall, to prohibit this regulation. Pregnant women should be able to assume that they are receiving complete medical advice from their doctors, whether they are treated in a federal clinic or a private doctor's office.

Bush has pledged to veto any effort to overturn the gag order. But congressional support is high and may be veto-proof, predicts Oregon Rep. Mike Kopetski, because many members of Congress acknowledge that this attack on abortion infringes on the sanctity of the doctor-patient relationship and intrudes on a doctor's professional speech.

Those are compelling reasons to lift the gag order. And for those same reasons, senators and representatives should resist any attempt to add a parental-consent clause or other restrictions on the information that doctors can provide their patients.

Although it is the subject of much debate, abortion remains a medically safe choice that is legally open to pregnant women. Doctors should not have to risk violating a federal law simply because they mention the word to their patients.

MILWAUKEE SENTINEL
Milwaukee, Wisconsin, November 12, 1991

As we said a month ago, the battle over parental consent for abortions for women under 18 would soon be joined in the Legislature.

As of last Tuesday, it was.

When the Assembly approved consent legislation more to the liking of anti-abortion groups, the stage was set for a critical vote in the Senate. It is a vote that could determine whether the most vulnerable among us — the 30% of all minors who have special needs — also shall have access to reproductive rights granted by the US Supreme Court.

In truth, the consent legislation passed by the Assembly is little more than a stalking horse for anti-abortion forces.

The bill passed by the Assembly, rather than establishing workable options to parental consent or judicial bypass, simply makes it harder for the truly troubled teen to obtain an abortion.

Furthermore, it ignores the reality that there will be cases where direct communication with parents will lead to the irreparable destruction of family relationships.

What the Assembly passed was a measure requiring girls under 18 to get consent before obtaining an abortion by persuading a parent, adult relative who had been raising the teen or a judge to approve.

The version favored by pro-choice factions and recommended by an Assembly committee was more workable. It provided a broader range of options to parental or judicial consent, including a professional counselor or member of the clergy, in addition to an adult relative who had not necessarily been involved raising the child.

That version recognizes that while 70% of minors experience little trouble in obtaining consent, another 30% have very special needs that, if ignored, could lead to tragically abusive situations within the family.

The example of pregnancy through rape or incest immediately comes to mind.

By rejecting blanket exemptions from consent in such cases, the Assembly would set up the machinery that could lead to abusive situations for the minor already living in an abusive environment.

By requiring, for example, signed statements and police reports of such incidents, the teen sets herself up for more abuse, especially in cases of incest. In many cases, the teens have already been abused and have never reported it. What are we asking them to do? Literally beg for more?

The Assembly bill is an anti-abortion bill with potentially dire consequences for the minor. It is not a consent bill. It must be amended by the Senate.

Los Angeles Times
Los Angeles, California, October 18, 1991

After forcefully vowing to uphold repugnant and counterproductive regulations that would bar even the mention of the abortion option to poor pregnant patients in federally funded clinics, there are signs that President Bush has finally begun to see the folly of his position.

The so-called "gag rule" is embodied in Reagan-era regulations that prohibit any discussion of abortion—even when patients specifically ask for such information or for referrals to a physician who might perform one. These absurd regulations were suspended while legal challenges proceeded. But last term the U.S. Supreme Court upheld their constitutionality, clearing the way for implementation. The court, in effect, sanctioned one standard of medical care for poor women—one that forces physicians to withhold medical information—and another for middle- and upper-income women.

The court's decision was so ethically unpalatable that it immediately galvanized the medical profession, free-speech advocates, a majority of the public and Republicans as well as Democrats in Congress. Legislation preventing implementation of the counseling ban swiftly passed both houses over the summer by veto-proof margins. These bills are now in conference committee.

Throughout the summer the President was steadfast in his determination to enforce this indefensible rule at all costs. In recent weeks, however, Bush has dispatched some of his domestic advisers to sit down with sponsors of the bills in an effort to avert a legislative showdown. The outcome of these negotiations is unclear; they could result in the Administration's withdrawal of the gag-rule regulations or in promulgation of new, more permissive ones. Regardless of the decision, any pragmatism from the Administration on this issue would be wise and welcome.

The Washington Times
Washington, D.C., November 11, 1991

Last week the president and Congress hammered out an accord on federally funded abortion: Government family-planning clinics will be allowed to refer women to abortionists, but only licensed doctors can do the actual referring.

The ostensible purpose of the deal was to end the Great Gag Rule Standoff. In 1988, President Reagan issued regulations denying federal funds to "family-planning" clinics that promoted or performed abortions. These regulations were in keeping with a much-abused 1970 law known as Title X that first created a program for federal family-planning grants. But since the Reagan rules were published they have been vehemently challenged in the courts and in Congress by the abortion-rights movement.

The abortion absolutists argued: 1) that the taxpayers must subsidize abortions for poor women because abortion is a "right"; 2) that the federal government violates the First Amendment right to free speech if it refuses to fund clinics that promote abortion; and 3) that the federal government violates the sanctity of the "doctor-patient relationship" if it refuses to subsidize doctors who discuss abortion with their patients.

In June, the Supreme Court properly concluded that these arguments were wrong. The government, it said, could constitutionally conclude that the interests of the state favored childbirth over abortion and could promulgate policies to that effect. The court thus dropped a public policy question of profound moral consequence back in the laps of the nation's elected policymakers: Should government use the money of taxpayers, many of whom believe that abortion is nothing less than the taking of a human life, to subsidize groups that promote abortion?

But President Bush and many members of Congress did not care to look at the issue in such stark terms. They looked at the so-called gag rule in much the same way they would look at a new tax package or an agreement on the defense budget. The political game was engaged, a compromise was struck.

Mr. Bush will now veto a bill from Congress that would have completely overturned the Reagan rules. That supposedly will make him look good with pro-life voters. Congress will not override the veto. But in trying, both pro-abortion and pro-life congressmen will presumably look good to their respective constituencies. The president has already sent a memo to Dr. Louis Sullivan, secretary of Health and Human Services, stating, "We must ensure the confidentiality of the doctor/patient relationship will be preserved and that the operation of the Title X family planning program is compatible with free speech and the highest standards of medical care." Wishy-washy politicians will point to this when they appeal to wishy-washy voters.

The worst abusers of Title X grants will not abide by even this "compromise" and will surrender their grants. Other grantees will leave the abortion pitching to in-house doctors. On the margin, there will be fewer abortions than there would have been had abortion-rights activists achieved an absolute victory.

The compromise is better than an overridden veto. But it speaks to the unwillingness of national leaders to take many political risks in opposition to abortion.

THE SPOKESMAN-REVIEW
Spokane, Washington, October 6, 1991

President Bush's veto pen is loaded with indelible ink, and he's waiting for Congress to test his anti-abortion resolve.

They will.

Sometime within the next couple of weeks, the House and Senate are expected to reach agreement on a 1992 appropriation bill for the departments of Labor and Health and Human Services and send it to the president.

A sliver of the $204 billion involved would go to family-planning clinics which, under existing federal rules that the Supreme Court affirmed on May 23, may not help a woman obtain an abortion. Not only are such clinics forbidden to perform abortions or even refer clients for abortions, they may not so much as mention that abortion is an option.

The House and Senate differ on some details of the appropriation package, but on one thing they see eye to eye. Both versions would end the repugnant gag rule that Bush's secretary of Health and Human Services, Louis Sullivan, slapped on federally funded family-planning clinics in 1988.

The question on Capitol Hill is whether there's enough support in Congress to override a veto that Bush has threatened for any legislation lending federal support to abortion.

Bush and Sullivan have lined up with the rigidly anti-abortion forces that would like to see the procedure outlawed again. They have a number of allies in Congress. They also represent, as poll after poll discloses, the minority view in the nation. Most people continue to favor a woman's right to make her own reproductive decisions.

That's why the focal point of this issue, for the next couple of weeks or so, isn't those who are settled in their ideology but those who are torn between personal conviction and political loyalty.

Primarily, that means pro-choice Republicans in Congress who may support overturning Sullivan's gag rule but will be pressured by the White House to back down when Bush's veto is on the line.

In the Bush White House the veto pen is a formidable political weapon. Not once in 22 opportunities has Congress overridden the president. This is a case where an exception should be made, but that will depend on congressional Republicans having sound reasons to part company with their president.

Hear are some to consider:

■ Independence. Federal lawmakers who ideologically oppose abortion and vote that way consistently are one thing. Those who have pro-choice beliefs but yield to White House arm-twisting when it really matters appear to be wishy-washy.

■ Fairness. Federally funded family planning clinics serve mainly the disadvantaged. Such a clientele is in the greatest need of solid information on which to base difficult, critical decisions.

■ Separation of powers. To uphold Sullivan's gag rule, the Supreme Court had to reject an argument that a counseling ban violated congressional intent in the family-planning law. The votes taken this year show where congressional intent really lies, but that will be immaterial if a presidential veto is sustained.

■ Freedom of speech. The ban on abortion counseling violates a First Amendment prohibition against stifling a specific form of expression, based on philosophy.

Lawmakers of both parties are sent to Washington to represent their constituents. If they merely let duty guide them, the family-planning clinics' gags will be removed.

CONCORD ⊕ MONITOR

Concord, New Hampshire, November 21, 1991

President Bush has made a moral and political misjudgment in imposing a gag rule on family planning clinics.

In vetoing a bill to allow staff members at federally financed clinics to discuss abortion, Bush ignored the prevailing view of the American public and dashed the hopes of moderates to find some accommodation for pro-choice views within the Republican Party. The president showed a willingness to go to nearly any length to please his party's extremists, even at the expense of free speech and the patient-doctor privilege.

All this from a man who gave signs of being a pro-choice moderate until his selection as vice president in 1980.

The gag order is an act of discrimination that will deny poor women the access to the same vital health care information available to women who can afford non-subsidized care. It is a violation of the trust between a health care provider and patient. The government has no business censuring the medical advice a doctor, social worker or nurse gives. To do so makes a mockery of free speech protected under the Bill of Rights.

The veto also indicates that Bush will continue to apply the same position with regard to foreign policy. Instead of becoming a leader in promoting population control, Bush, like President Reagan before him, has cut U.S. support for Third World non-governmental birth control programs that include abortion counseling.

Congress fell 12 votes shy of overriding the president's veto for the first time in two dozen tries. Both of New

Hampshire's congressmen, Dick Swett and Bill Zeliff, sided with the majority and were true to their campaign promise to vote pro-choice. As one of only 53 Republicans to buck the president, Zeliff didn't buckle under pro-life pressure.

Bush could have avoided a confrontation with Congress on this issue. The White House issued the gag order in 1988, under President Reagan. It has never been enforced, however, because of a court challenge that ended this year when the Supreme Court (shame on David Souter, a former Concord Hospital trustee) decided that the prohibition on discussing abortion did not violate the First Amendment.

Several conservative senators, Alan Simpson of Wyoming among them, had pleaded with Bush to compromise and avoid a veto, and indeed an agreement was close. Then Chief of Staff John Sununu intruded in the process and took a hard line. Negotiations fell apart. One can only presume Sununu became involved with the president's consent.

Congress's failure to override the veto shows that Bush has a virtual lock on vetoes, but this one could be costly. Pro-choice groups have been pushing to get the Supreme Court to decide next spring on a Pennsylvania case that promises to provide the long-anticipated definitive challenge to Roe vs. Wade. The Bush administration is in no hurry to get that case decided before the November 1992 election.

With his veto, Bush handed Democrats another issue to use against him a year from now.

THE TENNESSEAN

Nashville, Tennessee, October 22, 1991

NO gag on abortion counseling in federally funded family planning clinics is the best solution. A compromise may have to do.

The Bush White House finally has been made to deal on the silly gag order rule, requiring doctors to keep their mouths shut on abortion when advising pregnant women in federally funded clinics. The rule, promulgated under the Reagan administration and upheld this summer by the U.S. Supreme Court, was anti-intellectual rubbish designed solely to court rabble-rousing anti-abortion interests. It had absolutely no basis in medical practice and little support beyond anti-abortion groups. And the rule's victims were the poorest and least educated who seek assistance at the federally funded clinics.

Most Americans saw the rule for what it was — a gag on good sense, not a deterrent to abortion. It wasn't Congress or pro-abortion supporters who made the Bush administration look foolish on this position; it was the President's own friends in the medical community.

So unpopular is the rule that Congress

reportedly has a veto-proof majority to pass a bill overturning the gag order. That forced the administration to the bargaining table. Bush didn't want to ruin his record on vetos, plus he didn't want any debate on what has become a national embarrassment — a government telling doctors how to practice medicine.

In the compromise, doctors still couldn't favor abortion, except when the pregnancy endangered life. But it would permit doctors in counseling patients to at least mention abortion as one option for pregnant women.

There ought to be no restrictions on what doctors are allowed to discuss, but if the issue is now down to merely keeping a doctor from favoring abortion as an option, that's pretty mild.

A veto override may have served only to let the public forget which administration implemented the rule and which administration defended it. This way, there's enough of a remnant of the rule left to remind folks how dangerous the Bush administration is when it comes to medical matters, but fortunately, no one has to get hurt. ■

THE SACRAMENTO BEE

Sacramento, California, October 21, 1991

As expected, President Bush vetoed the appropriation bill that would have allowed free discussion of all medical options, including abortion, for pregnant women in federally funded clinics. Although the House voted by a large margin to override the veto — the vote was 276 to 156 — it fell 12 votes short of the two-thirds needed. Of the 29 women in the House, 27 voted to override. If there had been 50 women in the House, there would be no gag rule.

The gag rule was never intended by Congress and these votes leave no doubt that it's not what Congress intends now. Despite all that, the president will keep the gag rule, which the administration conjured out of prior law and which he says is not a gag rule. He also says that the restriction on providing full information to women in clinics — many of whom have no access to other medical advice — is not a violation of free speech or a requirement that practitioners violate their professional ethics and the trust of their patients.

That's baloney. Although the president said that he might revise the rule to let physicians talk about abortion — so far no revision has been drafted — most of the counselors in federally funded clinics are nurses and physician assistants. That Bush would only require midlevel practitioners to violate their ethical obligations hardly makes the rule acceptable; it only makes it more insulting.

The question now is how to proceed. The bill that eliminates the gag rule also contains major appropriations for the Departments of Health and Human Services, Education and Labor. If it's not passed and signed, funding for those departments will continue at the previous year's levels. That will put pressure on a lot of members of Congress to quietly vote for a bill without the prohibition on the gag rule.

But in a situation where the administration is infringing on the right to provide full medical advice, violating the plain intent of Congress, and violating the constitutional rights of both providers and patients, it's George Bush who bears the responsibility. That fact ought to be made clear to the country by whatever means possible. At a time when the nation is struggling to deal with hundreds of thousands of teenage births and unwed mothers, the idea that government itself should try to keep valid medical choices from women is an abomination.

The New York Times
New York City, New York, October 27, 1991

Laws, so the textbooks say, are expressions of majority will, enacted by Congress with the approval of the President. Or, in some cases, over his veto. Throw those textbooks out. The U.S. has just managed to enshrine the family planning clinic "gag rule" in national law even though Congress never dreamed of censoring doctors.

The gag rule is only the latest and most successful example of backward lawmaking — a series of usurpations, end runs and floutings of legislative authority engineered by the Reagan and Bush Administrations.

Year after year, the White House has evaded the confirmation process by making recess appointments to the Legal Services Corporation after Congress adjourned. And Reagan-Bush lawyers routinely ignored statutes and court decisions condemning their discriminatory handling of Social Security disability claims.

The Iran-contra affair was perhaps the ultimate end run. And just last week President Bush instructed his agencies to interpret the new civil rights law on the basis of a White House memo placed in the Congressional Record by the bill's *opponents*. Here's how the law ran backward in the gag rule case:

In 1988 the Health and Human Services Department, driven by anti-abortion ideologues, issued a regulation enforcing a 1970 law in a radically new way. The law said only that abortion could not be a method of family planning at federally subsidized clinics.

The regulation, however, said that doctors and health professionals at the clinics couldn't even mention abortion as an option. If a poor woman asked about abortion she was to receive the answer, technically accurate but mean and misleading, that "the project does not consider abortion an appropriate method of family planning."

This May the Supreme Court found the regulation constitutional and within the scope of the law Congress passed. Senate and House majorities profoundly disagreed and passed corrective legislation. The President vetoed the legislation and the House failed by a handful of votes to muster the two-thirds needed to override. The net result is that the Government, notwithstanding the will of Congress, is free to enforce this cruel gag order. That's undemocratic and threatens the rights of professionals and patients to exchange vital information.

Congress often sets broad policy and leaves detailed enforcement to executive agencies with the general understanding that the executive branch will honor Congressional intent. Yet both the gag rule and the Supreme Court decision upholding that rule represent a perversion of that process.

Writing for a 5-to-4 majority, Chief Justice William Rehnquist ruled that restraining professional speech in federally funded family planning clinics was simply a legitimate extension of the Government's clear right not to finance abortions. But that is not what Congress said.

Backward lawmaking thus fabricates oppressive orders and imputes the coercion to Congress. How can Congress protect itself? The Senate can be more careful about judicial nominees. And both chambers must keep trying to amass veto-proof majorities.

In the gag rule case there's one thing more that Congress can do. It can keep passing the corrective law until President Bush signs it, weary of the justified criticism from Americans who see through this illegitimate, malevolent lawmaking.

Lexington Herald-Leader
Lexington, Kentucky, November 21, 1991

There is no doubt the federal government can attach strings to the money it doles out left and right. It has always been, and ever will be, so.

But strings come in many sizes; and some of them even the federal government rightfully should shun, if the nation's Constitution is to have any meaning at all.

For instance, when the federal government hands out money for higher education, it might be expected to establish some standards for the institutions receiving that money. The most basic would be that the college or university be accredited.

But nowhere in those standards would you find the government telling a professor at a recipient school what he or she can or cannot say in the classroom. Such a blatant attempt to deny free speech would not be tolerated in this democracy.

Yet that is exactly what the federal government is doing in regard to family planning clinics. Thanks to the inability of the House of Representatives to override a presidential veto, workers in family planning clinics will be gagged.

The result, despite President Bush's false protestations to the contrary, is that millions of women in the United States will be denied full and complete information on their medical condition. By and large, these are poor women whose only access to medical care and advice during a pregnancy comes from such clinics.

Yes, we are dealing here with abortion — that most volatile and divisive of issues. Abortion is the word these clinic workers will not be allowed to speak. But, at least for the moment, abortion is still a legal medical procedure throughout this country.

Because abortion is legal, there is no constitutional justification for this gag rule. And only a dubious sort of morality can justify a public policy that deprives poor women of medical advice routinely available to their more affluent counterparts.

Aided by a wrongheaded U.S. Supreme Court decision and the blatant nonsense coming from the president's mouth, this rule tramples underfoot the most basic of individual liberties — freedom of speech. And because the speech being outlawed is medical advice, it needlessly puts millions of American women at risk.

Lincoln Journal
Lincoln, Nebraska, November 20, 1991

It wasn't so much that President Bush Tuesday afternoon once more prevailed in a veto override struggle with a Congress controlled by opposition Democrats as it was a demonstration that (1) House Speaker Thomas Foley is deficient counting votes or (2) a critical number of House members lied to Foley. Our guess is the latter.

Regardless, for the 24th consecutive time in an override confrontation, Bush triumphed. His formal objection to a bill doing away with the abortion-counseling "gag" rule instituted during the closing days of the Reagan administration in 1988 prevails.

Count the result yet another Washington victory for unconditional foes of abortion.

But count as well the result a further implacable squeeze on poor, pregnant females — those whose economic circumstances force them to seek medical advice and help from facilities in part financed by federal funds.

Not for an instant should any reliance be invested in the last-minute presidential memorandum purportedly taking the stinger out of the gag rule. That was cynically done to confuse the issue.

Bush said the directive he sent to the secretary of Health and Human Services "makes clear . . . that nothing prevents a woman from receiving complete medical information about her condition from a physician." Yes, lady, you are pregnant.

What the physican is still barred by regulations from adding is that abortion is an option which can be considered, if the female so desires and elects.

Speaker Foley hustled the override effort in an obvious belief "We have the votes." He/"we" didn't, it turned out, by a margin of just 12 votes.

The final quotation here belongs to a congresswoman from Maine and a member of President Bush's own political party, Olympia Snow: "Make no mistake about it. The failure to override will not be forgotten by the women of this country. . . . No male patient is affected by this gag rule. You are creating a situation for women only." A hostile situation, most especially for the poorest 4.5 million women in the nation..

The parochial solitary bright spot in all this is that Rep. Doug Bereuter was among those supporting the override.

The Record

Hackensack, New Jersey, November 22, 1991

NOW that the House of Representatives has failed — by 12 votes — to override President Bush's veto of the latest abortion bill, the situation regarding abortion makes less sense than ever.

Abortion in the United States remains legal, even though many believe the increasingly conservative U.S. Supreme Court may soon allow the states to ban abortion. As of now, however, women who can afford to go to private health clinics continue to obtain counseling about abortion.

But poorer women who use federally financed clinics may not receive any information about abortion at those clinics. Doctors and other trained advisers at these facilities are barred from even mentioning abortion, even if they consider it an advisable option.

Ironically, it is the poorer women, who don't get much information from newspapers and magazines, who probably know the least about abortion to begin with. Many of the people who come to the federally financed clinics are teenagers in desperate need of advice. The doctors are not able to mention abortion to them, even though they can continue to discuss abortion freely with their more affluent patients.

Is it fair to have these two categories of patients — one rich and one poor — and to treat them differently? Is this really what America is all about? Should doctors and counselors be free to provide their affluent patients with uncensored advice while being restricted by the federal government as to what they can tell poorer women? Polls show that most people in America think the answer is no, that all women should have equal access to such information and advice.

●

The Supreme Court allowed the restrictions on the federal clinics in a decision last May. While both the House and the Senate passed legislation to lift the restrictions, President Bush refused to back down on his threat to veto the bill. Supporters of free choice on abortion say they will raise the issue in the 1992 presidential campaign.

Certainly, Mr. Bush is entitled to his own opinion on abortion, but while abortion is legal in America, access to information about it should not be easily available to some women and denied to others.

The president insists that these regulations do not constitute a "gag rule" and do not hinder freedom of speech. But the fact is that a double standard exists, and that it is patently unfair.

> **A double standard exists, and it is unfair.**

Detroit Free Press

Detroit, Michigan, November 21, 1991

George Bush would be well advised not to take a lot of comfort from the fact that his veto of the abortion gag rule ban has been sustained. That fight, in which the House failed by a dozen votes to override the veto, revealed a new political fault line in the national debate over abortion rights.

A solid majority of the U.S. House, 276 members, **did** vote to override the veto. Many House members were ready not only to end the ban on abortion counseling at family planning clinics, but to confront the president to make the point. Mr. Bush had sought to undercut the veto override effort by issuing instructions saying that the regulations are not intended to keep doctors from talking with their patients about abortion. His effort kept his veto record intact, but it is clear that the abortion debate is more complex than the president seemed once to assume.

When the U.S. Supreme Court upheld the administrative ban on such counseling, the ruling touched a nerve. The ruling helped to focus the argument that many of us have tried to make over the years of the abortion debate: The issue of whether to have an abortion is too personal a choice, with too little consensus about what is the right thing to do, to be decided by anyone but a woman and her physician.

Unlike the issues of Medicaid-funded abortions, which entailed the use of tax dollars to pay for abortions, and of parental consent, which involved questions of parental authority, the gag rule controversy has helped to underscore that the issue is whether the state should impose its decision on people. The issue, in other words, is privacy.

That's what the Supreme Court said when it handed down the original Roe vs. Wade decision affirming a woman's right to choose to have an abortion. And that's why, despite the sustaining of the veto, the key issue will continue to be privacy.

THE KANSAS CITY STAR

Kansas City, Missouri, November 21, 1991

The fight for the ability and rights of poor women to obtain decent reproductive health care is not over, despite President Bush's veto of the abortion counseling legislation and the House's failure to override that veto.

The administration's "gag rule" on federally funded family planning clinics has not gone into effect. Clinics have yet to be notified as to when they have to decide either to stop taking tax money or cease providing even a whisper of information about abortion.

Legislation still is pending in Congress which would abolish the gag rule. Bills have passed both Houses. The legislation vetoed by the president was a labor and health appropriations bill which called for a one-year moratorium on putting the gag rule in effect. There still is time for Congress to pass something of a more permanent nature to continue this right.

The gag rule is a disastrous piece of bureaucratic over-reach. If it is allowed to go into effect, some clinics will close their doors. Many will lose physicians, nurses, social workers and others who cannot work in a system where they are denied the right to counsel patients on all options regarding dangerous or unwanted pregnancies. The violation of the physician-patient relationship and the clamp on free speech rights are the distinguishing hallmarks of this rule.

Those who will be hurt are the women who cannot afford to go to private physicians for reproductive health care. They will not merely be denied counseling about abortion. They will not have access to pelvic examinations, treatment of sexually transmitted diseases, cancer screening, breast exams and other lifesaving services which no longer will be available. They will not get contraception advice and supplies, and many will go on to unwanted pregnancies and abortions.

Some clinics will continue to operate but without the federal funds. This is the case with Planned Parenthood of Greater Kansas City, which earlier announced that it would forfeit the federal dollars rather than stop serving women who need it. But if federal dollars cannot be replaced with private donations, fewer clients can be served.

The repercussions from this veto and the failure to override it will be felt for a long time in increased health risks for poor women who will seek medically unsafe help. They also will be felt at the polls. Congressmen who voted to sustain the president from Kansas were Dick Nichols and Pat Roberts. From Missouri, those voting against reproductive freedom were Mel Hancock, Bill Emerson and Harold Volkmer.

People are angry about this. It is an issue which isn't going to go away.

St. Petersburg Times

St. Petersburg, Florida, November 21, 1991

For a former congressman who supported abortion rights, President Bush has claimed an odd victory. In bullying House Republicans to sustain his veto of a $205-billion spending bill for labor, education and health programs, Mr. Bush has aligned himself in a highly visible way with the nation's most extreme anti-abortion faction.

The bill the president vetoed, and the House sustained, had precious little to do with abortion rights. It did not establish further legislative protection for pregnant women. It did not appropriate money so that poor women have equal access to abortion. It did not address the family planning practices of clinics in other nations. What Mr. Bush vetoed was the right of doctors in 4,000 federally funded clinics to inform female patients of their medical options. He put an abortion gag on doctors.

As Rep. Nancy Pelosi, D-Calif., described it: "This . . . is not about who controls a woman's body. It is about who controls a woman's mind."

The president could easily have used the bill as an opportunity to create a little distance between himself and the doctrinaire Reagan politics on abortion, but he didn't. Instead he listened to chief of staff John Sununu, who has branded White House abortion philosophy with the insignia of the far right. In so doing, the president is taking an incalculable risk not only with the ethical practice of medicine but with his own upcoming election.

Mr. Bush already has used other vetoes to limit reproductive options for poor women in the District of Columbia and to take away abortion money for poor women who have been raped. He and his predecessor have all but assured the U.S. Supreme Court will overturn *Roe vs. Wade*, though the ruling is unlikely to occur before the election. What is the president now telling American women when he says doctors shouldn't be allowed to even tell them the option of abortion exists?

The House attempt to override the president's veto fell just 12 votes short, 276-156, and Democrats weren't the only ones to recognize the political implications. Rep. Olympia Snowe, of Maine, one of the 53 Republicans who refused to help the president, told her colleagues: "The failure to override is something women won't forget in this country, nor should they."

Though the president is now suggesting his administrative rules will give clinic doctors some flexibility in discussing reproductive options, he already has declared his position. In a debate that is at the outer fringe of abortion policy, Mr. Bush used his veto in ways that should offend even those who oppose abortion. He is not just insulting women, he is insulting medicine.

The News and Observer

Raleigh, North Carolina, November 22, 1991

It was an undeserved victory for anti-abortion forces and a sad day for women caught in unplanned pregnancy when failure by the U.S. House to override George Bush's 24th veto left a federal gag on family-planning counselors' mouths.

The victory was undeserved because American women have the right to know about and choose among all their options, not just some. Even in defeat, this view, firmly based in the ideal of individual responsibility, mustered almost 50 votes more than a simple House majority.

But in the government-by-veto that George Bush is running, forget what the majority wants. When push came to shove on the abortion-counseling gag rule, combined pressure from the White House and anti-abortion extremists pushed just enough votes across the line to block the two-thirds required to override.

Even if those 12 votes had gone the other way, no woman would ever have been compelled to listen to a pro-abortion pitch, let alone to have an abortion. All the measure aimed to do was untie the gag that prevents doctors and other counselors, in family planning clinics that receive federal funds, from mentioning abortion as among the choices and answering further questions if asked.

In human terms, not to allow that is worse than unkind, and impractical to boot. It means that a desperately scared teenager facing personal future shock, or a mother already burdened with all the children she can possibly care for, is barred from the full range of information she needs to make a sound decision in an agonizingly tough situation.

This president has let his awesome power be used to permit one minority's viewpoint, inspired largely by minority religious views, dominate and define a supposedly open and pluralistic society's approach to a difficult problem.

No matter how hard zealots try or how many restrictive laws are passed, the morality of abortion remains something that can never be legislated. Abortion, legal or not, will always be with us. Choices about it will always remain a matter for individual hearts and consciences. Everyone has the right to reject it as an option for themselves — or to base their views on variables like whether or not the fetus has reached the point of viability.

What is wrong is for some to presume to use governmental authority to foreclose others' free and informed choice. That is profoundly un-American, but it's what this Bush veto — and its upholding — will do.

THE SPOKESMAN-REVIEW

Spokane, Washington, November 22, 1991

Apparently the U.S. House of Representatives doesn't have as much spine as Speaker Tom Foley thought it had when he predicted President Bush's string of veto victories would end Tuesday.

Foley uncharacteristically went out on a limb and declared the House would cancel a White House rule forbidding federally funded family planning agencies from discussing abortion with their clients. Legislation to that effect passed easily in both House and Senate but the real trick would be to override the president's promised veto. When the votes were recorded Foley was a full dozen short of the two-thirds majority he needed.

As a consequence, the 4.5 million primarily needy women who go to such clinics every year will be denied information about abortion as one of the options open to them. That may be great news to those who oppose abortion on principle but it is disappointing to the majority of Americans who support a woman's right to make such choices on a personal level.

In Washington state it now appears that Initiative 120, which reinforces that right as a matter of state law, won a narrow victory in this month's general election. The thin margin is misleading, however. During the campaign, opponents of the measure conceded public support for choice but attacked the initiative through misrepresentations about what it would accomplish. A straightforward campaign on the question of abortion almost certainly would have passed by a comfortable margin.

Washington is not unlike most other states. Public-opinion surveys repeatedly show wide support for reproductive freedom.

That is why Tuesday's timid vote in the House is so disappointing. According to reports, several House members were prepared to vote for an override so long as they knew they would prevail, but they didn't want to stick their necks out in a losing cause. Credit Washington's House delegation with backbone. All eight members, including three Republicans, defied the president.

Overall, however, so many representatives were waiting for a clear reading that the tally on the House's electronic voting machine never got close enough to give them the assurance they wanted. They took the easy way out.

Before pregnant low-income women can expect to get the information they need, Congress will have to acquire the courage it lacks.

The Courier-Journal
Louisville, Kentucky, August 4, 1991

IF THE U. S. Supreme Court muzzled physicians who care for middle-income patients, voters would be outraged. In fact, they would insist that Congress reverse the ruling and stop any further meddling.

But of course the court hasn't restricted speech between physicians and their well-heeled patients. Its ruling is limited to their discussions with poor women. Specifically, the court said workers in federally funded clinics may not discuss abortion with their patients. Congress subsequently voted to strike down that ban. But it's unclear whether the support is strong enough to override President Bush's promised veto. It's unclear because the vote was by voice, not by hand.

Congress is perpetrating an even bigger dodge by framing the issues implicit in this ruling as a case about abortion. That's misleading.

Rust v. Sullivan is about the doctor-patient relationship. It's about the care people will get when the government pays the bill — by funding clinics, Medicaid and Medicare. The frightening implications are spelled out in a splendid essay by lawyer George J. Annas in the current *New England Journal of Medicine*. To help control the costs of health care, could the government limit the information physicians may give Medicare patients about alternative treatments? How could such regulations be enforced? Could videotapes of all doctor-patients conversations be required?

Congress needs to do more than strike down the abortion ban. It must include language in all future health-care bills specifically barring government agencies from restricting what physicians may tell patients. To do anything less would be untenable.

THE DENVER POST
Denver, Colorado, November 21, 1991

PRESIDENT George Bush has won another pyrrhic victory against the right of American women to make their own private decisions about abortion. But in so doing, the anti-abortion president ensured that his unreasoned and unpopular position will be a target of pro-choice voters in 1992.

The issue erupted in 1988 when the Reagan administration ordered workers in federally funded clinics not to tell women that the option of having abortions even existed. Bush continued that ban after his own election and the U.S. Supreme Court later upheld its constitutionality.

Congress, however, rebelled against Bush's anti-abortion crusade and attached a provision to a $205 billion spending bill for labor, education and health programs that would have stopped the administration from enforcing its ban. To save his ban on abortion counseling, Bush vetoed the entire bill. While the House voted 276-156 to reject Bush's position, that fell short of the two-thirds necessary to override the veto.

The pro-choice majority, however, has plenty of ways to keep Bush's feet to the fire on this issue. For openers, they should keep attaching the provision to bills that Bush needs — until they find one he can't afford to veto. Anti-abortion leaders regularly attached the anti-abortion Hyde amendment to unrelated legislation. Pro-choice legislators should give Bush a taste of the same medicine and tack the repealer of the counseling ban on everything in sight until the president is forced to back down.

Additionally, Congress should add its support to the appeal by Planned Parenthood and other pro-choice groups asking the Supreme Court to review the landmark Roe vs. Wade abortion rights decision this spring.

Bush has appointed anti-abortion judges to the Supreme Court at every opportunity, but cringes at the thought that the high tribunal might actually overturn Roe before the 1992 election — thereby making it a hot election topic.

However, abortion is an issue where Bush can run but he can't hide. Once a strong supporter of Planned Parenthood, Bush defected to the anti-abortion camp while seeking the GOP presidential nomination — and his record since being elected has been glaringly anti-choice.

A similar flip-flop on abortion helped defeat Bush protege Richard Thornburgh — once strongly pro-choice, now stridently anti-abortion — in the Pennsylvania senatorial election. Congress ought to seize every opportunity to spotlight Bush's own hypocrisy on the abortion issue and force the president to openly defend his anti-choice record in his 1992 re-election bid.

The Chattanooga Times
Chattanooga, Tennessee, November 21, 1991

Twice this week, on Monday and again on Tuesday, House Speaker Thomas Foley confidently predicted that the House would override President Bush's veto of legislation permitting doctors and workers in federally funded family planning clinics to discuss abortion. But Mr. Foley was wrong. When the votes were counted on Tuesday, he was 12 short of the 288 needed to override.

That puts Mr. Bush 24-and-0 in the veto stats. But on this issue, freedom of speech is 0-and-1.

The legislation was intended to overturn administration regulations — which the Supreme Court upheld last June — and was part of the $205 billion appropriations bill for the departments of Labor, Education, and Health and Human Services. Mr. Bush insisted the regulations didn't constitute a "gag" rule; that doctors were free to give pregnant women "*complete* medical information" (emphasis added) about their condition.

But of course under the regulations the medical information could not be complete. The rules were necessary, Mr. Bush said, because otherwise the federal family planning programs would become entangled with abortion.

As a practical matter, the House will now take out the provision to which Mr. Bush objected and pass the basic spending bill again. Other bills are still pending to change the law on such counseling. With less than a week remaining before congressional leaders expect to end this session, however, those bills are unlikely to be brought to a vote.

Although a key element in the debate involved freedom of speech — a doctor's right to give a woman all of the advice she needs regarding her pregnancy — Mr. Bush insisted otherwise. In his veto message, the president said there was no doubt the administration is "committed to the protection of free speech." He noted that the Supreme Court had ruled 5-4 in May that the regulations did not violate the Constitution's free-speech guarantees.

In fact, the decision did erode free speech. In dissent, Justice Harry Blackmun wrote that until that ruling, the court had never said that government can suppress speech about a certain viewpoint as a condition for accepting public money.

That set a dangerous precedent, which the House has now reiterated by failing to override the president's veto. To their credit, Tennessee's six Democratic representatives voted to override.

Does that mean they favor abortion? Absolutely not. Rep. Marilyn Lloyd's opposition to abortion is well-known. Her vote, like those of her Democratic and Republican colleagues, reflected the point that government has no business intruding into the confidential doctor-patient relationship by restricting the advice doctors can give to their patients. The House has now endorsed that intrusion — and an ominous restriction of free speech.

San Francisco Chronicle

San Francisco, California, November 8, 1991

THE OVERWHELMING margin by which the Senate voted to reverse an administration-backed ban on abortion counseling at federally funded clinics is heartening.

This ban is a gag rule, no matter how its purpose is rationalized. It interferes with full and proper dispensation of medical advice. And this kind of censorship has no place in a free society such as ours. The tally in the Senate was 72 to 25, more than enough to overturn a threatened presidential veto.

This gag rule on doctors should not stand

Just the day before, a vote in the House on the same issue also strongly rejected this policy — but was not as effective. The vote was 272 to 156, 14 votes short of the number needed to override a veto. But there was an appropriations measure attached to the bill, and that may have dissuaded some members from supporting it. The subsequent Senate surge could also bring back necessary "yes" votes in the House.

BUT THE BEST thing that could happen is a change of heart on the part of President Bush. The White House has already sent a letter to Health and Human Services Secretary Louis Sullivan saying that while the regulation prohibited doctors and other counselors from talking to women about abortion, it did not forbid doctors to give complete medical information to women. Why the weaseling equivocation? Why not just admit the ban is a bad idea?

ALBUQUERQUE JOURNAL

Albuquerque, New Mexico, November 8, 1991

President Bush's veto of a $205 billion spending bill for labor, education and health programs was a blow to poor women and young women throughout the nation. The veto was aimed specifically at a provision that would have lifted an administration-imposed gag on delivery of abortion information at federally funded family planning clinics.

The House failed to override the veto by 12 votes, 276 to 156. The Senate earlier passed the bill by a veto-proof 72-25 margin.

Bush's veto will affect 50 New Mexico family planning clinics that serve 30,000 women a year. The majority of these women are poor and live in rural New Mexico.

The gag rule, imposed by the Reagan administration in 1988 and continued by Bush, had been held in abeyance while Congress worked to end it. The rule can now go into effect immediately. It would reverse two decades of understanding that no federal funds would be used to perform abortions unless it was needed to save the woman's life, while allowing family planning clinics to provide a complete range of advice and referrals to pregnant women.

The president's veto was confusing. In a recent memo to Health and Human Services Secretary Louis Sullivan, the president said the ban should not prevent a doctor from giving a woman full medical information. He also said federally aided clinics could refer women to groups providing abortions unless the groups perform abortions as their principal activity. That position shows the president to be quibbling more about form than principle.

The principle the president should have supported is found in the First Amendment. It protects everyone's right to free speech, a right that is corrupted by the administration's gag order.

The State

Columbia, South Carolina, November 23, 1991

A REAGAN-ERA regulation barring federally funded family-planning clinics from abortion counseling is one step closer to implementation. Earlier this week, Congress again failed to muster the two-thirds majority to overturn President Bush's veto of legislation banning the so-called "gag rule."

The 1988 rule has never been enforced because of continuing court challenges. However, last May the U.S. Supreme Court said the abortion counseling ban was legal; the Bush administration delayed implementing until the battle within Congress was decided. Now the time, apparently, has run out, and the Adminis-

tration is expected to put the rule into effect at the 4,000 clinics that receive federal funds.

Here in South Carolina, family-planning clinic directors say the gag rule will not have much impact. The reason is that most of the state's 96 clinics are in county health departments that have several divisions. Usually, women who are already pregnant are referred to maternal-health divisions which are not bound by the federal rule, according to state Department of Health and Environmental Control officials.

But for low-income women in some other states, that's not so. Many receive a wide array of family planning services through federally supported clinics, and they will be deprived of full, candid information about their choices. As Rep. John Chafee, R-R.I., observed, this isn't an argument about the pros and cons of abortion. "The argument here is whether a poor woman is entitled to the same information any other woman could receive from her doctor," he said.

Until Congress musters the strength to act, the sad answer to that question is "no."

The Seattle Times

Seattle, Washington, November 9, 1991

PRESIDENT Bush has become a fanatic, slavishly following the agenda of anti-abortion lobbies. Now he's threatening to veto a law Congress passed last week that abolishes the federal rule preventing doctors at federally-funded family planning clinics from mentioning abortion.

The rule, created by the Reagan administration, makes it illegal for doctors in 4,000 clinics around the country to tell patients about abortion, even if they ask.

The gag rule has nothing to do with whether abortion should be legal. That question will be decided soon enough by the Supreme Court. Nor does the gag rule have anything to do with abortion funding – no federal money is used to pay for any abortions.

The only issue is whether a poor woman has a right to basic medical information that other women can obtain from their doctors. Bush says no: if you're poor, you only get half the facts. Medical professionals vehemently oppose this limit on their free-speech rights. They argue convincingly that the gag rule exposes them to more malpractice suits.

Getting rid of the gag rule is not a pro-choice position. Several Republican senators and representatives who oppose abortion voted to eliminate the rule on free speech and fairness grounds. The 72-25 vote in the Senate is sufficient to override a Bush veto, but passage in the House was 14 votes short of a veto-proof margin.

Bush seems intent on turning this narrow issue into a major political brawl. In fact, he may do it just to divert attention from a host of domestic issues – the economic recession, health care reform, education – for which he has no plan. Picking a fight over abortion is an easy distraction from the nation's real troubles.

Chicago Sun-Times

Chicago, Illinois, November 22, 1991

There was bad news for women and their doctors in the House of Representatives' failed attempt at a veto override Tuesday.

Pregnant women seeking complete information about their options will be the first to feel the impact of the so-called "gag rule," which prohibits counselors and other health workers at federally subsidized clinics from telling women where to go for an abortion, even if they are asked.

But federally subsidized clinics in inner-city or rural areas, where there may be no other place for women seeking birth-control or prenatal care to go, and patients without any interest in abortion also have been dealt a blow.

Congress' failure to block enforcement of the Reagan administration rule issued in 1988, but held up by court and legislative challenges since then, forces those clinics to decide whether to obey the rule or follow Planned Parenthood's lead in forgoing funds that defray the cost of health services for poor people.

The rule will limit counselors and other health professionals to answering questions about abortion with the response that the government "does not consider abortion an appropriate method of family planning."

Bush and his allies cheered the restrictions on counseling of pregnant women Tuesday.

They may not cheer long if family and free-speech advocates are correct in predicting more unwanted pregnancies, more abused children, more delayed (and therefore riskier) abortions and more incursions on First Amendment freedoms as a result.

St. Paul Pioneer Press & Dispatch

St. Paul, Minnesota, November 6, 1991

The new spirit of compromise at a pragmatic White House found itself at work this week on the odious abortion counseling gag rule. President Bush has received the message that he has lost the political ground on this extreme manifestation of abortion ideology and sent word Tuesday to the House that a deal is in order.

President sees room to move away from an extreme position.

That message is good news for legislation that has cleared conference committee and is up for House passage. The legislation reverses a regulation that forbids doctors and other care providers at federally funded family plannning clinics from even mentioning that abortion is a legal option for pregnant patients. Impetus for the overturn came in the last Supreme Court term when the regulation was upheld in the Rust vs. Sullivan decision.

We have argued before that the gag rule violates doctor-patient rights, that it discriminates against poor women who don't have access to private health care, that it's a plain insult to the fair administration of public policy.

Congress made the same points in gathering wide support for this legislation that cleanly addresses only the issue at hand: whether medical providers at clinics that get federal money can advise their patients of all their legal options.

The president, looking at the polls and at moderate voices within his natural constituency, sees room to move away from an extreme position. Even if that conversion comes late in the process, it should be welcome on Capitol Hill.

Unless Mr. Bush is trying another scam to work both sides of his political street, it seems possible that reason can triumph. It's time to make a deal that rescinds the gag rule and get on to constructive matters on the long and urgent national agenda.

DAILY NEWS

New York City, New York, November 22, 1991

Last Tuesday, Congress had its first real chance to override a Bush veto — and to stand up for freedom of speech to boot.

Instead, the House came down on the side of political cowardice. Only 276 members — a dozen too few — opposed the "gag rule," which prevents workers at federally funded health clinics from mentioning the word "abortion" to patients.

From now on, clinics that inform their clients (often young, poor women) that abortion is a safe, legal option will risk losing federal funds. Women, medical workers and all who cherish the First Amendment should be outraged. And Congress — and the President — can hang their heads in disgrace.

Idaho Sets Abortion Curbs; Guam Restrictions Enacted

The Idaho Senate voted March 22, 1990, to approve legislation that would ban most abortions in the state. The legislation, which was the most restrictive of any state in the U.S., had been designed as a vehicle to give the U.S. Supreme Court an opportunity to reconsider and possibly overturn its 1973 *Roe v. Wade* decision, which had legalized abortion.

The bill, which the Senate passed by a vote of 25–17, was sent to Gov. Cecil D. Andrus for signature. Andrus, a Democrat who opposed abortion, had not said whether he would sign the measure. The bill had been approved by the Idaho state House on March 9.

The legislation was described as a ban on abortion as a means of birth control. Specifically, it prohibited all abortions except in cases of rape reported to the police within seven days, incest involving a woman under age 18, "profound" fetal deformity or threat to a woman's physical health.

The bill had been crafted by members of the National Right to Life Committee, in the wake of a Supreme Court decision in July 1989 that had granted states wide latitude to restrict abortion.

Supporters of the legislation said it had been specifically designed to overcome the objections of Supreme Court Justice Sandra Day O'Connor, who had previously voted to uphold abortion restrictions, but whose opinions had stopped short of a declaration in favor of overturning *Roe v. Wade*. Abortion opponents believed that one of her chief objections to other abortion restrictions had been that those bills had included criminal penalties for women who obtained abortions. Therefore, the Idaho bill had been drafted in such a way as to avoid holding women criminally responsible for having an abortion.

Instead, the bill penalized doctors, making them liable for a fine of up to $10,000 and allowing individuals involved in a particular abortion case – including fathers of fetuses or parents of minor children who had an abortion – to file civil lawsuits against the doctor who performed the procedure.

Both supporters and opponents of legalized abortion said that the law, if it took effect, would outlaw about 95% of the abortions performed in the state. In 1988, there had been about 1,650 abortions in Idaho.

Abortion-rights supporters said that if Gov. Andrus signed the bill, they would immediately challenge it in the court, meaning that it would not take effect until all appeals had been exhausted.

Previously, Gov. Joseph F. Ada (R) of the U.S. Pacific island territory of Guam March 19 signed into law a measure that contained the most restrictive curbs in the U.S.

The law banned all abortions except in cases where pregnancy threatened a woman's life. In such cases, approval from two doctors was required for the procedure to be performed. The doctors' decision would be subject to review by a medical licensing board.

The law made it a third-degree felony to perform an abortion, and a misdemeanor to have an abortion or to "knowingly solicit" a woman to have an abortion.

The measure had been approved unanimously by Guam's unicameral legislature on March 8. It contained a clause calling for a referendum on abortion to be held during the next general election, on November 6. At that time, voters would decide whether to keep the new law.

Guam's attorney general, Elizabeth Barrett-Anderson, who believed the law was unconstitutional, filed charges March 20 against an American Civil Liberties Union lawyer, Janet Benshoof, who gave a speech in Guam advising women that they could obtain legal abortions in Hawaii. The case was intended to force a constitutional review of the new law.

New York City, New York, March 22, 1990

When the Supreme Court handed down its 1987 Webster decision, giving states more latitude to regulate abortions, it set in motion forces that have led legislatures to consider hard and harmful new restrictions on abortion. The most extreme — making abortion a crime — was signed into law Monday in Guam.

For the sake of the women in the U.S. Trust Territory in the Pacific, the first order of business must be to wipe the cruel new law off the books. That can be done by the courts or by the voters, who will vote Nov. 6, in an unusual referendum, to endorse or reject the law, which was signed by Gov. Joseph F. Ada despite his attorney general's opinion that it violates the U.S. Constitution. We hope Guam voters have more sense than the governor and say "no."

The law had been in effect only a day when Janet Benshoof, an American Civil Liberties Union lawyer from New York City, spoke at the Guam Press Club advising women where to go in Hawaii for abortions. Now she faces criminal charges of soliciting abortion. The ACLU intends to challenge the law's constitutionality and fight her case as well — all the way to the Supreme Court if necessary.

Guam's supertough law bans abortions except when the mother's life is in danger. A doctor who performs an abortion can be sent to jail for five years. A woman who has one can be sentenced to a year in jail. Benshoof could be imprisoned for a year for her words.

As America learned before women's right to abortion was guaranteed by the Supreme Court in Roe vs. Wade, laws against abortion don't stop it, they only drive it underground and make it dangerous. That happened in Romania, where abortion-related deaths surged 700 percent after abortion was restricted in 1966. If Guam's terrible law is not rejected by voters or the courts, women will die.

Guam's a dot in the Pacific; no similar law could pass *here*, right? Or could it? Guam's legislature was moved by the Webster decision and by the dominant Catholic Church's strong anti-abortion stance: Archbishop Anthony Apuron threatened to excommunicate any lawmaker who voted against the bill. Sounds familiar, doesn't it? Not long ago, a cleric told New York Gov. Mario Cuomo he'd go to hell for his abortion stance.

Is this what the Supreme Court wanted when it handed down Webster? Laws like Guam's that unconstitutionally muzzle free speech and privacy rights? Fifty state governments torn apart, arguing at the extremes of an emotional, polarizing issue? If the Guam law ever gets to Washington, the Supreme Court should strike it down. Meanwhile, as other abortion cases come before it, the court should recognize the uncertainties Webster has caused and use its first opportunity to make clear that abortion remains a constitutional right of American women.

The Des Moines Register

Des Moines, Iowa, March 24, 1990.

It's now a virtual certainty that the U.S. Supreme Court soon will revisit its 1973 decision legalizing abortion in the United States. First Guam, then Idaho, this week passed anti-abortion bills aimed specifically at forcing the court, with its Reagan-era conservative majority intact, to re-examine whether government can prevent a woman from obtaining an abortion in all but the most extreme cases.

Guam's law would prevent all abortions except those intended to save a mother's life. Idaho's would make abortions illegal except in cases where the mother's life or physical health is in danger, incest if the victim is younger than 18, severe fetal deformity, or non-statutory rape reported within seven days. Both laws may be subject to voter referendum, though anti-abortion forces appear to be in control in heavily Mormon Idaho and Roman Catholic Guam, where a church bishop said lawmakers voting against the bill would be excommunicated.

Of course neither approach will prevent abortions. Idaho women will drive to Oregon or Montana or Washington state. Women in Guam have a less attractive option — an expensive plane flight to Hawaii. In both cases expect more back-alley abortions, and more deaths. And if anti-abortion activists have their way, that will be the norm in every state and territory of the union.

The court's 1989 Webster decision was hailed in many quarters as providing a rational option for states to develop their own laws regarding abortion. But it instead removed for many American women their protection against government's interference into a decision affecting their own bodies. Rather than settling anything, it re-opened a nasty nationwide debate and reduced many political campaigns to single-issue politics.

Supporters of the Webster decision argued that individual states and territories should have authority to establish their own laws. But the inevitable result was an invitation to anti-abortion forces to re-impose their will on the entire nation. Nothing was gained; there now is much to lose.

The Honolulu Advertiser

Honolulu, Hawaii, March 21, 1990

In Boston, a federal appeals court has ruled that regulations to prohibit government-funded family planning clinics from discussing abortion with clients violate the Constitution's free-speech guarantees.

In Guam, the governor has signed America's most restrictive abortion law, passed unanimously by the island's 21-member legislature. It prohibits abortions except when a pregnancy endangers a mother's life and makes it a felony to perform or aid an abortion and a misdemeanor to have or seek an abortion or to advise a woman to have one.

Guam's attorney general warned that the law is unconstitutional. It is already being challenged and seems likely to be struck down. It would be a great hardship on Guamanian women, especially those too poor to travel.

What will happen to a planned November referendum on this issue is unclear. But the local archbishop's threat to excommunicate any senator who voted against the law will cast a shadow over any referendum among the overwhelmingly Catholic citizens of that Pacific island.

Meanwhile, in California, several candidates for governor favor abortion rights and at least one has made waves by calling for the state to test RU 486, the French pill that ends pregnancy within weeks of conception — simply, safely and privately.

While the nation's largest state could not approve the drug for interstate distribution, its testing there would force fast action by the federal Food and Drug Administration.

That won't end debate on abortion — a question to be decided by each woman based on her own religious and moral beliefs. But it would remove it from the public arena where it only makes for discord and divisiveness.

The Washington Post

Washington, D.C., March 22, 1990

THE TINY Pacific island of Guam is a U.S. territory, and the same constitutional limitations that govern state action here, apply to the local legislature, a unicameral body with 21 members. When *Roe v. Wade* was decided in 1973, the territory's antiabortion laws were nullified. But in the aftermath of last summer's *Webster* decision, legislators in Guam, like their counterparts in many states, decided to test the scope of *Webster* by placing restrictions on abortion. Unlike lawmakers here, however, the Guamanians didn't start out slowly with a limitation on public spending or a rule on parental notification. They banned abortion entirely except to save the life of the mother. For good measure they made it a crime to perform or to receive or aid in an abortion, *and* they outlawed speech in the form of "solicitation for abortion."

There was little debate on the measure, which was passed unanimously March 8. The island is 90 percent Catholic, and the local archbishop had weighed in with a heavy hand threatening to excommunicate legislators who voted against it. But at least one woman—Anita Arriola, who had recently returned home after practicing law in San Francisco for six years—was outraged. Undeterred by the fact that the author of the bill is her own mother, Sen. Elizabeth Arriola, the lawyer alerted the American Civil Liberties Union to what was going on. The drama came to a climax this week when Janet Benshoof of the ACLU flew from New York hoping to persuade the governor to veto the bill (he didn't see her) and was thereafter charged with violating the solicitation provision of the law because at a public meeting she pointed out that Guamanian women could still get abortions in Hawaii. A hearing on these charges has been set for April 2.

The voters of Guam will have an opportunity to decide on this new law themselves. There will be a referendum on Election Day in November. The chances that it will survive a constitutional test in the U.S. courts are remote. The attorney general of Guam, Elizabeth Barrett-Anderson, advised legislators that the law would be unconstitutional and has probably—wisely—chosen to prosecute Miss Benshoof on the hard-to sustain speech charges, as a good test case. But even if the law doesn't survive, the Guam experience is a good reminder of how bad things could get if *Roe* is overturned. Young American women have no personal experience of laws that criminalize abortion, laws that would jail women and doctors alike and that would justify the arrest and prosecution even of those who supply information and advice. No one expects that such repressive legislation would be enacted by many state legislatures in the absence of *Roe.* But the speed and ease with which territorial lawmakers acted is a chilling reminder of what is at stake.

Arkansas Gazette

Little Rock, Arkansas, March 24, 1990

Ever since Ronald Reagan's appointees created a new majority on the Supreme Court, and especially since that new majority invited the states to limit abortions, it has been inevitable that someone would challenge Roe vs. Wade head-on, despite the risk to the country. The Idaho legislature has claimed the honor.

Roe vs. Wade was the 1973 Supreme Court decision that said a woman had a constitutional right to an abortion. It was a "political" decision, to some extent, as the abortion issue raises questions — When does life begin? — that not even the most learned of judges can answer definitively. Many of the greatest court decisions have been political. A court that hides from real life, that is blind to the effect of its decisions, cannot perform the role in American government for which it was created. An overturning of Roe vs. Wade would be political, too, and religious.

Roe vs. Wade was not a perfect answer to abortion, there is no perfect answer, but it was a reasonable one that a majority of Americans could tolerate, a vast improvement over the mix of hypocrisy, discrimination and danger that prevailed before. But an earnest and aggressive minority of anti-abortionists could not tolerate the decision and have warred on it relentlessly. Their hopes now are with a bill just enacted by the Idaho legislature. In essence, the bill reverses Roe vs. Wade. It says that women *don't* have a right to an abortion, except under circumstances so restrictive as to disallow most of the abortions that are now performed. Idaho Gov. Cecil Andrus has not yet signed the bill, but is expected to. Then the legal battle will begin, and it won't stop short of the Supreme Court.

Justice Sandra Day O'Connor, who is part of the new majority but is also the first woman on the court, has said that she would never consider overturning Roe vs. Wade unless that consideration could not be evaded, unless there was no other way to resolve the matter that was before the court. The Idaho law is designed to block evasion.

The history of the court and the United States Constitution that it interprets is of extending rights to the American people. In a case challenging Roe vs. Wade, the court will be asked to take back a right it had previously granted, a regressive, mean-spirited and unprecedented action and one that would disrupt the country far more than it is now. Millions of people will not willingly give up a right that has been theirs for nearly 20 years. The Supreme Court as an institution, perhaps our most important institution, would be gravely damaged.

Would the court embark on such a perilous path? Some members of the new majority are radical enough or insensitive enough; some may not be. Justice O'Connor will be the most closely-watched justice in our history.

Idaho has sowed the wind. We preferred it when it sowed potatoes.

The Register-Guard

Eugene, Oregon, March 30, 1990

Idaho Gov. Cecil Andrus was born in Hood River and grew up in Eugene. He is a lifelong Democrat and projects a liberal image based largely on his environmental record.

But as events of the past few days have demonstrated, Andrus' liberal instincts have limits: He is strongly opposed to abortion.

At the moment, he is in a quandary because the Idaho Legislature has passed what would be the most restrictive abortion law in the country. It would also be unconstitutional under the 1973 Supreme Court decision in Roe vs. Wade. But the National Right to Life Committee wants the bill to become law knowing that it would be challenged, thereby becoming a vehicle that could force the present Supreme Court to reconsider and possibly overturn the Roe decision.

Basic provisions of the bill match Andrus' personal views. He opposes abortion except to save a woman's life and in cases of rape or incest.

Seventeen years ago, during his first term as governor, Andrus signed legislation that would have banned all abortions except to save a woman's life. Violators — women and their doctors — would have been subject to criminal prosecution and imprisonment. The law would only have become effective, however, if Roe were reversed.

The present legislation is milder than the 1973 version in that it would impose only civil sanctions. But Andrus has refused all along to say whether he would sign the bill. He has three weeks from Wednesday to decide, but most recently said he would make a decision by this weeked.

If the bill fits his own preferences, why is the governor finding it so difficult to make up his mind? Probably because he's not sure how the issue will play out in electoral terms at a time when militant anti-abortionists are on the political defensive around the country.

Andrus wants to be elected in November to an unprecedented fourth term as governor. He first won the office in 1970 as an "accidental candidate," as the Alamanac of American Politics puts it, after the original Democratic nominee died in a plane crash. He was re-elected overwhelmingly in 1974, and then went off to Washington to be Jimmy Carter's secretary of interior.

He re-entered the home political scene in 1986 and barely won the governorship again, defeating the Republican lieutenant governor 50 percent to 49 percent. He has since exhibited more conservative political behavior.

Some abortion rights advocates around the country have threatened to boycott Idaho potatoes if Andrus signs the bill. That's a stupid tactic, more likely to get the governor's back up than intimidate him.

But even among conservatives there is concern that the restrictive abortion law would stigmatize the state and produce a negative impact with economic as well as psychological ramifications.

It's an interesting political problem for the man who wants another four years of grappling with such things. We'd like to see him veto the bill. But given his personal leanings and the political complexion of his adopted state, no one should be surprised if he signs it.

The Miami Herald

Miami, Florida, March 31, 1990

HAVING cracked the door of privacy in its *Webster* decision last summer, the U.S. Supreme Court shouldn't be surprised that anti-abortionists are now pushing through it and demanding that state legislatures reassert government control over pregnant women. Nor should anyone else be surprised.

In Idaho, legislators have sent Gov. Cecil Andrus a bill that would ban 95 percent of all abortions. The legislation was written specifically to elicit a challenge that will force the Supreme Court to reconsider the 1973 *Roe vs. Wade* decision legalizing abortion.

In Guam, an American Civil Liberties Union lawyer read the Guam Press Club a list of abortion clinics advertising in the Yellow Pages. The lawyer is now charged with the criminal offense under a new law that forbids anyone "to solicit any woman to submit to any operation, or to use . . . any means . . . to cause an abortion."

In Maryland, legislators are deadlocked. A House committee rejected a confusing Senate compromise that would have passed contrary bills (1) to permit unrestricted abortions and (2) to limit abortion to instances in which a woman was raped, the victim of incest, or in danger of dying or suffering permanent health damage. The Senate would have voters repeal one or both.

In California and Texas, abortion has become a major issue in gubernatorial races. It is likely to become one in Florida. The Legislature reconvenes next week amid anti-abortionists' vows to amend any germane bill that comes up for a vote to prohibit the use of "abortion as birth control."

The broad-based attacks do not bode well for women. Depending on how abortion is defined, many of the anti-abortion proposals also reach out to prohibit birth-control pills and devices that prevent fertilized eggs from attaching to the womb.

Abortion is as complex an issue as exists. Nonetheless, experience demonstrates that pregnancy decisions are better left to the women involved than to state or Federal governments. It is increasingly clear too that the "women involved" must organize and stay organized to protect their civil right to make those decisions in private.

ST. LOUIS POST-DISPATCH

St. Louis, Missouri, March 25, 1990

The anti-abortion movement scored two victories last week when legislatures in Guam and Idaho enacted restrictive abortion laws. Both are meant to challenge *Roe vs. Wade.* Guam's law is already embroiled in court action. On Friday, U.S. District Judge Alex Munson issued a temporary restraining order, preventing the law from being enforced.

Guam, a U.S. territory, passed what must be considered the strictest abortion law on U.S. land. It outlaws all abortions, except to save the life of the woman. It also makes it a crime for doctors to perform abortions, for women to solicit abortions and for anyone to tell women about abortions. The Catholic Church exerted enormous pressure on legislators to ensure the bill's passage; Archbishop Anthony Apuron promised to excommunicate any Catholic lawmaker who failed to vote for the bill.

While the law in Guam might be described as the anti-abortionists' dream legislation, the bill passed by the Idaho Legislature, which waits for Gov. Cecil Andrus' signature, might be viewed as a vehicle for overturning *Roe vs. Wade.* The Idaho bill allows the standard exceptions — rape, incest, "profound" fetal abnormality and the physical health or life of the woman. Yet what makes this bill unique is that it was crafted by the National Right to Life Committee to address what the committee believes are the concerns of U.S. Supreme Court Justice Sandra Day O'Connor. By imposing penalties on doctors, instead of women, it is an explicit attempt to woo Justice O'Connor into the court's anti-abortion camp.

The anti-abortion movement has long proclaimed that abortion is a crime. These two pieces of legislation add what many in the anti-abortion movement have regularly downplayed — punishment, in the form of outrageous fines and even jail. Perhaps that's all for the better. The sympathy for women with problem pregnancies, sympathy that anti-abortionists have glibly mouthed, is revealed to be the hollow ruse and sham it always was.

The Providence Journal

Providence, Rhode Island, March 30, 1990

The politics of abortion, 1990s-style, has proved to be less volatile than expected. The pro-abortion position of the Democratic gubernatorial candidate in Virginia might have furnished his margin of victory in a very close election last year; the same could be said for the race in New Jersey — although the Republican candidate's abrupt change of heart on the issue might have done him more damage. But last year's Supreme Court decision in *Webster v. Reproductive Health Services* has neither opened the floodgates to anti-abortion measures nor turned abortion rights into a pivotal political issue.

Indeed, in Florida, where the governor dragged the legislature into special session to push restrictive measures, the scheme exploded in his face. And in Maryland, efforts to dramatically expand abortion rights were stymied by a filibuster, and remain at an impasse. Only in the state of Idaho and territory of Guam — two comparatively tiny constituencies — has real action been taken.

In both places the local legislatures have virtually banned abortion. The Guam measure is a direct challenge to the Supreme Court to overturn *Roe v. Wade* without apologies; the Idaho law is designed to appeal to Justice Sandra Day O'Connor, the conservative swing vote on the question, who seems to favor limitations on abortion except those that place an "undue burden" on women. Exactly what that means has never been clear, but even the Rehnquist court — which opened the door in *Webster* to state-by-state adjustments — is likely to find these mea-

sures too draconian to uphold.

While the territorial governor of Guam signed with enthusiasm, Gov. Cecil Andrus of Idaho, who was Jimmy Carter's secretary of interior and describes himself as pro-life, faces an agonizing decision. As with many politicians who personally deplore abortion but publicly choose to uphold the law, Mr. Andrus finds himself caught between moral conviction and political expediency. If he should veto the measure, he would probably be overridden, and lose status with the legislature. But if he should sign the bill, or allow it to become law without his signature, he faces a threatened boycott of Idaho agriculture (potatoes) and tourism, both of which contribute substantially to state income.

For what it's worth, we believe Governor Andrus should veto the bill. But what especially concerns us is the fact that several well-known advocacy groups — notably the National Organization for Women and some pro-life organizations — are calling for a boycott in the event of gubernatorial action. No matter what happens, neither Mr. Andrus nor the people of Idaho can win: If the governor should sign the measure, Idahoans who support abortion rights will no doubt suffer more than the legislators who drafted and passed the bill; and if he should exercise the veto, pro-lifers around the country will cause economic hardship for their allies in Idaho.

All of which reminds us that boycotts can be foolish and indiscriminate weapons, and that most Americans believe politics and abortion don't mix very well.

Los Angeles Times
Los Angeles, California, March 21, 1990

If its potential consequences were not so serious, it would be tempting to dismiss the constitutional drama now being played out in Guam as theater of the absurd. However, when the first legal action taken under the island's restrictive new anti-abortion statute seeks not to halt termination of a pregnancy but to prohibit speech, it is clear that what's in progress is comedy too dark for laughs.

Guam is a self-governing U.S. territory. Its residents, most of whom profess Roman Catholicism, are American citizens. Earlier this month, Guam's 21 territorial senators—all but one a Catholic—passed America's most restrictive anti-abortion legislation shortly after the island's archbishop threatened anyone who voted against the measure with excommunication. Monday, Guam's governor signed the bill into law, despite the opinion of his attorney general that the statute is patently unconstitutional. It prohibits termination of any pregnancy unless two doctors declare that the mother's life is in danger or that her health will be gravely impaired by giving birth. Under the law, anyone who performs an abortion can be prosecuted as a felon; women who undergo abortion face misdemeanor charges, as does anyone who advises or solicits terminating pregnancy.

Tuesday, during a speech to the Guam Press Club, Janet Benshoof, director of the American Civil Liberties Union's Reproductive Rights Project, advised pregnant women that they could leave the island and obtain abortions in Hawaii. She has been charged with soliciting abortion. If convicted, she may be jailed for one year and fined $1,000.

Cooler heads will sort out the grotesque muddle created on Guam, but not before the right to privacy established in Roe vs. Wade and delicate questions of free speech are put to a burdensome and dangerous test. If there is any value to this distasteful exercise, it is that it reminds us again that a woman's right to decide her fate in the private sanctuary of her own conscience and the right of any person to speak his or her mind are threads inextricably interwoven in the fabric of individual liberty. Pull one such thread away and the entire fabric frays to rags, leaving us all to shiver in the cold wind of tyranny.

The Idaho STATESMAN
Boise, Idaho, March 23, 1990

Dear Gov. Andrus:

What can we say? You've heard all the arguments, read all the mail, tallied the phone calls and endured endless questions and debate.

Now it's up to you. Just you, alone with HB 625, the ill-considered abortion-banning legislation sent to you by the House and Senate.

You're the last hope for thousands of Idahoans who don't want to see our beloved state mark its Centennial year by becoming embroiled in a fight on behalf of the national Right to Life movement.

Despite your long history of support for the pro-life cause, this decision won't be easy.

You don't need to be told the political costs. No one gets elected governor of Idaho three times without being able to count noses and read the pulse of the average Joe and Jane.

But there's going to be political fallout, no matter what you do. The new faces that probably will be around the Statehouse next year will be there in large part because of votes already cast in the House and Senate.

In any event, this decision isn't about politics. It's about what's right for Idaho.

It's about how best to preserve the diversity of religious and moral views in this state. It's about protecting freedom, privacy and dignity.

Keeping your pro-life views in mind, there are good reasons for you to veto HB 625.

There's evidence that several provisions, including the draconian rape and incest restrictions, won't pass constitutional muster. That could do more harm than good to the pro-life movement.

Besides, a long, messy fight all the way to the Supreme Court could take two years

and cost taxpayers up to $3.5 million.

That would buy a lot of schoolbooks, governor.

There might be some justification for signing an expensive, unenforceable bill if there was some certainty that an overwhelming majority of Idahoans thought it was worth it.

But that's not the case. Polls and the mail show no consensus that most Idahoans want to ban more than 90 percent of all abortions or to overturn Roe vs. Wade, both of which HB 625 is designed to do.

Let's view this from the outside looking in. How will the rest of the nation, which already focuses on the Aryan menace, see us now?

It's tragic that a pioneer state whose residents have long prided freedom and independence would even consider taking away a woman's right to exercise some control over her reproductive life.

Isn't it likely that many businesses will not be interested in setting up shop in such a state?

And what about doctors? Idaho needs more doctors, especially in rural areas. Few will want to move to a state where they will be subject to the legal harassment that's implicit in HB 625.

If that doesn't convince you, governor, consider Idaho women. Think of the wives and daughters who are being asked to give up control over what should be a private family decision, not a governmental one.

The bill is too extreme for many Idahoans and is fraught with costly legal entanglements.

Please veto HB 625. Do it for Idaho.

The Seattle Times
Seattle, Washington, March 25, 1990

THE Idaho legislature's passage of a law to ban 95 percent of all abortions is mob zealotry at work. It's all the more frightening when the zealots — paying no heed to individual rights — hold a few powerful seats in the state capitol.

Idaho was a target of the National Right to Life Committee, which has been shopping for a political arena supportive of its anti-abortion crusade. The Idaho legislature, commandeered by right-wing Mormon leadership, obliged with a crude attack on well-established privacy rights.

The law, which may — and should — be vetoed by Gov. Cecil Andrus, permits abortion only in cases of officially reported rape, incest if the victim is under 18, fetal deformity, or when pregnancy threatens a woman's physical health.

Any doctor performing an abortion for other reasons would face a $10,000 fine, and be subject to civil lawsuits by the father (even a rapist) of the fetus or anyone else establishing an interest in the case. Women caught trying to abort their own fetus would face the same penalties.

It's unclear whether the *people* of Idaho want to turn doctors and women into criminals. The law isn't an expression of political consensus; it's a tool fashioned by a narrow group to force the U.S. Supreme Court to reexamine the right to a legal abortion established in the 1973 Roe v. Wade decision.

The statute is aimed at Supreme Court Justice Sandra Day O'Connor, who anti-choice forces believe may be the swing vote to overturn Roe if given the opportunity.

The strategy could backfire: O'Connor has never stated she will vote to dismantle abortion rights. In fact, her sharp criticism of Minnesota and Ohio statutes requiring parental consent for teen-agers seeking abortions showed her uneasiness with laws far less restrictive than Idaho's. Decisions on those cases have not yet been issued.

Gov. Andrus can rescue Idaho from national ridicule by doing the reasonable thing: Veto the unconstitutional statute pushed through by a moralistic minority, and save Idaho taxpayers time, money, and needless grief defending a bad law.

THE SPOKESMAN-REVIEW
Spokane, Washington, March 23, 1990

It boils down to this: Idaho women give up their right to seek abortions. But, in exchange, the state gets a chance to have its name in a footnote to U.S. constitutional history.

A reasonable trade? Hardly. But that's the gist of legislation now headed to Idaho Gov. Cecil D. Andrus' desk. Idaho lawmakers have passed what, with abortion foe Andrus' signature, would be the most restrictive abortion law of any state.

In so doing, Gem State legislators are acting as handmaidens for the National Right to Life organization, which came up with the model law on which Idaho's bill is based and which longs for a constitutional confrontation in the U.S. Supreme Court.

Such a confrontation was invited last year when the Supreme Court indicated in a Missouri case, Webster vs. Reproductive Health Services, that states have some latitude in regulating abortions. The Webster decision eroded the landmark 1973 Roe vs. Wade opinion which held that an American woman's right to privacy extends to reproductive decisions, including whether to terminate a pregnancy.

Now, National Right to Life hopes it has, in Idaho, a vehicle to go after Roe vs. Wade altogether. The anti-abortion organization wants the more conservative Supreme Court of the 1990s to reverse the stand taken in 1973.

Unfortunately, Idaho lawmakers have supplied the vehicle — unless Andrus applies the brakes.

If enacted, the Idaho law would prohibit abortion except to save the mother's life or in cases of non-statutory rape reported within a week, incest when the victim is under age 18 or severe fetal deformity. In the case of an unintended, unwanted pregnancy, the mother would have no legal recourse. The pregnant teenager with no way to support herself or a baby would be stuck.

Or would she? Even if National Right to Life, using Idaho legislation for leverage, manages to pry open the shield around Idaho women's privacy, that would not affect other states unless their legislatures follow Idaho's lead. And that, public opinion surveys consistently indicate, would be unlikely.

Many Idahoans seeking abortions undoubtedly would find them in neighboring Washington, where state voters legalized the practice years ago. Thus, the impact of the Idaho law would not be to eliminate legal abortion as a means of terminating unwanted pregnancies, but rather, to limit it to those Idahoans who have the resources to travel out of state to obtain the procedure. As for those who don't, if the demand is high enough, some back-alley enterprise will meet it.

Andrus, in whose hands the bill's fate lies, has strong convictions against abortion. But he also has a commendable record of supporting equal rights for all state residents regardless of financial means. If he follows his anti-abortion convictions and signs the bill, it will be a symbolic but ineffective act. This is a case where fairness and compassion should be his guide.

THE ATLANTA CONSTITUTION
Atlanta, Georgia, March 24, 1990

For a glimpse of what the law will be like in some states if the U.S. Supreme Court reverses its 1973 ruling that gave women a right to a safe, lawful abortion, look to distant Guam.

The Pacific island, a self-governing U.S. territory whose residents are American citizens, has outlawed abortion unless two doctors testify that the mother's life is in danger or her health will be gravely harmed by giving birth. The law prosecutes anyone who performs an abortion as a felon and any woman who has an abortion as a misdemeanant. It even makes anyone advising or soliciting abortion subject to a fine or jail.

The provision against free speech is unconstitutional on its face and no doubt will be found so even by the current Supreme Court. (Though that's small comfort to the woman who already has been charged, after mentioning in a test-case speech to the Guam Press Club that women can fly to Hawaii for lawful abortions.)

It may well be, too, that most justices will want to deflect the Guam statute as a direct challenge to Roe v. Wade. Guam is overwhelmingly Roman Catholic. Twenty members of the 21-member Legislature are Catholic, and the anti-abortion law was passed after Archbishop Anthony Apuron threatened on television to excommunicate any lawmaker who voted against it.

A potentially key test of the right all American women have to safe, lawful abortion, has thus been created by the use of civil law to enforce one religion's doctrine on everyone, and it was enacted under open religious intimidation.

It is doubtful that even the justices President Reagan appointed to outlaw abortion will want to jump into a mess like that. As they shop for test cases, the law enacted a few days after Guam's by the Idaho Legislature is bound to strike them as more promising, precisely as national anti-abortion groups intended when they designed it.

The Idaho law will give the justices a slightly more respectable model for recriminalizing abortion; there's at least some consideration for rape and incest victims. But even if the court dodges Guam's law to accepts Idaho's, it would be eliminating any constitutional logic for barring Guam's law in the long run. Only if the wavering court finally sustains Roe v. Wade — and four of nine justices are committed to overturn it — will there be any constitutional protection from Guam-like extremes.

THE ⬥ SUN
Baltimore, Maryland, March 24, 1990

There was no glory to be found in the Maryland Senate's handling of the abortion issue, only shame. Instead of resolving the issue, senators chose a cowardly cop out: they passed two contradictory bills in hopes that both would be petitioned to referendum. When the going got tough, the Senate ran for cover.

What is the Senate's stance on abortions? It is for stringent restrictions and for liberalizing present law — both at the same time. Its position is actually no position at all. Most senators profess pride in this intentional obfuscation. They sought a crass political trade-off in order to end an increasingly mean-spirited and deadlocked filibuster. In the process, they made a mockery of representative government in Maryland.

Let's suppose that the U.S. Congress were to adopt the Maryland Senate's approach for dealing with delicate and highly controversial matters. Legislators could raise taxes and lower them, balance the budget and unbalance it, pass laws to clean up the environment and dirty it, declare war or declare peace — and then ask the voters to decide for them in a nationwide referendum.

What a ridiculous way to run a government!

Legislators in this country are elected to represent constituents in the making of laws. They are not supposed to abrogate that responsibility when pressure gets intense. They are elected and paid to make tough decisions and come up with difficult solutions to touchy social problems. That is what the Maryland Senate failed to do.

Perhaps what the state needs is a "new" Maryland Senate. Since our craven senators will not resign en masse, voters might want to consider making that decision for them in the fall elections.

It was fortunate that members of the House Environmental Matters Committee would have none of it. They killed off both bills last night. House leaders had the courage to make the tough calls that their Senate colleagues refused to make.

Unless the committee's action is reversed today on the House floor, the abortion issue is over for this General Assembly session. There will be no referendum in the fall. Instead, each side will target incumbents they feel are vulnerable.

Because of legislative inaction, Maryland remains in peril should the Supreme Court overturn its long-standing ruling on the legality of abortions. Women should not be denied the right to make a determination for themselves on an abortion during the early stages of pregnancy. Sadly, the General Assembly hasn't found the courage to deal with that issue directly and conclusively.

Louisiana Legislature Battles Gov. Roemer on Abortion Curbs

The Louisiana state legislature July 8, 1990 approved some of the nation's strictest curbs on abortion after failing to override Gov. Buddy Roemer's (D) veto of an even stricter measure.

Initially, the legislature had approved, on June 27, a bill that would have banned all abortions except to save the life of the mother. Doctors who performed illegal abortions would have been subject to prison terms of up to 10 years' hard labor.

Abortion opponents had pressed hard for passage of the measure so that it could be used as a challenge to the Supreme Court's 1973 *Roe v. Wade* decision legalizing abortion. The court had raised the hopes of abortion foes in 1989 with a decision that granted states wide latitude to restrict abortion. Since then, however, strict abortion curbs had been rejected in several states and blocked by courts in Pennsylvania and the U.S. territory of Guam.

Roemer vetoed the bill July 6 on the grounds that it made no exception for victims of rape or incest. "The rights of women must be protected against such horrible crimes," Roemer said.

Although the state House quickly voted July 6 to override the governor's veto, an override effort in the state Senate failed, July 7, when the measure was approved by a vote of 23 to 16 – three votes short of the two-thirds majority needed for an override.

In a last-ditch effort to pass some form of anti-abortion legislation during the current term, state senators and anti-abortion activists July 8 crafted a plan to gut a bill against flag desecration currently before the legislature and substitute language banning abortion except in cases of rape reported to the police within seven days, incest or threat to the mother's life. The revamped bill, which retained criminal penalties for doctors who performed abortions, quickly passed both houses of the legislature July 8.

Louisiana Gov. Buddy Roemer (D) July 27 vetoed the revamped bill as well. In vetoing the second bill, Roemer July 27 said, "I consider myself pro-life in the belief that abortion on demand must be, in the name of the unborn, sharply curtailed."

He added, "I have, however, grown in the personal belief that common sense, common decency and respect for women require exceptions" for victims of rape or incest. He said that although the legislature had succeeded in satisfying his concerns regarding incest victims, the requirement that rape victims report the crime within seven days in order to be eligible for an abortion was too restrictive. Roemer had asked for a reporting period of up to 30 days.

The Louisiana legislation June 18, 1991 adopted the most restrictive anti-abortion law of any U.S. state, overriding a veto by Gov. Roemer. The legislature had failed to pass an abortion bill over the 1990 veto.

The legislature was approved by the state Senate, 29–9, and by the House, 76–25. (A two-thirds majority of both houses had been needed to override Roemer's veto.)

The Louisiana law was expected to face an eventual Supreme Court challenge, as were strict anti-abortion laws passed by Utah and the U.S. territory of Guam.

FORT WORTH STAR-TELEGRAM
Fort Worth, Texas, July 10, 1990

Despite the bizarre twists and turns that gave it birth, a new anti-abortion law passed by the Louisiana Legislature could set the stage for the ultimate constitutional confrontation on *Roe vs. Wade*.

The Louisiana law, which would create the new crime of simple battery of abortion, undoubtedly will be challenged all the way to the U.S. Supreme Court, because its basic provisions strike at the core of the landmark 1972 Supreme Court ruling that struck down state laws infringing upon the constitutional rights of pregnant women.

Unlike new laws in some states that place restrictions on the right to an abortion after the first three months of pregnancy, Louisiana's new law would ban all abortions except in cases of rape, incest and endangerment of the life of the mother. In those cases, the abortion would have to be performed within the first trimester, and in the case of rape, the crime would have to be reported within seven days.

A physician convicted of simple battery abortion could face penalties of 10 years in prison and up to $100,000 in fines.

That anti-abortion law, which would be the toughest in the nation, was grafted upon the conceptual framework of a proposed anti-flag-burning bill after the legislature failed to override the governor's veto of a bill that would have banned all abortions.

The flag-burning bill would have made it a simple battery offense punishable by a $25 fine for beating up a flag burner. After the Supreme Court ruled that a federal statute banning flag burning was unconstitutional, a joke went around the nation suggesting that a law should be passed imposing an inconsequential fine for assault on flag burners.

Some members of the Louisiana Legislature took that suggestion seriously enough to introduce actual legislation to that effect, but proponents could not muster enough votes to pass it. That bill, with the flag-burning element eliminated, was transformed into the anti-abortion law.

Because of its evolution, some critics of the law have scoffed that the Lousiana Legislature went "from the most restrictive abortion bill in the nation to the most absurd."

Nevertheless, Louisiana's abortion law must be taken seriously everywhere in the United States because there is not room under the same constitutional umbrella for both the restrictive provisions of that statute and the theory of a basic right to privacy that is the legal essence of *Roe vs. Wade*.

The Times-Picayune
New Orleans, Louisiana, May 21, 1990

This week in New Orleans the voice of reason manifested itself in at least one troublesome aspect of the bitter nationwide struggle over abortion. It was the voice of a Municipal Court judge.

People on both sides of the controversial issue said they were pleased with a decision by Judge Bruce J. McConduit setting new guidelines for picketing at the city's abortion clinics. The ruling bars anti-abortion protesters from blocking access to the clinics.

The decision, which both the protesting groups and the clinics had asked for, resulted from charges against both sides stemming from a demonstration outside Orleans Women's Clinic at 211 Banks St.

The new guidelines also apply to three other clinics — Gentilly Medical Clinic for Women, New Orleans East Women's Clinic and Delta Women's Clinic.

Delta, at 1406 St. Charles Ave., has been the scene of many demonstrations by anti-abortion groups. The oldest abortion clinic in New Orleans, Delta opened shortly after the 1973 Supreme Court ruling in Roe vs. Wade judged abortions to be legal in the first three months of pregnancy.

In his decision, Judge McConduit restricted pickets to an area where they will not block access to the building. He said opposing pickets must stay at least five feet away, and prohibited demonstrators from touching any patient attempting to enter the building.

The decision contains specific instructions for each of the clinics. In that part relating to Orleans Women Clinic, Judge McConduit said, "Pro-life group shall be limited to, as you are looking at the building, the space between one foot from the driveway and three feet from the white brick wall closest to the sidewalk. Clinic escorts are to escort patient on the patient's left side to the entrance to the left of the building as you are looking at the building."

"It's a very ideal situation," said Michelle Gross, a co-chairwoman of Pontchartrain Organization for Women for Equal Rights. "It allows everyone to have their rights."

A "pro-life" representative also approved of the decision. "We're going to abide by it," said the Rev. Anthony Marquize, director of Gulf States United for Life. The minister gave credit to Judge McConduit for trying to be fair to both sides.

The appeal Judge McConduit's guidelines has for both sides indicates that his solution might well serve as a model for other cities with similar problems. It is a reasoned approach to an emotionally charged issue.

New Orleans has not been plagued by the kind of violence that has marked demonstrations at clinics in many other cities. There have been many arrests here, but the demonstrations have been relatively peaceful, clashes pretty much restricted to shouting, pushing and shoving.

Judge McConduit's guidelines draw a clear line in the dust both sides seem prepared to respect. Perhaps the agreement here can show that both sides can satisfy their purposes without changing the terms of the engagement from the issue itself to the way partisans behave.

The Washington Post
Washington, D.C., July 10, 1990

LEGISLATORS in Boise and Baton Rouge have put their governors on the spot this year on the question of abortion restrictions. In March, Idaho Gov. Cecil Andrus came under tremendous pressure to sign a bill that would have in effect outlawed abortion in Idaho. He vetoed it. Now Louisiana lawmakers have sent a similar bombshell to Gov. Buddy Roemer, who must decide within 20 days whether to veto, sign or let the bill become law without his signature.

The Louisiana law is even worse than the Idaho one. It would outlaw abortion except in cases of rape or incest reported promptly, or where necessary to save the life of the mother. Doctors performing abortions for any other reason would be subject to fines of $10,000 to $100,000 and one to 10 years in prison *at hard labor.* As originally passed, the Louisiana bill did not even contain an exemption for rape or incest, but that measure was vetoed by the governor, and his veto was sustained over the weekend. The amended version was passed in the final hours before adjournment Sunday and is now on the governor's desk.

Abortion opponents in Louisiana hope to present the Supreme Court with the most restrictive law in the nation as a test of the justices' fidelity to the underlying principle of *Roe v. Wade.* Certainly, a statute as sweeping as Louisiana's could not pass court muster unless *Roe* were repudiated. That is unlikely. The ACLU has announced its intention to test the statute if it becomes law.

Although Gov. Roemer describes himself as "a right-to-lifer"—as did Gov. Andrus—he sees the constitutional problems in approving the bill. He has raised procedural questions about the manner in which the bill was passed and substantive ones concerning requirements that victims of rape and incest must have reported the crime within seven days and received medical treatment. The attorney general of the state has voiced his objections. The governor is in a tough spot. Like Gov. Andrus, he comes up for reelection relatively soon, and he will have a lot of disappointed legislators on his hands if he exercises a veto. But if Gov. Roemer shows the same political courage as his colleague in Boise, he will reject this repressive and mean-spirited bill.

The Honolulu Advertiser
Honolulu, Hawaii, July 10, 1990

Louisiana Governor Buddy Roemer, who opposes abortion, may yet veto his state legislature's latest anti-abortion bill, as he did a previous stricter one.

But the Louisiana Legislature is clearly moving toward one of the nation's strictest anti-abortion laws. It would be used to challenge the Supreme Court's 1973 decision legalizing abortion nationwide.

Since the high court last year gave states more freedom to restrict abortions, some 350 abortion-related bills have been offered in more than 40 states. So far, only Pennsylvania, South Carolina, West Virginia and Guam have new, tighter laws. Others have come close.

The high court, as now composed, has balked at overturning the 1973 decision. But under its recent rulings, some states may allow women wide freedom of choice, as does Hawaii, while others may control the availability of abortion more tightly.

In anti-abortion states, women seeking abortions who can afford to travel, will. Those who cannot will find a doctor to break the law (at huge risk in some places), self-abort or have children they may be unable to raise. The result will be a legal crazyquilt.

Abortion is a sad last resort, but it's birth control women long have used and they will continue to do so. The question is whether they will be safe, clean, fairly priced procedures.

A new factor is the American Medical Association's call for testing of a drug which ends pregnancies of five weeks without surgery. RU-486 is used safely and effectively in France.

The "abortion drug" wouldn't end moral arguments. Some states may seek to outlaw it. But it would help return the debate where it belongs — the private, individual consciences of women, acting with advice of doctors and whomever they choose to consult.

The Record
Hackensack, New Jersey, August 1, 1990

The antiabortion bill passed recently by the Louisiana Legislature would have been the most restrictive in the nation. It would have imposed, for example, severe limits on the right of even victims of rape and incest to seek abortions. Governor Buddy Roemer was right to veto the measure. In the governor's words, "common sense, common decency, and respect for women" demanded no less.

Under the proposed law, abortion would have been allowed only in cases of rape or incest, or to save the life of the mother. And victims of rape and incest could not have obtained a legal abortion unless they had reported the crime and sought medical treatment within seven days. This meant, as Mr. Roemer put it, that "sheer trauma or ignorance would force a woman to bear and give birth to a child conceived in brutality." The vaguely worded bill also left it unclear whether relatives who paid for an abortion could be sentenced, like doctors who performed one, to 10 years of hard labor and fined $100,000.

"On issues like this," Mr. Roemer said, "the extremes speak the loudest and with the most concerted voices. I find that there are a multitude of families who don't classify themselves on either extreme." In issuing his veto, Mr. Roemer stood on the side of the moderation and decency of which he speaks.

The TENNESSEAN
Nashville, Tennessee, July 14, 1990

LOUISIANA legislators' zealous rush to enact anti-abortion legislation is a classic case of poorly conceived law.

Earlier this month Gov. Buddy Roemer vetoed anti-abortion legislation that would have denied all abortions except when the life of the woman was at stake. He said at the time that his main objection to the bill was that it did not allow abortions in the case of rape or incest.

Eager to satisfy Mr. Roemer's objections, Louisiana lawmakers quickly drafted another bill that puts more pressure on victims of rape. This bill allows abortion in instances of rape — if the rape is reported to authorities within seven days of its occurrence.

Such is the malicious mischief that can occur when lawmakers try to interfere in the most personal of decisions. Anxious to pass the "toughest abortion law in the country," Louisiana's lawmakers apparently are willing to ride roughshod over the most helpless in society.

The reasoning behind the rape notification provision is obvious. Without some evidence of rape, their law would be hard to enforce.

But Governor Roemer wisely withheld his immediate signature and indicated in an interview this week that he will probably not sign the bill. The idea of forcing women to report rape strikes at the very heart of privacy.

The governor also questioned the method used to pass the measure. The anti-abortion bill was actually an amendment to a bill that lessens penalties for people who attack flag-burners. The Louisiana Constitution prohibits lawmakers from attaching amendments that are not germane to the original bill.

Governor Roemer supports some restrictions on abortion. While his position on abortion may not be appreciated by all abortion rights supporters, his caution on the matter surely should be.

It would have been easy for him to just sign the second bill, which was rushed through the legislature after an override of his veto failed. His doubts about the legislation's fairness and its constitutionality show a restraint his eager legislators should emulate. ■

Arkansas Gazette.
Little Rock, Arkansas, July 27, 1990

Louisiana Gov. Buddy Roemer is being tested, and so far he's come through in great shape.

A few weeks ago, Roemer vetoed an irresponsible but politically popular bill that would have outlawed abortion even in cases of rape and incest. Wednesday, he vetoed a bill that would have required warning labels on recordings that deal with potentially offensive topics, such as drug abuse, sex and violence, and would have prohibited the sale of these recordings to persons under 17.

The labeling bill is a clear restriction on free speech, which is why Roemer vetoed it. As a parent, he objects to many of the recordings now sold, he said, but not enough to permit the government to infringe on individual rights. He said he hoped that a voluntary labeling system recently begun by the recording industry would succeed.

Tipper Gore showed her class by appearing with Roemer at a news conference. Mrs. Gore, president of the Parents Music Resource Center, has been a leading critic of what she considers dangerous recordings. But she also prefers voluntary labeling to government-imposed labeling, and proved it by her appearance with Roemer. Many of those who complain about recordings would rather the government take charge. They hate the First Amendment and seek ways to weaken it.

Under the bill Roemer vetoed, retailers, manufacturers and distributors would have been subject to jail terms and fines of up to $5,000 for violations — lighter punishment than murderers and drug dealers usually get, but more than savings and loan executives who stole millions.

Roemer has another test facing him. After he vetoed the abortion bill, the legislature slipped another one through in questionable fashion, tacking anti-abortion provisions onto another piece of legislation in the closing days of the session. This second bill is now before Roemer. It's not as bad as the first, but it's terrible and still would be the strictest anti-abortion law among all the states. Obviously the Louisiana legislature is out of its banks. Doctors performing abortions could be sentenced up to 10 years in prison and fined up to $100,000. Exceptions would be made only for rape, incest and to save the life of the mother.

Roemer has declined to say whether he'll veto the bill or allow it to become law. He has a hot streak of leadership going. Why not extend it with another veto?

The Dallas Morning News
Dallas, Texas, May 24, 1990

As emotional as abortion protests have become, there must be limits on how far any demonstration can go. Otherwise, the protesters' constitutional right to express themselves begins to infringe upon other people's right to get abortions. Three U.S. Supreme Court rulings this term, one which came this week, have defined what protesters may not do, as well as what they may do. Those guidelines now need to be observed.

As broad as the First Amendment may be, it simply does not allow someone to block an entrance to an abortion clinic. Nor does it permit a protester to unduly harass a patient or a clinic worker. Protesters, of course, still have every right to disapprove of abortion and to state their opposition in as vivid of terms as they may see fit.

The court hardly could have ruled any other way. As an appellate court judge wrote, "Blocking access to public and private buildings has never been upheld as a proper method of communication in an orderly society." In a nation such as ours, where the rule of law prevails, the circumstances under which a woman should be able to have an abortion is a question to be decided by lawmakers and jurists, not by protesters.

Rather than jamming themselves into doorways, abortion opponents would serve their cause far better by focusing their efforts on the political arena. Their message — that abortion is wrong and must be stopped — was not, in any way, encumbered by the high court. So long as they don't overstep the newly defined limits of protest, they are as free as ever to convey their sentiments to people in power or to those who seek it.

The Honolulu Advertiser

Honolulu, Hawaii, July 28, 1990

Louisiana Governor Buddy Roemer deserves praise — as did Idaho Governor Cecil Andrus a few months back — for not being railroaded.

Roemer, who says he is "pro-life," refused to sign an anti-abortion bill that was draconian in its harshness, particularly to rape victims. It was his second such veto this year.

No one favors abortion as an ideal method of birth control. But most Americans do believe it should be available as a last resort when a woman has legitimate reasons to end a pregnancy early in its term.

"One of the things that I've tried to become sensitive to is the voice of women on this issue," Roemer said. Only three of Louisiana's 144 state legislators are women.

Eventually, those legislators may pass a bill Roemer can sign in good conscience. Or they may break a strong historical precedent by overriding his veto in special session. Louisiana may yet become the most difficult place in the nation to obtain an abortion.

Especially if Roe vs. Wade is overturned by a Supreme Court with one or two new justices, such dramas as the one in Baton Rouge may be repeated in other state capitals. The result, unfortunately, will be a crazy-quilt of abortion laws that vary widely from state to state.

The losers will be the young, poor and ill-educated who can not travel to those states where a woman's right to make her own personal decisions on abortion is protected.

Los Angeles Times

Los Angeles, California, July 10, 1990

What a creative bunch those Louisiana state legislators are. Instead of spending their time shoring up a sagging state economy or increasing literacy, a single-minded faction of the Legislature has fixated on laying down the law on abortion. Why go after issues that require complex thought and planning when the political equivalent of a fistfight will do?

The proposed Louisiana law would outlaw abortion except in the cases of rape, incest or when the pregnant woman's life is in danger, and would institute an unprecedented penalty on doctors of up to 10 years in prison and a $100,000 fine.

It would be easy to disparage Louisiana for its backwardness. But actually, this bill is merely the most radical example of the continuing fallout from last year's confused Supreme Court decision on abortion. An indecisive high court was not quite willing to overturn the landmark Roe vs. Wade case legalizing abortion, but it was willing to throw it back to the states to renew debate on abortion restrictions. So the attempts to restrict abortions keep coming—from Idaho, where a stricter law failed, to Pennsylvania, where one succeeded.

The Louisiana law now is in the hands of Gov. Buddy Roemer, who said he favored an anti-abortion law but who now questions the constitutionality of this one. That's because the anti-abortion bill was transformed, whole cloth, from a bill that would have allowed a maximum $25 fine for beating someone who burned the flag.

"Only in Louisiana could you have a flag burning bill become an abortion bill," said one abortion-rights activist. Not so. Not anymore.

Quayle's Abortion Comment Stirs Widespread Debate

U.S. vice president Dan Quayle appeared July 22, 1992 on the Cable News Network interview show "Larry King Live." Host Larry King, alluding to the abortion issue, asked Quayle what he would do if his 13-year-old daughter "grew up" and got pregnant. "I would counsel her and talk to her and support her on whatever decision she made," replied Quayle, adding, "I'd hope that she wouldn't make that decision [for an abortion]."

The comment quickly became the subject of controversy since Quayle had always been a strong advocate of making abortion illegal.

Democrats accused the vice president of hypocrisy. "You can't make a distinction between your own blood and everybody else's daughter," said New York Gov. Mario Cuomo (D) July 23. Clinton the same day said Quayle had answered the question "as a father, not a vice president."

Quayle July 23 denied the comment signaled a change in his stance against abortion.

Quayle's wife, Marilyn, said their daughter, Corinne, had been "raised in a Christian household" and taught to behave responsibly. However, she added, "If she becomes pregnant, she'll take the child to term."

The San Diego
Union-Tribune.
San Diego, California, July 25, 1992

Vice President Dan Quayle took a deep breath and gave an answer from his heart on "Larry King Live" the other night.

Asked what he would do if his daughter became pregnant and decided to have an abortion, Quayle said he hoped she wouldn't make that decision and that he would counsel her, but that he would support her in whatever decision she made. It was the natural reaction of any conscientious father.

And his answer shed light on the abortion dilemma in America. Nobody likes abortion. But most Americans also do not relate to extremists on either side of the issue. Most Americans view abortion with gnawing ambivalence.

When asked whether abortion should be outlawed, most Americans say no. If asked whether they approve of the act of abortion, most Americans also would say no.

That's not wishy-washiness. When faced with a difficult moral question such as abortion, in which any decision carries serious life-long personal consequences, it's a natural human reaction to feel unsettled.

Quayle's honest answer helps remove the abortion debate from a doctrinaire straitjacket. People feel forced to choose sides on the issue when they don't really want to. In the political arena, Quayle has said he favors a constitutional amendment banning most abortions. And yet, when faced with abortion as an intensely personal question, he is much more irresolute.

Quayle should not back away from his statement. Nor should administration handlers scurry to try to make it appear consistent with his past positions on abortion. His words reflect the mainstream view on abortion: "I don't like it, but . . . "

The pro and con screaming outside abortion clinics has led many Americans to believe one side must be right, and the other side wrong. In truth, neither extreme is necessarily right.

If more people honestly confessed their ambivalence about abortion, like Quayle did on television, perhaps the nation could deal with this highly emotional issue in a calmer, more rational way.

LEXINGTON HERALD-LEADER
Lexington, Kentucky, July 25, 1992

Finally, Vice President Dan Quayle got it right.

In an interview on "Larry King Live," he forgot to don his politician's hat and failed to speak in Bush-Quayle rhetoric. In answering a question about abortion, he sounded like, well, a good father, a concerned one and, most important, one who understands that abortion is a difficult choice that ultimately belongs to the woman involved.

King asked what he would do if his daughter grew up and came to him "with a problem all fathers fear."

Quayle answered that it was a hypothetical situation, one that he hopes he would never have to deal with. "I would counsel her and talk to her and support her on whatever decision she made."

And if the decision were abortion? "I'd support my daughter," Quayle said. "I'd hope that she wouldn't make that decision."

His answer stood in contrast to his wife's the next day. If their daughter, now age 13, were pregnant, Marilyn Quayle said, "She'll take the child to term."

Afterward came the back-pedaling and the clarifications. Marilyn Quayle said she had been talking about what would happen if her 13-year-old daughter became pregnant now. (Her comments offered a glimpse of the difficulty the daughter would have in telling her mother she was pregnant and wanted an abortion. It simply would not be an option, so where would the daughter turn?)

For his part, Dan Quayle came back with a reminder that he had been talking about her as an adult. He went on to say that his remarks on King's show reflected no change in his position. "We are pro-life," he said. "We are opposed to abortion."

That's the politician talking, one who needs to re-examine his rhetoric on the issue and how it meshes with his comments on King's show. If choice is an option for his daughter, why should it not continue to be an option for all women in this country?

Quayle, the father, demonstrated respect for an individual's right to make the most personal of decisions. Quayle, the politician, could learn from his empathetic alter ego.

The Hutchinson News
Hutchinson, Kansas, July 25, 1992

The Quayle family's venture into the politics of abortion was revealing last week when Marilyn and Dan Quayle provided slightly different answers to questions concerning how they would handle abortion as a family matter.

Placing the abortion issue on a personal level, the Quayles were separately asked how they would react if their own teen-age daughter became pregnant.

Without equivocation, Marilyn Quayle insisted her daughter would bear the child. Her husband said he would support whatever decision his daughter made, an answer that infuriated anti-abortion conservatives.

While the Quayles were answering a hypothethical question, it is the question many American families are confronting today, both as a philosophical abstraction and as a harsh reality.

The Quayles' answers only emphasize the difficulties Americans are facing when it comes to the question of abortion. Dan Quayle's answer exposes the difference between espousing a particular political belief as opposed to personally confronting a real situation within the bosom of one's own family.

His answer reveals that while his political mind is made up, his mind as a parent is more flexible.

None of this is meant to criticize the Quayles. It is one thing to preach to a nation that a particular conduct is acceptable. It is quite another to confront the issue head-on and become so immersed in a family crisis that long-standing principles, once so clear in calm times, become less so when coming face-to-face with jolting reality.

This is less hypocrisy than it is the ambiguity of human nature, which generally tends to go to extremes when it comes to aiding our children, a tendency Dan Quayle innocently revealed in himself.

The national debate over abortion is often vicious and vile, a mixed bag of religious perceptions, moral underpinnings, social virtues and political planks. But in a home embroiled in the crisis brought on by an unwanted pregnancy, abortion is a whole other matter entirely.

Dan Quayle was speaking as a father, and while he ran for cover as a politician representing so-called conservative values, he told his own version of the truth, revealing that such personal matters may not belong in politics at all.

The Phoenix Gazette
Phoenix, Arizona, July 27, 1992

Vice President Dan Quayle is getting bashed over his own words again, this time on abortion. Democrats are howling about his comments on "Larry King Live" that he would support his daughter if she chose to have an abortion.

Quayle, a strong opponent of abortion, was asked: "What if your daughter grew up and . . . came to you with that problem that all fathers fear? How would you deal with it?"

"Well," Quayle responded, "it's a hypothetical question and I hope I never do have to deal with it. But obviously I would counsel her and talk to her and support her on whatever decision she made."

Those candid, painfully honest comments from a father have produced a swarm of protest from pro-choice activists. They suggest Quayle would deny choice for everyone except his daughter, the wealthy and powerful.

Which raises two ironic and contradictory points.

First of all, Quayle was speaking honestly, from the heart, and responding as a father, not as a calculating political candidate.

Why be so hard on him? Don't we want our elected leaders to acknowledge the complexity of these issues, the moral struggles involved? Is that not the first step to reasonable debate on such questions?

Indeed, wife Marilyn later contradicted her husband by insisting that if her daughter became pregnant, "She'll take the child to term." That answer is by far the more politically correct response for a conservative Republican in the 1990s.

But the vice president's response, we suspect, was more candid for a modern-day parent.

Second, the pro-choice activists make a valid point. The vice president's remarks run counter to his politics. But the critics might have drawn the irony more sympathetically to Quayle. Had they done so, they might have scored more points in this important policy debate.

Make no mistake, though. If, as the saying goes, a 1960s conservative was a liberal who had been mugged, then a 1990s liberal is a conservative with a teenage daughter.

The Hartford Courant
Hartford, Connecticut, July 27, 1992

Bill Clinton got this one right. What would he do, he was asked, if his 12-year-old daughter got pregnant? "I wouldn't talk to the press about it," he said.

Mr. Clinton was responding to a question raised after Vice President Dan Quayle became embroiled in a controversy that started on the "Larry King Live" show. What would he do, Mr. King asked the vice president, if his daughter, as an adult, became pregnant and decided to have an abortion? Mr. Quayle answered, quite rightly, that he would support his daughter.

The pro-choice forces started celebrating. "It sounds like choice to me," said House Speaker Thomas S. Foley. The National Abortion Rights Action League welcomed Mr. Quayle's "newfound respect for his daughter's freedom to choose."

Seeking to distance themselves from this interpretation of his remarks, Mr. Quayle and his wife, Marilyn, did some clarifying. If their daughter, as an adult, made the choice to have an abortion, they wouldn't like it but they would still support her. But if, as the 13-year-old she is now, she became pregnant, she would "take the child to term," said Mrs. Quayle.

This strange episode illustrates dramatically why abortion and politics don't mix, and why the issue should be a private one.

Of course the Quayles should support their daughter, even if she made a choice they disagreed with. But the fierceness, and the public nature, of their declaration about their 13-year-old, are upsetting. How must this poor child feel to have such a private, delicate matter, concerning her sexuality and her body, discussed in the national news media, and at such a vulnerable age? It's inappropriate and demeaning.

Mr. Clinton was right again when he said he thought Mr. Quayle had answered Mr. King's question "as a father, not as a vice president."

That's the point.

This is a decision any person has to make, or support, not as a politician or a judge or any other kind of public figure. It's a private matter, which individuals have to assess as private citizens: as parents, husbands, siblings and, most important, as potential mothers.

After the convention, there were rumblings about Mr. Clinton's and Sen. Albert Gore Jr.'s use of their family's traumas as public demonstrations of their political convictions — particularly Mr. Gore's use of the near-death of his son. Was this appropriate? some wondered.

Now it seems that Mr. Clinton, at least, knows where to draw the line. He refused to make his daughter's body a matter for public discussion.

The Quayles' willingness to sacrifice their young daughter's privacy for the sake of politics is worrying indeed.

Detroit Free Press

Detroit, Michigan, July 28, 1992

Vice President Dan Quayle spoke as a concerned parent, rather than a standard-issue politician, in his celebrated discussion of abortion last week. Such candor, even if unintentional, probably ought to be appreciated rather than censured by either advocates or opponents of abortion rights.

Mr. Quayle was asked in a television interview how he would react if his teenage daughter, as an adult, chose to have an abortion. His response: "... obviously I would counsel her and talk to her and support her on whatever decision she made ... I would hope that she wouldn't make that decision." Even that reasonable-sounding answer conflicts with the Republican Party's and Bush administration's highly restrictive posture toward abortion, and the vice president quickly reiterated his opposition to the procedure.

Yet Mr. Quayle's initial, unvarnished response seems more in keeping with the honest ambivalence felt by many people on both sides of the abortion issue. It was more helpful than the dogmatic assertion of the vice president's wife that if their daughter, as a teenager, becomes pregnant, " ... she'll take the child to term" — a position later seconded on the campaign trail by Mr. Quayle.

Abortion rights advocates have a point when they accuse the vice president of favoring choice for his own family, while denying it to everyone else. But it probably doesn't need to be pushed too far. If Mr. Quayle is guilty of anything, it may be inadvertent — but welcome — sincerity. There may be plenty of valid reasons for President George Bush to dump the vice president from his re-election ticket, but this isn't one of them.

The Detroit News

Detroit, Michigan, July 25, 1992

Vice-President Dan Quayle gave an honest, thoughtful answer to a hypothetical question about abortion and his daughter. Now he's reportedly caught up in a "storm" and is "under fire" because of his answer.

Baloney. The whole "controversy" is a phony, manufactured by a media-interest-group "controversy" machine that automatically overheats every time Dan Quayle's name is mentioned.

On CNN's *Larry King Live* Wednesday, Mr. Quayle was asked, "What if your daughter grew up and had a problem and came to you with that problem that all fathers fear?" To that very ambiguous and hypothetical question, Mr. Quayle answered in part: "I hope that I never have to deal with it. But obviously I would counsel her and talk to her and support her on whatever decision she made." Asked if the decision of his daughter were to abort, Mr. Quayle said: "I would support my daughter. I would hope that she wouldn't make that decision."

Of course. What pro-life father, dealing with a presumably adult daughter, as Mr. King's question implied, wouldn't have said exactly the same thing? This is the stuff of controversy?

Later, both the vice-president and his wife said that "under the present situation," their daughter would carry her child to term. The "present situation" is that the vice-president's daughter is a 13-year old. The statements are not at all mutually contradictory. Parents of young teens have much more control over their children than parents of adults. Can this be big news to pro-choice forces and Democratic Party officials?

Apparently. A Republican pro-choice official said the vice-president's remarks "seem contradictory" and House speaker Tom Foley said Mr. Quayle's answer "sounds like choice." Only if you are brain dead.

Bill Clinton attempted a subtle dig, saying Mr. Quayle "wasn't prepped" for the question and then reiterated his own abortion position. But he at least resisted further temptations to pile on.

All the vice-president did in his answer to Larry King's questions was indicate that he would not push his daughter out of his life if she did something he disagreed with. That is the mark of a loving parent. If this qualifies as a "gaffe," then no candidate can say anything reasonable or human about any delicate situation.

In this instance, there is no real "storm of controversy." Just a tempest in the media teapot. Where, of course, nobody ever misspells a word, writes a clumsy phrase or serves in the National Guard.

THE ARIZONA REPUBLIC

Phoenix, Arizona, July 25, 1992

ONCE again the thundering herd of independent thinkers has joined the partisan gunslingers in galloping off in hot pursuit of Dan Quayle, who had the timerity to suggest on *Larry King Live* that if his grown daughter became pregnant and wanted an abortion, he would try to talk her out of it but, failing in the attempt, would "support her on whatever decision she made."

"Sounds like choice to me," smirked House Speaker Tom Foley. It was "classic pro-choice," said New York Gov. Mario Cuomo. "You can't make a distinction between your own blood and everybody else's daughter."

Both gentlemen were allowing partisanship to cloud their powers of reason. As columnist William F. Buckley observes (see his column on the page opposite), a man may support his daughter in all manner of mistaken actions that he would regret to see either made legal or universalized.

Mr. Quayle was asked how he would respond if his daughter were to make, by his lights, a tragic mistake. What was he supposed to say? "As you know, Larry, I'm a gibbering idiot on the subject of abortion, and if my grown daughter refused to accept my judgment in the matter, I'd have no choice but to call in Marilyn, and together we'd just lock her in the basement until she came to term." Or, as Mr. Buckley suggests, he could have said that he'd tell her never to darken the door of the Quayle home again.

As it happens, Mr. Quayle responded as most pro-life fathers would have done. He would hope, he said, that his daughter would not choose an abortion. "I would counsel her and talk to her and support her on whatever decision she made."

To such fair-minded and reasonable people as Kate Michelman, president of the National Abortion Rights League, the vice president's position smacked of hypocrisy. "While we welcome Vice President Quayle's newfound respect for his own daughter's freedom to choose," gloated Ms. Michelman disingenuously, "we regret that he and President Bush want to take that same freedom away from everyone else."

What a hideous distortion. It is hardly hypocrisy to concede (a) that one's grown daughter has a right to avail herself of whatever legal options are available, however one might deplore certain alternatives and urge her to avoid them, but (b) that in any event she may rely on her father's support. The word for this is not hypocrisy, but devotion.

Tasting blood, some critics even tried to suggest that Marilyn Quayle, the vice president's wife, had undercut her husband by saying, at a news conference in Evansville, Ind., that their daughter, who is 13, "would have the child." In fact, Mrs. Quayle was speaking of a 13-year-old, whereas her husband had been asked how he would respond "if your daughter grew up and had a problem."

One thing more. Let the record show that in the midst of this feeding frenzy, Democratic presidential candidate Bill Clinton, offered a chance to join in the fun, behaved instead with decency and restraint. "My impression is he was asked a question he was not prepared for, prepped for," said Mr. Clinton. "He answered it as a father, not a vice president."

Exactly — demonstrating, as did Mr. Clinton, that not every politician is everywhere and on all occasions a fanatic.

THE BLADE
Toledo, Ohio, July 29, 1992

EVERY so often in most people's life, an agonizing choice must be made between principle and the protection and caring for loved ones. These crises of values usually pass unnoticed behind the closed doors of private homes. For a politician in an election year there is no such privacy.

The luxury of trying to balance what sometimes appear to be irreconcilable positions must be done in the glare of the cameras' lights and to the accompanying scribbling of reporters' pens.

In the last presidential campaign, Gov. Michael Dukakis was asked how he, as an opponent of capital punishment, would react if his wife were raped and murdered. He made a somewhat cold, stiff comment reaffirming his stand against the death penalty, and another nail was banged into his bid for the White House.

Last week, Vice President Dan Quayle, fresh from the controversy over *Murphy Brown* and his misspelling of "potato," was questioned on abortion by television interviewer Larry King. Mr. King didn't ask a question of principle. He asked a personal question. There are arguments as to whether such questions are appropriate, but having been asked, Mr. Quayle answered.

Asked what he would do if his daughter were grown up and came to him saying she was pregnant, Mr. Quayle said he would counsel her and support her whatever her decision. He and his wife, Marilyn, said that if the girl were still a juvenile, she would carry the child to term, and Mr. Quayle reiterated that he and his wife are opposed to abortion rights.

He answered as a father, not a vice president. He answered as a man concerned for the well-being of his daughter, wanting to support her. It would have been a rather touching response for a private citizen. For the vice president it was another land mine upon which he had stepped squarely.

The conundrum posed by the question was quickly picked up by proponents of abortion rights who argued that Mr. Quayle has a double standard, wanting one rule for his family, another for the rest of the American people. House Speaker Thomas Foley put it succinctly: "Sounds like choice to me."

Gov. Bill Clinton sidestepped the issue saying that if his daughter were in that situation, he wouldn't talk to the press. But he's talking apples and oranges. Mr. Quayle likely wouldn't talk to the press either if it were a real situation rather than a response to a hypothetical question.

By answering the question as a parent, Mr. Quayle underscored the danger in legislating to restrict abortion rights. If a constitutional amendment banning many abortions, supported by Mr. Quayle, were in effect, it wouldn't matter what his daughter decided. She wouldn't have a choice, and he wouldn't be able to counsel her because there would be nothing to counsel her about. Lawmakers who oppose abortion rights would have taken that woman's and that family's choice away from them.

Political analysts from both parties will be watching closely in the coming weeks to see how the vice president's comments play in the country at large. To some, he will be a more sympathetic figure for having spoken as a caring father; to his critics, it will be yet another example of the vice president opening his mouth only to change feet.

The Philadelphia Inquirer
Philadelphia, Pennsylvania, July 26, 1992

In an unguarded, apparently unscripted moment on a TV talk show last week, Vice President Quayle seemed to speak from the heart. The question on the table was what Mr. Quayle would do if his own daughter "came to you with that problem that all fathers fear."

Nice bit of delicacy there: We'd submit that the problem at issue (called *pregnancy* by the euphemism-impaired) is one that all daughters (and sons) fear as well.

The Vice President said he'd counsel his daughter and "support her in whatever decision she made." And if that decision was abortion? "I'd support my daughter," he said without hesitation. "I'd hope she wouldn't make that decision."

That brief, seemingly genuine exchange touched off a firestorm. From the abortion-rights side came predictable sound bites: "We are pleased to welcome Mr. Quayle to the pro-choice family," said Planned Parenthood. Even House Speaker Tom Foley weighed in: "Sounds like choice to me ... a respect for the woman's right to make the decision." Actually, it seemed like something larger — a parent's instinctive desire to support a child, right or wrong.

Soon enough, Second Lady Marilyn Quayle was beating back the flames: "If she becomes pregnant, she'll take the child to term," Mrs. Quayle declared, reasserting the ideological purity that, for a brief shining moment, her husband had seemed to abandon.

In that moment, Dan Quayle did unwittingly what the ideologues will not: He gave a human face to the abortion issue, opening a window on the deeply painful, personal dilemmas that unwanted pregnancy poses. That may be a gaffe in some camps. We see it as candor — and a rare and refreshing sighting at that.

The Chattanooga Times
Chattanooga, Tennessee, July 25, 1992

Vice President Dan Quayle probably didn't help his case for staying on the Republican ticket this fall by stumbling into a pro-choice position on abortion the other day.

That will hurt Mr. Quayle with archconservatives and the anti-abortion movement, which he has been championing, and seed more doubts about his intellectual merit for his office. But in saying he would support his daughter if she chose to have an abortion, he revealed a most natural parental reflex and, in a moment of candor, reinforced the foundational argument for the right to choice.

Mr. Quayle, as he and his wife later stressed, are officially against abortion. They say often it should be outlawed. And that position, which the Republican Party would propose as a constitutional amendment, will be adopted as part of the GOP platform at the party's convention next month.

But when it comes to his own daughter, in a straight-up, no-trick question on *Larry King Live*, Mr. Quayle takes the position that would come naturally to most parents whose love and longing for the well-being of their *own* children take precedence over official ideology they might preach for *other* people.

Q: What if your daughter grew up and had a problem and came to you with that problem that all fathers fear? How would you deal with it?

Mr. Quayle: Well, it's a hypothetical situation and I hope that I never do have to deal with it. But obviously I would counsel her and talk to her and support her whatever decision she made.

Q: If the decision was abortion, you'd support her?

Mr. Quayle: I'd support my daughter. I would hope that she wouldn't make that decision.

That is, in fact, a pro-choice viewpoint, much as the Quayles might now refute it. Most people, polls show, do not *favor* abortion; they simply think such decisions should be left up to the person whose life will be most affected and not made by state edict or government intervention into the most private aspects of one's life.

Pro-choice proponents say most people who are against the legal right to abortion accept three exceptions: rape, incest, and their own family. Mr. Quayle's unscripted candor reveals the concern from which that thesis springs. It might expose him to charges of hypocrisy, but it reveals the humanity that supports the right to choice.

■ The Cincinnati Post
Cincinnati, Ohio, July 25, 1992

Just this week we used this space to say that the vice president is a doofus and a bumbler and a drag on the GOP ticket. Dan Quayle has earned most of the criticism he has received over the last four years, but he doesn't deserve the latest rap against him.

Appearing on CNN's "Larry King Live" program, Quayle and King had the following exchange:

King: What if your daughter grew up and had a problem, came to you with that problem all fathers fear? How would you deal with it?

Quayle: Well, it is a hypothetical situation. I hope I never have to deal with it. But obviously—

King: What would you do?

Quayle: I would counsel her and talk to her and support her on whatever decision she made.

King: And if that decision was abortion, you'd support her, as a parent?

Quayle: I'd support my daughter. I'd hope that she wouldn't make that decision.

If Quayle erred, it was that he ignored a cardinal rule of politics: Never answer a hypothetical question. Michael Dukakis got clobbered during the 1988 presidential debates when he fumbled a similar question, and Quayle should have known better.

Abortion advocates jumped on Quayle's answer to try to prove that the vice president was waffling on his anti-abortion position, or that he was hypocritically supporting the right to choose for his daughter but not for others.
He was doing neither. He merely said what fathers should always say: When my child grows up, I hope she'll make the right decisions; but, no matter what she does, even if I disagree, I'll stay by her side.

Dan, you did good this time. For once, reality seemed to take precedence over the rhetoric. The pity is you felt compelled the next day to change your tune.

The Des Moines Register
Des Moines, Iowa, July 24, 1992

Poor Dan Quayle. Even when he gives a sensible, compassionate, almost touching answer to a question, he causes a political uproar.

Appearing on the "Larry King Live" show Wednesday night, the vice president was asked what he would do if his daughter became pregnant and sought an abortion. Quayle said he would counsel his daughter and would hope that she would not get an abortion, but would support her in whatever decision she made.

It was a warm, fatherly answer. But in the world of anti-abortion dogma, it was po-

DAN QUAYLE   **MARILYN QUAYLE**

litically incorrect. The GOP platform calls for a constitutional amendment to ban most abortions. The Bush-Quayle administration has tried to pack the Supreme Court with judges who will abolish the right of women to choose abortion.

Quayle was expressing support for his daughter's hypothetical decision to engage in what his party wants to make a criminal act. Moreover, anti-abortion zealots hold that abortion is murder. Surely not even a loving father like Quayle would support his daughter in an act of murder.

Obviously, he doesn't believe that abortion is murder. The vice president's remarks put him in the position of appearing to support choice for his daughter, while wanting to deny it to everybody else.

On a Des Moines radio show Thursday, Marilyn Quayle disagreed with her husband. She said if their daughter became pregnant, "she'll take the child to term."

The vice president on Thursday said his remarks reflected no change in his position on abortion. "We are pro-life," he said. "We are opposed to abortion."

A spokesman said Quayle did not mean that he would allow his teen-age daughter to have an abortion, but if she made that decision as an adult he would support her.

David O'Steen, executive director of the National Right to Life Committee, tried to put a good face on the vice president's seeming heresy. He was quoted as saying that "most right-to-life parents would give the same response" as Quayle.

If so, then a lot of right-to-life parents are closer to the abortion rights position than they've let on. The great debate raging in this country isn't whether abortion is right or wrong. Indeed, many "pro-choice" Americans believe that abortion is wrong. Others believe it is wrong in certain circumstances, acceptable in others. Hardly anyone "favors" abortion.

What they favor is the right to decide belonging to individual women, not to the government. Corinne Quayle, 13, has that right, which in her case would be exercised within the embrace of a loving family.

Not all women are so fortunate as to have such families, but they all should continue to have the same right to decide.

Minneapolis Star and Tribune
Minneapolis, Minnesota, July 24, 1992

The hullabaloo over Vice President Dan Quayle's remarks on abortion says more about the state of political discourse than it does about Quayle.

All Quayle did was allow the political mask to slip a bit. For a moment he was just a human being, a father. As nice as it would be if Quayle joined the abortion-rights ranks, he didn't, and no amount of clever construing of his answer can make it otherwise.

On the Larry King show, Quayle was asked: If your daughter grew up and became pregnant and came to you, what would you do? Quayle answered: "I would counsel her and talk to her and support her on whatever decision she made."

King then asked: "And if the decision was abortion, you'd support her as a parent?"

Quayle replied: "I'd support my daughter. I'd hope that she wouldn't make that decision."

That answer isn't for abortion; it's for a daughter. As someone pointed out, most parents, whatever
their position on abortion, would say the same.

And yet Quayle has been variously praised for finding the "prochoice" faith or condemned for gross hypocrisy. All that is baloney.

Larry King let the tough question go unasked. When Quayle said, "I'd support my daughter. I'd hope that she wouldn't make that decision," King might have asked: Should government let her make that decision? That's the guts of the abortion debate, and it would have been enlightening to hear how Quayle responded while his political mask was askew.

Few people actively extol the virtues of abortion. It represents failure. But failure happens, and it should be up to an individual woman finally to judge whether abortion represents the least horrible option for dealing with her situation. Let parents counsel against abortion, let ministers preach the sanctity of life, let antiabortion activists seek to provide alternatives. But let each woman decide, and then support her, as Dan Quayle would support his daughter, in that decision.

ALBUQUERQUE JOURNAL

Albuquerque, New Mexico, July 26, 1992

Rarely in the long and often vituperative abortion debate have so many sought to read so much into so little as they have into Vice President Dan Quayle's answer to a hypothetical question.

Quayle was asked what he would do if his daughter "grew up and came to you with that problem all fathers fear?"

"I hope I never have to deal with it," Quayle answered. "But obviously I would counsel her and talk to her and support her on whatever decision she made."

Pro-choicers pounced on his answer like hyenas on a lamb. An abortion rights group spokesman asserted Quayle's stance "smacks of a double standard," and Democratic presidential nominee Bill Clinton, an abortion rights supporter, said Quayle's remarks were in line with "my position that these matters should not be turned back into crimes."

Double standard? Crimes? Those responses were clumsy attempts to read ideological or political connotations into a loving father's simple affirmation of support for his daughter no matter what. Clinton, when asked a similar question about his daughter, evaded it by answering, "I wouldn't talk to the press about it."

Parents everywhere need only consider all the things their offspring have done despite strong parental disapproval — but which did not extinguish parental support and love. Then it would be obvious that Quayle's from-the-heart response was in no way a modification of or even an expression of his own personal opposition to abortion. A loving parent on either side of the abortion question should be comfortable with Quayle's response.

Perhaps Clinton answered more skillfully, in that he kept his daughter out of the abortion debate hypotheticals — which is where Quayle's daughter is entitled to remain, as well. But don't fault Quayle for being honest and open.

The Seattle Times

Seattle, Washington, July 24, 1992

IN a revealing moment on talk television, viewers caught a rare public glimpse of Dan Quayle, father, instead of Dan Quayle, political ideologue.

CNN's Larry King asked the vice president to ponder a hypothetical situation: What if his daughter were pregnant?

"I would counsel her and talk to her and support her on whatever decision she made," Quayle said.

"And if the decision was abortion?" King asked.

"I'd support my daughter," Quayle said again. "I'd hope that she wouldn't make that decision."

That was Wednesday night. By yesterday morning, Marilyn Quayle was busy repairing the gaping hole in her husband's conservative armor. "If she becomes pregnant, she'll take the child to term," Mrs. Quayle insisted.

Political damage control aside, there is no undoing the honesty of the vice president's unscripted response.

Dan Quayle's fatherly instinct gets to the heart of the abortion issue in a way his political rhetoric does not.

As a politician he has consistently supported severe government restrictions on a woman's right to choose. As a father he would support his daughter's decision regarding her pregnancy, even if she were to choose an abortion.

In one brief moment of fatherly concern and respect for his daughter, Dan Quayle revealed the simple truth about unwanted pregnancies: The decision is best made in the privacy of the home and ultimately rests with the pregnant woman.

Part III: Pro-Life v. Pro-Choice

The most impassioned arguments over abortion involve the moral, religious and medical issue of when life begins. The question of personhood and when, in the view of the Constitution, an individual starts to exist, is paramount in the debate involving fetal and women's rights. The right-to-life movement bases its activities on the belief that the "moment" of conception marks the beginning of personhood, and that every fetus has the right to be born. Pro-choice advocates maintain that freedom of conscience is upheld by the First Amendment and that limiting a woman's right to abort essentially restricts her right to religious and moral freedom.

Some radical elements of the right-to-life movement have taken the law into their own hands. As a result, clinics and hospitals that perform abortions, as well as individual medical practitioners, have been the targets of violence, including arson and bombings. Such acts are not, however espoused by the majority of anti-abortionists.

One of the more militant pro-life groups gaining notoriety in the 1990s is Operation Rescue. Its methods of passive resistance, borrowed from the Gandhi-inspired anti-war activism of the 1960s, included the blockading of abortion clinics to prevent women seeking abortions from entering.

In 1991, Operation Rescue's tactics focused national attention on Wichita, Kansas, where the group attempted to block access to the city's three abortion clinics. The month-long effort was met with equal forcefulness by local and federal law enforcement authorities who were ordered by the courts to arrest the protesters.

The leaders of Operation Rescue had selected Wichita for the protests because they felt the region would be receptive to their activities and because one of the Wichita clinics had a reputation as one of the only clinics in the U.S. that performed late-term abortions. Though the clinics closed down for a week to avoid confrontation, clashes between the rival camps ensued, prompting U.S. District Judge Patrick F. Kelly to issue a temporary restraining order barring protesters from blocking entrances to the clinics. Eventually, despite a wrangle with the Justice Department over the legality of the use of federal marshals, nearly 2,000 arrests of Operation Rescue members were made. Many of the arrests involved individuals arrested more than once.

In the spring of 1992, Operation Rescue targeted Buffalo, New York, staging a two-week-long protest against abortion clinics and doctors who performed abortions. Unlike the Wichita protests, there was little violence in Buffalo as pro-choice counterdemonstrators outnumbered and outmaneuvered their rivals. As a result, the area's six abortion clinics remained open despite the group's efforts to shut them down.

More moderate anti-abortion expression has taken place annually, on January 23 in Washington, D.C., where marchers numbering in the hundreds of thousands have demonstrated their belief that *Roe v. Wade* should be overturned.

Increasingly, however, the pro-choice movement has been able to garner similar levels of emotional – and financial – support for its side of the debate. Just as the pro-life movement had been galvanized by the *Roe v. Wade* decision, the pro-choice movement reacted to the results of the 1980 elections with an increased attention to campaign politics on the state and national levels. The growing effectiveness of the pro-choice movement's defense of women's rights has found expression in the movement's annual Washington, D.C. demonstrations supporting the right of women to make their own decisions about bearing children.

The battle over abortion is not, strictly speaking, between those who believe there should be abortions and those who believe they should be banned; there are no champions of abortion per se. Even the most radical of feminists have indicated that they prefer contraception to abortion, while defending a woman's right to make her own choice about terminating a pregnancy once conception has occurred.

It would seem that even between the adherents of the most extreme "pro-life" and "pro-choice" viewpoints, common ground could be found in a mutual effort to find more effective ways to prevent unwanted pregnancies and to channel financial support to those women who would carry their pregnancies to term if circumstances permitted. Some anti-abortion groups do in fact offer free prenatal care for pregnant women as well as adoption services.

But the Republican administrations of Ronald Reagan and George Bush, far from allocating additional funds for birth-control research or providing economic assistance for single mothers, have consistently sought to cut federal family-planning programs.

Many in the anti-abortion movement also oppose such efforts to reduce the number of unplanned pregnancies. Groups such as Operation Rescue and the National Committee for the Right to Life oppose the basic family planning program, Title X, arguing that it does little to prevent unwanted pregnancies and actually encourages sexual promiscuity among adolescents.

Church/State Debates on Abortion Intensify

The nation's Roman Catholic bishops, meeting in Baltimore November 6–9, 1989, adopted a major policy statement on abortion. The abortion resolution, adopted unanimously November 7 by the 300-member National Conference of Catholic Bishops, flatly ruled out the so-called pro-choice position as an option for Catholics. It underlined the issue as an "overriding concern" on the national agenda and specifically directed it to the attention of public officials, who, the bishops said, should work to end legal abortions.

"No Catholic can responsibly take a 'pro-choice' stand when the 'choice' in question involves the taking of innocent human life," the bishops declared.

New York Gov. Mario M. Cuomo (D) was assailed Jan. 23, 1990 by Roman Catholic Auxiliary Bishop Austin Vaughan of Orange County, N.Y. who said Cuomo was at "serious risk of going to hell" for his views on abortion.

Vaughan made his statements in an interview conducted at the Albany County jail, where he was serving a 10-day sentence for attempting to block the entrance to an abortion clinic in Albany, N.Y. in March 1989.

Cuomo, a Catholic, had often spoken out about the difficulty of reconciling the church's anti-abortion position with the responsibility of elected officials to uphold laws supporting a woman's right to an abortion. In a major speech at Notre Dame University in 1984, he had insisted that public officials must refrain from imposing their private moral beliefs on others.

The National Conference of Catholic Bishops announced April 5, 1990 that it had hired the public relations firm of Hill & Knowlton and a polling firm, the Wirthlin Group, as part of a campaign to influence public opinion against abortion.

"Abortion organizations have lost sight of fundamental values, such as the sanctity of human life, or they have tried to convince America that the main issue in the abortion debate is the right to choose rather than, as it really is, what is being chosen," said Cardinal John J. O'Connor, archbishop of New York City and chairman of the bishops' Committee for Pro-Life Activities. "Given the stakes – life itself – we can do no less," he added.

Although the bishops' conference had previously hired consultants to help with such events as the visit of Pope John Paul II to the U.S. in 1987, this was reported to be the first time they had done so in an effort to influence public policy.

Cardinal John J. O'Connor, June 14, 1990 warned Catholic politicians that they faced excommunication if they supported legalized abortion. In an article published in the archdiocese's weekly newspaper, O'Connor wrote that Catholics who supported the right to abortion "must be warned that they are at risk of excommunication." He said the threat applied not only to women who underwent an abortion and doctors who performed the operation, but also to those who helped to "multiply abortions by advocating legislation supporting abortion or by making public funds available for abortion." He stated that Catholic officeholders should be willing "even to accept political defeat, should such be the result, rather than sacrifice human life."

O'Connor's published remarks touched off a political outcry June 14-17.

Gov. Mario M. Cuomo (D, N.Y.) who had been widely seen as one of the targets of O'Connor's article, June 14 called O'Connor's statements "upsetting."

The biennial assembly of the 5.2-million member Evangelical Lutheran Church in America, meeting in Orlando, Fla., voted Sept. 3, 1991 to adopt a moderate policy statement on abortion.

The Evangelical Lutheran Church, founded in a merger of three Lutheran branches in 1987, was the largest Lutheran denomination in the U.S.

The statement adopted by the assembly read: "Human life in all phases is God-given and, therefore, has intrinsic value...The strong Christian presumption is to preserve and protect life. Abortion ought to be an option only of last resort."

THE ATLANTA CONSTITUTION
Atlanta, Georgia, September 1, 1991

Last year, in perhaps its worst decision, the U.S. Supreme Court seriously undermined the right of Americans to worship as their consciences dictate.

No longer does the government have to demonstrate a "compelling" state interest in order to overturn a religious practice. As long as a law is of general applicability and is not intended to discriminate, then it's OK. Thus it would be perfectly constitutional for a prohibition law to extend to sacramental wine.

In response, Rep. Stephen Solarz (D-N.Y.) has introduced the Religious Freedom Restoration Act. Backed by a broad coalition of religious bodies, this bill would simply require the government to meet the former, higher standard of proof in order to defeat a legal challenge based on the right to freely exercise one's religion. Unfortunately and for no good reason, the bill has been taken hostage by the abortion issue.

Led by the National Right to Life Committee, anti-abortion advocates have argued that the Solarz bill would favor a woman's right to obtain an abortion. The Catholic Church, which should know better, has gone along with this bogus argument.

It goes like this. If Roe v. Wade were overturned and a given state banned abortion, a woman could make the case that she is entitled to an abortion as an exercise of her religious freedom.

Such a case could in fact be made. For example, Orthodox Judaism holds that an abortion is required if the mother's health is at serious risk. It is not unlikely that an Orthodox Jewish woman, confronted with a serious health risk by carrying to term, would go to court to be allowed to have an abortion. The right-to-life lobby, believing it has the only morally legitimate position on abortion, wants to deny her the opportunity.

The point, however, is that her claim would not necessarily prevail under the "compelling interest" standard. Indeed, if the law defined a fetus as "life," the courts would doubtless find the state interest in protecting life sufficiently compelling to outweigh any claim of religious free exercise. (That's not to say the law should define a fetus as "life.")

By characterizing the Religious Freedom Restoration Act as a pro-choice bill, the right-to-lifers have intimidated some members of Congress into withholding their support. But recently, Rep. Robert K. Dornan (R-Calif.), one of the staunchest anti-abortion votes in the House, signed on as a backer.

With any luck, other anti-abortion members — and President Bush as well — will spurn the abortion red herring and sign on to a bill that will guarantee those religious liberties that lie at the heart of the American experiment.

THE DAILY OKLAHOMAN
Oklahoma City, Oklahoma, June 12, 1991

PERSONS of faith in all denominations applaud the decision of the Presbyterian Church (U.S.A.) to affirm biblical insights into human nature. The action came after weeks of dramatic debate, ending in a 534-31 vote in the church's General Assembly.

Traditionalists in other faith communities sympathized with their sisters and brothers among the Presbyterians, recognizing this debate as one occuring in their own churches.

Human insight about some problems can develop over time. The Bible does not contain explicit foreign policies, nor does it mandate that every social system be identical — although it certainly requires those who love God to seek justice. The Western tradition has reflected diversity in governance, with democratic and republican structures (and market economies) dominating in the modern era.

When it comes to personal morality, however, the Bible's message is not one of "diversity." The Good Book, as most Americans still regard it, is absolutely explicit about certain kinds of human activity, including adultery and homosexual behavior. Both the Old Testament and New Testament explicitly condemn such behavior by individuals. While there may be definitions of "justice-love" (as the "gay" activists and their allies labeled their cause) which promote morality, how can one reject biblical guidance and still be called Christian?

Perhaps adherents of traditional moral values in all the denominations have not directed enough care, understanding and forgiveness toward those who have fallen into these particular sins of behavior. Each community of faith must deal with that question in its own way.

That, however, is a separate question from the confrontation of recent weeks, an epic battle which saw adherents of non-traditional behavior asking for church approval of their "lifestyle." The Presbyterians are not alone. This one is playing itself out in all the churches.

Omaha World-Herald
Omaha, Nebraska, June 12, 1991

Members of some religious denominations have put up with a great deal in recent years. They have seen their ancient hymns reworded to reflect modern notions of political correctness. They have heard their heavenly father referred to as "she." At times they have gone to church for religious devotions and found themselves harangued by political activists.

This week, at least for members of the Presbyterian Church (U.S.A.), a milestone arrived in the struggle for the church's soul. Traditional values won out.

Delegates to the denomination's general assembly in Baltimore soundly rejected a committee report that would have charted a new course in matters of sexual ethics. The report called for erasing the centuries-old ban on sexual activity outside marriage and recommended the blessing of relationships based on "justice-love," including homosexual partnerships.

The 534-31 vote against the report seemed to reflect the outrage and dismay that had been expressed by congregations across the country after word of the committee's recommendations spread. The delegates even affirmed the sanctity of marriage, a statement that wouldn't have been newsworthy except that the existence of the committee's report made it so.

That isn't to suggest that contemporary concerns were ignored in Baltimore. The delegates called on the church to continue a discussion of sexual issues, including sexual violence, sexual misconduct by members of the clergy and sexual issues confronting the elderly, as well as gays and lesbians. They declared sexual equality to be a part of Presbyterian doctrine. And they took a strong stand for environmental responsibility.

Certainly such matters shouldn't be outside the realm of a religious body's concern.

But when the push for change reaches the point of redesigning the bedrock beliefs that have guided the church for centuries, it's something else entirely. A number of mainline Christians have voted with their feet in recent years, dropping out of churches that watered down their doctrine or lost sight of their heritage.

The Presbyterians who objected to the proposed changes in Baltimore found a different way. They said, "Enough, already," and they said it repeatedly and emphatically enough to preserve the faith of their forebears.

THE ARIZONA REPUBLIC
Phoenix, Arizona, June 13, 1991

THE theological avant-garde — those elitists who believe it is the duty of churches to accommodate their doctrine to every fad that sweeps through the radical-chic set — was dealt a setback this week when the Presbyterian Church (U.S.A.) overwhelmingly rejected a report on sexuality.

The denomination's General Assembly affirmed instead the sanctity of monogamous, heterosexual marriage. At this point, the titanic battle over extending the church's blessings to adultery, premarital sex, homosexuality and bisexuality fizzled.

The lopsided rejection surprised many observers. The assembly voted 534 to 31 to table the report, the work of a select committee of ersatz Calvinists. Such a resounding rejection suggests that the committee on sexuality was not within light years of rank-and-file Presbyterians.

As the popular country-Western song puts it, "You've got to stand for something, or you'll fall for anything." Sadly, mainline Protestant churches have stood for little in recent times and consequently have fallen for all manner of theological witchcraft.

It is true that they have stood up to apartheid in faraway South Africa, along with sexism, racism, agism and militarism closer to home. But the Gospel often has been reduced to a mushy inclusivism that made "intolerance," which is to say taking a principled stand for eternal verities, the cardinal sin.

This is why the Presbyterian vote may be a landmark. After three decades of experimentation, fadism and declining membership, the Presbyterians in the pew finally said no to the liberal vanguard. Could this presage a rebellion against those accommodationists who would contort Christianity to conform to the prevailing whims of the theological left?

The object of the controversy was a report that would have sanctified nearly all sexual unions — whether inside or outside marriage, homosexual, heterosexual or bisexual — so long as they took place within the context of "justice-love." This is a concept, previously unknown in Christian teaching, that recently has taken the fashionable by storm.

The issue goes far beyond attempts to elevate the traditional marriage over the gay "lifestyle." At stake is the nature of the Christian religion itself. Is the Gospel rooted in immutable, transcendent truths that defy cultural and temporal captivity, or must church doctrine be updated constantly in order to remain relevant? At least on one, narrowly focused issue, the Presbyterians have affirmed the permanence and divine authority of the faith.

ST. LOUIS POST-DISPATCH
St. Louis, Missouri, June 12, 1991

By definition, religions straddle this world and the next. Churches cannot be immune to the cares and struggles facing their members; at the same time, they must offer their members timeless truths, a vision larger and more enduring than the ephemera of everyday life. As each religion confronts this paradox, it is forced to decide what is essential to its creed and to a moral life — and what is not.

Over time, that means that religions change. What was permitted no longer is; what was not permitted now is. In Old Testament days, polygamy was allowed; now it's widely considered immoral. Consider the biblical injunction against usury, charging interest. Today, the prohibition is usually interpreted to mean a ban only on excessive interest. It is easier, of course, to see and accept changes already made.

It's a far different story when churches are caught up in social turmoil, as many are today. For denominations such as the Presbyterians, the Episcopalians and the Catholics, questions relating to women, homosexuals and human sexuality threaten to tear congregations apart — just as they do society.

In coming to grips with these issues, people on both sides of the fence have to engage in genuine soul-searching. Is a church's evaluation of a particular practice the result of custom and tradition, and thus subject to change, or central to the sect's theology, and thus immutable? Sometimes, it's not easy to tell. Slavery was once considered biblically ordained; now no U.S. church would uphold that view.

If unity on contemporary issues of personal and social morality is hard to come by within a religion, it is nearly impossible among religions. Indeed, one religion may ordain women, another may not — and both may use Scripture to justify their decisions. Such differences also make it difficult for any religion to stifle internal discussion on these issues.

The Presbyterian Church (U.S.A.) just rejected a report arguing that the church should liberalize its views on sexuality. The Episcopal Church is debating whether practicing homosexuals ought to be ordained. The Vatican has urged U.S. bishops to reclassify their pastoral letter on women. Yet no matter how these particular crises are resolved, these churches will not be off the hook. As long as society is grappling with these issues, religions will be, too.

TULSA WORLD
Tulsa, Oklahoma, June 12, 1991

THE PRESBYTERIANS, meeting in Baltimore, have reaffirmed the sanctity of matrimony and rejected a report that would have given the church's blessing to pre-marital sex, homosexuality and bisexuality.

Any other decision by the General Assembly of the Presbyterian Church (U.S.A.) would have been unthinkable a few decades ago. But it was major news when it happened in Baltimore Monday. Marriage is no longer taken for granted as the exclusive, approved sexual relationship.

The Presbyterian vote will be condemned by some feminists, the gay movement and others who see nothing special about the one-man-one-woman arrangement. But the Presbyterians were loathe to tinker with an institution — including appropriate restraints — that has been sanctified by religion, protected by law and encouraged by social convention since the dawn of history.

The vote was cautionary — and wise. Why mess with an arrangement that — given half a chance — works so well?

Marriage hasn't been around all these years because the church likes it. It no doubt began as a practical arrangement for raising children and avoiding sexual jealousies and quarrels. It probably wasn't invented, but grew out of a process of elimination. Other arrangements proved unstable and unworkable.

Critics can condemn the Baltimore vote as gay bashing or anti-freedom-of-choice or worse. In fact, it simply endorses a valuable institution that has served an imperfect human race very well and for which no satisfactory substitute has been found.

Good for the Presbyterians.

THE ANN ARBOR NEWS
Ann Arbor, Michigan, July 23, 1989

The continuing debate over abortion is guaranteed to generate a considerable amount of heat, especially when positions are polarized as "pro-life" and "pro-choice." But one expects more light than heat on the issue from someone who's been around for a while and who deals with sensitive matters all the time.

Rep. Perry Bullard, D-Ann Arbor, did not distinguish himself in abortion debate when he referred to the Catholic Church as an "illegitimate institution in the modern world" whose "all male hierarchy" takes its cues on the abortion issue from "an ideology that comes from the Middle Ages."

Bullard's remarks are poorly chosen, insulting and beyond the bounds of intelligent social commentary from a state lawmaker. One of the oldest institutions in Western civilization is the papacy of the Roman Catholic Church — the apex of that supposedly objectionable all-male hierarchy. Far from being an illegitimate institution, the church traces its history to the dawn of the Christian era and still speaks for millions of devoted followers on all continents.

The church's anti-abortion position reflects that body's reverence for life and centuries of the church's best thinking on the subject.

Perhaps emotions got the better of Bullard. Still, an apology for his tasteless comment is in order.

The Seattle Times
Seattle, Washington, October 9, 1989

THE fervent crusade by anti-abortionists continues unabated in various parts of the country. The most visible activity in recent days has been in Atlanta, where disruptive demonstrations at abortion clinics have tied up roughly one-fourth of the city's police force and resulted in hundreds of arrests.

Similar demonstrations on a smaller scale have occurred in the Greater Seattle area, some organized by Operation Rescue, the same national group involved in the Atlanta disorders.

Amid such furor, it is well that voices of reason be raised to lend balance to the seemingly endless debate over legal abortion, which has divided Americans like few other issues on the national agenda. Thus, a salute is due a local group of Christian, Unitarian and Jewish clergy for coming together in a recent collective expression of support for choice on the matter of abortion.

Responding to the anti-abortion demonstrations organized by Christian pastors, the group said such expressions are but one view of religious truth.

"We want you to know," said the Rev. Laurie Aleona, pastor of the Capitol Hill Methodist Church, "that they (the demonstrators) do not represent all religious people, nor are they the mainstream."

Rabbi Earl Starr, senior rabbi at Temple de Hirsch Sinai, said "I remember too many tragedies . . . because there was no choice. If choices no longer are available in our society, we are no longer the great democracy that all of our ancestors strove to create."

The Rev. Gary Kowalski, pastor of the First Unitarian Universalist Church in Seattle, said at this time there is no moral consensus in this community regarding abortion and that "in the absence of consensus, it would be wrong to attempt to impose one through social legislation."

Others in the group included the Rev. Bruce Parker, district superintendent for the United Methodist Church, who said his church supports the sanctity of unborn life, yet is "equally bound to respect the sacredness of the life and well-being of the mother, for whom devastating damage may result from an unacceptable pregnancy."

None of this will end the debate, of course, but it helps keep the issue in perspective at a time when elements of the "pro-life" movement are active on a wide front, including activities that have posed problems for the current United Way campaign here.

More voices should be raised to articulate the issue of choice, including those in women's groups, which have been strangely silent in the face of the mounting attacks from the other side.

'BAD ENOUGH, I SAY, TO HAVE WOMEN ORDAINED IN THE FIRST PLACE. NOW, WHAT WAS ALL THAT ABOUT ORDAINING SOME LEBANESE WOMAN? WHAT?'

The Washington Times
Washington, D.C., June 12, 1991

That old-time religion turned out to be good enough for the Presbyterian Church after all. For a short while there it looked like religious tradition was going to be a thing of the past. But at their convention in Baltimore this week, the Presbyterians rejected the preliminary findings of a panel of the denomination's more progressive thinkers, whose proposed code of sexual conduct seems to have its origins more in Madonna than in the Bible.

THE DAILY OKLAHOMAN
Oklahoma City, Oklahoma, June 11, 1991

USING the "bully pulpit" of the presidency to promote moral values was a hallmark of the Reagan administration. It is gratifying to see President Bush continuing the good fight.

Bush's appearance before Southern Baptists at their convention in Atlanta served to remind Americans of his belief in spiritual guidance. He used the occasion to underscore his commitment to initiatives that will "preserve faith and family."

Of special significance to Oklahomans was his renewed support for prayer in public schools. In urging passage of a constitutional amendment to permit voluntary prayer, Bush related the case of a Norman fifth-grader, Monette Rethford.

The 11-year-old girl upset school officials by praying and holding Bible studies during recess. They relented after her parents filed a federal lawsuit.

Bush also reiterated his opposition to abortion, specifically the use of federal funds for abortions except to save a mother's life.

Speaking of the "two fundamental pillars supporting our society, our families and our faith," Bush noted that in a recent survey 40 percent of Americans named faith in God as the most important part of their lives.

"Whatever we've learned over the last few decades, it's clear that America is a nation that no longer lacks a moral vocabulary," said Bush. "Ideals like decency and virtue are no longer subject to scorn."

In George Bush, the nation has a leader who recognizes the important role that religion has played in the country's development and how vital it is to allow people the freedom to follow their faith. For that, all Americans can be thankful.

Though it may have lacked spiritual integrity, the report's provocative conclusions were no snap judgment. The Presbyterian Task Force on Human Sexuality spent four years studying the mating habits of its congregation in order to prepare "Keeping Body and Soul Together: Sexuality, Spirituality and Social Justice."

The church's 2.9 million members were being asked to support a new sexual ethic that approves of adultery and homosexuality. The commandment "Thou shalt not commit adultery" would be packed away in obsolescence with the assurance that the church "will not condemn, out of hand, any sexual relations in which there is genuine equality and mutual respect." Under the new thinking, "What matters is not narrowly whether sexually active adults are married or not, but rather whether they embody justice-love in their relating." No hell to pay there.

But 96 percent of the church's commissioners decided there ought to be hellfire and damnation. They reaffirmed scriptural authority and the "sanctity of the marriage covenant between one man and one woman." Rev. William Jameson, a Pennsylvania pastor, noted that a new report adopted Monday, which affirms tradition, "may not have been prophetic but it reassured people that the Presbyterian Church (USA) believes in basic truths."

Human beings crave guideposts by which to live. Traditionally churches have offered those rules and have possessed the moral authority to enforce them. Society has been better off because of it.

Religious leaders who set standards for behavior based on a reading of the latest social trends are abdicating their responsibility to provide the kind of leadership the human character wants and needs. Religious leaders must be able to say what is right and what is wrong, and they must believe it. This is the best alternative to the seduction of permissiveness, which allows young people to practice a brand of feel-good ethics that can only leave them aimless and morally crippled.

That the Presbyterian assembly rejected the report of its study group is good news indeed.

THE ⬛ SUN

Baltimore, Maryland, March 12, 1987

As the technology for intervening in the birth process reaches awe-inspiring vistas, it raises questions so complex that they shake the foundations of traditional moral values. The array of procreative choices means single people and homosexual couples, as well as heterosexual couples, can have children. And the process may involve the storing of sperm in banks, the freezing or disposing of fertilized eggs, the union of sperm and ova in a petri dish, or — what in contrast appears relatively simple — surrogate motherhood.

The Vatican's response to this dilemma was a predictably stinging indictment. Its Doctrine of Faith builds on the church's position that from the moment when the nuclei of a sperm and egg fuse, that single cell is a human being with full identity and rights. Thus, the church condemns virtually all forms of artificial fertilization and embryo transfer. In the name of morality, it asserts that children can be conceived in only one acceptable way — through an act of love consummated in marriage.

The Vatican's position is understandable. The conflicting and often irreconcilable values involved beg for a simple resolution. But in reality, there is none. Since the 1968 encyclical banning artificial birth control, Vatican dogma has failed to commanded universal allegiance among the flock. Catholic couples who otherwise would be sterile most likely will make up their minds for themselves on this issue, as did those who have decided to use artificial birth control.

The church's teaching will be more troublesome for Catholic health care professionals. No force in history has been able to stifle the human thirst for knowledge. While Catholic physicians and hospital administrators are struggling with the dilemmas posed by the Vatican's position, research in secular institutions will forge ahead, impeding their ability to keep up with state-of-the-art developments.

The Vatican doctrine does not envision such divisiveness. It calls on governments to enact laws that embody its teachings. But the spirit of medical research and the economic impact of such restrictions mitigate against it. In the fuzzy realm of surrogate motherhood, liberal states will enact laws legalizing surrogate motherhood, regardless; conservative states will not. In states like Maryland, where legislators are unsure about what to do, the Vatican's edict will carry some weight. But so will the court decision in the Baby M case, public opinion and political arm-twisting.

Ultimately, science will press forward. And recommendations about how to deal with it will continue to be advanced. The question is not what dogma we should adopt, but whether a pluralistic system like ours, designed to accommodate deep-rooted moral differences, can weather this technological storm. We believe it can.

"UNCONVENTIONAL, BUT IT INVOLVES NO QUESTIONABLE METHODS"

The Orlando Sentinel

Orlando, Florida, May 4, 1987

Cardinal Joseph Bernardin of Chicago has performed a valuable service for both Catholics and the Roman Catholic Church with his comments on the Vatican's recent instruction on new birth technologies.

The instruction, you'll recall, affirmed the Vatican's opposition to virtually all forms of "artificial" reproduction, including such increasingly common methods as *in vitro* fertilization, surrogate motherhood and third-party sperm donors. That opposition is rooted in a fundamental tenet of Catholicism: that procreation must be achieved in marriage, through normal conjugal relations.

Without challenging that tenet, the cardinal maintained that married couples of any faith who desire to have a baby have the right to inform themselves about available technologies and then decide which, if any, they will use.

It's tempting to see the cardinal's comments as a crack in the wall of Vatican opposition to the new reproductive advancements. But measured responses of this sort from within the church should only strengthen the moral underpinnings of the instruction.

Categorical opposition by the church and its officials would put too many Catholic couples incapable of having children by approved methods in the position of poor children forced to stand forever outside the candy-store window while the display racks are filled with ever more tempting varieties of sweets. That's a cruel trick to play on people suffering enough already.

Instead, the cardinal suggests, Catholics should take time to understand the Vatican's moral concerns — the instruction is a very powerful moral document — and then make up their own minds.

Essentially he has told the couples to do what many of them would have done at any rate. This is not the Middle Ages; in the Western world in the last part of the 20th century, individual choice in such matters ultimately will prevail, whatever edicts get issued from high places.

The cardinal clearly recognizes that. In expressing his feelings, he should help ease the guilt of Catholics who follow the dictates of their consciences with regard to birth technology. Doing that shouldn't be a staging ground for endless guilt.

The News Journal

Wilmington, Delaware, March 20, 1987

THE 1960s are generally characterized as the onset of the sexual revolution. That's when reliable contraceptives lessened the pregnancy risk and cultural patterns made non-marital sex socially acceptable.

But even as sexual practices became more relaxed, open and public discussion of sex remained taboo.

However, we are now witnessing the second sexual revolution — discussion of sex and its implications is all around us. Teen-age pregnancy, AIDS and the Vatican's prohibition of technical fertility aids are constantly in the news. The word *condom*, once used only with great trepidation, is rapidly turning into a household word.

Societal and health-risk problems associated with promiscuous sex have been of concern for quite some time, but were not talked about in polite society. Now they are. And this new frankness, it is hoped, will advance efforts to reduce incidence of teen-age pregnancy, now more rampant in the United States than in any other developed nation.

AIDS, which has afflicted 32,000 persons in the United States alone, has even made the U.S. government candid about sex and health precautions that should be taken. And medical scientists around the world are racing to find a cure and an immunizing vaccine for this killer disease.

But it remained for the Vatican to bring to the fore the ethical implications of an aspect of sex that most have been viewing with admiration — the latest in medical techniques to help couples overcome fertility problems. In a doctrinal statement issued earlier this month, the Vatican condemns high-tech methods of conception as sinful.

Children should be conceived the natural way, it says. Test-tube babies, sperm and embryo banks, surrogate motherhood, artificial insemination — these are condemned by the church. And the church urges governments to adopt laws outlawing these procedures.

These new procedures treat human matter as "disposable" biological material. That is morally wrong, says the church.

The Vatican's pronouncement has caused quite a stir, and not just among Catholics.

Just as we have until recently shrunk from open discussion of sexual matters, so we have failed as a society to debate the ethical implications of modern medicine. For some years, we have been struggling with the question of when it is appropriate to withdraw mechanical life support from the hopelessly ill. We are slowly reaching a societal consensus on that issue.

But the debate over the ethics of surrogate motherhood, the creation of life in laboratories and genetic manipulation has barely begun. The Vatican's radical pronouncement should help push this debate to the forefront where it belongs.

Times-Colonist

Victoria, British Columbia, March 20, 1987

With genetic and medical researchers regularly developing startling new techniques, the legal and the ethical guidelines provided by lawmakers and religious philosophers are under constant challenge.

To address some of these issues, the Roman Catholic Church last week released a 40-page document, *Instruction on Respect for Human Life in its Origin and on the Dignity of Procreation — Replies to Certain Questions of the Day.*

The Vatican document condemns all forms of test-tube fertilization, surrogate motherhood and experimentation on living embryos and also rejects cloning of humans, attempts to fashion animal-human hybrids, and the freezing of human embryos or planting them in artificial or animal uteruses. Jean-Marie Cardinal Lustiger, Archbishop of Paris and a senior adviser to Pope John Paul II, didn't mince words either. All acts of human artificial insemination, he declared, are a "return to paganism."

The Vatican's determination to defend the sanctity of life is both understandable and commendable, of course, but so-called "test tube babies" hardly seem an appropriate target. These are infants of parents who could not have children (because of procreational abnormalities) without the sophisticated assistance of modern medicine. For these couples, the assistance of science in this way must seem divinely inspired.

The most distressing example of the Church's narrow view of the subject concerns artificial insemination involving married couples. While the Church permits artificial insemination of a woman with semen from her husband, the semen must be produced as a result of intercourse only. But that presents all sorts of practical difficulties. Still, the Church contends that a conceived child must be the "fruit of his parents' love." Most people will share the Church's abhorrence of human cloning and experiments aimed at creating animal-human hybrids. Experiments on living human embryos are undoubtedly immoral and disgusting. But to reject that part of the new technology which enables children to be born to a family when none could be before will baffle many lay people.

St. Louis Review

St. Louis, Missouri, March 10, 1987

Widespread discussion and considerable controversy greeted issuance of the doctrinal congregation's document concerning contemporary life issues. Specifically the document condemned as immoral surrogate motherhood, in vitro fertilization and non-therapeutic embryo experimentation.

At present, U.S. courts are being asked to determine custody in a number of cases involving surrogate motherhood. There are no laws which directly address this issue which has attracted widespread interest. The Catholic Church's condemnation of surrogate motherhood is consistent with its traditional ethical and moral point of view regarding human dignity, the sanctity of marriage and a humane and moral application of technology to human problems.

In asking that surrogate motherhood be outlawed, the Church is calling on the conscience of mankind to resist this technological reinstitution of slavery. Our courts and the people of the world must recognize and condemn surrogate motherhood for what it is — the sale of human beings.

That figment of the medical and legal profession which panders to the elitist clientele seeking such services, ought to be condemned by their peers for trafficking in human beings.

There is a terrible inconsistency on the part of those members of the medical and legal professions who support the annual destruction of millions of human beings through abortion while squandering time, talent and treasure to deliver customized babies for an affluent minority.

In the case of in vitro fertilization, the public is not informed of the wholesale destruction of human embryos in the preparation of a "suitable" embryo for implantation. The whole technology of in vitro fertilization generates a climate callous to the value of the individual person.

Essentially, the practices proscribed in the Vatican document are those which involve disregard for the values and dignity of the human person and which are not directly regulated by existing law.

In 1946 Pope Pius XII appealed to the world community against the testing and production of atomic, bacteriological and chemical weapons only to have his cautionary words ignored. Today, we are in danger of becoming impotent spectators in a society increasingly controlled by a science and technology which reject ethical considerations. The new Vatican document is an appeal for inclusion of a human and moral viewpoint in determining these vital issues.

Anti-Abortion Rallies Mark *Roe v. Wade* Anniversary

U.S. President George Bush addressed an anti-abortion rally in Washington, D.C., via telephone January 23, 1989 and told the assembled demonstrators that he would work to repeal the 1973 Supreme Court decision legalizing abortion.

The March for Life rally was an annual event held on the anniversary of the high court's decision in the case of *Roe v. Wade.*

The march, which attracted 65,000 participants, was reportedly marked by an atmosphere of growing optimism because of the Supreme Court's recent acceptance of a case that could open the way for a re-examination of *Roe v. Wade.*

Bush told the demonstrators that abortion on demand was "an American tragedy" and that he would support a constitutional amendment protecting the life of fetuses.

"After years of sober and serious reflection on the issue, this is what I think: I think the Supreme Court's decision in *Roe v. Wade* was wrong and should be overturned. I think America needs a human life amendment," Bush told the crowd. "I promise the president hears you now and stands with you in a cause that must be won."

President Bush addressed the annual rally of anti-abortion demonstrators in Washington, D.C. by telephone January 22, 1990 and reiterated his opposition to abortion.

The march was held annually on the anniversary of the Supreme Court's 1973 *Roe v. Wade* decision. Washington police estimated that 75,000 people attended the 1990 rally.

A smaller march by abortion-rights advocates was also held in Washington the same day.

The Wichita
Eagle-Beacon
Wichita, Kansas, January 14, 1989

THE U.S. Supreme Court agreed this week to review an appeals case that could allow the court to overturn Roe vs. Wade, the 1973 decision legalizing abortion. The newly conservative court, however, could do as much to erode the rights of American women through a backdoor approach — upholding portions of the Missouri abortion law under review — as it could if the 1973 decision were overturned entirely.

The case the court has agreed to review involves a 1986 Missouri law defining life as beginning at the moment of conception. If the Missouri law or portions of it were allowed to supersede Roe, it could prohibit the use of publicly funded hospitals for providing abortion services, deny the use of public funds to counsel women to have abortions, and require doctors to test for fetal weight and lung development if they believe a pregnancy to be at least 20 weeks along.

If the Missouri law were upheld, all state legislatures would be given the green light to apply similar restrictions on a woman's right to reproductive choice. Without Roe vs. Wade, no legal obstacle on the fed-

eral level would exist. It is even possible that Congress could enact legislation to ban abortion nationwide.

For legislatures or Congress to apply such restrictions would mean a return to the days, not so long ago, when women seeking abortions were killed and maimed, either by themselves or by clandestine abortionists. It also would mean a further victimization of this nation's poor, since only affluent women who wanted an abortion would be able to get one.

The effect all this could have, ultimately, is to restrict current providers of abortion services almost out of existence. By attacking hospitals, clinics and physicians that provide those services at their economic base, abortion opponents — with the help of the court — would be able to achieve virtually the same effect as would occur if Roe were overturned.

Women through the ages have sought and will continue to seek abortions, even when they put their own lives at risk. Regardless of how the court decides come June, the demand for abortions always will be present. The rights of women to control their reproductive and personal destinies, however, well may not.

The
Washington Post
Times Herald
Washington, D.C., January 19, 1989

RIGHT-TO-LIFERS were delighted when C. Everett Koop, a strong opponent of abortion, was appointed surgeon general in 1981; they felt an important policy outpost had been captured for their cause. But they and others with similar expectations have been disappointed. Called upon to choose between his views on such matters as abortion and his obligations as the nation's chief health officer, Dr. Koop has never hesitated. "I've always been able to separate my personal beliefs from my responsibilities as surgeon general," he said on television the other day.

This sort of thing is never easy. We live in a society that values and depends on compromise yet rightly admires people in public life who won't, the lonely ones who stand on principle, and moral principle especially. Too many people in government tend to temporize and duck, muddying the issues; yet government doesn't work unless these same people bend a little, and there is a point beyond which it is dangerous for government to moralize. All these contradictory things are true, and the fine line among them is hard to define, much less to walk. But our sense is that, in the issues that have come to him, Dr. Koop has done it pretty well. He has remained responsible to his profession.

The most notable example was perhaps the report that he produced on AIDS in 1986. Some keepers of the conservative social agenda were aghast. The head of the public health service was insisting on treating a spreading and fatal disease as . . . primarily a public health problem, rather than a moral issue. His critics felt his report was not reproving enough, dwelt too much on sex education and condoms at the expense of abstinence and monogamy and so put the government in the position of facilitating what it should condemn.

But he was right, and so again in the letter he sent to the president the other day, which said he had done a study requested of him and could not conclude that abortions do medical harm to the women who have them. He couldn't conclude they do not do such harm, either, he said; the data aren't conclusive either way.

Right-to-lifers complain that he flinched, but what he did was much more the opposite. It marks how far the country has come in the past eight years that his letter seemed so remarkable. Issues that ought to be left to conscience—abortion, prayer—have been rawly politicized; fervent orthodoxies have grown up in the two parties, which aspiring politicians ignore at their peril.

What Dr. Koop has stood for instead, when these high-voltage issues have come his way, is rational discourse. He has in fact been a good doctor and a good public policy maker in this, dispensing not just medical expertise but also common sense, when a little of that was badly needed.

AKRON BEACON JOURNAL
Akron, Ohio, January 26, 1989

THE ISSUE of abortion remains one of the most contentious policy questions of contemporary America. The 16th anniversary of the Supreme Court's *Roe vs. Wade* decision sparked rallies by those opposed to legalized abortion, prompted President Bush's unusual lobbying of the court to change its mind, and produced counterdemonstrations by those who support the right of women to decide, with their doctors, whether or not to have an abortion.

Polls show a majority of Americans support the free-choice decision approved by the court in 1973. A minority of Americans oppose the legalization of this private decision, and some opponents are adamant about it, holding demonstrations, taking part in politics, and accusing others of endorsing what they see as murder. In some cases, they intentionally break the law. But they are exercising their right of expression, as are those who demonstrate or petition in behalf of the 1973 ruling.

Some anti-abortionists see no room for compromise, rejecting even President George Bush's belief that abortion should be permitted in cases of rape, incest or to save a woman's life.

Now populated with a number of Ronald Reagan's appointees, the Supreme Court is believed in a mood to overturn or at least to alter *Roe vs. Wade*, possibly by throwing the issue of abortion back in the laps of state legislatures.

Whatever the court does, the whirlwinds of this emotional issue will not fade away.

To understand that, think back to pre-1973, when abortions were still illegal in much of the country. In 1962, for example, an estimated 1 million women underwent *illegal* abortions, often in medical conditions that could only be described as abominable. During the 1960s, as Carole Joffe, a professor of social work at Bryn Mawr College, recently recalled in the Philadelphia Inquirer, as many as 5,000 women a year died from backroom abortions and thousands more were injured yearly.

Now, the medical situation has changed. About as many abortions take place, perhaps 1.5 million a year, but they do so in medically acceptable conditions. Contrary to the opinions of some, the U.S. surgeon general reports there is insufficient evidence to show that women are psychologically hurt in any great number by having abortions. Some in the medical community are even more certain there are seldom mental side effects to the procedure.

If the current Supreme Court reverses or seriously alters *Roe vs. Wade*, as President Bush urges, the illegal abortion market will surely flourish once again. Women, especially poor women, will try self-abortion, with household chemicals, even coat hangers. Does the country really want to return to those practices and the risks to women they entail?

There is another medical issue looming on the horizon. French physicians have developed a pill, called RU 486, that can be taken with no apparent side effects within 10 days of a woman's missed period in the first month of pregnancy. With no reported discomfort and no other medical procedures, tests by volunteers show that the pregnancy is then ended for 95 percent of women involved. It is already reaching markets in European countries.

Some anti-abortionists call this pill "chemical warfare against the unborn." But is it? And even if that is the view of some, assuming it is safe medically, should it be banned? And even if it is banned, does anyone reasonably think that government can prevent a pill reaching thousands' of women wanting to terminate pregnancies?

Would those who would ban the use of such a medical breakthrough also propose today that condoms and other contraceptives be made illegal? All contraceptives were at one time illegal in some states, the rule of law thus tilting strongly against men and women, even husbands and wives, seeking marital relations with protection against pregnancy. Do we want a society that forces people to risk pregnancy when they have sexual relations, or do we want to leave that decision to individuals as a matter of choice?

Those are a few of the other issues in the continuing abortion controversy. Whatever the Supreme Court does will not stop abortions. The facts tell us that women will continue to seek ways to terminate unwanted pregnancies, especially those caused by the cruel crimes of rape and incest. If abortion is made illegal again, they will simply do so in unsafe and medically inappropriate circumstances.

And, advances in medical technology may make this issue moot, anyway, unless Americans are prepared to ban the new pill, thus implying a march backward to ban contraceptives as well. Is that the kind of society Americans and especially women want, or, as the Supreme Court said in 1973, aren't such delicate, difficult decisions better left to individuals to make in privacy with their doctors?

It is because of just such questions that the Supreme Court decided that, within certain medical bounds, the state should not interfere in such sensitive personal decisions. Given medicine's steady advances, such as the pill developed in France, the ruling in *Roe vs. Wade* seems even wiser today than it was in 1973.

Newsday
New York City, New York, January 29, 1989

The stage is set in Washington for a complete retraction of a woman's right to choose an abortion — not because of any dramatic change in the moral equation in the 16 years since Roe vs. Wade, but because Ronald Reagan's appointees have shifted the political balance of the Supreme Court.

That is not reason enough to dispose of this right, which is exercised by about 1.5 million women a year. That is not reason enough to send women to illegal abortionists to terminate unwanted pregnancies.

This is not to say that nothing has changed. Medical advances have made it possible for fetal life to be sustained outside the womb at an earlier stage of development than when Roe vs. Wade was handed down Jan. 22, 1973. These changes suggest it would be appropriate for the court to more strictly curtail late abortions. The effect would be modest since women and their doctors are curtailing late abortions themselves: Only 1 percent of legal abortions occur in the 21st to 26th weeks.

Attorney General Richard Thornburgh predicts that this Supreme Court will send the job of legalizing or banning abortions back to the states. But that would produce a patchwork quilt of laws, a situation permitting the well-to-do to travel to pro-abortion states but one that would send poor women in right-to-life states into the back alleys.

That would be bad enough. But the case before the court could permit a much worse, much broader ruling. It stems from Missouri's stringent anti-abortion law, which states that life begins at conception. If the new Supreme Court justices buy that, abortion will become murder. The procedure will be driven underground from coast to coast.

No one knows for sure what the Reagan appointees will do. Associate Justice Anthony Kennedy is the wild card; he has never ruled directly on abortion rights. But he, Sandra Day O'Connor and Antonin Scalia have shifted the court's balance to the right.

In the past 16 years, anti-abortion groups have seized the initiative. By the tens of thousands, they have lobbied passionately each Jan. 22 to ban abortion. Some politicians mistakenly think that, if the Supreme Court does their bidding, the tumult will finally end.

Wrong. If the Supreme Court reverses Roe vs. Wade, it will be the pro-abortion groups that roil the political waters — as they did around the country *before* Roe vs. Wade. Women who have terminated pregnancies legally will not accept the declaration that they have participated in 20 million murders.

Feelings on abortion go down to bedrock. Polls show that for years, 10 to 20 percent of people have believed abortion is morally wrong under all circumstances, and 20 to 25 percent have believed it should be available no matter what. In between is a wide range supporting abortion in some instances and opposing it in others.

The stage is set for the Supreme Court to ban abortion. But there is no scientific reason for a total ban, no practical reason for a total ban and no national consensus for a total ban. Abortion will remain a painful public issue no matter what is done. Let it be.

MILWAUKEE SENTINEL

Milwaukee, Wisconsin,
January 11, 1989

Yet another challenge has been raised to the landmark US Supreme Court decision in the Roe vs. Wade case, which essentially grants the right of freedom of choice to expectant mothers in the matter of abortions.

But if the court acts responsibly, that landmark decision won't be an issue.

Rather, the justices should exercise their option to act only on the constitutionality of the Missouri law which appears to be an awkward contrivance aimed at reviving the abortion issue in the high court.

Basically, the question should be whether the statute's preamble declaring it to be Missouri policy that life "begins at conception" squares with the Roe vs. Wade prohibition against a state adopting such a theory to justify regulating abortions.

That answer should be in the negative but, in any event, the court's decision should not apply nationwide.

From one end of the country to the other, and at the federal level, health and social welfare authorities are grappling with the problems — basically ignorance and poverty — that create a large market for abortions.

Closing off that option at this time will not solve the problem but drive it underground, jeopardizing the lives and welfare of the mothers involved.

A court ruling may outlaw abortions but it can't stop them. And, rather than opposing the responsible pro-choice advocates, sincere anti-abortionists should be working with them to provide pre-abortion counseling, ensure humane and competent medical treatment if abortion is chosen and promote prudent use of birth control methods afterward.

Only conscientious cooperation of this kind can lead to a situation where young people can and will make the right choice at a point before abortion is an alternative.

The Pittsburgh
PRESS

Pittsburgh, Pennsylvania, January 20, 1989

Although it is usually impervious to pressure, the U.S. Supreme Court can hardly fail to notice the sources of the latest push for a reversal of Roe vs. Wade.

Last week, both Ronald Reagan, who was president then, and Attorney General Richard Thornburgh went to bat for an overturn, adding their support to that of George Bush, who made his wishes known long before he took the oath of office today. The Supreme Court, you can be sure, got the message.

That message is to reverse Roe vs. Wade, the landmark decision that 16 years ago Sunday legalized abortion in the United States by prohibiting states from banning it.

Mr. Reagan was blunt. In a speech before a Roman Catholic group in New York last Friday, he called for an outright reversal and promised that he "won't leave the battle" just because he no longer will be in the Oval Office.

Mr. Thornburgh's comment was less pointed. In a broad hint to the Supreme Court, he predicted an overturn, saying it was his "guess" that the abortion issue will be turned back to the states.

Their messages are aimed chiefly at the two newest justices, Anthony Kennedy and Antonin Scalia, neither of whom has been involved in abortion decisions. Chief Justice William Rehnquist and Justice Byron White already are on the anti-abortion side. Justice Sandra Day O'Connor may provide the crucial fifth vote necessary to overturn.

What they will be voting on is an appeal of a Missouri law that aims to restrict abortion. It will be heard this spring and a decision is likely this summer.

The high court could return the issue to the states or reaffirm Roe vs. Wade. If given the chance, it is predictable that the Pennsylvania Legislature and Gov. Robert P. Casey would outlaw abortions.

Although a clear battle line has been drawn over the issue, the issue itself is less clear. Abortion is an enormously complex problem.

Passions, intolerance and inflexibility abound on both sides. But in the middle are millions of troubled Americans who sense that neither side has it quite right.

They, like us, are troubled by the nagging debate that has gone unresolved for centuries — at just what point does a human life begin?

Polls indicate that Americans overwhelmingly support abortion in cases of rape, incest or threat to the mother's life. Such abortions, however, account for only a fraction of the 1.6 million abortions performed annually.

Americans are less sure of abortion on demand but a majority, 56 percent, support a woman's right to have an abortion. A total of 77 percent think abortion is a private issue between a woman and her doctor.

But who are those 1.6 million women who had an abortion last year? Eighty percent are unmarried, the majority are under 25 and non-white. About two of every five had abortions before the one they had last year, providing validity to the argument that abortion has become a routine method of birth control.

That, it seems to us, is unsound for the country — physically and spiritually.

Ultimately, though, we must make the distinction between the legality and the morality of abortion.

Abortion, no matter how public the discussion, is not a public issue. It is a private issue, a very private issue, for a woman, to be debated only with her conscience.

What should be debated more in the public forum are teenage pregnancy, ignorance about contraception, unwanted children, child neglect, child care, poverty and malnutrition. These are public policy questions that have a great impact on why women seek abortions in the first place.

To ignore these questions and return the abortion issue to the patchwork system of state-by-state regulation isn't the answer. Well-to-do women would be able to choose states where abortions are legal and safe. Poor women, meanwhile, would have the choice of having an unwanted baby or a back-alley abortion.

The country cannot and would not stand for such a turning back of the clock. Our message to the Supreme Court — the message that is prevalent throughout the land — is that Wade vs. Roe should be reaffirmed.

The New York Times

New York City, New York, January 21, 1989

The Missouri abortion case the Supreme Court has accepted for review doesn't warrant the commotion it has evoked on all sides. As abortion cases go, it's no legal landmark. But Missouri, at the Justice Department's urging, has asked the Court to use the case as a vehicle for overturning the 1973 Roe v. Wade decision. The Court has rejected such invitations before and ought to do so again.

Like most recent abortion cases, this one involves an attempt to discourage abortions using regulatory powers the Court has left the states. The question is whether the state's rules intrude too deeply on a woman's right to choose abortion.

Missouri seeks to outlaw the use of any public funds or facilities for abortion and even for abortion counseling. That, pro-choice lawyers argue, exceeds the state's right to bar public funding of abortions for the poor. This point can be argued without a wrenching reconsideration of Roe v. Wade. Yet two days after the election, Solicitor General Charles Fried filed a gratuitous friend-of-the-court brief telling the justices that they were free to use the case

for a big showdown. He cavalierly appended an anti-Roe brief he filed three years ago and advised the justices, who ignored it then, to read it now.

Since the justices haven't indicated whether they want a full-scale revisiting of Roe, prudence requires both sides to offer full arguments. That's unfortunate because even the review is a step backward. It was just such distaste for opening old wounds that led many senators to vote against Robert Bork, who called the decision illegitimate.

If the full review is conducted anyway, the Court would be wise to adhere to its humane precedent. It held that a woman's freedom to choose whether to give birth is protected by the same Constitution that protected a married couple's right to practice birth control. The Court's ruling in Roe astutely accommodates the shifting interests of the woman, the fetus and the state as pregnancy proceeds. Beyond that, Roe v. Wade found that abortion is so personal, so consequential that the public has no right to decide for the burdened woman. That principle deserves to rest undisturbed.

The 🌳 State
Columbia, South Carolina, January 12, 1989

THE U.S. Supreme Court has agreed to hear another challenge to its 1973 ruling legalizing abortion. Abortion-rights leaders are understandably concerned that a reversal of the *Roe vs. Wade* decision would create political and social upheavals throughout the country.

This week, the high court said it would study a federal appellate ruling that struck down key provisions of a Missouri law regulating abortions. But U.S. Justice Department and Missouri officials have asked the court to go even further and overturn *Roe,* which held that women have a constitutional right of privacy to terminate early-stage pregnancies without government interference and to do so later under certain conditions.

Twice, in 1983 and 1986, the Supreme Court reaffirmed the '73 decision. But the '86 vote was 5-4, and since then a member of the majority, Justice Lewis F. Powell Jr., has retired and been replaced by the more conservative Justice Anthony Kennedy.

Justices Kennedy and Sandra Day O'Connor are expected to cast the pivotal votes this year. The former's views on abortion are unclear, while Mrs. O'Connor has criticized *Roe* but so far refused to vote to overturn it. Of the remaining justices, Harry Blackmun, William Brennan, Thurgood Marshall and John Paul Stevens support the '73 decision, while Byron White and Chief Justice William Rehnquist oppose it. Justice Antonin Scalia is expected to join forces with the latter.

In the Missouri case, the 8th U.S. Circuit Court of Appeals found several provisions of the state law unconstitutional, including one declaring "the life of each human being begins at conception," and others that banned abortions in publicly funded facilities, barred using public money for abortion counseling and required that doctors determine whether a fetus older than 19 weeks could live outside the womb.

Many legal experts predict that the Supreme Court will find some of those provisions constitu-

tional and will gradually erode the principles enunciated in *Roe* rather than overturn it completely. But William Bradford Reynolds, who as assistant U.S. attorney general pushed for a review of *Roe,* said he hopes the court "would go further and . . . correct the error that was made some years ago."

If the court does so, it would throw the question back to the states, which would probably enact a hodge-podge of laws dealing with abortion.

But pro-choice groups maintain that such a change would be disastrous. Kate Michelman, executive director of the National Abortion Rights Action League, said a reversal of *Roe* would "create firestorms all across this country. . . . Women and men alike will never accept going back to the day when women have to risk their lives, their health, their families' lives in order to seek an abortion."

She is probably right. Although anti-abortion groups have a substantial following, surveys consistently show that the majority of Americans believe the decision should be left to the woman.

Nevertheless, the time is drawing nigh to reconsider some aspects of the '73 case. For example, under *Roe,* states cannot deny a woman an abortion during the first three months of pregnancy and have limited regulatory powers over second-trimester abortions. During the final three months, abortions usually are permitted only for compelling health reasons. It would make ethical as well as common sense to give states the right to apply the stricter third-trimester standards to second-trimester abortions as well.

But it would, indeed, be tragic to force women in the very early stages of pregnancy to return to the days of backroom abortions performed by sleazy, unqualified individuals under medically dangerous conditions. Such a change would discriminate most against poor women, since the wealthy would be able to shop around, from state to state or even country to country, in order to obtain a legal abortion.

St. Paul Pioneer Press & Dispatch
St. Paul, Minnesota, January 21, 1989

It is one of the most painful, emotional and morally wrenching topics Americans face. And it is again headed for a Supreme Court review. Abortion.

Last week, the high court agreed to consider the constitutionality of a Missouri law that places limits on abortion rights. The case offers the court a chance to reconsider its 1973 Roe vs. Wade decision, decided 16 years ago Sunday, which established abortion as a right of privacy.

The court should reject this challenge as it has rejected those of previous appeals; the constitutional protection for abortion should be retained. Current law is the best balance between difficult competing and conflicting rights of women and the unborn.

We understand and respect the deep, adamant feelings expressed by both sides in the continuing abortion debate. Those who oppose

abortion view the practice as murder, compelling them to save lives. Yet the abortion-rights lobby raises legitimate concerns about a woman's right to choose, to have control over her own body.

The Missouri law now before the Supreme Court asserts that life begins at conception; outlaws the use of public funds, facilities and employees in abortions; and requires that any abortion performed after the 16th week (second-trimester) take place at a hospital, not a clinic. Two lower courts rejected the statute.

Those restrictions erode the edges of the law and effectively ban abortions for some women. If government participation is eliminated, many poor women lose their right to choose. That alone is reason enough to oppose the law.

Many abortion-rights groups are worried that the court will accept the Missouri limitations, in view of Reagan administration interest in reversing Roe, trends in lower court decisions and public controversy.

Composition of the Supreme Court has changed and decisions on abortion have grown closer over the years. Roe was decided on a 7-2 vote. In 1983, the court voted 6-3 to strike down a group of local legislative abortion restrictions. And the last major abortion decision was in 1986 with a 5-4 vote. Since then, one of the Roe-majority justices, Lewis Powell, has retired and been replaced by Anthony Kennedy whose views are untested on this issue.

Kate Michelman, executive director of the National Abortion Rights Action League, assessed the court challenges to Roe vs. Wade in a recent interview at the Women's Agenda Conference II in Kansas City. Michelman called the Missouri case of great importance as the first major abortion rights challenge to come before the new court.

"It is important for people to realize that Roe can be overturned without the court explicitly saying so," Michelman said, referring to the Missouri case and at least three others in which the court could narrow Roe without nullifying the decision.

Eroding the law opens the door to eliminating choices. The court should strike down the Missouri law.

THE BUFFALO NEWS

Buffalo, New York, January 12, 1989

THE U.S. SUPREME Court's 1973 decision legalizing abortion is now facing the most serious challenge so far with the court's acceptance for review of a Missouri abortion case. The addition of three conservative-minded justices to the court by President Reagan raises doubts whether there is still a majority on the court for the 1973 Roe vs. Wade precedent.

It would be hard to think of an issue that stirs more emotion or raises more profound moral and religious questions than the issue of abortion. But a decision on abortion is such a personal one that the Supreme Court in Roe vs. Wade rightly ruled that it should be made, not by the government, but by the woman and her doctor in accordance with their own convictions.

The court's position, however, may now be changing.

The Missouri case involves a 1986 state law that bans the use of public funds or buildings for counseling or performing abortions. A preamble to the law states that "the life of each human being begins at conception," an apparent violation of the 1973 ruling that a state may not justify its regulation of abortion by adopting a particular theory of when life begins.

Federal district and appeal courts declared most provisions of the Missouri law, including the preamble, unconstitutional, and the state is now appealing. The Reagan administration, which has long sought to overturn Roe vs. Wade, has filed a brief with the Supreme Court saying that the case "presents an appropriate opportunity" to reverse the 1973 ruling.

In agreeing to hear the case, the court gave no indication of how broadly it intends to delve into the precedents going back to 1973. Thus, it could support Missouri's limited restrictions on abortion without necessarily overturning Roe vs. Wade.

But the outcome is difficult to predict, since the makeup of the Supreme Court is vastly different from what it was when abortion was legalized in 1973 by a 7-2 vote. Since then, four members of the seven-man majority have retired: Chief Justice Warren Burger and Justices William O. Douglas, Potter Stewart and Lewis Powell.

The 1973 minority of two — Chief Justice William Rehnquist and Justice Byron White — could now be augmented by Reagan's three appointees — Justices Sandra Day O'Connor, Antonin Scalia and Anthony Kennedy — to create a majority, although they have not indicated precisely what their views are on Roe vs. Wade.

As the court hearings are held, we can expect the national forces on each side of the issue to make themselves heard. The president of the National Organization for Women, Molly Yard, said the potential threat to Roe vs. Wade created "a state of emergency for the women of America."

If Roe vs. Wade were to be overturned, several states could be expected to outlaw abortion and others would be likely to adopt new restrictions. The controversy, which appeared to be settled in 1973, would thus rage anew across the nation, inevitably curbing in at least some parts of the country a personal choice that most people thought had been firmly established.

THE TENNESSEAN

Nashville, Tennessee, January 12, 1989

THE U.S. Supreme Court's agreement to hear an abortion case has terrified abortion proponents and delighted its detractors.

The court announced that it will decide the constitutionality of a Missouri law, which was passed in 1986 at the urging of that state's anti-abortion faction. The law restricts any use of public money or public facilities in abortions. It also requires women seeking abortions after 20 weeks of pregnancy to have a doctor ascertain the fetus' weight and lung maturity.

Both a federal district court and a federal court of appeals have declared major portions of the law to be unconstitutional. The Supreme Court is expected to hear arguments in the case in April, and to issue a decision in July.

Obviously, Missouri needs a ruling on its law. But the greater concern now is not the Missouri law but is the court's opening up the abortion issue.

The landmark ruling of Roe v. Wade, which granted women the right to abortion, was made 16 years ago by a court considerably more liberal than the one now on the bench. The vote in the 1973 abortion case was 7-2. The last time the court heard a major abortion case was in 1986, and in that case the right to abortion was upheld by a 5-4 vote. Since then Justice Lewis Powell, a supporter of the right to abortion, has been replaced by Justice Anthony Kennedy, whose views on abortion are not clear.

Although the court has changed, the 14th amendment to the Constitution has not. It is that amendment that the 1973 court said protected a woman's right to privacy, including her right to privacy in making a decision regarding abortion.

After 16 years of legal abortion, any significant restrictions would be wrenching. Many abortion supporters today remember only too well the days when abortions were only legal in four states — New York, Alaska, Hawaii, and Washington — and only the wealthy could afford to make the trip to have a safe abortion. Women who weren't able to afford that expense were too often left at the mercy of a quack or, worse yet, their own devices.

The court could well decide the constitutionality of the Missouri law without laying a hand on the substance of Roe v. Wade. And that is exactly what it should do. ■

The Register

Santa Ana, California, January 11, 1989

Now that the US Supreme Court has begun a new round of reviewing laws on abortion, there is a chance it may reverse some of its previous bad decisions. This may include the 1973 Roe v. Wade decision, in which the court seized powers for itself that the Constitution's 10th amendment clearly had left to "the States respectively, or to the people."

One case under review is a Missouri law that reverses a policy in which taxpayers' dollars, including those of taxpayers strongly opposed to abortion, were used to subsidize abortions. The law also limits abortions after the fetus has lived for 20 weeks, and has a clause declaring that "the life of each human being begins at conception."

The Missouri law conflicts with the definition in Roe v. Wade in which an unborn child's life is divided into "trimesters," periods of three months each, during which the fetus supposedly becomes progressively more human. Such a notion is as absurd as saying that a person 20 years old is less human than someone 60 years old. And fetological research has advanced far in the past 16 years. We now have stethoscopes that let the mother hear her baby's heartbeat at just six weeks, well within the first "trimester."

As Walker Percy, a medical doctor — and one of America's best novelists — recently put it: "Any doctor can tell you that an unborn child is fully human. There is no difference between a child five minutes before birth and five minutes after birth. What about a month before birth? Same. How about eight months? How about one day after conception? Sure. It's a separate organism. Any doctor will tell you that it's all standard biology: the fetus is a separate genetic structure, a separate immune system ... a separate creature."

We also now have more evidence about how the Roe v. Wade decision was made.

> **❝ The Supreme Court has taken an immense burden on its shoulders. One can hope that in reviewing the legacy of 1973, this time it will base its decisions on better ethics, better science, and better law. ❞**

The woman involved in the case had said she was made pregnant by a rapist; in reality it was her boyfriend. Moreover, lies have cropped up in another landmark abortion case handed down the same day as Roe. The other case is Doe v. Bolton, and the Supreme Court used it to strike down a Georgia abortion law. The woman involved, Sandra Kay Race Bensing, now admits, "Mary Doe [her pseudonym] didn't have an abortion. Mary Doe won't ever have an abortion." This means that both decisive 1973 abortion cases were based on lies.

Evidence also is mounting of the immense psychological toll that abortion takes on the mother, in addition to physical risks, and risks to the woman's future children. When a recent government study on the matter proved inconclusive, Surgeon General C. Everett Koop urged that a more conclusive study be made. But a recent book, Aborted Women: Silent No More, contains the experiences of hundreds of women who have had abortions. It notes that "all these women feel that they were deceived and manipulated. Together, they are determined to save other women from the same fate."

The Supreme Court has taken an immense burden on its shoulders. One can hope that in reviewing the legacy of 1973, this time it will base its decisions on better ethics, better science, and better law.

ST. LOUIS POST-DISPATCH
St. Louis, Missouri, January 10, 1989

The Supreme Court has decided to review Missouri's law regulating abortions. That won't necessarily lead to a reconsideration of *Roe vs. Wade*, the 1973 court decision legalizing abortion nationwide, but neither is it a decision that people concerned with protecting privacy and reproductive rights can welcome. For the Missouri case itself revolves around some of the most fundamental, highly charged issues in the abortion debate.

Should, for example, abortions be performed in public hospitals? The Missouri law forbids this; a decision by the 8th U.S. Circuit Court of Appeals last July struck that provision down. Can a state require doctors to perform viability tests for fetuses when the pregnancy is beyond its 19th week? Missouri law requires this, in another provision the appeals court ruled against. What is the consequence of a state declaring that "the life of each human being begins at conception"? Missouri law declares this, in yet another provision thrown out by the appeals court.

In fact or in principle, upholding any of these provisions would severely restrict women's ability to exercise the freedoms granted in *Roe vs. Wade*. Nor has this escaped the attention of Missouri Attorney General William L. Webster. In his appeal to the Supreme Court, he noted that if Missouri's law cannot be squared with the 1973 decision, that decision "should itself be reconsidered." The U.S. Department of Justice, in supporting briefs, also sees the Missouri appeal as a wedge to open the way to a reconsideration of *Roe vs. Wade*.

Whether it develops in this fashion or not, the Missouri case is an important measure of the Supreme Court's respect for women's hard-won rights to privacy and reproductive freedom. They are rights that Attorney General Webster is blind to, but all Americans should hope the Supreme Court will continue to hold them in esteem.

The Honolulu Advertiser
Honolulu, Hawaii, January 15, 1989

It would be disastrous if the U.S. Supreme Court overturned Roe vs. Wade, the 1973 ruling that guarantees women the right to an early-pregnancy abortion.

Many find abortion morally objectionable (and they are entitled to that view), but it has become a widely accepted birth control practice. It's the least desirable technique, but one that should not be denied to women as a last resort.

If Roe vs. Wade were overturned, the abortion question would be left to the states. Every capitol would face an ugly debate between pro-choice and anti-abortion forces.

Some states would likely outlaw abortions. Others — including, it is hoped, Hawaii, the first state to legalize abortions — would permit them. The result would be a national patchwork of differing laws and liabilities.

Women who could afford to travel could find safe treatment. The poor, young and naive would be left to illegal back-alley abortions or dangerous self-abortion attempts — or to having children they are not equipped to properly raise and love.

It's unclear whether the more conservative "Reagan court," in agreeing to review a draconian Missouri anti-abortion law, has the bare majority needed to overturn Roe vs. Wade in the process. Action is not expected until July.

But the possibility the court could deny or further restrict the right to abortions, as Justice Harry Blackmun warned it might, is creating an understandable uproar among women's groups.

It is said that Supreme Court justices read election returns, and the choice of conservative, anti-abortion George Bush is a bad sign for Roe vs. Wade.

But it must also be hoped the justices heed public opinion. Repeated surveys show that, despite protests of a vocal minority, most people believe a woman has the right to control her body and have children when she wants them and is prepared to raise them properly.

St. Louis ⚔ Review
St. Louis, Missouri, January 13, 1989

Pro-lifers in Missouri and throughout the country are heartened by the U.S. Supreme Court's decision to review the constitutionality of Missouri's 1986 statute on abortions. The scope of the statute would afford the High Court the opportunity to review some of the fundamental points of the Roe vs. Wade decision.

The 1986 Missouri statute specified the ways in which Missouri would exercise its constitutional right to refuse to use public funds to pay for abortions. When major portions of the Missouri statute were struck down by the U.S. Eighth Circuit Court of Appeals, the state decided to appeal against this ruling to the U.S. Supreme Court.

The unique feature of the Missouri statute is that it declares that "the life of each human being begins at conception." The Eighth Circuit Court held this declaration unconstitutional on the premise that a state "may not adopt one theory of when life begins to justify its regulation of abortions."

In point of fact, the original Roe vs. Wade decision re___ ¹ to consider any of the medical or scientific evidence concerning the beginning of a human life. The data of science shows conclusively that the only difference between a human embryo and a fully developed human person is time and development. The entire chromosomal makeup of each human being is present when the ovum is fertilized. Thus, the declaration about the beginning of human life is not a theory but a scientific fact.

The court which refuses to consider the relevance of scientific data removes itself from the world of reality. The early Christian theologian, Tertullian, declared "that which is man-to-be, is man."

It is clear from a reading of the Eighth Circuit Court of Appeals' decision that it operated from the point of view that a woman has a virtually unrestricted right to abortion. It did not even consider how the Missouri statute attempted to intrepret and implement the suggested legal safeguards for a more developed human fetus, including the determination of its viability.

We sincerely hope that the U.S. Supreme Court will give the Missouri statute a very careful review. If it does so, there is every reason to hope that the high court's 1973 decision might be abrogated at least in part. We pray for the gift of wisdom for the justices as they approach this important task.

THE [logo] SUN

Baltimore, Maryland, January 24, 1988

Starting this week, if a family planning counselor so much as utters the A-word, he or she will jeopardize the facility's chances of getting federal Title X money. Credit President Reagan, who came into office promising to ban abortion and is trying to do the next best thing — make the procedure virtually unavailable to the 4.3 million people who depend on 3,900 federally funded family planning clinics.

For two decades, the rules governing Title X family planning funds specified that no government money be used for abortion. And it hasn't. Yes, Planned Parenthood, the largest recipient of Title X money, performs abortions. But those programs are privately funded. Audits by the General Accounting Office found "no evidence that Title X funds had been used for abortions or to advise clients to have abortions." Three health department secretaries have said there is no abuse.

That is not good enough for the president. His new rules do not allow any abortion-related activities. Period. If a program receiving Title X money wants to offer comprehensive counseling, it will have to open a separate facility at another location under a different name, share no telephone lines, receptionists or waiting rooms with its federally funded operation and not even have access to its own medical records — a proposition too cumbersome and costly to make it feasible.

Moreover, the new rules stipulate that once a woman is diagnosed as pregnant, she immediately becomes ineligible for Title X funds. That means service stops. Even if the pregnancy threatens her health, counselors at the government-sanctioned facility can do no more than send her to a prenatal clinic. This means she may never be informed of her legal and medical options. If she is, and if she does choose abortion, it will be farther along in her pregnancy when the cost and trauma are greater. This will hit the poor disproportionately; they make up 80 percent of the clients at federally funded facilities.

Far more is at stake. The president's rules force family planning programs to implement a policy that reflects his personal moral beliefs. That is like making heterosexuality or church attendance a precondition for Medicare coverage. Like it or not, abortion is legal; restricting that choice is wrong.

The News and Observer

Raleigh, North Carolina, January 23, 1988

Fifteen years after the landmark U.S. Supreme Court ruling that spelled out the abortion rights of women, most Americans remain committed to the basic legal principle of Roe v. Wade, even when they have uneasy personal feelings about abortion.

That a consensus has formed for preserving a woman's right legally to choose abortion — within particular time limits — stands out in a new national study. The opinion survey for the National Abortion Rights Action League shows that 88 percent of Americans favor retaining abortion rights in some form.

This is a strong response to politicians and groups who demand a constitutional amendment to overrule the Roe v. Wade decision. A convincing majority of Republicans, Democrats and independents in the survey voiced opposition to this course.

The ambivalence many Americans feel about abortion emerges from the study, too. Only 39 percent support a right to abortion for "any woman who wants one." Many who answered this question have a fear that abortion may become another kind of birth control — a substitute for sexual responsibility. But a disturbing survey finding is that men and women under 30 have no sense of the danger to health that many women faced from illegal abortions before the 1973 ruling.

While not a perfect answer to the dilemma of abortion, Roe v. Wade seems to be about as near a consensus on the issue as can be achieved right now in America. Undoubtedly there must be alterations in the law from time to time, for example, when medical advances permit earlier viability of the fetus apart from the mother's womb.

Still, a large American majority believes that women, not the state, must have essential control of their bodies and that women and physicians who agree on an abortion procedure should not face legal sanction. And that's true of many people who are convinced that they wouldn't choose abortion themselves. Americans need to live with their consensus on abortion while striving to minimize the unwanted pregnancies that bring much of it on.

SYRACUSE HERALD·JOURNAL

Syracuse, New York, January 22, 1988

Lawyers everywhere are probably rubbing their hands together in happy anticipation of the fat legal fees they will collect after the president institutes a regulation prohibiting the distribution of federal funds to family planning clinics that offer abortions or abortion counseling.

The administration says it is issuing the order because current regulations require women be told about abortion as an option to unwanted pregnancy. It maintains that such a policy is in direct conflict with a 1970 law that forbids the use of federal funds by clinics that suggest abortion as a method of family planning.

The administration, in other words, found a loophole to move closer to the goal Reagan has had since he took office seven and half years ago — to repeal the Roe vs. Wade decision that legalized abortion 15 years ago today.

The trouble is, the president hasn't been able to accomplish that goal through the highest court in the land. In 1973, the Supreme Court ruled there was an implied right of privacy in the Constitution, which in turn, gave women the right to opt for an abortion.

Since that landmark decision, it has consistently rejected anti-abortion arguments, and with the exception of restricting Medicaid to pay for life-threatening abortions only, it has favored the "pro choice" position.

The court has said they do not have to get their husband's consent for an abortion before the first trimester; a minor does not need parental consent for an abortion except in special circumstances; and that physicians do not have to tell abortion patients that a fetus becomes a human being when it is conceived.

Although the Justice Department may be able to justify its policy to deny Medicaid patients abortions except in life-threatening situations, it seems to be on shaky ground with the part of the new rule that involves abortion counseling.

Roe vs. Wade gives women the right to have abortions, which means they more than likely have the right to be counseled about abortions.

No matter how vehement the anti-abortion sentiment is in the Reagan administration, it has no business telling family planning clinics that if they offer abortion counseling, they cannot receive federal funds.

Already, there are abortion advocates talking about filing lawsuits on behalf of clinics when the regulation takes effect. They envision a whole range of areas that will serve as the basis for litigation: free speech violations; discrimination against poor women, who would be affected most by the ruling; and malpractice suits brought by women who became seriously ill or injured during a pregnancy, a condition that might have been avoided had they been given abortion counseling.

The president and the Justice Department will have to be prepared to fight this latest anti-abortion maneuver in the courts. In the meantime, they had better start looking for another loophole. This one's sure to fail.

©1987 MIAMI NEWS

Abstinence IS THE ONLY *REAL* ANSWER

ABSTINENCE CONDOM COMPANY
WEEHAWKEN, N.J.

THE ATLANTA CONSTITUTION
Atlanta, Georgia, January 20, 1988

The foolishness, even the cruelty, of the Reagan administration's efforts to undermine international birth-control programs that have so much as a secondhand associa-tion with abortion are dramatized by a report from the Washington-based Population Crisis Committee. The policy is bound to force desperate women to resort to illegal abortions, often deadly to the woman.

The issue is not really, in many cases, whether there will be an abortion when an unwanted pregnancy occurs. The issue is whether the abortion will be safe. Of the 28 million abortions performed yearly in developing countries, the report says, an estimated 20 million are illegal and thus inherently unsafe. In denying women access to birth control in the name of opposing abortion, the Reaganites are actually forcing women to abortion as a last resort.

The result for many is tragic. An estimated 100,000 women die worldwide annually from unsafe abortions. The United States is familiar with the phenomenon. In 1968, before abortion was made lawful here, abortion was the leading cause of maternal deaths — some 5,000 out of the 1 million illegal abortions that were performed yearly. The U.S. mortality rate now is just 10 per 1 million abortions.

The Reagan administration is withholding U.S. aid from international birth-control programs merely as a political sop to American anti-abortion groups, a busy part of the Reagan constituency and, increasingly, of the Republican constituency. In effect, the administration is sacrificing the lives of Third World women for its political convenience, while only increasing the number of illegal abortions abroad. Some policy.

The Miami Herald
Miami, Florida, January 24, 1988

PREDICTABLY, the Reagan Administration chose Friday's anniversary of the landmark 1973 *Roe vs. Wade* decision to reaffirm its plan to harass Federally funded family-planning agencies whose services include abortion counseling or referrals.

The Administration's own public-health officials seem reluctant to be the pawns in this political game. The White House is courting its right-to-life constituents by inviting a lawsuit that almost certainly will delay its proposals' implementation until next year and a new President. The White House is reaching back to a law predating *Roe*, and purporting to enforce it with unprecedented rigidity. This ignores both the Court and Congress's will as expressed in subsequent laws supporting a broad spectrum of family-planning efforts. The Administration seeks to bar clinics from even *mentioning* abortion.

Federal law now requires clinics that get Federal money to tell clients about all birth-control options, including contraception, abortion, and adoption. If the client asks, clinics also must refer her to a licensed physician who performs abortions, which the clinics themselves may not provide with Federal funds.

OF BIRTH-CONTROL CLINICS

The existing policy is both clear and correct: Once a woman asks about abortion, the public interest is served by referring her to a safe, licensed practitioner rather than leaving her to risk aborting herself or trusting an illicit, back-alley butcher. Americans dislike abortion, but they don't want a return to the days of coat-hanger deaths.

In fact, polls consistently reveal that public opinion is thoughtfully ambivalent toward the 1.5 million abortions done each year. Only 10 percent of the public shares the Administration's hard-line view, while 39 percent supports a woman's unlimited right to choice. The others support choice under varied circumstances. Most wish that women would avoid unwanted pregnancy.

That is a sensible, sensitive, and civilized view. Any President *ought* to embrace it wholeheartedly instead of relentlessly harassing those whose first goal is to prevent the unwanted pregnancies that make abortion necessary.

Operation Rescue Organizes Throughout Country

The U.S. Supreme Court June 27, 1988 affirmed the right of local government to ban picketing in front of a person's home.

In a 6–3 ruling, the court upheld an ordinance passed by Brookfield, Wis. after anti-abortion demonstrators picketed the home of a local doctor who performed abortions as part of his practice in several clinics.

The protesters called the doctor "a killer" and told a neighborhood child that "a man up the road kills babies."

A challenge to the law was brought by the demonstrators on their constitutional right to free speech.

Justice Sandra Day O'Connor, writing for the majority in *Frisby v. Schultz*, said the local law did not violate the free-speech guarantee since it banned picketing directly in front of a person's home but left many other avenues of expression open to protesters.

"General marching through residential neighborhoods or even walking a route in front of an entire block of houses is not prohibited by this ordinance," she said.

But, she said, "there simply is no right to force speech into the home of an unwilling listener."

She noted that the ordinance was not directed at picketing that would "disseminate a message to the general public," but rather at those who would "intrude upon the targeted resident, and to do so in an especially offensive way."

"The state's interest in protecting the well-being, tranquillity and privacy of the home is certainly of the highest order in a free and civilized society," O'Connor said. "One important aspect of residential privacy is protection of the unwilling listener."

Justice William J. Brennan Jr., in a dissent, joined by Justice Thurgood Marshall, said "a crowd of protesters need not be permitted virtually to imprison a person in his or her own house." But, so long as coercion was not a factor, he said, the state may not broadly prohibit picketing.

Justice John Paul Stevens filed a separate dissent.

Police arrested more than 400 people during a series of anti-abortion protests in Atlanta October 4-8, 1988.

The demonstrations, sponsored by Binghamton, N.Y.-based Operation Rescue, sought to disrupt activity at several clinics and prevent women from obtaining abortions. Most of the arrests were made when protesters attempted to obstruct clinic entrances or blocked the streets near clinics.

The protests, termed a "siege of Atlanta" by organizers, marked the second major wave of anti-abortion activity in the city in 1988. During the Democratic National Convention in July, some 754 protesters had been arrested.

Tom Pocock, deputy director of the Atlanta Corrections Bureau, October 10 said that 463 protesters had been arrested during the five-day event. Many of those taken into custody had refused to give their real names, calling themselves "Baby Doe" as a gesture of solidarity with aborted fetuses. Judges refused to release those who failed to identify themselves, and 282 protesters remained in jail as of October 10.

Clinic operators said the protests had little effect.

The Supreme Court May 21, 1990 let stand a federal court order issued in January 1989 that permanently barred Operation Rescue from blocking access to and from abortion clinics in New York City, Long Island and Westchester County, N.Y. The court, without comment, refused to hear the appeal, *Terry v. New York State National Organization for Women*. (In a 5–4 decision May 14, *Hirsch v. Atlanta*, the court had denied a stay of an injunction by an Atlanta court barring Operation Rescue from blocking access to clinics.)

THE
KANSAS CITY STAR
Kansas City, Missouri, November 2, 1988

If the protests and blockades at family planning clinics across the nation escalate any further, lives are likely to be lost. Already there have been bombings of clinics to make the anti-abortion point. Unsettled minds in this movement advocate and carry out death and destruction as their means to promote life.

In Kansas City, protesters can be found regularly at the clinics of Planned Parenthood. They argue that this is their constitutional right. But along with that go the tactics of fear—personal threats and intimidation have served to keep a family planning clinic out of Johnson County. There has been vandalism. What follows next for Kansas City? A recent opinion expressed by a special contributor in the Rockhurst College newspaper calls for bombings by a nationwide network of anti-abortion advocates, acknowledging that people could be injured, "but it would send a message to everyone to stay away from abortion clinics. . . ."

This kind of advocacy is what sets off the unstable. Not able to take away women's right to privacy through the courts, or by constitutional amendment, some members of the right-to-life movement try to accomplish the goal through terrorism. They are helped by the example of those who break the law in other ways, or who stir up the atmosphere with hate. Even lawful protests have limits—some are within constitutional rights of protest and some result in arrest and conviction for those carrying them out. Many times those who are subjected to them are not entering the clinic for an abortion at all, but for birth control or pregnancy testing.

Abortion will not be stopped in this country by tactics of fear and destruction. The real way to stop abortion is to make unwanted pregnancies a rarity. That will be accomplished through education and the availability of contraception. This is where all this misguided energy to fight abortion should be going.

THE BUFFALO NEWS
Buffalo, New York, November 11, 1988

CONTROVERSY is continuing over the Buffalo Police Department's handling of recent anti-abortion demonstrations. In contrast to what happened in many other American cities, demonstrators succeeded in closing an Elmwood Avenue clinic during regular hours for two successive days.

While anti-abortion protesters have a right to picket and demonstrate, it is clear that they have no right to block entrances to clinics performing lawful abortions and other services. Yet that is what happened in Buffalo on Oct. 28 and 29.

Buffalo police officials say they could not act sooner than they did because they did not have a written complaint from the clinic.

Maybe so, but that is only part of the story.

Even after arrests began on the second day, police used the slow course of taking demonstrators away two at a time in squad cars, instead of using buses for mass arrests. As a result, the clinic remained closed for an extended period.

Mayor Griffin said the city's goal was to avoid the mass arrests and harsh tactics that had been employed by police in Atlanta. Yet Amherst and Kenmore police were able to restore prompt access to clinics in their communities in an efficient and professional manner without any hint of ill treatment of protesters.

Buffalo city lawyers have asked the courts for instructions on how to protect the city from lawsuits and claims of false arrest in coping with future abortion protests.

Certainly false arrests must be avoided, but if legal guidance is needed, the city's Law Department should be able to provide it.

The mayor is clearly right in wanting "to see everybody treated with compassion and common sense." But that does not absolve him of his legal responsibility to prevent unlawful acts by demonstrators.

The issue here is not abortion, a matter on which Americans are deeply and sincerely divided, but the rule of law. At stake is Buffalo's reputation as a community that is capable of enforcing the law and protecting the legal rights of all.

Buffalo, New York, December 12, 1988

AFTER AN INCIDENT provoked by anti-abortion protesters, officials in the Town of Amherst are planning, very appropriately, to propose an ordinance that would ban the "selective picketing" of the homes of Amherst residents.

"Our residents have the right not to be harassed in their own homes because their beliefs happen to differ from someone else's," said Supervisor Jack Sharpe, expressing a widely shared sentiment.

What triggered all this was the picketing by a handful of abortion opponents in front of the home of Dr. Barnett Slepian, a physician specializing in gynecology and obstetrics, on Dec. 5.

At the time, Dr. Slepian, his wife and children were celebrating the religious holiday of Hanukkah. Dr. Slepian, accused of responding by hitting one of the pickets with a baseball bat, is free on bail, pending a Jan. 3 hearing on the case.

The right of free speech, fundamental as it is, should not extend to harassing and haranguing people at their own homes.

Nor does it. The Supreme Court, in a 6-3 decision last June, correctly ruled that a locality could bar picketing of a private residence without violating First Amendment guarantees of free expression. The decision flowed from a case — involving the picketing of a physician's home by anti-abortion protesters in a Milwaukee suburb — similar to the Amherst picketing.

In the majority opinion in that case, Associate Justice Sandra Day O'Connor noted that the protesters, prohibited from picketing "solely in front of a particular residence," retained ample alternative ways to communicate their messages. They could picket a doctor's office or commercial areas, for example, or even parade generally through a residential street.

But Justice O'Connor rightly argued that no one has the right "to force speech into the home of an unwilling listener." She placed heavy emphasis on prior court decisions that had recognized the special importance of "preserving the sanctity of the home, the one retreat to which men and women can repair to escape from the tribulations of their daily pursuits."

Thus, the nation's highest court decided, carefully drafted local ordinances could bar picketing in front of a particular residence without jeopardizing basic rights of free speech.

Amherst attorney James M. Nesper is preparing such an ordinance for consideration by the Town Board, a task eased by the constitutional guidelines already set down by the Supreme Court decision.

Picketing private homes for any reason is a repugnant tactic, whether the target is a private physician or a public official like County Executive Dennis Gorski, whose home was picketed by county sheriff's deputies last March.

Certainly people should be free to live with their families in their own homes without disruption and harassment from outsiders who happen to disagree with them, whatever the nature of the controversy.

In a sense, it is truly regrettable that such laws are required in order to protect the ordinary privacy of people in their own homes. Reasonable rules and rights of privacy ought to be accepted by all Americans. But the extremist tactics evident in Amherst now, as in the Milwaukee suburb earlier, render such legal limits necessary and proper.

THE INDIANAPOLIS NEWS
Indianapolis, Indiana, October 20, 1988

Abortion is an issue that evokes strong emotions.

One side passionately believes that abortion is murder, plain and simple, and that victims have no voice to defend themselves. The other believes, just as passionately, that no one should make the decision to end or to continue a pregnancy but the individual woman.

Such passions lead inexorably to conflict, as they have recently at the Affiliated Women's Services clinic on the city's Westside.

On Saturday, Marion County Sheriff's deputies arrested 57 at a mostly peaceful protest when they blocked an entrance to the clinic. On Sunday night, someone smashed a clinic window with a car battery.

The next night, the newly replaced window was smashed. This time, someone dropped a gas-soaked rag and lighted matches through the shattered glass. A deputy, responding to a burglar alarm, put out the fire.

Officials do not know whether the incidents of property damage and arson are connected with the protest group.

A spokesman for Operation Rescue, which staged the protest here and in Atlanta and other cities, said the group does not "condone this type of activity."

He does, however, vow to continue protests "until the laws are overturned."

Peaceful protest is the right of every American. Violence is not. Neither is interfering with the legal rights of others — including women who choose to have what is, under current law, a legal abortion.

Individuals who oppose abortion only damage their case by actions such as those at Affiliated Women's Services. There are far more effective — and legal — means to make their point.

Passion should be tempered with reason.

The Idaho STATESMAN

Boise, Idaho, October 8, 1988

The picture on the front page of Wednesday's newspaper was reminiscent of the 1960s' anti-war and civil rights protests. Except this time the photo showed an anti-abortion protester being carried away by police.

An anti-abortion group called Operation Rescue has been demonstrating in Atlanta ever since the Democratic National Convention was held in that city last July. So far more than 750 demonstrators have been jailed.

On Tuesday 250 protesters were jailed for protesting in front of an abortion clinic. Their aim was to shut the clinic down for the day, but some women entered the clinic anyway.

Some of the protesters screamed or cried as they were hauled off to jail. Many supporters watching the arrests sobbed or prayed quietly. Others sang hymns or songs from the civil rights movement.

It probably is not a coincidence that the right-to-lifers are taking this stand in the South, the site of the civil rights demonstrations and freedom marches of the 1960s and the home of the Rev. Martin Luther King Jr. They want comparisons drawn between their cause and the civil rights movement.

Like the civil rights marchers, these demonstrators see theirs as a moral cause, a fight for the lives of the unborn. Like the civil rights marchers, they are willing to go to jail for their cause.

One cannot argue with their right to demonstrate, to test their cause in the court of public opinion. That is what the civil rights demonstrators did two decades ago and it helped break the back of bigotry in the South.

But it would be better if Operation Rescue demonstrated before the U.S. Supreme Court, Congress or state legislatures, places where public officials can do something about changing U.S. abortion policy.

Demonstrating in front of abortion clinics does not put heat on public officials. It puts heat on women who have already made the tough decision to have an abortion. Crossing a picket line only adds to their trauma.

At least two demonstrators have been arrested because they assaulted a woman who was trying to enter the clinic. There is no room for such intimidation in a demonstration held to promote life.

Still, whether the cause is civil rights or right-to-life, the rights of Americans to demonstrate for their cause must be tolerated, especially by those who disagree with them.

The Charlotte Observer

Charlotte, North Carolina, September 6, 1988

Anti-abortion protesters in Atlanta have a right to protest. But the protest group, called Operation Rescue, goes beyond the limits of reasonable civil disobedience when it tries to prevent women from entering abortion clinics.

The group has been blocking the entrances to abortion clinics and engaging in other obstructive tactics since the Democratic National Convention in July. More than 700 demonstrators have been arrested. Now their tactics are turning other opponents of abortion against them.

The First Baptist Church of Atlanta has issued a two-page leaflet that calls abortions "an abomination before God" but opposes the Atlanta protestors' tactics. The leaflet says it represents the "carefully studied" view of pastor Charles Stanley — a former president of the Southern Baptist convention — the pastoral staff and deacons of the state's largest Baptist church.

The statement makes three important points:

● Protesters have been charged with criminal trespassing, obstructing rights of way and other violations, but are not directly preventing abortions.

● The 1973 Supreme Court decision legalizing abortion "neither requires abortions nor prohibits them, but makes them permissible with certain restrictions."

● Women are "free moral agents responsible before Almighty God for their actions, including the exercise of the rights of their innocent, unborn child."

Operation Rescue leader Randall Terry said the group is glad Mr. Stanley opposes abortions, but that the effort is "not about protest or civil disobedience. It is about saving the lives of babies scheduled to be murdered."

Civil disobedience has a long and effective history as a means of focusing public attention on moral and political questions. No doubt Mr. Terry is sincere. But no matter how sincere, he and his fellow protestors have neither the right to stop women from seeking counseling or abortion, nor the almighty power to judge them if they do.

Charlotte, North Carolina, October 9, 1988

The Atlanta anti-abortion protesters described in Observer Southern Editor Frye Gaillard's report today are undeniably sincere. However, their method of expressing their belief — by blocking entry to abortion clinics — is plainly illegal.

Atlanta police are pawns of the protesters' tactics, forced into the unwelcome role of oppressors who drag them off to jail. Understandably, the police are weary. But weariness is no excuse for abuse. The officers' job is to arrest and remove them, not to inflict physical punishment on them.

It is difficult for officers to remain civil in the face of adamant civil disobedience. But in Atlanta, of all places, authorities should understand the necessity of doing just that.

Most Americans oppose the protesters' call for a ban on abortion. In 1987 the polling firm Time/Yankelovich Clancy Shulman asked Americans which position represents their views about abortion. The responses:

● 51% said abortion should be legal only in certain circumstances, such as when a pregnancy results from rape or incest or endangers a woman's life;

● 34% said a woman should be free to get an abortion if she chose to;

● 12% said abortion should be illegal in all circumstances.

To summarize, 85% of those polled didn't support an abortion ban. Yet most of those polled apparently are troubled by the 1.5 million abortions performed in America each year, for 63% favored a more restrictive abortion policy. They disagree, however, on what to do.

The division does not follow traditional political lines. The 1988 Republican platform supports a constitutional amendment asserting that "the unborn child has a fundamental right to life which cannot be infringed." Vice President Bush, however, favors exceptions in cases of rape, incest and a threat to the mother's life. Many Republicans favor the degree of choice guaranteed by the U.S. Supreme Court.

We don't support the Atlanta protesters' tactics, or their call for an abortion ban. But they believe concern for life must not end at birth, and so do we.

We believe that, early in pregnancy, a woman should be free to choose abortion. We do not think the blastocysts and zygotes that are the earliest stages of life should have the legal protection that should be provided later in pregnancy. Yet we are troubled that so many women choose abortion.

The most effective way to reduce the incidence of abortion is to work on ways to help a woman choose motherhood, rather than force her to.

A pregnant woman is hardly encouraged to bear a child if she looks at her future and sees a struggle for food, housing and medical care, during pregnancy and for years afterward; inadequate day care or none; and sharply diminished opportunities to improve her life. Yet many opponents of abortion oppose government efforts to provide such help. And many oppose efforts to provide contraceptive education and devices.

That morally myopic view won't eliminate abortion, even if it leads to restrictive abortion laws. Remember, before Roe vs. Wade, American women in great numbers were having abortions — as many as 1 million a year, according to some estimates.

THE SUN HERALD

Biloxi, Mississippi, August 15, 1988

The millions of abortions performed in this country in recent years constitute a national tragedy. It is a sad commentary on our times that abortion has come to be regarded by many as simply another form of birth control.

Whether we believe abortion should be legal or illegal, surely none among us can be undisturbed by the staggering number of terminated pregnancies.

The issue is far from permanently settled, but the fact remains that for now, abortion within certain guidelines is the law of the land. Millions of people want to change that, and they have every right to pursue their cause through all legal means available.

The emphasis is on the word "legal." The other day, the Rev. Jerry Falwell called for a national campaign of non-violent civil disobedience by right-to-life activists with the goal of "shutting the country down" and forcing Congress to pass a constitutional amendment prohibiting abortion. This would be an unfortunate and misguided approach. It would likely prove ineffective; the kind of unlawful demonstrations and massive arrests Falwell advocates would almost certainly produce a public backlash harmful to the anti-abortion cause.

There are other avenues available. Anti-abortionists can lobby state legislators and members of Congress, work to elect those sympathetic to their cause, stage peaceful and legal demonstrations, use the courts and, perhaps most important of all, continue to work to change public opinion.

Polls indicate that a majority of Americans believe abortion should be legal. Legislatures and Congress aren't likely to act until that consensus is reversed. Fortunately for anti-abortionists, there is evidence that many Americans are having second thoughts.

Falwell compared his call for a national campaign for civil disobedience on the abortion issue to the civil rights demonstrations and sit-ins of the 1960s. There is an important difference: The state and local laws that those civil rights demonstrators sometimes violated were often in direct conflict with existing federal laws or court rulings. The civil rights demonstrators knew they had federal authority in many cases to back them up; the anti-abortionists, on the other hand, have no such legal leg to stand on if they choose to violate the law.

The kind of campaign Falwell proposes would be counterproductive. If the anti-abortionists stay within the legal process, are persistent, and keep the debate as civil as possible, they have a fighting chance to achieve their goals.

The Clarion-Ledger

Jackson, Mississippi, September 8, 1988

So far presidential candidates George Bush and Michael Dukakis are not generally speaking on the high plane of issues and principles American voters should expect, but neither do they deserve the intense heckling they encountered Tuesday.

Anti-abortionists shouted "baby-killer" at Democrat Dukakis in Niles, Ill., a Chicago suburb, while Republican Bush was confronted with ironworkers chanting "union buster" in Portland, Ore.

Dukakis shrugged off the interruptions by saying, "That's democracy." It may be a dark facet of democracy, although trying to drown out or silence a speaker is more akin to totalitarianism. It's certainly not what most people think of as the American way.

Displeasure with political speakers can be expressed through numerous routes. The "quiet treatment" is effective, and a restrained boo that doesn't interrupt the speech is not beyond the pale. Pamphleteering, writing letters to the press and sounding off from a soapbox are, among other things, avenues available to the nay-sayer.

Heckling is, of course, not new, even in this campaign, though the incidents Tuesday are probably the ugliest manifestations so far. One wonders if it reflects the mood of Americans. Are voters so angry, are minds so closed, are one-issue groups so powerful that candidates for the highest office in the land are not free to carry their campaigns to all corners of the country and get a decent hearing?

Perhaps the behavior of the throng of pipefitters, sheet metal workers and machinists in Oregon and of the protesting anti-abortionists is an aberration. But one is not encouraged by the director of the Chicago-based Pro-Life Action League saying the Niles protest was a continuing organized effort to disrupt Dukakis speeches.

The presidential campaign is sputtering along the low roads. Voters and candidates must both try to lift it to the higher level its great import deserves.

Jackson, Mississippi, May 17, 1988

Saturday's anti-abortion rally at a local medical clinic, which culminated in 64 of the approximately 150 protesters being arrested, might be viewed as a simple act of civil disobedience in order to call attention to a cause.

It was not. The actions of the group of abortion protesters were offensive, disruptive to the community and did little to further their cause.

The public should note that this is part of a national effort by radical anti-abortionists, designed to bring attention to themselves. There was more ego and self-righteousness demonstrated Saturday than effort for a cause.

They said their concern was for individuals, but their actions showed anything but concern. There are plenty of legitimate approaches to discouraging abortion, such as counseling or education. The actions of Saturday only hurt the credibility of their position and reflected on the legitimate groups doing work in this area.

The police did their job in controlling a mob breaking the law. That is the only way Saturday's "protest" should be viewed.

THE INDIANAPOLIS STAR

Indianapolis, Indiana, October 8, 1988

Later this year Operation Rescue, the anti-abortion group whose protesters have been arrested by the hundreds in Atlanta, will demonstrate in Indianapolis.

Protesters will sit in front of four clinics and try to keep women from entering, Robert P. Rust, an anti-abortion activist from Greeensburg, said.

Ernest C. Rosenthal, an Indianapolis activist who was among those arrested in Atlanta, will organize the demonstrations, Rust said.

The date could be Oct. 29, which Rust said Operation Rescue has declared a "national day of rescue."

Members of the Indiana Pro-Choice Action League will provide escorts to help women entering the clinics, the pro-abortion group's executive director said.

Indianapolis police hope to handle the situation with more finesse than Atlanta police used in their city, where over 400 demonstrators were arrested this week and nearly 800 were arrested in earlier protests.

Bob Fierer, an Atlanta attorney representing Operation Rescue, said police brutality lawsuits will be filed in Atlanta, where he said police broke the jaw of an Indiana minister, Doyle Clark, and kicked another man unconscious. An Atlanta police captain denied the charges. He said police "have to use whatever pressure is necessary and condoned by the Atlanta Police Bureau" to get demonstrators into police wagons.

Indianapolis demonstrators may be arrested on misdemeanor charges including criminal trespassing or obstructing traffic, Jon M. Bailey, Indianapolis Police Department legal adviser, said.

The abortion controversy is one of the most emotion-charged issues in the nation, possibly the most. More than 22 million abortions have been performed since the 1973 U.S. Supreme Court ruling overturning state anti-abortion laws.

It is being fought on moral and political ground at this point. Under the Pro-Choice ensign, pro-abortion people assert that women have the right to do as they choose with their bodies. It is also argued that if women are denied the right to legal abortions by qualified physicians, many will risk their health and lives by turning to "back-alley butchers," unqualified and inept abortionists.

Under a Pro-Life ensign, anti-abortionists maintain that abortion is murder and that they are struggling to save the lives of innocent unborn babies. They say that mothers who do not want children they have conceived should bear them and allow their adoption by couples who want children.

Reconciliation of such sharply opposed attitudes will require a rare blend of intelligence and wisdom if it is possible at all. Profound moral, social, philosophical and religious values are at issue. One side has the power of government and law behind it.

That power should not be used roughly against people whose motive is saving human life.

The Union Leader

Manchester, New Hampshire, August 19, 1988

Will history be kind to the anti-abortion protesters being arrested daily for the past month in Atlanta, the focal point of their effort to shut down the nation's abortion factories?

Who can know? Obviously, it depends on who writes the history.

But one wonders how history would have viewed demonstrations, had they been possible, outside the Nazi slaughterhouses where other innocents were exterminated, also by the millions, while the world looked the other way.

The Atlanta protesters understand the biological fact that life is a continuum and that man-made efforts to terminate lives simply because the state deems them to be socially undesirable constitutes a moral outrage. Only by using euphemisms — "freedom of choice," "enemies of the state" et al. — to describe the victims, only by declaring them non-persons, can the state rationalize the mass killings.

THE BUFFALO NEWS

Buffalo, New York, November 1, 1988

ANTI-ABORTION protests in Buffalo and around the nation have placed police departments in a difficult situation, all the more so because of the intensity of honest convictions on both sides of this contentious issue. Nonetheless, Buffalo police officials deserve criticism for allowing protesters to block entry to an Elmwood Avenue clinic for many hours before taking action and making arrests.

The Buffalo demonstration was part of a coordinated, nationwide protest against abortion. Locally, Police Commissioner Ralph V. Degenhart indicated that the department wanted to avoid mass arrests in order to prevent the kind of problems that had occurred earlier in Atlanta when police used rough tactics against anti-abortion demonstrators. That is understandable and indeed commendable. But the choice for Buffalo police officials need not and should not be between harsh measures on the one hand and, on the other, allowing protesters to block access to the clinic for an extended period.

Police have a responsibility to protect the right of abortion opponents to assemble and demonstrate, and everyone can be glad that the protests came off peacefully. But the right to protest does not extend to preventing access to lawful activities. Degenhart claims that the police needed a formal, written complaint before they could act. Whatever the reason, the failure to protect the rights of those denied access cannot be condoned.

The Miami Herald

Miami, Florida, August 5, 1988

JOAN ANDREWS is serving a five-year sentence in Broward for attacking a Pensacola abortion clinic in 1986. Despite the national pro-life movement's attempts to canonize the Delaware woman and get her paroled, she should serve that sentence unless she satisfies the usual requirements for clemency in this state.

Her supporters, who are expected to rally this week in Tallahassee, should appreciate that hers was not an act of nonviolent civil disobedience. Equipment was destroyed, two clinic employees were slightly injured, and she resisted arrest without violence. Furthermore, their imploring Gov. Bob Martinez to release Andrews because she also is "a loyal, practicing Catholic" is wholly irrelevant.

The judge properly levied the maximum sentence because Andrews wouldn't renounce her tactics. He also cited her record of more than 120 arrests and 17 misdemeanor convictions in several states. Also, at the time of her arrest, she was free on bail after invading the same clinic a month earlier.

The Ladies Center that Ms. Andrews twice attacked, and the offices of two gynecologists who performed abortions, were bombed on Christmas Day 1984. After four people were

ON ANTI-ABORTION FELON

convicted, anti-abortion groups targeted the center and its employees for protests. Andrews joined in.

If the anti-abortion movement wants to use her to make its stand, so be it. Until Florida, her longest jail term had been six months in St. Louis. There is a penalty to be paid for violating laws, and Florida's insistence on exacting it should be a warning to others who flout laws that they dislike. Jailers consider Andrews a discipline problem, unsuitable for early release. To cooperate, she has said, is to make peace with a murderous system. She is entitled to that view — and she warrants the full consequences of it.

Governor Martinez, who opposes abortion, couldn't free Andrews even if he wanted to. Only a cabinet majority that includes the governor can grant clemency. Apart from process, remorse is a standard requirement for leniency. Absent any display of remorse, Andrews should stay in prison until her tentative release date of Oct. 11, 1990.

The Providence Journal
Providence, Rhode Island, November 1, 1988

Saturday's anti-abortion demonstration in Providence proved that public sentiment on the question is now, and probably always will be, emotional indeed. Since *Roe vs. Wade*, the instrument of public demonstration and civil disobedience has been largely the province of the "pro-life" brigades, since "pro-choice" advocates have the law on their side. And Saturday's demonstration was one of the largest, and most volatile, in recent Providence history.

Of course, people opposed to abortion have every right, within the law, to advance their cause. They are encouraged to march, to write, to influence their legislators, to sing, to engage in dialogue, to shout, to demonstrate in public their deeply-held beliefs. They have the right to complain about abortion, and to picket those places where abortions are performed. These are basic civil liberties, enjoyed by all Americans.

But just as abortion opponents may exercise those rights, they must also consider the rights of fellow citizens. So it was not only ill-advised to descend *en masse* for a surprise demonstration, causing public disturbances and distracting the police, it was also simply wrong. Indeed, the demonstration was so explosive, and so clearly unexpected, that police were unable to perform their vital duties in other sections of the city.

If anti-abortion demonstrators seek to influence opinion, they would be well advised to avoid guerrilla tactics that endanger civil order. In Providence, as in other cities, the authorities did what they clearly had to do.

Civil disobedience is an honorable recourse, and people so attached to their various causes impress us with sincerity. No cause, however, raises its adherents above the law — and a demonstration aimed at disrupting the community (as well as its target) angers the public, and properly so.

TULSA WORLD
Tulsa, Oklahoma, July 15, 1989

REP. Bill Graves, R-Oklahoma City, a leading anti-abortion redhot in the state House, insists that abortion legislation be taken up during the August special session called by Gov. Henry Bellmon.

That despite the fact that Bellmon, Senate President Pro Tempore Bob Cullison and House Speaker Steve Lewis all have said they prefer the highly emotional and divisive issue not be considered in the Legislature until the U.S. Supreme Court finally resolves it.

But Graves persists.

"The right to life of the unborn child is, in the eyes of many Oklahomans, even more important than the issues you called for the consideration of," he said in a letter to the governor.

The issue that prompted Bellmon's call for a special session is, of course, education. That is, the education of children who have been born. Graves and others of like mind who would impose their religious beliefs on everyone else, might give some more thought to needs of complete, breathing children.

The tragic problems that face many children who are born — inadequate health care, abuse, lack of educational opportunity — must not be sidetracked by Graves preoccupation the abortion issue.

Many Oklahomans are sincerely concerned about the "unborn." But it isn't unreasonable to devote a legislative session to the immediate and desperate needs of "the born."

The Seattle Times
Seattle, Washington, July 21, 1989

THE Republican Party may very well end up the big political loser on the abortion issue. The party's two big constituencies — the religious right and prosperous suburban moderates — won't hold together on an issue that, though deeply divisive, has been quietly hushed up by state party leaders trying to keep the two groups allied.

Anti-abortion forces led by Doug Parris, a party committeeman from Snohomish County, have called for a resolution to ask Attorney General Ken Eikenberry to enforce a 1970 state law that prohibited abortions after 16 weeks. The old law, which permitted early abortion, was struck down by the Supreme Court decision in Roe v. Wade.

The aim is to coerce party leaders such as state chair Jennifer Dunn to carry out the objectives in the Republican national platform, which is strongly anti-choice.

Washington Republicans have a lot to lose by giving in to the vocal right-to-life minority. Passing an anti-choice resolution would be foolhardy, providing lethal ammunition for moderates and liberals at the polls. Voters in this state have been consistently pro-choice and have strongly supported public funding of abortions for low-income women.

It's time Republican leaders, instead of hiding from the issue, openly acknowledge that this state's political history (Washington being the first in the nation to permit abortion by referendum prior to Roe v. Wade) honors reproductive freedom.

By waffling, Dunn and other Republicans may find themselves in the ridiculous position of being led by the folks who delivered this state to Pat Robertson in the 1988 presidential primary.

The Charlotte Observer
Charlotte, North Carolina, November 16, 1988

The crush of election season delayed us a bit in saying what everyone surely felt after last weekend's anti-abortion protests here: The Charlotte Police Department handled the matter with great professionalism and sensitivity.

Charlotte police officials had seen what had happened in Atlanta, where police were widely criticized earlier this month for twisting the arms and gouging the necks of hundreds of anti-abortion demonstrators who were non-violently resisting arrest. The commitment to make sure nothing like that would happen here was clear in the careful planning and in the statements of police spokesmen.

Before Saturday's attempts to block entry to abortion clinics, Charlotte Assistant Police Chief Ronnie Stone put the department's position plainly: "Our policy," he said, "will be to use the least amount of force necessary. We have no animosity toward any of the participants." And he defined the role of police officers in such situations in words that should be required reading for law enforcement officers everywhere: "Our role as police officers is not to pick sides. Our role puts us in the middle. We represent the rights of both parties."

On Saturday morning, Charlotte police arrested 71 anti-abortion protesters for trespassing, and in doing so kept Chief Stone's promise.

District Attorney Peter Gilchrist made a sensible and sensitive decision in choosing not to prosecute the trespass offenses — this time. But he clearly — and properly — implied he might not be so lenient if the offense is repeated. These protesters are sincere people, but in their attempt to block entry to clinics they commit a crime. Next time it should be treated as one.

Justice Department Intervenes In Wichita Operation Rescue Protest

The Justice Department August 6, 1991 filed a friend-of-the-court brief in a court case in which anti-abortion protesters were seeking to overturn a federal judge's order prohibiting them from blocking the entrance to two abortion clinics in Wichita, Kan. The Justice Department argued that the federal courts had no jurisdiction in the matter.

The episode had begun on July 15, when members of the militant anti-abortion group Operation Rescue began to stage protests and block access to Wichita's three abortion clinics. Operation Rescue leaders had selected Wichita for the protests because they felt the region would be receptive to their activities and because one of the Wichita clinics, Women's Health Care Services, operated by physician George R. Tiller, had a reputation as one of the only clinics in the U.S. that performed late-term abortions.

The clinics closed down for a week to avoid confrontation. On July 23, however, Tiller's clinic filed a lawsuit in U.S. District Court in Wichita, seeking an injunction to prevent the protesters from blocking access to the clinic. The suit was joined July 29 by a second clinic, Wichita Family Planning Inc. In arguing for the injunction, the clinics cited the Civil Rights Act of 1871, a Reconstruction-era law originally designed to protect blacks from racial harassment. The clinics maintained that the law should be used to protect clinic patients and staff members from harassment by the protesters.

U.S. District Judge Patrick F. Kelly, who had been appointed by President Jimmy Carter, July 23 issued a temporary restraining order barring protesters from blocking entrance to the clinics. After two weeks in which police arrested hundreds of protesters, Kelly July 29 ordered U.S. marshals in to Wichita to assist police in carrying out his order.

Operation Rescue officials then filed a motion seeking to lift the restraining order. They also filed an appeal with the U.S. Court of Appeals for the 10th Circuit, in Denver, asking it to overturn Kelly's order.

The Justice Department filed its brief in Wichita, in connection with Operation Rescue's attempt to have the restraining order lifted. The department, in collaboration with the U.S. Attorney's Office in Wichita, argued that the legal issues involved in the case—trespass and loitering—were state and local matters, not federal ones. The brief also maintained that the 1871 civil rights law did not apply in abortion cases and that additional orders issued by Kelly, directing the actions of the U.S. marshals, infringed the marshals' prerogative to decide how to enforce court orders.

Justice Department officials noted that they had made similar arguments in a case involving anti-abortion protests in Alexandria, Va. That case was scheduled to be heard by the Supreme Court in October.

Judge Kelly agreed to allow the Justice Department to file its brief, but said, "I am disgusted by this move by the United States." In an appearance on the television program "Nightline" August 6, Kelly blasted the Justice Department's intervention, saying it had "given an imprimatur to what, in my view, is a license for mayhem."

Between July 15 and August 7, more than 1,900 arrests had been made. Many of them involved individuals arrested more than once.

Some members of the Bush administration August 7 sought to soften the impact of the Justice Department's action and to distance themselves from the politically controversial decision.

THE PLAIN DEALER
Cleveland, Ohio, August 21, 1991

Violence is intolerable in any society governed by the rule of law. Anti-abortion protesters, no matter how sincere they claim to be, can only repel fair-minded Americans by using physical intimidation as they besiege three women's health clinics in Wichita, Kan. It is astonishing that the Bush administration has chosen to give political and legal support to the Kansas lawbreakers.

About 2,000 protesters have been arrested by federal marshals as they tried to deny patients access to three Wichita reproductive-health centers. Goaded by Operation Rescue, a New York-based group of anti-choice militants, the demonstrators have made Wichita a test case of their crusade: to deny each woman her right to choose the option of carrying her pregnancy to term — a right that remains a constitutional guarantee.

Worse, some of the protesters have threatened to kill federal Judge Patrick Kelly, who is trying to maintain law and order in Wichita. Militants have used the most vicious tactics to intimidate the judge: provoking street-corner shoving matches with Kelly and sending his family graphic letters about how he will be killed and mutilated. The violent wing of Operation Rescue has abandoned any claim to peaceful, "pro-life" idealism.

The demonstrators are within their rights to protest the sad reality of abortion. Their lawyers are entitled to argue against the landmark 1973 ruling, the case of Roe vs. Wade, that found abortion is included within the Constitution's right of individual privacy. Those courses of action are legal and proper; threats of physical violence are contemptible.

Needlessly inflaming the dispute, the Bush administration recently intervened in court on behalf of the demonstrators. The Justice Department, supported by President Bush, has filed an appeals-court brief supporting Operation Rescue's claim: that the federal courts have no jurisdiction to act in the local Wichita dispute. The militants are forum-shopping, hoping to return the case to state courts (which might coddle them) from federal courts (which have taken a law-and-order hard line).

"Disgusted" by the Justice Department's intervention on the protesters' side, Kelly says the Bush administration has "given [its] imprimatur to what, in my view, is a license for mayhem." Indeed, recalling earlier eras of civil disobedience, it is impossible to imagine the Justice Department intervening in court on behalf of lawbreakers after protests turned violent. Would the Kennedy administration have defended club-wielding segregationists? Would the Johnson administration have defended Ku Klux Klan bombthrowers?

At best, Bush and his aides have shown the greatest insensitivity in supporting the Wichita lawbreakers. It would be deplorable if Bush or his advisers had any political motive in this decision, throwing a pre-election sop to the anti-choice movement to swell Bush's re-election margin in 1992. It is surely suspicious, however, that Attorney General Richard Thornburgh — a lame-duck time-server who is planning his next step up the electoral ladder — sided with the anti-abortion protesters only a week before he begins running for the Senate seat from Pennsylvania, a state where the anti-abortion movement is virulent.

Reasoned debate over the right to choose should occur in the courts and at the polls, not amid mobs in the streets. Anti-abortion forces have only discredited themselves by choosing the threat of violence over the rule of law.

The Hartford Courant

Hartford, Connecticut, August 16, 1991

Remember outside agitators? Back in the Sixties they had long hair and wore feathers and bells. They whipped up American college students, inciting them to demonstrate and boycott classes and take over deans' offices. Huge rallies and protests were not really an indication of national will, just the work of a troublesome few, America's leaders insisted. Those few needed to be dealt with severely, especially when their activities involved breaking the law.

How times have changed! Now outside agitators are God-fearing grannies, truck drivers, solid Americans, mostly with jobs and short hair. But in support of their cause — the fight against abortion — they are also breaking the law. And the nation's leaders are strangely silent.

There is little in the tactics of Operation Rescue protesters that was not also part of the protest movements of the Sixties. They travel from one trouble spot to another. They seek to raise the political temperature wherever they go. Their tactics are often illegal. They are divisive and fanatical. They regard multiple arrests as a badge of honor.

Faced with such tactics, Richard M. Nixon, Spiro T. Agnew and a host of fellow Republicans delivered blistering condemnations and called for the restoration of law and order. The groups became the objects of constant surveillance and harassment by the FBI and other covert agencies.

Many of our leaders appear to be tongue-tied about this new group of outlaws. Perhaps it is because they don't feel so threatened, since the targets of the protesters' wrath are simply individual women trying to exercise a constitutionally guaranteed right, rather than corporations and government agencies.

Whatever happened to the official fury unleashed 20-odd years ago at those who crossed state lines to incite riot? Have our leaders become more mellow in the intervening years? Or are some lawbreakers more equal than others?

ST. LOUIS POST-DISPATCH

St. Louis, Missouri, August 27, 1991

The battle raging in Wichita is over abortion, but the real war is the conflict between modernism and traditionalism. Within this context, Operation Rescue can be seen as the shock troops of the hysterical fringe of the anti-abortion movement. Like traditionalist fanatics anywhere, the adherents of Operation Rescue virulently reject the essential components of modern society: compromise, negotiation, pluralism, tolerance. They do not obey the law because they are moved by a "higher law." They are absolutists.

They are also ineffective. Despite claims to the contrary, Operation Rescue has stopped few, if any, abortions, although it has blocked many a clinic. Operation Rescue is better described as Operation Reschedule, to borrow a phrase from Kate Michelman of the National Abortion Rights Action League. And, needless to say, in the 18 years since abortion has been legal, Operation Rescue has never been in the forefront of doing anything that might reduce the need for abortion. The real world of unwanted pregnancy seems to be outside its moralistic universe.

For the followers of Operation Rescue, stopping abortion really means stopping the clock and returning to a nostalgic version of the past in which women stayed home, raised children and were subservient to their husbands. As sociologist Kristin Luker documented, women who are actively pro-choice tend to be career women, while women who are actively anti-abortion tend to be homemakers. (Interestingly, the leadership of much of the anti-abortion movement, including Operation Rescue, is male.) In the traditionalist view, abortion allows women to reject their "natural" roles, thus causing the further breakdown of the family.

In a speech to a crowd of 25,000 anti-abortion activists, Pat Robertson, the TV evangelist, summed up the traditionalist agenda: "And we will not rest until this land we love so much is once again truly one nation under God" — though not necessarily one with liberty and justice for all.

THE KANSAS CITY STAR

Kansas City, Missouri, August 27, 1991

The growing violent tone of the anti-abortion protests in Wichita should be moderated with jail terms. U.S. District Judge Patrick Kelly has shown remarkable restraint given what he has had to deal with in recent weeks in that beseiged city — violations of his orders and the law. The fact that the protesters have become even more flagrant means increased risk to people and property. A rush Tuesday by protesters over the fence and into the complex of one clinic was the most aggressive to that date, but if this kind of tactic is allowed to succeed, what is next?

The federal judge has attempted to get financial information from Operation Rescue leaders in deciding on fines or bond amounts. The group always has prided itself on keeping this information secret. It would be most interesting to learn where these people are getting their money and how they use it.

Operation Rescue needs some holes poked in its facade of being a do-good organization only concerned with saving babies.

The disruptions in Wichita are one way the public sees the real nature of this group. It is not by accident that the group's leaders are men — they don't want women in leadership roles, even within their own group. Their public statements on birth control and women's roles show they are out of step. Their tactics show it as well — encouraging children to endanger themselves as human blockades is not something reasonable people would do. They cannot be allowed to succeed in ignoring the law and in denying other people their rights.

The Evening Gazette

*Worcester, Massachusetts
August 16, 1991*

A Massachusetts judge has sent a strong message to radical anti-abortion groups: Blocking access to clinics is a violation of civil rights on a par with the actions of segregationists who barred black children from schools.

Middlesex Superior Court Judge Peter M. Lauriat last week ordered a permanent halt to the blockades in a ruling against Operation Rescue Boston, the Pro-Life Action Network and 38 individual defendants.

Lauriat's comparison of anti-abortion extremists to fanatic segregationists was part of an extended denunciation of the illegal protest tactics:

"A woman choosing to have an abortion should not have to assault a citadel of human blockaders ... to exercise her constitutionally protected rights," he wrote. "Threats, intimidation and coercion of pregnant women have no place in the arena of public debate and discourse on the issue of abortion."

He's right. The systematic violation of women's civil rights is unconscionable.

The deliberate lawbreaking has worked as a publicity gimmick for a handful of individuals and groups at the outer fringe of the anti-abortion movement. However, the extremists undercut the credibility of more responsible pro-life groups.

Lauriat's ruling makes permanent a preliminary injunction issued in May 1990. Violations carry a maximum penalty of 2½ years imprisonment and a $5,000 fine, giving the courts a powerful tool to protect women who choose to exercise their legal rights.

Lauriat's message is both welcome and clear: The right of anti-abortion groups to call attention to their views through public protest does not extend to actions that cruelly violate the civil rights of others. Indeed, lawbreaking has no part in this or any political debate.

The Providence Journal
Providence, Rhode Island, August 16, 1991

Although his harsh rhetoric has been ir-responsible and counter-productive, US District Judge Patrick Kelly has been correct in principle to issue — and then to enforce by means of federal marshals — a restraining order against members of Operation Rescue. Until the marshals arrived last week, dozens of members of the anti-abortion organization had been illegally blocking three clinics providing abortion services in Wichita, Kansas, for two weeks in violation of Judge Kelly's order.

It should be emphasized here that it is Operation Rescue that has been breaking the law, and not the abortion clinics, which have been providing services that have been clearly permitted by the US Supreme Court since its *Roe v. Wade* ruling 18 years ago.

There are several culprits in this case, among them the mayor of Wichita and the city's police department, both allies of Operation Rescue who deserve rebuke for effectively urging on the demonstrators in their lawlessness by failing to keep access to these clinics open. This is a dangerous kind of demagoguery, apt to lead to violence, and particularly disturbing when practiced by those sworn to uphold the law.

The Justice Department has not acquitted itself so brilliantly, either. It seems to have been playing to the grandstands when it filed a redundant brief last week supporting the protesters' efforts to overturn the judge's order (by moving the case into state courts). That brief probably has more to do with scoring points with abortion opponents than expediting legal matters. For one thing, Judge Kelly's order is already on appeal; for another, Justice had already stated its jurisdictional interpretations in *Bray v. Alexandria Women's Health Clinic*, a case that the Supreme Court will hear in a few months.

President Bush might have done some good in this instance by stepping in sooner and clearer on the side of the law.

It is entirely possible that the clumsy fashion in which Washington has handled this case might be due to the organizational confusion spawned by the departure of Attorney General Richard Thornburgh for a Pennsylvania senatorial race, and to President Bush's removal to Kennebunkport for his annual vacation. But whatever the explanation, the Justice Department and White House should have made it clearer from the start that they don't condone violation of the law, whatever the administration's views on this agonizing social issue.

Indeed, the issue of abortion is much too important a matter to be allowed to play itself out on the streets. It belongs in the courts, whose decisions law-abiding citizens, including government officials, must obey — and urge others to do the same.

The Clarion-Ledger
Jackson, Mississippi, August 20, 1991

The Bush administration's policies on abortion haven't helped the nation deal with this difficult issue very much, but at least he has offered a voice of reason concerning the protests in Wichita, Kan.

"I disapprove of breaking the law," Bush said. "I don't think it helps the cause. ... the American people get turned off by the excesses, the denial of rights of others. ... That's clear."

He's right. The lawless, offensive tactics of Operation Rescue have only further hurt people and have polarized the issue in a damaging manner. The Wichita protests have not furthered the anti-abortion cause.

At least, the president has had the courage to say it. Perhaps the Operation Rescue leaders will listen to their pro-life president. But, then again, they're not known for listening to reason.

The Hutchinson News
Hutchinson, Kansas, July 26, 1991

If the anti-abortion activists visiting Wichita hoped for publicity, they are successfully receiving some.

Their tactics are atrocious.

Walking, chanting and blocking roadways is one thing, but robbing people of their right of privacy is another thing.

This action rises well above civil disobedience and raises the specter of facism.

A young woman, already six months pregnant, was prohibited by anti-abortion protesters from entering a Wichita health clinic Wednesday. The woman, who by all accounts visited the clinic in search of medical advice and aid, was denied entry into the clinic by protesters.

There seems to be much concern and debate over the abortion question, but very little concern for adult, pregnant women.

Pregnancy is a stressful, often difficult time, especially when the term is complicated by physical or mental problems. Pregnancy often transforms an otherwise strong, healthy woman into a more fragile version of herself. She needs care and attention.

None of this was displayed Wednesday in Wichita.

A pregnant woman felt compelled to justify her visit to the clinic by explaining her medical condition. It's a wonder the protesters aren't insisting American citizens carry visas and passports as they travel.

Debate is to be encouraged. But the actions of the Wichita protesters leave no room for debate, not if they invade the privacy of fellow citizens at the drop of a hat.

Additionally, no other anti-abortion groups have raised objections to the tactics of the Wichita visitors, leaving the impression that Wednesday's tactic — the hassling of pregnant women — is an approved plank in the political platform of the national movement. That is news, indeed — very depressing news.

Hutchinson, Kansas, August 22, 1991

U.S. Sen. Bob Dole looked over the record of the protesters at Wichita and concluded the anti-abortionists struck out.

Dole said he thought the protesters have added "a lot of harm" to the cause.

He's right about that.

Overall, however, the zealots at Wichita have done a great and good service to the nation the past month. They have shown the nation in no uncertain terms that religious zealotry is intolerant of rights that belong to other people, and is indifferent to laws, the majority, or democracy itself.

The past few weeks will not destroy the fanatics' efforts. Their movement now, however, is stripped bare of any claim to justice or to democracy.

The movement began with timid politicians such as Wichita Mayor Bob Knight and Kansas Gov. Joan Finney comforting those who would violate the nation's laws and destroy the rights of others. The movement will wind down with understanding of zealotry that would not have been possible without the zealots' arrogance.

Not even Joan Finney has much to say about lawbreaking these days. She's diverting attention from her earlier gaffes by dropping in unannounced at various places in Kansas as far removed as possible from the streets of Wichita.

The protesters' sales pitch came with all the glorious media attention that it could have expected a month ago. Now, the show's over. The sales pitch failed.

San Francisco Chronicle
San Francisco, California, August 28, 1991

THE ANTI-ABORTION activists who recently wound up a six-week drive to make Wichita, Kansas, an "abortion-free city" assert their actions have rekindled national support on this controversial issue. This is a doubtful claim.

Their confrontational tactics — shouting, blocking doorways and generally trying to intimidate both workers at family-planning clinics and nervous, would-be clients — are not the kind of approach that appeals to most Americans' sense of decency and fair-play. Indeed, polls in the Wichita Eagle-Beacon showed that Operation Rescue is not winning converts: More than two-thirds of those recently polled rejected the group's hostile style.

We have a good example here in the Bay Area of how such a situation may be resolved with reason and intelligence.

In a case involving the right of protest at a Daly City clinic, U.S. District Judge Stanley Weigel, noting that the nation is currently threatened from within by "widespread lawlessness, violence, ugly confrontation, intolerance, hatred, and, in general, disregard of rights of others," suggested the parties had a "unique opportunity" to demonstrate recognition of the right to disagree "vigorously but peacefully."

THE SETTLEMENT order worked out under Judge Weigel's aegis did just that. It set up a "protected zone" to reduce confrontations between protesters and women visiting the Planned Parenthood clinic.

Whatever one feels about the abortion issue, this kind of decree can serve as an exemplar for resolution of similar situations: Allow demonstrations, of course — but insulate patients from direct harassment. The Wichita protesters, in their disturbingly passionate readiness to confront others and to career headlong into the law, undercut their own cause.

THE SAGINAW NEWS
Saginaw, Michigan, August 14, 1991

It was bound to happen that the extremes in the abortion debate would meet up somewhere, some time. It happened this summer in Wichita.

Well, what's the matter with Kansas?

It could have been Michigan. In fact, Operation Rescue says Detroit might be next.

But Wichita was where that fervently anti-abortion group found a clinic that performs third trimester abortions.

In accordance with its revulsion at abortion in any case, and invoking a "higher law," adherents of Operation Rescue tried to block all access to the clinic.

In accordance with his oath of office, U.S. District Judge Patrick Kelly gave the protesters a choice: go home, or go to jail.

It was a classic American standoff. It might as well happen in the American heartland.

And this is one that goes to the heart of the issue.

To Operation Rescue, abortion is murder. To women, patronizing such a clinic is their right — in the seventh month of pregnancy, a desperate right, perhaps, but absolute just the same.

So said the U.S. Supreme Court in Roe vs. Wade.

But that was 1973. In 1991, a different court will almost certainly face the question once again, in a case out of Kansas or an even more blunt challenge from the Louisiana legislature. To let the issue lag invites the social anarchy of a clash of extremes.

Meanwhile, the law stands. Where is the U.S. Justice Department in all this?

It came out on the side of the lawbreakers — provoking Kelly to go public last week with his outrage, an unusual step for a judge, but justified in this instance.

Regardless of political or moral differences, a guiding principle of the United States is the rule of law and the protection of established rights. Until the Supreme Court revises or rejects Roe vs. Wade, abortion remains one of those rights.

The Justice Department, of all agencies, should stand behind judges who stand by their oath of office. President Bush did no better, saying the courts should "sort it out" but letting his people undercut those courts.

Operation Rescue has every right to express its views. Civil disobedience is a time-honored American method of calling attention to perceived injustice. But the duty of the national government is to back the officers of the law of the land.

In Kansas or anywhere else, that is still the American way.

DIARIO LAS AMERICAS

Miami, Florida, October 8, 1991

An extraordinary demonstration of morality, civicism and lofty public spirit, took place all around the U.S. at two p.m. on Sunday, October 6th, in defense of the integrity of life, under the slogan "Abortion Kills Children". Without a single act of violence, that would have hurt the event's image, people of all ages went out in their cities in solidarity with the fair and necessary movement that has been launched throughout the whole world and particularly in the United States of America against abortion and, fundamentally, in defense of respect for human life.

It is important that the immense number of millions of civilized individuals who are pro-life and who, specifically, are against abortion, express their sound moral and ideological convictions on this issue. This is not only an issue of the Catholic Church. Individuals who are not Catholic share this same opinion out of human sensibility and of general moral convictions.

Here in Dade County the demonstration involved an impressive amount of people, just as in the rest of the country. It is really encouraging for noble causes to see so many thousands bearing posters, with their spirits and consciences on high, condemning abortion as an instrument to kill children.

Rockford Register Star

Rockford, Illinois, June 27, 1991

A federal court in Chicago was entirely correct to dismiss a lawsuit that accused anti-abortion groups of violating racketeering and anti-trust laws by demonstrating at abortion clinics. At stake in this case were nothing less than First Amendment freedoms of speech and assembly.

The suit had special relevance to Rockford because of the many protests outside the abortion clinic here. However, it is not yet clear what effect the ruling in Chicago will have on a lawsuit filed by the landlord of the Rockford clinic seeking to limit demonstrations here.

The lawsuit dismissed in Chicago was filed five years ago by the National Organization for Women and alleged that anti-abortion demonstrators have violated racketeering and anti-trust laws by seeking to close down abortion clinics. According to the plaintiffs, the protestors are, in effect, committing economic crimes.

That's nonsense. Yes, the protestors want to see all abortion clinics closed down. After all, what else would be the ultimate objective of people who are morally opposed to abortion? But this goal, as U.S. District Judge James F. Holderman notes, is a political goal, not an economic one.

In cases where anti-abortion demonstrators assault passersby, damage property, trespass, or block traffic, there are plenty of laws to to deal with such conduct. Witness the many prosecutions in Rockford and around the country for such offenses.

Nobody on either side of the abortion issue should be free to violate the legitimate laws intended to protect the rights of others. But neither should the rights of free speech on either side be abridged under the guise of fighting racketeering or anti-trust violations.

On the issue of abortion, this newspaper's editorial policy is pro-choice. But that doesn't mean we countenance the stifling of anti-abortion protests. Our highest priority is the cause of political freedom, even for those with whom we disagree.

Edmonton Journal

Edmonton, Alberta, September 18, 1991

D r. Henry Morgentaler's new abortion clinic in Edmonton is here to stay. It will operate with the full sanction of Canadian law. Sidewalk crusaders should not be allowed to harass the women who turn to the clinic for help.

One of the clinic's first patients had to endure that abuse on Tuesday. As she walked into the building, a middle-aged man shouted to her: "You'll have no friends among men once you kill your baby. Don't let them talk you into killing your baby."

It's easy to imagine the woman's distress at these remarks, as if she didn't have enough anguish already. And yet her tormentor would call himself a Christian.

Alberta's anti-abortion lobbyists have served notice of their intention to hold demonstrations at the Morgentaler clinic. In a free society, they have every right to assemble in protest on public property. They can state their point of view that all human life begins at conception, and they can attempt to convince people that abortion is immoral.

There are reasonable limits to their freedom of expression, however. The anti-abortion protesters can't be permitted to intimidate the clinic's patients or staff, to deface or vandalize the building or to interfere with the normal business of the neighborhood.

The clinic's opponents should recognize the difference between legal and illegal forms of protest, but not all of them do. Unknown individuals vandalized the building four times before it opened. Certain members of the anti-abortion lobby harassed tradespeople who worked on the project, and even picketed an architect's office. Biblical graffiti is sprayed across the back wall.

"We'll be making sure all hell breaks loose in that neighborhood," said the protesters' spokesman, Gerard Liston, earlier this week. He added that his group will use "the weapon of non-violence" to oppose abortion.

That's good to hear. But does Liston recognize that violence can take many forms? The abusive shouts that rain down on women as they enter the clinic, the chanting insults that follow the doctors and nurses, are a kind of violence. They inflict their own damage.

Edmonton police are investigating the vandalism, and they promise to act promptly against any illegal harassment. This city should not tolerate even a mild imitation of the demonstrations in Wichita, Kan., this summer when 2,400 people were arrested for demonstrations outside three abortion clinics. (Protesters directed children to lie down in front of vehicles trying to enter the clinic; other demonstrators knocked down barricades, and blocked traffic.)

Fortunately, the Morgentaler clinic's first day of operation in Edmonton did not inspire this degree of extremism. Protest organizers predicted that 200 people would barricade the clinic on Tuesday, but only about half that number appeared for a relatively quiet demonstration. Perhaps this is the best that could be anticipated.

Alberta women who have fought hard for the decriminalization of their reproductive decisions will not surrender those choices now to the strangers who would condemn them.

Protesters at the Morgentaler clinic are free to judge abortion as evil. They are not free to sit in divine judgment of women who seek abortions, or to intimidate law-abiding citizens with abusive behavior.

St. Petersburg Times
St. Petersburg, Florida, August 21, 1991

The cynical and disruptive tactics of radical anti-abortion protesters in Wichita, Kan., have begun to create a strong public backlash, even among many Americans who oppose abortion. President Bush and his pollsters have noticed the shift in public opinion, and the president is belatedly trying to prevent Operation Rescue's confrontational strategy from creating a larger political backlash that hurts him and the Republican Party as well.

Mr. Bush took time out from yet another golf game during the weekend before the Soviet coup to criticize the protesters who have blocked entrances to abortion clinics for more than a month, and who have placed small children on the dangerous front lines of their showdowns with police. "I think breaking the law is excessive," the president said. "I don't think it helps the cause, whether the cause is anti-abortion or pro-abortion . . . When you hurt somebody else's rights, that's what I disagree about."

Mr. Bush's blunt words of criticism over the weekend must have come as a shock to anti-abortion organizers in Wichita. After all, the Bush administration also has gone to what many people would consider radical lengths to deprive women — especially poor women — of their legal right to an abortion.

Earlier this month, the Bush Justice Department took the highly unusual step of filing a brief that challenges the jurisdiction of U.S. District Judge Patrick Kelly, who ordered an end to the

Wichita blockades last month. And only hours after his criticism of Operation Rescue, the president made good on his vow to veto a spending bill for the District of Columbia that would have allowed a relatively small amount of money to be used in the nation's capital to help finance abortions for women who cannot afford them.

For President Bush, whose views on abortion have always bent with the political winds, the awkward snub of Operation Rescue leaders over the weekend represents a case of the chickens (or the eggs) coming home to roost. Mr. Bush had a solid pro-choice record until 1980, when he conveniently changed his position as part of a larger effort to make himself a more compatible running mate for Ronald Reagan. Over the past decade, though, Mr. Bush and his political advisers have assiduously cultivated the support of the very anti-abortion activists whose representatives were denied an audience with the president in Kennebunkport last weekend.

With the abortion issue creating a widening ideological division within the Republican Party, the president now finds himself scrambling to find a more politically palatable middle ground. He is not the first politician to discover that playing politics with abortion can be far more treacherous than taking a principled position on the issue and sticking with it, regardless of temporary shifts in public opinion.

Minneapolis Star and Tribune
Minneapolis, Minnesota, August 16, 1991

Out of the abortion battle in Wichita, Kan., come two radically different images of contemporary justice in America. One — the brave conduct of U.S. District Judge Patrick Kelly — is heartening. The other — political pandering by the U.S. Justice Department — is worrisome.

The catalyst for this judicial showdown was the effort by Operation Rescue, a fanatical antiabortion group, to close down two Wichita clinics where abortions are performed. More than 2,000 arrests have been made for trespassing and assorted other charges since the group laid siege to the two clinics July 15.

Operation Rescue participants and their supporters like to draw parallels between their actions and civil-rights efforts of the 1960s. But their behavior more resembles that of George Wallace and Lester Maddox, governors determined to reject federal law and deny equality to blacks. Roe vs. Wade, the 1973 Supreme Court abortion decision, is federal law. It doesn't grant a privilege to women; it articulates a right. It is neutral on abortion but firm that each woman has the right to make her own decision.

When the two Wichita clinics sued in federal court to keep Operation Rescue from shutting them down, Judge Kelly issued a court order prohibiting demonstrators from blocking clinic access, then dispatched federal marshals to ensure his order was honored. When it wasn't, he began meting out

jail sentences — often suspended if demonstrators promised future deference to Kelly's order.

Kelly is a lifelong Catholic who refuses to talk about his feelings on abortion. The only evidence is from his law career, when he counseled daughters of several clients to complete their pregnancies and give their babies up for adoption. It seems likely that in his heart he disapproves of abortion. But, he told the New York Times, when people ask him how a Catholic judge can preside over this case, he replies, "It's simple. I have a duty to carry out the law, and Roe is the law." Amen.

To its discredit, the U.S. Justice Department doesn't agree. The department has joined with Operation Rescue in challenging Kelly's order, thus supporting those breaking the law against the judge who is trying to uphold it. The department's intervention was a provocative political act, designed, we'd guess, to cement the antiabortion vote for George Bush. This is the same Justice Department that intervened to prevent lifting of the ban on travel to the United States by foreigners with AIDS — a ban vigorously opposed by American and international public-health communities.

Those running the department seem determined to make it into the U.S. Department of Injustice. Thank heaven for the countervailing courage and clear legal thinking of men and women like Judge Kelly.

THE DAILY OKLAHOMAN
Oklahoma City, Oklahoma, August 17, 1991

MANY people may have mixed feelings about the ugly turn of events in Wichita, where an anti-abortion group has been demonstrating in front of a clinic that performs late-term abortions.

More than 2,000 arrests have been made for alleged violations of a federal judge's injunction against blocking access to the clinic. One man has been sentenced to a year in jail for civil contempt.

The demonstration, led by a group called Operation Rescue, has lost some sympathy because of its tactic of allowing children to lie down in front of automobiles, along with the adults. One of the group's leaders said minors who feel "morally compelled" to protest abortions and have their parents' permission should be allowed to do so.

People who oppose abortions and sympathize with what the demonstrators are trying to accomplish may feel uneasy about placing children in harm's way. The rationale that "14-year-olds are getting abortions, so 14-year-old kids should be involved" might not be so convincing to the parents of a child accidentally run over by an automobile.

Other sympathizers of Operation Rescue may conclude, reluctantly, that, while they are sickened by the deliberate taking of life in such clinics, abortions are still legal, at least for the present. Thus, the demonstrators have no right to block access to them, even when they know in their hearts, the abortions performed there are for the most part merely a form of birth control.

Until now right-to-life forces have limited their demonstrations to peaceful efforts to persuade women about to patronize the clinics that better alternatives to abortion do exist. In many cases that strategy was effective.

But with the abortion issue heating up, they may feel passive resistance is no longer useful. It's strange to hear them condemned when the tactics they employ are not much different from those used in the past by anti-war, homosexual and civil rights demonstrators.

THE KANSAS CITY STAR
Kansas City, Missouri, August 17, 1991

Abortion is an emotional issue. But there is nothing in it that should stir crackpot members of Congress or anyone else to threaten U.S. District Judge Patrick Kelly with impeachment over his role in the Wichita abortion protest.

If there is a question of jurisdiction, there is a remedy. It is in the courts, not in Congress, not in the streets.

Impeachment under federal law is not intended to oust a judge for legal views and rulings. In fact, judges are sworn to uphold the law as they read and interpret it. Kelly or any other judge would be derelict to stop short of that.

In this instance, Kelly enforced a court order to halt a human blockade at a medical clinic where abortions are performed. Individuals should not, in this instance, be impeded from access to an operation that is legal. To do less would invite anarchy.

The federal courts and lifetime appointments for judges are established in the Constitution and the law. The purpose is to insulate them from the hot political winds of the moment. The other two branches, the executive and legislative, are elected and are designed to respond to the will of the people.

Thus the judiciary is meant to function as an independent, co-equal arm of the government. Independence means that the judiciary should be beyond the undue influence of the other two branches of government or the direct influence of a majority of the citizens.

This enables judges to make decisions free from fear of political retaliation.

Even with these powers, judges have certain limitations. They must avoid misconduct. The Constitution directs that grounds for impeachment are "treason, bribery, or other high crimes and misdemeanors."

In its dealing with impeachment, the record shows that Congress considers these offenses to include criminal violations, severe abuse of power and seriously questionable conduct in office.

The anti-abortionists in Wichita and elsewhere can pursue their cause in the courts, as they are doing. They can seek redress in the legislatures. The judiciary should be left to make decisions grounded in the law.

FORT WORTH STAR-TELEGRAM
Fort Worth, Texas, August 23, 1991

Lawlessness is lawlessness, regardless of how noble those responsible for it believe their cause to be.

In staging increasingly violent protests in Wichita, Kan., militant abortion opponents are deliberately violating the law and endangering public safety, and the harsh punishment being meted out there by a federal judge is fully justified.

Clear and legal avenues of protest are in bountiful supply in this country, but the ugly confrontations being instigated by protesters in Wichita exceed the bounds of acceptable behavior and have transformed the legitimate national debate over the appropriateness of abortion into a mob scene.

The struggle in Wichita is no longer over abortion but over the rule of law. Even President Bush, whose anti-abortion views are well documented, was moved to criticize the mob-mentality behavior of the Wichita rowdies.

Some of those in the vanguard of the demonstrations claim that what they are doing represents "civil disobedience" and compare themselves to the civil rights marchers of the 1950s, but it won't wash.

There is nothing civil about the actions of the Wichita mob, and they do a monumental disservice to the civil rights movement with their comparison.

When people break the law with impunity, they are outlaws and should be treated accordingly.

THE TENNESSEAN
Nashville, Tennessee, August 27, 1991

WHEN members of the anti-abortion Operation Rescue came to visit President Bush on his vacation, the President refused to see them.

Wichita, Kan. didn't have that luxury. In fact, President Bush's Justice Department intervened on behalf of Operation Rescue's law-breaking protesters and against law-abiding women who were seeking a legal abortion.

Now the President finally acknowledges that the protesters acted above the law. He's a little late.

Bush wants it both ways on abortion. When he was running against Ronald Reagan in the Republican primary 12 years ago, he was for abortion. Bush then abruptly changed his views to win conservative support.

He demonstrated in the Wichita protests that he's willing to use the Justice Department to support the effort of abortion protesters. Yet when asked about the protesters' tactics, he scolded them for going beyond the law.

Now he's got a Supreme Court that may be willing to overturn *Roe v. Wade*, so that Bush can again stand at arms length from the issue.

George Bush has used the abortion issue as cynically as any politician in America. In Wichita, the President supported people who threw their own children into the streets to block cars. He allowed them to block a legal business. He let them harass women who were exercising their legal rights. He let protesters break the law.

The President may not care to speak to Operation Rescue members. Who can blame him? But he owes the American public one hell of an explanation. ■

DAYTON DAILY NEWS
Dayton, Ohio, August 24, 1991

The Wichita abortion protest has been done by the numbers:

1) Get every anti-abortion group in the country focused on one event.

2) Pick the most politically vulnerable target you can find (in this case, a clinic that does late-term abortions).

3) Get some people arrested.

4) Complain about the manner in which they are treated.

5) Manipulate the media, (A): Complain early that they are not covering the event enough.

6) Manipulate the media, (B): Have demonstrators call their home-town newspapers to jinn up publicity.

7) Manipulate the media, (C): Try to get a meeting with the president.

8) Manipulate the media, (D): Claim that any criticism leveled at the demonstrators comes out of a double standard (it wouldn't be leveled at civil-rights demonstrators) and shows bias on the part of critics.

(This last dictum was undercut a bit when President Bush — who opposes abortion rights — criticized the tactics of the group.)

The demonstrators are both professionals and zealots, a volatile combination.

THE
DENVER POST

Denver, Colorado, August 15, 1991

THE ILLEGAL and sometimes violent tactics of "Operation Rescue" have isolated it from the mainstream of the anti-abortion movement, since most "pro-life" groups have scrupulously obeyed the law. But Operation Rescue's apologists continue to argue that their illegal actions somehow place them in the same moral league with Mahatma Gandhi or Martin Luther King because King and Gandhi also practiced civil disobedience.

That's a logical fallacy equivalent to saying that Jack the Ripper and heart surgeon Dr. Christiaan Barnard were morally identical because they each used scalpels to remove human hearts.

The fact is, neither King nor Gandhi advocated civil disobedience when society offered them legal alternatives to seek justice. King modeled his movement after Gandhi's philosophy of *Satyagraha*. Gandhi turned to civil disobedience because Indians were denied the right to vote under British rule. Once India achieved independence, Gandhi happily abandoned civil disobedience for the democratic process.

Likewise, the great fight of King and other civil rights leaders in the

'60s was aimed at winning political rights for black people. King and his colleagues swiftly turned to legal channels after passage of the Voting Rights Act because they then had a much more effective and morally justifiable tool to win justice — their ballots.

That is completely different from Operation Rescue — or its true moral equivalents, the demonstrators who have periodically tried to illegally disrupt operations at Rocky Flats. People who want to outlaw abortion, or outlaw nuclear weapons, have the same right to vote that people who want to keep them legal have. The problem is simply that the extreme anti-abortionists — like the extreme anti-nukers — aren't willing to abide by the decision of the democratic process. They believe that they, and they alone, are endowed with a moral superiority that gives them the right to trample the rights of their fellow citizens.

So, where King and Gandhi fought to expand the democratic process to include their people, Operation Rescue seeks to overturn its results by force. That's not the theory of civil disobedience embedded in *Satyagraha*. It's the logic of a *coup d'etat*.

The Register-Guard

Eugene, Oregon, August 15, 1991

Patrick Kelly is the kind of judge who could give politics a good name.

He is the federal district judge in Wichita who has been doing his best to maintain control over a volatile situation caused by the radical anti-abortion organization, Operation Rescue.

Kelly has angered the protesters by applying an 1871 law that prohibits conspiracies against the exercise of constitutional rights. Noting the Supreme Court-decreed right of women to obtain an abortion, Kelly has enjoined Operation Rescue militants from blocking access to local abortion clinics. And he has used federal marshalls to arrest and jail those who defy his orders.

Kelly was an active Democrat as a practicing attorney and a friend of Jimmy Carter. He helped organize the Carter for President Committee in Kansas in 1975. His reward came five years later when the outgoing president appointed Kelly to the federal bench.

It was overtly political, as are all

such appointments in some measure. But some turn out better than others, judicially.

Kelly has developed a reputation as a good, fair, firm judge. In this case, the irony is that he is a lifelong Roman Catholic whose use of the law irritates many fellow Catholics who oppose abortion. He has said he can't even attend church because of the anger of some of his fellow communicants.

But the judge simply separates abortion and the questions raised in his court by the anti-abortionists who have invaded his hometown. He refuses to discuss his personal views on abortion or Roe vs. Wade, the 1973 Supreme Court decision that established the right of abortion nationally.

"People ask, 'How can a Catholic judge sit on this kind of case?'" he said. "It's simple. I have a duty to carry out the law, and Roe is the law. . . . This is not a religious issue. It's a legal one."

Would that all judges — especially at the politicized federal level — saw things as clearly.

St. Petersburg Times

St. Petersburg, Florida, August 8, 1991

White House press secretary Marlin Fitzwater was quick to claim Wednesday that President Bush was not involved in — but supported — the Justice Department's decision to intervene in a court dispute on the side of radical anti-abortion demonstrators in Wichita, Kan. If that's true, then the president *should* get involved. If the Justice Department is playing abortion politics on its own, to the detriment of the federal courts, Mr. Bush ought to set his lawyers straight.

Operation Rescue began daily demonstrations at three Wichita clinics on July 15. Its announced goals were to close down the clinics and to establish in Kansas a beachhead of grassroots anti-abortion sentiment that would spread across America.

The protesters have turned sections of Wichita into a war zone. About 1,200 people turned out for one demonstration at sunrise. In the struggle of demonstrators to block the entrance to the clinic and that of police to keep it open, more than 1,900 demonstrators have been arrested.

The protesters have every right to demonstrate on public property. That is assured them by the First Amendment in its sections protecting free speech and the right to assemble peaceably. But they have no right to try to put a clinic out of business, or to attempt to deny any woman her legal right to an abortion, or to trespass on clinic property. That is why so many protesters have been arrested and why U.S. District Judge Patrick Kelly ordered Operation Rescue leaders not to block entrances to the clinics or to harass staff and patients.

Last year the U.S. Supreme Court let stand a similar order in New York against Operation Rescue, and a $70,000 fine. The Supreme Court agreed in February to hear a Virginia case in which the court of appeals upheld a district judge's order against Operation Rescue's trespassing and blocking entrance to a clinic. The Justice Department earlier joined that case on the side of Operation Rescue.

In Wichita, Judge Kelly was not amused at seeing the Justice Department oppose his effort to keep the peace. The judge said he was "disgusted by this move of the United States, that they would now put an imprimatur on this conduct." The judge also said the Justice Department's involvement was a political move.

If Mr. Bush doesn't know what his Justice Department is doing, at least he knows the players well. In January, he took time out from supervising the war in the Persian Gulf to speak by loudspeaker to anti-abortion demonstrators in Washington, joining Sen. Jesse Helms, R-N.C., and Operation Rescue leader Randall Terry in his praise for their efforts.

The Wichita
Eagle-Beacon

Wichita, Kansas, August 3, 1991

Abortion evokes such powerful emotions in those who oppose it that it's sometimes difficult for them to focus on this fundamental point: The law is the law and must be enforced.

In this case, the law allows doctors, staff and patients to enter Wichita abortion clinics and conduct business. The abortion protesters who abhor that business claim a divine right to violate the law, in the interest of preventing abortion. Thus, they step beyond the bounds of their legal right to assemble on public ground near the clinics and demonstrate their abhorrence of abortion. They block clinic entrances and harass people trying to enter.

City authorities need now to ensure that these willful lawbreakers experience the full consequences of their actions. On July 23, U.S. District Judge Patrick Kelly issued a court order saying abortion protesters must respect the legal rights of doctors, staff and patients and allow them to enter the clinics. Those who violate that order are subject to jailing for contempt of court, and stiff, escalating fines. Mr. Kelly's order is read to everyone the Wichita Police Department arrests for blocking the clinic entrances. If such a person is arrested for blocking the clinics a second time, he or she is in contempt of court.

The need now is to enforce Mr. Kelly's court order to its fullest extent. Citing the protest leaders with contempt hasn't gotten across the message that the clinics cannot and will not be blocked. If every single person who blocks the clinics is cited for contempt, jailed and fined, chances that the message will get through should improve considerably.

Blocking an abortion clinic is legally no different from blocking a school to prevent children and teachers from entering, blocking a supermarket to prevent workers and customers from entering or blocking someone's home to prevent him and his family from entering. It's an unlawful act and cannot be tolerated. In the case of the clinics, it makes no difference that the person doing the blocking doesn't like what's going on inside.

The mayor and city manager have taken the position that police cannot prevent people from breaking the law, and can only arrest them after they do. Therefore, the police are not allowed to use affirmative action — such as barricades — to keep the clinics open. That's not only nonsense — of course police have the duty to stop violations of the law in advance — but is also hypocrisy of the foulest sort because it cushions those city officials at the expense of the legal rights of all citizens.

The city's leaders have a duty to keep the legal clinics open. It's tragic that it apparently will take a federal judge to inform them of that duty. But if that's what it takes, Judge Kelly should do so.

Wichita, Kansas, August 8, 1991

Wichita needs closure on the current round of abortion protests. So much energy and emotion has been spent — so many harsh words have been said and so much bitterness has been generated — that the community needs to decide if it wants to change the law on abortion.

The best way to achieve that catharsis is through a referendum, as proposed by City Council member Frank Ojile, through which voters could decide whether or not they want an ordinance limiting abortions within the city.

For the past few weeks, Operation Rescue has made Wichita the national center of the abortion issue. People not part of the community have used Wichita as a convenient soapbox to promote their political and religious goals, and they have drawn national media attention to the city.

The continued protests threaten to shred the community's social fabric. Neighbor is being pitted against neighbor, workplace colleague against workplace colleague, church member against church member. At risk is the sense of community togetherness that makes Wichita more than a collection of houses and businesses.

By the nature of the issue, abortion never will be totally resolved to many people's satisfaction. But, as regards the local political system, Wichita needs to confront — then get beyond — the abortion issue.

While the wording of a referendum hasn't been worked out, Mr. Ojile has one available model in the measures he pushed before the City Council last month. Those elements included a declaration that life begins at conception and a ban on late-term abortions performed within the city.

A vote on an ordinance would be in the best tradition of local democracy. Each side would be able to present its case in the full glare of public debate. Given the passions of abortion, a knock-down political campaign could strain civility, but Wichita could show the rest of the country how to fight fairly on a wrenching social issue. The nation could use such a positive example, especially if the U.S. Supreme Court overturns the Roe vs. Wade ruling and makes abortion subject to local and state laws.

Pro-lifers and pro-choicers should support Mr. Ojile's referendum proposal. After all, people opposed to abortion can't picket in front of clinics indefinitely; they need an outlet for the intensity that Operation Rescue has fueled. Likewise, abortion rights advocates can stop feeling frustrated by the clinic demonstrations and put their energies into a meaningful political effort.

Although an abortion referendum would be heated, ultimately it could have a healing effect on the community. It would give all voters a chance to express their opinion. It would remove a difficult issue from the local political agenda, which it threatens to dominate until it is settled.

Wichita faces a great many challenges, including the revitalization of downtown and a faltering education system. Abortion politics shouldn't be a constant undertone as those challenges are taken up.

Wichita, Kansas, August 9, 1991

The interlude of relative calm at the city's abortion clinics is no accident. It exists because of Judge Patrick Kelly's injunction against blockades and because the radical national leaders of Operation Rescue have left town, at least for the time being.

During this time of reduced tension while the court system weighs the validity of Judge Kelly's order, this community's pro-life advocates show signs of taking charge of their movement. That's encouraging, because it can lead to the permanent restoration of lawfulness without limiting the movement's campaign.

Among the awakening local forces are pro-life ministers who plan a retreat to consider what to do now. The ministers say they want to think beyond the immediate situation and consider how they and their congregations can become more of a political force in the community. Such contemplations should lead them to conclude that such physical tactics as blocking the free movement of other citizens is a bankrupt one, particularly for a group that wishes to work within the democratic system.

Reaching that conclusion, it will then be appropriate for them to tell the national Operation Rescue people, politely, that they are no longer wanted or needed. The national leaders are not, nor have they ever been, in favor of peaceful persuasion. Staying within the law does not bring them the national media attention they thrive upon both psychicly and fiscally. It is time, in short, for Wichita's issues to be decided by Wichitans, who are by nature and habit law-abiding.

The ministers and other abortion opponents can draw support in their determination to protest lawfully from more respectable leaders, including Mayor Bob Knight, Gov. Joan Finney and President Bush. All espouse the pro-life position, but each has said with varying degrees of emphasis in recent days that the law should be obeyed while the issue is settled politically and judicially.

Such support of the rule of law in a democracy should be automatic, but in the emotional crucible of abortion politics, where every tenet seems subject to partisan rationalization, their firm statements are both necessary and welcome.

Should a higher court overrule Judge Kelly, responsibility for what happens in the streets of Wichita will fall squarely upon the shoulders of pro-life leaders. If their ambition is to become a force in the democratic process, they could make no better start than to declare that they will work within the system, not endanger it with willful and deliberate violation of the law and the legal rights of other citizens.

The Seattle Times

Seattle, Washington, August 13, 1991

THE U.S. Justice Department puts itself on the wrong side of public safety by intervening on behalf of Operation Rescue protesters in Wichita.

Since July 15, more than 2,000 anti-abortion demonstrators have been arrested for blockading three medical clinics in that city. The radical group is not merely engaging in free speech, it's threatening and preventing clinic patients from exercising their constitutional right to chose abortion.

U.S. District Court Judge Patrick Kelly issued a restraining order barring the protesters from their abusive demonstrations. The court asserted jurisdiction under an 1871 federal law that prohibits groups from conspiring to deprive others of their civil rights.

Operation Rescue argues that the federal court has no right to hear the case because the 1871 statute does not apply to abortion protests. Whether or not the law applies will be decided by the U.S. Supreme Court this fall in a Virginia abortion-protest case.

In the meantime, the Justice Department, pushing the Bush administration's anti-abortion agenda, has jumped into the explosive Wichita situation with a brief to the court supporting Operation Rescue. Outgoing Attorney General Dick Thornburgh says the department doesn't condone the protesters' tactics, just their legal arguments.

That may be, but the symbolism is rotten. Judge Kelly was rightly "disgusted" by the administration's move. These outlaw demonstrators take aid and comfort in knowing Thornburgh is backing them up.

The distress caused by their violent behavior has been enormous. The community has had to pay nearly $500,000 in police overtime to control the mob. The last thing Wichita needs is for the Justice Department to add fuel to the fire.

THE EMPORIA GAZETTE

Emporia, Kansas, August 6, 1991

IT is time for the abortion protesters to leave Kansas. What began as a group's passionate effort to stop late-term abortions at a Wichita clinic has turned into a circus. The protesters have lost sight of their mission to save lives and have turned a city upside down. They have become a nuisance. Extending their stay will only anger those people who believe in their cause.

Since Operation Rescue moved into Wichita in mid-July, the protesters have diverted the attention of the city's police force and clogged the court system. Nearly 2,000 arrests have been made for trespassing and violating court orders. Special arrangements have been made to handle the flood of court cases.

In the meantime, police have had little time to deal with other important cases. The Wichita Eagle reported last week on a series of attempted abductions of children in a city neighborhood. Police were too busy with Operation Rescue to give the case the attention it needed. Paperwork was delayed and parents were having to spread the word of the danger themselves.

The newspaper published another alarming story on Friday. A protester came to Wichita from Russellville, Ark., and brought his four children, ages 9 through 17. When he was arrested for wrapping himself around a car tire as it tried to enter the women's clinic, he neglected to tell police about the children.

He was so upset that a woman might be trying to end a pregnancy that he abandoned his own children. A kindly man in the crowd took the children into his home to care for them while their father was in jail.

Abortion is a topic that has no middle ground. It always will be that way, regardless of how many bloody pictures of fetuses Operation Rescue members circulate.

The fight in Wichita is not about being for or against abortion. It is a fight about common decency — the decency to let a city get on with its life.

Operation Rescue members have worn out their welcome. They need to take their money and energy and devote it to helping the children who are born — those who are hungry, abused or homeless.

San Francisco Chronicle

San Francisco, California, August 8, 1991

THE JUSTICE Department's intervention on behalf of anti-abortion protesters who have blocked access to abortion clinics in Wichita cannot be dismissed as a mere "jurisdictional dispute," as Attorney General Richard Thornburgh and President Bush have tried to portray it.

The use of U.S. civil rights law to protect the constitutional rights of individuals when threatened by possible violence has a long and proud history in numerous cases similar to the Wichita abortion controversy, and it is dismaying to see its application now come under attack from the Justice Department for what seem to be ideological reasons.

U.S. District Judge Patrick Kelly's order to federal marshals — now contested by the Justice Department — to ensure access to the clinics and to arrest protesters who block such access is reminiscent of federal court actions to guarantee black children access to formerly segregated schools 30 years ago, when racist mobs and a governor stood in the doorway.

WE MUST COUNT ourselves fortunate that attorneys general then did not take the same "states' rights" view of civil rights enforcement as today's Justice Department.

In acting to block the judge's order, the attorney general is resorting to flimsy legalities in avoiding its solemn duty to uphold civil rights and liberties.

TULSA WORLD

Tulsa, Oklahoma, August 8, 1991

FEDERAL appeals courts will decide whether U.S. District Judge Patrick Kelly is wrong in ordering protesters to stop blocking abortion clinics in Wichita. In the meantime, the protesters should obey the law as defined by Judge Kelly. If they don't, the judge should use whatever power he can summon to enforce his order.

He should be able to count on the full force and power of the United States government. Apparently he won't. The Bush administration has jumped into the case on the side of the protesters and obviously doesn't intend to enforce the judge's order.

Whatever its position on abortion, the administration should not condone illegal behavior on the part of the protesters.

U.S. history is full of examples of judges and public officials enforcing laws that they personally did not support. President Eisenhower sent federal troops to Little Rock to enforce the law. Judge Kelly, a Roman Catholic, might not be in favor of abortion. But he knows the law allows it and that abortion clinics are due protection.

The Bush administration has indirectly condoned very bad behavior at the least and terrorism at the worst. Its action can only encourage zealots all over the nation to use protest as an excuse to physically stop abortion clinics from functioning.

Perhaps appeals courts will reverse the judge; maybe the abortion laws will be changed. At this point, the administration has sided with those who would take the law in their own hands.

It is, as Judge Kelly said, disgusting.

LEXINGTON HERALD-LEADER
Lexington, Kentucky, August 8, 1991

If you're a believer in civil disobedience, you've got a new and unusual ally. The United States Justice Department has joined the ranks of those who think they have no obligation to pay attention to a court decision with which they disagree.

That's the only way to interpret the department's decision to side with anti-abortion protesters in Wichita, Kan. For weeks, the protesters have been harassing women on their way to the clinic for abortions. The harassment continued even after U.S. District Judge Patrick Kelly ordered protesters to stop.

Now, the Justice Department has joined in the appeal of the decision. The department argues that the question should be left to state and local courts, not federal ones.

That's a dubious notion, given that women's right to obtain an abortion stems from a decision by the United States Supreme Court. It's even more dubious in the context of this case, since the department opposes Kelly's order requiring U.S. marshals to help protect women from harassment.

In the circumstances, it's hard to view the Justice Department's position as anything other than a political ploy. Apparently, Attorney General Richard Thornburgh is perfectly content to take the side of the protesters, whom Kelly correctly calls "lawbreakers."

That's a questionable standard for the attorney general of the United States to set for the nation. But then, President Bush's spokesman said yesterday that the president supports the department's decision. So what would you expect?

Richmond Times-Dispatch
Richmond, Virginia, August 9, 1991

The Bush Justice Department has come under heavy fire from abortion rights activists and its friends in the media for daring to file a friend-of-the-court brief in a case involving a now month-long protest at a Wichita abortion clinic. The Justice Department acted after a seemingly out-of-control District Court Judge Patrick Kelly called in U.S. marshals to keep Operation Rescue protesters away from the clinic and ordered the group to post a $100,000 bond in order to continue its protest.

Judge Kelly promptly went on "Nightline" to call the Justice Department filing "illegal," which the Jimmy Carter appointee should know is absolute hogwash. But that is not the only manner in which Judge Kelly's vision of the American legal system is a bit twisted.

Whatever the cause, protesters must operate within the bounds of the law or face the legal consequences. But as long as the First Amendment remains a part of the Constitution, no law can prohibit protest marches or impose the kind of prior restraint ordered by Judge Kelly with the $100,000 bond.

But Judge Kelly hardly seems concerned with the law. Instead of limiting his comments to bench rulings on the issues at hand, he has held multiple press conferences, gone on television and given interviews with newspapers. His biases are evident when he calls Operation Rescue members "lawbreakers" and "violators." At one of his press conferences he said of Operation Rescue: "I don't believe they're [at the clinic] just to make a statement. It seems to me it's more than that." To Judge Kelly, a group of citizens exercising their right to freely assemble is some sort of grand conspiracy. It is, to say the least, an unusual way for a judge to conduct himself.

Until Judge Kelly entered the case, Wichita city officials seemed to have things well in hand. If protesters actually blocked entrances to the clinic, which they targeted because third-trimester abortions are performed there, police arrested them. But the judge wants police to arrest people *before* they have broken any laws.

And that is where the Justice Department entered the scene. In keeping with its filings in a similar case to be heard by the Supreme Court, the Justice Department has taken the sensible position that the case belongs in a state or local court, not a federal one, because no federal laws have been broken.

This current controversy, of course, is a logical result of the completely illogical ruling of the Supreme Court in *Roe vs. Wade,* which federalized abortion law. Judge Kelly apparently views this case as being under his jurisdiction simply because the protest involves abortion.

We hope the U.S. Court of Appeals has a clearer and more fair-minded view. If Operation Rescue or anyone else wants to use civil disobedience tactics, let them do so. And also let them suffer punishment for any violations of state or local laws they may commit. But as Operation Rescue's Randall Terry points out, Judge Kelly has taken the law into his own hands, levying penalties against pro-life activists that no federal judge ever imposed on civil rights activists in the 1950s and 1960s. The rule of law must prevail.

Arkansas Gazette
Little Rock, Arkansas, August 9, 1991

Periodically throughout the nation's history, Kansas has been the theater of confrontation. Before the Civil War, it was where the slavery debate frequently erupted in violent clashes, giving rise to the nickname, "Bleeding Kansas." It also provided a stage, in Dodge City, for some of the wild west's most legendary showdowns.

The battleground imagery is being revived now by a skirmish in Wichita involving two abortion clinics and the militant anti-abortion group, Operation Rescue, which has been blocking access to the clinics.

A federal judge has ordered the protesters to stop it, maintaining that their right to free expression does not include prohibiting a woman from entering an abortion clinic. As U.S. District Judge Patrick Kelly correctly recalls, *Roe vs. Wade,* which legalized abortion, is still the law of the land.

Operation Rescue is appealing Kelly's order — a move too predictable and routine to be upsetting — but what is alarming is the U.S. Justice Department's role in the case. It has intervened, claiming the matter should be handled by local and state courts, instead of federal.

That is a decoy, of course. The Justice Department is using the jurisdictional issue as a cover for its real intent: To give as much aid and comfort to the anti-abortion movement as possible without stomping on the Constitution.

Shrewd, perhaps, but preposterous too. So much so that Judge Kelly has become publicly defiant and critical — an unusual posture for a federal judge, especially one with a live case. Kelly has put Operation Rescue and the Justice Department on notice that he will not be deterred by either legal action or personal threats.

He has also made it clear that he believes the government's position is transparently political, which he finds repulsive. "I am disgusted with this move by the United States," was how Kelly put it.

Attorney General Dick Thornburgh denies that his agency's involvement is politically primed. And President Bush has taken an out by noting that he is vacationing in Maine and didn't know the Justice Department was planning anything.

But, then, what else could they say? The truth — that the anti-abortion Bush administration is not above twisting the law or the Constitution to advance its agenda — would be too honest for so cunning a crew.

THE SPOKESMAN-REVIEW
Spokane, Washington, August 9, 1991

Most of the country is tired of demagogues who chain themselves to doors and keep other people from engaging in lawful, though controversial, activities. But the protesters take themselves as seriously as ever.

Thank goodness for a firm judge who is willing to crack down on the self-righteous zealots and show them he means business.

Such a judge is Patrick F. Kelly of Wichita, Kan., where an intense anti-abortion demonstration has been waged in the past month. Kelly said he didn't care if it was the governor of Kansas or the Roman Catholic bishop of Wichita, the federal judge expected U.S. marshals to arrest and jail anyone who defied his order to keep two abortion clinics in Wichita open.

In Wichita, as in a lot of other places, a national anti-abortion organization known as Operation Rescue has found that just airing its pro-life message is not enough to deter women from seeking abortions at targeted clinics. So they have taken bolder steps by blockading the clinics and intimidating — sometimes physically — the clients who seek access there.

Their ruffian methods are common in the extreme reaches of the pro-life movement, though not unique to it. Foes of U.S. foreign policy in Central America, for instance, have employed it often.

The ideology doesn't matter. What does matter is the dividing line that must exist between one group's right to preach its message and another group's right to reject it.

In Wichita, in a pattern that has become too familiar in the abortion debate, Operation Rescue has trampled on the rights of other citizens. Its members and sympathizers have interfered with the clinics' right to engage in a lawful business and, worse, with the patients' right to seek health care of their own choosing.

Clinic operators did what law-abiding citizens do in such cases. They turned to the courts to referee.

Kelly then issued an injunction against activities that prohibit access to the clinics and vowed to fill up jails across Kansas if that's what it took to get his point across. Some 1,900 arrests later the judge has shown how serious he is.

Interestingly, national leaders of the group went through the formalities of arrest, then obtained release by meeting Kelly's demand that they promise not to violate his injunction again. They then left town, hypocritically leaving it to Wichita locals to test Kelly's resolve further.

Before leaving for his home in Binghamton, N.Y., Operation Rescue founder Randall Terry ranted that never had he seen a judge so out of control, so "lawless."

Or so . . . effective. May there be many more like him.

THE BUFFALO NEWS
Buffalo, New York, August 9, 1991

THE BUSH ADMINISTRATION pursues a reckless course in the legal battles surrounding the abortion controversy in Wichita, Kan. The Justice Department's gratuitous entry on the side of the protesters' legal case abets those extremists who abuse the right of peaceful demonstration and defy federal court orders.

No one questions the right of people, protesters or the president, to oppose abortion and try to get laws changed to reflect their views. It is hardly a secret that Bush favors anti-abortion policies.

What offends here is that the protesters, in weeks of aggressive tactics that have brought 1,900 arrests on charges of trespassing and loitering, tried to block workers and clients alike from entering three clinics operating perfectly legal services.

Ugly harassment and intimidation have marred these militant protests conducted by Operation Rescue. The U.S. district judge handling the case, Patrick F. Kelly, has received threats of death and dismemberment and been confronted on the street while walking with his wife.

And what was his grave failing? A court order that barred protesters from blocking entrances to these legally operating clinics or physically harassing their staffs and patients. That order, which would not bar protest that didn't infringe on others' freedom of movement, sounds eminently fair and reasonable to everyone involved.

Bush says the Justice Department intervened only because of jurisdictional issues: namely, that these cases should come before local or state, not federal, courts.

But that technical question was already under review, posed and framed by lawyers for Operation Rescue, and it still is.

So from a legal standpoint, Justice's intervention was unnecessary. That raises suspicions of grandstanding politics in a high-visibility dispute that teeters on the edge of violence, a dismaying course for anyone in authority to follow.

No wonder this intervention, so eagerly sought by the administration's Justice Department, while granted by Judge Kelly, also provoked his disgust with the federal government for putting "an imprimatur to what in my view is a license for mayhem."

The courts can be trusted to sort out the jurisdictional angles here. Maybe there is federal jurisdiction, maybe not. Meanwhile, the administration's ill-considered action helps polarize and divide, rather than helping to reconcile, Wichita and the nation.

And to what constructive end?

Legal businesses and services have the right to operate without harassment. Clients and customers have a right to go in and out without being prevented, intimidated or harassed.

Those who object must do so within the liberally permissible boundaries of law in a free, civilized society.

The Washington Post
Washington, D.C., August 10, 1991

THE JUSTICE Department has gratuitously intervened in a volatile situation involving antiabortion demonstrations in Wichita. The Kansas city has been the scene of disruptive protests for weeks, and local police have arrested more than 2,000 demonstrators who tried to block access to three abortion clinics. Worse, the federal judge who has been attempting to reestablish order and protect the rights of those entering the clinics has been physically harassed at his home and has received what are described as credible death threats. Into this explosive situation lurches the Justice Department, challenging the authority of the judge and siding with demonstrators on an important procedural point.

The siege of Wichita began when Operation Rescue descended on the city intent on shutting down the three clinics. All citizens have the right to picket and protest so long as their activity is peaceful, but the Wichita demonstrators turned nasty. Owners of two clinics went to federal court seeking an order to end harassment and the blocking of access. Judge Patrick Kelly issued that order and later directed federal marshals to enforce it. His action was premised on a federal Reconstruction-era statute outlawing conspiracies formed to deny civil rights.

The Justice Department contends that this statute, passed to protect blacks, does not protect the rights of women seeking abortions. The entire Wichita dispute, government lawyers maintain, belongs not in federal but in state court. This is still an unsettled legal question, but the Supreme Court is about to consider it in a case from Virginia. The Justice Department has presented its view in a brief filed in the Supreme Court. There was no valid reason to intervene and make the same argument in a lower court in Wichita.

It would be unfair to assume that the government, in taking this action, has sanctioned the demonstrators' tactics of harassment and obstruction. Pending appellate court review, Judge Kelly's order remains in effect and is being enforced by U.S. marshals. The problem is that by *unnecessarily* weighing in with this procedural argument, the department has undermined the judge's authority, fostered uncertainty in a dangerous situation and allowed Operation Rescue to be seen at this critical stage as an ally of the federal government.

The legal issue here over federal jurisdiction will be settled soon in the Supreme Court. The department's position on the question is well known and on the record. Considering the potentially explosive situation in Wichita, the intervention was not only unwarranted but cynical.

The New York Times

New York City, New York, August 9, 1991

For three weeks in Wichita, Kan., this is what has greeted the terrified teen-ager, the poverty-stricken mother, the woman who could die in childbirth. Members of Operation Rescue, a group on the fringes of the anti-abortion movement, have been blocking the doorways to three clinics. Clogging the sidewalks. Flinging themselves under cars. Crawling beneath police horses. Making it all but impossible for women to exercise a right granted them by the Supreme Court of the United States.

And now, with mischievously poor timing, the Justice Department has filed an amicus brief supporting the protesters' efforts to overturn a judge's order barring any further blocking of the clinics. The Department says it's merely raising a jurisdictional issue and does not condone the demonstrators' goals or tactics. But the effect of its message is to endorse the mob.

The restraining order was issued last month by a Federal district judge, Patrick F. Kelly. For two weeks the order was largely disobeyed, leading to mass arrests, and this week Judge Kelly strengthened it by telling Federal marshals not to tolerate any delaying tactics.

Operation Rescue appealed, arguing that the case belongs in a state court, and the Justice Department quickly flew to the group's aid. Judge Kelly granted the Government's request that it be permitted to file an amicus brief, but not without a parting shot. "I am disgusted by this move by the United States," he said in court. Later, on ABC's "Nightline," he charged that Attorney General Dick Thornburgh had "given an imprimatur to what, in my view, is a license for mayhem."

His anger is justified. What the Justice Department purports to be doing is simply restating its interpretation of the 1871 Federal civil rights law on which Judge Kelly based his ruling. But what it's really doing is furthering its anti-abortion agenda by championing a band of zealots shunned by mainstream anti-choice groups.

Furthermore, the Department's brief seems gratuitous. The judge's order is already on appeal and the appellate panel is expected to rule shortly. In addition, the department has already staked out its position on jurisdiction in another case, Bray v. Alexandria Women's Health Clinic, that will be heard by the Supreme Court in October. So what conceivable judicial goal is it serving by intervening now?

Judge Kelly has behaved with far greater honor. When asked his personal views on abortion, he replied that it would be improper to state them or allow them to influence his interpretation of the law. "I have my constitutional duty to carry out and to follow the law," he said, "and Roe is the law."

Contrast that with the Justice Department, which has thrown its considerable weight with those who have shown contempt for a Federal order.

The Philadelphia Inquirer

Philadelphia, Pennsylvania, August 8, 1991

Two weeks ago, Randall Terry, the former used-car salesman who heads Operation Rescue, showed what he thought of a federal judge's order to stop blocking entry to legal abortion clinics in Wichita, Kan. Already, hundreds of anti-abortion protesters — the movement's "shock troops" — had been arrested. Mr. Terry denounced the injunction as "judicial tyranny," wadded it up and threw it to the ground: "We have an injunction in the Bible," he said, "that commands us to rescue innocent children."

The arrests have gone on; the city has edged toward chaos. Police on horseback waded in one day. Another time, 200 protesters did a *crawling* assault. Now a West Coast *pro-abortion-rights group* says it's coming to town to even up the sides — to unblock clinic doors by force.

Against this unraveling backdrop, the U.S. Justice Department committed an outrage Tuesday. It threw its weight behind Operation Rescue's challenge of the order, arguing that there was no federal jurisdiction.

What a moment for Mr. Terry to find he's got a friend in Attorney General Dick Thornburgh, the nation's chief law officer — and very-soon-to-be Pennsylvania's GOP Senate candidate: The federal judge, Patrick Kelly, is being subjected to physical confrontation; the city's mayor has grossly mishandled the whole affair; local officials, including Gov. Joan Finney, have played to the anti-abortion crowd. With a scent of anarchy thickening, the judge felt compelled to take to national TV to defend his own authority — and to invite Mr. Thornburgh to stop playing politics. Indeed, to stop courting bloodshed.

Were Judge Kelly waltzing into the case absent precedent — or if he was squashing free speech (he isn't) or protest rights (he isn't) — we might think differently. But he is relying on an 1871 anti-Klan law that courts have used to protect vulnerable groups from being violently denied their rights. The law was applied against Operation Rescue in New York and upheld on appeal.

The precedent is by no means safe, as the Supreme Court will take up the issue this fall. But by gratuitously intervening in *this* highly charged case — Operation Rescue's lawyers were capable of arguing alone — the Justice Department emboldens law-breaking, undermines a beleaguered federal judge and helps keep Wichita in an uproar.

THE ARIZONA REPUBLIC

Phoenix, Arizona, August 8, 1991

WHEN the U.S. Justice Department intervened on behalf of Wichita abortion protesters, contesting a federal injunction against them, U.S. District Court Judge Patrick Kelly was, shall we say, displeased. "I am disgusted by this move by the United States," the judge told U.S. Attorney Lee Thompson.

Later in the day the judge appeared on ABC's *Nightline* and amplified on his pique. "If my order is set aside (and) these marshals are removed," he fumed, "the pro-choice folks will be here (and) there will be bloodshed. And it's just ludicrous to believe that somehow our government puts an imprimatur (sic) and agrees to that."

Federal judges, let it be said, ordinarily conduct official business in court, where contending points of view can be aired in an orderly manner, not on television, where the rules of procedure do not apply. But "King Kelly" is no ordinary federal judge, and he evidently feels no need to hear other points of view. He already has determined that the Wichita protesters — "these lawbreakers" he calls them — are entitled to none of the usual presumptions and protections.

It would be easier to believe that the judge was concerned about the risk of violence, as he alleges, except for his vengeful attitude toward the protests, organized by Operation Rescue. Not only does he denounce the demonstrators as lawless people, but he also has ordered federal marshals to put them under arrest if, when ordered to disperse, they move with less alacrity than the judge expects.

Criticism of Judge Kelly, it needs to be emphasized, is not the same as support for violent demonstrations or for physical interference with clients of Wichita-area abortion clinics. If pro-life forces want to stay out of jail, they should keep their protests strictly within legal bounds. If civil disobedience is their aim, they should expect to suffer the consequences, which may entail jail time.

Even so, the Justice Department is entirely within its rights to urge Judge Kelly to back off, because federal jurisdiction is unclear. The judge has acted under a Reconstruction-era civil rights act prohibiting conspiracy for the purpose of denying any person or class of persons equal protection or equal privileges and immunities. This law, the Justice Department argues, does not protect women seeking abortions. Local authorities, it says, should be policing the Wichita abortion protests.

This jurisdictional dispute is shortly to be decided by the U.S. Supreme Court, which has agreed to rule on a similar case arising out of anti-abortion protests in Alexandria, Va. It might be judicious for Judge Kelly, instead of lambasting the Justice Department on television, to lift his injunction until the court can decide.

The Chattanooga Times
Chattanooga, Tennessee, August 8, 1991

The 33 men and women charged with trespassing as a result of their anti-abortion protests at the Chattanooga Women's Clinic in 1989 are understandably elated that the state agreed to dismiss the charges. But the dismissals don't mean a green light for similar protests at the clinic in the future, chiefly because of an appellate court decision on another case involving anti-abortion protests.

No one questions the sincerity of the protesters' opposition to abortions performed at the clinic. In fact, given the depth of their feelings on the subject, they had — and have — a clear constitutional right to protest, even though abortion is legal.

They erred, however, in trespassing on the clinic's property, a tactic used in numerous other protests around the country. In some cases, protesters have chained themselves to clinics and defied police orders to leave. Their purpose, they say, is to "rescue" the potential victims of abortion — the unborn children.

Upon arrest, the "rescue" protesters invoked the "necessity defense," which attorney Hoyt Samples said means that it may be appropriate to violate one law to prevent an act that might create a greater harm. In this case, the "greater harm" was the clinic's performance of abortions after the first trimester of pregnancy. Under state law, such abortions may not be performed at a clinic but are allowed under certain circumstances at a hospital. The clinic's attorney said second-trimester abortions have not been performed there since a judge ruled they should not be.

If such abortions are being performed illegally, however, it is up to the state — that is, law enforcement agencies — to take action, not individual protesters. No such action by the state has been taken here.

The common law defense of necessity says it is justified if "the person reasonably believes the conduct is immediately necessary to avoid imminent harm; and the desirability and urgency of avoiding the harm clearly outweigh . . . the harm sought to be prevented by the law proscribing the conduct."

In other words, a citizen could freely violate the law — by assaulting someone in the act of rape in order to protect the victim, for example. The Sentencing Commission that recodified Tennessee criminal law noted, however, that such situations are "exceedingly rare."

So rare, in fact, that the Tennessee Court of Criminal Appeals rejected the "necessity defense" in a case from Bristol that involved anti-abortion protesters who trespassed at an abortion clinic and were arrested.

In upholding the protesters' convictions on trespassing charges, the appellate court included this significant comment:

"It is an unusual and difficult occasion for the court to rule as a matter of law that individuals are not protected by general necessity when acting illegally albeit in furtherance of a heartfelt belief that they must do so to discontinue infanticide. Nonetheless, the enduring clashes of beliefs in this fractious dispute must be resolved not by physical confrontations at the front line, but rather through the legislative and judicial framework created for the very purpose of undertaking the sometimes formidable tasks of choosing between extreme positions and competing values."

And it added: "The defense of necessity simply cannot be utilized when the harm sought to be avoided is abortion, which remains a constitutionally protected activity and the harm incurred is trespass, which is a violation of the law." The court noted that while some trial courts have accepted the necessity claims of some protesters, "the appellate courts have uniformly held that abortion clinic protesters are precluded, as a matter of law, from raising a necessity defense."

In fairness, it was not alleged in the Bristol case that the abortion facility was acting illegally by performing second-trimester abortions. Mr. Samples said, however, that it is proper to infer from the decision that if such illegal acts were taking place, then the necessity defense is permissible. Given the Chattanooga clinic's changed policies, however, the Bristol decision would seem to preclude the use of that defense in future protests here.

Chattanooga, Tennessee, August 10, 1991

Operation Rescue is back in the news again, and this time it is taking no prisoners. "Rescuers" have been trying since mid-July to shut down three abortion clinics in Wichita, Kan., employing their usual tactic of blocking access to the clinics by patients and staff members. Now, the mood has turned ugly. The federal judge overseeing the protest has become the target of death threats and is being guarded by federal marshals.

Also, in a move shot through with political overtones, the Bush administration has jumped in on the side of the protesters.

The issue here is not abortion, although that practice is the target of the "rescuers'" ire. Even though abortion is legal, opponents have the constitutional right to demonstrate against it. Harassment of patients and staff, and blockades of clinic entrances, however, reflect a willingness to ignore any law they believe hinders their crusade.

The Bush administration's craven eagerness to demonstrate solidarity with the "rescuers" is only slightly less contemptible than its argument that this is simply a disagreement over jurisdiction.

Two of the clinics asked U.S. District Judge Patrick F. Kelly to end the blockades and the protesters' harassment. To justify coming into federal court, the clinics invoked a federal law passed during the Reconstruction era to protect blacks from harassment by such racist organizations as the Ku Klux Klan. The law, they said, was a logical vehicle for protecting patients and clinic staff members.

Three weeks ago Judge Kelly temporarily barred protesters from blocking the clinics' entrances, but his order was ignored. This week he toughened the order with specific guidelines for marshals to use in arresting trespassers. But last week the administration filed a dissenting petition, asserting the Reconstruction-era law isn't applicable. It says the issue belongs in a state court.

That's something an appeals court will have to decide, and it could have done so without the administration getting involved. It was unnecessary for the administration to align itself with a group whose contempt for the law contradicts the moral tone of its beliefs. That moral underpinning was weakened further by reports of death threats telephoned to Judge Kelly, and by one of the anti-abortion protesters who confronted the judge personally and engaged in a shoving match.

The Bush administration opposes abortion, except under certain circumstances, which is its right. But the administration still has a responsibility to avoid actions that suggest it condones violation of a court order, which is what the "rescuers" have done. Even more important, the administration must never appear to favor violation of the law, even when the protesters' target is a legal — but in their eyes objectionable — activity. The administration's attempt to portray its intervention as merely procedural is an insult to the intelligence.

The Phoenix Gazette
Phoenix, Arizona, August 9, 1991

The incendiary issue of abortion exploded in Wichita, Kan., recently after U.S. District Judge Patrick Kelly's preliminary injunction that barred opponents of abortion from blocking the entrances to two Wichita clinics.

The protesters come from Operation Rescue, an organization sympathetic to the use of physical intimidation in preventing women lawful access to abortion clinics.

In the midst of the high-tension and unsavory protests that followed Kelly's decision — including threats made against the judge and his family — the U.S. Justice Department joined Operation Rescue's legal machinations seeking to have Kelly's injunction reversed, as a "friend of the court."

"I am disgusted with this move by the United States, that they would now put an imprimatur on this conduct, and I will ask you please to report that to the attorney general personally and have him view some tapes," said Kelly, apparently referring to videotapes showing protesters preventing women legitimate access to medical facilities of their choice.

Operation Rescue founder Randall Terry has spent time in prison for his assaults on the freedoms of others, and the U.S. Supreme Court has already granted a permanent ban on Operation Rescue demonstrations in New York.

Operation Rescue is under similar injunctions in other cities across the country because of its abuse of women, its violent attacks on family counseling centers, its willing trespass on private property and the rights of others.

Now, the U.S. Justice Department rushes to the aid of this unsavory organization, challenging Kelly's jurisdiction, an intervention engineered by George Bush's attorney general, Richard Thornburgh.

Bush, on vacation in Kennebunkport, Maine, said his administration was "not judging (the abortion dispute) at all . . . It's a jurisdictional dispute. Whether it's state (or) federal (jurisdiction), let them sort it out . . . This isn't a matter for the president to be concerned about, particularly on the first day of his vacation."

If the president really believes what he says — and he should — then he ought to tell the people who work for him to shut up and butt out of Wichita, Kan.

The Wichita
Eagle-Beacon

Wichita, Kansas, August 27, 1991

More than 25,000 people showed up for Sunday's "Hope for the Heartland" rally against abortion. That impressive turnout should convince Wichitans who oppose abortion that the political process — not illegal tactics such as blockading abortion clinics — is the best way to advance their cause.

Most of the speakers at Sunday's rally applauded this summer's blockades, now entering their eighth week, as expressions of heartfelt Christian repugnance at the destruction of life. Certainly, those tactics and the attendant mass arrests of abortion protesters have given the anti-abortion message a higher profile — both locally and nationally — than it had enjoyed before.

But the blockades are counterproductive to the cause of rendering abortions illegal. Many who oppose abortion hope that the conservative majority on the U.S. Supreme Court will overturn Roe vs. Wade, the 1973 decision that barred states from outlawing abortion. If it does, abortions to preserve the physical or mental health of the mother — that is, most abortions — still would be legal in Kansas, under a law passed by the Legislature in 1969. The only hope of changing that law would be to elect a pro-life Legislature. Right now, the Kansas Legislature is decidedly pro-choice.

As a recent Wichita Eagle survey showed, the blockades, if anything, have hardened the attitudes of the majority who believe that the decision whether to have an abortion should lie with the woman in question. Politically speaking, then, the blockades are counterproductive.

Sunday's rally, however, shows that the anti-abortion forces have a large political base upon which to build. But if local anti-abortion leaders wish to succeed, they need to urge the Operation Rescue outsiders to leave town, then begin vying for the hearts and minds of local voters. That not only would sweeten the bitter local atmosphere considerably, but improve the local anti-abortion movement's chances for success at the ballot box.

The local pro-choice contingent, of course, has taken this summer's activities as a wake-up call to action to protect abortion rights. It, too, will be vying for the hearts and minds of the voters.

Especially if Roe vs. Wade is overturned, the city and state seem doomed to a long season of single-issue politics, during which other critical issues may not get the attention they need. Continued disagreement over abortion, in short, seems inevitable. But if the anti-abortion forces realize the futility — and impracticality — of illegal action, and renounce it, the abortion debate won't continue to polarize the community.

Wichita, Kansas, July 6, 1991

When governing bodies are divided into camps of approximately the same size on a question, it often falls to one member to decide whether the answer is to be yea or nay. On the abortion question facing the Wichita City Council earlier this week, that uncomfortable duty fell to council member Rip Gooch.

In answering nay, Mr. Gooch assured that city government won't get into the dicey business of attempting to regulate abortions — a task to which it is ill-suited. It can't have been an easy decision for him.

Mr. Gooch has refused to state his personal views on abortion, as is appropriate considering that the issue has nothing to do with city government. But he was one of a coalition of seven City Council and County Commission members who in 1989 voted to deny Planned Parenthood federal block grant money, on the ground that that organization does abortion counseling. While it may be risky to infer from that one vote that Mr. Gooch is pro-life, the vote does suggest an antipathy toward abortion.

Regardless of his reason for voting no on the abortion ordinance proposed by council member Frank Ojile, Mr. Gooch did the city a favor. It isn't for council members to decide when life begins, as the proposed ordinance would have required. And it would have been pointless for the city to ban third-trimester abortions, or to ask physicians who perform abortions to notify parents if teenage girls seek abortions.

The reach of any ordinance stops at the city limits. To be effective, laws that attempt to regulate abortion must be passed by governments of larger scope.

The hope must be that Mr. Gooch's courageous vote puts the abortion question to rest in Wichita. As he undoubtedly knows, the City Council has a full enough plate as it is, and didn't need to get involved in an issue that's beyond its power to resolve.

Wichita, Kansas, August 20, 1991

The patience of Wichita police, U.S. marshals, U.S. District Judge Patrick Kelly and local citizens will be tested this week as Operation Rescue counts down to its weekend rally and orchestrated big moment in the national spotlight.

Operation Rescue's imported protesters are obviously intent upon continuing to violate the law and the rights of others by blocking access to legal abortion clinics. Given events in the Soviet Union over the weekend, their lust for national attention may cause them to escalate their physical activities, hoping to invite a more physical response from the beleaguered police and marshals, who have handled their provocations with admirable forbearance.

It's a shame that just as local pro-life leaders are beginning to understand the dangers and divisiveness of confrontation, the national leaders will be tempted to escalate it. Again, it's time for local leaders to take full charge and strongly invite Randall Terry and his people to leave.

As this countdown week begins with all its possible perils, Kansans should keep in mind several points:

■ It is not a peaceful tactic to physically occupy space to which someone else has a legal right. It is intimidation.

■ The issue of abortion is not going to be settled in the streets of Wichita. It will be settled in the courts and voting booths, as appropriate in a democracy.

■ Free speech is not the issue, nor has it been since Operation Rescue arrived. No one is being denied the right to peaceful protest.

■ If violence occurs, understand what started it. Under Judge Kelly's order, police and marshals are charged with maintaining access. They are doing that by establishing police lines and cordons on private property. Any contact that occurs between officials and protesters clearly will be initiated by the protesters.

Wichita, Kansas, August 29, 1991

It will come as a relief to many Wichitans, both pro-life and pro-choice, that Operation Rescue's "Summer of Mercy" campaign appears to be winding down. The city badly needs a period of calm so that residents can sort out their feelings about abortion and — more important — refocus on other issues needing resolution.

Both U.S. District Judge Patrick Kelly and Operation Rescue deserve credit for the tailing off of abortion clinic blockades that, during this fractious summer, have brought more than 2,600 arrests and unleashed a blizzard of intemperate rhetoric.

Mr. Kelly offered to release three jailed Operation Rescue leaders in return for the group's promise to stop blocking access to two clinics. At the same time the judge wisely said anyone arrested for blockading a clinic wouldn't get a second chance before suffering the legal consequences of violating his court order that the clinics remain open for business.

Operation Rescue denies promising to cease the blockades in return for the release of the three leaders. But its leadership did say that blockades won't be likely to occur again soon. Continuing the battle against abortions in Wichita, they say, now is the responsibility of local activists.

That's as it should be. And the hope must be that local anti-abortion leaders understand that political action is the best way to advance their cause. Illegal action brings jail and fines. And it hardens the attitudes of the very voters whom the anti-abortion movement must court if it's to gain legislative passage of abortion restrictions.

Blockading the clinics dramatized the intensity of the protesters' belief that abortion is murder and created a political base upon which the movement can build. If the local anti-abortion leadership uses the period of calm now beginning to plot legal political strategy, it has a chance at changing the law. But if it opts for further illegal action, failure is certain.

The Wichita
Eagle-Beacon

Wichita, Kansas, August 24, 1991

Much that's destructive has happened in Wichita during the almost seven weeks of the Operation Rescue demonstrations. But this weekend's major rallies by both sides of the abortion issue need not, and should not, fall into that tragic trap.

The rallies are exactly what each camp should be doing to advance its cause.

Pro-choice forces will start their weekend at 9 a.m. today at A. Price Woodard Park next to Century II. A number of national figures in the choice movement — including Patricia Ireland, executive vice president of the National Organization for Women, and Kate Michelman, head of the National Abortion Rights Action League — will speak. Thousands of local and national supporters are expected to jam the banks of the Arkansas River.

The big pro-life rally, which starts at 2:30 p.m. Sunday, has been dubbed "Hope in the Heartlands." Christian broadcaster Pat Robertson will be the featured speaker.

Pro-life leaders say their supporters will number more than 13,000.

These are what demonstrations on the abortion issue should be: supporters coming together, speakers arguing their cases, people promoting their causes through free speech and assembly, folks asserting their rights and beliefs without trampling on the rights and beliefs of others.

The only danger is that the demonstrators will clash, one group attending the other's rally and baiting the opposition into an ugly, perhaps violent, confrontation.

But if city leaders lead, if local leaders of the pro-life movement spread their message of community healing, if pro-choice people continue to keep their cool, that won't happen. What will happen is two passionate but peaceful rallies in the great tradition of democracy.

This weekend can be, and should be, the best that pro-choice and pro-life supporters have brought to Wichita.

Wichita, Kansas, September 4, 1991

The long summer of abortion protests in Wichita has degenerated into a campaign of hatred and personal attacks by people on both sides of the issue.

The latest tactic is to picket the homes, businesses or offices of individuals who have taken a high profile stance on abortion. It's gotten to the point that even the most innocent actions are viewed as politically significant. Witness the Wichita McDonald's that lent coolers to a church group. The coolers later were seen at an Operation Rescue demonstration; in response, pro-choice marchers were out in force at the restaurant.

Meanwhile, pro-lifers set up their lines Monday in front of the home of a physician who performs abortions.

The Wichita Eagle also has been targeted because some people object to the paper's news coverage and editorial comment on the abortion controversy.

Civility and decency have been among the first casualties of the abortion battle.

Activists on both sides have demonized their adversaries, instead of recognizing them as fellow citizens with whom they might have much in common on other issues.

Fortunately, there have been some positive role models. On the op-ed page of last Sunday's Eagle, for example, members of the clergy on both sides presented their views in an intelligent, persuasive manner that didn't demean their opponents.

The clergymen showed that even on an issue as explosive as abortion, it's possible to disagree without being disagreeable, to attack someone's ideas without resorting to personal insult and invective.

Yet, on the street level, the abortion debate too often is marked by simplistic sloganeering, bumper-sticker logic, harassment and intimidation. That's hardly the kind of discussion abortion deserves.

It's time to put away the signs. To call off the rallies. To give Wichita a chance to heal the wounds from a rough summer.

Wichita, Kansas, September 7, 1991

U.S. District Judge Patrick Kelly's effort to end the city's summer-long abortion dispute, while understandable, simply wasn't acceptable. His proposed compromise court order would have required women entering abortion clinics to submit to 15 seconds of harassment from Operation Rescue sidewalk counselors. His proposal also would have required Dr. George Tiller to open his clinic to an inspection by a "neutral third party."

Dr. Tiller was absolutely right to reject the judge's proposal as a violation of his rights and his patients' rights. As his attorney, John Cowles, told Judge Kelly during a hearing Thursday, Operation Rescue picked this summer's fight over abortion, and employed illegal tactics for advancing its cause. To reward Operation Rescue for doing so would have been ludicrous.

As a result of Dr. Tiller's refusal to accept the compromise, Judge Kelly's original order forbidding abortion protesters from

blocking access to the clinic or interfering with staff and patients trying to enter remains in effect. That leaves the clinic staff and patients and abortion protesters in a more confrontational mode than would have existed if Dr. Tiller had accepted the judge's offer, and raises the possibility of more attempts to blockade the clinics.

Better that distasteful prospect, though, than a situation requiring a legal business to operate under constraints that favor lawbreakers. The principle upon which Judge Kelly constructed his original order — that the legal rights of the clinics and their patients must be upheld — is too important to be undermined for expediency's sake.

The Operation Rescue leadership now is in the position to claim it's Dr. Tiller's fault if more clinic blockades occur. But thoughtful Wichitans will see such rhetoric for what it is: a blatant example of blaming the victim for his own misery.

Wichita, Kansas, August 22, 1991

The time has come for Wichita leaders on all sides of the abortion issue to take back the city from Randall Terry and Operation Rescue. Doing so will require a new level of political and religious courage, because the earnest pro-life people of Wichita have a large emotional investment in their effort to curb abortions.

But the time has arrived, hurried along by the escalating violence of protests at three local clinics. What began as peaceful protest turned first to physical obstruction and, this week, has become outright assault on law enforcement people charged with maintaining access to the legal clinics.

The escalation was inevitable. Operation Rescue's national leaders, knocked from the front pages and network news by events elsewhere and aiming to crown their invasion with a huge rally Sunday, are instructing their followers in guerrilla tactics that can result in physical injury.

Before that happens, Mayor Bob Knight and other political and religious leaders have a duty to firmly and directly call upon Wichitans to act in the community's interests and avoid increased violence. The best way to do that is to avoid the clinic demonstrations. But those who feel they must be present should urge their fellow pro-lifers from outside to act like good guests and not further harm this community.

Operation Rescue leaders have used the heartfelt beliefs of hundreds of Wichitans to make their point about abortion. They should not be allowed to abuse those beliefs and endanger those bodies in the name of their own fanaticism.

At some point Operation Rescue will be gone. Wichitans on all sides of the issue will then be left to try to put the pieces back together, while Operation Rescue's leaders find another community to exploit. This community is bruised enough. It cannot afford a legacy of physical strife atop the backlog of divisive emotions.

The least our leaders can do is to ask that Wichitans of good will isolate the outsiders and not get dragged further into the turmoil that Operation Rescue is determined to manufacture. The wounds from further physical confrontation will last long after the flesh has healed.

Mr. Knight, the Rev. George Gardner, the Rev. Gene Williams and others who hold or are moving into positions of leadership cannot stand by and watch further escalation. Regardless of how they feel on the issue itself, the immediate potential for violence between Wichitans and their law enforcement officials overrides such concerns. The Eagle believes that those leaders can have an important quieting effect and that they are obliged in the name of the city's future to do so. Wichitans will listen to a unified call for a respite from confrontation. We also believe that our leaders' failure to do so will be read by many as condoning violence against each other and against law and order.

Operation Rescue chose Wichita, not the other way around. It's time for the city, behind its moral leaders, to choose not to tolerate Operation Rescue's rough tactics.

Operation Rescue
Targets Buffalo, N.Y.

The national anti-abortion group Operation Rescue staged a two-week-long protest against abortion clinics and doctors who performed abortions in Buffalo, N.Y. April 20 to May 5, 1992. Unlike Operation Rescue protests staged in Wichita, Kan. in July 1991 and August 1991, there was little violence in Buffalo, and the area's six abortion clinics remained open despite the group's efforts to shut them down.

The Buffalo protests, called the "Spring of Life" campaign, resulted in 597 arrests. Almost all of those arrested were anti-abortion protesters charged with disorderly conduct, trespassing and resisting arrest. A handful of abortion-rights advocates were also arrested.

Observers said that two factors made the Buffalo protests different from the events in Wichita. First, abortion-rights volunteers in Buffalo provided a physical barrier between anti-abortion protesters and the clinic doors, allowing the clinics to remain open. Second, in February, a U.S. District Court in New York State had issued an injunction restricting anti-abortion supporters from having more than two "sidewalk counselors" approach patients arriving at clinics. Other anti-abortion protesters were required to stay at least 15 feet from any person entering a clinic.

As the protests began April 20, hundreds of supporters on each side of the abortion debate massed in and around Buffalo. Regional Operation Rescue leader Rev. Keith Tucci led a rally of some 1,000 supporters late April 20. On the pro-choice side, Eleanor Smeal, leader of the Feminist Majority Foundation and a former president of the National Organization for Women, told protesters, "There will never be another Wichita."

Rev. Robert Schneck, an Operation Rescue leader, was arrested April 21 and charged with disorderly conduct for allegedly pushing what he said was an aborted fetus at abortion-rights activists. Schneck's bother, Rev. Paul Schneck, was also arrested in connection with the incident. Buffalo newscasts quoted by the *New York Times* April 22 said the Erie County Attorney's office had reported that a medical examination had determined the fetus to be a stillborn male about 20 weeks old.

The greatest number of arrests in a single day, 194, came April 22, when anti-abortion protesters tried to close down a clinic in suburban Amherst, N.Y., outside Buffalo. Four news photographers and a television news cameraman were among those arrested in the crowd. One escort, who was trying to help a patient enter the clinic, was also arrested.

Other protests, dubbed Operation John the Baptist, focused on the homes and offices of private doctors who performed abortions.

Operation Rescue officials April 29 announced that they had suspended the Buffalo campaign and would hold a period of "prayer and fasting." National and local leaders made contradictory statements about when the protests would begin again and who would make the decision on resuming the campaign.

Observers perceived the rift as evidence of the national group's failure to gain support in the Buffalo area, saying the group's tactics alienated residents who agreed with their anti-abortion stand.

Abortion-rights supporters, who for the most part had outnumbered Operation Rescue protesters at the Buffalo clinics, hailed the suspension as a sign of victory.

Abortion opponents resumed demonstrating May 1. More than 100 protesters were arrested that day after rushing the back of a clinic in Amherst.

The Idaho **STATESMAN**
Idaho Falls, Idaho, April 27, 1992

Last week in Buffalo, a minister threw what was alleged to be an aborted fetus at abortion-rights protesters who chanted: "Anti, anti, go away. You're all liars anyway."

Meanwhile, in Washington, spectators crammed the U.S. Supreme Court building to hear arguments for and against a Pennsylvania law designed to limit abortion rights guaranteed under *Roe v. Wade.*

As the nation waits for the court's July decision in the Pennsylvania case, the angry encounters and political rhetoric are likely to heat beyond the boiling point. Drowned out in the din of protest is the woman who faces the very real, very private and sometimes very frightening prospect of an unwanted pregnancy.

Let's not forget her. Regardless of what the anti-abortion forces say, she is unlikely to be seeking an abortion because she wants to select the sex of her child. And she is unlikely to be using abortion as a convenient means of birth control.

She is likely to be poor. She often is young. And she often has good reason to want to keep her pregnancy confidential.

If the court upholds the Pennsylvania law, women seeking abortion in that state will be required to: prove they have told their husbands about the pregnancy if they are married; obtain consent from a parent or judge if they are a minor, and put off the procedure for 24 hours once they have decided on abortion.

Their doctors will be required to counsel the women about fetal development and keep detailed records of all abortions performed. Those records would be subject to public disclosure.

With the exception of the parental consent requirement, which seems reasonable given the fact that a parent's consent is required before a minor undergoes every other medical procedure, the Pennsylvania law sets up unreasonable obstacles.

In most cases, it is a good idea for women to tell their husbands before they undergo an abortion. But that's a private discussion, and one which the state has no business forcing.

The same can be said for the 24-hour waiting period. Of course it's wise for women to consider abortion carefully. Most women recognize that abortion is a serious decision.

The law's provision requiring the doctor to keep detailed records is especially disturbing. It will have a chilling effect, and will likely discourage many doctors from doing abortions.

The U.S. Supreme Court may use the Pennsylvania case as an opportunity to throw out *Roe v. Wade.* But even if justices simply allow states to write their own abortion regulations, the decision could be disastrous.

It will allow the nation to return to a patchwork of abortion laws, forcing women to seek out states where abortion is safe and legal. It may take a deadly toll, especially on young girls and poor women.

The Providence Journal
Providence, Rhode Island, April 24, 1992

The Supreme Court listened to arguments this week about a Pennsylvania law that would, to some degree, restrict the right to an abortion held by American women since *Roe v. Wade* in 1973. The conventional wisdom seems to be that *Roe*, in its present form, will soon be history: that it will not be overturned outright, but abridged by stages in a series of test cases.

That is too bad — and, as we noted last week, if the Supreme Court sees fit to send the abortion issue back to the states for revised judgment, Rhode Island would do well to duplicate *Roe* at the local level.

In the meantime, however, Operation Rescue, the militant anti-abortion organization, has arrived in Buffalo, determined to repeat the campaign of civil disobedience it launched in Wichita last year. Demonstrators are targeting abortion clinics, picketing, blocking sidewalks, seeking to prevent women from entering the premises, sometimes even storming the clinics themselves. Operation Rescue has been met on the streets by equally militant pro-choice organizations, disrupting their rivals' meetings, marching, chanting and sometimes assaulting their opposite numbers.

The poor Buffalo police, of course, are caught in the middle. So, for that matter, are the American people.

If the public opinion polls tell us anything about abortion in the United States, it is that most Americans have deeply ambivalent feelings on the subject. Most Americans, it is true, are very uncomfortable with the idea of abortion; but at the same time, they do *not* wish to see abortion outlawed. They support — indeed, they would welcome — some middle ground between the two extremes of doctrine and opinion. This is what might be called the fundamental wisdom of the American people. And as usual, it puts most Americans squarely between the two camps now fighting and shouting and squaring off in Buffalo.

Abortion is a complex, sensitive, emotive public issue, informed on all sides by testimonials of anguish, serious conviction and deep-seated religious beliefs. If the Supreme Court should impose limitations on *Roe v. Wade*, it should be understood that the only way a mature society can resolve such troubling issues is through civilized discourse, and mutual respect for differing opinions: the knowledge that no one side is absolutely correct, that views can be held for disinterested reasons, and that violence, coercion and inflammatory rhetoric will aggravate America's self-inflicted wound.

THE PLAIN DEALER
Cleveland, Ohio, April 22, 1992

Violence and physical intimidation have no place in a reasoned society's debate, especially on the most sensitive issues of individual liberty. Today, as the Supreme Court hears arguments in another case involving the nation's most inflammatory legal topic — every woman's fundamental right to choose the option of abortion — the threat of violence is creating a climate of fear in a Great Lakes city targeted by anti-abortion militants: Buffalo, N.Y.

The right to demonstrate peacefully is surely guaranteed to all those who feel strongly about such social issues, on all sides of the debate. But as anti-choice absolutists besiege health clinics in Buffalo, intent on harassing women who seek to exercise a right implicitly guaranteed by the Constitution, there must be no tolerance for any type of physical intimidation. America's agonizing debate over abortion rights can only be settled by compassion in the courts and moderation at the ballot box, not by angry mobs' agitation in the streets.

All too often, violent tactics have marred the activities of the group that is victimizing Buffalo, the self-styled "Operation Rescue." Thousands of its members were arrested last summer during the group's siege of health clinics in Wichita, Kan., where anti-choice militants used the most contemptible tactics: provoking street-corner shoving matches, sending death threats to a federal judge and physically interfering with law-abiding doctors, nurses and patients. Single-issue crusaders, no matter how sincere they claim to be, sacrifice any pretense of idealism when they intimidate others.

As Buffalo braces for possible violence, Washington this week is again weighing legal threats to abortion rights — and this time, the issue comes before a Supreme Court whose majority seems openly hostile to a landmark of liberty, the Roe vs. Wade decision of 1973. That ruling is challenged by a Pennsylvania law that clamps severe restrictions on women's access to abortion. Even if the Rehnquist Court does not completely overturn Roe vs. Wade when it decides the Pennsylvania case, it may approve draconian limits that undermine citizens' ability to exercise their right to choose.

The principles of privacy and liberty that undergird Roe vs. Wade remain, and should remain, the law of the land. Last week, a federal appeals court sensibly struck down a severe anti-abortion law from the U.S. territory of Guam, asserting that its limits on access to abortion violated the Roe vs. Wade standard. That welcome decision sets the right tone for this week's Supreme Court deliberations.

Each woman's decisions about her reproductive freedom should be free from interference — by any Big Brother government and by any group of militants who would impose their choices on others. Reason, not violence, should govern the Buffalo protesters. Liberty, not the state's power, should guide the Supreme Court justices as they consider abortion rights, an individual liberty that must not be infringed.

THE SPOKESMAN-REVIEW
Spokane, Washington, April 21, 1992

The pro-life and pro-choice demonstrators who are trading taunts in Buffalo make good theater but the lasting policies governing abortion continue to be shaped in the courts and the legislatures.

On Wednesday a 1989 Pennsylvania law placing a number of restrictions on a woman's right to obtain an abortion will be examined in the U.S. Supreme Court. The philosophical complexion of the current court indicates that when the ultimate ruling comes down, probably this summer, it will further erode the 1973 ruling in Roe Vs. Wade which made abortion legal in the United States but which seems to be destined for reversal.

Other cases on the horizon point toward greater and greater authority for states to severely restrict or even outlaw abortion. Cases from Guam, Louisianna and Utah all are in the pipeline to the Supreme Court where the prevailing view toward abortion is hostile.

The upshot, as has been becoming more apparent with each case, is that the place for securing women's rights to make their own choices about reproductive freedom is the respective state legislatures.

That may be of little comfort to women in Missouri, Pennsylvania, Utah, Louisianna and others where lawmakers are inclined to restrict their options.

However, it underscores the importance of Washington voters' approval last fall of Initiative 120.

The initiative affirmed and updated a 1970 referendum legalizing abortion in Washington state.

Initiative 120 was put on the ballot last year in anticipation that new faces on the Supreme Court would put Roe vs. Wade in serious jeopardy.

In conspicuous contrast to the relatively orderly way lawmakers and judges deal with the issue, however, are the sidewalk escapades being staged at present in Buffalo and last summer in Wichita. Anti-abortion activists in such places persist in trying to impose their own moral views on others, even if it means scorning the law and trampling on individual rights.

If the protections embodied in Roe Vs. Wade are indeed on borrowed time, defenders of the right to choose face a major challenge that will have to be met in every state capital.

The Buffalo News
Buffalo, New York, April 21, 1992

THE LONG-PLANNED confrontation over legal abortions here got off to an inauspicious start on Easter weekend. When pro-choice militants jostled, mocked and spat upon the Rev. Paul H. Schenck while he read a Bible outside a downtown abortion clinic, they crossed a line of behavior early that should never have been crossed at all — by either side.

The shoving of Schenck, a local anti-abortion leader, contributes to a climate of extremism that threatens violence.

Such violence would rip aside the hopes of the community at large and contradict the professions of local leaders on both sides of this emotional issue in favor of peaceful conduct during Operation Rescue's demonstrations at Buffalo-area abortion clinics scheduled for the next couple of weeks.

The idea of lawful protest and lawful response is not enhanced by last weekend's words of the militants, often voiced by those here from outside Buffalo, on either side.

"Society is willing to fight (for abortion rights)," said Sara Lolar, a spokeswoman for the militant National Women's Rights Organizing Coalition. "Violence is a necessary fact. Sometimes it is needed."

On the other side, Randall Terry, preaching on Good Friday, likened state Attorney General Robert Abrams and U.S. District Judge Richard Arcara to Pontius Pilate in powerful but particularly misguided religious symbolism as he sought to rouse his followers.

All this can quickly fuel a perilous assumption on the street in the next several days: That the ends of preventing abortions, on the one hand, or protecting the right to them, on the other, justify any means, including lawlessness and violence.

Abortions are legal. American women have a right to privacy and to choose, within an appropriate legal framework defined by the courts, to end a pregnancy. Women using Buffalo-area clinics, many of them very young and very frightened, must be allowed to exercise that constitutional right.

They must not be overlooked in this confrontation, and it is the duty of the law-enforcement community to see to it that their personal rights are protected. They must keep the clinics open despite the intentions of anti-abortion forces to try to blockade them.

But the responsibility for enforcing the court orders and the laws does belong to the police. It does not belong to private individuals or some vigilante kind of sidewalk faction.

This a difficult time for our community. But our free society permits people to make their arguments peacefully and within the law.

After the regrettable Schenck incident, a minimum level of civility needs to be restored. It is a perishable civic commodity. And it's one especially desirable here now.

Buffalo, New York, April 23, 1992

BUFFALO is suddenly the center of national attention, and it's not a comfortable spot to be in. The region that had hoped to make a national splash in a positive way, as host of the 1993 World University Games, is finding it is getting publicity effortlessly and much sooner in a way it would never have asked for.

As abortion demonstrators from around the country choose our city to show off their most polarized views and confrontational tactics, Buffalonians might well feel — as Wichita residents did last summer when it was their turn with Operation Rescue — that they are being used.

The TV networks and the national news organizations are here. The organizers are getting what they wanted — their faces and voices and opinions splashed around the nation. But what does Buffalo get?

What's appearing on TV has nothing to do with the real life of our city. It is bringing Buffalo disruption, confusion and expense. At times it doesn't even seem to have much to do with abortion. It is a stage presentation, in which some organizers clearly relish making themselves the stars, that could have been played out anywhere.

It is easy to understand the tactic of the anti-abortion demonstrators who chose our city for their moment of glory. Targeting one confined area at a time is the most effective way to push what is essentially a minority point of view. It's a way to make a splash with small numbers.

Now it is clear that an equally militant faction from the fringe of the other side of the conflict — a group that believes in confrontation bordering on violence to push its own views — has been attracted to Buffalo for its own purposes as well.

Many Western New Yorkers with strong pro-life or pro-choice convictions are horrified to see the distortions that glory-seeking extremists can bring to what should be a civil discussion of an issue.

The ugliness of some of the shouting and shoving matches, the obscene gestures, the spitting, the shoving of preserved fetuses in people's faces, the lecturing and hectoring, the grandstanding are not pleasant to watch. And those who engage in them, on either side, do nothing to add to the credibility of their cause.

Mayor Griffin, whose own house was targeted for one reprehensible tactic — residential picketing — made an ill-considered move when he suggested several months ago that he'd like to see Operation Rescue's national organization come to town. That invitation alone might not have been enough to bring the current spectacle down on us. But it certainly didn't help.

It was also, we believe, entirely misleading. Mayor Griffin may welcome Operation Rescue. But that's his opinion. Thousands of his neighbors, watching the blockades, slugfests and waste of police time and funding, fervently wish that the bullying histrionics would end and the opportunistic out-of-towners who care nothing about our city and its welfare would pack their bags and go home.

The Atlanta Journal
AND
THE ATLANTA CONSTITUTION
Atlanta, Georgia, April 30, 1992

When Operation Rescue moved its traveling circus to Buffalo, N.Y., the city was not amused. More than 400 anti-abortion activists had to be arrested to maintain the peace, consuming police and court time as well as jail space, before organizers called a halt.

In the siege of Buffalo, like that imposed on Wichita, Kan. last summer, Operation Rescue activists tried to use physical force to stop people from entering legal abortion clinics. But Buffalo marked the first time that pro-choice activists organized in roughly equal numbers to confront Operation Rescue protesters and keep the clinics open.

Pro-choice groups realized that government cannot defend civil liberties unless it has support and assistance from the public. That realization mirrors a similar change in the larger debate over abortion.

In the past, the debate has been more monologue than discussion, with anti-abortion groups waging a one-sided battle to overturn a woman's right to choose. Pro-choice voters felt confident that government would protect their interests, and so stayed out of the fray.

No longer. Just as hundreds of pro-choice activists volunteered to protect clinics in Buffalo, millions of those who support a woman's right to choose are coming to understand that unless they are prepared to use their vote, they will concede the debate, and the battle, to the anti-abortion crowd.

Part of the credit for that transformation may belong, ironically, to Operation Rescue. Anti-abortion activists have seen Operation Rescue as a way to demonstrate the depth of their conviction, and it's done that.

But it has demonstrated something else: a dangerously anti-democratic attitude that stirs up deep suspicions among many Americans.

The Operation Rescue folks act out of absolute conviction in their moral superiority. They see themselves as good pitted against evil, the forces of God against those of Satan.

As one Operation Rescue leader put it, dismissing a court order for his arrest on grounds of violating a judge's injunction:

"I have an injunction from God to rescue children from death."

That kind of talk has been heard throughout history. And typically, those who believe they are acting on God's orders recognize no legitimate obstacle to getting their way.

Yet democracy, if it is to work, requires citizens to accept the possibility that they might be wrong. Americans know that, if only intuitively. And they share an instinctive distrust of groups that fail to demonstrate the necessary respect for the opinions of others.

Operation Rescue has proved itself such a group.

The Virginian-Pilot

Norfolk, Virginia, April 22, 1992

How much does the confrontation staged in Buffalo between anti-abortionist and pro-choice forces reflect national sentiment? Not much.

How helpful is such confrontation in resolving the reservations most Americans have about abortion? Not helpful at all.

So if militant feminists make good their threat to "militarily defeat" the demonstrators of Operation Rescue, they will harm more than help their cause precisely as anti-abortion extremists hurt theirs.

The shrill, in-your-face tactics that Operation Rescue prefers to characterize as prayerful guidance are maddening. But the resort to similar tactics by pro-choice forces won't change the minds of anti-abortionists. It will instead alienate the thoughtful citizens who realize that criminalizing abortion is no way to lessen the need for it, who must be mobilized against the antis' effort to reverse abortion rights by adjudication and legislation if they can, by intimidation if they cannot. The fight to retain abortion rights must be for the support of the vast and vastly more tolerant middle, who are unhappy with abortion as birth control — but unhappier with self-appointed, self-righteous strangers claiming authority to decide what any and every pregnant woman may or may not do.

Several pro-choice groups in Buffalo have the better idea: They have spent past weeks planning how to help clinic staffers and clients maneuver through Operation Rescue's physical and psychological obstacle course.

This week's confrontation with the potential to throw far greater obstacles between women and abortion takes place today between lawyers at the Supreme Court of the United States. The Pennsylvania attorney general, joined at President Bush's behest by the U.S. solicitor general, will argue to preserve his state's restrictive abortion law; to preserve it, that is, at the expense of *Roe vs. Wade*, the landmark 1973 ruling that established a constitutional right to abortion. His opponent will argue to preserve *Roe* and, by the oddsmakers, lose.

Do not bet the tax refund on that. And do not bet that even such a loss in the high court leaves anti-abortionists triumphant. A ruling by this conservative court that states *may* restrict an abortion right the federal Constitution does not guarantee is not a ruling that says states *must*. To ensure that states *do not*, pro-choice groups must drum up those pro-choice votes that drum out — from Congress, state legislatures, candidate forums and national convention halls — the lawmakers who disagree.

THE ☁ SUN

Baltimore, Maryland, April 21, 1992

With the drums of combat in Buffalo between abortion opponents and supporters sounding ominously in the background, the Supreme Court tomorrow will take up a case that offers it the opportunity to overturn *Roe vs. Wade*, the landmark 1973 abortion rights decision.

Six years ago this spring, the court overturned a somewhat similar Pennsylvania law. In so doing, Justice Harry Blackmun reaffirmed what he had written in *Roe*. A woman's right to an abortion is fundamental and constitutional, involving individual liberty, and no state may regulate that except for a compelling state interest.

Only last week a federal appeals court in San Francisco, stating that *Roe*'s principle is still the law of the land, overruled a Guam anti-abortion law. But does *Roe* prevail? The new Pennsylvania law is back before the Supreme Court because an appeals court in Philadelphia ruled last year that while the Supreme Court has not expressly said so, its tinkering with *Roe* has in effect undone it: Women now have only the right to object to laws that place an undue burden on their decision regarding abortion. The state's goal must be "reasonable," but not "compelling."

That's quite a difference. So much so, in fact, that many pro-choice leaders say they would like to see the court go ahead and overturn *Roe* explicitly, rather than just deal narrowly with counseling, spousal notification, parental consent and the other elements of the Pennsylvania law. The present court might go to the extreme of flatly overturning *Roe*. It has been asked to by the Bush administration. In upholding *Roe* in the earlier Pennsylvania case, Justice Blackmun spoke for a bare majority of five justices. Three of those are now retired, replaced by one Ronald Reagan and two George Bush appointees. *Roe vs. Wade*, which was decided on a 7-2 vote, could very well be overturned on a 7-2 vote, only 19 years later. There may be a precedent for such judicial volatility, but we can't think of one that directly involves so many individuals and so much political passion.

Perhaps this won't happen. Perhaps even justices who are troubled with *Roe* will, when the moment of truth comes, have second thoughts. We hope so. As we contemplate the events in Buffalo, and recall those like it in Wichita last year that got so ugly, and as we anticipate the referendum fight in Maryland over this state's new abortion laws (more or less codifying *Roe*, in anticipation of its fall), and as we see the sort of harsh and unhealthy laws like Guam's, Louisiana's and Utah's (criminalizing almost all abortions) — as we add all this up, we are reminded anew just how wise *Roe vs. Wade* was in striking a humane balance between a woman's rights, society's rights and the rights of the unborn. If and when *Roe* goes, no one can predict the political turmoil and individual grief that will be the direct result.

The Evening Gazette

Worcester, Massachusetts, April 23, 1992

During last summer's abortion fight in Wichita, it hardly seemed the confrontation could be any nastier or more irrational. However, the current siege in Buffalo, invited by Mayor James Griffin, could make Wichita pale by comparison.

The confrontational mood was set by the sign — darkly paraphrasing the line from "The Wizard of Oz" — that greeted arriving anti-abortion demonstrators: "You're not in Kansas anymore."

Unfortunately, some pro-choice activists seem determined to meet Operation Rescue's tactics of unlawful obstruction, trespass and intimidation with similar tactics of their own.

The folly of that strategy became clear after members of the National Women's Rights Organizing Coalition roughed up an anti-abortion minister. The incident succeeded only in undermining the pro-choice cause.

It should go without saying that violent tactics on either side are indefensible.

For the pro-choice side it is also politically ill-advised. A recent poll in Buffalo indicated that Operation Rescue's lawbreaking is a major factor in residents' objection to the group. Only 7 percent welcome Operation Rescue, but 50 percent say they'd welcome the organization if its members obeyed the law.

Moreover, pro-choice advocates have no need of the illegal tactics. The law and public sentiment clearly favor women's right to choice. The strategy of pro-choice activists must be to defend that right peacefully and legally — not to create martyrs for the other side.

ST. LOUIS POST-DISPATCH
St. Louis, Missouri, April 28, 1992

If the fanatics of Operation Rescue cared about babies or women, they wouldn't block the entrances to abortion clinics or terrorize the people who work in them. They would be doing something productive, such as trying to stop the need for abortion. But zealots have little patience with the hard work of improving the lot of children and women. They would rather parade around in front of clinics and harass women, doctors and nurses while they pretend they are stopping abortion.

Indeed, in the 19 years since *Roe vs. Wade*, anti-abortion groups haven't contributed a whit to making it easier for women to get cheap and effective contraceptives to help avoid pregnancy; they can't claim credit for pushing social reforms that help women to balance family and work, such as family leave policies or affordable day care; they haven't organized against the discrimination that keeps women earning 64 cents for every dollar men earn.

Scores of studies document the deplorable conditions of life for too many American kids, yet the anti-abortion activists, content to keep their blinders on, consider the real-life quality of life for children and their mothers a distraction from the "real" issue. It's precisely by ignoring the complexities of life that people in Operation Rescue, for example, can self-righteously demonize those who are pro-choice as "murderers," for all the good that that does.

The issue for them is not life; it's abortion — and the changing role of women and sexuality. Certainly, though, Operation Rescue, Lambs of Christ and like groups have every right to express their opposition to abortion in peaceful and legal ways. They do not, though, enjoy the right to harass people and to prevent women from exercising what is, at least for the moment, a constitutionally protected right.

Newsday
New York City, New York, April 21, 1992

Having invited, even entreated, trouble to come to his city, Buffalo Mayor James Griffin could qualify for any number of ad hominem designations -- fool being the least of them. However, preserving public safety — not Griffin's imprudence — is the issue of the moment, and the mayor of Buffalo isn't the only elected official in the State of New York charged with that responsibility.

To his credit, Attorney General Robert Abrams recognized his duty long before the abortion activists, pro and con, began their current dangerous round of confrontations in front of Buffalo's abortion clinics. Early last month, Abrams filed a suit in U.S. District Court seeking an order that would bar any blockade of clinics or harassment of patients or staff. What's more he asked for significant penalties — fines beginning as high as $10,000 and doubling every day. Considering what happened last year in Wichita, Kan., the attorney general's proactive response is appropriate, timely and prudent.

His suit was filed against Operation Rescue, the national anti-abortion organization, which created havoc last year in Wichita. During the group's effort to block access to clinics there, police and federal marshals made more than 2,700 arrests.

The court order, backed by federal marshals, can't come quickly enough because the situation is even more explosive in Buffalo, where a strong contingent of abortion-rights advocates vows to do whatever is necessary to keep the clinics open. Emotions are running so high that Buffalo police have obtained permission from the governor to use a downtown armory as a detention center.

Pending the arrival of federal marshals, Gov. Mario Cuomo must stand ready to do more than open an armory. He should put the New York National Guard on alert status. Although the two sides have pledged themselves to nonviolence, anything can happen. The issue just now is not abortion. It's public safety. It must be preserved.

AKRON BEACON JOURNAL
Akron, Ohio, April 26, 1992

The national debate over abortion heated up again last week, in shouting and shoving in the streets of Buffalo and in legal arguments before the U.S. Supreme Court. The latter forum is where this issue that has so long divided so many is most likely to be decided again in any substantive way.

We continue to believe strongly that the question of whether or not to have an abortion is a matter of personal conscience best left to a woman and her doctor. Those who take an opposing view have every right to their beliefs and every right to use the American political process to try, if they wish, to impose their views on others.

In a nation committed to individual liberty and privacy, it has long been our belief that the question of abortion is a matter of individual decision and privacy, and that that is where the issue should be left by governments, legislatures and courts.

The anti-abortion demonstrators in Buffalo are, clearly, people of conviction. But as the leaders of this particular group, Operation Rescue, have shown in the past, they are willing to break the law to deprive others of their legal rights. In Buffalo, that has sparked counteractions by some who defend abortion rights. The situation has been nasty, but kept under control by police. Women have not been physically denied access to clinics where abortions are performed.

In deciding the legality of new anti-abortion laws passed in Pennsylvania, the Supreme Court, shaped over almost 12 years by Ronald Reagan and George Bush, could well reverse or at least seriously alter the court's earlier *Roe vs. Wade* decision that gave all American women the right to privacy and individual decision-making over abortion.

We believe the court would best serve the country and the rights of women if it did not tamper further with *Roe vs. Wade*. Given the ideology of the Reagan-Bush court, that may not happen.

If the court overturns *Roe vs. Wade*, abortion as a right will not automatically disappear across the country. The issue will surely then be fought out in the legislature of each state. That is why, on this issue, the choices made by voters in filling state legislative offices in this election year will be important.

In those states where abortion is outlawed, abortions will not end. They will simply move once again into medicine's back alleys, and women will be at medical risk dealing with unskilled practitioners and unsanitary conditions and those willing to break the law for profit. Those who want or need abortions should not be subjected to coat-hanger quackery.

In the meantime, it is still instructive to note that every known poll taken of American attitudes on this question of abortion shows that a majority of Americans supports the basic right of choice for women. It is a private decision by a woman about her own body that should not be prohibited by lawbreakers in the streets or legislators unwilling to permit women their basic rights.

Herald ☰ News
Fall River, Massachusetts, April 23, 1992

The circus has begun anew.

Just as Wichita was brought under seige last summer by Operation Rescue forces backed by the Bush Administration, Buffalo, N.Y., has become the arena for still more senseless posturing and needless antics.

Yesterday, police arrested at least 150 anti-abortionists at a women's clinic in Amherst, N.Y. The arrests occurred on the second day of large-scale abortion demonstrations in the Buffalo area by Operation Rescue.

No reasonable person would deny those on either side of the abortion issue the right to express their views. But you have to wonder just what the protestors in the Buffalo suburbs were attempting to communicate.

If it was that they could collectively act as irrationally and childishly as a 2-year-old staging a full-blast temper tantrum, then perhaps they accomplished their objective. (Indeed, the habit of protestors to go limp and await the tug to the paddy wagon is reminiscent of a toddler's misbehavior.) But if they were striving to sway public opinion in their favor or stop abortions at clinics, they failed miserably.

There may be people out there who have yet to make up their minds about abortion and it's possible that the arguments of either faction could influence them. But it's hard to believe that making a spectacle of oneself is an aptly persuasive maneuver, unless it's to dissuade. Wouldn't it be far more effective for abortion opponents to offer thoughtful, measured explanations of their beliefs?

Despite their ill-conceived strategy, abortion foes were not successful in stopping any abortions, either. The office manager for the Amherst clinic said demonstrators had not stopped any women from getting into the clinic for abortions.

It seems the only thing in which demonstrators were successful was costing taxpayers a chunk of money in overtime pay for police who had to deal with the petulant ranks.

No doubt, the circus is fine entertainment. But it's of little value otherwise. Theatrics have no place in the very real drama surrounding the abortion issue in this country. If demonstrators on either side wish to make lasting impressions or real change, they must take their arguments out of the center ring and into the realm of reason.

Rockford Register Star
Rockford, Illinois, April 21, 1992

The targeting of Buffalo, N.Y., for massive anti-abortion protests by Operation Rescue beginning this week raises a question that ought to trouble even the staunchest of pro-life forces: Will this campaign be politically counter-productive?

Aside from the moral aspects, abortion is a political issue. Even if the U.S. Supreme Court overturns the *Roe vs. Wade* ruling, the continued legality of abortion will be a matter of politics at state and local levels. Hence, we would think that anti-abortion forces would want to avoid losing political ground.

The anti-abortion movement suffers from some of its own tactics.

Last summer, Operation Rescue hit Wichita, Kan., with waves of civil disobedience resulting in thousands of arrests. The net effect was a loss of sympathy with the anti-abortion movement among Americans in general and Kansans in particular. The current scene in Buffalo suggests that Operation Rescue learned nothing from its Wichita experiences.

The right to protest is sacred in this country. There is even a moral right to engage in non-violent civil disobedience. But when such tactics only narrow your political base, how wise is it to persist in them?

What happens in Buffalo in the coming days probably won't prevent a single abortion. And it likely will give a political boost to pro-choice forces. Thus, we can only conclude that with friends like Operation Rescue, the anti-abortion movement doesn't need enemies.

Pro-Choice Rallies Target Supreme Court

Several hundred thousand people marched in Washington, D.C. April 9, 1989 to demonstrate their support for "safe and legal" abortion and to urge the Supreme Court not to overturn the 1973 *Roe v. Wade* decision that had recognized a woman's right to an abortion. The court had recently accepted a Missouri case that observers said could pave the way for a reversal of *Roe v. Wade* or for tighter restrictions on abortions.

The rally, which had been sponsored by the National Organization for Women (NOW), was one of the largest political demonstrations ever held in the capital. The official crowd estimate was 300,000, but organizers insisted that the march had drawn more than 600,000 people. In contrast, an annual anti-abortion rally held in January had attracted 65,000 demonstrators.

NOW President Molly Yard, in a pre-march press conference April 8, said that the gathering was intended as "a statement to the political leadership of this country – to President Bush, the Congress of the United States and the Supreme Court – that the women of this country will not go back."

THE ROANOKE TIMES
Roanoke, Virginia, April 11, 1989

THE SUPREME Court is supposed to read the Constitution, not public-opinion polls. It is supposed to listen to legal arguments, not to the voice of the crowd. So, ideally, the presence of 300,000 people, more or less, marching in support of *Roe vs. Wade* should not influence the court's decision on whether to overturn the 1973 decision that staked out for women the right to control of their bodies, even when another life was involved.

That decision should be based on an objective answer to the question: Does the United States Constitution imply a right to the privacy of one's body — a right that transcends the right to life for a developing fetus that may or may not be a human being, depending upon how you define humanity?

The issue before the court is not moral or philosophical. It is not a question of whether abortions violate the Ten Commandments, the Christian writings or the Judeo-Christian moral code. It is a question of whether state bans on abortions violate the Constitution.

The question is hard to answer. Whenever something is *implied*, it is, by nature, ambiguous. It's hard enough sometimes to agree on what an *explicit* provision means. When the provision is *implicit*, it means that the arguments must be prosecuted on shifting terrain.

"The Constitution," said Charles Evans Hughes, "is what the judges say it is." And what the judges say and believe will vary with the times and with public attitudes. The Constitution, for instance, forbids "unreasonable search and seizure." When does it become "unreasonable" for the state to require an individual to produce and surrender to its custody a vial of urine to be analyzed for illegal drug content? It depends upon your definition of "reasonable," and that definition will vary from mind to mind.

So the legal questions regarding *Roe vs. Wade* have no "right" or "wrong"

answers. They depend upon the perspectives of the justices who must resolve the questions. And those perspectives derive from the moral and social environments in which the justices have lived their lives. It is fair to say that, eventually, constitutional interpretation comes around to the consensus view, or else the Constitution is altered by amendment.

So the outpouring of sentiment in Washington has long-range significance, whatever its effect on the immediate outcome of the case before the court. It helps to confirm what opinion polls seem to show: that most Americans, regardless of their personal views on abortion, believe a woman should be able to decide for herself whether to carry a fetus to full term.

Justices don't need to check public opinion to decide how they'll rule. They don't have to worry about re-election or reappointment.

But the politicians who appoint the justices will take note. American voters have twice in a row elected presidents who have endorsed the "right-to-life" principle. If their stances are at odds with the views of most Americans, there's a reason. The "right-to-life" voter is more likely to base his choice on a single issue — abortion.

The depth of commitment shown by the marchers in Washington suggests that pro-choice advocates might also become single-issue voters should they perceive that the right to an abortion is in jeopardy. It takes a long time to change the complexion of a Supreme Court, but in the end, the court does follow election results.

If the Supreme Court does overturn *Roe vs. Wade*, the pro-life forces should not consider the victory won. For in the long run, the law is likely to reflect the convictions of the majority of Americans. What happens in the courtroom this month will be a major battle. But the war will be won in the heart and mind of the American public.

St. Petersburg Times
St. Petersburg, Florida, April 11, 1989

WASHINGTON — The celebrities may have been in the front line, festooned in yellow sashes that proclaimed them "honored guests," but the real story in Sunday's March for Women's Equality/Women's Lives is the ordinary people who demonstrated calmly in the spring chill for what they believe.

What they believe is that a woman's decision whether to have an abortion should be her own. The real story is that so many women, men and children traveled to the nation's capital to express that belief to the Supreme Court, President Bush, the Congress and state lawmakers.

Regardless of whose crowd estimate is accurate — federal authorities say 300,000, the organizers say twice as many — the march was one of the largest ever in Washington, certainly the country's largest ever in support of women's rights.

As people squeezed into state delegations on the Ellipse north of the Washington Monument before the march began, their deep commitment was as palpable as the dampness on the grass underfoot. A sweat shirt declared one woman's purpose: "I am here for granddaughter Jennifer, daughter Dr. Marshall and all the women I love."

The colossal grassroots response of Sunday's march is an overwhelming sign of how much Americans do care about the pro-choice position. "We will not go back," a common message of rally banners and chants, referred to the time before 1973, when the Supreme Court ruled in *Roe vs. Wade* that a safe and legal abortion was a woman's right.

That right is back in the hands of the court as it prepares to hear a Missouri abortion case later this month that could result in a reversal of *Roe*. Of course, the court is not supposed to be swayed by political sentiment, but to the extent it already may have been influenced by the extremism of those who wish to take away a woman's right to choose, the powerful, non-violent statement made by the marchers on Sunday may help draw the court back to the neutral ground from which it should function.

The marchers' determination should be plain even to President Bush, who earlier this year welcomed a much smaller contingent of anti-abortion demonstrators to Washington. Even if Bush didn't look out his White House window Sunday, he would have had to feel the presence. State politicians had to feel it, too. If the court's next move on abortion rights is to rescind or even limit them, the fight will not be over.

Sunday in Washington, those ordinary people with extraordinary convictions made that fact perfectly clear, and did so in a rational manner that contrasted strikingly with the arson that leveled a women's health clinic in Ocala the same day.

Failing to recognize the significance of Sunday's march, the conviction expressed by the hearts and footsteps of the hundreds of thousands gathered in Washington, would seem humanly impossible.

The Courier-Journal
Louisville, Kentucky, April 11, 1989

THE DIVISIVE debate over abortion took another dramatic turn Sunday when 300,000 or more people marched on the nation's Capitol demanding preservation of the 1973 Supreme Court decision legalizing abortion. It was an impressive display of support for a precious liberty — a woman's right to personal privacy.

The need for many to demonstrate their support for *Roe v. Wade* was made critical by the clout and visibility of such anti-abortion groups as the National Right to Life Committee, whose formation was stimulated by the decision now under attack. The strength of Right to Life, which has 2,500 local chapters, is estimated at 7 million.

Abortion foes have financed political action committees that toppled many politicians' candidacies, and they have engaged in high-pressure lobbying campaigns.

ILLUSTRATION BY ELEANOR MILL

Nothing wrong with that — both tactics are an established part of the American political scene. But some anti-abortion zealots have overstepped the law — and shamefully disregarded all boundaries of human decency — by harassing individual women seeking legal abortions, by burning abortion clinics and by issuing bomb threats.

It is ironic that abortion clinics have become the lightning-rod for anti-abortion sentiment. After all, one of the most profound occurrences since *Roe* legalized abortion in the early stages of pregnancy has been the development of relatively uniform public health standards, making it possible for medical personnel to provide safer abortions.

Foes of *Roe v. Wade* have jabbed at the decision over the years, sometimes successfully, and now their hopes for a reversal rest on the constitutionality of a 1986 Missouri law. It limits a woman's access to abortion and is, quite possibly, the most restrictive legislation now on the books. Depending upon whether the justices rule narrowly or broadly, the case could be used to limit or reverse *Roe*.

Members of the high court will hear the Missouri case April 26. In anticipation of that event, marchers gathered in Washington to show the justices that the anti-abortion groups do not speak for everyone. Far from it.

The marchers, including many from Kentucky and Indiana, powerfully bore witness to the hopes of millions. Like those they represent, they are relying on the court to honor its precedents and to sustain a woman's right to choose the course that she and her doctor conclude is best for her.

THE INDIANAPOLIS STAR
Indianapolis, Indiana, April 16, 1989

The clash between pro- and anti-abortionists has long been a struggle between conflicting outrages, and instead of losing its fervor, it gets meaner as time goes on.

An estimated 300,000 pro-choice demonstrators marched in Washington last Sunday to oppose efforts to overturn the Supreme Court's 1973 decision legalizing abortion.

"This is the first step of an outpouring of outrage against President Bush — how dare he overturn our rights?" shouted Molly Yard, head of the National Organization for Women.

In Florida, on the eve of the protest, arsonists torched abortion clinics at Fort Myers and Ocala. It is easy to jump to the conclusion that the arsonists were anti-abortionists. But what if they were pro-abortionists out to befoul their enemies' cause?

Legitimate concern for the unborn does not totally invalidate the argument that if abortions are made illegal, as they were in many states before *Roe vs. Wade*, many women will try to perform abortions upon themselves or have them performed by unskilled, unsanitary "back alley" practitioners.

Yet no one can truthfully deny that an abortion is the deliberate taking of human life. There is tremendous moral force to the anti-abortionists' assertion that innocent, unborn children have a right to life and that this right is entitled to defense.

Anyone is on marshy ground who maintains law should waive this right for convenience's sake. And it is arguable that by terminating a pregnancy, a woman is making a choice that involves only her own body.

The conflict between the two sides is not likely to end in this century. The Supreme Court's pro-abortion decision did not end it. A Supreme Court decision returning authority to the states would not end it.

One side finds it an outrage that abortion should be denied. The other finds it an outrage that abortions have taken more than 22 million lives of the unborn since abortion was legalized nationally.

A solution satisfactory to both sides seems impossible. Yet reasonable men and women should not give up on the task of striving for a meeting of the minds and an alternative to the current endless confrontations of outrage.

The Charlotte Observer
Charlotte, North Carolina, April 13, 1989

Sarah Weddington, the Texas attorney who argued and won the 1973 Supreme Court case that legalized abortions, will speak at the Great Hall of Myers Part Baptist Church at 8 p.m. today. Admission is free; the public is invited.

Dr. Weddington also served as a Texas state representative, as general counsel for the U.S. Department of Agriculture and as an assistant to President Jimmy Carter. She will speak on the future of legal abortions.

With the U.S. Supreme Court considering a Missouri case that could overturn Roe vs. Wade, the debate over abortions is more heated now than ever. Opponents of abortion include a wide range of people, from conservative religious fundamentalists to leftist pacifists, both of whom view abortion as murder. Proponents are equally diverse, from those who simply view abortion as a woman's right to control her own body to those who view it as part of a wide range of social concerns, including care for unwanted children, safe and effective birth control, better health care for pregnant women and better child care.

Dr. Weddington's lecture and the discussion to follow will not settle the abortion debate. But it should provide an excellent opportunity to hear the issues aired by someone who entered the legal debate on the ground floor.

The Philadelphia Inquirer
Philadelphia, Pennsylvania, April 9, 1989

The legal world will little note nor long remember what Ernie Preate contributed to the upcoming Supreme Court case on abortion. The attorney general of Pennsylvania merely signed another state's argument that basic abortion policy should be set by each state. Mr. Preate calls the step consistent with his official duty to defend a contested 1988 Pennsylvania law that somewhat limits abortion. It's consistent all right, but it also seems gratuitous.

Admittedly, Mr. Preate has long expressed his opposition to abortion rights. But in his current position, he serves as the lead lawyer not only for the state's government, but for all of its nearly 12 million people — who are deeply divided on this emotional issue. The millions of Pennsylvanians who support the current right to abortion can reasonably suspect that, were it not for Mr. Preate's personal opposition to abortion, he might well have kept the commonwealth on the sidelines.

The case itself involves a Missouri law, which is the latest challenge to the Supreme Court's 1973 ruling in Roe v. Wade that legalized abortion nationwide based on a woman's constitutional right to privacy. On this point, the words of Justice Harry A. Blackmun still resonate: "Few decisions are more personal and intimate, more properly private, or more basic to individual dignity and autonomy than a woman's decision ... whether or not to end her pregnancy."

The Supreme Court's 7-2 decision was controversial from the start, not only because of the deep divisions over abortion itself, but because of the court's highly creative interpretation of the Constitution. But whatever one thinks of the court's reasoning in 1973, there is a well-established legal doctrine that inclines the court to abide by its past decisions.

That doesn't mean that every word of Roe v. Wade should be inviolate. Instead of throwing the issue back to the 50 states, the high court might reasonably find that medical advances dictate changing the way in which rights and responsibilities vary in each of a pregnancy's three-month segments, or "trimesters."

Roe v. Wade held that, starting with the third trimester, the child's right to be born is paramount over the mother's right to choose. But because medical science now sometimes can save the lives of babies born more than three months prematurely, the court could expand this right into part of the second trimester.

Granted, much of the abortion debate is about proper policy, rather than constitutional law. As a practical matter, handing this issue back to the states would create a patchwork whereby a few states retain abortion rights, some states keep abortion legal in cases of rape, incest or saving the pregnant woman's life, and some simply criminalize it. In Pennsylvania, where the old law defined abortion as a crime and subjected an abortionist to up to five years in prison, women would probably see this right ended or sharply curtailed. But they would still probably be able to get a legal abortion in Washington, D.C., or New York.

For desperate women with little money, illegal abortions would undoubtedly be available. After all, there were an estimated one million illegal abortions annually before 1973 — a number that gives some perspective to the "right-to-life" movement's outrage over the 1.5 million legal abortions performed in the U.S. each year. The wide availability of legal abortion undoubtedly encourages some people to play sexual roulette, but the soundest way to change that is through education and suasion, not by letting many states redefine abortion as a crime.

As a prelude to April 26, when the Supreme Court will begin to hear the Missouri case, there will be a huge "pro-choice" demonstration in Washington today and a smaller "pro-life" counter-demonstration. Neither side's clarion rhetoric is likely to acknowledge that most Americans have conflicted feelings that fall somewhere in between.

According to polls, the average American believes that in many circumstances abortion is a moral wrong that nonetheless ought to be left up to a woman in consultation with her doctor.

That's the way it is today in Pennsylvania. And that's how it should stay.

The Register-Guard
Eugene, Oregon, April 13, 1989

Ironies abound in the fight over government policy on abortion.

Some were reflected in Sunday's march in Washington, D.C., and concurrent rallies in Eugene and elsewhere. The turnout made the Washington march a huge success for its organizers. Yet, while the technique — a large public demonstration — was familiar, the message and its targeted recipients were not.

These were not radicals demanding change. They were conservatives in the classic sense, seeking to preserve and maintain what exists. Nor were their appeals aimed at the customary chief policy-makers — Congress and the president. Rather, the marchers were speaking primarily to the lady and eight gentlemen of the U.S. Supreme Court.

Why this massive display of support for the status quo? Because the status quo is threatened. The court may soon overturn or heavily encumber the right to abortion that it effectively created in deciding *Roe vs. Wade* 16 years ago.

Normally, a political/social change of this magnitude could result only from a great shift in public opinion. But in this instance, no such shift has occurred. The right of a woman to choose to have an abortion is favored by roughly two-thirds of the American people, according to opinion surveys. Support for the right has risen rather than declined since the Supreme Court's 1973 decision.

No, the threat in this case has been created simply by change in the composition of the court — change made by a president who strongly opposed abortion and factored that into his choices in filling three court vacancies during his time in office.

Ronald Reagan was out of step with the majority of Americans on this issue, yet he was elected twice with ease. His successor, George Bush, holds similar views on abortion. Those ironies may confuse the court if it tries, in Mr. Dooley's phrase, to "follow the iliction returns."

Four members of the present court are considered safe votes in support of *Roe vs. Wade*. Three favor overturning that decision or greatly modifying it. The preferences of two justices, Sandra Day O'Connor and Anthony Kennedy, are in doubt. They could produce a majority to undo the 1973 decision.

A vehicle presenting that opportunity is on the court's current docket, *Webster vs. Reproductive Health Services*. Arguments will be heard this month, with a decision possible by July.

The case concerns a Missouri law which declares that life "begins at conception." The law tightly restricts access to abortion. A federal circuit court of appeals declared it unconstitutional. But in agreeing to hear this case, the Supreme Court agreed to a Justice Department request to consider "whether *Roe vs. Wade* should be overruled."

Roe vs. Wade should not be overruled, or even noticeably disturbed. As the Washington marchers proclaimed, the status quo on this issue is fine. Elimination of constitutional protection for the right to have an abortion would return the question to each state legislature and produce a national patchwork of differing laws and regulations.

Women would still have abortions, as they did before 1973. But doing so would be safe, easy and legal only for those who lived in or could go to the states with liberal laws. The burdens of forced child-bearing or risks of health damage and criminal prosecution would fall, as before, on the poor.

The final irony is that the question of proper public abortion policy eventually will be resolved not in a court or a legislature but in the laboratory. Pills that induce abortion are already being manufactured and sold in France. It is generally expected that a safe pill of this type will be available everywhere before long.

Once that becomes a reality, the decision on abortion will truly rest where it morally belongs — with each woman who becomes pregnant, beyond the practical reach of interfering government.

THE ATLANTA CONSTITUTION
Atlanta, Georgia, April 11, 1989

It was the largest women's rights protest in history. It may have been the largest march in Washington for any purpose. Even police put the number of people marching for abortion rights Sunday, conservatively, at 300,000 — more than the seemingly endless throngs that heard the late Martin Luther King Jr. deliver his "I have a dream" speech, or that marched against the Vietnam War, in the 1960s.

Of course, the popularity of a cause isn't always a predictor of its success, much less a sure guide to its worth.

Still, this march, if nothing else, gave the lie to the myth that abortion protests would end with Betty Friedan's generation. The gray-haired author of "The Feminist Mystique" was joined by her 32-year-old daughter in a procession headed by the likes of Whoopi Goldberg and Morgan Fairchild and in which the average age seemed to be closer to 20 than 60. There were delegations from more than 450 colleges, many of whom had traveled all night; and entire young families marching together, many pushing baby carriages, in what many said was their first protest.

This was a source of great pride to Ms. Friedan, who had been unable to interest her own daughter in attending a women's rights event in almost 20 years, and surprised the opposition, which had doubted the organizers' ability to generate so much enthusiasm among the young for keeping abortions legal.

But it is the next generation that has the most at stake in a case under consideration by the Supreme Court, which has been asked to use a constitutional challenge to a Missouri law declaring that "life begins at conception" as a vehicle for overturning *Roe v. Wade*, the 1973 ruling that legalized abortions. It is the young who stand to lose control over their own bodies if they remain on the sidelines.

It was only a matter of time before that sunk in.

ST. LOUIS POST-DISPATCH
St. Louis, Missouri, April 6, 1989

A federal appeals court has upheld the part of Missouri's 1986 abortion law that requires a doctor performing abortions to have privileges at a hospital providing obstetrical and gynecological services. The reasoning behind the decision is sound; the state should have the right to regulate surgical procedures. In the case of abortion, the condition that the doctor performing it be able to admit patients to a hospital that can provide needed services in an emergency is not unreasonable or onerous.

As the majority opinion of the court noted, the law has not restricted Missouri women's access to abortion — even though it might have limited the practice of Dr. Bolivar Escobedo, the physician who challenged the requirement.

This provision is part of the same 1986 law that is now being challenged before the Supreme Court in the case of *Webster vs. Reproductive Health Services*. Among the contested provisions are the prohibition on abortions in public hospitals; the requirement that physicians test for fetal viability beyond the 19th week of pregnancy; and the declaration that the life of each human being begins at conception — a dubious premise but one that, if accepted, leads logically to granting the fetus "protectable rights," as the Missouri act does.

If the Supreme Court adheres to the criterion invoked in the appeals court's decision — that is, whether the law places unwarranted limits on women's access to abortion — it would have to conclude that the contested provisions of the 1986 law do indeed infringe on women's rights as affirmed in the earlier Supreme Court decision in *Roe vs. Wade*. One can only hope that the justices are guided by the same wisdom as the lower court.

BUFFALO EVENING NEWS
Buffalo, New York, April 11, 1989

ANTI-ABORTION demonstrators have made themselves felt and heard in recent months. But Washington felt and heard the other side of this national controversy when an estimated 300,000 marchers jammed the nation's capital with their pro-choice message.

This massive throng, one of the largest ever to march in Washington, offered a visible manifestation of what public opinion surveys have long indicated — that a large majority of Americans support the right of women to choose whether to have an abortion or not.

The constitutional right of women to make this choice in the early stages of pregnancy was asserted by the U.S. Supreme Court in its landmark Roe vs. Wade ruling in 1973.

That the controversy over the decision still rages attests to the profound depth of feeling and honest conviction on both sides of the issue, both then and now.

The message mobilized by the Washington marchers was directed at Congress and the Bush administration — and most especially at the Supreme Court. That is because the high court on April 26 is scheduled to hear arguments in a Missouri case that could, depending upon the court's decision, narrow or even overturn the rights granted in Roe vs. Wade.

The thrust of the marchers' message was simple: Preserve the right of women to decide freely for themselves, and without government interference, the intensely personal issue of whether to have an abortion. As a popular sign at the march asked: "Who decides? You or them?"

A significant distinction surfaces on this point. Surveys show that Americans do not necessarily equate support for a woman's right to choose an abortion with support for abortion itself. Many who support the right of women to choose also abhor abortions personally. It is the choice, not the abortion, that wins backing.

That assumes critical importance, it seems to us, and defines a distinction that the Supreme Court should not slight.

On a topic so disputed as this one — with society deeply divided at many different levels of emotion and thought, and in terms of religious belief, morality and philosophy — the 1973 court wisely limited how far the government could intrude into personal decisions, into the personal privacy of women faced by such an intimate, wrenching decision.

Significantly, Roe vs. Wade requires no woman to have an abortion. Nor, in early pregnancy, does it prohibit women from having one. Along with her physician, this is her decision to make. She is free to decide on her own, according to her personal convictions and circumstances, without government intrusion into that choice.

We have some concern about marchers seeking to pressure the Supreme Court to decide any issue before it one way or the other. But former President Reagan helped politicize the abortion issue with his efforts to nominate only anti-abortion judges, and as Chief Justice William H. Rehnquist has indicated, judges cannot remain wholly isolated from their own societies and times.

Similarly, a New York Times analysis noted that Paul A. Freund, a retired Harvard law professor and expert on constitutional law, said that judges "should not be influenced by the weather of the day, but they are necessarily influenced by the climate of the age." The Washington march is part of the climate of our times.

Whatever one's personal views on abortion, there is good reason for the Supreme Court to accept the core holding of Roe vs. Wade as a settled constitutional precedent.

THE ATLANTA CONSTITUTION
Atlanta, Georgia, April 19, 1989

The stage is set for a demonstration of the national mood on abortion. If it doesn't rain in Washington today, and if there is as much support for freedom of choice as organizers of the "March for Women's Equality, March for Women's Lives" contend, it should not be hard to top the anti-abortion rally in which 67,000 marched last January.

In fact, it has already been done. In 1986, the last time abortion-rights advocates marched on the Capitol, they drew 85,000. This time, they are expecting at least 100,000 from 478 organizations, 450 college campuses and the casts of some of the most popular prime-time TV shows to take part.

"When you take away a woman's right to her own body, she has nothing," according to a member of a Georgia contingent estimated at 2,000.

But if public opinion alone guided the administration and the Supreme Court on abortion, no rally would be necessary. The overwhelming majority of Americans, 81 percent, favored keeping abortions legal under some (57 percent) or all (24 percent) circumstances in an October 1988 Gallup poll, as they have in every major public opinion survey since 1973, when the Supreme Court made them legal.

Even when the question was asked in another way, in January 1989, most (58 percent) said they would be opposed to the reversal of *Roe v. Wade* and 5 percent said they had no opinion.

Pro-choice sentiment also runs deep within the ranks of the administration, which — officially, at least — opposes it. On Tuesday, petitions signed by more than 200 attorneys in the U.S. Justice Department were delivered to Attorney General Richard L. Thornburgh, criticizing their boss's "interference with this basic right." Mr. Thornburgh has urged the court to use its upcoming review of a highly restrictive Missouri law as a vehicle for overturning *Roe v. Wade*.

Since 1981, the White House has proved more responsive to the vocal minority, which has characterized itself as "pro-life" and abortion as murder. In fact, opposition to abortion became a standard for the selection of Supreme Court candidates by former President Reagan, who appointed three conservatives to the high court and named one as chief justice. President Bush also opposes abortion.

Thus, the stakes have not been higher, nor the possibility of a reversal likelier, in 16 years, as the center of action moves to the Supreme Court. It will hear oral arguments on the Missouri case, in which it has received an unprecedented 78 briefs — more evidence of the extraordinary interest in the issue — in 17 days.

Today's events are aimed not just at the justices but at what the organizers believe is a complacent majority that does not yet see a basic right as threatened; a force which, if aroused, could mount such a groundswell in the next two weeks that not even the court could ignore it.

As Faye Wattleton, president of the Planned Parenthood Federation of America, put it recently, "The court is not sequestered on another planet. They do hear the voices of the American people."

The New York Times
New York City, New York, April 9, 1989

On April 26, the State of Missouri will ask the Supreme Court to overturn Roe v. Wade, the historic 1973 ruling that left most decisions about abortion up to individual women and their doctors. Today, thousands who hope the Court reaffirms that right to decide will gather in Washington. Like the anti-abortionists who demonstrated in January, they seek to make an impression with their numbers, passion and witness.

The justices, who do not rule by referendum, are doubtless discomfited by the mass lobbyings. But they can put the controversy to rest by reaffirming the constitutionality of Roe v. Wade. There is strong reason for even those justices who would not have voted with the 1973 Court to let the precedent stand.

•

Neither the demonstrations nor the dozens of legal briefs now on file before the Court would have been necessary had the Reagan Administration not persuaded Missouri's lawyers to ask the Court to overturn the law. Until then, Missouri had merely wanted to argue that its law regulating abortions, struck down by lower Federal courts, was consistent with Roe v. Wade — a question that could have been decided without raising anew the validity of the 1973 decision.

If the present furor has any redeeming feature, it is the quality of the briefs filed by other interested parties. Some 885 law professors argue the soundness of the original ruling. It balances a woman's interest with a state's concern for the health of the fetus, a concern that deserves growing respect during pregnancy. Briefs filed by members of Congress argue against returning to pre-Roe turmoil in state legislatures. Women's rights groups argue that men and women alike share strong concerns for the autonomy of women.

In still another brief, a group of doctors disposes of a major complaint about Roe v. Wade: that it draws lines differentiating between early stages of pregnancy when a woman can choose abortion without restriction and later stages when she must begin to yield to the state's right to protect a fetus.

One important line was drawn at about 24 weeks — the point of "viability," when the fetus could survive outside the womb. Justice Sandra Day O'Connor and others argue that advances in medical science have made earlier viability possible and have exposed the intellectual weakness of a constitutional rule that seems vulnerable to technological change.

The scientists, however, insist that such advances simply haven't happened; the fetus is not becoming viable any earlier. What medicine has done, they say, is to increase the survivability of the fetus *after* viability. Viability thus remains a logical and natural place to identify the point at which the state begins to acquire a legitimate interest in fetal health.

Today's demonstrators do not proclaim abortion for abortion's sake; they proclaim choice and freedom. They hope to preserve a hard-won liberty. The Court's proper choice is fidelity to its own honorable precedent.

The Honolulu Advertiser
Honolulu, Hawaii, April 12, 1989

Sunday's massive march in support of women's right to abortion was a success beyond organizers' fondest hopes.

It confirms what opinion polls show again and again: While hardly anyone favors abortion as a birth control method of choice, the overwhelming majority believes there are times when women must have access to legal abortion, and the question of whether to terminate a pregnancy in the early stages should be made by the woman.

So the huge march (backed by smaller demonstrations like the one at the State Capitol last week) sends an important message to all those who have to wrestle with this hard-to-compromise controversy.

The Supreme Court is supposed to be isolated from politics and public opinion, but Congress and state legislatures are not.

The march makes it clear that overturning Roe vs. Wade after abortion has been legally accessible for nearly a generation would create tremendous social strife as the issue is fought out across the country.

When the discord ended, the outcome would be a legal crazy quilt — with abortion illegal in one state and legal in the next, publicly funded in one and reserved for the wealthy with private doctors in another.

There would likely be women again dying from back-alley or self-administered abortions; doctors, nurses and perhaps needy women in jail; and many more children who are unloved and perhaps abused.

Clearly, the nation needs a uniform basic law on abortion and it should protect women's privacy and their right to control their lives.

Most people would also agree that the 1.6 million legal abortions a year in this country are too many. Half the women surveyed said they were not using birth control in the months before conception.

But the answer is not to make abortion illegal. It is to improve incentives for adoption (a small but useful part of the solution), upgrade contraceptive research to find safer, simpler techniques, and increase knowledge about and availability of better techniques of birth control.

The Philadelphia Inquirer
Philadelphia, Pennsylvania, April 11, 1989

As Americans marched down Constitution Avenue Sunday by the hundreds of thousands, they seemed to recast the debate over abortion. By the children at their side, by the coat hangers on signs (and on some people's heads), these supporters of the right to abortion sent a powerful message that they are no less "pro-life" than the minority of Americans who want to make abortion a crime.

In the 16 years since the Supreme Court ruled that abortion was a woman's constitutional right, opponents have skillfully marketed their viewpoint as a matter of fundamental morality, while defining legal abortion as an immoral convenience. The huge outpouring on Sunday put a human face on the argument for keeping government out of this deeply personal issue.

There was the retired Marine with a crewcut and a quavering voice, who told a Saturday-night crowd that his mother had been warned that having another child would endanger her health — and had died from an illegal abortion. And on Sunday, there was the placard with the jarring image of the human toll from illegal abortions. It showed the bloody, naked corpse of a woman in New York City who had died from trying to do her own abortion.

This is what the other side ignores while waving its gruesome pictures of fetuses. And it's what the future will look like if abortion is once again made a crime, and as before, hundreds of thousands of women turn to illegal abortions.

With signs and symbols, speeches and song, the marchers also rebutted the "right-to-life" side's pose as the true repository of religious faith, family values and basic American rights. Standing before the Capitol, Judy Collins expressed her support for free choice with a soaring rendition of "Amazing Grace."

Time and again, speakers at the Capitol shared the spotlight with their children and the ensuing words about why women shouldn't be forced to bear children seemed redundant. But speak they did, saying that such government coercion would create human suffering for infants and their mothers — and reinstitute a basic component of women's inequality in America.

Not long after the first marchers had reached the Capitol, Melissa Manchester stood in front of the growing crowd, near an American flag snapping in the wind, and sang "America the Beautiful." Before her was a mile-long panoply of marchers, many of them women wearing the white, purple and gold worn by the uppity suffragettes who 70 years ago had finally got Congress to approve a woman's right to vote.

It was a poignant way of claiming this cause for the political mainstream, of proclaiming that rights, once gained, should not be taken away.

THE SUN
Baltimore, Maryland, April 11, 1989

The march on Washington in support of the right of women to have abortions was among the largest demonstrations seen in the national capital. Pro-choice marchers reclaimed the headlines from their adversaries, the right-to-life movement. In doing so, they symbolically reminded the nation that most Americans favor a woman's right to an abortion. Two recent national polls showed Americans support the Supreme Court decision legalizing abortions. (Harris: 56-42, January, 1989; Gallup: 58-37, December, 1988.)

Somehow this pro-choice sentiment has not been translated into political influence. Pro-choice and pro-life lobbyists agree that if the states could write laws regarding abortion, almost all would forbid or sharply restrict them. No more than five states (Maryland is not among them) are thought likely to keep pro-choice laws on the books if the 1973 pro-choice Supreme Court decision, *Roe vs. Wade*, is overturned or significantly weakened — as it might be.

The reason for the march Sunday was that the Supreme Court will hear an appeal this month in an abortion case that gives it a chance to change course. If the court shifts, strict anti-abortion laws might be written in most states. In some cases, the reaction would be immediate. Five or six states already have laws with a trigger — pulled when *Roe* is overturned. In two dozen states, including Maryland, unconstitutional restrictions on abortion remain on the books, presently unenforced, and might go into effect right away.

The Supreme Court is often said to be unimpressed by public opinion, but justices don't deny that they are affected by the times they live in. Numerous "friend of the court" briefs are often as much an expression of public opinion as they are of legal and constitutional thinking — and the justices recognize them as such. Justices are concerned about the consequences of their decisions, and they should be.

In our view, *Roe vs. Wade* was correct. There *is* a constitutional right to privacy which encompasses most abortions. It is also our belief that given developments over the past 16 years, overturning *Roe* would be a revolutionary act. It would surely provoke a counter-revolutionary response from pro-choice activists and voters. In the few states where the pro-choice forces would prevail, and in the many states where they would not, the politics would be bitter and devour other issues — not just in 1990, the election year in which both sides recently vowed to fight it out if the court invites them to — but for the rest of the century.

St. Petersburg Times
St. Petersburg, Florida, April 4, 1989

Two sides are trying to get their messages across about abortion, but you've probably noticed only one of them.

It's the side that's willing to descend upon women's health clinics by the hundreds, blocking the entrances and denying women access to medical care.

It's the side that's willing, usually in the name of religious morality, to set up displays of tiny caskets and doll parts and hand out pictures of aborted fetuses to women trying to get into the clinics for any reason.

It's the side that, on the extreme, has set fire to health facilities where abortions are performed.

This is the side you usually hear, fueled by the nationally organized Operation Rescue which staged massive clinic sit-ins in South Florida last weekend and in California the weekend before. These anti-abortion forces are energized by the U.S. Supreme Court's agreement to hear an appeal of a case that struck down a Missouri law restricting abortion. They are strengthened by the U.S. Justice Department's quest to use this case as a fulcrum for overturning *Roe vs. Wade*, the 1973 Supreme Court decision that legalized abortion. With such bully tactics and developments that are tantamount to the government sanctioning them, you can scarcely hear the other side.

Next weekend it will be the other side's turn.

Sunday, April 9, hundreds of thousands of people who believe in the ruling that guaranteed a woman's right to decide for herself about abortion and also her right to a safe and legal procedure, are expected to converge on Washington, D.C. for the March for Women's Equality/Women's Lives. Their message to the Supreme Court, President Bush, his administration and the Congress will be unmistakable: Americans will not stand for a reversal of those rights.

The nationwide show of support will be diverse and powerful, with potential to rival in number and impact the historic march for civil rights in 1963. Delegations are being organized from more than 450 colleges. Bus loads of high school students are expected. Mothers are taking their daughters; daughters are taking their mothers. Florida, and the Tampa Bay area, will be well-represented at this peaceful demonstration of women and men who believe that refusing a woman the right to make decisions concerning her own body is the same as enslaving her.

People who believe in choice have no penchant for firebombing buildings or flaunting outrageous handbills and posters. Their intent, in a calm, reasoned show of conviction, is strictly to fight what would be a devastating erosion of women's rights.

Which side's approach to this emotional, deeply personal issue more truly represents the sentiment of the American public? A national poll conducted by the *Los Angeles Times* shows that even among those who oppose abortion on moral grounds a majority (74 percent) believe that the decision must be a woman's choice. A majority (62 percent) also firmly oppose a constitutional amendment to outlaw abortion. By 50 percent to 34 percent, respondents are against returning to the pre-*Roe* system of allowing states to determine whether abortions are legal.

This prevailing mindset is also reflected in petitions signed by at least 50 lawyers within the Justice Department criticizing the administration's attempt to use the Missouri appeal as a pretext to overturn *Roe*. It is encouraging that these government employees are willing to resist their administration's high-pressure campaign to outlaw abortion.

There is solid support, even in the most unlikely places, for protecting this crucial decision, but it's hard to discern over the fanatic roar of the anti-abortion movement. Will that fanaticism end before a firebomb gets tossed into a clinic that is not empty?

The March for Women's Equality/Women's Lives will be a historic affirmation of the simple human right to privacy, a right that a woman should be allowed to exercise by the light of her own conscience and religious beliefs, free from governmental intrusion and the presumption of those who would impose their own morality upon her.

The march will be hard not to notice.

Omaha World-Herald

Omaha, Nebraska, April 12, 1989

The abortion rights demonstration in Washington Sunday put on display a warped, dangerous view of how public policy ought to be made in this country.

Even people who are sympathetic to the pro-choice cause could only have been horrified at the blatant attempt to intimidate government by sheer numbers.

There are forums for advancing a political cause. But sending traffic-stopping throngs into the streets is the least-effective way of winning people over to one's cause.

One of the abortion rights demonstration's organizers said that a goal of the demonstration was "to close Washington down." Another said afterward that "we took over the city."

How is "closing Washington down" or "taking over the city" any different from mobocracy — rule by the mob?

The focus of the demonstration was to persuade the U.S. Supreme Court to uphold its 1973 decision that established a woman's right to have an abortion.

Molly Yard, president of the National Organization for Women, discussing the decision to lobby officials in the legislative and executive branches of government as well, said: "Do you think the leadership in this body (Congress) doesn't talk to the Supreme Court? Sure they do. Do you think members of the Bush administration don't talk to the Supreme Court? Sure they do.

"Nobody in public office isn't affected by a huge outpouring."

Comments by others who participated made it equally clear that the idea was to get the Supreme Court's attention. Referring to the Supreme Court justices, actress Jane Fonda said: "They're human, they're political animals, and I think we can make a difference."

Sen. Robert Packwood, R-Ore., said: "You never know what may have an effect, but clearly the size of this march, we hope, has got to have some effect."

Never mind, apparently, the standard of judicial impartiality or the principle that America is a nation of laws, not of men.

Judges have a sacred obligation to decide the law based on facts. A judge couldn't be faithful to the principles he is sworn to uphold if he took his cues from street demonstrations.

To take to the streets in an attempt to influence the outcome runs the risk of alienating people who support the right of abortion. Indeed, those non-demonstrators who believe that women should have the option of legal abortion now have to hope that the cause wasn't hurt by the demonstration, with its talk of trying "to close Washington down."

No matter how well-disciplined a street demonstration might be, or how sincere its participants, the tactic lacks credibility. Admittedly, 300,000 people, including a contingent of Hollywood celebrities, showed up for the Washington event. But their opinions are no more important than the opinions of the 180 million American adults who stayed home that day.

The Wichita Eagle-Beacon

Wichita, Kansas, April 11, 1989

"OUR law's in jeopardy," said Norma McCorvey, the plaintiff in the landmark 1973 Supreme Court decision, Roe vs. Wade, that established a woman's right to abortion. More than 300,000 people converged Sunday on Washington, D.C., to show their support for keeping intact that decision, which may be reconsidered by the Supreme Court later this month. Should Roe vs. Wade be overturned or substantially altered, the question of abortion could become even more volatile than it is today.

If the 1973 decision is overturned in a case from Missouri, Webster vs. Reproductive Health Services, abortion rights would be fought again in the halls of every state legislature. The turmoil of the abortion debate would be a part of every legislative session in every state capital until the state-by-state rights of women to abortion services were either confirmed, sharply restricted or outlawed altogether. Indeed, it is doubtful that the issue ever would be put to rest, politically.

Such an endless fight over abortion would severely damage the ability of state governments to respond to the severe challenges facing them. As never before, state governments must make difficult fiscal and social policy decisions that have an immediate impact on their citizens. Moving the highly charged abortion debate to state government would take the issue out of the courts and put it into the political arena.

As the performance of the Kansas Legislature this session indicates, achieving consensus over politically divisive issues is difficult enough already. After the 90-day session's first adjournment, no definitive progress has been made on the state's response to prison overcrowding, highway maintenance and improvement, or funding for the state water plan.

Attaching abortion riders to every piece of legislation in coming sessions would put an unhealthy and unwelcomed political dynamic on every bill. Such actions — and they should be expected — in the wake of the court's overturning the Roe vs. Wade decision could virtually shut down the state legislative process. That's a possibility that the Supreme Court would do well to consider as it deliberates the Webster case.

The Star-Ledger

Newark, New Jersey, April 12, 1989

It was a scene vividly reminiscent of the activist civil rights movement. Several hundred thousand persons demonstrated, brought together by a deep concern that legal abortions face an uncertain fate in the latest challenge to a controversial court decision that continues to arouse strong passions.

There were veterans of various causes, but this was a widely representative assemblage that included many youthful newcomers who wanted to be involved with an issue that could have an adverse impact on their generation. They had come to the nation's capital to publicly appeal to the Supreme Court to keep abortions legal and safe.

Sixteen years after the historic Supreme Court decision that established the right to abortions, that right is imperiled once again. The court will hear arguments later this month in a Missouri test case that could significantly narrow or even overturn the ruling.

The challenge comes at a time when the pro-life movement has been staging vigorous protests against abortions—a stand that has been staunchly supported by the Reagan and Bush administrations. Concern has been heightened by the conservative cast of the Supreme Court, where swing votes of one or two justices take on crucial importance in the court's reassessment of the Roe vs. Wade ruling that recognized rights to abortion.

Historically, the Supreme Court is not swayed by public opinion, addressing legal issues in an impartial constitutional manner. But it would be naive to assume that in such volatile social issues as legal abortions the court operates in a cocoon—hermetically sealed off from swelling public expression that is forcefully evident in the sharply differing advocacies in this case.

Opinion polls have consistently shown that most Americans believe that abortions should remain available. This week, a Star Ledger/Eagleton Institute poll showed an overwhelming 80 percent of New Jersey respondents believed the decision to have an abortion is a private matter that a woman should decide without government intervention.

While abortions are the crucial point of difference between pro-lifers and activists who support these operations, the central issue is really one of personal choice—the right of a woman to decide whether or not she wants to abort a pregnancy.

That right was clearly affirmed in the landmark decision by the Supreme Court—a ruling that has lost none of its constitutional relevance in the intervening years. It should be a compelling factor to reaffirm the court's original ruling.

Newsday

New York City,
New York, April 11, 1989

For 16 years, opponents of women's right to choose abortion have filled the streets of Washington each Jan. 22, the anniversary of the Supreme Court's ruling in Roe vs. Wade. In recent winters, when abortion foes marched past the White House by the tens of thousands, their friend the president — first Ronald Reagan and later George Bush — cheered them on. And now, thanks to Reagan's appointive powers, they have new friends where it counts: on the Supreme Court.

On Sunday, a very different crowd filled the parks, hills and sidewalks of Washington. Some 300,000 supporters of women's right to choose abortion insisted that the Supreme Court hang tough when it hears a new challenge to Roe vs. Wade. If the annual right-to-life marches had left the impression that only one side was speaking out on abortion, this demonstration, one of the largest ever in the capital, must have dispelled it. Good.

We believe that Roe vs. Wade should be sustained. Women should have the legal right to choose to end unwanted pregnancies. Each year, 1.5 million women do so. When abortion is illegal, as it was before Roe vs. Wade, it doesn't vanish; it just becomes illicit, dirty and deadly. That mustn't happen again.

Nor should it become a matter for states to decide. That would guarantee a crazy quilt of laws and endless battles in legislative halls.

But the nine Supreme Court justices will not, and should not, be swayed by street rhetoric and crowd counts. When they hear arguments April 26 in Webster vs. Reproductive Health Services, they must decide whether a woman's constitutional right of privacy — which in 1973 was found to protect her right to choose abortion — no longer exists.

What could have happened in the past 16 years to make that right vanish? Nothing.

Granted, medical science has made it possible for fetal life to be sustained outside the womb at earlier stages of development, but that's no reason to ban abortions: Less than 1 percent of legal abortions occur in the last 12 weeks of pregnancy. Not even public opinion has changed much: A majority still views abortion as a sad but sometimes necessary option.

All that has changed is the composition of the Supreme Court. That's not reason enough to sentence as many as 1.5 million women a year to back-alley abortionists.

DAILY NEWS

New York City, New York, April 11, 1989

Some say it was 300,000, others say 600,000. However many, it was one of the largest outpourings in the history of Washington, Americans marching Sunday to express opposition to further government intrusion on women's rights to control their own reproductive functions, including the liberty to have abortions.

Such are the passions about abortion, pro and con, that it is unlikely a single mind was changed by the march, or by the words spoken there. Nor are many, if any, minds swayed by the arguments of abortion opponents — of whom a few hundred were in Washington Sunday. Does that mean there is no good purpose in such demonstrations, such arguments? Not at all. The debate over abortion is one of the most personally profound in America. It is healthy to vent the passions. It is constructive to expose to sunlight the arguments and the intensity of feelings. At the least, a degree of personal respect for the seriousness of differences may emerge from that process.

The pro-choice side of the argument made a powerful statement Sunday — in their numbers and their intensity and their capacity to organize. That was moving testimony to the convictions of Americans who believe questions of abortion and birth control rightly must be left to individuals rather than be seized by the heavy hands of government.

The Seattle Times

Seattle, Washington, April 14, 1989

LATELY, anti-abortion groups have taken to invoking the names and legacies of Gandhi and Martin Luther King Jr. to justify their blockades of medical offices. They describe their unlawful activities as civil disobedience. There is, however, a difference between these demonstrators and those whom they claim to follow.

Civil disobedience, by definition, involves committing illegal acts. It is the exercise of conviction over the fear of the consequences of breaking the law. The practice should command respect, if not for the beliefs of the actors, then for their willing sacrifice.

Yet not all lawbreakers can lay claim to that honorable but perilous tradition. Missing from the current protests is the basic premise of civil disobedience: resistance against the actions of the state.

The civil-rights movement was propelled by the refusal to comply with segregationist laws. By contrast, the anti-abortion groups aren't resisting state authority. Their sole aim is to prevent individuals from exercising personal rights that they don't agree with.

Recently, the protesters who barred entrance to clinics in King County were convicted of criminal trespass. To their surprise, Bellevue District Court Judge Joel Rindal sentenced one defendant to the maximum penalty of one year in jail and a $5,000 fine when that defendant refused to refrain from breaking the trespass law for the next two years.

Rindal later withdrew that sentence to give the individual and the other 49 defendants time to reconsider their position.

Rindal's initial sentence may seem draconian, but civil disobedience – as the protesters call their conduct – is not a gentle act.

By their increasingly drastic activities, the anti-abortion demonstrators have raised the stakes. They should realize that the consequences will be greater than an afternoon in the paddy wagon.

WHAT A REVERSAL OF ROE VS. WADE WOULD HANG ON

The Union Leader
Manchester, New Hampshire, April 12, 1989

The sight of Jesse Jackson warmly greeting, with his traditional bear-hug, Norma McCorvey, the "Jane Roe" of the U.S. Supreme Court's controversial 1973 Roe v. Wade ruling, at last Sunday's pro-abortion rally in Washington served only to highlight the man's opportunism.

On this great moral issue of the Twentieth Century the Reverend Jackson, like former abortion foe

JESSE JACKSON

Senator Ted Kennedy, has played whatever side of the issue he thought would advance him toward his ultimate goal: the Presidency.

The Jesse Jackson who now says that women must have the freedom to *"make a choice about one's body"* under a *"right to privacy,"* as if only one body were involved in that "choice," is the same Jesse Jackson who went about denouncing abortion **four years after** Roe v. Wade.

Then, Jackson was contemptuous of those who resorted to the clever ruse of using euphemisms to conceal ugly reality, scornfully charging:

"Those advocates taking life prior to birth do not call it killing or murder. They call it abortion. They further never talk about aborting a baby because that would imply something human."

In 1977, Jackson was sensitive to the hypocrisy inherent in the "right to privacy" argument, protesting:

"There are those who argue that the right to privacy is of a higher order than the right to life. . . . That was the premise of slavery."

Indeed, it was part of the premise of the Supreme Court's controversial Dred Scott decision of 1857, which in effect declared slaves non-persons, mere property belonging to their masters, sub-humans denied the rights of U.S. citizenship in the same sense that today's "slaves," unborn children, are dehumanized and deprived by Roe v. Wade.

When the Supreme Court chooses, it can always discover some new "right" to justify its ideological and social predilections. In the Dred Scott ruling, Chief Justice Roger Taney argued for the majority that since slaves are property, Congress could not forbid slavery in the territories without violating a slave-owner's "right" to own property.

Similarly, **those who run and those who serve the nation's profitable abortion abattoirs claim that since the unborn child in the mother's womb is the property of the mother, abortion-on-demand cannot be outlawed or controlled without violating the mother's "right" privately to dispose of said property if she finds his or her continued life inconvenient.**

But as in the case of the Dred Scott decision, which was effectively rescinded in 11 years with the 1868 adoption of the 14th Amendment extending citizenship to former slaves and granting them full civil rights, the immoral premise of Roe v. Wade will eventually bore deep into the public's consciousness.

At which time one may expect Jesse Jackson and Ted Kennedy to be knocking each other down in their eagerness to be the first prominent convert to the new cause.

The Charlotte Observer
Charlotte, North Carolina, April 6, 1989

Women all over the country are gearing up for a March for Women's Equality, Women's Lives to take place in Washington April 9. The march is planned to draw national attention to the threat to legalized abortions and to the need for passage of the Equal Rights Amendment (ERA).

Roe vs. Wade, the 1973 Supreme Court decision guaranteeing women the legal right to abortions, will be challenged in the next few months as the Supreme Court hears new arguments in a Missouri case, Webster vs. Reproductive Health Services. Whatever the problems with Roe vs. Wade — and there are some — the Missouri law is not the solution. It says human life begins at conception, forbids abortions in public hospitals and clinics and bans the use of public funds to counsel a woman to have an abortion.

The struggles to preserve a woman's right to have a safe, legal abortion and to secure passage of the ERA will not be easy. But the problem is less in the attitude of Americans than in the attitudes of — and pressures on — America's elected and appointed officials. Most Americans are female. Most of the people who write and interpret America's laws aren't.

Polls consistently show that a majority of Americans don't want the government to take away a woman's right to choose whether to have an abortion and do want an amendment guaranteeing equal rights for women. The march on Washington is one way to make the voice of the majority heard.

The Providence Journal
Providence, Rhode Island, April 11, 1989

Sunday's march in Washington reminds us that tremendous public support persists for the principles established by Roe vs. Wade. And as columnist William Safire points out elsewhere on this page, there is a political paradox at work as well: Most Americans support a woman's right to an abortion, even if most Americans have also supported and elected presidential candidates who are skeptical about Roe vs. Wade. Few people have changed their pro-abortion or anti-abortion views in the intervening years; and reconciling that bitter truth has proved nearly impossible, dividing our nation.

So let us look take a second look at things. For several years now the focus of public attention has been on the anti-abortion movement: Mass marches in the nation's capital, intensive lobbying in states and municipalities, television programs, civil disobedience at abortion clinics and medical offices. This weekend's pro-abortion gathering was peaceful, well-attended, and from a public relations point of view, singularly effective. While some are likely to dissent from the curious assortment of political causes and attitudes represented by many speakers, few can fail to be impressed by the fervor and dedication of these citizen-petitioners.

Still, just as we would dread to think that anti-abortion demonstrations might intimidate the Supreme Court, it is doubtful that the numbers and enthusiasm of pro-abortion marchers will make much difference in the court's deliberations. That is not the way our democracy works; the justices are political creatures, but their function is to judge the constitutionality of issues, not to respond to public pressure.

We hope and expect that Roe vs. Wade will be upheld this term. But suppose that it is not. The political firestorm that is likely to ensue must not be allowed to overwhelm one fundamental fact: The most that the Supreme Court can do is return this issue to the individual states. That would not necessarily erode civil liberties; it would, however, concentrate the elements of the debate, and mandate legislative action at the level of the states.

If we have learned anything in the 16 years since Roe vs. Wade, it is that abortion is a many-sided question. It is not just a political issue, but a religious problem as well; and not just a medical phenomenon, but a scientific, ethical, and philosophical symbol of discord for all Americans, female and male, rich and poor, spirited and meek. Let us hope that Sunday's march was part of the process by which understanding, and reconciliation, might usefully begin. For in a democracy, it is talk, as well as action, that shapes our destiny.

Rally Backs Right to Choose

At least half a million people marched in Washington, D.C. April 5, 1992 in support of abortion rights and to impress upon lawmakers the importance of women's votes in the 1992 presidential campaign.

The rally came at a time when advocates believed that abortion rights were threatened. The Supreme Court had recently agreed to hear challenges to a Pennsylvania law that sought to limit access to abortion through a variety of restrictions. The case was viewed as a chance for the court to overturn the 1973 *Roe v. Wade* decision, which had recognized a woman's right to an abortion.

The March for Women's Lives, sponsored by the National Organization for Women and dozens of other groups, was one of the largest political gatherings ever held in the capital. Police estimated the number of marchers at 500,000, while organizers placed the figure between 700,000 and one million. A similar demonstration in 1989 had drawn 300,000 people.

Following a rally on the Ellipse in front of the White House, demonstrators marched to Capitol Hill.

The event drew college students, professionals, clergy and Hollywood celebrities including Joanne Woodward, Jane Fonda and Morgan Fairchild. As in previous rallies, participants were predominantly white women.

Democratic presidential candidates Edmund G. (Jerry) Brown and Gov. Bill Clinton (D, Ark.) appeared at the march, as did Paul E. Tsongas, who had suspended his campaign. President George Bush was at his presidential retreat in Camp David, Md.

"The reality is that we're tired of begging men in power for our rights," NOW President Patricia Ireland said in an interview April 5. "If the courts won't protect them, then Congress has got to enact laws to protect a woman's rights. And if Congress doesn't, then we're going to elect pro-choice women to Congress."

About 200 pro-lifers staged a counterdemonstration on the West Lawn of the Capitol.

St. Petersburg Times
St. Petersburg, Florida, April 4, 1992

The hundreds of thousands of people expected to gather in Washington Sunday for a march in support of abortion rights are driven by an even deeper sense of urgency than in years past. It is nearly certain that *Roe vs. Wade*, the 1973 case that legalized abortion, will be dismantled this summer by the Supreme Court.

The protection guaranteed women by that decision has been eroding since the court's 1989 decision in *Webster vs. Reproductive Health Services* gave a green light to states to restrict access to abortion. Louisiana, Utah and Guam have passed laws that would ban, with limited exceptions, virtually all abortions; all have been challenged in court. It is such a challenge by Planned Parenthood against the Pennsylvania Abortion Control Act that is scheduled to be heard by the court April 22, with a decision expected by July.

Florida's Supreme Court has affirmed that the state constitution's right to privacy applies to a woman's right to obtain an abortion, but even the weight of that invocation has not thwarted attack. At least 12 states have considered or are considering legislation that would protect abortion rights in the event of the demise of *Roe*.

Barring conversion of a majority of the Supreme Court justices, that demise is the likely outcome of the Pennsylvania case. It would be wrong, however,

to rely on a patchwork of state-by-state protections to take *Roe*'s place. That is why support for two pieces of federal legislation is crucial.

The Freedom of Choice Act, which will write the protections of *Roe* into law, and the Reproductive Health Equity Act, which addresses the Bush administration's restrictions on federal funding of abortion for poor women, have been introduced in Congress and are worthy attempts to repair the damage inflicted by the Reagan and Bush administrations.

This is a critical year for abortion, not just because of the court threat but also because of its role in election politics. President Bush, trying to fashion a campaign lifeline that would snag him the support of both anti-abortion and abortion-rights voters, amended the restriction on abortion counseling at federally funded health clinics to allow doctors to discuss the subject, but not nurses, counselors and other personnel responsible for most patient advising.

Mr. Bush should realize no one will fall for so transparent a political move. He should be taking notice of the building sentiment of Americans such as those converging on Washington this weekend. They are voters, and they won't tolerate a return to the days when abortion was illegal, when women's rights and lives were unsafe.

The Evening Gazette
Worcester, Massachusetts, April 9, 1992

The success of the recent pro-choice rally in the nation's capital indicates the issue of abortion won't go away any time soon. The presence of half a million people served notice that a woman's right to choose may determine political careers.

The first pro-choice march in Washington in three years turned out six times as many demonstrators as the last pro-life gathering. With little advance fanfare, thousands of people, from grandmothers to graduate students, sent a warning to politicians, judges and bureaucrats.

President Bush didn't address the crowd as he usually does pro-life rallies, and presidential candidates were requested not to speak. Instead it was the voters, present and future, who marched and chanted. Geraldine Ferraro, '84 vice presidential candidate now running for the Senate from New York, declared: "For the record, this is a pro-choice nation."

The message is aimed not only at politicians but also at the U.S. Supreme Court, which soon will consider a Pennsylvania case that pro-lifers hope will overturn Roe vs. Wade, the landmark decision that made abortion legal.

Politicians, from President Bush to candidates for state legislatures, would be wise to take notice of what happened in Washington. The strength and tone of the rally showed that backers of free choice will not fold their tents and fade away if Roe vs. Wade is weakened or overturned.

The fight for women's choice to decide how to handle pregnancy will move to state legislatures, unless Congress protects the right through legislation.

Just like equal opportunity, choice is a constitutionally protected right in this country. The clock cannot be turned back.

The Washington Post
Washington, D.C., April 7, 1992

EXPECTING the Supreme Court to limit or reverse *Roe v. Wade* this term, and unwilling yet to mount a state-by-state effort to preserve abortion rights, a half-million marchers came to Washington last weekend seeking congressional action. They want federal legislators to enact a statute protecting the rights guaranteed in *Roe* even if the court rules these are no longer guaranteed by the Constitution. A very simple bill has been introduced in both Houses that prohibits a state from restricting the right of a woman to choose abortion before fetal viability, or even later if her life or health is at risk.

This bill to protect abortion rights is right and necessary. Opponents have raised objections in two areas, constitutionality and scope. Some scholars believe that Congress cannot preserve abortion rights by statute but only by amending the Constitution. Others say Congress does have authority to legislate in this area even though abortion has traditionally been regulated by the states. Either view could be proved right, but since there is at least a reasonable argument on the side of constitutionality, legislators have cause to proceed under that assumption. In practical terms, abortion rights proponents have no alternative because they do not have the votes needed for a constitutional amendment.

Does the bill go beyond *Roe*? Its proponents are divided. Some, primarily litigators representing abortion rights groups, say it does. They would be happy to wipe out a series of Supreme Court decisions interpreting *Roe* that authorize parental involvement, for example, or allow states to refuse Medicaid funding for abortions. Others more directly involved in the political process of getting the bill passed say the drafters do not intend to disturb this line of cases and will accept restrictions already approved by the courts.

But this is not clear in the bare-bones language of the bill, and that has led to misunderstandings and provided ammunition to the bill's opponents. A House subcommittee, for example, did vote in 1990 against an amendment that would have protected doctors and nurses who refused to perform abortions for reasons of conscience. The bill's proponents say they did so because the language was unnecessary. That kind of informal explanation may not be enough to win the votes of moderates. If necessary, the bill should be clarified to reassure those who don't want to go beyond codifying *Roe*.

Neither the House nor the Senate is expected to act on this legislation before the end of the Supreme Court term, and if the court's ruling in the critical abortion rights case from Pennsylvania is as restrictive as abortion rights groups fear, the political momentum for passage will gather strength. President Bush has already promised a veto, but by the summer that could be a high-risk position for any candidate. Republican lawmakers who would be pressed to sustain a presidential veto a few weeks before the election cannot be pleased by the prospect. Fortunately this increases the chance that an important bill will become law.

The Washington Times
Washington, D.C., April 7, 1992

MAYBE you guessed something about the half-million or so marchers who thronged into Washington this weekend in support of abortion rights when you saw some of the glitterati who were leading them. Jane Fonda was there, as were former Congresswoman Bella Abzug, the Rev. Jesse Jackson and professional feminist Betty Friedan. If you thought that maybe these people, despite their numbers, don't represent the run-of-the-mill American, you go to the head of the class.

The Washington Post, in addition to a front-page lead story that was breathlessly sympathetic to the march, the marchers and the marchers' cause, did a little profiling of the men and women who participated, and the results show that for all their zeal and energy, the people who marched for more liberal abortion laws are not exactly your Joe and Jane Sixpacks.

For starters, 78 percent of the participants were women and only 22 percent men, as opposed to the 51 percent women and 49 percent men who make up the real population of the United States. Only 35 percent of the marchers came from the District, Maryland or Virginia, while 65 percent hoofed it all the way from four other states: New York (36 percent, the largest single source), Pennsylvania, New Jersey and Massachusetts. But nobody seems to have shown up from California, Tennessee, Texas, Idaho, Michigan or any other state that, despite the conceits of the Northeast, are also part of America.

The marchers also happened to be white (94 percent); only 5 percent were black, as opposed to 12 percent of the real America. In religious profession, 15 percent identified themselves as Roman Catholics, who make up 23 percent of the whole population, 25 percent as Protestants (32 percent of the American people) and 21 percent Jewish (2.3 percent of the population).

Politically, the marchers described themselves as Democrats (59 percent) and 79 percent as "liberal" — 49 percent "liberal" and 30 percent "very liberal" — and only 4 percent called themselves "conservative" or "very conservative." In age, 76 percent were between 18 and 44.

It's also notable that 57 percent reported their annual incomes as being $30,000 or more and that 35 percent had incomes of more than $50,000. These are the people who are supposed to have done so well under Ronald Reagan while everybody else was getting poorer, and they're usually the first to complain.

Rich, white and liberal — except for the gender, it could have been Congress. But America it wasn't. If there's any doubt, look at what the marchers actually believe about abortion rights as opposed to what most Americans think.

Asked about the circumstances under which they believe abortion is permissible, the marchers gave answers that show them to be noticeably different from the majority of other Americans on the issue. Thus, while 87 percent of Americans think abortion is all right when the life of the mother is in danger, 99 percent of the marchers think so. But that's as close as they come to each other. On abortion when pregnancy is the result of rape or incest, 100 percent of the marchers believe it's permissible, though only 79 percent of the population agrees.

On abortion when there's "a chance" the child will be deformed at birth, 97 percent of the marchers are in favor, as opposed to 63 percent of the population. If the parents "cannot afford" to have the child, 96 percent of the marchers say abort the fetus, though a mere 39 percent of Americans say so; and if the parents just don't want "another child," 95 percent of the marchers favor abortion, against a mere 32 percent of the population. In other words, while most Americans believe in abortion under some circumstances that affect the child's or the mother's safety, the marchers believe in abortion under virtually all circumstances, and they believe in it overwhelmingly.

The whole purpose of the abortion rights march, as of any mass demonstration, was to manipulate public opinion and the votes of lawmakers. That's a perfectly legitimate goal and a legitimate means of trying to achieve it, but both the American people and their elected leaders should realize that what poured through the streets of Washington this weekend was not the American people or even a representative sampling of it but rather an elite — affluent, white, liberal, female and largely at odds with what most Americans believe about abortion and about public issues in general — and both people and leaders should consider that when they form their own views on abortion in the future.

The Philadelphia Inquirer
Philadelphia, Pennsylvania, April 7, 1992

When at least half a million women march down Washington streets in support of abortion rights, as they did on Sunday, lawmakers on both sides of the aisle have to take notice.

The march's importance lies not just in the numbers, which added up to one of the biggest demonstrations the capital has ever seen. It also signaled — as both political parties now understand — that the abortion issue has the potential to play a pivotal, and unpredictable, role this election year. Conservative Republican women like Linda Chavez have warned their party that its anti-abortion position will cause it to lose ground at the state level.

In part the sense of urgency that galvanized so many women arose from the fact that *Roe v. Wade*, the landmark 1973 Supreme Court decision establishing a woman's right to abortion, is in jeopardy. The Supreme Court is preparing to hear arguments later this month on the restrictive Pennsylvania abortion law, which many see as a potential vehicle for overturning Roe. Some other states have adopted even stricter limitations, giving a preview of the odds that would face women seeking abortions if the ultimate power to grant them were left to state legislatures.

But the unease generated by the abortion issue among politicians and the public goes even deeper than that, because of the very nature of the debate. The half-million women in Washington demonstrated peacefully. In contrast, the anti-abortion forces have been dominated by the radical fringe, those who physically threaten doctors, patients and clinic directors.

Intimidation and violence often limit women's ability to get abortions, even as growing federal and state restrictions increase the travel, cost and risk of exercising what remains a legal right. And those with an eye on some middle ground — keeping abortion legal while working to decrease the numbers — usually fall afoul of the take-no-prisoners school of anti-abortion protesters.

But this kind of intimidation, which is the antithesis of democratic debate, may finally boomerang. Many politicians are beginning to worry that their position on abortion will affect the support they get from women, even women who would never have an abortion themselves. The complexity of public attitudes is reflected in one large nationwide poll in which 74 percent of the respondents said they believed that women should have the right to an abortion, even though they personally felt it was morally wrong. Sunday's demonstration was a wake-up call for politicians to rethink their positions on choice.

The Star-Ledger

Newark, New Jersey, April 13, 1992

The huge throng of a half-million or more that demonstrated in Washington reflects not only the strength of the pro-choice movement but a political dilemma that has become increasingly relevant. The vital question that must be answered is: What will follow a decision by the U.S. Supreme Court to further modify or even annul the nearly two-decade-old Roe vs. Wade decision that first legalized abortion across the nation?

In the light of the increasingly conservative nature of the high court, an end to the Roe vs. Wade ruling is quite likely. In fact, pro-choice advocates have sought to have the court take a stand on the issue soon so that the process of finding other means than a court decision to legalize abortion can be started.

There is no need for a high court ruling to begin these efforts. The path that most pro-choice advocates seek to follow is to have Congress enact a statute that will have the same effect that Roe vs. Wade does—guaranteeing a woman's right to make her own reproductive decisions.

It is possible that even now a congressional majority could be assembled in support of a reproductive choice bill. But President Bush would almost certainly veto such a measure to avoid alienating the conservative Republicans who have voted for challenger Patrick Buchanan. At this point, Mr. Bush's veto could not be overridden.

But next year, conditions may be different. There will be wholesale replacements in congressional ranks and this should favor the choice forces. Many Republican congressional candidates are adopting pro-choice positions. And if a Democrat should defeat Mr. Bush, he would certainly sign such a measure into law because the Democratic presidential candidates are pro-choice.

Another battleground in post Roe vs. Wade America would be state legislatures. Here, too, pro-choice factions have made dramatic gains. In New Jersey, it would be almost impossible for an anti-abortion measure to become law.

Pro-choice politics are becoming increasingly important in America. This could well emerge as an important issue in the upcoming presidential campaign.

Detroit Free Press

Detroit, Michigan, April 7, 1992

The peaceful gathering of at least 500,000 abortion-rights proponents (an estimated 7,000 from Michigan) in Washington over the weekend illustrates that safeguarding reproductive choice remains politically salient for huge numbers of Americans. That is an important and encouraging reminder, particularly in an election year.

The timing of the demonstration — one of the largest of its kind in history — highlighted the threats posed to Roe vs. Wade, the 1973 U.S. Supreme Court ruling that defined a nationwide constitutional right to abortion during the first months of pregnancy. The general diversity of the marchers, partisan and demographic, seemed to belie attempts by opponents of abortion to dismiss choice advocates as a narrow, unrepresentative special interest.

The Supreme Court is to rule this term on a Pennsylvania law supported by the Bush administration that sharply restricts access to abortions. One of its provisions requires women who seek abortions to notify their husbands, even abusive ones. Another — also embodied in a bad bill before Michigan's Legislature — imposes a 24-hour waiting period for abortions. Yet another, mandating parental or judicial consent for minors' abortions, is law here.

Many fear — or hope — that the Pennsylvania case could become the conservative high court's vehicle for overturning the landmark Roe decision entirely. If that happens, the responsibility of elected officials, in Washington and Lansing, to defend against an utter revocation of abortion rights becomes even more pressing.

So it's appropriate that abortion is emerging as a defining issue in this year's presidential campaign. The major Democratic candidates support abortion rights. George Bush, who at one time expressed some freedom-of-choice sentiments, has worked assiduously as president to restrict abortion counseling at federally funded family planning clinics, among other things. Congress has failed to override the president's anti-abortion vetoes.

Choice also is likely to become a crucial issue in state and local elections, in our state and elsewhere. Michigan already has imposed abortion restrictions on poor women and young women; a further erosion of rights for *all* women is next on the anti-abortion agenda in Lansing.

The Washington march suggests that there will be a political price to be paid if the right to safe and legal abortion is taken away. More important, though, would be the broader price that potentially would be paid by all American women — and men, too — in lost privacy, foreclosed life options, health threats, and greater subjugation by government.

Fortunately, this week's march also suggests that the abortion-rights debate can't be considered over just yet.

The State

Columbia, South Carolina, April 8, 1992

ABORTION-RIGHTS supporters managed to pull together a half-million or more demonstrators in the largest rally in the nation's capital since an anti-Vietnam protest 21 years ago. Their message was clear: We don't want "those guys" in Washington telling us what we can do with our bodies.

In truth, however, their fight was against a conservative Bush administration and U.S. Supreme Court. The majority-Democrat Congress is pro-choice. Indeed, Congress probably will approve this year the Freedom of Choice Act, a bill to guarantee the federal right to choose abortion.

But President Bush has promised a veto, which is likely to kill the legislation. He has taken a hardline conservative stand on this issue and has offered verbal support to anti-abortion groups. Recently his Administration promulgated regulations that would bar most health professionals at federally supported family-planning clinics from even discussing abortion with clients.

At the same time, the Supreme Court seems headed toward a reversal of the 1973 *Roe vs. Wade* decision that granted women the right to an abortion. The court is expected to rule this summer in a Pennsylvania case that could be the vehicle for overturning or sharply limiting the abortion rights granted in *Roe.*

On the other side are most Democrats. Democratic Presidential hopefuls Bill Clinton and Jerry Brown attended Sunday's abortion-rights rally with bells on, while Mr. Bush took a trip to his retreat at Camp David, Md.

And speakers at the rally, from feminist leaders to movie celebs to students, promised that abortion will be *the* burning issue in the 1992 elections. "We can, and we must, elect pro-choice officials from the statehouse to the White House," said Kate Michelman, head of the National Abortion Rights Action League. ". . . We're not talking to the court; we don't trust the court. We're talking to every officeholder and every office seeker."

But while both sides of the abortion issue want to puff up their headcount at rallies and imply that abortion will be a burning issue in the November elections, polls indicate it is not so important as the economy and other pocketbook factors.

In a recent nationwide poll by *The Washington Post*, two of every three voters said the abortion issue will have no impact on their vote for President this year. However, of those who said it would matter, 14 percent said they were more likely to vote against Mr. Bush while only 9 percent said they were more likely to vote for him.

That small difference could be crucial in a close election. In any event, it should give Mr. Bush pause to think before he vetoes, if Congress passes the Freedom of Choice Act.

THE SUN
Baltimore, Maryland, April 7, 1992

A rally of a half-million people is the sort of demonstration of public opinion in action that legislators and presidents — if not judges and justices — have to heed. That is true even if, as was true Sunday in Washington, the people attending the rally are *not* a slice of American life statistically speaking, since rallies tend to attract those most committed to a cause.

In this case, the cause is the right to an abortion. The March for Women's Lives was organized by the National Organization for Women and several other groups. Its goals were to demonstrate the strength of the pro-choice movement and to energize and enlarge the movement. We suspect those goals were met.

The *Washington Post* interviewed some 900 of those attending the rally. At least 95 percent favored a woman' right to an abortion in all circumstances. Pollsters have consistently found that except in the case of rape or incest or a threat to the health of the mother, public opinion is much less monolithic in support of abortions. Most Americans oppose abortions for reasons of convenience or economics, for example.

But even in those situations, public opinion is solidly on the side of choice. *The Sun* polled 1,210 state residents last February. That random sample represented true public opinion better than did the 500,000 attending the Washington rally. By 57-31 percent, those polled said they favored a woman's right to have an abortion up to the point of viability of the fetus — and even after that in certain cases.

Another good indication that Sunday's huge rally was on the side of the majority of the public is that last year the Maryland General Assembly passed by solid majorities (60-plus percent of the members of the state Senate and of the House of Delegates) a bill that would in effect codify *Roe vs. Wade*, the 1973 Supreme Court decision asserting that women have a basic, if unenumerated, constitutional right to an abortion.

Still another indication that the public wants *Roe* left intact is a recent Gallup Poll that shows Americans want the decision left intact by 64-30 percent.

The Supreme Court will hear a case this month that could lead to overturning or severely restricting *Roe*. Justices may or may not pay attention to 500,000 people marching down Pennsylvania Avenue. (In our view they shouldn't.) But elected officials do (and should). Bill Clinton, Edmund G. Brown Jr. and Paul Tsongas showed up in Washington Sunday. Choice may be primarily a Democratic issue. Democrats outnumbered Republicans by 12 to 1 at the rally, and a whopping 79 percent of all marchers said they were liberals. But President Bush ought to take note of the energy and enthusiasm of that crowd — and of the fact that fully one-fifth were moderates and conservatives and over one-fourth were independents.

Herald News
Fall River, Massachusetts, April 9, 1992

It's sadly ironic that while half a million abortion rights supporters gathered in the nation's capital Sunday for the mother of all rallies, they were absent from a forum in which they might have affected a real difference.

As celebrities, activists and ordinary folks unleashed their collective fury on Capitol Hill to bemoan the anticipated reversal, or gutting, by the Supreme Court of the Roe vs. Wade decision granting women the right to legal abortions, they seemed blinded by their own passion as to what the real issue was.

Is it any wonder that eight years of Ronald Reagan and nearly four of George Bush have yielded a Supreme Court that would reverse Roe vs. Wade in a heartbeat? Have those same 500,000 marchers monitored carefully how the current presidential candidates stand on abortion?

As candidates, Reagan and Bush were both vocal in their opposition to abortion. Did those who support legalized abortion fail to make the connection between a president's stand on abortion and his propensity to nominate Supreme Court justices who concur with it?

Do they understand that participation in the political process underway in this country right now will have a more profound and lasting effect than anything yelled through a bullhorn on the Capitol steps? How many of the young Americans proclaiming the right to control their own destinies actually cast votes toward that future?

Sunday's rally, by sheer numbers alone and perhaps in spirit as well, was reminiscent of the civil rights marches of the 1960s. But there's one important difference. Presidents Kennedy and Johnson, both exemplary supporters of civil rights, were in office then, able to sustain the preferences of voters.

That's not the case now. Even if a pro-choice president is elected, the Supreme Court will remain largely conservative for many years to come, with no conservative justices likely to retire anytime soon.

All the indignation in the world won't change that.

* * *

It is likewise odd that so many gathered Sunday to fight for a right that is essentially an admission of failure. Whether pro-choice or pro-life, most people would admit that no one really *wants* to have an abortion. Ending up on a clinic gurney is almost always the result of a failure to use contraception or of contraception to work or of careful forethought about sex.

Whether you believe its right or wrong, or whether you believe a fetus is a person or only tissue, there's no disputing that abortion is the ending of the beginning of a life.

That's a strange thing to rally round. But as organizers approach something resembling glee over the turnout at Sunday's protest it seems that's just what they're celebrating.

Part IV: Health, Youth & Abortion

Although more than half of all abortions in the United States are performed on women in their twenties, much of the debate surrounding preventative birth-control measures has centered upon sex education and contraceptive use and their effect upon teenagers. The pregnancy rate among minors in the U.S. is certainly very high, with teenagers accounting for 30% of all abortions. But measures such as the Reagan administration's "squeal rule," which required clinics to notify parents when teenagers received birth control devices, seem to their opponents to defeat the primary goal of preventing unwanted pregnancies by making it difficult for teenagers to practice contraception.

Abortion exists largely because unwanted pregnancies occur. For that reason, sex education and birth control figure prominently in the abortion controversy. While many people argue that the increased use and availability of contraceptives would reduce unwanted pregnancies, others feel it would only increase sexual promiscuity, particularly among teenagers.

Perhaps the most significant recent development regarding medicine and abortion is the introduction of the controversial French abortion pill, RU-486. It was said to be 80% effective in terminating a pregnancy by causing a miscarriage. When taken in conjunction with a second drug – the hormone prostaglandin – the success rate rose to 95%. Though the drug has been cleared for use in France and several other countries, its use in the U.S. has thus far been legally prevented.

Another scientific breakthrough that influenced the abortion debate concerned the use, in research and therapy, of human fetal tissue obtained from legal abortions. Fetal tissue was of scientific interest because it did not carry the full complement of immunities that adult tissue did. Early research suggested that fetal tissue transplants offered hope in the treatment of Parkinson's disease and other brain disorders. Though backed by abortion rights groups, such research was opposed by anti-abortion groups

Certainly the medical community's stand on abortion was muddied when former Surgeon General Dr. C. Everett Koop told then-President Ronald Reagan in a letter that he would not issue a planned report on the health risks of abortion, because the scientific data were inconclusive. Though a long-time opponent of abortion, Koop surprised both liberals and conservatives with his announcement.

Despite Dr. Koop's personal positions on abortion, he had previously spearheaded various efforts to promote birth control and "safe-sex" techniques.

Throughout the 1980s and early 1990s the controversies surrounding abortion rates and birth-control issues intensified. This was dramatized in two developments.

The first was the new rules issued by the Department of Health and Human Services in 1988. The rules barred federally funded family planning clinics from engaging in abortion-related activities. Most family planning clinics received federal funds. At the time the rules were issued, federally funded clinics were already barred from using federal money for abortions. The new regulations also barred the clinics from advising a woman, even indirectly, that getting an abortion was a legal option for handling a pregnancy.

Furthermore, a clinic was not allowed to refer a woman directly to an outside facility performing abortions even if she asked for one. Instead, the woman would simply be given a list of outside facilities providing prenatal care. Such a list could include facilities that performed abortions but not facilities "whose principal business is the provision of abortions."

The rules seemed to disregard a report issued by the National Academy of Science's Institute of Medicine and National Research Council.

As a result of the failure to make new, more effective and more convenient methods of birth control available, the report concluded, the rate of abortion in the U.S. was much higher than necessary. According to the report, about half of the approximately 1.5 million abortions performed in the U.S. each year resulted from failure to use birth control methods properly or, more rarely, from contraceptive failure.

In addition, the panel noted that 17 major firms in the U.S. had been carrying on research and development into new birth control methods up until the early 1980s. Since that time, a combination of factors had combined to cut the number of active developers to one. According to the report, these factors included a rise in liability lawsuits against contraceptive manufacturers, political pressure from anti-abortion forces, federal drug approval policies that considered only the risks of new birth control methods and not the benefits, and a lack of government funding.

Concurrently, a federally funded study on black, inner-city teenagers had found that pregnant teens who had had abortions did better economically, educationally and emotionally than those who had given birth.

Laurie Schwab Zabin, one of the study's chief researchers, said, "Clearly the abortion experience is not setting these kids back."

Sullivan's HHS Appointment Stirs Wide Controversy

President-elect George Bush continued his smooth transition to power by naming five more members of his cabinet December 22, 1988. Bush made five appointments, including four cabinet members, December 22. There was controversy over one of them, as Bush chose a medical administrator who was thought to be sympathetic to abortion rights as his secretary of health and human services. But the nominee, Dr. Louis W. Sullivan, managed to satisfy the antiabortion forces that he would heed their wishes. Bush had the electoral support of antiabortion activists.

Sullivan had a strong reputation as a physician, academic administrator and fund-raiser, having built a medical school from scratch at Atlanta's predominantly black Morehouse College.

Sullivan was not active in politics, but he had struck up a friendship with the Bushes in 1982. He had named Barbara Bush, the President-elect's wife, to the medical school's board of trustees and had been chosen to introduce Mrs. Bush to the Republican National Convention in August 1988.

Sullivan met with anti-abortion activists and congressional foes of abortion December 21. Two Republicans who were leaders of the anti-abortion forces in Congress, Sen. Orrin Hatch (Utah) and Rep. Vin Weber (Minn.) proclaimed him acceptable. Hatch said he believed Sullivan had been "misunderstood" by the press, and Weber said Sullivan had assured him that "he would have strong pro-life people in the department."

But John C. Wilke, president of the National Right to Life Committee, said there were "many questions remaining...Either Dr. Sullivan had been totally misquoted or he has changed his position in the last few days."

At his introduction December 22, Sullivan read a statement saying, "I wish to emphasize that in the areas of abortion, my personal position is that I am opposed to abortion except in the case of rape, incest of threat to the life of the mother. I'm also opposed to federal funding for abortion except in the case of a threat to the life of the mother.

"This position is the same as that of President-elect Bush, with whom I agree completely."

The U.S. Senate March 1, 1989 confirmed Sullivan as secretary of health and human services, by a vote of 98–1. The lone vote against Sullivan came from a Republican, Sen. Jesse Helms (N.C.).

Arkansas Gazette.

Little Rock, Arkansas, January 1, 1989

The militant anti-abortionists are tireless and reckless agitators, as they have just proved once again. Even a heavy charge of common sense fired into their midst will disperse them only temporarily.

Arkansas Right to Life tried to pick a fight over a proposed school clinic last week, but the effort fizzled quickly. Julie Wright, executive director of the anti-abortion group, held a news conference at the Capitol to denounce the state Health Department for allegedly setting up school clinics without local school board approval. She used Osceola as an example. The anti-abortion zealots are opposed to school clinics because they fear the clinics will provide family-planning services and information about abortion.

Wright proved wrong in all important particulars. Members of the Osceola School Board and school administrators said they knew all along of the plans for the clinic, which is scheduled for another discussion at a Board meeting Jan. 10. The clinic will not provide family-planning services or abortion counsel-

ing and was never intended to. In short, there was no controversy, as far as local officials were concerned.

State Sen. Mike Bearden of Osceola pointed this out to Wright, rather forcefully, at a legislative committee meeting the next day, adding that all Osceola was trying to do was provide free health services in a school system with a high percentage of low-income students. Most reasonable people would take the point.

★ ★ ★

But not the "Right to Life" crowd. Their one issue is more important to them than all others. They would gladly block basic health care in the schools to assure that no family planning is taught. Local control of the schools? Away with it. Wright testified against a bill to give local school boards authority to establish clinics and determine what services they will offer.

What wouldn't these people sacrifice to the anti-abortion cause? It is an unsettling question, and one the rest of us must keep asking.

The News and Observer

Raleigh, North Carolina, January 25, 1989

One-issue political activists are like one-note singers. They suffer from limited range, they are monotonous and they can cause problems.

President Bush faces a problem with one such group over his nomination of Dr. Louis W. Sullivan to head the Department of Health and Human Services. Dr. Sullivan, who would be the only black in the new Cabinet, is well-qualified for the job — president of Morehouse School of Medicine in Atlanta, experienced physician and researcher.

But the nominee faces opposition from a single-issue bloc, the anti-abortion forces who say he is not sufficiently forceful on the one topic that consumes their energy. Never mind that he has said he supports Mr. Bush's views — opposition to abortion except in cases of rape, incest and when the life of the mother is threatened. That pledge is not good enough for the anti-abortion people.

The people who say they are "pro-life" — although their concern with life often seems to begin with conception and end with birth — complain that Dr. Sullivan is waffling and telling congressmen privately that he does not want the 16-year-old Supreme Court decision legalizing abortion to be reversed.

It's another example of how many of the anti-abortion activists see the world in cut-and-dried, either-or terms. There is no room for disagreement or qualification. Yet, for most people, abortion is an agonizing question that is not susceptible to easy or certain answers.

The Department of Health and Human Services has an enormously complicated mission — dealing with a host of maladies from AIDS to poverty, not just with abortion. It is essentially the federal government's "people department," and it needs a leader who can offer a combination of education, experience and empathy, someone who can bring harmony out of a chorus of often conflicting goals.

Dr. Sullivan appears to possess those qualifications. It would be a mistake if Mr. Bush were to give less than full support to his nominee because of opposition from a Johnny-one-note, single-issue lobby.

DESERET·NEWS
Salt Lake City, Utah, January 29, 1989

In a way, an injustice is being done to one of this nation's top public health experts, former Utahn James O. Mason.

That's because of the rationale being given for Dr. Mason's new appointment as the top aide to Secretary Louis O. Sullivan of the U.S. Department of Health and Human Services.

The word is that Mason is being brought into the post to appease those who are unhappy with Sullivan's views on abortion. Consequently, attention is focusing on Mason's views as an opponent of abortion.

But, important as abortion is, Dr. Mason is anything but a man with just one issue on his mind or with a narrow range of expertise. On the contrary, he is has a broad background in the medical field and has a wide spectrum of concerns.

His impressive background includes service as director of the National Centers for Disease Control in Atlanta, director of the Utah Department of Health, commissioner of the Health Services Corporation for The Church of Jesus Christ of Latter-day Saints, and administrator of the federal Agency for Toxic Substance and Disease Registry.

An effective and far-sighted administrator who recognizes public health problems before they become crises and anticipates the best solution to them, Dr. Mason is also a nationally-respected authority on infectious diseases who has published many scientific articles.

Among the major challenges he sees Health and Human Services facing in the next few years are finding a cure for AIDS, working to reduce infant death rates, and setting health goals for the year 2000.

Let's hope HHS adds at least a couple of other items to that list. One of them should be getting Americans to smoke and drink less. Tobacco kills as many Americans every 46 days as AIDS has killed in six years. Alcohol is by far the most abused drug. Another challenge for any federal operation as big as HHS is to recognize that problems are best solved not by bureaucrats holding down a desk in Washington but by those closest to the problems.

In any event, the toughest jobs ought to be filled by the most able people. That's exactly what the U.S. Department of Health and Human Services is getting in Dr. James O. Mason.

The Union Leader
Manchester, New Hampshire, January 26, 1989

What's done is done. It's time to move on.

Instead of looking on the flip-flopping on the abortion issue of Dr. Louis W. Sullivan, President George Bush's nominee to head the Department of Health and Human Services, solely as a problem for his new administration, the President might as well view it as an opportunity to prove to skeptics that his vaunted support for the anti-abortion cause does indeed go beyond mere lip service. Moreover, having just lectured his White House staff on the importance of avoiding ethical problems, Bush now has an opportunity to demonstrate that he simply will not tolerate Sullivan's deception of himself and the public on this issue.

When Sullivan told the Atlanta Journal last month that women should have the right to an abortion, the angry feeling of betrayal that welled up in opponents of the killing of the innocent unborn was assuaged somewhat by assurances, arranged through the Bush transition team, that Sullivan actually held the same position toward abortion as did then President-elect Bush.

Even Congress' leading foes of abortion held their fire, opting to give Sullivan the benefit of the doubt.

But now it is reported, without denial, that Sullivan has been telling members of Congress that he opposes the overturning of the conroversial 1973 Roe vs. Wade ruling of the U.S. Supreme Court that legalized abortion.

Thus, he has turned his back not only on what some view as Bush's most important campaign pledge but also on the Republican Party platform's clear position on this life-and-death issue.

Bush's choice, while a painful one, seems clear: Either pull the plug on Sullivan or pull the plug on Presidential credibility among voters who took seriously Bush's unequivocally stated opposition to Democratic Presidential candidate Michael Dukakis' avowedly pro-abortion stance.

In any event, if retaining Sullivan is more important to President Bush than retaining his good standing among foes of abortion, who were perhaps his most fervent supporters during the recent Presidential campaign, then it's better that the latter know it now.

The Star-Ledger
Newark, New Jersey, January 9, 1989

The early signal sent out by the transition team of President-elect George Bush was that he planned to broaden his administration to be more inclusive of blacks. He also pledged to name a black as a member of his Cabinet.

The transition team cast a wide net in its search for black appointees and found Atlanta educator Louis Sullivan, named to become health and human services secretary. Mr. Sullivan, president of the Morehouse School of Medicine and a strong administrator, is the first black to be tapped for service by Mr. Bush.

Dr. Sullivan is a long-time advocate of improved health care for disadvantaged Americans, and his nomination fulfills Mr. Bush's campaign pledge. The nominee holds impressive teaching credentials in addition to his administrative skills.

The nomination of the Atlanta educator had been long anticipated, but was met with a last-minute outcry from anti-abortion forces. Their objections were triggered by a newspaper interview in which Dr. Sullivan said he supports a woman's right to seek an abortion, though he opposes federal assistance for it.

He later clarified his position to say he is "opposed to abortion except in cases of rape, incest and where the life of the mother is threatened," a statement that mirrors the President-elect's view.

Abortion will be but one of many controversial matters that Dr. Sullivan will have to confront when he steps into the Health and Human Services Department.

As an advocate of health care services for the poor, which have often been among the first to be pared when the budget ax begins to fall, Dr. Sullivan will surely have his hands full trying to advance his precepts.

There are those who believe that if anyone can come to grips with the Health and Human Services Department in this time of limited resources, it is Dr. Sullivan. Mr. Bush is openly confident this is so, and his choice of Dr. Sullivan seems to signal a departure from the Reagan administration approach to this sensitive agency.

THE ROANOKE TIMES
Roanoke, Virginia, January 27, 1989

IF LOUIS Sullivan holds ambivalent views about abortion, welcome to the crowd.

So does the president who wants to make Sullivan his secretary of health and human services.

So does the Editorial Page of this newspaper.

So do the American people.

Maybe it's because the issue itself is rife with ambiguities: more ambiguities, anyway, than zealots on either side of the question are willing to concede.

We can't be sure, because so far it's all come second- and third-hand, but Sullivan's position seems to be: (a) personal opposition to abortion; (b) personal opposition to overturning *Roe v. Wade*, the 1973 Supreme Court decision that found in the U.S. Constitution the right of a woman to have an abortion; and (c) willingness to swallow his personal views and support the administration's position.

Points (a) and (b) are in tension, but are not necessarily contradictory. It's possible to be against abortion as a moral wrong, but at the same time to oppose making it a legal wrong. This is Ambiguity No. 1.

Conversely, it is possible to possess no great qualms about abortion but at the same time to see *Roe v. Wade* as judicial error, on the ground that the Constitution neither states nor implies a right to an abortion. This is Ambiguity No. 2.

As for point (c), it's possible for administration officials — indeed, it's expected of them — to make their personal views subordinate to the president for whom they toil. Let's call this Ambiguity No. 3, though technically it's not unique to the abortion issue.

But just what is George Bush's position?

As a candidate during the campaign debates, he seemed not to have thought much about it. He opposed abortion, but not in all cases. There ought to be a law against it, and if there were, obviously, the women who demanded abortions should be subject to criminal penalties.

Just as obviously, Bush's comment was impolitic, and his handlers went to work: Any penalties ought to be imposed on the physicians who perform abortions, a clarifying statement said the next day, but not on the women for whom they are performed. Thus, Ambiguity No. 4: It's OK to throw those slimy abortionist-doctors in jail, but not the women (and their sexual partners) whose behavior is the cause of it all.

This week, Bush assured thousands of anti-abortion demonstrators in Washington that he strongly supports overturning *Roe v. Wade*. But what does he mean by that?

If that's all he wants, then it won't make abortions illegal. Rather, it would be up to each state to do so. Rest assured, some states wouldn't. Ambiguity No. 5.

Or does the president want a constitutional amendment outlawing abortion? Nothing ambiguous about that — until you consider the practical result. Too many Americans have come to see little or nothing wrong with terminating a pregnancy for an anti-abortion law to be enforced on anything but a sporadic basis.

Some pro-choice advocates fear that criminalizing abortions would result in a return to back-alley butchery. (Yes, Virginia, there *were* abortions — a lot of them — before 1973.) More likely, the result would be further erosion of respect for the law, and a constitutional amendment more scorned than honored.

If that's Ambiguity No. 6, then in the political aspects of the abortion issue lies Ambiguity No. 7. Not only does the idea of criminalizing abortion lack the sort of overwhelming consensus that any criminal statute must have to be effective, but — assuming the public-opinion polls are correct — it also lacks the support of even a majority of Americans. Yet it is generally to a politician's benefit to oppose *Roe v. Wade*. That's because the anti-abortion forces are likelier than the pro-choice forces to be single-issue voters.

Would President Bush play politics with the abortion issue? Did President Reagan? Perish the thought.

Suffice it to say that Reagan could engage in strong anti-abortion rhetoric and then do nothing about it, because that was his style and nobody much minded. But Bush, a more energetic man, may feel compelled to act decisively on his anti-abortion beliefs. If he does, he could find that decisiveness without regard for ambiguities has a way of turning into failure.

The Kansas City Times
Kansas City, Missouri, January 2, 1989

It wasn't the most famous quote involving Dr. Louis W. Sullivan, but George Bush said he and his choice for secretary of the Department of Health and Human Services "see eye to eye on the critical issues facing the next secretary of HHS."

Only one issue has been heard. But most enlightening information should come out of confirmation hearings as Sullivan's ideas are drawn out on everything from AIDS to how the nation's nursing home bills will be paid the rest of the century, from the integrity of the Social Security system to Medicaid eligibility for welfare families. They're also in HHS.

The discussions will be most welcome. An array of bread-and-butter issues are the province of the prospective cabinet officer. Sullivan, a black professional who is also president of the Morehouse School of Medicine in Atlanta, has been attended since his nomination only about his views on women's right to abortion. Any place else but in this country where protagonists' intimidation volume rather than reason influences the setting of an agenda, Sullivan would not be judged so narrowly.

Unless the law has been quietly changed in the witching hour, Sullivan's personal preference — and Bush's, for that matter — are irrelevant. The right to abortion is a matter of fact. Present arguments are exhausted; move on to other delicate questions that are also matters of life and death in the agency.

What's to be done about the one in five children living in poverty? From pre-natal care to substance abuse programs, funding is inadequate and in many cases, programs aren't working.

At least 32 million Americans lack health insurance. What's the federal responsibility?

Last year Congress added coverage of catastrophic illness to Medicare. It's limited and narrowly defined. It's also so expensive through a tax on upper income elderly that efforts already are being made to postpone or repeal it. But how are the increasing chronic health and custodial needs of frail, dependent elderly Americans to be covered?

Do the president-elect and Sullivan have any "eye to eye" visions of making adult day care a viable alternative to institutionalization? Can leadership from Sullivan be expected on a national, comprehensive long-term care policy?

The nation deserves to know more about Sullivan's attitudes toward and abilities to deal with the gamut of social concerns.

The Register-Guard
Euegene, Oregon, January 27, 1989

Louis Sullivan, nominated to head the Department of Health and Human Services, has recently placed himself on both sides of two questions: Should a woman have the right to an abortion in most circumstances? And should *Roe vs. Wade*, the Supreme Court abortion decision, be reversed?

Sullivan is the only black chosen for the Bush Cabinet. Even anti-abortion conservatives are reluctant to offend blacks by scuttling his appointment.

Some defenders have explained that Sullivan just isn't used to Washington. If they wanted to, they could use another excuse based on precedent: George Bush once opposed reversing *Roe vs. Wade*. He changed his mind when he joined the Republican presidential ticket in 1980.

The 🌳 State
Columbia, South Carolina, January 3, 1989

LOUIS Sullivan got himself into hot water with the anti-abortion forces even before President-elect George Bush named him to head the Department of Health and Human Services. And so far, he has done little to endear himself to folks on either side of this emotional issue.

The controversy started when Dr. Sullivan, founder and president of Morehouse College of Medicine in Atlanta, said in a newspaper interview that he supports a woman's right to choose abortion.

Predictably, his statement raised the hackles of myriad right-to-life groups, and Mr. Bush then delayed the announcement of his nomination to the Cabinet post until Dr. Sullivan "clarified" his stand.

At that point, the good doctor conveniently flip-flopped and issued another statement saying, "I am opposed to abortion except in cases of rape, incest and where the life of the mother is threatened."

Where does Dr. Sullivan really stand?

No doubt he will be questioned closely on the issue during Senate confirmation hearings. And pro-life, pro-choice and welfare reform advocates will be listening intently.

After all, the massive health and welfare agency is responsible for propounding not only the new regulations governing the vast changes in entitlement programs for the poor, such as Aid to Families with Dependent Children, but also those governing Medicaid, Medicare, medical research and health-care policies.

Last year, for example, the Department of Health and Human Services issued restrictive regulations, now being challenged in the courts, to deny federal funding to clinics that offer abortion counseling.

In effect, the department's rules would prevent many poor women from having easy access not only to abortions but also, more importantly, to family planning information.

Under current law, abortion during early pregnancy is legal. But the Health and Human Services Department has, in effect, taken an anti-abortion stand in doling out federal funds.

Planned Parenthood and other agencies that counsel poor women on birth control can no longer receive federal grants if they share space, personnel, medical records, names, phone numbers, waiting rooms or even entrances and exits with a privately funded abortion clinic.

Does Dr. Sullivan agree that these regulations are reasonable and fair? Does he have the backbone to stand up if he disagrees with them? If not, then Mr. Bush's first black Cabinet appointee will be tacitly perpetuating a federal policy that condones one standard of health care for the wealthy, who can afford private doctors, and another, lower standard for the nation's poor.

the Charleston Gazette
Charleston, West Virginia, January 25, 1989

MOMENTUM is growing among Reagan-Bush forces and the fundamentalist New Right in an all-out effort to take away the right of American women to choose abortion.

U.S. Attorney General Dick Thornburgh brought action before the U.S. Supreme Court in an attempt to overturn the 1973 Roe vs. Wade ruling. President Bush and Vice President Quayle embraced the anti-abortion camp Monday and backed a constitutional amendment to outlaw abortion.

If their push succeeds, America will take a step backward to grimmer times when government had greater control over people's private lives.

Most other nations give pregnant women the right to make this difficult decision themselves. They may consult their doctors, their ministers, their husbands or lovers — but, ultimately, it's up to the woman involved. Why should the United States revoke this freedom that has existed for 16 years?

Do Americans really want to return to the days of back-alley abortions? Do they really want to force unlucky 14-year-old girls to become mothers? Do they really want to make criminals out of desperate women? Do they really want to let fundamentalists and other rigid moralists dictate the choice for everyone?

We think the national upheaval over abortion is a minority matter. TV preachers and other one-issue zealots are loud and powerful, but they speak for only a small part of America.

A *New York Times*-CBS poll this month found that 61 percent of people surveyed felt that pregnant women and girls should be allowed to decide. The rate of approval is even higher if the pregnancy was caused by incest or rape, if the mother's life is in danger, or if she's unable to support and raise a child.

In October, a poll by the Planned Parenthood Federation found that most people favor U.S. distribution of RU-486, the new European pill that is taken when a menstrual period is missed, terminating any pregnancy.

Nobody thinks abortion is attractive. It's traumatic and sad. But sometimes it's the lesser evil for pubescent girls and women trapped by circumstance.

It's a grim choice that should be decided by the women themselves — not by extremists and politicians wanting their votes.

THE BLADE
Toledo, Ohio, January 30, 1989

LIKE most Americans we are inclined to go along with new presidents, at least until the policy directions of their administrations have become clear. However, President Bush has made a serious tactical and perhaps a strategic error in urging that the Supreme Court's 1973 decision legalizing abortion should be overturned.

He is entitled to his views, as is everybody else. And that's the problem. There plainly is no grand consensus in this country on what ought to be done about abortion; many Americans are ambivalent on the issue, perhaps not favoring abortions in principle but unwilling to insist that all others adhere to their viewpoint on such an intensely personal issue.

Mr. Bush's comments were made to anti-abortion demonstrators by telephone, thus avoiding direct contact with them. But his timing is deplorable because the matter is before the Supreme Court, an independent branch of the government. His comments look like an attempt to bludgeon the Supreme Court into a reversal of its earlier decision.

Eventually the Roe decision will be reviewed and perhaps modified, although we believe that would be the wrong public-policy course. If the Supreme Court does modify its own 1973 decision, it would probably result in a state-by-state patchwork of abortion laws which will work an immense hardship on many poor women unable to travel to a state where the law is more receptive to abortions.

Mr. Bush's view that adoption is preferable to abortion is true, in theory at least. However, many babies are not easily placed in new homes because of one factor or another, and many unwanted children grow up in families where poverty or child abuse are common. This is an issue never really addressed by right-to-life (or perhaps one should say right-to-birth) groups.

Abortion is not an issue that requires early presidential attention such as decisions about the budget, the deficit, or other matters on the legislative agenda. A reversal of Wade vs. Roe would put pressure on many state legislatures to outlaw abortions and thus create a whole new class of status criminals — women who attempt to have abortions and who will in countless numbers resort to backyard butchers for abortions under unsafe conditions.

Such a decision by the Supreme Court would stir up large numbers of people who now are relatively quiescent on the issue, but do not believe that the state should intrude upon the right of women to make decisions about their own reproductive destinies. If right-to-life groups believe defiance of the law is justified, it seems safe to say that the turmoil over this issue would increase many times over if abortions were outlawed.

MILWAUKEE SENTINEL

Milwaukee, Wisconsin, January 26, 1989

The outstretched hand President Bush extended to erstwhile opponents in his inaugural address Friday apparently did not reach out to pro-choice factions on abortion.

Rather, the president chose to publicly take sides in a legal appeal that asks the Supreme Court to overturn its 1973 edict granting what opponents call "abortion on demand."

What's going on here?

Bush is convincing in his statements opposing abortion. But it is obvious that the issue provides the president with an opportunity to revalidate conservative credentials that may have been frayed by the stress he placed in his inaugural address on such matters as the hungry and the homeless.

In the process, however, the president has rekindled opposition to the controversial appointment of Bush's only black cabinet nominee — Louis W. Sullivan, whom he has tapped for the post of secretary of health and human services.

Sullivan, who waffled in pre-appointment interviews on the question of whether he was pro-choice, now reportedly has expressed opposition to overturning the landmark pro-choice case of Roe vs. Wade.

While Sullivan's nomination may not be in jeopardy, the situation could cast doubt on his credibility as an administration spokesman if he is approved. Bush must wonder if his own outspokenness did more harm than good.

In addition, the president already may have raised the hackles of court members who might look upon his statement as an attempt to meddle in court business, regardless of their disposition on Roe vs. Wade.

They justifiably might suspect that Bush is hoping to claim part of the credit if the pro-choice ruling were overturned.

Significantly, Bush's attack on Roe vs. Wade did not necessarily change his pre-election stance opposing abortion except in cases of rape, incest or when the health of the mother was threatened — limitations by which Sullivan said he could abide.

And instead of politicizing this controversial case with his pre-trial remarks, Bush should have let the appeal run its course without any coaching from the White House.

THE ATLANTA CONSTITUTION

Atlanta, Georgia, January 30, 1989

If there was any doubt about the rigidity of President Bush's position on abortion, he removed it Monday with his ringing denunciation of *Roe v. Wade.*

"I think the Supreme Court's decision ... was wrong and should be overturned," he told an anti-abortion rally on the 16th anniversary of the ruling that legalized abortion. "I promise you that the president hears you now and stands with you in a cause that must be won."

It was no less than abortion foes had been led to expect by his campaign demurrers and his party's platform rhetoric on abortion. Still, it was disconcerting to see him pick up the cudgel right where Ronald Reagan had left it and, in his predecessor's very words, deplore the "American tragedy of abortion on demand."

A former pro-choice advocate, Mr. Bush was embarrassed during last year's presidential debates by a question about the practical effect of a ban on abortions. He said at first that the women who sought them should be jailed, then a day later apologized for not having thought it through, saying, to the outrage of the medical profession, that it was the doctors who should face criminal penalties.

Yet, the questions of who should be punished if abortions are outlawed after 25 million have been performed legally — and how severely — are still wide open and deserve complete, and well-reasoned responses before the new president plunges the nation headlong down the same blind alley.

The overwhelming majority of Americans who, according to the latest Louis Harris poll, continue to support *Roe v. Wade,* do not expect any succor from the Bush administration. But the election was not a referendum on abortion. Many of *them* voted for Mr. Bush, too.

They do expect to be heard and to have their concerns addressed — and that is not too much to ask now that Mr. Bush is president of us all.

The New York Times

New York City, New York, January 29, 1989

George Bush once said that he wanted to be President of "all the people" of the United States. Since this is a country with a remarkably, and often unnervingly, diverse citizenry, that's a tall order but an indispensable duty.

Among the issues that now divide Americans, none is more tormenting than abortion. Sometimes the dissension has provoked violence; always it has provoked an avalanche of words. Strip the issue of rhetoric, however, and it comes down to a simple question: Does society have the right to force a woman to incubate a fetus against her will?

Sixteen years ago this month, the Supreme Court settled the question in the case of Roe v. Wade. The court neither endorsed abortion nor declared that one side had the superior moral claim. Instead, Justice Blackmun, who wrote the opinion, held that a woman's right must be weighed against the fetus's growing *potential* for life.

Therefore, he reasoned, the state's interest in protecting life increases as the fetus grows. Accordingly, the decision left up to a woman and her doctor the choice to continue a pregnancy, at least during the first trimester. It allowed the state to impose some limitation on abortion in the second trimester, and allowed stronger limitation in the third.

To millions of Americans the Supreme Court's decision was wise, humane and in the finest tradition of tolerance. But to others it was anathema, denounced, sometimes with arson, and bombs, at abortion clinics. Those who disagree with Roe v. Wade are free to speak out, even to line the entrances to abortion clinics and hiss the patients. What they refuse to do is grant to others what they have granted themselves: the freedom to make their own choices.

In this refusal they have two allies: former President Reagan — and his successor. The right-to-life movement is, in fact, so certain — rightly or wrongly — of its claim on Mr. Bush that one of its leaders had no qualms about calling him to heel last week. "Unfortunately, the White House staff chose to put in a one-way communication line," Nellie Gray complained after Mr. Bush greeted Monday's abortion protest by phone. "He spoke to us but he could not hear us. That was not an adequate way to deal with our pro-life march."

Most Americans are never called upon to balance public tolerance and private morality. But a President, especially one who wants to be the President of "all the people," has a responsibility to do so. By declaring himself determined to overturn Roe v. Wade, Mr. Bush, like his predecessor, expresses his indifference to the deepest views of millions. No one "likes" abortion, especially not the woman who must make so painful a decision. But to deny her the right to make it is to traduce tolerance and infringe freedom.   copyright © The New York Times 1989

THE INDIANAPOLIS STAR
Indianapolis, Indiana, January 1, 1989

Almost without exception the newspaper and TV commentators who notice such things congratulated President-elect Bush on his nomination of Dr. Louis Sullivan of Atlanta as secretary of health and human services.

The plaudits were not so much for Sullivan as for Bush — because Bush had the courage or the smarts not to knuckle under to anti-abortion activists who contended that Sullivan was soft on abortion.

In truth, it is hard to say just where Sullivan stands. He is on record as strongly supporting a woman's right of free choice — unhindered and unlimited freedom of choice. He is also on record as opposing abortion except in cases of rape, incest, or imminent danger to the life of the mother.

Either Sullivan is trying to be all things to all women, or he is embarrassingly ambivalent on an issue that to many people is the most politically charged moral dilemma of the decade. Or, he may have very strong feelings that he is willing to suppress for a Cabinet post.

Sullivan's supporters argue, and correctly so, that abortion is, after all, only one of the many crucial interests to be dealt with by HHS. Yet if a secretary is indecisive or confused on abortion, he may well lack direction and commitment to principle on other public health interests.

In all the backing and filling on the Sullivan appointment, however, one sentiment was almost unanimous among the major media. Bush was strong, wise and courageous to ignore the anti-abortion activists. Had he heeded them, of course, he would have been weak, stupid and foolhardy.

Like beauty, the merit of a political appointment is in the eye of the beholder.

The Wichita
Eagle-Beacon
Wichita, Kansas, December 23, 1988

THE conservative ideological litmus test has appeared, unfortunately, at the doorstep of the Bush administration a month before the inauguration. Even though during his campaign Mr. Bush promised no litmus test for Supreme Court appointees, the country's pro-life interests seem eager to administer the test to possible Cabinet appointees on Mr. Bush's behalf.

The test is abortion and the subject is medical educator Dr. Louis Sullivan, Mr. Bush's appointee as secretary of health and human services. Dr. Sullivan managed to pass the test by changing his answer from pro-choice to no choice.

To win the endorsement of the Republican Party's conservative right wing, Dr. Sullivan — and Mr. Bush before him — reversed their positions on abortion rights. In both cases, it might be argued that qualifications and experience became far less important to a dogmatic right wing than jumping through the proper ideological hoops.

Considering the complexities of HHS — which deals with programs as diverse as Social Security, drug and alcohol recovery services and child support enforcement — applying the litmus test to a qualified candidate such as Dr. Sullivan is truly unfortunate. The secretary of health and human services is a key Cabinet position and a potential appointee's administrative qualifications should take precedence over personal beliefs.

Mr. Bush could have stood up to the pro-life community and spared Dr. Sullivan this needless posturing. As long as abortion is a legally protected right in this country, Dr. Sullivan's position on abortion — and Mr. Bush's, for that matter — is irrelevant. As secretary of health and human services, it would be Dr. Sullivan's responsibility to uphold the law, as it will be President Bush's.

Far better that the test of a potential Cabinet member's fitness for office limit itself to the qualifications and experience a candidate would bring to the post. This litmus test proves nothing and means nothing.

THE SACRAMENTO BEE
Sacramento, California, December 22, 1988

As he campaigned for the presidency, George Bush tried to make clear that he opposes abortion and wants the Roe vs. Wade decision, which made abortion a constitutional right, overturned. But he also said that abortion ought not be used as a litmus test for political appointments. His commitment to that position is itself now being tested in the attack of right-to-life groups on his intention to appoint Louis W. Sullivan, the president of the Morehouse School of Medicine, as secretary of health and human services.

If Bush doesn't stick to his course, his assurances about the litmus test — and confidence in Bush's own ability to resist special-interest pressure groups — will be undermined even before he takes office. Equally unfortunate, he'll lose a good candidate and exclude hundreds of others from high federal office.

The source of the controversy is a statement Sullivan made to the Atlanta Journal-Constitution last weekend that while he opposed federal funding for abortions, he personally believed that a woman had a right to make her own choice. That brought a storm of protest from anti-abortion groups, which declared that their entire program would be jeopardized if Sullivan were appointed. Subsequently, Sullivan declared that he supported Bush's position on abortion, and that he personally opposed abortion except in cases of rape, incest or where a mother's life was in danger.

What's been nearly forgotten in this controversy is that Sullivan appears to be such a good choice. Given his record — in turning what had been a marginal medical program into a respected medical school; his commitment to training doctors for community service rather than high-paying specialties; his familiarity with state and federal health policies and with the problems of medical care; and his exemplary personal history, as a young man from a rural Georgia town, the son of a black undertaker, who has become one of the nation's most influential medical educators — the flap about abortion rights is stupid and demeaning. Bush certainly understands that; he should act accordingly.

French Abortion Pill
Stirs Worldwide Debate

The French company Roussel Uclaf S.A. October 26, 1988 announced that it would suspend distribution of a new drug used to induce abortion. The drug, RU-486, had been approved for use in France and China.

Roussel said that it was withdrawing the abortion pill, marketed under the trade name Mifepristone, "in the face of emotion on the part of public opinion in France and abroad." There had been periodic protests against the pill at Roussel's Paris headquarters and at the French ministry of health.

(Abortion had been legalized in France in 1975 after a bitter political debate. Since 1984 the health system had reimbursed abortion expenses.)

Antiabortion groups in the U.S. had also protested against the pill and had threatened boycotts of Roussel's products and those of Hoechst AG, the West German company that owned a majority of Roussel. The French government held a 36.25% stake in the pharmaceuticals firm.

The drug had been cleared in France September 23 to be administered at medical facilities to women in the first 49 days of pregnancy. It was said to be 80% effective in terminating a pregnancy by causing a miscarriage. When taken in conjunction with a second drug – the hormone prostaglandin – the efficiency rate rose to 95%.

The first large-scale study of RU-486 had found the pill to be as safe and effective as surgical abortion, according to a report published in the March 8, 1990 *New England Journal of Medicine*.

The study, which had been performed by the drug's manufacturer, Roussel-Uclaf, had found that among 2,115 women in France who were given the drug, 96% succeeded in terminating their pregnancy, a rate comparable to that for surgical abortion. (The remaining 4% of RU-486 user were subsequently given surgical abortions.)

Virtually all the women in the trial reported heavy menstrual-like bleeding that lasted for an average of nine days following administration of the drug. Many women also reported abdominal cramps following an injection of the hormonal substance prostaglandin, which was used to improve the efficiency of RU-486. About one-third experienced nausea or vomiting, although the effects were said to be mild.

A federal judge July 14 ordered the government to return the pills to the woman, but an appellate court the same day blocked the judge's order. The Supreme Court July 17 denied the woman's request the get the pills back.

The woman was Leona Benten, 29, an unmarried social worker from California. Volunteering for the activist group Abortion Rights Mobilization, which sought to legalize RU-486 in the U.S., she had traveled to London to obtain the drug and flown back to Kennedy Airport. The group notified Customs officials of her arrival, and they seized from her luggage 12 pills – the precise dosage required to terminate her six-week pregnancy.

Benten planned to have a surgical abortion if she could not get the pills back. But she said she was frightened to do so, having undergone the procedure once before.

THE
DENVER POST

Denver, Colorado, July 22, 1992

ORDINARILY, it would seem highly improper for Congress to play politics with science by ordering the Food and Drug Administration to approve a specific drug for use in the United States.

The FDA, after all, is supposed to serve as the public's first line of defense against untested, ineffective or downright dangerous remedies, whether they're produced here or imported from abroad. Nobody would fault the agency for rejecting a new version of thalidomide or laetrile, for example.

But in the case of the French-made abortion pill, RU-486, it seems apparent that the FDA itself has been playing politics with science. The agency's refusal to allow Americans to bring the drug into this country is based on purely ideological opposition, rather than a reasoned medical analysis.

As a California woman argued in a futile attempt to overturn the policy last week, more than 100,000 women in Europe have used the pill to safely end their pregnancies since it was introduced in 1986, with no indication of any serious side effects.

In short, the FDA position seems to be a direct result of the Bush administration's "zero tolerance" approach to abortion, as evidenced by the president's mindless veto of a critically needed bill that contained funds for fetal tissue research.

This is not to say that RU-486 is entirely risk-free. Like other powerful drugs, it should be used only under a doctor's supervision. But outlawing it, especially at a time when many states may be making it harder to obtain a conventional abortion, will only invite women to buy the pill on the black market and use it without any professional guidance at all.

Congress should put pressure on the FDA to lift its ban. As U.S. Rep. Pat Schroeder of Colorado has rightly pointed out, the agency is "being held hostage" by the anti-abortion lobby, and thousands of American women are losing the opportunity to exercise a legitimate choice as a result.

The Philadelphia Inquirer
Philadelphia, Pennsylvania, July 27, 1992

Leona Benten did a public service by trying to bring the French-made abortion pill RU 486 into this country for her own use. When her pills were confiscated at Kennedy Airport early this month, that focused attention on the reason why there is an embargo against the pill, and why the pill is not available in this country. The reason is the same in both cases: the Bush administration's obeisance to anti-abortion zealots.

Even though access to this particular abortion method may seem like a secondary issue compared to the fight over the very right to abortion, both sides in point of fact consider the abortion pill extremely important. By providing abortion with pills, not surgery, this method diffuses (and defuses) the abortion business. Simply put, if pregnant women no longer have to go to an "abortion mill," where does Operation Rescue go to harass them? With no venue for confrontation, the issue will, literally, vanish.

In a technical sense we have really only had Round One of this case. In it, the Supreme Court refused Ms. Benten's bid to reclaim the pills while the case is pending — which had the practical effect of forcing her to undergo a surgical abortion. (The abortion pill, which induces a miscarriage in which the fertilized embryo is discharged from the woman's body, is recommended for use only within the first nine weeks of pregnancy.)

The court has yet to rule on the basic claim in her case — that the abortion pill does not belong on the Food and Drug Administration's "import-alert" list of drugs that customs personnel should be seizing. However, the Supreme Court's unwillingness to intervene indicates that there's a good chance she'll ultimately lose. That being the case, Congress should go ahead and pass a bill by Rep. Ron Wyden (D., Oregon) that would stop the FDA from listing this drug for seizure.

The abortion pill — which has been used by more than 100,000 women in other countries — doesn't fit any of the usual reasons for being on the FDA list. In particular, there's no evidence that it's unsafe or ineffective for most women. On the contrary, this FDA policy seems to have been triggered by letters from people who call the abortion pill "chemical warfare against the unborn," ignoring the fact that abortion is legal.

Mr. Wyden's bill would apply only to this single special case, where political factors have so clearly obliterated the medical considerations that normally would determine the outcome. The bill would have no effect on the FDA's efforts to protect American women from foreign-made drugs that may be risky.

But even if this quarantine against the abortion pill is ended, access to it will be very limited because most women can't afford to jet off to Paris or London to pick some up. The real question is why the FDA hasn't tested and approved the abortion pill for sale in America, and the answer at present is simple: The manufacturer hasn't submitted it. The company's reluctance to do so is understandable in light of the Bush administration's extreme antagonism to abortion rights.

The company is prudently waiting until the federal government is willing to judge the abortion pill on its medical merits. That won't happen before the presidential election, but it could happen soon after.

The Wichita
Eagle-Beacon
Wichita, Kansas, July 17, 1992

The U.S. Supreme Court last month reaffirmed the constitutional right of American women to abortion. It's ridiculous, therefore, that the Bush administration is still making a political football of the French abortion pill, RU486.

The issue came up again when a California woman returned from France with one dose of the pills for her personal use. Customs agents in New York seized them, triggering a court battle over the administration's long-standing failure to recognize and approve RU486.

It's bad enough that the administration's attitude toward the French pill has discouraged U.S. pharmaceutical companies from applying for a license to manufacture the drug here. It's downright cruel that the administration seeks to thwart Americans from venturing abroad to secure pills for personal use. The pill has proved to be a generally safe, effective way to end unwanted pregnancies, and the FDA does allow Americans to bring home foreign drugs for treating AIDS and some forms of cancer.

The appeal of RU486 is that it ends pregnancies without invasive surgical procedures, which can be dangerous. Moreover, it makes abortion a private act. It doesn't subject women to the publicity and harassment that can accompany a trip to abortion clinics.

The FDA ban on RU486 has nothing to do with safety, and everything to do with abortion politics. It's sad that an agency supposedly dedicated to science and objective research has been enlisted in a political cause.

As long as abortion is a constitutional right, it makes no sense to deny women a safer, less costly and less drastic alternative to surgery. That the Bush administration refuses to see it that way is a disgrace and an embarrassment.

The
Des Moines Register
Des Moines, Iowa, July 18, 1992

If there is a moral from the story of Leona Benten's trip to England to obtain the French abortion pill, and her subsequent run-ins with the U.S. government over her right to keep it, it is that in the contentious climate surrounding abortion, even personal decisions become ammunition in a political battlefield.

Benten, 29 and pregnant, volunteered to be a test case in an abortion-rights group's challenge to the ban on importation of the drug, RU486, which is used in Europe to end pregnancies. The drug is not approved for use in the United States. The U.S. Customs Service seized Benten's supply to make a political point. And the FDA, which has the right to make exceptions to its import ban, refused to do so. One federal judge ordered the pills returned to Benten, but an appeals court overruled, sending the case up to Supreme Court Justice Clarence Thomas. On Friday, the entire Supreme Court rejected Benten's plea to regain possession of the pills.

None of this would have happened if the drug were approved for use. But the Bush administration's antipathy toward abortion rights and threats from abortion opponents have intimidated European distributors from even seeking approval to market the drug in the United States. That has prevented access to a promising new drug by thousands of American women. In the three years since its introduction in France, some 110,000 European women have used RU486 as a safe, effective alternative to clinical abortion. The drug can be used as early as the morning after conception and up to 47 days later. It also has shown promise in treating glaucoma, breast cancer, Alzheimer's disease, AIDS and other illnesses.

California and New Hampshire have passed resolutions inviting RU486 research in those states. Clinical testing of the drug here is favored by the American Medical Association and many other medical and scientific organizations.

But the manufacturers chose Canada over the United States for studying RU486's effectiveness in breast-cancer treatment, citing the U.S. anti-abortion movement. It's a tangible fear, considering anti-abortion forces have successfully boycotted companies with the most tenuous links to abortion providers.

The FDA could signal U.S. receptiveness toward research into RU486 by relaxing the import restrictions to encourage clinical trials, and by making exceptions for personal use. In its behavior toward Benten, it makes little attempt to conceal its outright hostility toward the drug.

The Oregonian

Portland, Oregon, July 24, 1992

The introduction of private-relief legislation Tuesday by Rep. Patricia Schroeder, D-Colo., that would have released the French abortion pill RU 486 to the woman who tried to bring it into this country was a largely symbolic act. The first of two deadlines for the woman to have safely taken the single dose had passed three days earlier.

Schroeder's challenge to the Food and Drug Administration was to take the politics out of its policies. It follows legislation introduced last year by Rep. Ron Wyden, D-Ore. Wyden's bill would lift the FDA's import alert, which seizes prescription drugs imported for private use.

Schroeder's and Wyden's bills shouldn't be necessary. The FDA, on its own, ought to resolve any implication that its import ban is politically motivated by treating RU 486 like any other drug.

FDA policy allows individuals to bring drugs that have been approved in other countries into the United States in small quantities for personal use. Drugs to fight AIDS and cancer frequently enter this country under this policy.

The agency's official position is that its concern with RU 486 is that it can pose a health hazard if taken without a doctor's supervision. How does that differ from other drugs that are available only by doctor's prescription?

In ruling in the woman's favor last week, U.S. District Judge Charles P. Sifton said politics did appear to be behind the ban and called the controversy "a lawsuit waiting to happen." Higher courts reversed him.

The effect of the controversy has been to keep the drug from entering the customary testing loop for foreign drugs. The manufacturer, Roussel Uclaf of France, has said it would not seek approval for the drug here until the government changed its policy and the threat of boycotts or violence by abortion opponents decreased.

Wyden says the recent attention focused on RU 486 should help generate additional support for his bill, pending in the health and environment subcommittee of the Energy and Commerce Committee.

If the FDA is unable to base its RU 486 policy on science, then Congress should remove the drug from the politically steeped agency's jurisdiction.

The Washington Times

Washington, D.C., July 22, 1992

The ongoing controversy over the French abortion pill RU-486 brings the U.S. Food and Drug Administration full circle. Once pressured to resist approval of a 1960s drug linked to birth defects, the agency is now under the political gun to approve a chemical that threatens both life and limb.

This week Rep. Patricia Schroeder introduced legislation to force the FDA to return RU-486 pills it took from a woman earlier this month. Leona Benten, a pregnant woman who wanted a nonsurgical abortion, brought the pills back from Great Britain, where the drug is legal. She had intended to use the drug in this country, where it is not legal, but the FDA confiscated the pills at the airport.

When the Supreme Court refused to make the agency return the pills, Mrs. Schroeder stepped in with her legislation. She said the agency was discriminating against Miss Benten because the agency doesn't always stop people from bringing drugs into this country that they intend to use on themselves. "For example," she said, "AIDS and cancer patients often go to other countries and bring medicine back with them."

Mrs. Schroeder may have revealed more by her analogy than she intended. It's not every day that one hears somebody compare pregnancy with, say, AIDS or cancer. Nor does one expect to hear a drug whose explicit purpose is death described as "medicine," not at any rate in a field where the guiding principle is: First, do no harm. Of course, if you like Dr. Schroeder's nonfamily practice, you'll love her legislation.

A more illuminating comparison is between the RU-486 controversy today and the thalidomide controversy of 30 years ago. West German drug manufacturers developed thalidomide as an "ideal sedative," one that pregnant women could also take to relieve morning sickness. Physicians later came to link the drug to so-called thalidomide babies, those with arms missing, with deformed legs or worse. The toll ran into the thousands.

The FDA never got around to approving the drug for use in this country, and its inaction in that case was later rewarded with a presidential medal. Then-FDA medical officer Dr. Frances Kelsey received the gold medal for distinguished federal civilian service from President John F. Kennedy. Shortly afterward, drug experiments involving pregnant women were cut back sharply.

Today, the thalidomide case comes up almost any time FDA officials want to expand their oversight of the nation's food and drug laws. Editorials here have often argued that the oversight creates such uncertainty in the drug approval process that the nation loses the benefit of many experimental drugs produced by companies financially unable to run the FDA gantlet.

But there is no uncertainty about the intent of RU-486. It is supposed to kill the fetus. That is not medicine, and the FDA has every right to keep it out.

The Virginian-Pilot

Norfolk, Virginia, July 22, 1992

Leona Benten lost a battle last weekend when the Supreme Court decided, 7-2, that the Food and Drug Administration and the U.S. Customs Service legally seized her cache of RU-486. Ms. Benten brought "the abortion pill" from France, where it is approved for use, to the United States, where it is not. But the fight for choice is far from lost, and that court decision turns on a spiteful irony most Americans do not laud.

The Bush administration argued, and the court agreed, that RU-486 does not qualify under either of the usual FDA exceptions for admittance of an unapproved drug; that is, RU-486 is neither ineffective nor innocuous; and alternative treatment, surgical abortion, is available here. The irony is that surgical abortion would *not* be available here if the Bush administra-

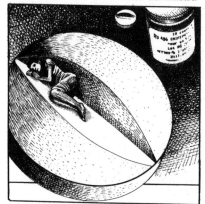

tion and that small band of anti-abortionists to whom it gives undue ear had their way. And no safe alternative will be available if they can continue to intimidate the French manufacturer out of undertaking FDA approval.

These anti-abortionists reject this pill for the very reasons advocates of choice support it. As prescribed by physicians, RU-486 safely induces early abortion (that is, within eight weeks of conception) in the privacy of a woman's home. It takes women who choose abortion off the sidewalks and out of the clinics. It thus deprives the anti-choice zealots of their prized tactic: the gantlet of psychological and, at times, physical abuse they set up outside clinics. It thus threatens their latest tactic: thrusting fetuses in the faces of Bill Clinton and other politicians and, via campaign ads which federal law forbids networks to censor, onto every TV screen.

That tactic may well backfire, and should. For some time now, it has been clear that most Americans are increasingly uneasy with abortion late in pregnancy, when the fetus may be viable outside the womb. They dislike a woman's resort to abortion as birth control. But they dislike even more permitting government and anti-abortion activists a veto of this most private decision.

RU-486 offers early abortion, safely, privately. It offers as well promise of another method of contraception, the best preventive of abortion. *Benten vs. FDA* may not have the ring of *Roe vs. Wade*. It will reverberate in the battle nonetheless.

THE SACRAMENTO BEE
Sacramento, California, July 27, 1992

It's unfortunate that Leona Benten's highly publicized effort to bring 12 RU-486 abortion pills into this country couldn't have been a clearer test of the government's suppression not just of abortion technology but of important medical research in other areas. Not much will be lost for those who support choice and unfettered research. But not much has been gained either.

There's little doubt that the administration's actions in blocking import even of individual doses of the French pill for personal use – something that's permitted in the case of some other drugs not licensed for sale here – were based as much on political as on medical grounds.

But it hardly took this case to demonstrate that. The Reagan and Bush administrations, blindly marching with anti-abortion extremists, have put barriers in the way of even the most desirable research – on Parkinson's disease, for example – if it involved aborted fetal tissue. And they have so vigorously discouraged research in better methods of contraception – an area in which this country is far behind the rest of the Western world – that the maker of RU-486 has not even applied for permission to test the drug in this country.

Benten's efforts may remind some people of those facts. They also helped make clear that sooner or later, if government policy doesn't change, there is likely to be a black market in RU-486 in this country. The more some states, abetted by a conservative Supreme Court, make it hard or impossible to get legal abortions, the more widespread that black market will become.

But even in the countries, like France, where RU-486 is widely used, it's not used without medical supervision. The Benten challenge ignored that consideration. While there would no doubt be physicians who might have supervised Benten's use of the drug, it's not at all clear what their legal responsibilities would have been in such circumstances. And since there are risks and side-effects associated with RU-486, the FDA's formal opposition to its import, even for personal use, could not be flatly dismissed merely as political. Unlike AIDS patients, who face imminent death and for whom even risky remedies are justifiable, Benten, who has many other abortion options open to her, could not claim this was a matter of desperation.

Because of that, her challenge may have done as much to conceal the blindness of the government's policy as to highlight it. The real issue with things like RU-486 is not that they're unavailable for private use by people who can afford to go to Europe to bring them back, but that the government has been so resistant even to legitimate tests, not just of new contraceptive options but of a host of other medicines to deal with everything from breast cancer to Alzheimer's. That's the real consequence of this stupid policy.

The Washington Post
Washington, D.C., July 21, 1992

THE COURT fight over RU-486, the abortion pill, is just one example of the larger tensions that tug at the Food and Drug Administration. Prime among those tensions, especially now, as the agency gains visibility under an activist administrator, is the seeming strain between two differing FDA roles that each played a part in the RU-486 case: approval, which certifies drugs and devices as safe and effective and clears them for use, and enforcement, which uses nationwide muscle to track down and stop abuses. In his push to make the FDA a more aggressive player in health regulation, administrator David Kessler has concentrated mostly on enforcement, with campaigns on such disparate matters as breast implants, tranquilizers and drug promotional campaigns. This has led not just to the predictable outcry from affected companies but also to the more complicated argument that in strengthening enforcement muscle, the FDA is letting the approval side of its roster slow down too far.

Is there a correct balance somewhere that isn't being struck? One problem with that argument is the distance, practical as well as political, between the agency's approval and enforcement apparatus. The former requires mostly scientists and experts to put drugs through the tests; the latter, mostly on-site investigators. Drug approval policy is a complex field of its own, whose extremes are often invoked by two shorthand examples, thalidomide and AIDS. The first, the British-made drug that produced birth defects in the 1960s, is the classic case of a drug cleared too easily; the second has been the engine for special streamlined procedures when sufferers have nothing to lose and can't wait.

The enforcement side, of drugs, devices and practices already cleared and in use, is even more complicated. Dr. Kessler's first high-visibility campaigns after taking office—nutrition labels that might mislead, breast implants that might be unsafe, a promotional campaign for a drug that violated FDA drug advertising rules—were designed to curb specific abuses but also to project the image of an FDA that would go aggressively after violations.

The strategy is needed because the health and medical markets are so sprawling and difficult to police that without the psychological jolt they could absorb nearly infinite resources. Last week the consumer group Public Citizen complained in a letter to the FDA that the agency had been lax in prosecuting medical-device manufacturers who fail to meet FDA rules on reporting deaths and injuries—the argument being that, without consistent follow-through, that message isn't convincing. That implies that the largest investment of time and manpower comes now, at the start, and that easing it too soon would be a mistake.

Portland Press Herald
Portland, Maine, July 21, 1992

The Bush administration was too busy last week to cut the nation's $4 trillion debt. It was too busy to help hundreds of thousands, perhaps millions, of homeless people find housing. It was even too busy to expand affordable medical care.

What was it so busy doing? Reaching into the life of a California woman, Leona Benten, 29 and eight weeks pregnant.

By a vote of 7-2, the U.S. Supreme Court told her last week: Sorry, lady, if you want an abortion, you cannot take a pill that is safely used abroad. If your pregnancy is to be ended, it must be surgically done.

The Bush administration had urged the court to say exactly that. Why? Because the French abortion pill RU486 has become a pawn in this country's politics of pregnancy and abortion.

The U.S. Food and Drug Administration has not approved the pill, developed in the 1980s and used successfully abroad. It hasn't been asked to. The manufacturer, Roussel Uclaf, has been understandably chilled by 12 years of presidential opposition to abortion here.

All of which brings us to Leona Benten. She bought a small amount of RU486 in Europe and notified Customs she would be bringing it into this country. The point was to test whether RU486 would be treated like many other foreign medications, or singled out for special censure.

Now Benten has her answer. While Americans traveling abroad can bring home small quantities of medications for personal use, even when the medicines are not approved in this country, they cannot bring home abortion pills.

RU486, taken with the hormone prostaglandin, allows a woman to end a pregnancy in its early weeks in her own home. Privacy replaces politics. Confidentiality replaces confrontation, and personal morality, not public doctrine, governs.

RU486 can take abortion out of the public arena. Sadly, the Bush administration, politically bound to abortion opponents, refuses to let it go.

St. Petersburg Times

St. Petersburg, Florida, July 21, 1992

In letting the Food and Drug Administration keep the controversial abortion pills it seized from a California woman, the Supreme Court shed some faint light on its new standard for judging government obstacles to obtaining abortions. Abortion rights advocates had arranged for Leona Benten to bring the French abortifacient RU486 from London in order to challenge the government's ban on importing the drug for personal use. Since Benten was only days away from the cutoff point for safely taking the pills, the court ruled in emergency session.

Benten's attorneys argued FDA procedural violations, but two dissenting justices were willing to say that its actions placed a so-called "undue burden" on Benten's right to end her pregnancy, the criterion that emerged from the court's recent high-profile decision in *Pennsylvania vs. Casey* ; but their colleagues either didn't agree or were understandably loath to encourage such end-runs around the normal judicial appeals process and executive branch regulatory authority.

That probably wasn't encouraging to those who fear the court's new standard doesn't amount to much protection of abortion rights, but the court still acted wisely in sending Benten's lawsuit back for calmer arguments before lower courts, where it might yet prevail in principle. Benten's need for an abortion was real but her emergency was admittedly contrived.

Nonetheless, the suit focused attention on the fact that abortion politics, not science, is playing a role in the Bush administration's handling of RU486. The result is that in seeking to exercise a legal right, women like Benten are needlessly condemned to more invasive surgical procedures.

The FDA certainly needs wide discretion to safeguard public health with limited resources, but the agency only weakens its credibility when it uses that authority to do the opposite. Its handling of RU486 flies in the face of the administration's own stated goal of streamlining the drug approval process, including more receptivity to reliable research data produced outside the United States.

The drug is hardly an unknown quantity. It's legally available in several countries, and respected nations such as Britain and France have ample data showing its safe use by more than 100,000 women. The agency has allowed people to import more questionable drugs for cancer and AIDS for their use under its personal-use exception rule. Yet RU486 has languished under a personal import ban since 1989 that even has researchers complaining of inability to get a reliable supply line from its French manufacturer in order to study the drug.

RU486 is a promising drug for treatment of many vexing diseases, and its use as an abortifacient must not stand in the way of exploring that promise. If our regulatory system were working in the interests of science instead of politics, we wouldn't have the spectacle of a member of Congress introducing a bill to prescribe a drug for a pregnant woman.

TULSA WORLD

Tulsa, Oklahoma, July 30, 1992

OPPONENTS of the U.S. government's ban on the French abortion pill RU-486 have found new arguments. In addition to the pill's value in terminating pregnancy, they say, it holds promise as a treatment for a variety of illnesses.

The claims, if true, add urgency to the need to get this pill approved for use in this country.

But the argument that RU-486 might be useful in treating certain tumors and glandular disorders does not change the basic issue.

The issue is whether the safe drug laws can be used to promote a certain religious view — call it a bias — against a safe and valuable drug.

The argument is not whether this pill is safe or whether it can or cannot be useful in treating disease. If there is any question about safety, that could be determined by further testing.

The reason the pill is being kept out of the United States is because it offers a safe means of abortion.

Not that the Federal Drug Administration has specifically outlawed RU-486 because it can be used to induce abortion. The FDA hasn't done much of anything. The company licensed to produce the pill in France has shown no interest in bringing it to the United States. Rep. Ron Wyden, D-Ore., says that's because of a "hostile climate" in this country, the result of the Bush administration's alliance with the anti-abortion lobby.

If this pill offers hope to victims of cancer or other diseases, then there is all the more reason to approve it for use in the United States as quickly as possible.

But the fact that it offers a safe alternative to surgical abortion is reason enough to stop the stalling. Federal policy on pharmaceuticals should be based on safety and usefulness — not the religious views of anti-abortionists.

The Seattle Times

Seattle, Washington, July 17, 1992

LEONA Benten's private drama shows RU-486, the abortion pill, is the next battle ground in the abortion fight.

Her lawyers appeared before U.S. Supreme Court Justice Clarence Thomas Wednesday to ask for the return of RU-486 pills confiscated from Benten two weeks ago. If federal customs officials do not release the pills by tomorrow, Benten will have to seek a surgical abortion.

Benten acquired the drugs in England for personal use. The pills, manufactured by a French pharmaceutical firm, can cause a non-surgical abortion by preventing a fertilized egg from implanting in the uterus.

Since the drug became available in 1988, it has been used by more than 110,000 women in France and Britain. It is effective if taken very early, usually prior to the eighth week of pregnancy. Benton will reach that threshold tomorrow.

The case is the first to test the Food and Drug Administration's prohibition against importing RU-486 to this country. The drug has not been approved for sale here and can be barred at the border. But the FDA frequently allows in other unapproved drugs for personal use.

There is no safety reason to treat RU-486 differently; the difference lies in the Bush administration's abortion politics. The FDA rule is intended to discourage the drug's manufacturer from opening a U.S. market.

The anti-abortion camp's opposition to RU-486 is not surprising. The pill literally removes abortion from the public arena. Access to the pill means women will be able to get abortions early, safely, and at home. Abortion as a privacy right will become truly a private act.

RU-486 could diffuse the political controversy. It also could change the role of government and the courts. Restrictions on doctors intended to discourage abortions would have less impact. Waiting periods would become meaningless. And anti-abortion protesters would lose their stage — they can't chain themselves to every woman's home.

Banning RU-486 will not alter the fact that 1.5 million abortions are performed in the U.S. each year. Yet the administration's opposition to the drug has caused a perverse outcome. Benten was prevented from getting a safe abortion at six weeks. And now she may have to undergo surgery.

Washington, D.C., July 21, 1992

OPPOSING VIEW **This could be a chemical time bomb; nothing is known about long-term side effects.**

Friday's Supreme Court ruling on RU-486 sent a clear message that drug use in this country will not be dictated by the ideological agenda of abortion advocates intent on making an election-year splash.

In France, the RU-486 abortion technique is used only on women five to seven weeks pregnant. Contrary to numerous inaccurate press accounts, an RU-486 abortion does not destroy a "fertilized egg" but kills a living human embryo. When the Supreme Court denied Leona Benten's petition, she was eight weeks pregnant; her unborn baby's heart had already been beating for over two weeks.

RU-486 must be administered with another powerful hormone, prostaglandin, also not approved for sale in the

By **Richard Glasow**, education director of the National Right to Life Committee.

USA. This powerful two-drug cocktail has killed one woman and caused three life-threatening heart attacks and other serious short-term complications. The manufacturer in Britain has acknowledged that 9% of women have "very heavy bleeding" and 30% will require narcotics for pain. Most women experience vomiting, nausea and dizziness.

The president of Roussel Uclaf, manufacturer of RU-486, has called the technique "an appalling psychological ordeal." RU-486 could be a chemical time bomb because nothing is known about possible long-term adverse side effects.

Even some RU-486 supporters have acknowledged in recent interviews the inherent danger of using RU-486 without close medical supervision and emergency medical facilities available. For that reason, the American Medical Association said in 1990 the Food and Drug Administration "acted responsibly in issuing import restrictions."

Pro-abortion advocates want to trivialize abortion as a method of birth control. In this case, they've been willing to intentionally expose a woman to a dangerous, unapproved drug to promote their extreme pro-abortion agenda.

Rockford Register Star

Rockford, Illinois, July 18, 1992

In an incident that seemed stage-managed from the outset, a pregnant California woman brought a dose of RU-486, the French abortifacient, into the United States from Britain. No sooner was she off the tarmac than U.S. Customs seized the pills.

This drug should not be held hostage to political sentiment.

A federal judge ordered the drugs returned to the woman, but an appeals court stayed that ruling. A battle now rages over the applicability of a federal regulation permitting importation for personal use of drugs that are legal in the country of origin.

But whether Leona Benten —whose seven-week pregnancy may now be beyond the safe reach of RU-486 anyway — can keep her abortion pills is not the central issue.

More to the point is the Bush administration's political sensitivity to RU-486, which has been under a Food and Drug Administration "import alert" since 1989. That means that the drug, widely available in Britain and France, cannot be brought into the country for personal use. Even though there is no ban on import of the drug for scientific research, the controversy over RU-486 in this country has effectively dried up supply. The French manufacturer wants to stay out of the political firestorm.

By most reports, RU-486 is a safe and effective means of abortion for up to seven to nine weeks of pregnancy. But without sufficient research in the United States it's impossible to judge performance of the pill, beyond anecdotal evidence from other countries. One thing's for sure: It may be a much less traumatic means of terminating a pregnancy, but it's not a trouble-free one. Taking the drug requires at least three visits to the doctor, and it's only 96 percent effective.

All the medical facts about the French pill may never be known to American women, though, unless the FDA loosens its grip on a drug that deserves legitimate and thorough testing.

IF BUSH GOT PREGNANT, RU486 WOULD BE LEGAL.

Post-Tribune

Gary, Indiana, July 19, 1992

The Honolulu Advertiser

Honolulu, Hawaii, July 20, 1992

Not wishing to take the heat alone, Justice Clarence Thomas passed to the full Supreme Court the decision on a woman's quest to bring an unapproved, early-pregnancy "abortion pill" into this country for her own use.

The court said no, with two liberal justices dissenting.

Abortion rights advocates brought this legal test on purpose, alerting authorities that the woman was carrying the drug.

They want the drug, called RU-486, available as an alternative to surgical abortion in the first eight weeks. They argue that a drug which made any other legal procedure, like heart surgery, unnecessary would be welcomed.

But the Bush administration not only argued against allowing the woman to have the drug for her own use, as allowed by the Food and Drug Administration in some cases, it also refuses to have the FDA test RU-486 for American use.

The French manufacturer of the drug has not asked for approval to sell it here, fearing reprisals and boycotts of its other products. In France, the health minister had to order the company to put the drug back on the market, calling it "the moral property of women."

The pill (which actually prevents gestation, as the IUD does) is used safely under doctor supervision in France, Britain and China. There's no medical reason it should be dangerous here.

Many people in this country feel there are too many abortions; we agree. To deal with that, better sex education, encouraging more personal responsibility and better availability of pre-conception birth control may help.

But depriving women of the results of medical progress is mindless and backwards. Ultimately, it will be futile in stopping abortions.

The timing of Leona Benten's pregnancy could not have coincided better with the need to begin to resolve the important issue of women controlling their own bodies.

Benten is the Berkeley, Calif., social worker challenging the federal government to allow her to terminate her pregnancy with a drug already legal in parts of Europe, but illegal here in the land of the free.

Our opinion

The federal government has extended the political argument over abortion in blocking the abortion pill from usage.

In the wake of the U.S. Supreme Court's decision to let states heavily regulate abortions, it would be wise for the U.S. government to let the controverisal RU486 pill be governed by the same rules as the medical procedures for abortions.

The moral question of abortion has been talked to death. And the talking has produced different laws in different states, but abortion is still legal in this country. Instead, having lost the fundamental argument over choice in the legislatures and courts of the land, the Bush administration has taken its anti-choice position one step further by banning certain methods.

Where does the government get off saying that a method safer than many clinical approaches — one approved of in England and France — ought to be illegal? The question of choice has been resolved, but the government persists in its intrusions by trying to select the methods. This, too, is a matter of choice.

Who is in control of women's bodies and their right to choose? More importantly, why has a question of medicine become a question of morality and been tied up in politics?

There should be no political considerations here. Those have been addressed by the states and the courts.

RU486 has been safely administered to  more than 110,000 women in Europe and is widely accepted. Yet it remains off the shelves here because of the Bush administration's conservative anti-choice stance, and apparently for that reason alone. Solicitor General Kenneth Starr admitted as much last week in arguments before Supreme Court Justice Clarence Thomas when he said the Food and Drug Administration allows some unapproved drugs into the U.S. but bans others in a manner more arbitrary than reasoned.

This is a screen of smoke billowing from a political pipe. It is not sound policy.

Opposition to this drug is rooted in politics, not in a sound medical determination. It is time to take abortion out of the political arena. The questions of rights and of control over one's body should not be political.

Those questions have been answered by the courts already.

The debate is important because it addresses the place we give to women in our society. But it is tiring just the same because it seems repetitive, because it shouldn't need to take place anymore and because it is such a simple question. Women's rights to privacy and self determination are elementary and they are guaranteed. That should be the end of it. Why must some people continue to make it so hard?

The Hartford Courant

Hartford, Connecticut, July 16, 1992

Often, drugs that are approved for sale in other countries may be imported in small quantities into the United States provided they are not used commercially. That is, someone may bring in the drugs for personal use, as Leona Benten tried to do on July 1.

In a well-planned legal challenge to the Bush administration's ban on the French-made abortion pill RU486, she brought one dose — 12 tablets — which was promptly confiscated by customs agents at Kennedy International Airport.

The Food and Drug Administration, encouraged by the administration, had removed RU486 from the list of drugs that could be imported in small quantities for personal use.

But the FDA should have held a hearing or published its decision to remove the exemption for limited use of RU486. So U.S. District Judge Charles P. Sifton ruled Wednesday that the government had seized Ms. Benten's pills illegally.

The 2nd U.S. Circuit Court of Appeals temporarily blocked Judge Sifton's ruling, however, at the request of the U.S. Justice Department, which wants time to prepare a full-fledged appeal.

This case probably will be decided by the Supreme Court.

The FDA's claim that RU486 could pose a risk is vigorously contested by scientists. Some 110,000 women in Britain and France have used this pill. As Judge Sifton noted, "the decision to ban the drug was based not from any bona fide concern for the safety of users of the drugs, but on political considerations."

Only an administration zealous in its determination to deny women choice carries its policies to such an extreme. Confiscating one dose of pills from a pregnant woman at Kennedy airport is insane.

AKRON BEACON JOURNAL
Akron, Ohio, July 25, 1992

One word goes to the heart of the debate over the importation of the so-called "abortion pill," RU-486: politics.

On one side are the anti-abortion Reagan and Bush administrations, which have sought to pack the Supreme Court with justices who would reverse *Roe vs. Wade*. While the court hasn't done that, it did last week uphold U.S. Customs' confiscation of the drug from a pregnant, California women. This, in spite of the Food and Drug Administration's common practice of allowing individuals to import personal doses of drugs approved in other countries.

On the other side is Leona Benten who allowed herself to be the public foil for an attempt by abortion-rights groups to breach the importation ban even though the 12 aspirin-sized pills could have been carried unnoticed through Customs in her purse.

Because politics all too often prevails in the abortion issue in the United States, the French pharmaceutical firm Roussel Uclaf has not sought FDA licensing of RU-486 for the potentially lucrative American market.

Lost in the politics of abortion is the possibility that RU-486, which works to prevent the implantation of a fertilized egg, also holds promise in the treatment of such diseases as breast and cervical cancer, brain tumors, diabetes and hypertension. Roussel Uclaf recently buckled under the political heat and halted shipment of the drug to the University of Southern California in Los Angeles, which was conducting clinical tests.

Politics in the United States is also keeping RU-486 from women in other nations, 150,000 of whom die each year from complications of legal and illegal abortions. The World Health Organization receives 25 percent of its funding from the United States; it won't buck its biggest donor.

It's more than unfortunate that something that keeps private a woman's decision to end a pregnancy and that could help in other debilitating, even fatal illnesses, is caught in such political combat.

The Phoenix Gazette
Phoenix, Arizona, July 25, 1992

RU-486 will be back.

Though the Supreme Court denied Leona Benten the pills she needed to end her pregnancy, her attempt to bring RU-486 into the United States is just an initial skirmish along the battle line of forces that have not yet begun to fight.

U.S. District Judge Charles P. Sifton agreed with Benten that the U.S. Food and Drug Administration "acted illegally" in implementing its ban on RU-486 without public notice or comment, but the 2nd U.S. Circuit Court of Appeals blocked Sifton's ruling and the Supreme Court sustained the ban.

The focus here was narrow and ought not give much comfort to the forces of ignorance and fear, those who believe RU-486 to be the devil's gift.

The courts simply ruled that Benten failed to demonstrate that there was a substantial likelihood she might win in court during a full hearing of the case.

While that victory was sufficient to deny Benten access to the pills and compelled her to seek a surgical abortion, dissenting Justices Harry A. Blackmun and John Paul Stevens held that the government's action did place an undue burden on her right to an abortion.

"There is no evidence in this record that this applicant faces any ... risk (from the pills)," said Stevens. "I am persuaded that the relevant, legitimate federal interest is not sufficient to justify the burdensome consequence of this seizure."

In fact, according to *The New York Times,* the drug, manufactured by the French company Roussel-Uclaf, is reported to be "as safe as prescription drugs go, and perhaps safer in some respects than standard surgical abortions. More than 110,000 women have used it and it is rapidly becoming popular where it is legal."

Further, French doctors say RU-486 is 96 percent effective and shows promise for use in treating other diseases, including a form of breast cancer and AIDS.

As we have said before, to answer whatever questions remain about RU-486 in the United States, thorough testing must be encouraged — which is precisely what several major medical and scientific organizations have proposed.

At its June 1990 meeting, the American Medical Association's House of Delegates adopted a resolution that said, "The American Medical Association support the legal availability of RU-486 for appropriate research and, if indicated, clinical practice."

This does not mean the AMA endorses widespread access to the drug. It does mean the AMA hopes the drug "can be made available and research can be conducted in this country to determine if the drug is safe and effective for its known uses and whether its use may be appropriate for other medical treatments."

Though Leona Benten probed the ban against RU-486 and was turned back, there will be other legal assaults, including attempts at federal legislation permitting RU-486's right to land on American soil. The AMA's prudent approach to research should help in that eventual touch-down.

Newsday
New York City, New York, July 24, 1992

It's a shame Leona Benten lost her courtroom fight to end her pregnancy by taking the drug called RU-486 instead of having a surgical abortion. The result is that this safe and effective "abortion pill" is still not cleared for use in the United States. even when a woman brings it in from a country where it's legal — as Benten did — solely for her own use under a doctor's supervision.

True, Benten's challenge to the Food and Drug Administration policy that allowed customs officers to seize her 12 pills at Kennedy Airport isn't over yet. Although the Supreme Court denied her plea to have the pills returned, as U.S. District Court Judge Charles Sifton in Brooklyn had ordered, the FDA still might lose its appeal of his ruling that its procedures in cases of this kind are illegal.

There's more politics than science in the FDA's policy on "compassionate use" of drugs that it hasn't officially approved for use in this country. Typically they're tolerated for life-threatening diseases such as AIDS or cancer, when normal considerations of safety and effectiveness become irrelevant, or for mild conditions such as a skin rash, when it hardly matters whether a medication is effective as long as it doesn't make matters worse.

Since Benten's medical condition was neither life-threatening nor trivial, the FDA — arguing that the alternative of a surgical abortion was easily available to her — exercised its discretion to narrow her choices rather than to widen them. That's not acceptable. Sifton was right to order a review of FDA procedures for reaching such decisions.

But even if those procedures are eventually changed, enabling a limited number of women to import RU-486 is an inadequate response to the need for safe, noninvasive abortions.

The manufacturer of RU-486, Roussel-Uclaf, wouldn't have marketed it in France without a push from the government. It's going to need some kind of push here to overcome the company's fear of a boycott of other products by anti-abortion activists.

Maybe the threat of a boycott by abortion-rights supporters would provide that push. The Bush administration certainly won't.

Los Angeles Times
Los Angeles, California, September 6, 1991

The debate over abortion in this country has been described as the politics of symbolism. The symbols invoked are powerful and jarring: aborted fetuses, bloody coat hangers and chanting protesters who block public access to medical clinics.

Mindful not only of the power of symbols to effect change in this escalating debate but also of the power of medical science to improve lives, the state Assembly last week approved a resolution urging that research on the French abortion pill, RU-486, be conducted in California. Authored by Assemblywoman Jackie Speier (D-South San Francisco), the resolution is similar to one adopted by the New Hampshire Legislature in May. The Appropriations Committee of the California Senate is expected to take up the Speier measure, possibly today. We urge passage.

Developed by the French pharmaceutical firm Roussel-Uclaf, RU-486 appears to be safer and less painful than surgical abortions. It is approved as an abortifacient in Britain and France; in France it has been used on as many as 100,000 women. The drug has also shown great promise in treating some forms of cancer, Cushing's syndrome and other serious diseases.

But despite its potential, RU-486 has become a casualty—and yet another powerful symbol—in the fractious abortion war. Foes fear that the drug will make abortion too easy and painless. Responding to these fears, the Bush Administration in effect halted testing of the drug in 1989 by banning its importation for personal use.

In France, Roussel-Uclaf took this action as a signal of official U.S. policy on abortion and now refuses to make RU-486 available for research by the federal Food and Drug Administration. Assemblywoman Speier hopes that her resolution, which urges the President to lift the "import alert" on the drug and encourages Roussel-Uclaf to undertake research in California, will send a strong, countervailing signal.

But in the meantime, the right of choice is increasingly constricted. Last week, as the California Assembly passed Speier's important resolution, Ohio Gov. George V. Voinovich signed a bill mandating a 24-hour wait for abortions during which women must be given material explaining fetal development and listing alternatives to abortion. Once again, government seeks to intrude on a woman's right to make such a deeply personal and difficult decision.

St. Petersburg Times
St. Petersburg, Florida, July 8, 1991

Britain last week became the third major country to approve use of the RU-486 abortion pill, behind France and China. Meanwhile the United States, which ought to be leading the way in research on a drug that shows promise for treating a variety of serious maladies, remains under the thralldom of the anti-abortion lobby, which persuaded conservative politicians effectively to ban the pill in 1989.

Opponents claim they've only succeeded in blocking use of the drug for abortions, not for research on its therapeutic potential for such painful or fatal illnesses as brain cancer, breast cancer, AIDS, Cushing's syndrome, endometriosis, diabetes and hypertension.

That argument is disingenuous.

It's true that the Food and Drug Administration has not technically banned RU-486 importation for research, having issued a dozen or so permits for clinical testing. But it has banned importation of RU-486 by private individuals for personal use, and the uncertainties of satisfying the FDA's terms puts a damper on scientists' willingness to commit to research projects. It restricts their ability to get funding and the French manufacturers' willingness to supply the drug under uncertain liability conditions in the United States. Researchers complain that their counterparts in places such as India, Hong Kong and Cuba have an easier time getting a reliable supply of the drug.

What's really needed is for the FDA to lift its import alert on RU-486. Until that happens, anti-abortion groups must answer for obstructing potentially life-saving research in the name of banning a drug that wouldn't increase or decrease the 1.6-million abortions that occur each year, but might make many of them safer, cheaper and less invasive physically.

Even if the Supreme Court eventually overturns *Roe vs. Wade*, that probably would not mean the end of all legal abortions in some states. Since it is irrational to deny new medical technology for those abortions that will take place anyway, the whole rationale for slowing the research on this drug to a snail's pace falls apart.

The Gazette
Cedar Rapids, Iowa, June 1, 1991

ADVENTURESOME New Hampshire again is living up to its motto, "Live free or die." The Legislature there recently established the state as a testing ground for RU486, the French abortion pill. That means a controversy featuring religious conviction, ethics, medical safety and politics.

Development of RU486, a synthetic steroid, is an apparent breakthrough. By blocking naturally produced hormones, RU486 causes a woman's uterus to shed its lining along with a fertilized egg. Pregnancy is terminated (without surgery) so early that few people equate the process with taking human life. What's more, the drug may be useful in treating several diseases, such as hypertension, breast and brain cancer, diabetes and acquired immune deficiency syndrome (AIDS). We hope RU486 is proven safe.

At the same time, we are glad New Hampshire, not Iowa, is this nation's first test site for the drug. For all its promise, RU486 is still unproven. Though it has been used for about 65,000 abortions in France, authorities there have banned its use for smokers and women over 35. The action came two months ago following the death of a woman using the pill.

The U.S. Food and Drug Administration has banned RU486 imports, though it allows medical testing for battling cancer and other illnesses. If RU486 passes muster in New Hampshire and with the FDA, it almost surely will continue to draw fire from the National Right to Life Committee. While not disputing the drug's potential value in fighting disease, the organization opposes its use in terminating pregnancy. "We oppose this pill because it kills unborn members of the human family," said Doug Johnson, the committee's legislative director.

We expect RU486 to spark controversy the rest of this decade.

The Hartford Courant

Hartford, Connecticut, December 14, 1990

First the federal regulators flipped and then they flopped: A year ago, they banned all U.S. research on the French abortion pill RU 486, which shows promise in the treatment of some forms of breast cancer, brain cancer, diabetes, high blood pressure and a rare pituitary gland disorder called Cushing's syndrome.

The outcry from patients and physicians was loud, but the government was more sensitive to the anti-abortion lobby, which wants to ban the importation, production and testing of RU 486.

Now, however, Food and Drug Administration officials say the research ban was an oversight. Researchers, the officials explained, had been inadvertently included in the ban on personal importation or use of the drug.

That's a cover story. FDA officials issued a total ban on RU 486 shortly after receiving a letter from a dozen anti-abortion members of Congress. President Bush's opposition to abortion undoubtedly figured in the decision.

The sweeping ban was imposed even though no evidence existed that RU 486 was being imported into this country illegally. In their search for an excuse, the regulators said they feared anti-abortion demonstrators might disrupt the flow of the drug to researchers and upset both patients and scientists. Better to keep the drug out of this country, was the rationale.

Even FDA officials now admit the unconvincing quality of their previous arguments.

Opponent of abortion still object. Doctors and patients who oppose the ban on RU 486 research are tools of those who want to import the drug without restriction, according to Dr. Richard Glasow, educational director of the National Right to Life Committee.

Research on all uses of RU 486 should go forward in the United States, and federal approval should be granted as soon as the drug is found safe. If the FDA flip-flop has increased pressure on the Bush administration to stop playing politics with the drug, so much the better.

The San Diego Union-Tribune

San Diego, California, December 6, 1990

Medical science increasingly presents us with moral questions for which there are no easy answers. The debate over the French-made medication, RU-486, the so-called abortion pill, provides the latest example.

Eighteen months ago, the Food and Drug Administration saw fit to issue an "import alert" prohibiting individuals from either bringing RU-486 into the country or receiving it in the mail. At the time, the FDA also told medical researchers they could not import the drug, although the agency has since backed away from that stance.

Meanwhile, various researchers have found RU-486 to be a promising treatment for such conditions as breast cancer, endometriosis (a uterine disorder), meginioma (a strain of brain cancer) and Cushing's syndrome (an adrenal gland disorder). Taken together, these ailments annually account for more than 50,000 deaths in the United States.

Further research into the medical benefits of RU-486 is jeopardized, however, by lack of an adequate supply of the drug in the United States. The French manufacturer, Roussel-Uckaf, is reluctant to ship larger quantities to this country for fear of being thrust into the middle of the American abortion debate. This is a very real prospect in the wake of the FDA's highly publicized 1989 ban.

The FDA originally banned RU-486 on the pretext that the drug might cause profuse bleeding in women. However, the experiences of 65,000 French women who have used the drug since it became available in France in 1988 have demonstrated that this concern was vastly overstated.

Consequently, the only objection to RU-486 that the FDA raises at this point is against its primary function of inducing abortion. But however FDA authorities may feel about this extremely divisive issue, it is not their mandate to dictate American social policy. The FDA's determination of whether RU-486 should be permitted in the United States should be based on medical rather than political considerations.

If judged by that criteria, the weight of evidence dictates recision of the ban on RU-486. One vital moral-medical question that should not be overlooked in this debate it is that a possible lifesaving treatment is being withheld from hundreds of thousands of Americans who suffer from one of the medical conditions mentioned above.

Approval of RU-486 is not tantamount to endorsement of abortion. Indeed, there are surely thousands of Americans who are opposed to abortion, but who would use the drug for its other valuable functions. But as long as abortion is legal in the United States, does it make sense to require women to undergo surgical procedures when there is a safer alternative — namely, the abortion pill?

Perhaps more than anything, the RU-486 debate reveals what can happen when a government agency oversteps its regulatory bounds in an attempt to ordain social policy. The FDA should never have banned RU-486 in the first place. It should take immediate steps to correct its mistake.

> The RU-486 debate reveals what can happen when a government agency oversteps its regulatory bounds.

Detroit Free Press

Detroit, Michigan, December 11, 1990

RU 486, the so-called abortion pill, may be excellent therapy for a number of illnesses that have nothing to do with abortion. But the "right-to-life" crowd has so poisoned the political waters that federal policies have impeded medical testing of the drug in this country. We have called for thorough testing of the drug as an abortifacient, but the possibility that the drug has other uses makes testing crucial.

RU 486 is already available in several other countries. Some tests indicate that it is safer, when used properly, than surgical abortions. Now the drug's proponents say it also can be helpful in treating breast cancer, brain tumors and other maladies. Maybe some of the claims are hype, but we won't know until full testing is allowed. Anti-abortionists say they only want to stop testing of the drug as an abortion pill. Their actions suggest otherwise.

The anti-abortionists have bludgeoned the weak-kneed manufacturer into keeping the drug out of this country, and have threatened any U.S. company that tries to license it here. Opponents of the pill have threatened the French company and its German parent with a worldwide boycott of all products the companies make if RU 486 is sold here. (Why unborn French or British babies are of less concern to the American right-to-lifers is unclear to us.) Meanwhile, a potentially useful drug is unfairly kept away from people it might benefit.

The U.S. Food and Drug Administration should stop caving in to this pressure. It should lift its partial ban on the import of the drug, and should encourage full-scale testing. Otherwise we will see the emergence of a black market in RU 486. If anyone wants to see women get hurt — something the anti-abortionists claim they want to prevent — a black market would be a fine way to begin.

Arkansas Gazette.

Little Rock, Arkansas, November 26, 1990

The militant anti-abortionists would rather wipe out abortion than cancer. That's one reason they're a minority, but they gain a disproportionate strength through the weakness of public officials.

Anti-abortion politics continue to keep the French abortion pill RU 486 out of this country, even when it's sought only for research on its ability to treat and prevent disease.

RU 486 is a safe, effective, non-surgical method of abortion. The French manufacturer, Roussel-Uclaf, has declined to market it in the United States, for fear of an anti-abortionist economic backlash against other of the company's products.

However, American researchers were, for a time, able to obtain the pill for purposes other than abortion. RU 486 blocks progesterone, a hormone that plays a key role in early pregnancy and also contributes to the growth of some breast cancers. Evidence exists that RU 486 can halt some tumor growth and block pain in breast cancer victims.

RU 486 also has shown great promise in the treatment of Cushing's syndrome, a disorder in which excess secretion of a hormone called cortisol causes many potentially fatal complications.

The Food and Drug Administration adopted a policy last year that U.S. citizens can't import RU 486 for personal use, because of safety risks. The drug has not been approved for use in this country (the manufacturer has not sought approval) and FDA officials said they feared women might use the drug for an abortion without a doctor's supervision. In France, the drug is administered in a physician's office and follow-up visits are required to assure that the abortion is complete and that no complications have occurred.

American researchers say that because of the FDA policy, and the French manufacturer's timidity, they can no longer obtain the drug for study of its non-abortion properties.

(The FDA policy against importation for personal use won't hurt the wealthiest American women, the kind this administration cares most about. They'll still be able to obtain the pill for abortion, even if they have to go to France.)

The FDA cannot force the French manufacturer to seek approval to market RU 486 widely in the United States. But it can work out some sort of agreement so that the manufacturer can supply American researchers. The agency should use its considerable leverage to do just that, and Americans should demand that it do so. Anti-abortion politics cannot be allowed to block what could be invaluable research in the treatment of cancer and other diseases.

The Philadelphia Inquirer

Philadelphia, Pennsylvania, November 26, 1990

There's a gaping hole in American research efforts aimed at finding ways to combat cancer and AIDS. U.S. researchers find they are not able to do work with a French drug that has shown promise in dealing with these dangers and others. Researchers are neglecting this drug because it's hard to get. It's hard to get because of the political games the Bush administration is playing because it has a controversial use.

The drug is RU486, and it has been known mainly because of its demonstrated effectiveness in causing an abortion without surgery. Abortion opponents have decried that use, and U.S. officials have pandered to them, making the drug hard to obtain even for research unconnected with abortion.

To be fair, anti-abortion leaders say they oppose the drug's use for abortion, and only that. They should be taken at their word. But the stifling of this research could have deadly consequences for some people with cancer and other high-risk conditions. That's outrageous.

Last year, the Federal Drug Administration added the French drug to the list of drugs that not only can't be sold within the country, but can't legally even be brought across the border in small amounts (except for approved research projects). The policy was widely seen as a gesture on behalf of anti-abortion activists who were crusading against the drug as "chemical warfare against the unborn."

This policy, which addressed a non-problem (no efforts have been made to bring the drug in illegally),

seems to have made the manufacturer less willing to supply the drug for research. The FDA should rescind it, and the administration should advertise its support for research into the drug's lifesaving potential.

But we should also be clear as to where we stand on the use of the pill to induce abortions. If it successfully undergoes review by the FDA for safety, this drug should be made available to American women. Abortion is legal, and American women should have access to what appears to be the safest, least intrusive method yet devised. That's what abortion opponents fear, and in view of the drug's results in France, it's easy to understand why. More than 60,000 French women have taken RU486, in conjunction with another drug that induces contractions, to end pregnancies in the early stages.

Because it is so easy to use, the drug has the capacity to quell the volatile abortion debate. Although the drug is now administered only in clinics or hospitals, its safety record may develop to the point that women will be able to take it at home.

At present, the manufacturer hasn't begun the process of getting FDA approval for this drug. For now, the company won't try introducing it in countries where abortion is as controversial as it is here. Since part of the company's hesitation comes from President Bush's antagonism toward abortion rights, we can only recall that he flip-flopped on this matter of principle in 1980, and suggest that he do so again.

Los Angeles Times
Los Angeles, California, December 3, 1990

Washington's effective ban on imports of a French-made steroid that can induce abortions is wrong. That's one issue.

But there's another issue. That's banning imports for the purpose of further testing the drug RU-486—which shows great promise for treatment of some forms of cancer and other serious disorders. That's worse than wrong; it is heinous.

In one preliminary test, for example, RU-486—also known as mifepristone—reduced tumors in one of every five patients with advanced breast cancer that had not responded to such treatment as chemotherapy.

THE BARRIERS: Yet politically motivated federal efforts to keep the drug out of this country are stalling research that could save countless lives. The presidential oath may be silent on curing disease, but the silence does not sanction interference with the responsibility of doctors under the Hippocratic oath.

President Bush should order the federal Food and Drug Administration to sweep away any rulings that can even be interpreted as barriers to imports of the drug for research. Secretary Louis Sullivan's Department of Health and Human Services should use its influence to persuade the drug's European manufacturers that threats of retaliation by anti-abortion activists are not sufficient reason to continue to curtail exports to the United States.

The drug is manufactured by Roussel-Uclaf of France, a German-owned pharmaceutical firm. It has been used without adverse effects by 65,000 women in France as an alternative to surgical abortion. Britain, Sweden and even the Soviet Union are either on the verge of approving use of RU-486, are using it in tests or are about to start tests.

The vision that anti-abortion activists portray of abortion pills on every drugstore shelf is not even valid in France. It is a prescription drug that can be taken only in a clinic under medical supervision. Each pill is registered and must be accounted for. There is no reason to suppose that Roussel-Uclaf would make pills for export without similar restrictions.

But in 1989, in an obvious attempt to appease the anti-abortion movement, the FDA put RU-486 on a short list of "import alert" drugs that cannot be brought into the country for personal use. Technically, researchers could apply for a license to import the drug for testing, but the alert has had such a chilling effect that no applications have been submitted since it was posted.

THE CONSEQUENCES: The agency can argue, perhaps even brag, that its action is stopping abortions. But is it not also prompting some women to use other methods that are clearly more life-threatening than the professed concerns about profuse bleeding that the FDA used to justify the alert?

Look at the list of other uses for RU-486 that the agency is blocking. Federal regulatory recalcitrance means, as we have noted, no tests of the drug on advanced breast cancers. The drug has also been effective in treatment of inoperable cases of meningioma, a non-malignant brain tumor, but that cannot even be tested in the United States. It shows promise as a drug for high blood pressure, diabetes, osteoporosis, even AIDS.

As Dr. William Regelson noted in an August issue of the Journal of the American Medical Assn.: "It is tragic that in this country 43,000 victims die of breast cancer each year, while abject surrender to abortion politics delays clinical studies that might help them."

Doctors and patients alike have a right to use RU-486 both as a safe alternative to surgical abortions and to explore its healing potential.

The FDA is a partner in medicine, certifying scientists' claims for their new drugs. As such, it shares the responsibility of physicians to provide help. In this case, the agency is hiding, not providing, and the White House must set it straight.

The Miami Herald
Miami, Florida, November 27, 1990

A MISTAKE. Inadvertent. No one really meant to curb experimentation using a drug that could treat certain cancers and metabolic and hormonal problems. It just so happened that when some members of Congress objected to the importation of this drug last spring, the U.S. Food and Drug Administration (FDA) clamped down so hard that research on those problems stopped.

The drug is RU 486. It was developed in France, where it is used for inducing abortions early in pregnancy. It is that link to abortion that has ensnarled RU 486 research in the United States. FDA officials told a congressional subcommittee that the import ban wasn't intended to interfere with research. Medical researchers, though, told the subcommittee that promising inquiries into cancer and into Cushing's syndrome had been disrupted.

The drug blocks the impact of the hormone progesterone. In doing so, it disrupts early pregnancy, causing the uterus to shed its lining much as in a regular menstrual period. Because it involves only injections and oral medication, not surgery, it is less

BY RU 486 OPPONENTS

intimidating than surgical abortion.

Anti-abortion activists call it "chemical warfare" and a trivialization of the process. They have put RU 486 squarely into the political arena — where the FDA does not belong. The perniciousness of permitting politics to warp scientific judgment is terribly clear in this instance.

For example, use of this drug appears to inhibit the growth of breast-cancer tumors. Victims of Cushing's syndrome have shown dramatic improvement with its use. Cushing's is a disease that causes wasting of muscle and bone and attacks mostly women. Other research has focused on diabetes, hypertension, and a major contributor to female infertility, endometriosis.

Abortion is a legal medical procedure in the United States, and so is research into breast cancer and other diseases. Yielding to those who claim to protect life has put the FDA, deliberately or inadvertently, in the position of denying potentially life-saving medicine to others.

THE PLAIN DEALER
Cleveland, Ohio, November 21, 1990

When is a medicine not a medicine? When one of its ends gets confused with its means.

That seems to be the case with RU486, the miracle French drug that can turn off a hormone in the same way one turns off the tap. By shutting down progesterone, it causes a woman's body to act as if she were not pregnant. The fetus is sloughed off along with the uterine lining that would have supported it in gestation.

Yet RU486 is much more than a so-called abortion pill. Progesterone plays an as-yet unexplained role in certain cancers. It is also a key player in a debilitating disease, known as Cushing's syndrome, that can cause death if untreated. Using RU486 to control Cushing's has proved promising in tests by the U.S. National Institutes of Health — even though federally supported research on RU486's considerable potential as an anti-gestational drug is banned because of the prevailing anti-abortion hysteria in Washington.

Now, however, NIH will have to abandon its Cushing's research. The disease's sufferers must take the drug in large daily doses, so the institutes' clinical trials require substantial supplies that the drug's French manufacturer is now unable or unwilling to guarantee. In fact, when anti-abortion protest greeted RU486's original introduction, the French manufacturer, Roussel-Uclaf, halted distribution. It took threats by the French government — whose researcher, Etienne-Emile Baulieu, made the medical discovery that led to RU486's development and which owns 36% of Roussel-Uclaf — to get the drug back on the market.

Roussel-Uclaf, unfortunately, has reason to be fearful. Although RU486 promises privacy, economy and ease to women seeking abortions, it has proven safe and effective only when used within a couple months of conception and with repeated doctor's visits. It is easy to guess it wouldn't be very safe if a teen-ager tried to abort a six-month-old fetus using this method.

Yet the genie is out. Now that the theory Baulieu used to find the drug has proven correct, other anti-progesterone drugs will no doubt follow. Marketing of the Roussel-Uclaf drug elsewhere in Europe appears imminent.

Baulieu has repeatedly expressed dismay that his discovery has fallen victim to politics. It is indeed sad, given RU486's potential to save lives. In developing countries, deaths from botched abortions — both at home and in poorly staffed clinics — are common. The World Health Organization estimates they claim the lives of 200,000 yearly.

Even if that estimate is high, it is a sad commentary that anti-abortion hysteria should guide the research agenda of this nation's scientists, or determine the well-being of the 1% of Cushing's sufferers for whom there is no other treatment option.

It's understandable that politicians and pharmaceutical firms get cold feet about offending a highly organized minority. But it's not morally defensible to turn a collective back on research that already promises substantial medical relief to thousands. The fate of the NIH Cushing's research should prompt the nation's medical research community, including the NIH and its parent, the U.S. Department of Health and Human Services, to re-examine its approach.

Abortion Rates Surveyed; Birth Control Issues Debated

Two studies reported October 16, 1988 indicated that abortion was common among all racial, economic and religious groups in the U.S.

According to the surveys, which were conducted by the Alan Guttmacher Institute of New York City, nearly 3% of American women of childbearing age had an abortion in 1987. The rate for white women was 2.3%, while those for Hispanic and nonwhite women were 4.3% and 5.3%, respectively. Women who described themselves as Roman Catholic matched the average national rate, while Protestant and Jewish women reported lower than average abortion rates.

A study by the Alan Guttmacher Institute in New York, reported April 25–26, 1991, found that the overall abortion rate in the U.S. had declined by 6% between 1980 and 1987.

According to the institute, a private foundation that did research on abortion and family planning, there had been about 1.6 million abortions in the U.S. in 1987 (the latest year covered in the study). That number had remained level since 1980, but it represented a decline in the overall abortion rate, since there had been an increase in the number of women of childbearing age during the same period.

The study found that there had been 27 abortions per 1,000 women of childbearing age in 1987, down from 29 abortions per 1,000 women in 1980. Abortion rates had increased among some groups, however, including all girls under age 15 and minority girls between the ages of 15 and 19.

The 1987 abortion rate varied from state to state, with Washington, D.C. posting the highest rate (84.4 abortions per 1,000 women), followed by California (45.1), Hawaii (43.8) and New York (42.2). The states with the lowest rates of abortion were South Dakota (9.0), West Virginia (9.7) and North Dakota (10.2).

The Guttmacher study found that 51% of all abortions were performed before the eighth week of pregnancy, 40% between the ninth and 12th weeks, 8.5% between the 13th and 20th weeks and fewer than 1% later than the 20th week.

Researchers cited two possible reasons for the drop in the abortion rate: a decline in the number of doctors performing the procedure and changing social attitudes concerning unwed motherhood.

The U.S. was decades behind many other countries in the development of new birth control methods, according to the conclusion of a report issued February 14, 1990 by the National Academy of Science's Institute of Medicine and National Research Council. The institute noted that many European countries were years ahead of the U.S. in the development of new contraceptive devices, including a long-term implant, injectable contraceptives, male contraceptives, intrauterine devices and several pills, including the French abortion pill, RU-486.

As a result of the failure to make new, more effective and more convenient methods of birth control available, the report concluded, the rate of abortion in the U.S. was much higher than necessary. According to the report, about half of the approximately 1.5 million abortions performed in the U.S. each year resulted from failure to use birth control methods properly or, more rarely, from contraceptive failure.

The panel noted that 17 major firms in the U.S. had been carrying on research and development into new birth control methods up until the early 1980s. Since that time, a number of factors had combined to cut the number of active developers to one.

According to the report, the factors behind the decline were a rise in liability lawsuits against contraceptive manufacturers, political pressure from anti-abortion forces, federal drug approval policies that considered only the risks of new birth control methods and not the benefits, and a lack of government funding.

THE TAMPA TRIBUNE
Tampa, Florida, November 18, 1991

Lots of people cringed three months ago when Gov. Lawton Chiles said he'd like to see every community in Florida with a high-school health clinic that provides birth-control services.

Not that he wanted to tell communities what to do, Chiles said, but he would encourage it as part of his crusade to lower infant mortality rates. Chiles and health-care professionals agree that most low-birthweight babies — babies at risk of death — are born to teen-age mothers.

In Hillsborough County, the reaction was swift and simple: Not here. Maybe other Florida communities are ready to pass out condoms to teenagers but this community is not going to accept birth control on high-school campuses. Not the talk of it and certainly not the distribution of it.

More importantly, school officials worried that if the subject were even broached with some parents, it could jeopardize the good work that is being done already at Hillsborough schools. Programs aimed at students from homes where medical care may not be a priority or is not affordable are under way, and they are too important to risk losing.

But this is not the time for panic. This is the time to take very seriously the subject of teenage sex and take some preventive action.

The latest available figures on Hillsborough births show 2,074 of the almost 14,000 babies born in 1989 were to mothers younger than 20. Seventy-five percent of 17-year-olds in Hillsborough are sexually active, according to the Planned Parenthood Association of Southwest Florida.

School health workers now can give only information about birth control and refer students to other services to obtain it. Hillsborough school board members need to start asking themselves if that is enough or if more is needed.

They could start off small, with a pilot program at one or all three of the schools — Tampa Bay Vocational-Technical School, Hillsborough High and Middleton Junior High — where clinics are already in place.

Especially since Magic Johnson's revelations, it's clear this is not just a discussion about promiscuity. It's about life and death, the lives of babies and the lives of teen-agers.

We, perhaps like you, would prefer young people, for a host of reasons, to abstain from sexual activity. But many will not. Thus, there is hardly a more important reality for the school board to deal with than the consequences of unguarded sexual intercourse among our youth.

The Des Moines Register

Des Moines, Iowa, December 13, 1990

This week's Food and Drug Administration approval of the first new contraceptive system to be marketed in the United States in three decades is good news for millions of American women.

The new contraceptive, Norplant, consists of six matchstick-sized silicon-rubber capsules surgically inserted in a woman's upper left arm in a simple, quick procedure that can be performed in a doctor's office. The implants remain effective for up to five years, continually releasing a synthetic of the female hormone progesterone at a rate far lower than the quantity contained in birth control pills, thereby minimizing side effects to users.

There are minor risks such as irregular menstruation and spotting, particularly during the first year of Norplant's use. And the cost could be as much as $600 to $1,000, similar to or less than other forms of contraceptives when spread over a five-year period, but a one-time payment that may discourage some women from using Norplant.

But the advantages are clear. The implants can be removed, restoring fertility almost immediately. Norplant also is less costly than surgical sterilization, more effective and less a bother than oral contraceptives or barrier systems such as condoms or diaphrams. Those factors may make Norplant a particularly attractive option for women wanting to delay the start of a family, or those who no longer want children.

The availability of options is key to limiting birth rates, say population experts. Each new contraceptive advance expands the use of birth control. A major advance such as Norplant, under development for 20 years, is certain to mean more women will opt for contraception. That means a reduction in pregnancy rates and fewer unwanted births.

It seems unfair that, yet again, women are being asked to take on the burden of contraception — the inconvenience and the biological intrusion, however minor. Yet researchers say it's easier to prevent fertility in women than in men.

That matter aside, the FDA's long-awaited approval of Norplant — an effective, relatively safe, long-lasting and reversible contraceptive — is a most important development.

THE SPOKESMAN-REVIEW

Spokane, Washington, June 7, 1991

You remember Norplant. It's the five-year contraceptive implant that stirred up a three-week controversy early this year. The flap was over a markedly stupid comment printed by a Philadelphia newspaper about using the implant to fight poverty among people of color.

Then there was a legislator in Kansas who proposed paying welfare mothers $500 to use Norplant, and a judge in California who included Norplant in the sentence of a child abuser.

Those instances made for good headlines and outraged talk show hosts.

But the attention didn't last long. Norplant has faded from the front page. But as doctors and nurses get the necessary training to implant the device, it is becoming available to women in the Inland Northwest. Even low-income women.

That's not the case everywhere. Low-income women in Washington and Idaho are lucky. The two are among just a handful of states to help low-income women with costs of the five-year contraceptive.

Norplant is not a wonder drug. It has significant side effects — primarily irregular bleeding. It's not going to be the one and only contraceptive of the 21st century. But one of the great things about it is the relatively low cost.

The hormone implants, which were developed by the non-profit Population Council, have been priced at $350. Add the cost of insertion and a woman is looking at $500 for five years of protection. That's less than the cost of birth control pills, which cost $20 per month on average.

Ironically, it's the very convenience, the one-stop aspect of Norplant that can put it out of reach of those who want it: $500 in one shot is way out of reach for a lot of people.

The irony continues. Although Idaho and Washington have approved Medicaid payment for Norplant, Planned Parenthood may not be able to give its clients any break on the device. Planned Parenthood usually uses a sliding fee scale for its services. But the agency, which counts heavily on federal funding, doesn't have money budgeted for Norplant implants. So, it's likely that Planned Parenthood clients will have to pay the full $500.

None of this is as sensational as the outrage over some of the uses proposed for Norplant. But getting this device into the hands (or arms, literally) of women who want it is the real story.

Washington and Idaho deserve congratulations for their part in the process.

Arkansas Gazette.

Little Rock, Arkansas, July 21, 1991

Questions have been raised about the legality of the state Health Department's plan to provide the contraceptive Norplant in the department's school-based health clinics, but there remains hope that all problems can be overcome and the program proceed. It could do much to ease the grave problem of teen-age pregnancy in Arkansas.

Dr. Joycelyn Elders, director of the Health Department, said Monday the department would "hard sell" Norplant to pregnant women who visit the department's clinics, including the school-based clinics that furnish contraceptives. Not all school-based clinics do; local authorities make the decision. Norplant will not end a pregnancy but it will prevent others, for as long as five years. The decision to provide Norplant only to women who are pregnant or have been pregnant was intended to placate an anti-contraceptive faction that believes contraceptives encourage sexual activity. Elders said that Medicaid funds could be used to buy Norplant.

But Tom Butler, the Health Department administrator, says he doubts that Medicaid could be used for Norplant in the school-based clinics. Medicaid is funded jointly by the state and federal governments, and a state law prohibits the Health Department from using state money to buy contraceptives for its school-based clinics.

Butler says a different way to pay for the Norplant, using all federal money, can be found. But opponents of the school clinics threaten litigation, arguing that state and federal money for the clinics is so intermingled that it would be impossible to prove no state money was involved in the distribution of Norplant. They are poised to harass Elders as she attempts to lower the number of unwanted babies born to unmarried teen-age mothers. ∎

Birth control is important to this state, and the Health Department must keep looking for ways to provide it. If that means going to court to defend a Norplant program, so be it. Opponents cannot be allowed to crush the program through intimidation. It's highly unlikely that they will, with Elders directing the department. She does not intimidate easily.

THE SACRAMENTO BEE
Sacramento, California, December 18, 1990

Norplant, the long-lasting contraceptive implant that's just been licensed by the Food and Drug Administration, is a welcome new option for all American women. Its greatest promise may be in enhancing the reproductive choices of women who — because of their youth, personal habits or social circumstances — have difficulties using existing birth control. With proper social policies, it will make for better lives and fewer unwanted births to drug addicts and teenagers.

Norplant, which is already in use in 16 countries, is implanted by a physician under the skin of a woman's arm in 15 minutes or less. It works similarly to oral contraceptives, by preventing ovulation. But by releasing its progesterone-like hormone over time, it's effective for up to five years, or until the woman chooses to have the thin capsules removed. It represents the first major new contraceptive device to be approved for use in the United States in 25 years.

Like other contraceptives, Norplant has its side effects, causing irregular menstrual bleeding in some women. In addition, there is concern among some family planning services that if a woman uses Norplant she will not come in for regular medical checkups as she would if she were on conventional contraceptive pills, for which she has to get a new prescription every few months. Finally, while Norplant is cheaper than the pill over the five-year period of its effectiveness, the device, which will probably go on the market at $250, plus the physician's fee for inserting it, carries a far larger up-front cost.

Nonetheless, Norplant is more reliable than the ordinary pill. More important, it represents a promising new option, both for individual women who have difficulty managing other means of birth control and for a society concerned about the enormous social and medical damage — not to mention the cost — that drug-addicted babies and other unwanted children represent.

When he was a candidate last year, Gov.-elect Pete Wilson proposed compulsory drug treatment for women who bring addicted children into the world. But a more promising approach, particularly with Norplant, is to offer such women a technology that makes it far easier to not have babies. That means that the state will have to be willing not merely to fund the relatively high up-front cost of the device, but to promote its use as imaginatively as possible. It will be worth many times its cost.

The Seattle Times
Seattle, Washington, December 12, 1990

NORPLANT, the contraceptive implant approved this week by the Food and Drug Administration, is the first birth-control improvement in the United States since development of the Pill in the early 1960s.

In the past three decades, this nation has lagged woefully behind other countries in developing new contraceptives. Norplant is a desperately needed option that has been available for several years to women in Finland, Sweden, and 14 other countries.

Norplant's great advantage is that once embedded under the skin of a woman's upper arm, it will give safe, continuous, and nearly failure-proof contraception for up to five years. Unlike other birth-control methods, its effectiveness is not dependent on a user's behavior.

If made widely available at an affordable price, the new method could reduce significantly the number of unwanted pregnancies (about 2 million annually in the United States), and the number of abortions. The benefits to women's welfare could be enormous.

Yet, as with many medical advances, the benefits — in this case, complete effectiveness and convenience — raise issues that didn't exist before. Some medical ethicists and women's health advocates worry that Norplant will be used by courts and employers to take reproductive decisions away from some women.

Indeed, it's easy to imagine disturbing scenarios in which a judge orders a Norplant implant for a drug-addicted mother or a troubled teen, or an employer allows women to work at jobs that pose high risks to fetuses only if the women agree to take the implant.

Such abuse can be avoided without diminishing the obvious benefits of Norplant. There is a bright line between encouraging use of an effective birth-control method and coercing that use. Courts, employers, and government agencies can heed the line by respecting an individual's absolute right to control her own reproductive life.

The Augusta Chronicle
Augusta, Georgia, December 8, 1990

Science is about to accomplish what no law, court or politician could achieve in a million years — largely defusing the emotionally charged abortion issue.

Within days, the U.S. government is expected to approve a new system of contraception — already in safe, widespread use in 16 countries — that can prevent pregnancies up to five years, yet can be easily reversed at any time the woman so chooses.

The procedure is done with a local anesthetic and is 99 percent effective. Called Norplant, it involves implanting six tiny silicone rubber tablets in a woman's upper arm. The tablets, invisible to the naked eye, release on a timely basis an anti-pregnancy substance into the body.

The hormonal implant virtually immunizes a woman against pregnancy, but it does not act like an "abortion pill," which outrages pro-lifers. Instead it works on the same principle as the familiar contraception pill that has been available for decades. However, it is far more efficient because women don't have to remember to take it every day.

If used widely, it should cut the horrendous abortion rates dramatically, even putting many "abortion mills" out of business. That should make pro-lifers happy. But it is also good news for the pro-choice crowd. It gives them the most effective option yet in preventing pregnancies.

Indeed, the implant, even as it dampens one controversy, is likely to heat up another. Should unwed women, especially teen-age girls who repeatedly get pregnant and can't support their offspring, be compelled to undergo the procedure?

The courts may eventually have to make that thorny decision.

It's no easy matter, to be sure. But it is at least a conventional civil rights issue that can be decided on its legal merits rather than trying to decide whether life in the womb has the same civil rights as life outside the womb.

The Wichita
Eagle-Beacon
Wichita, Kansas, December 18, 1990

The United States has almost reached third-world standards in birth control. With government approval of Norplant, American women will have a contraceptive option that has proved effective, safe and is widely available around the world.

Norplant is the first new contraceptive the federal Food and Drug Administration has OK'd for the American market in 30 years. The product has been extensively tested and gives women another option to prevent pregnancy.

The method is to implant six matchstick-size capsules filled with the hormone progestin into a woman's upper arm. The chemical is slowly released, offering contraceptive protection for five years. Normal fertility returns upon Norplant's removal.

Cost is a potential problem in making the product widely available. Even though the initial cost of $500 is cheaper than a five-year supply of birth control bills, the outlay may make Norplant too expensive for many low-income women and teenagers.

The solution is for federal-and-state financed family planning clinics to provide Norplant for their clients. While the upfront cost may be expensive, Norplant is a bargain if it can prevent unwanted pregnancies that cost millions of dollars annually and lower the abortion rate.

As Congress debates reauthorization of the Title X family planning act, it should ensure adequate funding for Norplant. A safe, long-lasting and reliable contraceptive method is just what the country needs.

The Miami Herald
Miami, Florida, December 18, 1990

IF THE PILL is a bother, and a diaphragm even more so, many women will find the newly approved implant contraceptive a godsend. Goodbye hassle, farewell fumble, hello spontaneity.

In the matter of choice, women in this country have just been given another one. And with it comes another measure of sexual freedom that should be exercised with confidence and self-possession. But with that freedom, women — in partnership with men and medical researchers — would do well to maintain greater care and assume responsibility for safe sexual practices.

The new contraceptive, recently approved for use in this country by the Food and Drug Administration, was 25 years in the making. Six matchstick-size rods are inserted in the woman's arm through a tiny incision. For up to five years, the rods release a pregnancy-blocking hormone into her bloodstream.

That's it. No muss, no fuss, no baby. The implant is 99.8-percent effective, so only sterilization or abstinence work better.

If the woman decides to conceive, the

IMPLANT CONTRACEPTIVE

implants can be removed easily. Conception is possible 48 hours after that.

But times such as these demand that sexual responsibility go far beyond the use of a contraceptive. This implant in no way can protect against the AIDS virus, syphilis, and other sexually transmitted diseases. Safe sex should be foremost in both mind and habit.

The introduction of the Pill 30 years ago was a watershed event in medical science's contribution to the sexual revolution. But it had dubious side effects, such as an increased risk of heart attack and stroke.

Though the side effects of the new implant have been declared minor, medical research must be ever willing to re-examine this product. There has to be some lesson learned from the IUD tragedy.

This implant's availability does not lessen the imperative that its users' husbands or boyfriends participate fully and responsibly in the discussion and practice of birth control. It does, after all, take two.

THE BUFFALO NEWS
Buffalo, New York, December 17, 1990

FOR THE FIRST time in 25 years, the federal government has approved a new form of contraception. It's about time.

While it has surged ahead in other technical fields, the United States has been lagging in research on birth control, and the federal government has given the field little encouragement. Norplant, the method just approved, is not new. It has already been used by 355,000 women elsewhere and is now on the market in 14 countries.

The most revolutionary aspect of the new method, in which hormones are released slowly from tiny tubes inserted under the skin, is that it lasts for five years. There is a relatively high initial cost; but once the investment is made, the implant remains effective for that extended time without anything new to buy or to do.

If the woman decides she wishes to become pregnant, Norplant can be removed and normal fertility restored.

Contraceptives are about choice — about the freedom of individuals to decide when they will have babies and when they won't. They are about families that are planned for, children who arrive when parents are most willing and best able to care for them. A five-year method is a great advance for many who want this kind of choice.

There is a clear need for new methods of contraception. Among the industrialized nations, the United States has a high pregnancy rate and a high abortion rate.

Critics may fear that this device will lead to increased teen-age sexual activity. But no contraceptive should be kept off the market, away from the use of all women, because of such fears.

And young boys and girls should be discouraged from sexual activity through education about its emotional and physical consequences for them, not punished for their missteps with pregnancies for which they are woefully unprepared.

THE ATLANTA CONSTITUTION
Atlanta, Georgia, December 12, 1990

Norplant, the new contraceptive that can prevent pregnancies for five years, has the potential to be a major help in cutting back the U.S. birthrate, the highest among the Western democracies and driven mainly by unwanted and teenage pregnancies (often one in the same). Its potential, however, depends upon access — and that depends in equal parts upon information and economics.

The price — from $200 to as much as $500 if physician's fee is included — is about half that of a five-year supply of birth-control pills but still prohibitive to many women, particularly to the young and, of course, the poor. And the United States remains peculiarly reticent about making birth-control information easily available.

Public interests will be poorly served if Norplant's potential is, like that of other birth-control methods, allowed to go unfulfilled. Yet federal policy has been distorted by the Reagan and Bush administrations from its traditional support for family planning. Funding has been cut and put on a year-to-year basis; it had previously been allocated long term.

The deference of both administrations to televangelists and other social conservatives has impacted policy in other ways, too.

The Food and Drug Administration, always cautious in approving new medicine and medical technologies, has become glacial in assessing contraceptives. Norplant had been in use in more than 40 other countries before it finally was cleared in the United States. Several other birth-control options also are available overseas that are still forbidden here. The atmosphere of political repression is partly to blame, too, for the fact that only two U.S. drug companies are still conducting birth-control research. In the past, most were involved.

The ability of public agencies to offer the option will be further and sharply narrowed if Wyeth-Ayerst Laboratories declines to sell Norplant to clinics at a discount. That's the usual practice in the industry, but the company has so far refused to say it will follow the practice in this instance.

The potential for Norplant and other contraceptives to contribute to personal and social health continues to be limited not just by cost and government hesitation but also by the refusal of most television outlets and many publications to carry contraceptive advertising. Advertising is one of the chief instruments of information in this country. Its effective denial to contraceptives places a higher social priority on mere prissiness than on the prevention of unwanted pregnancies. Few other countries are any longer so foolish.

The Philadelphia Inquirer
Philadelphia, Pennsylvania,
December 12, 1991

Two stories from yesterday's newspaper:

• The U.S. Food and Drug Administration approves Norplant, a contraceptive that can keep a woman from getting pregnant for five years.

• A black research organization reports that nearly half the nation's black children are living in poverty — and that the younger the child, the more likely he or she is to be living with a single mother on welfare. "Growing numbers of them will not succeed," the study's author says.

As we read those two stories, we asked ourselves: Dare we mention them in the same breath? To do so might be considered deplorably insensitive, perhaps raising the specter of eugenics. But it would be worse to avoid drawing the logical conclusion that foolproof contraception could be invaluable in breaking the cycle of inner city poverty — one of of America's greatest challenges.

The main reason more black children are living in poverty is that the people having the most children are the ones least capable of supporting them. (The black middle class is growing, but its birth rate is very low.) This trend, as Children's Defense Fund president Marian Wright Edelman has said, "practically guarantees the poverty of the next generation of black children."

Now there are many ways to fight back — from better prenatal care to better schools. But it's very tough to undo the damage of being born into a dysfunctional family. So why not make a major effort to reduce the number of children, of any race, born into such circumstances? (More whites than blacks live in poverty, though poor blacks make up a higher percentage of people who are more or less permanently on welfare.)

No one should be compelled to use Norplant, which involves a doctor implanting matchstick-size capsules in a woman's upper arm. But there could be incentives to do so. What if welfare mothers were offered an increased benefit for agreeing to use this new, safe, long-term contraceptive? Remember, these women already have one or more children. And they can change their minds at any point and become fertile again. (This is not Indira Gandhi offering portable radios to women who agree to be sterilized.) At the very minimum, Norplant, which will probably cost $600 to $1,000, should be made available for free to poor women.

All right, the subject makes us uncomfortable, too. But we're made even more uncomfortable by the impoverishment of black America and its effect on the nation's future. Think about it.

Pittsburgh Post-Gazette
Pittsburgh, Pennsylvania, February 2, 1991

The timing could lead to some skepticism about motivation, but the state Senate's overwhelming approval of a $2 million appropriation for family planning is welcome, whatever the political considerations behind it.

This is the first time since state funding for birth-control counseling was cut off in 1980 that either house of the Legislature has even considered funding family planning, let alone approved the expenditure.

For all these years the issue has been inextricably bound with abortion in the minds of most lawmakers. That is because most family-planning agencies offer "options counseling" for women who are dealing with an unplanned or unwanted pregnancy. Among the options discussed — neutrally, according to those involved in the field — is abortion. Some agencies also perform abortions.

Most family-planning advocates feel that as long as abortion remains a constitutionally protected option, they would be professionally remiss if they refused to offer information about it just as they would about any other legal alternative.

Anti-abortion forces feel otherwise and have been successful in limiting state and federal funding for family-planning services over the last decade. More than a year ago, the U.S. Department of Health and Human Services promulgated a rule making it illegal for a family-planning agency to discuss any aspect of abortion if the agency receives federal funds. The 2nd U.S. Circuit Court of Appeals in New York recently upheld the rule, but it remains enjoined from taking effect while appeals are being considered in other circuits. The rule has not been implemented in Pennsylvania.

Efforts to append a similar restriction to the $2 million state appropriation in the Senate bill were defeated.

How did it happen that the first state to approve restrictions on abortion after the Supreme Court gave states more power to regulate the procedure is now defying the anti-abortion lobby on what it views as the related issue of family planning?

It is possible that the lawmakers suddenly saw the light and realized the absurdity of opposing birth-control counseling, which if effective could reduce the number of unwanted pregnancies and hence the number of abortions in the state.

More likely is the explanation offered by Sen. Robert Greenwood, the Bucks County Republican who sponsored the bill. In his view, the Supreme Court's abortion decision last year in a Missouri case breathed new life into the abortion-rights movement — a view supported by the results of several recent elections.

"It will not be acceptable anymore to be so extreme in your views that you are not only against abortion but also against access to birth-control information," Sen. Greenwood said.

Now the House and Gov. Casey should recognize not only the necessity of funding family-planning services (either in a supplemental appropriation or in next year's budget) but also the political wisdom of such a stand.

The Providence Journal

Providence, Rhode Island, August 20, 1990

Consider many of the social problems facing our nation, especially those prevailing in our inner city neighborhoods: The increasing proportion of women and children living in poverty, the unacceptably high dropout rates, the substance abuse and other disorders that hamper learning in the schools, the rise in serious crimes committed by youths.

Such a list could be lengthened without effort, but let's stop there. And then ponder these findings from a recent study issued by the National Center for Health Statistics in Washington: In 1988, the last year for which nationwide data are available, one out of every four American infants brought into the world was born to an unmarried woman. Among blacks, nearly two out of every three births were to single women. The corresponding figure among Hispanics was one out of three, and for whites one out of five.

Just ponder for a moment what this means: Twenty-five percent of our children are now born to unwed women. As a result, in the year 1988 alone, roughly one million American infants were added to the sad and growing company of youngsters who are at great risk of having to experience the tragic social pathologies mentioned above.

In fact, those pathologies have already become so widespread, and so much more resistant to reform, in large part because the rate of illegitimacy has soared in recent decades. The 1988 figure for out-of-wedlock births was 50 percent higher than the equivalent number in 1980, and the illegitimacy rate for 1980 was astronomical compared to that in the 1940s or '50s.

This woeful development can be tracked in the official data for Rhode Island, whose experience mirrors that of the nation as a whole. Here is the trend in our state, using the percentage of out-of-wedlock births for every fifth year between 1947 and 1987 (the last year for which Rhode Island data are available): 1947 (2.3), 1952 (1.9), 1957 (2.8), 1962 (2.9), 1967 (5.4), 1972 (8.0), 1977 (13.6), 1982 (16.1), 1987 (21.7).

That looks very much like the portrait of a state — and a society — that is simply asking for trouble. One of the most perplexing aspects of this phenomenon is that the rate of illegitimacy was lowest *before* sex education was introduced into the schools, modern methods of birth control were made widely available, and abortion was declared a constitutional right. This problem obviously involves moral issues. So while we certainly support sex education, birth control and abortion rights, it would be naive to suggest that these will do much to stem the soaring numbers of children born out of wedlock, or alleviate the resulting social pathologies.

The TENNESSEAN

Nashville, Tennessee, December 19, 1990

SINCE the 1960s, people have been looking for new options in birth control. The approval of the Norplant contraceptive provides such an option.

Norplant, which involves the implant of a set of tubes into a woman's arm for up to five years, gained the approval recently of the Food and Drug Administration.

The success rate of Norplant is impressive. Birth control pills, the last breakthrough in contraception, reportedly fail 6% of the time. But the new implant fails only one-tenth to one-twentieth of that rate. It also appears to be cost effective. Although it will bring a fee as high as $500, the five-year cost of birth control pills is now about $900. The device is already on the market in 14 countries.

Norplant, which contains a hormone which is gradually released, can be implanted at a doctor's office in about 15 minutes using a local anesthetic. An incision of only a tenth of an inch is made and the match-size tubes are inserted. They are not visible but can be felt under the skin.

The implant can be taken out at any time at the woman's request.

Some side effects have been reported, such as irregular periods and a higher failure rate in women weighing over 150 pounds. It should also be noted that the implant does not protect against sexually transmitted diseases.

All factors should be weighed in deciding about the use of contraceptive devices. But the Norplant provides people who have looked for options in contraception in recent years with another choice. ∎

THE BLADE

Toledo, Ohio, December 26, 1990

THE reproductive freedom of women was enhanced recently when the Food and Drug Administration approved Norplant, a contraceptive that can prevent pregnancy for up to five years. It is implanted in six silicone rubber capsules under the skin of a woman's inner arm. The capsules slowly release a hormone. Removal is a simple procedure.

Already approved in 16 other countries, Norplant marks the major step forward in contraceptives in the United States in many years. While said to be safe and effective, it does have side effects. One of them is scar tissue. The decision will be up to a woman and her physician, and that is appropriate.

For married couples, whether before starting a family or when no more children are wanted, Norplant may be a boon. Also, through its ease of implantation and continuing efficacy with no further thought on the part of the user, it should do much to reduce the number of unwanted pregnancies and abortions in this country.

Conversely, this no-fuss, forget-about-it ease of use should in no way lull any women into a false sense of security about sexually transmitted diseases or AIDS. The contraceptive will protect against pregnancy, but the use of a condom still is vital for non-monogamous couples.

The one issue that the introduction of Norplant in February will not resolve, of course, is why it is that with the exception of the condom, contraceptive efforts concentrate on women.

Providence, Rhode Island, August 31, 1990

A revolutionary new contraceptive may soon be on the market and change the terms of the birth-control debate, especially as it applies to abortion. The Food and Drug Administration is expected to approve Norplant, an implantable contraceptive, by the end of the year. That will make an extraordinary development in contraceptive technology generally available to American women.

With Norplant, a physician implants six small plastic capsules filled with a synthetic hormone called levonorgestrel under the skin on a woman's arm. These implants continually secrete tiny amounts of the hormone, and the device can prevent conception for as long as five years. The 10-minute procedure can be done in a doctor's office under a local anesthetic and does not require stitches. And particularly convenient will be the fact that the capsules can be easily removed at any time.

Norplant doesn't seem to carry the increased risk of stroke or heart attack associated with current birth control pills, which must be taken daily. Indeed, there has been only one major complication found in Norplant tests performed so far: Some cases of irregular menstrual bleeding. Having said that, of course, we should remember that there could very well be unforeseen hazards that only time and trial can disclose.

It might also be mentioned here that RU-486, the controversial French-developed pill that induces early abortions — it's often called 'the morning-after pill' — may ultimately be used to *prevent* conception. Researchers in Sweden believe that a monthly dose might enable women to do just that. And scientists think it could perform this function more safely than does the current generation of birth-control pills. Of course, it should be borne in mind that childbirth itself poses more medical risks than does any contraceptive now on the market.

(Doctors also suggest that RU-486 may be useful in treating some cancers and other conditions; and there are several studies underway to determine if RU-846 may have other, as yet unknown, medical uses.)

The widescale availability of Norplant and other new contraceptives may soon result in a dramatic drop in the number of elective abortions performed. That development, in turn, may serve to cool the heated moral and political debate on the subject. Of course, it's also likely that some people who object to abortion actually oppose *any* form of artificial birth control because, among other things, of the sexual license associated with it. And it goes almost without saying that the increased convenience provided by new contraceptives may also be accompanied by new epidemics of sexually transmitted diseases.

In a complex society, nothing about birth control is simple, and so the battle over it will continue — even as the rhetoric is revised as fast as the technology.

San Francisco Chronicle
San Francisco, California, December 12, 1990

APPROVAL OF the new implantable contraceptive called Norplant by the Food and Drug Administration is a welcome development. Expanding contraceptive choice for American women is clearly a constructive act. The result will be fewer unwanted births — and fewer abortions.

The dismaying side of this good news is that it also represents the first new birth control method to be made available here in 30 years. As Faye Wattleton, president of the Planned Parenthood Federation of America, noted, this "major breakthrough" comes at a time when American women have fewer options for birth control than their European counterparts. Surely they deserve better from a laggard government.

The new contraceptive has been extensively tested, and is already in use by 500,000 women in 15 countries. Reports so far proclaim it be both convenient and effective. In a simple procedure, the device is implanted in the recipient's arm and works for five years.

THE PROCESS IS also easily reversed and fertility returns promptly. There are no daily pills to remember, no problems with intrauterine devices and no necessity for dealing with diaphragms or spermicides.

The new method may be no panacea. But it does represent an important addition to options for family planning that must be available for this most personal — and essential — of decisions.

The Des Moines Register
Des Moines, Iowa, August 19, 1990

The infants of unmarried mothers and fathers are generally, with many exceptions, born into less supportive situations than are youngsters whose parents have made the legal commitment of marriage. That's why the concern over the startling rise in out-of-wedlock births in Iowa should be focused on the welfare of children, not on moralizing.

More than one out of every six Iowa births in 1988 occurred out of wedlock, compared to one in 10 in 1980, says a report by the Iowa State University sociology department. That means more babies must have help to get off to a good start. If Iowans fail to pay attention to their needs now, the cost will be even higher later for services provided by schools, hospitals and other public institutions.

Lack off prenatal care is one of the chief obstacles to good health for some infants born out of wedlock. Their mothers may not be knowledgeable about the importance of good nutrition during pregnancy or may delay seeing a doctor until close to delivery because of uncertainty over how to pay for regular office visits. Once born, their children may continue to miss out on proper health care, including a good diet, because of their parents' lack of resources.

Solutions to these problems include better education of boys and girls while they are in school about the responsibilities of parenthood.

More children and pregnant women should be covered under the Medicaid program. The federal Women, Infants and Children's food program, which lacks the money to meet the needs of all the malnourished, should be expanded. Preschool needs to be available statewide in the public schools. The state and the federal government need to ensure better child-care options for low-income, working families so that they can establish themselves financially.

Such aid is needed by many parents, whether their babies are born in or out of wedlock, though the latter category is more likely to find people needing assistance. This is everyone's responsibility, because children are the community's future.

Though three of four black infants in Iowa were born out of wedlock in 1988, it is a serious error to assume that out-of-wedlock birth is common only among black teen-agers. The vast majority of out-of-wedlock births — about 87 percent — involved whites. An increasing number of older women, in their 20s and 30s, had children outside of marriage.

The bearing of children outside of marriage is a trend throughout Iowa and the nation, among black and white, all levels of society. Like it or not, that's the reality, and the institutions of society simply must adjust to cope with it.

Lincoln Journal
Lincoln, Nebraska, October 8, 1990

The ambiguity often found in the way Mexicans view the continuing relationship with their giant neighbor to the north was evident again in Lincoln last week.

Carlos Fuentes, Mexico's distinguished writer-diplomat, made it clear to an audience attending the first in the 1990-91 E.N. Thompson Forum series on world issues. Fuentes' countrymen want to be included in an expanded North American commercial free trade zone. At the same time, as a proud people, they strongly resist being pushed around by the United States.

Actions reflecting cultural, if not political, imperialism exerted almost unconsciously by the United States, with its particular values and society, feed ancient tensions when in conflict with the controlling culture of Mexico. On that point, Fuentes cannot be contradicted. But he

might be a bit idealistic saying the people of Mexico don't want to accept greater wealth at the expense of social justice. That theory awaits testing.

Mexico remains a land of too much poverty. Fuentes is to be applauded saying one fundamental line of attack on that problem is exclusively Mexico's responsibility.

It must convince a predominately Roman Catholic population to adopt family planning practices and use contraceptive devices, going directly contrary to instructions of the Catholic clergy. One admires Fuentes' hopeful prescription:

"They can be persuaded to be good Catholics in other areas and still use birth control."

It's possible. That very behavioral model exists among Catholics in major numbers north of the Rio Grande.

ST. LOUIS POST-DISPATCH
St. Louis, Missouri, February 10, 1990

"In the '80s, Iran and the United States were the only two countries that really went backward in family planning," said U.S. Rep. Patricia Schroeder, a Democrat from Colorado. Rep. Schroeder would like to see that changed; she is campaigning hard for a bill to allocate $77.2 million over five years to establish five research centers to tackle the problems of birth control and infertility. But success is not guaranteed just because her proposal makes sense and addresses a pressing concern of millions of women. Anti-abortion forces, ever alert to any development that might offer women control over their own reproduction, are waging a battle against Rep. Schroeder's bill.

A brief glance at the numbers indicates the sorry state of research in this country into fertility and infertility: One out of every six American women is infertile; 3.4 million women find themselves with an unplanned pregnancy each year; the No. 1 contraceptive in this country, used by 13.8 million women, is sterilization, which is safe and effective but generally irreversible. In many respects, the pill, introduced 30 years ago, was the last major breakthrough in birth-control technology in this country. It is the second most popular contraceptive in this country, even though all the questions about its safety have not been answered definitively.

Private pharmaceutical companies have been reluctant to pursue research into contraceptives. Developing new contraceptives takes millions of dollars. If they prove to be harmful — as did at least two intrauterine devices — settling lawsuits may take millions more.

The anti-abortion movement's opposition to birth control is well known. It was behind efforts to ban federal funds for research into birth control that works after conception; it has worked to block RU 486, the French abortion pill, from entering the American market. But the anti-abortion movement also opposes certain research into infertility; it has been against in vitro fertilization, for example, because of the issue of unused embryos.

Rep. Schroeder's bill may benefit from the new political atmosphere surrounding the abortion issue. Certainly, any improvements in birth control would reduce the need for abortion. Beyond that, though, this bill deserves passage. The quality of each woman's life is immeasurably improved when she can take advantage of safe and effective methods to have — or not have — children.

The Charlotte Observer
Charlotte, North Carolina, January 12, 1989

The evidence about possible links between oral contraceptives and cancer is so inconclusive that the U.S. Food and Drug Administration decided it didn't warrant the requirement of warning labels. Still, the evidence was sufficiently compelling to keep FDA officials in an all-day meeting before making that decision.

Two recent studies demonstrate the problem. One, conducted in this country, found that women who had used birth control pills for fewer than 10 years were twice as likely to develop breast cancer by age 45 as women who had never taken the pill. And women who had taken the pill for more than 10 years were four times as likely to develop breast cancer by age 45 as women who had not.

However, another study, conducted in England, found no overall increase in breast cancer among women who had taken the pill, though it did find a threefold increase in cancer among women age 30 to 34 who were former users of the pill.

Though the results are conflicting, one message is clear: The studies should spur aggressive research for safer contraceptives and more effective cancer treatments.

Research in both areas has slowed significantly in recent years. Drug companies say liability risks, the high cost of research and the relatively low potential for profits keep them from developing new contraceptives. And budgets for cancer research are jeopardized as more funding goes to AIDS research. This year, 25% of new cancer research proposals deemed worthy of federal funding are expected to receive it, compared to 60% in the mid-1970s.

Yet cancer continues to be the No. 2 killer of Americans, striking almost 1 million each year and killing more than 500,000. Last year there were 135,000 new cases of breast cancer; 42,300 resulted in death. By contrast, there have been 80,996 recorded cases of AIDS in the United States and 46,678 deaths since 1981, according to the Centers for Disease Control.

Persons with breast cancer, when treated, have one of the best survival rates of any cancer patients. With aggressive research, even greater survival rates are possible, for all kinds of cancers. But the better alternative is to reduce the incidence of cancer. At least some researchers believe that can be done with breast cancers if safer contraceptives are developed.

The Wichita
Eagle-Beacon
Wichita, Kansas, January 8, 1989

A federal panel did little last week to calm the health jitters of the 13.2 million American women who take birth control pills. The group of experts assembled by the Food and Drug Administration said it has found no conclusive evidence connecting oral contraceptives to cancer — but added that more study is needed.

To be sure, the medical consensus is that the birth control pill is not particularly risky. "Overall, if you look at long-term pill use as a whole, the preponderance of the evidence is that there's no effect whatsoever," said Dr. Bruce Stadel of the FDA.

Worries about the safety of birth control pills have arisen periodically over the past 25 years since widespread use of oral contraceptives began. The latest concern focuses on possible links between birth control pills and breast cancer in women under age 45. Again, researchers have found no clear cause and effect between the pill and cancer.

The issue, however, has raised fears among many women about the safety of contraceptives. It also is a reminder of how severely limited Americans are in their choices of birth control options.

The situation in other countries is much different as people have a greater choice in the ways to avoid contraception. In several European and Third World countries, for example, women have access to small implants that guard against contraception for up to five years. Also available elsewhere but not in the United States are contraceptive injections.

Indeed, once a leader in contraceptive research, the United States is doing virtually nothing to develop new, more effective means of birth control. Part of the reason is fear by manufacturers of lawsuits in case something goes wrong with their product, as happened with the Dalkon Shield intrauterine device.

Moreover, pressure from anti-abortion groups has led to cuts in government research funds for new family planning efforts. That means many promising methods, including the much sought male contraceptive, are not being developed as rapidly as possible.

Ensuring safe, reliable contraception should be a national health priority. Americans should not have to worry that they are jeopardizing their lives to avoid pregnancy.

The New York Times
New York City, New York, January 17, 1989

American women fear breast cancer, and with reason: one in ten can expect to get it someday, and it will kill 30 percent of those that do. Now comes evidence that using birth control pills might increase the risk. What's a woman to do?

More than 13 million American women are probably asking themselves that question. The pill is, after sterilization, the most frequent form of birth control in this country. Should they switch immediately to another, less effective method, thus heightening the risk of an unwanted pregnancy? Or should they first weigh the uncertainty of the risk data against the proven benefits of the pill? Common sense suggests the second choice.

The new evidence, presented to an advisory committee to the Food and Drug Administration, comes from three studies that found the pill increased breast cancer risk in those who started taking it when they were young.

But the first study found the risk in women who never had children; the second in women with one child; the third in all women. All those studied had taken oral contraceptives when these contained much higher doses of estrogen and progestin. A comparable study of women who take today's lower-dosage pills has yet to be undertaken.

In any case, breast cancer is not, like lung cancer, a disease with one clear risk factor. Instead it appears to have links with early first menstruation, late first motherhood and late menopause — all of which are associated with a high standard of living. In that sense breast cancer is, as Dr. Melvin Konner put it, "a disease of civilization." It seems also to run in families and is especially prevalent in countries with high-fat diets.

In short, the link to the pill so far is not strong and the links to other factors are. That gives individual women who use the pill some basis for rational decision. But even as they answer the question for themselves, another question arises: "When it comes to birth control, why is it always women who have to do the worrying?"

The choice of contraceptives is limited. Information about methods and services is spotty and inconsistent. Research and development is limited not simply by insufficient funds but by the howls of those who perceive most contraceptives as causing or facilitating abortion. For millions of women the pill has been a blessing, and it's reasonable to hope that it will remain so. But as this alarm makes all too clear, it's not enough. American women need more choices; so do American men.

Planned Parenthood Program Loses Corporate Support

The AT&T Foundation of American Telephone and Telegraph Co. had withdrawn its long-standing support of a Planned Parenthood program to fight teenage pregnancy, because of Planned Parenthood's support for abortion rights, it was reported April 5, 1990.

"Our support for Planned Parenthood's educational programs has become impossible to separate from Planned Parenthood's advocacy activity," said AT&T Foundation President Reynold Levy in a March 12 letter to Planned Parenthood.

"Over the past year, AT&T's philanthropic support of Planned Parenthood has given rise to an unprecedented number of expressions of concern from employees, customers, suppliers and shareowners. Essentially, these parties believe that by virtue of its assistance to Planned Parenthood, AT&T funds abortions," Levy added.

In the latest year, AT&T had given Planned Parenthood $50,000 for use in its teenage pregnancy prevention program. None of the money had been used to provide abortions.

AT&T's decision had reportedly been made in response to a letter-writing campaign by several anti-abortion groups, which had threatened to boycott corporate sponsors of Planned Parenthood unless they withdrew their support.

"AT&T, a major American concern, has been brought to its knees by a fringe group and has allowed fanatics to dictate its corporate policy," charged Faye Wattleton, the president of Planned Parenthood. "If AT&T bows to pressure on a program it claims to be committed to, who will fall next?"

In a full-page newspaper advertisement, Wattleton urged individuals to "voice their opposition to this act of corporate cowardice" and donate AT&T stock shares to Planned Parenthood, so that the organization could influence AT&T's policies.

THE BUFFALO NEWS
Buffalo, New York, June 6, 1991

IT'S ALWAYS refreshing to see someone stand up for something besides money. Or in spite of money. So directors of Planned Parenthood of Buffalo and Erie County earn a pat on the back for deciding to forgo up to $200,000 in federal aid rather than accept it along with a scruffy gag rule on abortion information.

Had Planned Parenthood accepted the money, its counselors would have been forced not to ever mention abortion to those who sought counseling at one of its three clinics. If the patient brought the subject up, counselors would have to tell them the clinic "does not consider abortion an appropriate method of family planning and therefore does not counsel or refer to abortion."

Not only the idea but the exact phrasing has been dictated by the Reagan and Bush administrations and approved by the Supreme Court, all conservatives who demean a political philosophy that once abhorred any notion of centralized government dictating the details of the daily lives of its citizens or invading the ethics of professional health-care professionals.

So Planned Parenthood here has rightly said: Keep your money. We will continue to give our clients the whole story, and not half truths.

Unfortunately, the same cannot be said for Erie County's three Reproductive Health Clinics, all in Buffalo and serving lots of low-income clients. They will continue to accept federal funds. Worse yet, the new gag rule approved by the Supreme Court doesn't change anything at the county clinics: Under long-standing policy, counselors there haven't mentioned abortion in discussing family planning with their 1,200 clients a year, many from low-income circumstances.

One can only wonder what purposes family planning clinics, public or private, really serve when they cannot even mention a procedure that is perfectly legal throughout the United States — and when they can't answer a question straightforwardly.

Aside from that, at least two lessons spring from the Reagan-Bush policy and its destructive validation by the Supreme Court.

First, never delude yourself that federal money comes free of strings. It doesn't. In some cases, those strings can strangle free speech, professional ethics and responsible performance of the task at hand.

Second, everyone who values such qualities in a free society should press Congress to overturn the bizarre executive policy that led to the court decision.

Meanwhile, those who want to get full information from their doctors and other health providers might want to avoid government clinics and their gag rules. Better to visit Buffalo's Planned Parenthood clinics and get the whole story.

Minneapolis Star and Tribune
Minneapolis, Minnesota, June 10, 1991

When the abortion gag rule recently affirmed by the U.S. Supreme Court takes effect next month, federally funded family-planning clinics will start clamming up. Unless they want to forgo government support, they'll be forced to keep mum whenever clients ask about ending an unwanted pregnancy. Even some abortion foes see the folly in that policy: It keeps clinics from telling the simple truth about a legal procedure, and might very well spark an abortion boom. Lawmakers can avert that prospect by untying the gag.

The fault lies with the Reagan administration, which sought to accomplish by fiat what Congress refused to require by statute: Prohibit staff members at federally funded family-planning clinics from even mentioning the abortion option. The court deserves billing as a co-conspirator: Its May decision upholding the gag rule shrugged off troubling curbs on free-speech and abortion rights.

The coming silence on abortion won't be golden. The unanticipated upshot could be a disintegration of the nation's network of birth-control clinics: Forced to choose between cash and candor, many clinics say they'll decline federal money. But without federal support, the shrunken clinics likely won't be much help to the poor women they've served in the past. Denied access to contraception, those women may be headed for preventable pregnancies and abortions.

All of this misfortune could be averted if Congress asserted itself and canceled the gag rule. The Senate Labor and Public Welfare Committee took the first step last week when it voted 12-5 for a bill sponsored by Sen. John Chafee. The Chafee bill does more than permit clinics to talk about abortion: It requires such talk. Any clinic that accepts federal money would be obliged to alert pregnant women to the full range of alternatives available to them. House Democrats hope to push a similar plan next week.

Such a change isn't as dramatic as it appears: It would simply emphasize the original intent of Congress in funding family-planning programs. President Bush promises to veto the measure, which he says would promote abortion. But the bill would do no such thing. It would simply free the clinics to dispense relevant information along with contraception to the poor women they treat. The bill thus promotes honesty, not abortion. It deserves prompt passage, and Bush's signature.

The Burlington Free Press
Burlington, Vermont, March 28, 1989

A woman who wants to prevent an unwanted pregnancy needs information and she needs birth control. In Vermont, that often means she needs Planned Parenthood, particularly if she is poor.

Members of the Vermont House earned applause for sound social and fiscal priority-setting this month when they voted $185,000 in new funds for the family planning organization. If the Vermont Senate can find an additional $85,000 to fund Planned Parenthood's full request, it should.

Planned Parenthood already provides Vermont's only government subsidized family planning at its 15 clinics, serving thousands of women who might otherwise go without assistance. With the new money from Montpelier, Planned Parenthood can hold down the size of its fees, serve more low-income women and expand its community health education outreach to towns like Morrisville, Newport and Middlebury.

Family planning ought to be a financial priority of government because prevention saves money. Planned Parenthood estimates that for every dollar spent to help a low-income woman prevent an unwanted pregnancy, Vermont saves $4.70 on health and welfare services to child and mother. Since teen-agers are particularly likely to bear low-birthweight babies and to require extended public assistance, society has a selfish as well as an unselfish interest in helping them avoid pregnancy.

Family planning education and services ought to be a social priority because they offer a solid bridge over the chasm of abortion. Pregnancy prevention is preferable to abortion. Vermont Right to Life argues that subsidized family planning has failed to reduce the teen pregnancy rate. To us, this demonstrates the need for more education and services, not less.

Last year, Vermont spent more than $400,000 on intensive medical care for the baby of a single teen-age Medicaid patient. Stacked up against that staggering figure, the money for Planned Parenthood seems an extremely modest investment in prevention.

The Union Leader
Manchester, New Hampshire, April 11, 1989

"In the future, we'll have to be more sensitive to how the public feels about these things," said one Laurel Brownell, spokesman for Planned Parenthood of Northern New England, after the group canceled a safe-sex dance it had planned for next month.

"These things" refers to such examples of decadence as relay races involving condoms and bananas and putting a human-sized condom over a volunteer's body —all in the name of the "sex education" of teenagers and young adults who were to have been invited to a dance in the Vermont community of Burlington to kick off a May 13th conference on family-life education.

Credit the dance cancellation not to the acquisition by Planned Parenthood of some newly discovered sensitivity, but rather, to fear that the Vermont Right To Life organization, which had denounced the event, would exploit this orgy of poor taste and imbecility as illustrative of the mind set of the conference organizers.

Never mind. The point has already been made.

The real affront to society of which these Planned Parenthood radicals, ever determined to seek out new ways to exploit the AIDS scare, are guilty is that they display no manners. In his March 29th commentary on this page on the so-called Great Condom Race at Dartmouth (student participants put a condom on the wooden pole of a toilet plunger, sprint across the room unfurling it and then ram it on the wooden pole), Professor and syndicated columnist Jeffrey Hart made the point that sponsors of such depraved activities *"are the enemies of taste and style and also of ordinary norms"* who thumb their noses at *"normal expectations of behavior."*

Their pretension to the status of "educators" of young people is an absurdity. With minds apparently unable to expand beyond their fixation with genitalia, they themselves are in dire need of education in basic civility and common sense.

——Jim Finnegan

Birmingham Post-Herald
Birmingham, Alabama, July 29, 1989

Just about anyone to the left of Phyllis Schlafly recognizes that information is the most important weapon society has in the war against teenage pregnancy, infant mortality, venereal disease, AIDS, unwanted pregnancy, abortion and other problems of human sexuality.

The sticking point, however, is how to disseminate that information in helpful ways that don't confuse more than inform, or inflame political conflicts more than they solve social problems.

With its "Facts of Life Line," Planned Parenthood of Alabama has found one way around the sticking point.

The program is a free telephone service that enables callers to hear tape-recorded messages on such subjects as reproductive health, contraception, sexually transmitted diseases, pre- and post-natal care and AIDS. About 70 taped messages are contained in a device aptly called "The Communicator." Callers hear a recorded index of the messages and choose each one by number.

While the messages couldn't possibly be comprehensive in scope, they are an effective means of disseminating reliable, unbiased and non-judgmental information. Many of the messages refer callers to other sources for more in-depth material, and they suggest that callers seek guidance from professionals.

"Facts of Life Line" is a program that should be widely promoted in schools, youth groups, health clinics and other organizations that serve people who need this type of information. It's one small light in a woefully dark field.

The Hartford Courant

Hartford, Connecticut, June 4, 1988

It may come as something of a shock to learn that American women have higher rates of abortions than women in many other industrialized countries.

A study by the Alan Guttmacher Institute, an organization in New York that studies reproductive issues, contains that and other disturbing findings, including the fact that U.S. women appear to use contraception less than women in most other Western nations.

In the United States, women of childbearing age averaged 2.56 pregnancies and 0.76 abortions, according to the study, which used 1983 figures, the latest available.

More than 51 percent of pregnancies in the United States in 1983 were unplanned. That figure compares with 31.8 percent in Britain, for example, and 17 percent in the Netherlands.

Some method of contraception was used in 1982 by only 54 percent of U.S. women between the ages of 15 and 44 — a low ranking, near that of Portugal and Spain.

Even the most fervent advocate of a woman's right to choose abortion must feel chagrin, if not sorrow, that such is the state of reproductive affairs 25 years or so after the development in the United States of the birth-control pill.

The pill was supposed to make unwanted pregnancies and abortions virtually obsolete. The problem is that the pill, like some other forms of contraception, is a problem. It is unsuitable for use by many women, especially many who are older than 35 or who have medical histories contraindicating their use of the pill.

Some contraceptives, such as the Dalkon Shield intrauterine device, have been deemed unsafe and taken off the market. Acceptable, effective hormonal or other biological male contraceptive methods have yet to be developed — there is no male pill. Sterilization is a good option only for those who are certain they want no more children. The condom, while effective, is rejected by many couples. Abstinence is an option for some people, certainly, but not all.

Many contraceptives used in Europe and elsewhere are not approved for use in the United States, and the significance of that fact is obvious. The range of demonstrably safe contraceptive choices for American women and couples is limited.

A woman's right to choose abortion should not be limited, but neither should abortion be used as a form of birth control. Yet to decrease abortion, unwanted pregnancies have to be prevented.

With better public education about the advantages of using contraception, increased commitment by men and women to use it, and more research into safe and effective birth-control methods, the goal might be realized.

Los Angeles, California, June 2, 1988

The Arizona judge who sentenced 18-year-old Debra Ann Forster to spend the rest of her child-bearing years on birth control was trying for a reasonable answer to a terrible situation. Forster had left her two young boys alone without food and water for three days. The judge could have sentenced her to 30 years in jail, but because of Forster's childish intellect, decided instead on probation, with the birth-control condition. This takes the courts from the role of deciding who gets and who loses custody of children, to who can conceive. It's a dangerous, and unnecessary, intrusion.

More than 40 years of Supreme Court rulings have held that government must not force people to undergo abortion or sterilization, nor can it prevent people from exercising these options. Reproduction is rightly viewed as a realm for strictly private, personal decisions. Though the judge's benign intention was to prevent an unfit person from bearing more children, her order opens the door for courts to determine standards for parenthood.

The precedent seems even more unreasonable when one notes that Forster is Catholic; the court thus requires that she violate her religion's tenet against contraception.

Even at a practical level, the decision solves nothing. How can a woman who has proved entirely irresponsible be made diligent about birth control? The judge can expect to see her back in the courtroom, pregnant, facing imprisonment for violating probation.

It doesn't have to be this way. Society and the courts have established sensible means for handling such cases. Counseling, training and community service could be made conditions of probation. Unless Forster gains a tremendous amount of maturity and judgment, any future children she brings into the world could also be taken from her.

It's tempting to try to prevent the birth of children who won't get adequate maternal care. Dealing with such children, however, is a small problem compared to facing the specter of a society in which the government and its courts say who may, and who may not, reproduce.

The Charlotte Observer

Charlotte, North Carolina, November 11, 1988

We are strong supporters of the local Planned Parenthood. Nevertheless, we think there is some validity to questions raised about the use of Planned Parenthood's FOCUS drama group as part of the new AIDS curriculum in Charlotte-Mecklenburg Schools.

The central issue is not the quality of the FOCUS program, which uses teen actors to dramatize issues of family communication. The FOCUS program is excellent. Over the years it has been highly regarded throughout the community, and has presented programs in a variety of settings, including churches and public schools. In this instance, the system is taking pains to assure the appropriateness and effectiveness of the presentations for eighth-grade assemblies. There will be a preview for parents, who can have their children excused from the program. The emphasis of the overall AIDS curriculum is abstinence. Nobody is being careless or irresponsible.

But it strikes us as a mistake for the schools to rely on an outside advocacy group to provide part of a state-mandated, systemwide AIDS curriculum. The curriculum deals with topics so sensitive that the state requires the schools to give parents an advance look and a chance to have their children excused from the classes. In local schools, the rest of the material will be presented by school and health professionals. The schools should want that clear and direct control throughout the AIDS curriculum, simply as a matter of being accountable and prudent.

The system shouldn't shrink from teaching the facts about AIDS, or contraception or anything else. But public schools in a diverse society have some special obligations. One of them is to take care that the message not be overwhelmed by controversy over the messenger.

However excellent the FOCUS program, Planned Parenthood is a partisan in a long-running, bitter fight. There would be similar questions if the school system were proposing to turn assemblies on AIDS over to a troupe sponsored by a conservative group such as Concerned Charlotteans. It's difficult enough for the schools to achieve a sensitive, balanced approach to controversial topics when they use their own staff and others perceived as neutral and professional; when they use an outside advocacy group, the difficulty is multiplied.

As the school board talks about this issue and the policies on use of outside groups to supplement the curriculum, it should proceed carefully. There is a lot to be gained in many subject areas from outside resources, including Planned Parenthood and some other groups that are closely identified with one side or the other of a public debate. The board needs workable policies that provide accountability and direction, without stifling initiative.

A danger in curriculum battles in that the schools will choose to shun controversy, in practice if not in policy, and thus become as vapid as some of their textbooks. The greatest risk of this may lie not at the top — where a strong superintendent is willing to fight the battles — but out in the schools, where teachers and principals may decide that venturing beyond the text is too complicated, if not too dangerous.

BOSTON HERALD
Boston, Massachusetts, October 8, 1988

WHY it has taken researchers so long to ask women exactly why they abort their unborn — considering that abortion has been hotly controversial for far longer than it's been legal — is curious. In all of the words and all of the battles about the *ethics* of this medical procedure, too few people have bothered to listen to the *reasons* why women chose to abort rather than to give birth.

Now the results of two national surveys conducted by the Alan Guttmacher Institute, a private non-profit research organization in New York, have been published. Its findings, though interesting and informative, are shocking.

More than 11,000 women seeking abortions in health facilities nationwide were asked to fill out a questionnaire about their religious affiliation, marital status, ethnic background, age, employment status, and income level. They were then asked why they were having abortions.

Three-fourths said that having a baby would interfere with their careers or their school plans; two-thirds said they couldn't afford a child; half said they didn't want to be single parents or were involved in troubled relationships.

Catholic women had abortions at a rate 30 percent higher than Protestant women. Poor women had more abortions than wealthy women. The majority of women claimed they'd attempted to use some kind of birth control during the month they conceived.

There are some lessons here.

First: For many couples, a better form of birth control — more effective or easier to use — is clearly necessary.

Second: The Catholic Church, passionate in its opposition to abortion, is either failing to inculcate that passion in many of its adherents, or failing to make alternatives to abortion as easily obtainable as that drastic step.

Third: Most women are having abortions because it suits their personal convenience.

Seventy percent of the women surveyed acknowledged that they plan to have children in the future. In other words, it isn't the idea of a baby but the *timing* of a baby that leads most women to abort.

Think of it: A million and a half abortions performed every year because having that baby would be *inconvenient*. That is nothing short of scandalous.

If abortion is legal — and for the last 15 years, it has been — then it's legal for all reasons. Rape. Or health. Or convenience. In the eyes of the law, the reason is irrelevant — all reasons are alike.

But law and morality are different words — and often different worlds.

The Charlotte Observer
Charlotte, North Carolina, November 1, 1988

Major drug companies have virtually abandoned efforts to develop new drugs for contraception, and some anti-abortion groups are claiming credit for stopping them, according to a recent New York Times report.

Ironically, that claim comes at a time when anti-abortionists are stepping up their efforts to stop women from having abortions, by literally blocking the entrances to abortion clinics around the country.

Most anti-abortionists say they oppose only those birth control methods that act to prevent implantation of a fertilized egg. But if their claims are valid, they have helped stop the development of *any* new contraceptives.

Drug manufacturers dispute those claims, of course. They say the high cost of research, liability risks and the relatively low potential for profits are the major reasons they are reluctant to develop new contraceptives.

Nonetheless, if anti-abortionists see stopping the development of contraceptives as part of their strategy for stopping abortions, they are at best unrealistic. If safe, reliable contraceptives are not available, the only way to stop abortions is to stop women from engaging in sex. And while abstinence has its place, especially for adolescents, it is not a solution for the millions of married and other sexually active adult women who have chosen either not to have a child or not to have another child.

If stopping abortions is the goal of anti-abortionists, then stopping unwanted pregnancies should be the primary objective. Safe and available choices in contraceptives is one of the best ways to do that.

THE SACRAMENTO BEE
Sacramento, California, June 5, 1988

Presumably, if Debra Ann Forster had been given a choice between 30 years in prison and 30 years of birth control, she would have chosen the latter, but that doesn't make this novel sentence recently handed down in an Arizona court any more humane — or just.

Forster had pleaded guilty to attempted felony child abuse of her two infant sons, whom she abandoned without food or water in a hot apartment for nearly three days because, she said, she "couldn't cope." The babies were in critical condition when rescued and had to be hospitalized eight days. Arizona's maximum sentence for that crime is 30 years in prison, but the judge instead put the 18-year-old mother on lifetime probation, prohibited her from ever again seeing the children or a baby girl born to her in jail and — the inventive addition to this sentence — required her to use birth control for the rest of her child-bearing years.

The judge seemed to think this punishment fit the crime. But Forster's crime was not having children; it was abandoning, indeed nearly killing, them. The birth control sentence is probably unconstitutional — being arguably cruel and certainly unusual, as well as a violation of Forster's constitutional right to privacy in the conduct of her sex life — but even more disturbing, the sentence was utterly irrelevant to the crime committed.

Birth control will neither rehabilitate this woman nor prevent her from mistreating any child left in her care in the future. And as sheer punishment, it is either too trivial an inconvenience to avenge a crime of this seriousness or too personally invasive a retribution to exact for any crime — or perhaps both.

Biology is not destiny. It is not conception that made — or in future might make — Forster a danger to society. And a society that begins to think so is not far from punishing rapists with castration or robbers by cutting off their hands and otherwise deluding itself with notions that such barbarism offers either mercy to the criminal or protection to society itself.

THE KANSAS CITY STAR

Kansas City, Missouri, July 10, 1988

Vice President Bush needs to make clear his position on international family planning. This is one of many areas where the record of pre-Reagan George Bush differs sharply with that of Vice President George Bush, and no one knows where he stands.

The voters should know whether the likely GOP nominee plans to continue President Reagan's policies of abandoning U.S. aid to Third World countries which are trying desperately to control their burgeoning populations, or whether Bush will endorse the position he held as a congressman from Texas and as this country's representative at the United Nations. For the future of the world if he is elected, it should be the latter.

During his earlier years of public service, Bush was a strong advocate of international family planning and population control, and of helping women at home obtain birth control services. In one public writing, published in 1973, Bush said that one of the major challenges of the decade will be "to curb the world's fertility." That is even more true in this decade.

Since then, however, he has been silent as the top man in Washington has cut off money to the United Nations Population Fund, which provides help to developing countries, and reduced funding to private international agencies. Perhaps as vice president, Bush did not feel he could differ with Reagan. However, Bush as a presidential candidate has an obligation to the voters to make his position clear.

The two Democratic contenders for president, Michael Dukakis and Jesse Jackson, have issued clear statements on this issue. In response to inquiries by members of The Population Institute, both said they would reverse the current administration's policy and make the U.S. once again a leader in international family planning.

Without family planning in developing countries, those nations most unable to feed and house their populations will find conditions of starvation and environmental degradation exacerbated. Where will these people go when their own food runs out?

The answer has implications for everyone in this country and in the rest of the developed world. This nation's leadership can provide important inspiration in the population control effort. Bush needs to endorse that effort wholeheartedly once again.

The Boston Globe

Boston, Massachusetts, August 27, 1988

The double standard that has long ignored the role of adolescent boys in teen-age pregnancies deserves greater attention. Boys should be encouraged to go beyond the nascent image of manhood that they associate with awakened sexual activity, and the responsibilities of parenthood should be stressed to them.

Because of a decline in the teen-age population in the United States, the number of teenagers giving birth has dropped to 478,000 a year – 120,000 fewer than in 1970. At the same time, however, far fewer teen-age mothers are getting married today than did a decade ago.

Unsurprisingly, social research has documented that teen-age girls know more about sex at an earlier age than teen-age boys do. Although teen-age boys use contraception less often in early sexual encounters than their partners, the boys fail to take precautions for a different reason than the girls: they do not know much about contraception. Yet, sex-instruction programs almost always are geared toward adolescent girls.

Studies by the Children's Defense Fund show that many of society's assumptions about teen-age sex and pregnancy are wrong. Generally, the study found, teen-age boys do not assume any significant responsibility for avoiding pregnancy or supporting the baby.

As would be expected, teen-agers with the least-promising options for employment, education and even recreation are the ones most likely to become teen-age parents.

Though some expectant fathers do try to shoulder their responsibility in a teen-age pregnancy, their efforts have found little support in the past.

One Children's Defense Fund's recommendation for preventing pregnancy during adolescence is to modify boys' attitudes about what manhood really means. Boys should be provided with more responsible sex information. They also should be helped along the road to manhood – the hard and fulfilling work of life – through better education and job opportunities.

The Wichita Eagle-Beacon

Wichita, Kansas, June 7, 1988

THE United States is a world leader in abortion. Not surprisingly, the United States also is a world laggard in the availability and practice of birth control.

Those facts are part of a new study of pregnancy rates in industrialized countries conducted by the Alan Guttmacher Institute in cooperation with the federal Health and Human Services Department.

The report found that among 17 Western countries only Greece and Italy had higher abortion rates than the United States. Almost 30 percent of U.S. pregnancies — about 1.5 million annually — end in abortion.

The high U.S. abortion rate is linked to the fact that the United States is one of only three among the countries surveyed where unplanned pregnancies outnumbered planned ones. That suggests thousands of American women got abortions because they didn't use contraception.

Sex education and easy access to birth control services are key to reducing the number of abortions. For example, in the Netherlands, which stresses sex information and makes contraception widely available, abortion and unplanned pregnancy rates are about five times below those of the United States.

Indeed, American women are less likely to use birth control than women in most other countries. That is partly because of a lack of sex education programs in many schools, and a low priority given to family planning by government and the nation's health care system.

The tragic irony is that people most opposed to abortion could boost the U.S. abortion rate. In an attempt to appease the right-to-life movement, the Reagan administration has tried to cut off funding for Planned Parenthood and some other organizations that promote family planning. If successful, such efforts undoubtedly would raise the number of abortions.

Ideally, all pregnancies should be joyous events and none should be terminated. But until the country gets serious about sex education and birth control, abortion will remain a sad part of the American social reality.

ST. LOUIS POST-DISPATCH

St. Louis, Missouri, June 7, 1988

There is no reason the United States should have the highest abortion rate in the industrialized world. Public officials and the medical profession have a special responsibility to help bring that rate down.

Researchers for the Alan Guttmacher Institute, an organization dealing in population issues, found that countries where a wide variety of contraceptives is available and easy to obtain have fewer unplanned pregnancies and fewer abortions than countries where the selection is limited and less accessible. The United States falls into the latter category. In 1983, the institute said, 51.2 percent of U.S. pregnancies were unplanned. In Great Britain, 31.8 percent were unplanned; in the Netherlands 17 percent. In contraceptive use, the United States ranked with Portugal and Spain.

Based on current abortion rates in the United States, the researchers projected that among every 100 women there eventually will be 76 induced abortions — a shocking figure. This contrasts with Canada, where researchers predict 36 induced abortions among every 100 women.

Ironically, one explanation for the high American abortion rate can be found in the political influence of the anti-abortion forces. Largely through their efforts, the Reagan administration has impeded the wide and easy dissemination of contraceptives and has discouraged educational programs on contraceptive use.

The lesson here is twofold. First, contraceptives must be more readily available and their use encouraged through educational programs. Second, attitudes must be changed so that abortion becomes a last resort, not a routine form of birth control.

Minneapolis Star and Tribune

Minneapolis, Minnesota, June 6, 1988

Three years ago the Alan Guttmacher Institute, a population-research organization, shocked Americans with a study which showed that U.S. teenagers had the highest pregnancy and abortion rates among industrialized countries. A new Guttmacher study finds that the problem does not end with the teen years. American women of childbearing age have more unplanned pregnancies and rely more on abortion to control family size than in most developed countries. The culprit remains the same: inadequate education about birth control and poor access to effective contraception.

The U.S. pregnancy rate — the average number of pregnancies, including births and abortions, per woman during her childbearing years — is 2.6, surpassed only by Greece and Ireland among the 20 countries studied. But the U.S. fertility rate — the average number of births per woman — is 1.8, only slightly above average. An abortion rate of .8, second only to Italy's, accounts for the difference.

The abortion rate reflects a high number of unplanned pregnancies, which in turn reflects a low rate of contraceptive use, particularly of the most effective methods such as the pill. The problem is concentrated among women under 25, but even couples who want families frequently have children sooner and closer together than desired.

The United States' family-planning shortcomings have many causes: legal and regulatory problems that have driven most IUDs from the market and inhibited the development of new contraceptive methods, a health-care system that stresses expensive specialization over general practice, prohibitions on contraceptive education and services in schools, a welfare system that rewards premature parenthood, societal disputes over abortion that spill over into contraception. The net result is that many Americans have less information about, less access to and fewer choices of affordable, effective contraception than people in other countries.

Other developed countries have shown the benefits of providing more and better family-planning information and of lowering financial and physical barriers to contraceptive services. Information produces more responsible decisions about sexuality and parenthood. Contraception reduces unwanted pregnancies and abortions. Americans of childbearing age need better access to both.

©1991 HERBLOCK
Washington Post

'Dr. Bush and Dr. Rehnquist will see you now.'

Federally Funded Family Clinics Limited by HHS

The Department of Health and Human Services January 29, 1988 issued new rules that would bar federally funded family planning clinics from engaging in abortion-related activities. The new rules were the final version of a policy formulated by the department in August 1987 at the behest of President Ronald Reagan.

Most family planning clinics received federal funds. In the most recent fiscal year, the federal government had provided some $142.5 million for family planning services used by some 4.3 million people, of whom 85% were low-income women, according to the *New York Times*. The average clinic received an average of about 30% of its funds from the government.

Federally funded clinics were already barred from using federal money for abortions. The new regulations, which would take effect March 3, would also bar the clinics from advising a woman, even indirectly, that keeping a baby, putting it up for adoption or getting an abortion were all legal options for handling a pregnancy.

Furthermore, a clinic would not be allowed to refer a woman directly to an outside facility performing abortions even if she asked for one. Instead, the woman would simply be given a list of outside facilities providing prenatal care. Such a list could include facilities performing abortions, but not facilities "whose principal business is the provision of abortions."

Reagan administration officials said the new rules were intended to limit the role of the clinics to such prepregnancy services as contraceptive and fertility advice.

The Courier-Journal

Louisville, Kentucky, September 15, 1988

THE PRESIDENT has won a small victory by threatening to veto a huge spending bill if Congress permitted Medicaid to finance abortions for victims of rape or incest.

He got help from House members who made offensive arguments such as this: to abort in cases of rape or incest "is to kill a baby because his father committed a crime." Reducing the argument to that level is an insult to women victimized by such atrocities.

But what could one expect from Mr. Reagan? His administration eagerly has held a woman's right to an abortion hostage — hostage to her pocketbook.

Vice President George Bush and Sen. Dan Quayle were conveniently absent during the final key vote. By not having to break a tie vote in the Senate on whether to accept a House version, the Vice President spared himself possible embarrassment because he has differed with President Reagan and his own party platform on the issue. Mr. Bush has said he wouldn't oppose abortions for victims of rape or incest but thinks Medicaid should pay only for abortions to save a woman's life. By missing the vote, he can continue to duck the issue of whether a rape victim's right to an abortion should hinge on income.

Mr. Bush says a candidate's stand on abortion should not be a litmus test, and he's right. But it's tough to imagine voting for someone who puts a price tag on justice.

Portland Press Herald

Portland, Maine, September 14, 1988

It is difficult to think of women more desperate than those pregnant as the result of rape or incest. For women with money, abortion is an option; for poor women it is not. In such rare and compelling cases compassion alone suggests the government — through Medicaid — should make abortions available to the poor.

Until 1981 federal law permitted use of Medicaid money to fund abortions for poor women in such instances or whenever the pregnancy threatened the woman's life. Then Congress limited Medicaid abortion funding only to cases where the woman's life is endangered.

Now Congress is reconsidering the issue. The Senate has already approved a measure, supported by both Sens. William S. Cohen and George J. Mitchell, to permit — in those states that agree — Medicaid funding of abortions in cases of pregnancy caused by rape or incest.

But the House refuses to budge. Last week it defeated the measure by a 216-166 vote. Again, both of Maine's representatives, Olympia J. Snowe and Joseph E. Brennan, voted to expand Medicaid abortions for victims of rape and incest.

The unanimous support of the measure by the Maine congressional delegation reflects both wisdom and compassion. Pregnancy under such grotesque circumstances is shattering. Indeed, it is likely that many of those who oppose abortion generally would nonetheless make an exception for rape and incest cases.

The House should reconsider and join the Senate. Government should not require, by tightening its purse strings, women who have been so cruelly assaulted to bear the children of their assailants.

Detroit Free Press

Detroit, Michigan, September 9, 1989

IN A VERY real sense, Barbara Listing is absolutely right about this fall's Medicaid abortion funding ballot question. Ms. Listing, chairwoman of the Committee to End Tax-Funded Abortions, says: "This is an abortion funding issue . . . not whether abortions are right or wrong."

That goes to the heart of the question. The ballot issue will not affirm or repeal the U.S. Supreme Court's decision that whether to have an abortion is a choice best left to the woman herself. What will be decided is whether poor women, dependent for medical care upon the Medicaid system, will be denied funds to pay for their abortions.

The question is whether the state, unable or unwilling to challenge the right of women to seek abortions, is going to deny poor women the right to make that choice. No one has yet sought to repeal other forms of tax-paid abortions. State employees and public school employees, for instance, would continue to have medical insurance that provides funding for abortions. The decision not to attack that kind of choice was deliberate. It is easier to single out the poor women who must depend on Medicaid.

We do not doubt the validity of the polls on which Ms. Listing bases her comments.

There undoubtedly is a group of voters that supports abortion but opposes state funding for abortions. Some of that group may be people who are simply hostile to women on welfare or against Medicaid *per se*. Others may be taking the position that, yes, it's your choice, but no, don't use my tax money to support you in your choice.

In the end, though, we hope that people will come to see that this is a question of fairness. If you believe that abortions should be a matter for individual decision, then we think you will want to vote against cutting off state funding for abortions through Medicaid and, hence, you'll want to vote no on Proposal A. It is encouraging, rather than discouraging, that Ms. Listing wants to frame the issue in this way.

We believe that when people see that the denial of Medicaid funding is in reality an assault on the principle of equity, the voters of Michigan will reject the ban. That has been our central point in the long argument over funding of Medicaid abortions: The choice about whether to have an abortion is one that should be made by the individual involved, and the state should not deny that choice to poor women simply because they are vulnerable.

The Salt Lake Tribune

Salt Lake City, Utah, September 7, 1988

With Congress' summer recess now over, members of the House will soon be expected to break a deadlock over federal funding of abortions for poverty stricken victims of incest and rape. While there's only a remote chance of changing current policy, fairness and common decency would dictate that representatives side with the Senate on this issue.

Since 1976, Medicaid coverage — federally subsidized health insurance for the poor — has been restricted to abortions performed to save the life of the mother. The House upheld the policy in its spending bill for the departments of Labor, Health and Human Services and Education and their related agencies.

However, the Senate voted July 27 to extend coverage to victims of rape and incest as long as the crimes were promptly reported. A House-Senate conference committee has been unable to compromise on the abortion measure, and President Reagan has threatened a veto if the Senate prevails.

Abortion is clearly a difficult issue of conscience, but one the U.S. Supreme Court has determined is the mother's legal decision to make, within certain parameters. Because of congressional prohibitions against federally funding abortions, though, certain women are cruelly denied that decision. Those are the women who cannot afford the $250 it may cost to obtain an abortion, let alone the countless dollars it would cost to provide for a child.

The discrimination is largely the consequence of public ambivalence about abortion. In 1985, according to a Gallup poll for Newsweek, 55 percent of the population felt abortion should be legal under only certain circumstances. The remainder were split between allowing it in "all circumstances" and none at all. Almost every debate on abortion in Congress and other public arenas is consumed by emotional argumentation, pro and con.

There is considerably less disagreement about a sexual assault victim's right to abortion, however. The National Opinion Research Center, University of Chicago, reported in a 1987 survey that 81 percent of Americans believe pregnant women should be able to obtain an abortion if the pregnancy is the result of rape. Presumably, cases of incest would be categorized as rape.

If such a woman can pay for an abortion in this country, she can get one. But for those on welfare or earning as little as $5,000 a year, a $250 abortion represents more than half the family's monthly income. Their only alternative may be to give birth to an attacker's offspring.

The Senate would let states decide whether to make exceptions for rape and incest victims who immediately report the sexual assaults to the proper authorities. Those limits would exclude some women, including residents of states with conservative abortion laws and those reluctant to report a relative's assault to police. But the amendment would carry the country another step closer to its goal of equalized justice.

The Washington Post

Times Herald

Washington, D.C., September 9, 1988

AS IS ALWAYS true at the end of a session, Congress is now working its way through conference reports on appropriations bills. One that is ready for House action is the bill appropriating money for the Departments of Labor, Education and Health and Human Services. While conference reports are usually accepted by both Houses—they are the end product of months of compromise—the human services money bill may hit a snag because of abortion.

For three years after the Supreme Court decision in *Roe v. Wade*, Medicaid programs paid for abortions for the poor. But in 1976, Congress eliminated this funding except in cases of rape or incest or where the life of the mother was in danger. In 1981, even this exception was narrowed, and now federal funds can be used only for those abortions required to save the life of a mother. Fourteen states and the District of Columbia have voted to continue abortion funding using only their own money, but in all the others, no public funds of any kind are available to help women whose pregnancies are the result of violence and assault. Planned Parenthood estimates that one poor woman in five is unable to obtain a desired abortion when public funds of some kind are not available.

In July the Senate passed an appropriation bill that would allow states to use federal Medicaid money to pay for rape and incest abortions. The House bill did not contain this provision, but the conferees accepted it and the change is now in the final version of the bill. There may be objection on the House floor, but it should be overridden. Even among those who disagree with *Roe v. Wade*, a majority would probably accept an exception for cases of rape and incest. And for poor women in 36 states, finding the money to exercise their rights when they have been the victims of brutality is a terrible problem. A vote to allow the use of federal funds in these special cases would provide a modest and badly needed assistance to women in great need.

Fetal Tissue Use Sparks Medical, Ethical Debates

An advisory committee of the National Institutes of Health September 16, 1988 concluded that it was ethically acceptable to use human fetal tissue obtained from legal abortions for medical research and therapy.

Fetal tissue was of scientific interest because it did not carry the full complement of immunities that adult tissue did. Early research suggested that fetal tissue transplants offered hope in the treatment of Parkinson's disease and other brain disorders.

The 21-member advisory panel included medical, religious, legal and ethical experts. It was appointed by the Department of Health and Human Services in July after the government suspended federal financing of new research involving fetal tissue.

The panel's vote was 19–0, with two abstentions. The recommendation was nonbinding.

The panel concluded that any use of fetal tissue obtained from voluntary abortions was equivalent to using other cadaver tissue that would normally be discarded. But the committee suggested developing guidelines that would separate any decision about having an abortion from any considerations of medical use of the tissue, to prevent the possibility that medical demand might influence decisions to abort.

Shortly before the panel's report was released the White House was reported September 9 to have drafted an order forbidding all federally financed research on tissues from aborted fetuses. The order, which the White House said was merely a draft, was written by Gary Bauer, the assistant to the President for policy development and a conservative noted for his strong anti-abortion stance.

Secretary of Health and Human Services Otis R. Bowen said September 15 that despite a White House request for rapid action, he would not impose new curbs on fetal tissue research until advisory groups had completed their work.

A National Institutes of Health advisory committee December 14 voted, 21–4, to accept a report from a panel of scientific and ethical experts that concluded that using tissue from aborted fetuses in medical research was "acceptable public policy." Meanwhile the American Academy of Neurology recently had adopted a position statement urging "great caution" in proceeding with such experiments, it was reported December 9. But a Colorado doctor, Curt Freed of the University of Colorado Health Center in Denver, underscored the swift pace of research by telling an audience November 15 that he had on November 8 performed a fetal tissue transplant into a 52-year-old man with Parkinson's disease.

The U.S. House of Representatives July 25, 1991 voted to allow the use of aborted fetuses in federally funded research. The measure was part of a $4.4 billion National Institutes of Health reauthorization bill, which was approved on a vote of 274 to 144.

The measure, if passed by the Senate and signed by President George Bush, would overturn a three-year moratorium on the use of fetal tissue in federally funded research. Many researchers said fetal tissue was a promising source of treatments for Parkinson's disease, Alzheimer's disease, diabetes and other ailments.

But such research was opposed by anti-abortion groups. "It is unworthy of us, as a national to kill our unborn children and then cannibalize them for spare parts," complained Douglas Johnson, legislative director of the National Right to Life Committee, July 25. Rep. Robert K. Dorman (R, Calif.) called the action a "Nazi Hitlerian nightmare."

Kate Michelman, executive director of the National Abortion Rights Action League, said July 25, "Medical research must not be held hostage by a small, vocal, anti-choice minority."

The Augusta Chronicle
Augusta, Georgia, August 5, 1991

At first nobody really thought much about the Reagan administration's ban on federal funding for research involving the transplantation of fetal tissue, which was renewed by the Bush administration.

This summer, though, a group of congressmen led by Rep. Henry Waxman, D-Calif., got the House to overturn the moratorium in legislation reauthorizing the National Institutes of Health (NIH).

A healthy national debate has ensued, so we might as well join in. A few thoughts:

■ Medical researchers claim that tissue from aborted fetuses could be useful in developing treatments for Parkinson's and Alzheimer's, among other diseases. And, though they don't talk much about it publicly, researchers and doctors performing abortions work closely together to cull this tissue.

■ According to the *Washington Times*, this year more than 100 research projects across the country received approximately $8 million for experiments. Even with the moratorium, researchers can continue with private funding and, so long as they refrain from transplantation to humans, they can keep their NIH grants.

All of this focuses, of course, on a moral question.

What is at stake is treating human tissue, and thus human beings, as a means to an end. How can Congress overturn the moratorium if this is a nation and culture that preaches about the rights and dignity all human beings should enjoy?

A June poll by *Time* magazine found only 36 percent of all Americans feel it is morally acceptable to harvest humans for body parts. So it would seem the Bush administration's ban has strong public backing.

As one congressman underscored during floor debate, medical researchers have to understand that there are limits to what they can do to human beings.

Los Angeles Times
Los Angeles, California, July 25, 1991

With the House of Representatives scheduled to vote today on a bill lifting the three-year federal ban on fetal tissue transplant research, the Bush Administration finds itself in the uncomfortable and unfamiliar position of defending a medical research policy that is devoid of scientific or ethical merit.

Fetal tissue grafts have shown rising promise in the last 20 years as a treatment for Parkinson's disease, Alzheimer's disease, diabetes, spinal cord injuries, muscular dystrophy, hemophilia and a host of other disorders. In grafts the tissue grows so fast it can replace damaged or dying cells before the body rejects the transplanted material.

But such tissue comes from aborted human fetuses. For that reason, the Bush and Reagan administrations, because of their opposition to abortion, have objected to all transplant research using the tissue. In conse-quence, and contrary to the recommendation of a prestigious scientific advisory panel, the federal government has denied funds for research since 1988. And so research has withered in the United States, even as it flourished abroad.

Moreover, the Bush Administration deployed the fetal tissue issue, like the broader issue of abortion, as a "litmus test" for federal appointees. For example, the directorship of the National Institutes of Health, which fund most biomedical research in the United States, was vacant for almost two years while the Administration searched for an ideologically acceptable candidate. After some candidates for the post were angered by questioning about their views on abortion, the White House said it was dropping this so-called litmus test. But when Dr. Bernadine Healy—previously an active advocate of such research—was nominated as NIH director last spring, she suddenly changed her mind and came out against the research.

The heavy-handed tactics by the Administration may have backfired. A remarkable political shift has recently occurred. Last year Rep. Henry A. Waxman (D-Los Angeles) failed in his effort to tack onto the annual NIH reauthorization bill language that would have lifted the research ban. Since then, the American medical profession has stepped forward, strongly denouncing the ban as contrary to the principles of scientific research and the health of Americans with potentially treatable diseases.

House passage of this year's NIH reauthorization bill—with language lifting the fetal tissue ban identical to that in last year's bill—is assured. The White House is watching quietly to see whether the vote is veto-proof. We strongly hope it is.

Newsday
New York City, New York, September 14, 1991

Imagine the scorn that would be heaped on officials of a nation who — solely because of political ideology — prevented scientists at an important medical research lab from using a pioneering research method that could lead to better treatment, or even a cure, for deadly diseases. If that happened in a dictatorship, Americans would probably be repulsed.

Yet that is what's happening with the U.S. government's own ban on research involving fetal tissue at the National Institutes of Health, the nation's premier public research facility. Congress has an opportunity to overturn this mean-spirited policy in just a few weeks, when it considers legislation to reauthorize the NIH. In the interest of the nation's health, it must repeal the ban.

Anti-abortionists have made the ban on fetal tissue research a cause célèbre. It was these zealots within the Reagan administration who imposed the ban in 1988. The Bush administration extended it indefinitely.

The anti-abortionists' complaint is that more women will have abortions in order to provide tissues for research. That argument ignores that there are now 1.5 million legal abortions performed annually — all of them, it's safe to say, for personal and medical reasons that have nothing to do with what happens to the fetal tissue. Right now, that tissue becomes incinerated garbage. Its scientific value literally goes up in smoke.

Yet scientists believe experiments using fetal tissue holds promise for treating such common and life-threatening ailments as diabetes, Parkinson's disease, AIDS and a wide variety of neurological disorders.

Finally, Congress is moving to do something about this perversion of medical priorities. The House voted in July to eliminate the ban. Now the Senate Labor and Human Resources Committee, which is to begin work on its version of a bill to reauthorize NIH programs later this fall, has the chance to do the same. That is the only scientifically sound choice.

The News and Observer
Raleigh, North Carolina, July 27, 1991

The House vote to lift a federal ban on use of fetal tissue in medical research on dread degenerative diseases represents a small scrap of ground regained for reason in its struggle against hysteria.

The gain is temporary. President Bush, whose veto stamp must be wearing out from heavy use, is expected to use it again here. He has never missed a chance to cater to the extreme wing of the anti-abortion movement, one of whose spokesmen says the bill would "kill our unborn children and then cannibalize them for spare parts."

That is language aimed at the viscera, not the brain. Cooler heads will recall that millions of adult Americans have ordered that their bodies be given to science and/or organ donation upon death. Is that "cannibalizing for spare parts?"

Cooler heads realize that millions of legal abortions are performed each year in this nation and will continue to be performed as long as the United States keeps abortion legal. Further, they know that if the Supreme Court finds a way to overturn its own precedent and make abortion illegal again, there will be millions of illegal abortions.

The question is not whether fetuses will be aborted. They will.

Parkinson's disease is a scourge of aging. Victims dying in the last year include actor Robert Cummings, football immortal Harold "Red" Grange, artificial intelligence pioneer Arthur Samuel, guitarmaker Guy Fender, and Appalachian activist writer Harry Caudill. Those are only the best-known. Nearly every family knows if not numbers a victim.

Tissue from fetuses, research doctors already know, can relieve Parkinson's symptoms without rejection. Such tissue also holds promise in relation to childhood and other leukemias, Alzheimer's disease, diabetes, Huntington's disease and perhaps spinal cord injuries. Yet fetal tissue use has not been allowed in federally funded research since 1988.

How many thousands of living sufferers could have benefited if that ban had not existed, no one will ever know. To continue the ban is worse than anti-science, it is anti-compassion. When good demonstrably can come from sadness, this nation ought to let it come.

THE INDIANAPOLIS STAR
Indianapolis, Indiana, August 25, 1990

It's bad timing and a worse idea.

Earlier this month Rep. Henry A. Waxman, D-Calif., introduced legislation to remove the ban on federal funding of fetal tissue research. In itself, the proposal is nothing new. Various biomedical scientists have urged the ban be lifted, arguing that research in transplanting fetal tissue holds promise in treating Parkinson's disease, Alzheimer's disease, diabetes and other disorders.

The ban, instituted in 1988, prohibits funding only of research involving tissue that is obtained from induced abortions.

What is new about the Waxman legislation is that it would also give the National Institutes of Health permanent authority to fund such research so long as it complied with ethical guidelines. Further, it would prohibit the secretary of Health and Human Services from refusing funding based solely on ethical grounds unless a special advisory panel concurred with the judgment.

Proposal will further muddle the abortion controversy.

The latter is a slap at Louis W. Sullivan, HHS secretary, who last year extended the ban indefinitely, even though an advisory panel recommended it be lifted.

Waxman's proposal is bound to stir protests and further muddle the abortion controversy. In the testy debates ahead, it should be emphasized that no funds does *not* mean no research. Privately sponsored experiments will continue.

Nor does the ban rule out funding for research using tissue from spontaneous or involuntary abortions. Since an estimated 750,000 to 1 million non-induced abortions occur each year, there would seem to be no lack of fetal tissue as such.

How medically useful such tissue might be is uncertain. But the same can be said of the tissue remaining from the 1.6 million induced abortions reported annually.

Waxman's proposal appears to be inspired more by the election clock than by any demonstrated research needs. That's a pity. There is already an excess of abortion-related politicking. Waxman is only adding fuel to the fury.

The Register-Guard
Eugene, Oregon, September 24, 1990

Solomon would have approved.

The Tennessee Court of Appeals has overturned a lower court ruling and granted joint custody of seven frozen, fertilized embryos to a divorced couple. The court's decision was the only fair way out of an impossibly complex dilemma posed by the law's inability to keep pace with reproductive technology.

The case, involving Mary Sue and Junior Davis, began when the couple — after years of unsuccessfully trying to conceive a child in the traditional way — turned to in vitro fertilization. Nine of Mary Sue's eggs were fertilized with Junior's sperm in a petri dish. Two years ago, two of the eggs were implanted in Mary Sue but failed to develop. The remaining seven were frozen so they would be available for later implementation.

Shortly after, Mary Sue filed for divorce. The frozen embryos presented the divorce court with a unique custody/property issue. Mary Sue, who has since remarried, demanded custody of the embryos so that she could have one or more implanted in hopes of becoming pregnant. Junior demanded custody so that he wouldn't be forced into parenthood against his will. The stance each party took was eminently defensible.

In sorting through all of this, however, the trial judge leaped well beyond a question of custody by declaring the eggs to be "children" and awarding custody to the "mother," Mary Sue. Junior appealed the ruling.

Mary Sue later returned to court seeking permission to donate the frozen embryos to one or more childless couples. Junior objected, on the perfectly justifiable grounds that if he didn't want to become a father against his will, he certainly didn't want to become a father by having the eggs he fertilized implanted in a stranger.

Predictably, given the trial judge's declarations about "children" and "mother," there were attempts to link the abortion issue to the Davis' dispute over the frozen embryos. Fortunately, the appeals court didn't buy into that argument.

In awarding joint custody of the embryos, the appellate court went straight to the heart of the issue: "It would be repugnant and offensive to constitutional principles to order Mary Sue to implant these fertilized ova against her will . . . It would be equally repugnant to order Junior to bear the psychological, if not the legal, consequences of paternity against his will."

Not only is joint custody the simplest solution to a complex struggle, it is the best. Now, Junior and Mary Sue will each have a voice in what happens — and, as important, what doesn't happen — to the frozen embryos. In this instance, joint custody carries with it a veto power.

This case is just one of many around the country that are arising out of a shortage of legal, ethical and even moral guidelines regarding reproductive technologies. It is well past time for state legislatures, bioethicists, the legal and medical communities, counselors, biological researchers, childless couples and religious groups to work in concert toward establishing guideposts and outlining consequences for people like Junior and Mary Sue. Without them, technology will continue to outpace the tempering influences of the law.

The Miami Herald
Miami, Florida, September 21, 1990

KING SOLOMON couldn't have done it better, even though he never envisioned the technology that would bring a divorced couple into court over ownership of seven embryos that were frozen and stored during their marriage.

Wisely, the Tennessee Court of Appeals has ordered a lower court to award the former husband and wife joint custody of the frozen embryos. A lower-court judge had catapulted the case into the abortion-rights debate by ruling that the embryos were "children *in vitro*" and granting sole custody to the woman, Mary Sue Davis Stowe.

Ms. Stowe wanted to implant them in herself or donate them to a childless couple. Junior Davis, her ex-husband, protested that he should not be made a father against his will. The appeals court heeded that common-sense view. Ms. Stowe, now remarried, says that she will appeal to the state supreme court.

This case is one of many that exposes the

AS LEGISLATURES DUCK

failure of state legislatures to face the complexities of modern fertility technology. Baby M was the first, and its resolution remains unsatisfying. The baby's father and his wife have custody, but the mother who conceived and bore her under a surrogacy contract has visitation rights. A new issue arises in the California case in which a surrogate mother who agreed to be implanted with the fertilized egg from a married couple now wants to keep the baby, which she had no part in conceiving but is about to bear.

Legislatures, including Florida's, have an obligation to address these issues. When they duck in hopes that the courts will produce a Solomonic decision, they force the kind of judicial activism that most lawmakers resent.

THE TAMPA TRIBUNE
Tampa, Florida, January 18, 1989

When the artisans of technology push science to new frontiers, their advances threaten to push all of us to the edge of morality.

Consider news from the abortion front. According to the New York Times, 20 percent of medical geneticists approve of performing prenatal diagnosis for sex selection. This chilling practice is made possible when legalized abortion and quick, sensitive labwork are paired. Doctors do the test; parents acquire the information; the fetus of the "wrong" sex is aborted. Most often the wrong sex is female.

In the past, mothers and fathers learned the sex of their offspring the old fashioned way — some time after the child's first husky cry but before the counting of the fingers and toes. Today, many parents become informed without drama, months before delivery. Amniocentesis, performed for medically indicated reasons, pinpoints chromosomal abnormalities in the fetus. It also determines fetal sex. Still, until recently, that news was an almost throwaway piece of information, relevant only to the choice of color for the nursery, pink or blue.

By contrast, fetal sex is *all* that is relevant when prenatal diagnosis for sex selection is performed. If *Roe v. Wade* delivers abortion on demand for women, prenatal diagnosis yields baby boys on demand for families. How ironic that state-of-the-art technology provides the tools to act on a primitive if not strictly Stone-Age impulse: the desire for sons.

Rejecting the practice of producing what John Leo in *U.S. News & World Report* calls "baby boys, to order" does not require condemning people who believe in the greater worth of males. It demands a moral depth we sometimes seem less possessed of as, technologically primed, we march toward the 21st century.

The strongest argument against prenatal diagnosis is the simplest: Whether a child is wanted defines his existence. To thrive, a child must be wanted — unconditionally. There the simplicity ends. The fuzzy interface of technology and morality begins. Of the 20 percent of medical geneticists who approve of prenatal diagnosis for sex selection: "How could they not?"

Leo asks in his *U.S. News* column.

"Since abortion on demand is the law of the land, on what grounds could they logically and legally withhold test results? An overwhelming majority, of course, still refuse to go along if they suspect sex selection is the real aim of the test, but their stance already seems hopeless and rear guard."

That need not be so. Much of civilization is the act of drawing lines. No person of conscience can afford to sit out the task. Things could get ticklish for the National Organization for Women, which views abortion on demand as a woman's absolute right. But, according to Leo, "A few feminists are gingerly using the term *femicide*, a rare appearance of the suffix *-cide* in a movement that tends to regard abortion as the simple shedding of an unnecessary body part...."

Doctors and scientists who employ cutting-edge technology bear as much responsibility as anyone for debating the scrupulousness of its use. Reportedly, one reason carefully neutral physicians employ diagnostic tools upon request is that they are weary of the old, discredited mantle of paternalism. But they had better be wary of operating in a moral vacuum. Medical geneticists, after all, *must* provide counseling. It is an integral part of the services they render. Even abortion clinics, if reputable, will reject an abortion candidate who is discovered to be weakly motivated.

How ironic and yet how inevitable that legalizing abortion would set society on a slippery slope that falls away to an abyss.

Turning thumbs up or thumbs down on a fetus based on sex gives the phrase "planned parenthood" a ghastly new twist. Femicide may never be practiced so routinely that we will be inspired to ask, "Where have all the daughters gone?" But clearly we are perilously close to becoming architects of a society in which no one is born who has not been selected. The consequences of *that* are unknowable. We do know that, if even one daughter in utero is expended for the purposes of sex selection, the morality of the world is incalculably diminished, not just for the son but for us all.

THE ATLANTA CONSTITUTION
Atlanta, Georgia, September 12, 1988

In a rash concession to anti-abortion groups, the Reagan administration is preparing an executive order to ban all research using tissue from aborted fetuses.

An appropriately narrow prohibition is already in effect. It forbids the use of fetal tissue in transplant procedures that some doctors believe could help patients suffering from Parkinson's disease, Alzheimer's disease, juvenile diabetes and leukemia. Also, fetuses that survive abortions, and babies so premature they are expected to die, cannot be used for research. The prohibitions are wise for the moment; they cover the areas of research that raise the most troubling ethical and legal questions.

The administration's directive would go much further. Only tissue from a fetus that miscarried would be eligible for research. That could effectively end even the kinds of research that helped scientists develop safe vaccines for children and techniques for saving the lives of dangerously premature babies. It is almost never possible to use a spontaneously aborted fetus because the tissue dies quickly.

The current, sensible ban expires at the end of this month, perhaps another reason the administration is moving so quickly. Even so, there is no reason to rush. A special advisory committee of the National Institutes of Health is scheduled to convene this week in Washington to examine the sticky legal, ethical and moral questions surrounding fetal-tissue research.

Among the toughest of those questions is whether a way can be found to allow research involving transplants without encouraging women to become pregnant, and undergo an abortion, to make fetal tissue available for the treatment of a loved one.

Any action by the White House should await the outcome of that gathering, which is expected to draw medical ethicists, legal scholars and researchers from across the country. Their input could help the administration devise clear, proportioned guidelines that might allow the nation to benefit from fetal research as much as possible, while managing the tough legal, ethical and moral ramifications in a responsible way.

Koop's Abortion Stand Stirs Wide Debate

U.S. Surgeon General Dr. C. Everett Koop January 9, 1989 told President Ronald Reagan in a letter that he would not issue a planned report on the health risks of abortion, because the scientific data were inconclusive. Koop, a longtime opponent of abortion, surprised both liberals and conservatives with his announcement.

In his letter, the surgeon general stated that none of the studies that had been done on the physical or emotional effects of abortion had provided conclusive information to support either the pro-life or the pro-choice position.

He noted that although some women had experienced physical problems such as damaged cervixes or premature births after having had an abortion, it was difficult to prove that those problems had been caused by the abortion.

The Burlington Free Press
Burlington, Vermont, January 17, 1989

President Reagan dispatched Surgeon General C. Everett Koop to find a smoking gun to clinch the argument against abortion. The doctor in Dr. Koop reported this month that he couldn't find any gun. The politician in him promised to keep looking.

Anti-abortion advocates have insisted that women who choose abortion can face serious emotional problems five to 10 years after the fact. It's one of the arguments the advocates use for outlawing the operation.

When Reagan (a staunch opponent of abortion) asked Koop (another staunch opponent) to review the evidence, anti-abortion advocates hoped for the best. But Koop is known for putting science before politics. After a lengthy review, he told the president that the scientific evidence is inconclusive.

That's another way of saying that he could find no studies that demonstrated long-term pyschological problems. Anti-abortion advocates insist that anecdotal evidence proves otherwise. Certainly, some women later regret the decision to have an abortion, just as some women regret other major life choices: to put a child up for adoption, to have a child, to get married, to get divorced.

But more than 20 million women in the United States have had abortions. Were there some sort of "post-abortion syndrome," the results would be evident in crowded counseling and pyschiatric offices.

The American Pyschological Association has reviewed more than 100 studies on the mental consequences of abortion. The organization agreed with Koop that none of them was solid enough to draw hard, scientific conclusions. There is consistent evidence, however, that the stress accompanying both pregnancy and abortion fades quickly as time passes, the APA concluded.

"Temporary guilt, regret, stress and sadness are not unusual after difficult decisions and more importantly are not psychological disorders," the APA said.

Koop wasn't satisfied. He promised a five-year, multimillion dollar search for the elusive smoking gun.

But to be truly balanced, such a study would have to examine not not only the pyschological consequences of abortion, but the consequences of the alternatives. What are the long-term effects on a woman who places her child for adoption? What are the consequences of giving birth for a 15-year-old unprepared for motherhood?

Koop's successor has a simpler choice: shelve plans for the study and devote the money to research on heart disease, breast cancer and Alzheimer's disease — illnesses already known to devastate millions of American women.

The Record
Hackensack, New Jersey, January 29, 1989

Surgeon General C. Everett Koop has proven once again that he's a master at separating personal beliefs from his duties as the nation's chief public-health officer. Dr. Koop strongly opposes abortion. But that didn't prevent him from deciding, after a lengthy study, that there's little or no scientific evidence of physical or emotional injury to women who undergo an abortion. He could not say abortions don't cause such harm, Dr. Koop asserted, but the evidence is not conclusive either way. Anti-abortionists are outraged, but Dr. Koop has done no more than show he won't fudge the facts to suit his own politics.

Some of former President Reagan's aides hoped Dr. Koop would paint a picture of trauma that could help lay the ground for a successful appeal of Roe vs. Wade, the Supreme Court opinion that legalized abortion across the country. There was ample reason to think so. As John B. Judis reports in The New Republic, Dr. Koop had written two books and co-produced a movie strongly denouncing abortion. He called abortions "a bewildering nightmare" that create "hard people" and "stamp out motherliness." He still opposes abortion. But he's now convinced that there's insufficient evidence of post-abortion trauma.

At a time when some anti-abortion activists are resorting to bombings and angry demonstrations to press their point, Dr. Koop showed courage and a willingness to let the facts overcome ideology. It's far from the first time. Regarded as a mainstay of conservatism when he was appointed, he quickly caused an uproar with an aggressive campaign against smoking. Some tobacco state conservatives such as Sen. Jesse Helms, R-N.C., howled, as did many ideologues in the Reagan administration. But Dr. Koop has stuck to his drive against smoking. And so he should. His job is to protect the public health.

Dr. Koop next broke with conservative orthodoxy when he issued his 1986 report on AIDS. Conservatives hoped for a document that would stress sexual abstinence and condemn homosexuality. Instead, Dr. Koop, while emphasizing the advantage of abstinence for unmarried persons, advocated measures to fight the spread of AIDS, such as education in elementary schools and the use of condoms. He also urged compassion for those afflicted with AIDS. Some Americans, he wrote, believed that "somehow people from certain groups 'deserved' their illness. Let us put those feelings behind us. We are fighting a disease, not a people."

It would have been all too easy for Dr. Koop to use his office to promote an agenda based on his personal beliefs, and to ignore conflicting evidence. He hasn't done that. Dr. Koop has demonstrated over and over his overriding commitment to protecting the public health. He has shown his respect for scientific inquiry. President Bush should reappoint Dr. Koop when his term runs out in November.

The Union Leader
Manchester, New Hampshire, January 12, 1989

So it *is* possible for anti-abortion and pro-abortion groups to arrive at a point of agreement —i.e., that it would be ludicrous to spend an estimated $10,000,000 to $100,000,000 on a five-year study, proposed by Surgeon General C. Everett Koop, to determine whether the performance of an abortion can harm a woman's physical and-or emotional health.

Why waste taxpayers' money on a study that will only provoke a new controversy over methodology and, at best, determine that, yes, some women seem to remain healthy and happy after an abortion, while others, *their* plight a matter of indifference to the pro-abortion news media, suffer ill effects —sometimes many years after the fact?

Why waste taxpayers' money determining what is *already* known —i.e., that some women, having easier consciences than others, are able to ignore or rationalize the biological fact that abortion does constitute the termination of a human life, however euphemistically the act itself is described?

The avoidance of that simple truth is nowhere more evident than in the pro-abortion groups' tactic, in cooperation with the news media, of hiding behind the buzz word *"pro-choice"* to the exclusion of the fact that they allow the 1,500,000 annual victims of abortion-on-demand as much choice as the victims of the Nazi Holocaust —that is, **no choice.** (Incidentally, propaganda to the contrary notwithstanding, *fewer than 1%* of these 1,500,000 abortions are performed to save the life of the mother.)

Save the taxpayers' money. The costly study Koop proposes is irrelevant to the central issue.

Just as the immorality of the extermination of an estimated 6,000,000 Jews at Dachau, Buchenwald, Bergen-Belsen et al. does not depend on the mind set of the extermination camp directors who claimed to be "just following orders," so also does the basic immorality of the extermination of the innocent child in the mother's womb — by whatever euphemism that human life is designated — not depend on the sensitivity of the mother who instructs the physician to perform the deed.

The Kansas City Times
Kansas City, Missouri, January 19, 1989

Looking more like a hero than a bureaucrat, Surgeon General C. Everett Koop has been a champion of solid consumer positions in an administration that has often had other priorities. He's been a bright spot of leadership in an office where power is limited.

If his successor is a professional in the manner of Koop, undetracted from promoting public health by ideology or political alliances, the nation will be lucky. Koop has spoken out often on controversial matters, sometimes in conflict with others in the administration.

A most notable example was his recent report to President Reagan on how abortion affects a woman's mental and physical health. No scientific evidence exists to draw conclusions, Koop said.

This took courage. The administration's abhorrence of abortion is common knowledge. So are Koop's personal anti-abortion sentiments.

Other delicate issues have been well handled by Koop in the seven years he's been in the top Public Health Service job. He developed a plain-language pamphlet on AIDS, then promoted its distribution to 107 million households.

Koop has taken positions unpopular among some people on drinking and driving, violence in the home and cigarette smoking. Last spring he stirred a hornets' nest by pronouncing the nicotine in tobacco addictive, similar to heroin and cocaine.

Even the most benign of surgeons general could not escape criticism from those espousing extremist positions in public health policy, whether in conservative or liberal directions. Koop has gotten a goodly share. But in light of the mushy kind of individualism practiced in the Washington political arena in the 1980s, C. Everett Koop stands out as a man of integrity and a professional of value.

Minneapolis Star and Tribune
Minneapolis, Minnesota, January 16, 1989

It doesn't take a costly study to prove that reactions vary among women who have chosen abortion. Some remember it as a moment of liberation, others as a sad but necessary relinquishing; some eventually come to regret their choice. Now Surgeon General C. Everett Koop has acknowledged that apparently wide array of attitudes: No credible evidence shows, Koop said last week, that abortion has a predictable, distinct psychological effect.

That forthright appraisal is all the more welcome because of its source and its timing. As the Reagan administration's top medical officer, abortion-opponent Koop was directed to prepare a report on abortion's psychological consequences. Among Reagan's advisers, Koop noted, the notion that abortion inflicts distinct emotional harm was "a foregone conclusion." Some advisers hoped the expected findings would spur the Supreme Court to reverse its 1973 ruling legalizing abortion, which last Monday the court unwisely agreed to reconsider.

But Koop declined to embrace a theory his survey could neither certify nor confound: "The data do not support the premise," he wrote to the president, "that abortion does or does not contribute to psychological problems." The way to settle that question for good, the surgeon general said, is to launch a definitive government study.

But such a study is most likely to verify what casual observation suggests: that abortion reactions run the spectrum from relief to despair. In that way, abortion is little different from life's other weighty decisions. Most of them — from marriage to career change to divorce — yield unpredictable and occasionally negative emotional results.

A study makes sense only if the government intends to act on the results. But even a finding that abortion sometimes wreaks emotional havoc would be no reason to bar women from choosing it. The choice remains as legitimately private as other medical decisions — many of which can have unintended side-effects. Like all human choices, abortion inevitably carries different consequences for different people. The inescapable risks are no reason for government or the court to intervene.

INDEX

203